THE CRIMINAL LAW OF SCOTLAND

THE CRIMINAL LAW OF SCOTLAND

by

SIR GERALD H. GORDON
C.B.E., Q.C., LL.D.
Formerly Sheriff of Glasgow and Strathkelvin
and
Formerly Professor of Scots Law
at the University of Edinburgh

THIRD EDITION

Volume I

Edited by

MICHAEL G. A. CHRISTIE
M.A., LL.B, Solicitor
Formerly Lecturer in Law
at the University of Aberdeen

Nemo sine crimine vivit
Dicta Catonis, i.5

Published under the auspices of
SCOTTISH UNIVERSITIES LAW INSTITUTE LTD

W. GREEN
EDINBURGH
2000

First published 1967
Second Impression 1968
Second Edition 1978
Third Edition 2000

Published in 2000 by W. Green & Son Ltd
21 Alva Street
Edinburgh EH2 4PS

Typeset by Dataword Services Limited, Somerset

Printed and bound in Great Britain by MPG Books Ltd, Bodmin, Cornwall

No natural forests were destroyed to make this product;
only farmed timber was used and replanted

A CIP catalogue record of this book is available from the British Library

ISBN 0 414 010566

First and Second Edition
Dedicated

TO MARJORIE

PREFACE FOR THIRD EDITION

The simple aim of this new edition of Sir Gerald Gordon's classic text has been to reflect changes in the law since 1978. This task has been greatly facilitated by the comprehensive updating notes contained in the original author's *Second Cumulative Supplement to the Second Edition* of 1992, which incorporated the amendments detailed in his *First Supplement* of 1984. The editing work has, therefore, been sparse in order that the collateral purpose of preserving the bulk of this highly respected and familiar work might be realised. Nevertheless, the total size of the book has increased to the point where publication in two volumes was considered desirable. Volume I thus covers Part I, "General Principles", of the immediately former edition, whereas Volume II will relate to "Specific Crimes". The order and numbering of chapters follow exactly the pattern set in former editions. Chapter 2, "The Concept of Responsibility", remains virtually unchanged in the new edition, which may disappoint many readers: the editor considered, however, that the limited scope and purpose envisaged for this chapter had already been fully realised in both former editions, and that a more detailed exposition of the philosophical concepts involved — taking into account all modern variants and theories — was not justified in the context of the work as a whole.

It is hoped that this volume reflects the scope of Scots criminal law as of June 1, 2000. Sir Gerald has read and commented upon the text of all major revisions to the chapters of Volume I; but responsibility for the revisions, both major and minor, and for the final state of the text including the inevitable inaccuracies and omissions, remains solely that of the editor.

In the second edition of 1978, Sir Gerald quite correctly drew attention to the difficulties which were involved at that time in addressing the general principles of Scots criminal law. He particularly emphasised the dearth of scholarship and court reporting in relation to Scottish criminal matters, as also the lack of transparency in prosecutorial decisions affecting the substantive law itself. In respect of at least some of those matters, however, there have been significant developments over the past 20 years.

Scholarship and Criminal Cases

The position noted in the second edition[1] was that the criminal law had long been neglected by Scots lawyers and that there had been no extended discussion of principles since Hume, the only systematic modern treatment being that of Professor T.B. Smith in three short chapters of his *Short Commentary*.[2]

The facts that important criminal cases had often gone unreported, and that points of law and principle had often to be gleaned from directions given to juries by trial judges were also tellingly narrated.

[1] Gordon, *Criminal Law* (2nd ed., 1978), para. 0–02, pp. 3–4 (2nd ed., 1978).
[2] T.B. Smith, *A Short Commentary on the Law of Scotland* (Edinburgh, 1962), pp. 116–238.

Scots criminal law scholarship and case reporting have enjoyed something of a renaissance, however, since 1978.

There have, for example, been significant contributions to criminal law theory, particularly in the publications of Professor Lindsay Farmer[3] and Professor R.A. Duff.[4] The "Criminal Law" title of the *Stair Memorial Encyclopaedia* has also fairly recently attempted a restatement of the principles of Scots criminal law;[5] and articles in the *Juridical Review*, *Scots Law Times* and *Journal of the Law Society of Scotland* by various authors[6] have added much to the ways in which Scots lawyers look at their law. There has also been published at least one set of essays devoted to Scots criminal law issues.[7] In addition, a series of monographs on (*inter alia*) items of Scottish criminal law has appeared;[8] whilst the needs of law students have been served by the publication of not one but two relevant textbooks.[9]

The reporting of criminal cases in Scotland received a much needed boost in 1981 when the first parts of the specialised series known as *Scottish Criminal Case Reports* were published.[10] Over the last 20 years or so, the longer established sets of court reports[11] have doubled if not trebled their coverage of criminal cases in order to compete with the new series — such that there is now almost an embarrassment of reporting in this field of law. It is obvious too from many modern decisions of the Criminal Appeal Court that Scottish judges are far more willing to consider basic principles of the criminal law than was formerly the case, even ten years ago: in particular the Court during the tenures of Lord Justice-General Hope and Lord Justice-General Rodger not only has frequently discussed and reinterpreted the criminal law and its principles,[12] but also has been most willing to seek appropriate comparative material in the jurisprudence of foreign systems of law.[13]

---

3 *See, e.g.*, his *Criminal Law, Tradition and Legal Order: Crime and the Genius of Scots Law, 1747 to the Present* (C.U.P., 1997), which advocates an approach to criminal law theory which is both radical and intellectually challenging: it is also critical of the approach to criminal law taken in Gordon's *Criminal Law*.

4 Professor Duff holds the Chair of Philosophy at Stirling University, and his articles and books (*e.g.*, *Criminal Attempts*, Oxford, 1996) on Anglo-American criminal theory have undoubtedly brought to a wider audience some of the Scottish criminal cases and ideas to which he quite often makes reference.

5 *The Laws of Scotland: Stair Memorial Encyclopaedia*, Vol. 7 (Edinburgh, 1995), paras 1 *et seq*.

6 In particular, P.W. Ferguson, Advocate.

7 R.F. Henderson (ed.), *Justice and Crime: Essays in Honour of the Rt. Honourable the Lord Emslie* (Edinburgh, 1993).

8 Of the volumes so far published in this "Scottish Criminal Law and Practice Series", the following have been particularly well received: C.H.W. Gane, *Sexual Offences* (Edinburgh, 1992); and P.W. Ferguson, *Crimes Against the Person* (2nd ed., Edinburgh, 1998).

9 R.A.A. McCall Smith and D. Sheldon, *Scots Criminal Law* (2nd ed., Edinburgh, 1997); T.H. Jones and M.G.A. Christie, *Criminal Law* (2nd ed., Edinburgh, 1996).

10 This series, edited by Sir Gerald Gordon, continues to the present day, as a joint publishing venture by the Law Society of Scotland and the law publishers, Butterworths.

11 *Justiciary Cases*, and *Scots Law Times Reports*.

12 See, *e.g.*, *Ross v. H.M. Advocate*, 1991 J.C. 210 (reconsideration of automatism in Scots law); *Byrne v. H.M. Advocate*, 2000 S.C.C.R. 77 (which, after years of confusion, clarified the law on fire-raising).

13 See, *e.g.*, *Moss v. Howdle* 1997 S.C.C.R. 215, where there is citation of persuasive authority from England and Canada. The ready availability of foreign legal material, including case reports, on the internet makes such citation a much more practicable proposition at the beginning of the present century than was the case at the close of the 20th century.

It remains true, however, that discussion of the principles of criminal law is somewhat clouded by the nature of Scots criminal procedure. The conduct of prosecutions, and the decision whether or not to prosecute, or for what crime to prosecute in any case, lie almost entirely with the Crown Office. The prosecutor in any case can, and often does, accept a plea of guilty to part of the indictment; or to a lesser crime than that charged, such as culpable homicide on a murder charge, or reset on a charge of theft; or to attempting to commit the crime charged. In all these ways the Crown Office can materially alter the law in practice while leaving it unchanged literally. Whilst it is the case that the Crown Office have made considerable effort to be more open and accommodating[14] than in former times, it is still difficult to find out and state the principles on which the Office act, and very difficult to predict their actions. For the decisions of the Crown Office are in the last resort administrative decisions: like those formerly taken by the Secretary of State in considering the commutation of death sentences, they may be based on precedent and general rules,[15] but the precedents and rules are private. This system makes Scots criminal law flexible, and has many practical advantages, but it also makes it difficult to state and discuss the law from a theoretical standpoint.

Development of the criminal law: Scottish Parliament, Law Commission, European Convention on Human Rights

Development and reform of the criminal law in England has largely been led by the Law Commission in recent years. The Scottish Law Commission has thus far not been nearly so active in the field of criminal law as its English counterpart, although it has published a number of consultative papers[16] and a report on *mens rea*.[17] It is likely, however, that the Scottish Law Commission's future programmes will include more crime-related matters, since the Scottish Parliament will inevitably look to the Commission for advice in relation to development and reform of the law through legislation.

The Scottish Parliament was set up in Edinburgh in 1999 under the authority of the Scotland Act 1998[18]; and it is much more likely that a local legislature, such as this, will undertake reconsideration of the criminal law in Scotland than the United Kingdom Parliament at Westminster. The new Scottish Parliament, however, cannot enact legislation which relates to reserved matters[19]; and neither the Scottish Parliament nor the Scottish Executive[20] can act in a way which is

---

[14] It publishes, *e.g.*, an annual report, and has permitted academic research into some aspects of its operations.

[15] *Report of the Royal Commission on Capital Punishment*, 1953, Cmd. 8932, para. 49.

[16] See, *e.g.*, Consultative Memoranda Nos 60, "Mobbing and Rioting" (1984), and 61, "Attempted Homicide" (1984).

[17] *Report on the Mental Element in Crime*, (S.L.C. No. 80, 1983). See also, *e.g.*, reports on *The Law of Incest* (S.L.C. No. 69, Cmnd. 8422, 1981) and *Art and Part Guilt of Statutory Offences* (S.L.C. No. 93, 1985).

[18] See ss. 1(1), 28(1) and (6).

[19] See s.29(2)(b).

[20] This term includes the First Minister, ministers appointed by him, and the Lord Advocate and Solicitor General for Scotland: collectively, they are known as "the Scottish Ministers": Scotland Act 1998, s.44; see also s.57(2).

incompatible with "Convention Rights" or Community law.[21] Whilst reserved matters include treason, drugs offences, firearms offences and (generally) road traffic offences,[22] a large slice of the criminal law in Scotland has been devolved to the Scottish Parliament, to order as it sees fit. "Convention rights" are those rights which originate in the European Convention on Human Rights, and which have been brought into domestic law by the Human Rights Act 1998.[23] Not only is it incompetent for the Scottish Parliament or Scottish Ministers to act in violation of those rights, but it is also unlawful for the Scottish courts (as "public authorities"[24]) "to act in a way which is incompatible with a Convention right".[25] Since these rights have been subject to interpretation by the European Court of Human Rights (and the now defunct Commission) over many years, Scottish courts are directed, in cases where Convention rights are involved, that they "must take into account" the jurisprudence of the European Court and Commission.[26] The Scottish courts are in addition required to interpret domestic legislation (primary and subordinate) "in a way which is compatible with Convention rights".[27]

Certainly, the ways in which Convention rights will confront the criminal law in Scotland can at present be little more than speculation[28]; but that a period of challenge lies ahead, especially for a system of common-law-based criminal law, is beyond question.

A note on criminal charges

Although this book does not deal with procedural matters it may be useful to say a little about the forms in which criminal charges are made in Scotland. Trials in the High Court and, since 1887, jury trials in the sheriff court proceed on an indictment at the instance of the Lord Advocate for the time being. The charge in this indictment is sometimes called a "libel", and it is common to speak of "libelling" particular averments, aggravations or previous convictions. In summary proceedings the charge is brought by way of a "complaint" at the instance of the procurator fiscal for the court concerned, or in private prosecutions at the instance of the private prosecutor.

---

[21] Scotland Act, ss. 29(2)(d) and 57(2).

[22] *ibid.*, s.30(1) and Sched. 5, Pt II, Head B, B.1, B.4; Head E, E.1.

[23] See *ibid.*, s.1(1); Sched. 1.

[24] *ibid.*, s.6.

[25] *ibid.*, s.6(1) and (3).

[26] *ibid.*, s.2(1). The courts must inevitably become familiar too with the rules and conventions which the European Court of Human Rights has evolved for interpretation of the rights themselves: for example, that many terms used in the various rights have 'autonomous' meanings; that the Convention is interpreted 'evolutionarily', and, where competing interests are involved, proportionately. The European Court also recognises that individual States in the way in which they apply or safeguard the various rights must be allowed a certain degree of discretion (*i.e.*, a 'margin of appreciation'). On all of these rules, see P. van Dijk and G.J.H. van Hoof, *Theory and Practice of the European Convention on Human Rights* (3rd ed., The Hague, 1998), pp. 71 *et seq*.

[27] Human Rights Act 1998, s.3(1)and (2)(a).

[28] See, *e.g.*, A. Ashworth, *Principles of Criminal Law* (3rd ed., Oxford, 1999), pp. 62–66.

Prior to 1887 indictments were in "syllogistic" form containing a major and a minor premise and a conclusion, although the conclusion was not always stated expressly. The basic form of the indictment was "Whereas X is a crime and ought to be punished": major premise, "nevertheless you A.B. did a, b, c, . . .": minor premise, with the conclusion that A.B. is liable to punishment for having committed X. The importance of the minor premise was that a, b, c, etc., which are the acts alleged to have been carried out by the accused must have constituted the crime set out in the major premise.

For an indictment to be relevant it was necessary that both the major and the minor premise should satisfy certain requirements as to relevancy. The major premise had to set out a crime recognised by the law. In the normal case this was done simply by using what is called a *nomen juris*, such as murder, theft or rape, and a major premise which contained such a *nomen juris* was necessarily relevant. Difficulties regarding the relevancy of the major premise of an indictment arose in connection with allegedly criminal situations which did not have a *nomen juris*, and which had therefore to be described by reference to their particular circumstances. Crimes of this nature, crimes without a name, are called "innominate offences". Where the major premise purported to set out such an innominate offence it was for the court to decide whether the situation libelled did constitute a crime, either because it described a situation which could be regarded as analogous to one of the nominate crimes or because the court was prepared to exercise its power to declare that the facts set forth in the major premise, although not previously regarded as criminal, should now be a crime. Once a particular major premise had been held to be relevant it could of course be repeated in future indictments, and indeed could be said to have become the *nomen juris* of the new crime. But in practice the new crime was still called an innominate offence. From the point of view of pleading, the important thing about descriptions of innominate offences was that they had to include a reference to the essential element(s) of the crime. Decisions on the relevancy of such major premises are therefore decisions regarding the definitions of the innominate offences. The innominate offences are thus more clearly defined than the nominate ones.

Since 1887 indictments have not been in syllogistic form and no longer contain a major premise. Section 5 of the Criminal Procedure (Scotland) Act 1887[29] provided that it should not be necessary to specify by a *nomen juris* the crime charged in any indictment but that it should be sufficient to set forth facts which constituted a crime. This, it should be stressed, affects only the system of pleading. It does not affect the substantive law, nor does it affect the principle that in order to be relevant an indictment must set forth facts which constitute a crime, whether that crime is a nominate one or a recognised innominate one. The 1887 Act relieved the prosecutor from having to state which crime he is charging; it did not relieve him of the necessity of setting out a relevant charge. In practice most modern indictments do contain what amounts to a *nomen juris*, and convictions are still normally regarded as convictions for named offences. An indictment for murder is distinguished from an indictment for culpable homicide because in the former case the charge concludes "and

---

[29] See now 1995 Act, Sched. 3, para. 2: this provision also applies to complaints.

did murder him", while in the latter it concludes "and did kill him". The only difficulty which arises in modern practice is in relation to new forms of old crimes, which may be left without either a name or a recognised description and which are therefore very difficult to describe on a list of previous convictions. For example, the crime of giving false information to the police, exemplified in *Kerr v. Hill*,[30] is sometimes referred to as "giving false information to the police" and sometimes as "public mischief", and it could equally be described as "wasting the time of the police by a false story". Prior to 1887 in order to obtain a conviction at all on indictment it was necessary to obtain a conviction for the charge set forth in the major premise. Section 60 of the 1887 Act,[31] however, provided that where any part of what is charged in an indictment constitutes in itself an indictable crime it is to be deemed to be separable to the effect of making it lawful to convict of such a crime. This means, for example, that if a person is charged with extorting money by threats and by assault it is possible to convict him either of the whole charge, or of extortion by threats only, or of the separable crime of assault.

There is, however, authority to the effect that where the Crown choose to libel a *nomen juris* the indictment is irrelevant if it does not set forth facts which constitute that *nomen juris*, even although they constitute a different crime. In *H.M. Advocate v. Grainger and Rae*[32] the accused were charged with having intercourse with an unconscious woman and the charge concluded "and did ravish her", which is the accepted conclusion in a rape charge. The defence objected to the relevancy of the indictment on the ground that the facts set forth constituted clandestine injury to woman, a recognised innominate offence, and not rape. This objection was upheld by Lord Anderson partly on the ground that the penalties for rape were necessarily higher than those of clandestine injury, partly on the ground that a charge of clandestine injury could have been brought in the sheriff court, and partly on the ground that the Crown having chosen to charge rape were bound to set forth facts constituting rape. It may be doubted whether this decision fully recognised the spirit of the 1887 Act, and it is submitted that it would have been proper for a conviction of clandestine injury to have been recorded on the indictment in *Grainger and Rae*.[33]

The importance of the minor premise in pre-1887 indictments was twofold. In the first place it had to conform to the legal requirements of "specification", that is to say, it had to give proper notice of the facts which the Crown proposed to prove and it had to be sufficiently specific in its statement of the time and place of the offence. These requirements still apply to modern indictments although the amount of specification required has been much reduced by the provisions of the 1887 Act,[34] and by the short forms of charges which currently appear in Schedule 2 to the 1995 Act.[35] The minor premise also had to be relevant in the sense

---

30 1936 J.C. 71.

31 See now 1995 Act, Sched. 3, para. 9(2): this rule also applies to complaints.

32 1932 J.C. 40.

33 *Supra*. It may be that a conviction for rape would have been incompetent since in the absence of any averment of facts amounting to rape the Crown might have been precluded from proving the necessary elements of rape, such as the use of force or the deliberate rendering of the woman unconscious for the purpose of intercourse.

34 Now the 1995 Act, Sched. 3, which applies both to indictments and complaints.

35 These forms also apply to complaints, together with the forms in Sched. 5 to the 1995 Act.

that it had to set forth facts which amounted to the crime libelled in the major premise. This meant, for example, that an indictment whose major premise libelled theft, but whose minor premise set forth facts amounting only to embezzlement, was irrelevant although each premise in itself might have been unassailable.

There is now no substantial difference between the rules regarding complaints and those regarding indictments, and the wording of the charge in each is subject to virtually identical provisions.[36]

Michael Christie
September 30, 2000

[36] See 1995 Act, Scheds 2, 3 and 5.

PREFACE TO SECOND EDITION

THE period since the publication of the first edition of this book has been one of considerable activity in the field of criminal law. Some of this activity has been largely formal, by way of consolidating and revising legislation which while it does not change the law does make work for writers and editors even if, which is sometimes doubtful, it makes the law easier to find. Most of the substantial legislative changes made during that time by Parliament such as the Theft Act 1968 do not, of course, affect Scotland. But the contributions of the Law Commission and the House of Lords are of interest and importance on both sides of the Tweed, and they have been very considerable, including as they do papers and decisions on such general topics as *mens rea,* attempt, coercion and intoxication. The High Court of Justiciary itself has been much readier in recent years to issue written opinions (many of them reported) on matters of criminal law than was formerly the case. There has also been a resurrection of such forgotten offences as piracy, and a resurgence of the crime of conspiracy. It would be a very bold writer who today would characterise any common law offence as obsolete.

The principal aim of this edition has been to take account of these changes in the law, although the reader will also recognise that the author's views on certain matters, such as recklessness and insanity, have undergone a change over the years, a change which on the whole, I believe, brings them more into line with the practical and flexible genius of Scots criminal law which seems increasingly of recent years to be relying on concepts such as wickedness and evil intent (see *e.g. Cawthorne v. H.M. Adv.,* 1968 J.C. 32; *Smart v. H.M. Adv.,* 1975 S.L.T. 65; *Brennan v. H.M. Adv.,* 1977 S.L.T. 151) to distinguish conduct which is criminal from conduct which is not, a development which strangely enough is not without parallel in England (see *e.g. R. v. Feely* [1973] Q.B. 530; *R. v. Majewski* [1977] A.C. 443) despite the more academic approach of the Law Commission and, at times, the House of Lords (see *e.g. R. v. Hyam* [1975] A.C. 55: *R. v. Smith (Roger)* [1975] A.C. 476).

I am indebted to many people for assistance in preparing this edition. The hospitality of the Centre of Criminology and the Faculty of Law of the University of Toronto gave me an opportunity to collect my thoughts during the year I spent there prior to starting work on it. Like all academic writers I owe more than I can calculate to discussions with colleagues and students. I have also been fortunate in having had the benefit of discussions with practising members of the profession, and I am grateful to them and to the officials of Crown Office and Justiciary Office for keeping me up to date with the law, and for patiently and generously satisfying my importunate requests for unreported material.

I owe more than the usual author's debt to The Easter Press for their preparation of my MS. and for their care and attention in printing the book. The publishers, W. Green and Son Ltd., have as ever been helpful and understanding throughout. The Carnegie Trust for Scotland and the Scottish Universities Law Institute have once again provided sponsorship and financial assistance.

The thankless task of transforming my scribbled thoughts into workable MS. was undertaken by my wife, who also prepared the index. The tables of cases and statutes were prepared by Mr. R. R. Shaw.

I have tried to state the law as at 31st December, 1977, save that I have, perhaps rashly, assumed the coming into force of Acts passed by that date. I have tried to state all penalties in as up-to-date a version as I could, without burdening the footnotes with their legislative history. This includes, so far as I could absorb them, the provisions of section 193A and 289A to 289D of, and Schedules 7A, 7B and 7C to, the 1975 Act, as inserted by Schedules 11, 1, 5 and 6 to the Criminal Law Act 1977, provisions which are as realistic as they are readable. Their main effect is to make the maximum fine on summary conviction of an indictable offence £1,000 (or such higher figure as may be fixed in future by statutory instrument), and to remove all limits on the maximum fine on conviction on indictment. The only express exceptions to this undiscriminating blanket provision are in the case of certain drug offences, primarily in connection with cannabis, but other exceptions are created by making certain offences (including offences connected with drink and driving and offences against the Conspiracy and Protection of Property Act 1875) no longer indictable. In addition there are certain specific increases in the fines for some offences, and a general increase in all fines of under £50 provided in enactments passed before 1949 or which re-enact "with or without modification" enactments passed before that date.

GERALD H. GORDON.

Glasgow.
January 1978.

PREFACE TO FIRST EDITION

THIS work has taken a very long time to write, and my debts of gratitude are correspondingly many and great.

In particular, I am deeply indebted to the institutions and persons who are mentioned in this preface.

Most of Book I and the bulk of part 2 of Book II were originally written when I was a Faulds Fellow in Glasgow University; the remainder of the work was written under the auspices of the Scottish Universities Law Institute and the Carnegie Trust for Scotland without whose sponsorship and financial assistance in preparing the work for publication and in underwriting the actual publication it could never have appeared. Professor D. M. Walker has acted in a supervisory and advisory capacity throughout, and this has involved him in reading the entire manuscript at least once; Professor T. B. Smith has been a continual source of encouragement and assistance both personally and in his capacity as director of the Scottish Universities Law Institute.

The Hon. Lord Kilbrandon found time from his many other activities to read the whole of the proofs and offered many helpful criticisms and suggestions. Other friends and colleagues who have read parts of the text and given me the benefit of their knowledge and experience include Professor A. H. Campbell and other members of the Faculty of Law at Edinburgh University, Professor B. Beinart, Mr. Angus MacLeod, Procurator Fiscal, Edinburgh and his deputes, Mr. S. Bowen of Crown Office, and Mr. D. J. Stevenson, Clerk of Justiciary. The officials of the Justiciary Office and the Crown Office showed great patience in answering many importunate questions and were always very ready to trace and make available unreported material. Without the help of these and other colleagues this work would contain many more errors than it does; for the opinions expressed in it I am of course alone responsible, as I am for the errors, omissions, inconsistencies and infelicities which remain.

Mrs. E. Rodger and several other typists accomplished the difficult task of transforming a confused manuscript into an acceptable typescript; Mrs. S. Edwards helped in that task and also gave secretarial help of all kinds in the final stages of preparing the typescript and correcting the proofs; Dr. G. R. Thomson, of W. Green & Son Ltd., showed great helpfulness and patience to a tyro author; and the staff of The Eastern Press Ltd. showed their customary diligence and attention in the printing of the book.

Mr. Brian Gill prepared the index, and Dr. Ann Smith prepared the tables of cases and of statutes and the bibliography, and also gave unsparingly of her wise counsel at all stages of preparing the work for press.

Lastly, but by no means least, I must record my deep thanks to my wife who has not merely borne patiently with the presence of this work as an all too visible rival throughout her married life, but who also unselfishly helped to check the entire typescript and much of the proofs.

It was originally intended that this work should include a section on punishment by Sheriff J. V. M. Shields, Q.C., but this was unfortunately rendered impossible by his illness and untimely death.

I have tried to state the law in the text as at 31st July 1966.

GERALD H. GORDON.

Edinburgh University
February 1967.

CONTENTS

TABLE OF CASES

TABLE OF STATUTES

ACTS OF THE PARLIAMENT OF SCOTLAND

STATUTES OF THE PARLIAMENT OF ENGLAND

STATUTES OF THE PARLIAMENT OF GREAT BRITAIN

ACTS OF THE SCOTTISH PARLIAMENT

TABLE OF STATUTORY INSTRUMENTS

LIST OF ABBREVIATIONS

(Excluding standard journals and law reports)

Alison	*Principles and Practice of the Criminal Law of Scotland*, A.J. Alison (2 Vols: Vol. i, *Principles* (Edin., 1832); Vol. ii, *Practice* (Edin., 1833).
Anderson	*The Criminal Law of Scotland*, A.M. Anderson (2nd ed., Edin., 1904).
Beccaria	*An Essay on Crimes and Punishments*, Marquis Beccaria, (5th ed. in English; London, 1804).
Bentham, *Principles*	*Introduction to the Principles of Morals and Legislation*, J. Bentham, W. Harrison (ed.) (published with *A Fragment of Government*) (Oxford, 1948).
Burnett	*A Treatise on Various Branches of the Criminal Law of Scotland*, J. Burnett (Edin., 1811).
D	*The Digest of Justininan*, T. Mommsen (ed.) with P. Krueger, with English translation ed. by A. Watson (University of Pennsylvania Press, 1985).
Draft English Code	Law Commission, *A Criminal Code for England and Wales*, Vol. 1 (Report and Draft Criminal Code Bill); Vol. 2 (Commentary): Law Com. No. 177, H. of C. No. 299, 1989.
Ersk.Inst.	*An Institute of the Law of Scotland*, J. Erskine, J.B. Nicolson (ed.), 2 Vols (Edin., 1871).
Gl. Williams	*Criminal Law: The General Part*, Glanville L. Williams (2nd ed., London, 1961).
Hall	*General Principles of Criminal Law*, J. Hall (2nd ed., Indianapolis, 1960).
Hall and Glueck	*Cases on Criminal Law and its Enforcement*, L. Hall and S. Glueck (St. Paul. Minn., 1st ed., 1940; 2nd ed., 1958). (References are to 2nd ed., unless otherwise stated.)
Hume	*Commentaries on the Law of Scotland Respecting Crimes*, Baron Hume, 4th ed., B.R. Bell (ed.), 2 Vols. (Edin., 1844).
Inst.	*Institutiones Justiani*, J.B. Moyle (ed.) (12th ed., Oxford, 1912).
Kenny	*Kenny's Outlines of Criminal Law*, C.S. Kenny, 19th ed., J.W.C. Turner (ed.) (Cambridge, 1966).
L.C.W.P.	Law Commission Working Paper. Series of Working Papers published for the English Law Commission (H.M.S.O.).
Macaulay	*Notes on the Indian Penal Code*, Lord Macaulay (published in *Collected Works of Lord Macaulay*, Lady Trevelyan (ed.) (London, 1866, Vol. VII)).
Macdonald	*A Practical Treatise on the Criminal Law of Scotland*, J.H.A. Macdonald (Lord Kingsburgh), (1st ed., Edin., 1867); 3rd ed., by the author assisted by N.D. Macdonald (Edin., 1894); 5th ed., J. Walker (later Lord Walker) and D.J. Stevenson (eds) (Edin., 1948). (References are to 5th ed. unless otherwise stated.)

Mackenzie	*The Laws and Customs of Scotland in Matters Criminal*, Sir G. Mackenzie, (2nd ed., Edin., 1699).
Model Penal Code, T.D.	American Law Institute: Model Penal Code — Tentative Drafts (Philadelphia, 1956-61).
Model Penal Code, P.O.D.	American Law Institute: Model Penal Code — Proposed Official Draft (Philadelphia, 1962).
Model Penal Code, O.D.	American Law Institute: Model Penal Code, Official Draft (Philadelphia, 1985).
Modern Approach	*The Modern Approach to Criminal Law*, L. Radzinowicz and J.W.C. Turner (eds) English Studies in Criminal Science, Vol. IV (London, 1945).
N.E.D./O.E.D.	*Oxford English Dictionary*, J.A.H. Murray (ed.); 2nd ed., J.A. Simpson and E.S.C. Weiner (eds) (Oxford, 1989).
R.C.	Report of Royal Commission on Capital Punishment, 1953, Cmd. 8932.
R.C.Evid.	Report of Royal Commission on Capital Punishment: Minutes of Evidence, London, 1949-51.
Renton & Brown	*Criminal Procedure according to the Law of Scotland*, by R.W. Renton and H.H. Brown, 6th ed., G.H. Gordon (ed.) assisted by C.H.W. Gane (Edin., 1996).
Sayre	*A Collection of Cases on Criminal Law*, F.B. Sayre (Rochester, N.Y., 1927).
Smith and Hogan	*Criminal Law*, J.C. Smith and B. Hogan, 9th ed., Sir John C. Smith (ed.), (London, 1999).
T.B. Smith	*A Short Commentary on the Law of Scotland*, T.B. Smith (Edin., 1962).
Stair Inst.	*The Institutions of the Law of Scotland*, by Viscount Stair, ed., J.S. More, 2 Vols (Edin., 1832).
StGB	Strafgesetzbuch (German Penal Code).
1995 Act	Criminal Procedure (Scotland) Act 1995.

VOLUME I

GENERAL THEORY

PART I

INTRODUCTORY

CHAPTER 1

CRIMES, OFFENCES AND THE DECLARATORY POWER

THE DEFINITION OF "CRIME"

Crime, criminal law and criminal procedure

The terms "crime" and "criminal law" are well known but it is not easy to give a comprehensive definition of them, or to state clearly the difference between criminal and civil law. The now repealed Summary Procedure Act 1864 divided the jurisdiction of summary courts into civil and criminal, and described the criminal jurisdiction as that where "the Court shall be required or shall be authorised to pronounce Sentence of Imprisonment against the Respondent, or shall be authorised or required in case of Default of Payment or Recovery of a Penalty or Expenses, or in case of Disobedience to their Order, to grant Warrant for the Imprisonment of the Respondent for a Period limited to a certain Time, at the Expiration of which he shall be entitled to Liberation."[1] This Act was repealed by the Summary Jurisdiction (Scotland) Act 1908 and neither that Act nor its successors define civil or criminal procedure. **1.01**

The later Acts do, however, define the term "offence," and follow the 1864 Act in laying stress on the treatment of the offender. An offence is "any act, attempt or omission punishable by law".[2] This definition does not indicate the type of punishment envisaged, and does not specifically require the possibility of imprisonment desiderated in 1864. This may be because the number of offences normally dealt with by fining the offender has greatly increased since 1864, or may be merely because every fine now carries with it the possibility of imprisonment in default of payment.[3] **1.02**

The possibility of imprisonment. There are difficulties in regarding the possibility of imprisonment as the decisive factor. The requirement specifically made in 1864, that the imprisonment must be for a fixed period, would have served to distinguish criminal imprisonment from civil imprisonment for contempt of court until 1981[4]; but there does not **1.03**

---

[1] s.28.

[2] 1995 Act, s.307(1).

[3] 1995 Act, s.219. It was held under the 1864 Act that proceedings against a company for a penalty for breach of the Factory and Workshop Act 1901 were civil and not criminal, because a company could not be imprisoned: *Lauder v. Hurst Nelson and Co. Ltd* (1904) 4 Adam 413.

[4] When s.15(1) of the Contempt of Court Act 1981 came into force.

seem to be anything contradictory in the idea of a crime for which the offender cannot be imprisoned or, indeed, punished at all in the ordinary sense of the word. Many offences are in fact visited not by punishment but by other forms of treatment such as probation or absolute discharge.[5] These methods of treatment can, it is true, follow only on behaviour which is punishable in the conventional ways, but if a class of criminal acts, such as sexual offences, or all first offences, or all offences by children,[6] were to cease to be punishable and come always to involve some other form of treatment, they would not therefore cease to be crimes. And conversely a child sent to a residential establishment as being in need of care under one of the "non-offence" provisions of section 52 (1) of the Children (Scotland) Act 1995 has not committed any crime. It seems, therefore, that "crime" must be defined independently of the manner in which the offender is dealt with; but that the definition will probably have to take into account the procedure by which he is dealt with, or rather, in view of the provisions for child offenders,[7] the procedure by which he is liable to be dealt with, or by which he would be dealt with were he an adult.

1.04 *Criminal Procedure.* A definition of criminal law as the subject-matter of criminal procedure, or in terms of the jurisdiction of criminal courts, is not wholly satisfactory. Its apparent circularity is not of great importance; the members, officers and proceedings of the High Court of Justiciary can be defined more or less ostensively — they can be shown to anyone who wishes to see them, and the same is true of the sheriff court although the differences between civil and criminal courts and procedures are not so obvious there. The difficulty is caused by certain anomalous matters which are not criminal but which are dealt with by the criminal courts. Appeals from the Small Debt Court, for example, used to be heard by judges of the High Court, wearing criminal robes, sitting in criminal courtrooms, aided by the permanent officials of the Justiciary Office, although they were governed by a peculiar procedure.[8] Appeals against imprisonment for contempt of a civil court used to be dealt with by the High Court, perhaps because of the analogy with criminal imprisonment, though such imprisonment is not a criminal matter.[9] The jurisdiction of summary courts to deal with statutory penalties and certain orders *ad factum praestandum* has also created difficulty.[10]

The distinguishing feature of criminal law is often said to be the interest taken by the state in crime. The state has, of course, an

---

[5] 1995 Act, ss.228 (as amended by the Crime and Punishment (Scotland) Act 1997, Sched. 1, para. 21(27)), 246(2),(3)); see also ss.234J, inserted by the Crime and Disorder Act 1998, s.94(1), and 245D, inserted by the 1997 Act, s.5; *cf.* T. B. Smith, p.124.

[6] *cf.* Social Work (Scotland) Act 1968, s.31; Children (Scotland) Act 1995, s.52.

[7] Children may be prosecuted for offences: 1968 Act, s.31(1), but are normally dealt with by civil, or at any rate quasi-civil, proceedings: Children (Scotland) Act 1995, ss.56 and 65 *et seq.*; *McGregor v. T. and P.*, 1975 S.C. 14.

[8] Small Debt (Scotland) Act 1837, s.31; repealed by Sheriff Courts (Scotland) Act 1971.

[9] *cf. Graham v. Robert Younger Ltd*, 1955 J.C. 28. But see now *Cordiner, Petr.*, 1973 J.C. 16, and *Newland, Petr.*, 1994 J.C. 122.

[10] 1995 Act, s.133(2). *cf.* Renton and Brown, para. 1–15. The case of *James Dunlop and Co. Ltd v. Calder*, 1943 J.C. 49, is an example of an anomaly created by the interaction of various statutory enactments and repeals as a result of which the only appeal from an order by a court of summary jurisdiction removing a checker from his position in a coal mine was by the criminal procedure of a stated case, though the procedure for removal "is more analogous to civil than criminal proceedings": L.J.-C. Cooper at 58.

increasing interest in many forms of civil litigation such as actions to recover taxes. But if the interest of the state is combined with the use of criminal procedure, it is possible to arrive at a definition which, while it is by no means perfect, is sufficient for most purposes. The state as prosecutor in a criminal trial is normally distinguishable from the state as pursuer in a civil action. Definition in terms of the state as prosecutor is made easy in Scotland by the extreme rarity of private prosecutions, though these remain anomalous. Almost all prosecutions in Scotland are at the instance of the state, either in the person of the Lord Advocate, the official public prosecutor at common law and in many statutory offences, or of his deputies, or in the person of a prosecutor "in the public interest"[11] such as an official of the Customs and Excise Department.[12] The criminal law is probably, therefore, sufficiently defined as that branch of the law which deals with those acts, attempts and omissions of which the state may take cognisance by prosecution in the criminal courts.[13]

The formal nature of crime

The definition offered makes no reference to the content of the criminal law, or to the factors which determine which acts are made crimes. It is a purely formal definition applying only to the criminal law as it is, without reference to what it should be, or to why it is as it is. It embodies the view that murder and selling drinks outside licensing hours are both crimes for the same reason — they are forbidden by the criminal law.[14] In the words of an American work, "The criminal law is the formal cause of crime . . . Without a criminal code there would be no crime . . . the question involved in the formulation or amendment of a criminal code can be stated as what crimes do we wish to cause."[15] There is as yet no criminal code in Scotland, and the criminal law may still be capable of some extension by judicial decision,[16] but the declaration as criminal by a court of an act not formerly so characterised is not in this regard different from the enactment by a legislature of an addition to a criminal code. Both court and legislature will be influenced by various moral and social considerations, but the act once made criminal will be criminal because it has been so made by court or legislature and not because it is immoral or anti-social, or because of whatever other reason moved the court or legislature to make it **1.05**

---

[11] 1995 Act. s.307(1).

[12] See Renton and Brown, para. 3–05 in particular and Chap. 3 in general.

[13] *cf.* Gl. Williams, *Textbook of Criminal Law* (2nd ed., 1983), pp.27–29. In *R. v. Hull Visitors, ex p. Germain* [1979] Q.B. 425, at 452A Shaw L.J. spoke of "the essential characteristic of a criminal cause or matter, namely, that it is a penal proceeding for the infraction of a requirement relating to the enforcement and preservation of public law and order." For the purposes of Convention rights (*i.e.* those rights under the European Convention on Human Rights referred to in the Human Rights Act 1998, s.1(1)), 'criminal offence' has an autonomous meaning; this means that although the classification of an act or omission as a crime by the domestic law of a contracting State is conclusive of that fact, the classification by that law of an act or omission as something other than a crime (*e.g.* as an 'administrative' offence) will be subject to scrutiny and re-appraisal by the European Court of Human Rights: see P. van Dijk and G.J.H. van Hoof, *Theory and Practice of the European Convention on Human Rights* (3rd ed., The Hague, 1998), pp.77, 407–418.

[14] *cf.* T.B. Smith, p.123; *Mitchell v. Morrison*, 1938 J.C. 64, Lord Moncrieff at 72.

[15] J.Michael and M.Adler, *Crime, Law and Social Science* (London and New York, 1933), 5.

[16] See *infra*. paras 1–43 *et seq.*

criminal. "Acts are criminal not because they *are* harmful, but because they are *deemed* harmful by those who make or interpret the law."[17] The criminal law is amoral in itself, however immoral or moral any of its provisions may be.

> "The criminal quality of an act cannot be discerned by intuition; nor can it be discovered by reference to any standard but one: Is the act prohibited with penal consequences? Morality and criminality are far from co-extensive; nor is the sphere of criminality necessarily part of a more extensive field covered by morality — unless the moral code necessarily disapproves all acts prohibited by the State, in which case the argument moves in a circle."[18]

Crimes and offences

1.06 The definition offered makes no distinctions within the class of acts which the state may prosecute. Scots law has two common terms for criminal acts: "crime" and "offence"; but the terms are not clearly distinguished, and indeed are often used interchangeably,[19] and even statutory uses and definitions are unhelpful.

The Interpretation Act 1889 tried to use them to translate into Scots legal language the rigid English distinction between felonies and misdemeanours, but did so very confusedly. "Felony" was defined as "high crime and offence" and misdemeanour as "offence".[20]

The Prevention of Crimes Act 1871 designated certain types of conduct as "crimes", and defined an "offence" as "any act or omission which is not a crime as defined by this Act, and is punishable on indictment or summary conviction."[21] Section 7 of the Act made it punishable for certain persons to be found in certain places "about to commit . . . any offence punishable on indictment or summary conviction."[22] In *Strathern v. Padden*[23] the accused was charged under section 7 with being found about to commit theft by housebreaking, one of the acts designated as a crime. It was held that the term "offence" in section 7 included acts defined by the Act as crimes. Lord Sands said that the term "offence" had been intended by the legislature for "something which was not so serious as crime but which could be punished on indictment or summary conviction. . . . Every crime is an offence, but every offence is not a crime."[24]

---

[17] M.R.Cohen, *Reason and Law* (Glencoe, Ill., 1950), p.25.

[18] *Proprietary Articles Trade Association v. Attorney-General for Canada* [1931] A.C. 310, Lord Atkin at 324. *Cf.* Lord Devlin, *The Enforcement of Morals* (London, 1965), 20: "The criminal law is not a statement of how people ought to behave; it is a statement of what will happen to them if they do not behave."

[19] *cf.* T.B. Smith, p.122.

[20] s.28. (The 1889 Interpretation Act was repealed and replaced by the Interpretation Act 1978, which did not re-enact the terms of s.28 of the former Act.) It may have been the intention of the 1889 Interpretation Act that Scots courts should read "felony" as "high crime and offence" wherever it appeared in U.K. statutes, but this did not happen, and the words "high crime and offence" have never been part of the ordinary vocabulary of our criminal courts — but see *Gallagher v. H.M. Advocate*, 1937 J.C. 27, esp.L.J.-C. Aitchison at 32. Hume frequently uses the word "feloniously", but this means "wickedly" or "criminally", and does not refer to any specific category of crime. It appears that in earlier times, "felony" was used to describe an assault with intent to kill or do serious injury, but this use is long obsolete: see Hume, ii, 239n.

[21] s.20.

[22] Section 7 was repealed by the Civic Government (Scotland) Act 1982, Sched. 4.

[23] 1926 J.C. 9.

[24] At 14.

The word "offence" is used in this way in ordinary, and often in legal, language, but there is no rule for using the two terms, and no list of crimes or offences.

Certainly the two terms are not used consistently to denote greater and lesser breaches of the criminal law. "Crime" is defined by the 1995 Act, for example, as meaning "any crime or offence at common law or under any Act of Parliament . . . and includes an attempt to commit any crime or offence." No further explanation of "crime" is offered, but "offence" is said to mean "any act, attempt or omission punishable by law."[25] As it is difficult to imagine in what ways "crime" can differ from the proffered definition of "offence", it is tempting to think that the difference must be one of degree. Yet the same Act has a section which forbids District Courts from trying "any of the following offences — (i) murder, culpable homicide, robbery, rape".[26] It must be apparent, therefore, that the two terms do not have any effective differences in meaning; the general rules of the criminal law apply to all breaches of criminal law, whether they are described as crimes or as offences.

MALA IN SE AND MALA PROHIBITA

The view that all breaches of the criminal law are formally equal is not **1.07**
held by the only authoritative modern Scottish textbook on the subject.[27] Macdonald restricts his treatise, as he is entitled to do, to crimes punishable by death or by imprisonment without the option of a fine. But he goes on to say of the offences thus excluded that "Many such offences are not truly crimes, being made punishable to secure the health or comfort of the community."[27a] The criminal law is regarded as divisible into two sections; one deals with "true" crimes, like murder, robbery and rape, while the other is concerned with what are commonly called public welfare offences. The latter are offences created by statute and designed, not directly to preserve life or property or even public order, but to ensure, for example, that only clean food will be sold to the public, or that there will be an equal distribution of certain commodities in times of scarcity. The "true" crime is thought of as something evil in itself — *malum in se*, while the public welfare offences are thought of not as evil or immoral, but as being at best only technically crimes, punishable because they are forbidden by statute — *mala prohibita*.

The legal validity of the distinction

The division of crimes into these two classes is a very old one in the **1.08**
history of criminal theory and must be considered in any study of criminal law, although it has been condemned by some writers as untenable and unfortunate in its effect[28] and as "unscientific and fallacious"[29]; and although the outlook it represents is more the concern of the sociologist than of the lawyer.

---

[25] s.307(1).
[26] s.7(8)(b)(i).
[27] Macdonald, p.1.
[27a] *ibid.*
[28] See J. Hall, *General Principles of Criminal Law* (2nd ed., Indianapolis, 1960), pp.337–341.
[29] C.S. Kenny, *Kenny's Outlines of Criminal Law* (19th ed., J.W.C. Turner (ed.), Cambridge, 1966), para. 17.

1.09 *Mala in se and natural law.* The distinction is not of great importance to the lawyer because its terms are so vague as to be unusable. The idea of *malum in se* is not a legal idea at all, but a moral one. It belongs to the era of natural law theories when certain rights and duties were regarded as absolute, and as a necessary part of any valid system of law.[30] Certain acts were thought of as being absolutely and immutably bad because they were contrary to the "law of nature". These acts, it was thought, must be disapproved of by any society, and might therefore be treated by any society as punishable, even if there were no specific law against them. This view has not merely become outdated because of the great growth in the number and scope of statutory offences; it is untenable in itself. There is probably no act which is absolutely and universally bad. "Deliberate killing is not always murder; sexual intercourse by force and without the victim's consent is not always rape; the taking of another's property without his consent is not always theft; as witness the legally justifiable killing of a condemned criminal by an executioner, the exposure of Australian aboriginal women to sexual attack for violation of the sexual code, or the seizure of an allegedly immoral book by a customs officer."[31] Such acts are, however, fairly generally agreed to be criminal unless there are special circumstances removing their criminality. Once one passes from such basic crimes one finds that ideas of what acts are wrong vary from society to society and from time to time. As Hume pointed out, the "general spirit" of the criminal law "will always, in some measure, be bent and accommodated to the temper and exigencies of the times; directing its severity against those crimes which the manners of the age breed a direct abhorrence of, or which the present condition of the people renders peculiarly hurtful, in their consequences to private or to public peace."[32]

It must also be remembered that there may be acts which are abhorred by a society and yet, for one reason or another, are not made crimes. The criminal law does not include even all the local and contemporary *mala in se* of any time and place. It is not a crime in Scotland to refuse to pay your debts, or to trade as a prostitute, or to commit adultery (though this last was once criminal).

1.10 *Common law crimes and statutory offences.* The use of the phrase *mala prohibita* to describe crimes not *mala in se* suggests that the distinction is between crimes made illegal by statute and crimes recognised as wrong by the common law. But the suggestion that all common law crimes are *mala in se*, and all statutory offences not *mala in se*, will not bear even cursory examination. The moral attitudes to incest are not dissimilar in Scotland and England, and indeed incest is considered wrong in almost every society. The Incest Act 1567 which made incest criminal might have been regarded as merely declaratory of the common law, especially as it incorporated the eighteenth chapter of Leviticus,[33] but incest was not a crime in England until made so by statute in 1908.[34] Moreover,

---

[30] *cf.* W. Friedmann, *Legal Theory,* 5th ed. (N.Y., 1967), Pt. 2.

[31] A. Morris. "The Concept of Crime" in *Criminology*, Vedder, Koenig and Clark (ed.) (New York, 1953), p.22.

[32] Hume, i, 2.

[33] *cf. Neill McColl* (1874) 2 Couper 538. *Cf.* also the modern law in the Criminal Law (Consolidation) (Scotland) Act 1995, ss.1–4, re-enacting the Incest and Related Offences (Scotland) Act 1986 which repealed the 1567 Act.

[34] Punishment of Incest Act 1908, now Sexual Offences Act 1956, ss.10–11.

incest between bastard relations was not criminal in Scotland until 1986[35] but had been criminal in England since 1908, and conversely intercourse between uncle and niece has always been incestuous in Scotland but not in England.[36]

"True" crimes and public welfare offences

The distinction between crimes *mala in se* and crimes only *mala prohibita* cannot, however, be dismissed summarily simply by pointing out its inconsistencies. It has persisted because it forms a convenient way of focusing a widespread and persistent attitude.[37] This attitude is shown in an insistence that certain types of conduct punishable by the law do not deserve to be called crimes, and that those who behave in such a way do not deserve to be classed as criminals. The first meaning of "crime" given in the O.E.D. is "An act punishable by law, as being forbidden by statute or injurious to the public welfare. (Properly including all offences punishable by law, but commonly used only of grave offences)." It is the common usage which is important here, and it approximates more closely to the dictionary's second definition: "More generally: an evil or injurious act; an offence, a sin; *esp.* of a grave character." The typical crime is a dastardly act causing hurt to someone in his person or his property, perpetrated by a rogue or a ruffian. In the words of the old Scots indictments a crime is something which "by the laws of this and of every other well-governed realm" — note the suggestion of *malum in se* — "is of an heinous nature, and severely punishable." **1.11**

The problem of the trivial offence. This usage breaks down when faced with the modern law. The words "crime" and "criminal" seem out of all proportion excessive when applied to petty statutory offences like parking one's car on the wrong side of the street. Common usage revolts at saying even that "it is, for purposes of technical classification, no less a crime to be without an ash-bin of the pattern prescribed by the County Council than to blow up the Houses of Parliament."[38] The law itself recognises this problem. "There is a particular reluctance to use the expressions 'crime' and 'criminal' with reference to summary offences. This is because of the strongly emotive nature of these words, which makes them unsuitable for minor transgressions. Statutes creating summary offences use the less condemnatory term offence."[39] Someone who **1.12**

---

[35] Alison, i, 565; Incest and Related Offences (Scotland) Act 1986, s.1(2)(b), now re-enacted in the Criminal Law (Consolidation) (Scotland) Act 1995, s.1(2)(b).

[36] *cf.* Criminal Law (Consolidation) (Scotland) Act 1995, s.1, and Sexual Offences Act 1956, ss.10–11, re-enacting the Punishment of Incest Act 1908, s.3. And marriage between uncle and niece is prohibited in both Scots and English law (see Marriage (Scotland) Act 1977, s.2(1), Sched. 1, para. 1; Matrimonial Causes Act 1973, s.11(c)(1), Marriage Act 1949, Sched 1, Pt. I) but not in Jewish law; *De Wilton v. Montefiore* [1900] 2 Ch. 481; *Cheni (orse. Rodriguez) v. Cheni* [1965] P. 85.

[37] See P.J. Fitzgerald, "Crime, Sin and Negligence" (1963) 79 L.Q.R. 351.

[38] C.K. Allen, *Legal Duties* (Oxford, 1931), p.240.

[39] Gl. Williams, "On the Definition of Crime" (1955) *Current Legal Problems*, 107 at 111. But it should be noted that modern statutes now invariably refer to the crimes they create as "offences" irrespective of the level of seriousness involved: see, *e.g.*, the Misuse of Drugs Act 1971, where some of the "offences" created carry a maximum punishment of life in prison (see ss.4(2), 4(3) and 5(3) offences, and their corresponding maximum penalties (where Class A drugs are concerned) in Sched. 4, as these have been amended by the Controlled Drugs (Penalties) Act 1985, s.1(1)); and the Road Traffic Act 1988, s.1 (as amended by the Road Traffic Act 1991, s.1) where the "offence" of causing death by dangerous driving carries a maximum penalty of 10 years in prison (Road Traffic Offenders Act 1988, Sched. 2, Pt. I as amended by the Criminal Justice Act 1993, s.67(1)).

commits a crime is a criminal, but someone who commits an offence is only an offender, which is much less reprehensible. Most people today are prepared to admit that they might be, or even have been, offenders, but would be indignant at the suggestion that they were criminals.

1.13 *The problem of the respectable offender.* The matter is more serious than one of linguistic hyperbole, of using the steamroller word "crime" to crush the peanut of the parking offence. A man who steals five pence may be regarded as a true criminal and a man who cheats the income tax of £100 as perfectly respectable. The attitude represented by the distinction between the two types of crimes is important because it resents public welfare offences being treated as crimes; and in this context "public welfare offences" covers all offences which it is still considered respectable to commit. Though the denotation of the term will vary with the person using it, it would fairly generally be thought of as including, for example, smuggling, failing to pay one's social security contributions, dealing in at any rate certain types of black market, driving a motor-car without a licence. The crux of the matter is a breakdown in *rapport* between public opinion and the law. It is not so much a question of the seriousness or triviality of the respectable offences as of their being somehow different in kind from the basic, "old-fashioned" crimes. One result of this difference is that they are committed by respectable people, and so long as respectable people can behave in a particular way without thereby losing their respectability, it will be difficult to regard that kind of behaviour as "criminal". This attitude may even affect offences which would be considered "true" crimes if committed in non-respectable circumstances by what a past generation might have described as "members of the criminal classes."[40] The law itself allows much greater carelessness on the part of motorists without charging them with culpable homicide than it does on the part of housebreakers, or than it did in the nineteenth century on the part of engine-drivers.[41] And even when charges of culpable homicide are brought against motorists convictions are difficult to obtain. Juries feel in such cases that "There, but for the grace of God, go we"; and they also feel, as defending counsel emphasise, that it would be unfair to convict the careless motorist of culpable homicide, because to do so would be to brand him as a "killer", albeit only as a killer by negligence. The legislature eventually recognised this state of affairs and created the statutory offence of killing someone by reckless (now "dangerous") driving,[42] in the hope that juries who were unwilling to convict of the common law crime would be prepared to convict of the statutory offence, an offence which carries with it a maximum penalty as high as, if not higher than,[43] that normally awarded when juries do convict motorists of culpable homicide.

Culpable homicide has special features, but the difficulty with public welfare offences generally is that they are crimes which the community

---

[40] *cf.* Lord Young's refusal in *Campbell v. Maclennan* (1888) 1 White 604 to treat a rich man who gave found money to a beggar as guilty of theft by finding: at 608.

[41] *cf. Paton v. H.M. Advocate,* 1936 J.C. 19; *Wm Paton and Richd McNab* (1845) 2 Broun 525; see Vol. II, Chap. 26.

[42] Road Traffic Act 1956, s.8, now Road Traffic Act 1988, s.1 (as substituted by s.1 of the Road Traffic Act 1991).

[43] The original maximum penalty of five years was increased to 10 years by the Criminal Justice Act 1993, s.67(1).

as a whole does not consider "criminal". There will perhaps always be groups of people who do not consider it reprehensible to commit certain crimes, or who even consider it laudable to do so. For example, at one time the Mormons committed bigamy as a religious duty,[44] and many religious and political groups have considered it laudable to break laws discriminating against them; on a lower moral level, groups like soldiers or factory workers[45] may consider certain forms of dishonesty as permissible, or even as something in which they have a right to engage. But public welfare offences present the problem of a group of many heterogeneous offences which are not considered reprehensible by the bulk of the community, including those people who are looked on as "pillars of respectability".

The moral attitude to crimes

The main reason for the distinction between the true crimes and the respectable offences is that the latter are too different in content from the former to attract the same moral disapproval. Murder, robbery, rape and the like present simple and easily appreciated moral situations. We are all glad of protection against marauders, we all disapprove of rape, we all sympathise with the old lady who has her bag snatched by a young hooligan. As the philosopher David Hume pointed out, sympathy with the victim is to a large extent the base of our moral disapproval of the criminal and his misdeeds.[46] The origin of such sympathy is an imaginative identification with the victim; in Shelley's phrase, "the great instrument of moral good is the imagination". We disapprove of assault because we know what it would be like to be assaulted and can imagine the victim's pain. This imaginative identification becomes very difficult when the victim is not an individual, and where it is difficult to see where the pain or loss is being suffered. The typical "true" crimes are crimes against individuals, their persons, property or honour. Even treason was originally a breach of fealty to the King as an individual feudal lord.[47] Imaginative sympathy with the needs of the bureaucratic state, or of a bank, is difficult, and it is almost impossible to feel such sympathy with a town plan or with the purpose of an export control order, especially when these deprive particular individuals in whom we are interested of their property or livelihood. Instead there can only be a reasoned view, arrived at after an intellectual appreciation of the situation, that the law is worthy of approval.[48] Many people are not capable of making this appreciation, and even those who are are not affected by it as strongly as by their instinctive feelings about the simple crimes. And the longer the chain of reasoning the weaker the final reaction. **1.14**

We are used to the idea of stealing from a bank, but this is sufficiently like stealing from an individual for us to be able to carry over our disapproval of stealing to stealing from a bank. When we apply our minds to the similarities between stealing from a bank and from an individual we feel that stealing from a bank is a "true" crime. But if we

---

[44] *cf. Reynolds v. U.S.*, 98 U.S. 145 (1878).

[45] See H. Mannheim, *Group Problems in Crime and Punishment* (London, 1955), pp.23–24.

[46] Hume, *Treatise on Human Nature* III, iii, 2.

[47] See Treason Act 1351; C.S. Kenny, *Kenny's Outlines of Criminal Law* (19th ed., J.W.C. Turner (ed.), Cambridge, 1966), para. 400.

[48] I am not concerned here with the problem of the morally bad law, but with a law which is *ex hypothesi* worthy of approval.

consider instead that the thief may be in dire need of the money, that the bank will not notice an odd few hundred pounds, that the bank will be insured against theft, and that it can always print new notes anyway, this clarity is somewhat dimmed.

And if the bank is defrauded and not robbed the initial analogy will lose some of its force — cheating is not on the whole considered to be as bad as stealing, just because it is more complicated and less brutal.[49]

Moreover, banks and insurance companies are remote institutions, unlike the little old lady next door. As Hume pointed out, "the imagination is more affected by what is particular than by what is general . . . we sympathise more with persons contiguous to us, than with persons remote from us."[50] We are moved more by the sight of a beggar on our doorstep than by the thought of the starving millions of India.

The gap need not be spatial, it can also be consequential, as is illustrated by the common attitude to commercial or revenue offences.[51] People who commit such offences view their acts in isolation, and do not consider their consequences on society in general, or what would happen if everyone behaved as they do — if indeed they consider their acts at all from a moral point of view.

This failure in public response to parts of the criminal law is not in itself something new, brought into being by modern public welfare regulations. It seems in one form or another to be inherent in any complex society, which suggests that, at any rate in the modern world, the existence of public welfare offences may be almost as universal and necessary as that of "true" crimes. Beccaria, writing in 1775, said of smuggling:

> "This crime being a theft of what belongs to the prince, and consequently, to the nation, why is it not attended with infamy? I answer, that crimes, which men consider as productive of no bad consequences to themselves, do not interest them sufficiently to excite their imagination. The generality of mankind, upon whom remote consequences make no impression, do not see the evil that may result from the practice of smuggling, especially if they reap from it any present advantage."[52]

It is because public welfare offences do not excite moral indignation that they do not bring social disgrace to those who commit them. These people do not consider themselves criminals; if anything, they consider the law itself to be "criminal," and indignation is directed against the law which makes the crime, and not against the crime. And when they seek

---

[49] The tendency to concentrate on the individualistic nature of crime is illustrated by the case of *Foster v. H.M.Advocate*, 1932 J.C. 75, where it was held that a wife who forged her husband's name on a cheque had committed a crime against him, in the same way as if she had stolen money from his pocket. The court seized on this idea of individual loss in order to invoke the rule allowing a husband to give evidence against his wife where she has committed a crime against him, and even defending counsel does not seem to have taken the point that the crime was really one against the bank which would presumably be liable to credit the husband's account with the amount of the forged cheques. It has been said in England that a spouse is not a competent witness in such a case because the crime is one against the bank: *e.g. R. v. Algar* [1954] 1 Q.B.279, Lord Goddard at 285–286.

[50] Hume, *op.cit.* III, iii, 1.

[51] *cf.* on this aspect of the matter, E.H. Sutherland, "White Collar Criminality" in *Criminology*, Vedder, Koenig and Clark (ed.) (New York), 1935, p.406.

[52] Marquis Beccaria, *An Essay on Crimes and Punishments* (5th ed., in English; London, 1804), pp.133–134.

some theoretical justification for their attitude the offenders may turn to the distinction between *malum in se* and *malum prohibitum.* This distinction reflects a difference not in legal quality but in public attitudes, and as such it is one which the legislator must bear in mind. To create a large number of offences which do not excite moral indignation may weaken general respect for the law and weaken the feeling, based in part on the coincidence of the basic crimes with moral prohibitions, that it is morally wrong to disobey the criminal law. The absence of public indignation may also make it inexpedient to punish public welfare offences in the same way as other crimes are punished, even if it is necessary to make them offences, and courts may moderate their sentences accordingly. For "By inflicting infamous punishment, for crimes that are not reputed so, we destroy that idea where it might be useful."[53]

On the other hand, punishing public welfare offences in the same way as other crimes may lead the public to regard the public welfare offences as serious matters, and to feel indignant about them. Such a change in attitudes may presently be taking place with regard to certain road traffic offences such as dangerous or drunken driving.[54] These matters, however, are the concern of the legislator, the sociologist and the penologist, rather than of the legal theorist.

It should be noted, too, that the fact that conduct does excite moral disapproval is sometimes given as a reason for treating it as a "real" crime, even though it is prohibited only by statute, the effect of this being that the courts will, wherever possible, ensure that persons are not convicted of the statutory offence in the absence of *mens rea*.[55]

The Declaratory Power of the High Court

1.15 In Scotland, however, the legal theorist could not until recently ignore questions of criminal legislation altogether. For the High Court of Justiciary appeared to retain a power to create new crimes. The power was described by Hume as "an inherent power . . . to punish . . . every act which is obviously of a criminal nature",[56] and its continued existence was affirmed in comparatively recent times[57] although the extent of its actual exercise was always problematic.

General objections to the exercise of the declaratory power

1.16 There are a number of objections to any exercise of such a power, and these objections have greater practical force when directed against the

[53] *ibid*. 139.

[54] In the English civil case of *Marcel Beller Ltd v. Hayden* [1978] 1 Q.B. 694, at 707D Fay J. said that even if an insurance policy's exclusion clause, which made reference to the injured person's 'own criminal acts', was confined to crimes of moral culpability or turpitude: "I am satisfied that the offences of dangerous driving and driving while under the influence of drink are sufficiently serious to qualify."

[55] See *e.g. Sweet v. Parsley* [1970] A.C. 132; *infra*, para. 8.06; *cf.* W.G. Carson, "The Sociology of Crime and the Emergence of Criminal Laws" in *Deviance and Social Control,* Rock and McIntosh (ed.) (London, 1974).

[56] Hume, i, 12.

[57] *Grant v. Allan*, 1987 J.C. 71, L.J.-C. Ross at 77; *Sugden v. H.M. Advocate,* 1934 J.C. 103, L.J.-C. Aitchison at 109; *Logue v. H.M. Advocate,* 1932 J.C. 1, L.J.-G. Clyde at 3; *cf.* T.B. Smith, pp.126–129.

creation of public welfare offences than when directed against the creation or extension of crimes thought of as *mala in se* and generally regarded with moral disapproval.

(i) *The principle of legality; nullum crimen sine lege.* The main objection is that the exercise of such a power infringes the principle that no one should be punished for an act which was not legally proscribed at the time he did it. It is not necessary that the accused should have known the act was criminal if in fact it was recognised by the law as criminal so that the accused could have known it had he inquired — from this point of view the principle of legality is a corollary of the maxim *ignorantia juris neminem excusat.* The principle probably also requires that each crime should be capable of fairly precise definition so that its application to any particular set of facts can be seen clearly. A man contemplating a course of action is entitled to due notice of the fact that it is criminal; otherwise it is unfair to punish him for having broken the law. The fiction that the courts merely discover what has always been the law is here disregarded in favour of the reality of judicial legislation; and indeed the fiction does not seem to have been called in aid by the High Court to justify its former exercise of the power. The principle of legality requires that penal legislation should not be retrospective, but the decisions of British courts are always retrospective.

The principle of legality has great force when applied to administrative offences, social regulations and the like. It has much less cogency when applied to acts which arouse wide and strong disapproval. A good part of the strength of the principle rests on the assumption that had the accused known his act was criminal he would not have acted as he did; that he acted in the belief that he was not breaking the law, or at least in ignorance of the fact that he was. This may be said plausibly of an act like celebrating a clandestine marriage which involves "no injurious consequences to person or property, and constitutes no distinct or palpable violation of public morals",[58] and which is not "so grossly immoral and mischievous on the face of it, that no man can fairly be ignorant of its nature, or settled by a course of experience, and become notorious, that such is its nature."[59] But the argument rings a little hollow when advanced by a man charged with violating the chastity of a sleeping woman,[60] or with bribery.[61] The weakness, and indeed the danger, of the principle of *nullum crimen* can be seen when it is used, as it has been, to attack the propriety of the conviction of Nazi leaders for acts condemned as utterly evil by all civilised societies, and characterised as "crimes against humanity".[62]

1.17 (ii) *The danger of turning the law into a political instrument.* There is a fear that if the courts have wide powers to declare acts criminal because they are materially dangerous to public welfare, the law may become an arbitrary instrument of political power. If it were the law that any act thought by the court to be contrary to public welfare was *ipso facto* criminal, the position would not be very different from that in totalitarian countries where courts may declare an act unlawful if it is

[58] *John Ballantyne* (1859) 3 Irv. 352, L.J.-C. Inglis at 360.

[59] *Bernard Greenhuff and Ors* (1838) 2 Swin. 236, Lord Mackenzie at 268.

[60] *Chas Sweenie* (1858) 3 Irv. 109.

[61] *Logue v. H.M. Advocate*, 1932 J.C. 1.

[62] See, *e.g.*, W.J. Bosch, *Judgement on Nuremberg* (North Carolina, 1970), *passim*; *cf.* P. Papadatos, *The Eichmann Trial* (London, 1964), pp.63–71.

"socially dangerous"[63] or contrary to the "Gesundes Volksempfindung".[64] This fear is perhaps not of practical importance in a parliamentary democracy with an independent judiciary but it underlies the almost instinctive dislike of a system which disregards the principle of legality. And it is perhaps worth remembering that the High Court declared combinations of workmen to be illegal in 1813[65] after a series of differences of judicial opinion, only thirteen years before Parliament declared them legal.[66]

(iii) *The usurpation of the function of Parliament.* Where there is a parliamentary democracy the main objection to the power is that it constitutes a usurpation by the court of the functions of Parliament. It might, of course, have been argued at one time that rapid action by the High Court, in criminalising matters of (*e.g.*) pressing social concern, was required in view of an alleged lack of attention to Scottish matters by a Parliament which sat in Westminster and which was dominated by members representing English constituencies: but the advent of the Scottish Parliament in 1999 has made such argument almost untenable in the general field of criminal law.[67] **1.18**

The common law today has evolved sufficiently to include all "grossly immoral and mischievous conduct",[68] and complex matters of social control are better dealt with by a Parliament guided by a government or executive with access to relevant information not available to the courts, and with the right of an elected sovereign body to impose restrictions on the citizen's activities. Conversely, even where acts are generally recognised as wrong and worthy of public disapproval there may be reasons for not making them crimes. "If Parliament is not disposed to provide punishments for acts which are upon any ground objectionable or dangerous, the presumption is that they belong to that class of misconduct against which the moral feeling and good sense of the community are the best protection."[69] As Lord Reid said in his dissenting speech in *Shaw v. D.P.P.*,[70] "where Parliament fears to tread it is not for the courts to rush in."[71] **1.19**

---

63 Russian Penal Code, 1926, referred to in J. Hall, *Principles of Criminal Law* (2nd ed., Indianopolis, 1960), p.48. Soviet law eventually accepted the principle of legality: see, *e.g.* Criminal code of R.S.F.S.R., 1960, Art. 3.

64 German Act of June 28, 1935; see Hall, *op.cit.*, p. 48.

65 *Arthur Ferrier* (1813) Hume, i, 496.

66 Combinations of Workmen Act 1825, s.4; *cf.* Hume. I, 496–497.

67 See the Scotland Act 1998, s.1: most of the criminal law is devolved to the new Parliament, but *cf.* Sched. 1, Pt. II for reserved matters.

68 T.B. Smith, p.125.

69 Report of Royal Commission on the Draft Code, 1879, C–2345, 10.

70 [1962] A.C. 220, at 275.

71 See also *H.M. Advocate v. Semple*, 1937 J.C. 41, L.J.-C. Aitchison at 46; Lord Fleming at 47; and Lord Moncrieff at 49 (although the decision prompting the relevant dicta was overruled in *Docherty v. Brown*, 1996 S.C.C.R. 136); *Quinn v. Cunningham*, 1956 J.C. 22 (overruled, but not *quoad* the relevant issue — *viz.* the standard of carelessness required for a common law crime, by *H.M. Advocate v. Harris*, 1993 J.C. 150); *Grant v. Allan*, 1987 J.C. 71, L.J.-C. Ross at 77–78; *H.M. Advocate v. Forbes* 1994 S.L.T. 861, L.J.-G. Hope at 864C; *R. v. Bhagwan* [1972] A.C. 60, Lord Diplock at 82; *R. v. Knuller (Publishing, etc.) Ltd* [1973] A.C. 435, Lord Reid at 457–458; Lord Simon of Glaisdale at 490; *R. v.Withers* [1975] A.C. 842. *Cf. R. v. Clegg* [1995] 1 A.C. 482, Lord Lloyd of Berwick at 500F-G.

The Evolution and Application of the Declaratory Power

1.20 *The declaratory power before Greenhuff.* Little of value is to be gained by considering the exercise of the declaratory power before the leading case of *Bernard Greenhuff.*[72] Up to the time of Hume the law was still in its formative period, and in the absence of much legislation had to be developed by the courts. The main trend of development appears to have been by way of extending the scope of attempt by the creation of preventive crimes,[73] but Hume himself deprecated this and took the view that it was for Parliament to create preventive crimes.[74] There are, however, two nineteenth century cases in which the court created crimes of this kind. In *Chas Macqueen and Alex. Baillie*[75] it was held that housebreaking with intent to steal was a crime, although attempted theft was not then indictable. In *John Horne*[76] it was held to be a crime for a forger to sell forged notes, as forged, to an accomplice, because, *inter alia*, "In itself, such a dealing was a criminal act, and one of a dangerous as well as a base nature." The court vacillated between regarding this as a new crime and regarding it as a form of attempted uttering, but it represents an extension of attempt beyond what is consonant with general principle, and as such may be regarded as an exercise of the declaratory power.[77]

1.21 *The case of Greenhuff.* The classic case on the declaratory power is *Bernard Greenhuff*, in 1838.[77a] The charge was of keeping a public gaming house, and the High Court held by a majority, Lord Cockburn dissenting, that this was a crime, as having "a tendency to corrupt public morals, and injure the interests of society,"[78] and as an example of acts "by the law of God, and the laws of morality *mala in se.*"[79] The most interesting and important judgment is that of Lord Cockburn, and his dissent was at one time regarded as expressing the modern law.[80] This division of opinion, following as it did on the legalisation by Parliament of workmen's combinations which the High Court had declared illegal,[81] must have brought the exercise of the declaratory power into some disrepute, and made the court very chary of using it in future. Workmen's combinations at least had conjured up the spectre of Jacobinism, but it is difficult to believe that people who had lived in Regency Edinburgh regarded gambling with any great moral indignation; nor was it clear why public gambling should be *malum in se* and private gambling innocuous.

Lord Cockburn objected strongly to the view that everything dangerous to public morals should be indictable, pointing out that there are

---

[72] (1838) 2 Swin. 236.

[73] See Lord Walker, "The Growth of the Criminal Law," 1958 J.R. 230.

[74] Hume, i. 29.

[75] (1810) Hume, i, 102.

[76] (1814) Hume, i, 150–153.

[77] Alison, i, 406, and Macdonald, p.69, regard selling forged notes as forged to an accomplice as an independent crime. *Cf.* also *Chas Costello* (1882) 4 Couper 602 where a charge of sending explosives with intent that they should explode and cause bodily injury was held to set forth an innominate offence. But in fact bodily injury was caused, although this was libeled only as an aggravation of the innominate offence.

[77a] (1838) 2 Swin. 236.

[78] (1838) 2 Swin. 236, L.J.-C. Boyle at 261.

[79] Lord Meadowbank at 262.

[80] T.B. Smith, *loc. cit.*

[81] *supra*, para. 1.17.

"innumerable notorious overt acts . . . deeply injurious to individuals, and to the public" which are not crimes.[82] Lord Cockburn's own view is summarised in the following extract:

> "It has been said, that it is in the power of this Court to declare, that is, to *introduce*, new crimes; and that if it be in our power, it is our duty to do so on fitting occasions. I dissent utterly from this doctrine; and, if a proper occasion for discussing it shall ever arise, I shall endeavour to explain why I do so. I may only say at present that I am far from holding that the Court can never deal with anything as a crime, unless there be a fixed *nomen juris* for the specific act, or unless there be a *direct precedent*. An old crime may certainly be committed in a new way; and a case, though never occurring before in its facts, may fall within the *spirit* of a previous decision, or within an established *general principle*. . . . But this is not the meaning of the doctrine, as usually announced, when it is said that this Court can declare new crimes. There is no such declaration, nor the exercise of any extraordinary power needed, in the Court's merely determining that an act that has never presented itself before, *comes within the range of a known term, case, or principle*. The meaning of the doctrine is this, — that though vice may invent a *totally original offence*, — never heard of before, — and for which law has not only no name, but which is not included within any known penal description or principle, *but which is in its whole nature entirely new,* — still, *if it imply wickedness and be hurtful,* the Court of Justiciary, *treating it as an entirely unheard of thing*, may, in virtue of what is termed its *'inherent powers'*, introduce it as a new crime. *"It is from this that I dissent."*[83]

In this passage, Lord Cockburn confuses two things when he puts together previous decisions and general principles. It will be readily accepted that a new mode of committing an old crime is clearly criminal and does not need to be declared so, but the matter is more difficult when one passes to conduct falling under a known principle. If a principle is expressed sufficiently widely many different forms of conduct may fall under it, and the addition of a new form of conduct will amount to the creation of a new crime. This may have been a legitimate exercise of the declaratory power, as opposed to the kind of exercise criticised by Lord Cockburn, but it was nonetheless an exercise, and it is submitted that Lord Cockburn was wrong in denying this. For example, theft in Scots law involves an intention to appropriate another person's goods, and it is therefore quite a different crime from *furtum possessionis*, although both fall under the recognised principle of dishonest dealing with other people's property rights. It may be legitimate to use this principle to make *furtum possessionis* a crime, but to do so is to declare a new crime, and not merely to punish a new way of committing theft.[84] **1.22**

The difference between recognising a new mode of committing an old crime and creating a new crime is often largely one of degree, but some more modern examples of the exercise of the declaratory power have important affinities with creation. Where the old crime is something specific and easily defined, like theft by housebreaking, there is little

---

[82] At 277.
[83] At 274.
[84] See Vol. II, Chap. 14.

difficulty in deducing that a particular set of facts constitutes a form of committing it, without seeming to create a new crime. To decide that it is not housebreaking to enter by using a key found in the lock, but that it is housebreaking to use a false key[85] requires nothing more revolutionary than the exercise of logical deduction. This is merely interpretation of the meaning of "housebreaking." But where the "old" crime is described in very general terms as, for example, "shamelessly indecent conduct",[86] the decision that a certain type of conduct falls under the definition is not so much a question of logic as of public policy, or of the moral attitude of the members of the High Court.[87]

1.23 *The other nineteenth century cases. Greenhuff*[88] was followed by a case which illustrates these distinctions. In *John Barr*[89] the charge was of making a false oath in a declaration required by the Reform Act as a condition of voting in an election. The court had no difficulty in holding that this was a crime. Lord Mackenzie referred specifically to *Greenhuff*[90]; Lord Moncrieff regarded it a form of the *crimen falsi*,[91] which is not *a* crime in Scots law but a description of a class of crimes; Lord Cockburn regarded it as coming under the recognised principle exemplified by perjury that the "deceptive invasion of the rights of others" and the obstruction of legal proceedings "by the solemn asseveration of falsehood" were criminal.[92] But the crime was not perjury, since the statutory oath did not contain the appeal to the deity then considered essential for perjury, and the court were creating a new crime, although the creation may have been legitimate because they were able to place the crime in a known category, albeit they were not agreed as to which was the appropriate category.

1.24 The most important post-*Greenhuff*[92a] case in the nineteenth century is *Wm Fraser* in 1847,[93] in which the accused contrived to have sexual intercourse with a woman by pretending to be her husband. He was charged with "Rape; as also [Assault with intent to ravish]; As also Fraudulently and Deceitfully obtaining Access to and having Carnal Knowledge of a Married Woman, by pretending to be her husband". All the judges were satisfied that this act though "hitherto . . . unknown in the annals of this Court"[94] was a crime. The only difference of opinion was whether it was rape or fraud, and the majority of the court held that it was fraud.[95] The circumstances are more like rape than fraud,[96] and one would expect them to be treated either as a way of committing rape or as a new crime. The judges, however, were in a dilemma. They were

---

[85] See Macdonald, pp.26–29.
[86] *McLaughlan v. Boyd*, 1934 J.C. 19.
[87] *cf. R. v. Withers* [1975] A.C. 842, Lord Simon of Glaisdale at 863D-G, 872A-D.
[88] (1838) 2 Swin. 236.
[89] (1839) 2 Swin. 282.
[90] *ibid.* at 310.
[91] At 314.
[92] At 317.
[92a] (1838) 2 Swin. 236.
[93] (1847) Ark. 280.
[94] Lord Medwyn at 307.
[95] Or at least was conduct which was criminal because it was analogous to fraud; see Vol. II, Chap. 18.
[96] Parliament later declared them to be rape: Criminal Law Amendment Act 1885, s.4, now Criminal Law (Consolidation) (Scotland) Act 1995, s.7(3), as amended by the Crime and Punishment (Scotland) Act 1997, Sched. 1, para. 18(3).

unwilling to characterise the accused's actings as rape because rape was then still technically a capital crime, and they were unwilling to extend the scope of the death penalty. But they did not want to create a wholly new crime, because they accepted Lord Cockburn's view that "We are not entitled to create, or to aggravate, crimes by fanciful analogies or speculative expedience."[97] The analogy between Fraser's actings and fraud may appear at first blush to be more fanciful than that with rape, but the court relied on the view that "Any deceit that injures and violates the rights of another, is clearly punishable."[98] In the result Fraser was convicted of what was at least a new species of fraud, and was sentenced to 20 years' transportation.[99] In this way the difficulties were reconciled — no new crime was created, no extension was made of the scope of the death penalty, and Fraser received his just deserts.

A similar problem arose in *Chas Sweenie* in 1858[1] where the charge **1.25**
was of rape or alternatively of "wickedly and feloniously having carnal knowledge of a woman when asleep, and without her consent". This is sometimes called "clandestine injury to women",[2] but that is only a shorthand label; *Sweenie*[2a] did not create a new crime of clandestine injury, or indeed any new crime at all. For the same reasons as applied in *Fraser*[2b] the majority of the court refused to regard the facts as amounting to rape.[3] They did not, however, say that they formed a new crime; they said instead that they were a way of committing an old one, although they were not over-happy about which old one, and safeguarded themselves by saying that the facts could be brought within the scope of more than one known crime.[4] On the whole, thy seemed to think it was a form of indecent assault,[5] but did not consider the argument that an indecent assault involving penetration is rape.

In the following year the High Court had no hesitation in refusing to **1.26**
declare the celebration of a clandestine marriage to be a common law crime. Lord Justice-Clerk Inglis said:

> "[I]t is difficult to imagine anything less answering the description of *malum in se*, than the mere non-observance . . . of a form or ceremony which is required for the sake of decency and order, but the omission . . . of which is followed by no injurious consequences

---

[97] At 307.

[98] Lord Cockburn at 312.

[99] Ark. 329.

[1] (1858) 3 Irv. 109.

[2] Macdonald, 120; *H.M. Advocate v. Grainger and Rae,* 1932 J.C. 40, Lord Anderson at 41.

[2a] (1858) 3 Irv. 109.

[2b] (1847) Ark. 280.

[3] See L.J.-C. Aitchison in *H.M. Advocate v. Logan,* 1936 J.C. 100, 102.

[4] Lord Deas at 146; L.J.-G. McNeill at 154.

[5] Lord Ardmillan at 138; L.J.-G. McNeill at 154; *cf. H.M. Advocate v. Logan*, 1936 J.C. 100, L.J.-C. Aitchison at 102. It now seems accepted that to have intercourse with a woman too drunk to give or refuse consent, where she has not been made drunk by the accused, is to commit indecent assault, and the same would apply to intercourse with a sleeping woman: *Sweeney v. X.*, 1982 S.C.C.R. 509 (see Vol. II, Chap. 33). Nevertheless, charges of 'clandestine injury to women' are occasionally brought; and the statutory restrictions on evidence relating to sexual offences are applied to offences which include both 'clandestine injury to women' and 'indecent assault' — Criminal Procedure (Scotland) Act 1995, s.274(2)(c) and (e): see also the Sex Offenders Act 1997, Sched. 1, para. 2(1)(a).

to person or property, and constitutes no distinct or palpable violation of public morals."[6]

The idea that the declaratory power was restricted to injury to person or property appears again in *H.M. Advocate v. Coutts*,[7] itself an example of the recognised crime of violating sepulchres, in which Lord McLaren described the exercise of the power as "not an attempt to make a species of facts hitherto well known into a crime, but a crime consisting in some mode (hitherto unknown) of dealing unlawfully with the person or property of another."[8]

1.27 The only other nineteenth-century case which requires to be noted is *Holmes and Lockyer*[9] in which Lord Justice-Clerk Patton, sitting alone as a trial judge, held that it was a crime at common law to "open, intercept, or detain" a letter in the post. Lord Patton justified his decision partly by reference to an unreported case in 1826[10] in which a charge of detaining letters obtained by fraud had been sustained, and partly by describing the offence as "a breach of the law of property"; but he also regarded it as a breach "of a law of society requiring that [post office letters] should be sacred in the name of delivery", since the Post Office is an institution of the state "and the protection of communications entrusted to the Post-office is of the highest importance to society."[11] The decision in *Holmes and Lockyer*[11a] can easily be justified by reference to the fact that one of the accused was a postman; breach of duty by a public official is a common law crime, and there is authority for its application to postmen,[12] although the charge in *Holmes and Lockyer*[12a] was not libelled as breach of duty. But the language used by Lord Patton with its reference to the interests of society and the institutions of the state has an uncomfortable ring to it.

1.28 *The twentieth century cases.* The continued existence of the declaratory power has been asserted in recent times,[13] but the power has not been explicitly used in any twentieth-century case. On the contrary, there are cases in which the court has expressly refused to exercise it. In *H.M. Advocate v. Dick*[14] Lord Young held that a charge against a magistrate of soliciting a bribe did not amount to an attempt to take a bribe, and said that if there were grounds for thinking that the public interest required more protection against the misconduct of magistrates than the common law provided, it was for the legislature and not the courts to consider this.[15] In *H.M. Advocate v. Semple*[16] the court refused to create the crime

---

[6] *John Ballantyne* (1859 3 Irv. 352, 359–360; *cf.* Alison, i. 624: "By the common law every new crime . . . becomes the object of punishment, provided it be in itself wrong, and hurtful to the persons or property of others."

[7] (1899) 3 Adam 50.

[8] At 59.

[9] (1869) 1 Couper 221.

[10] *Alexander Barland*, June 5, 1826.

[11] At 237.

[11a] (1869) 1 Couper 221.

[12] Alison, i, 635; *Donald Smith* (1827) Syme 185.

[12a] (1869) 1 Couper 221.

[13] *e.g., Sugden v. H.M. Advocate*, 1934 J.C. 103, L.J.-C. Aitchison at 109; *Grant v. Allan*, 1987 J.C. 71, L.J.-C. Ross at 77.

[14] (1901) 3 Adam 344.

[15] At 353.

[16] 1937 J.C. 41.

of administering abortifacients to a non-pregnant woman with intent to cause an abortion, holding that to declare even such obviously immoral conduct to be criminal would be to usurp the function of the legislature,[17] yet such conduct clearly falls under a "known principle" in the sense used by Lord Cockburn in *Bernard Greenhuff.*[18] In *Quinn v. Cunningham,*[19] Lord Justice-General Clyde observed that it was for Parliament and not the courts to make it a crime to ride a pedal cycle recklessly.[20] In *H.M. Advocate v. Martin*[21] Lord Cameron explicitly stated that in treating an attempt to defeat the ends of justice by arranging the escape of a prisoner from a working-party outside the prison walls as criminal he was not exercising the declaratory power. Further, in *Grant v. Allan,*[22] the court declined to create the crime of taking copies, without lawful authority, of confidential information belonging to one's employer with intent to dispose of those copies to trade rivals for profit, Lord Justice-Clerk Ross and Lord McDonald holding that there were too many practical difficulties involved in the creation of such a crime and that in any event the correct place for consideration of such issues was Parliament.

Despite this strong body of authority there are a number of cases in which what was done was an exercise of the power, although ostensibly the power was not exercised — most of the cases started as summary complaints — and no explicit reference was made to it. Many of the cases concern offences against the administration of justice, and the courts have dealt with the conduct brought before them by treating it as a form of the crime of hindering or "attempting to pervert" the course of justice. It will be argued, however, that hindering the administration of justice is not *a* crime, but a quality of certain acts which may make them criminal, and that accordingly in declaring conduct to be criminal because it possessed this quality the court was in effect creating new crimes.

STRATHERN V. SEAFORTH.[23] This case is the clearest example of an **1.29**
exercise of the declaratory power in this century although the power was not referred to by any of the judges.[24] The accused had taken another person's motor car away clandestinely and in the knowledge that the owner would not have permitted him to do so, but with the intention of returning it after a short while — *i.e.*, without any intention of stealing it, as the law of theft then stood.[25] Defence counsel argued that the facts constituted *furtum usus*, a recognised type of conduct which was not

---

[17] "It may be reprehensible conduct; it may be injurious to private and public morality; it may be conduct which ought to be criminal conduct; but that will not make it a crime by the law of Scotland": L.J.-C. Aitchison at 45–46.

[18] (1838) 2 Swin. 236, *supra,* para. 1.21.

[19] 1956 J.C. 22.

[20] At 25; Parliament did make it criminal in the Road Traffic Act 1956, s.11, now Road Traffic Act 1988, s.28, which, as amended by s.7 of the Road Traffic Act 1991, applies only to dangerous cycling as therein defined.

[21] 1956 J.C. 1.

[22] 1987 J.C. 71, L.J.-C. Ross at 77–78, Lord McDonald at 79. See also *H.M. Advocate v. Forbes*, 1994 S.L.T. 861, where the court held that no such crime as housebreaking with intent to commit rape existed, and that if such a new preventative crime was needed, this was best left to the legislature.

[23] 1926 J.C. 100.

[24] The case was later referred to by L.J.-C. Aitchison in *Sugden v. H.M. Advocate,* 1934 J.C. 103, 109, as an exercise of the power.

[25] See Vol. II, Chap. 14 for the modern law of theft.

criminal by the law of Scotland,[26] but the court did not rely on the analogy with *furtum usus* and did not decide whether *furtum usus* was a crime in Scotland.[27] The decision that the facts constituted a crime depended not so much on their being a species of dishonesty as simply on the necessity of stopping people from behaving as the accused had done — *i.e.* very nearly on the ground that such actings were contrary to the public interest. As Lord Justice-Clerk Alness said, "In these days when one is familiar with the circumstances in which motor cars are openly parked in the public street, the result [of holding that the facts did not constitute a crime] would be not only lamentable but absurd. I am satisfied that our common law is not so powerless as to be unable to afford a remedy in circumstances such as these."[28] This decision anticipated section 28 of the Road Traffic Act 1930,[29] a fact which may be regarded either as a justification of the decision, or as an indication that the courts were usurping the function of Parliament. It is true that the offence was one against property, but the facts can hardly be said to constitute a new way of committing an old offence - if it was not a crime to borrow a horse and cart without the owner's permission, and no authority was produced in *Strathern v. Seaforth*[29a] to suggest that it was, to make it a crime to borrow a car without permission was to create a new crime. No doubt the car-borrowing involved stealing the petrol used on the "joy-ride"[30] but that was not made part of the charge.

Although the reason for the decision in *Strathern v. Seaforth*[30a] was a desire to put a stop to joy-riding, the case goes much further than this, and is authority for the proposition that the clandestine taking and use of another's property without his permission is a crime.[31] In a subsequent case[32] a fishmonger was charged with clandestinely taking possession of a number of fish boxes and using them to transport his fish to market. He was acquitted because his actings were not clandestine, but it was not disputed that if they had been clandestine he would have been guilty of a crime. *Strathern v. Seaforth*[32a] is not relied on much in practice now that joy-riding can be dealt with under the Road Traffic Act and that unlawful borrowing for an indefinite period may be charged as theft,[33] but charges of this kind have been brought in connection with boats and pedal cycles. There is therefore some ground for suggesting that *Strathern v. Seaforth*[33a] did not merely create a new crime, but a new principle which is wide enough to embrace the use of fish boxes as well as the driving of vehicles.[34]

---

[26] At 101.

[27] T.B. Smith, p.194; *Peter Alston and Alex. Forrest* (1837) 1 Swin. 433, L.J.-C. Boyle at 465. There are some cases dealing with the borrowing of books to copy secrets: *Dewar* (1777) Burnett 115; *H.M. Advocate v. Mackenzies* (1913) 7 Adam 189: see Vol. II, Chap. 14; but although these were cited by the Crown in argument they are so special that they are not really in point.

[28] At 102.

[29] Now s.178 of the Road Traffic Act 1988.

[30] *cf.* Lord Hunter at 102.

[29a] 1926 J.C. 100.

[31] L.J.-C. Alness at 102.

[30a] 1926 J.C. 100.

[32] *Murray v. Robertson*, 1927 J.C. 1.

[32a] 1926 J.C. 100.

[33] See, *e.g.*, *Fowler v. O'Brien*, 1994 S.C.C.R. 112, although there was an absence of clandestinity in the case.

[33a] 1926 J.C. 100.

[34] On the limits of this crime, see Vol. II, Chap. 15.

MCLAUGHLAN V. BOYD.[35] In this case there were two groups of charges, both arising out of homosexual conduct. The first consisted of charges of indecent assault, and as to these there is no dispute. The second group consisted of charges of using "lewd, indecent and libidinous practices" by seizing another man's hand and "placing it" on the accused's private parts. The language even of this second group is suggestive of assault, as is that of Lord Justice-General Clyde in denying that it is the law that "indecent conduct committed by one person upon another only constitutes a crime when the victim . . . is below [the age of] puberty."[36] But the decision that the charges in the second group were relevant and constituted common law crimes was reached by adopting a statement in Macdonald that "all shamelessly indecent conduct is criminal".[37] Although the facts constituted an offence under the Criminal Law Amendment Act 1885,[38] this was not regarded as evidence of their criminality; on the contrary, it was argued that the creation of the statutory offence showed that the behaviour was not criminal at common law. The existence of the statutory offence may, however, have made it easier for the court to regard the accused's behaviour as criminally indecent. **1.30**

The only other reference to authority was to Hume's "broad definition of crime — a doleful or wilful offence against society in the matter of 'violence, dishonesty, falsehood, indecency, irreligion' "[39] which is no more than a description of the characteristics of the specific acts which are (or, rather, were in Hume's day) regarded as criminal. It does not follow from the fact that all crimes are offences against society in one of the ways listed (assuming that this is the case) that any offence against society in one of these ways is a crime.

McLaughlan v. Boyd[39a] is open to the objections that it is a usurpation of the function of Parliament, and that its *ratio* is so wide as to infringe the principle of legality. Whilst it is true that indecent conduct arouses moral indignation, it is notorious that there is no general agreement on what forms of sexual behaviour are indecent. Parliament has now declared that private sexual activity between consenting adult males is not criminal[40]; but other examples of sexual, or sexually related, conduct have fallen foul of the common law by the expedient of treating Macdonald's statement adopted in the case not merely as some vague maxim of the criminal law, but rather as if it was a description of a broadly based offence in its own right. **1.31**

Shameless indecency indeed was long thought of, in a somewhat limited fashion, as at best a description of certain forms of behaviour between two or more persons, present together in one place, with at

---

35 1934 J.C. 19.

36 At 22. Lord Clyde also expressed the view that the findings in fact were inconsistent with consent on the part of the "victims": at 23.

37 Lord Clyde at 23. The passage appears in the first — 1867 — edition of Macdonald at 229 so that it can be said that *McLaughlan* did nothing new. But Macdonald gave no authority for the statement.

38 s.11, now Criminal Law (Consolidation) (Scotland) Act 1995, s.13.

39 Lord Clyde at 23; Hume, i, 21.

39a 1934 J.C. 19.

40 Criminal Law (Consolidation) (Scotland) Act 1995, s.13, re-enacting the Criminal Justice (Scotland) Act 1980, s.80 as amended by the Criminal Justice and Public Order Act 1994, ss.145(2), 146(2), 148.

least one of them indulging in some kind of sexual behaviour directed towards the other or others. Lord Maxwell said in *Dean v. John Menzies (Holdings) Ltd*[41] that he supposed "that in the past the crime usually concerned actual physical conduct of the human body"; and, on the supposition that shameless indecency is *a* crime, it did concern itself with that. The crime has, however, been extended to cover quite different situations. The process began in *Watt v. Annan*[42] where what the accused had done was to exhibit an obscene film to a number of adult males, *i.e.* run a stag movie night, and he was charged with conducting himself in a shamelessly indecent manner and exhibiting "a film of an obscene or indecent nature which was liable to create depraved, inordinate and lustful desires in those watching it and to corrupt the morals of the lieges." Macdonald's dictum was approved, and it was said that it was for Parliament and not the courts to set limits to it. The converse argument, that any application of the dictum (which technically could have no authority other than as a generalisation of common law decisions) to behaviour of a kind so different from that envisaged by Macdonald could be made only by Parliament, clearly did not find favour with the court. Lord Cameron said[43]:

> "Whether or not conduct which is admittedly indecent or obscene is to be held criminal will depend on proof of the necessary *mens rea* and upon the facts and circumstances of the particular case. It would be impracticable as well as undesirable to attempt to define precisely the limits and ambit of this particular offence, far less to decide that the nature of the premises or place in which the conduct charged has occurred should alone be decisive in transfering conduct which would otherwise be proper subject of prosecution into conduct which may do no more than offend the canons of personal propriety or standards of contemporary morals. If it were considered desirable or necessary that this was a chapter of the criminal law in which precise boundaries or limits were to be set then the task is one which is more appropriate for the hand of the legislator."

The only limitation on the crime of shameless indecency is, as Lord Cameron put it,[44] that:

> "It was accepted, and rightly so, in the submission for the Crown that the conduct to be criminal, in such circumstances as the facts in the present case disclose, must be directed towards some person or persons with an intention or knowledge that it should corrupt or be calculated or liable to corrupt or deprave those towards whom the indecent or obscene conduct was directed."

The offence was further extended in a series of cases[45] so as to apply to circumstances virtually indistinguishable from those of the statutory

---

[41] 1981 J.C. 23 at 38.
[42] 1978 J.C. 84.
[43] *ibid.*, at 89.
[44] *ibid.*, at 88–89.
[45] See *esp. Robertson v. Smith*, 1980 J.C. 1, and also *Scott v. Smith*, 1981 J.C. 46; *Ingram v. Macari*, 1982 J.C. 1; *Ingram v. Macari*, 1983 J.C. 1.

offence of selling or exposing for sale obscene material,[46] the purpose of the Crown in seeking such an extension being apparently to circumvent the smallness of the penalty then prescribed by Parliament for that statutory offence.[47] The crime in such a case is described as selling, exposing for sale and having for sale, indecent and obscene books likely to deprave and corrupt the morals of the lieges and to create in their minds inordinate and lustful desires. The view of the court was that simply to expose for sale material known to be obscene, *i.e.* corrupting, constituted shameless indecency.

Despite its rapid and apparently successful development,[48] it may be that this offence does not have much of a future. Its practical use is much limited by the decision in *Dean v. John Menzies (Holdings) Ltd,*[49] that it cannot be committed by a corporation, and the need to resort to it has been much reduced by the provision of substantial penalties for the statutory offence of dealing in obscene materials.[50] The *John Menzies* case also disturbed the theoretical basis of the whole development. Lord Cameron, who gave the opinion of the court in *Watt v. Annan*[50a] and *Robertson v. Smith,*[51] said in *John Menzies* that the shamelessness libelled in an obscenity case was objective, consisting of conduct known to be corrupting, and so was something with which the moral obliquity of the actor had nothing to do.[52] The majority, however, while accepting *Robertson v. Smith,* held that all forms of shameless indecency did indeed require shamelessness and indecency in a subjective sense. The accused must, said Lord Stott, be "so lost to any sense of shame" as to authorise the sale of the material[53]; and Lord Maxwell said that a finding of guilt implied that the accused had used his judgment and discretion in deciding to sell the material "in an indecent and shameless fashion".[54] If these are requisites of shameless indecency it becomes difficult to support *Robertson v. Smith,* and perhaps only a little less difficult to support *Watt v. Annan* — certainly they make the crime more difficult to prove than would the approach of Lord Cameron which requires no more than is needed to prove that the accused knowingly sold articles held by the court to be obscene.

The result of *John Menzies (Holdings) Ltd* may be, therefore, to introduce some common sense into what was described by Lord Stott in

---

[46] At that time, an offence under Local Acts, or generally under the Burgh Police (Scotland) Act 1892 s.380(5) which, as amended by the Criminal Procedure (Scotland) Act 1975 s.289C, fixed a maximum penalty of 60 days in prison or a fine of £25 (instead of the original £10). The present statutory offence, found in s.51(2) of the Civic Government (Scotland) Act 1982, now carries a maximum punishment (s.51(3), as amended by the Criminal Justice and Public Order Act 1994, s.87) of six months and/or the prescribed sum on summary conviction, or three years and/or a fine of any amount on conviction on indictment.

[47] A similar argument by the Crown found favour with the court in the virtual shameless indecency case of *Batty v. H.M. Advocate*, 1995 S.C.C.R. 525.

[48] See G.H. Gordon, "Shameless Indecency and Obscenity" (1980) 25 J.L.S. 262; G. Maher, "The Enforcement of Morals Continued", 1978 S.L.T. (News) 281; J.B. Stewart, "Obscenity Prosecutions", 1982 S.L.T. (News) 93; I.D. Willock, "Shameless Indecency-How Far Has the Crown Office Reached?" (1981) 52 SCOLAG Bul. 199.

[49] 1981 J.C. 23.

[50] Civic Government (Scotland) Act 1982, s.51(2),(3): see n.145, *supra*.

[50a] 1978 J.C. 84.

[51] 1980 J.C. 1.

[52] 1981 J.C. 23 at 32.

[53] *ibid.*, p.36.

[54] *ibid.*, p.38.

that case as "an area of law in which (as is perhaps indicated by the archaic and faintly ludicrous wording of the complaint) common sense is not noticeably at a premium."[55] Lord Maxwell in that case expressed sympathy with the view that "in the realm of what is in substance censorship of certain types of magazines, literature, films etc. on the grounds that they are socially unacceptable, it would perhaps be preferable that the matter be dealt with by statute rather than the existing common law, which was I think designed to meet rather different problems."[56] It may be that the strange eruption of shameless indecency into the already peculiar field of obscenity will come to be seen as merely a temporary crop which withered and died under the attack of *Dean v. John Menzies (Holdings) Ltd.*

In *Sommerville v. Tudhope*[57] the High Court declined to hold that it was a crime for a wholesaler to possess obscene material for distribution to retailers, on the ground that the public did not resort to wholesale premises so that no affront to public decency or morals was involved. It was said that the penalisation of the mere possession of pornography, as distinct from its exposure for sale, involved "issues of public and social policy which . . . are for the legislature to resolve, but not to be resolved by an unwarranted extension of the common law."[58]

In *R. v. H.M. Advocate*[59] the High Court held that any sexual relationship between parent and child constitutes the crime of shameless indecency as being behaviour which is repugnant to society, even where it does not involve sexual intercourse; and in *H.M. Advocate v. R.K.*[60] Lord MacLean decided at a preliminary hearing that sexual intercourse (and other sexual behaviour) between a man and his foster daughter was for similar reasons shamelessly indecent — certainly when she was between the ages of 16 and 18, and possibly so after she attained the age of majority.[61]

In the most recent cases, however, the High Court has shown itself keen to halt the extension of 'shameless indecency' by confining its ambit to positive conduct directed at another,[62] and by refusing to allow conduct which would have been non-criminal at common law (male person having sexual intercourse with a girl of 13 years) to be received as a relevant charge.[63]

---

[55] 1981 J.C. 23 at 37.

[56] *ibid.*, at 38.

[57] 1981 J.C. 58.

[58] *ibid.*, at 64.

[59] 1988 S.L.T. 623.

[60] 1994 S.C.C.R. 499.

[61] This was despite the fact that Parliament had not criminalised sexual intercourse in such circumstances, where the child in question was over the age of 16: Criminal Law (Consolidation) (Scotland) Act 1995, s.3 — re-enacting s.2C of the Sexual Offences (Scotland) Act 1976, as inserted by the Incest and Related Offences (Scotland) Act 1986, s.1.

[62] See *Paterson v. Lees*, 1999 S.C.C.R. 231, where permitting young children to continue watching an indecent video recording was considered not to be a crime at all, although it had been charged as a matter where the accused had conducted himself in a shamelessly indecent manner towards the children involved.

[63] *H.M. Advocate v. Roose*, 1999 S.C.C.R. 259. The time limit on prosecuting such an offence under statute had expired: see the Criminal Law (Consolidation) (Scotland) Act 1995, s.5(3) [as substituted by the Crime and Punishment (Scotland) Act 1997, s.62(1), Sched. 1, para 18(2)(b)], (4). The Crown's argument that the charge was relevant seems to have involved the fact that the accused was some 20 years older than the girl and that this somehow demonstrated the breach of an implied trust.

ATTEMPT TO PERVERT THE ENDS OF JUSTICE. One way in which the criminal law has been extended in modern times without explicit reference to the declaratory power has been by treating "attempt to pervert (or defeat) the course of justice" as a specific crime, and holding certain forms of conduct to be criminal because they are modes of committing this crime. An intention to pervert the course of justice has long been accepted as an aggravation of other crimes, especially of intimidation, extortion, and fraud, and "crimes against the course of justice" form a well-recognised class of crimes, like "crimes against property" or "crimes against the person", and include such specific crimes as perjury and prison-breaking. But the appearance of "attempt to pervert the course of justice" as a specific crime is a fairly modern phenomenon.[64] The standard forms of indictment for perjury or prison-breaking, for example, libelled the crime of perjury or prison-breaking, and not the crime of attempting to pervert the course of justice by swearing a false oath or escaping from prison, as the case might be.[65] In *Logue v. H.M. Advocate*[66] a charge of bribing a member of a licensing court was laid simply as one of corrupting a judge by bribery without any mention of "the ends of justice", and although reference was made to the declaratory power,[67] recourse to the power was unnecessary in order to decide that a member of a licensing court was a judge within the meaning of the common law crime. **1.32**

A case involving subornation of perjury was charged as an attempt to pervert the course of justice in *Scott (A.T.) v. H.M. Advocate*[68] but there was no dispute as to the relevancy of the charge, and the use of "attempt to pervert" as a *nomen juris* was mere surplusage. The first modern case to deal with the question was *Dalton v. H.M. Advocate.*[69] D was charged with pretending to a girl who was an eye-witness to a crime that he was a friend of W who had been charged with the crime, and that it would be to W's advantage if she refrained from picking out a man McG at a police identification parade, McG being also suspected of the crime. D. was charged further with threatening the girl that if she did pick out McG she would be assaulted. The crime libelled was attempting to intimidate the girl and attempting to pervert the course of justice, and the whole averments were run together in one charge. It may well be that but for the element of intimidation no charge would have been brought, but the Crown failed to prove the intimidation and the jury convicted only of an attempt to pervert the course of justice by attempting to induce the girl to refrain from identifying McG. **1.33**

The Crown argued that as this was an attempt to pervert the course of justice it was criminal, since any such attempt constituted a crime,

---

[64] Although Hume and Alison recognised that certain forms of fraud and interference in relation to evidence were punishable, they regarded them as extensions of subornation of perjury or as contempts of court rather than as modes of a crime of "attempting to pervert the course of justice": see Hume, i, 383 *et seq.*, Alison, i 488. See Vol. II, Chap. 18.

[65] *Turnbull v. H.M. Advocate*, 1953 J.C. 59, in which the charge was of effecting an escape to the hindrance of the course of justice, represents an interesting halfway house between the old type of charge and the new type exemplified in *H.M. Advocate v. Martin*, 1956 J.C. 1 where the effecting of an escape was narrated and was then charged as an attempt to defeat the ends of justice.

[66] 1932 J.C. 1.

[67] L.J.-G. Clyde at 3.

[68] 1946 J.C. 90.

[69] 1951 J.C. 76.

whatever form it took. The court did not in terms go so far as to accept this argument, although *Dalton's*[69a] place in the development of the law is an example of an attempt to pervert the course of justice. Lord Justice-Clerk Thomson and Lord Patrick delivered very short opinions in which they held that the facts constituted the recognised crime of attempting to destroy in advance evidence which might tend to incriminate someone on a criminal charge.[70] But elimination of evidence is a concept applicable only to real evidence, and not to tampering with witnesses — the only way one can eliminate oral evidence is by killing the witness. And even the elimination of real evidence had in the past been indicted only when what was involved was a fraud on a creditor by destroying a document of debt, and it had been charged as fraud and not as attempt to pervert the course of justice.[71] Interference with potential witnesses is punishable as contempt of court, even when matters are at as early a stage as they were in *Dalton*[72] but *Dalton*[72a] was not a contempt case. The effect of *Dalton*[72b] is probably that anything which is punishable as a contempt of court on the ground that it constitutes an unwarranted interference with criminal process is also indictable as attempt to pervert the course of justice, but this was not said explicitly.[73]

1.34 The view that anything done in order to pervert the course of justice is criminal was accepted in the later case of *H.M. Advocate v. Mannion*.[74] The indictment there charged a husband and wife that:

> "you did form a criminal purpose to hinder and frustrate the course of justice, in pursuance of which you, knowing that you were

---

[69a] 1951 J.C. 76.

[70] L.J.-C. at 79; Lord Patrick at 81.

[71] *e.g. Walter Murray and Margt Scott*, Bell's Notes 66; *John and David Reid* (1835) *ibid.*

[72] See Hume, i. 384, ii. 140; *Stirling v. Associated Newspapers Ltd*, 1960 J.C. 5. *Dalton* was followed in *Dean v. Stewart*, 1980 S.L.T. (Notes) 85, where it was held to be an attempt to pervert the course of justice to give the police false information as to the identity of the driver of a car which had failed to stop after an accident. See also *Fletcher v. Tudhope*, 1984 S.C.C.R. 267 (assisting a person to evade a police search); *Waddell v. MacPhail*, 1986 S.C.C.R. 593, which is again similar to *Dalton*; *Watson v. H.M. Advocate*, 1993 S.C.C.R. 875, giving false information and attempting to dispose of real evidence relative to police investigations into an "incident"; and *Johnstone v. Lees*, 1994 S.C.C.R. 687, false statement in a reply form to a complaint that the accused knew nothing about the charge libelled, his alleged intent being to induce the prosecutor to drop same.

[72a] 1951 J.C. 76.

[72b] *ibid.*

[73] There may be said to be some authority for this view in Alison's statement that "All practices tending to procure false evidence are punishable, though not falling exactly under the description of subornation or attempt at subornation": i, 488, but the cases cited by Alison are cases of false accusation or destruction of real evidence. *Dalton* could have been treated as an extension of subornation of perjury to false information to the police: *cf. John Barr* (1839) 2 Swin.282, *supra; Scott (A.T.) v. H.M. Advocate*, 1946 J.C. 90 esp.Lord Carmont at 93, but this was not done. It might even have been argued that D. was guilty of instigating the girl to give false information to the police, and that by extension of *Kerr v. Hill* — 1936 J.C. 71, see *infra* — giving false information to the police is criminal whether or not it incriminates anyone, although that would be a considerable extension of what is at best a dubious crime. The facts are also redolent of fraud. The pretence, if pretence it was, that D was a friend of W. and wished to help him played no part in the decision, but it could again be argued that he was instigating the girl to commit the fraud of inducing the police to refrain from prosecuting McG by herself pretending that he was not concerned in the crime. This, again, would make it a crime to tell lies to the police in circumstances not involving false incrimination or allegation, and the courts have not so far treated this as fraud despite the protean nature of that crime.

[74] 1961 J.C. 79.

required to give evidence for the prosecution in the trial of . . . did leave your . . . house and go into hiding . . . for the purpose of avoiding giving evidence . . . and the diet of said trial having been deserted . . . and a new diet appointed . . . you, again knowing that you were required to give evidence as aforesaid, continued to hide for the purpose aforesaid until said . . . had been tried . . . all with intent that your evidence would not be available to the prosecution and with intent to hinder and frustrate the course of justice, and you remained in hiding until . . . you were apprehended by officers of police, and you did attempt to defeat the ends of justice."

In this case no question of contempt of court arose, because the accused were never cited to attend as witnesses — their crime consisted in making themselves scarce so that the police were unable to cite them, nor was there any suggestion in the charge of anyone else conspiring with or inducing them to keep out of the way. Their sole offence was that they had hidden away with intent to pervert the course of justice. In holding the indictment relevant Lord Justice-Clerk Thomson delivered a very short opinion in which he said that there was nothing revolutionary in deciding that it was criminal to take steps to remove oneself from the possibility of being called to give evidence before one had actually been cited. He concluded:

> "It seems to me to be clear that if a man, with the evil intention of defeating the ends of justice, takes steps to prevent evidence being available, that is a crime by the law of Scotland. Evil intention, of course, is of the essence of the matter and must be established."[75]

Lord Thomson's choice of language suggests that, as in *Dalton v. H.M. Advocate*,[75a] he was thinking of the crime of destroying evidence. Taking steps to prevent evidence being available is, however, an odd way of describing what the Mannions did, and would be better suited to a charge of hiding someone else away.

The charge in *Mannion*[75b] was libelled as an attempt to defeat the course of justice, and unless the case is regarded as an example of such an attempt, it must be treated as a completely new crime, in which case Lord Thomson should probably not have decided the question himself, but have reported the matter to a *quorum* of the court to consider whether the declaratory power should be exercised.[76] *Mannion*[76a] therefore raises sharply the questions which were glossed over in *Dalton*[76b]: whether attempt to pervert the course of justice is *a* crime, and whether, if it is, there is any real difference between creating a new crime and treating conduct as a *modus* of the crime of attempt to pervert the course of justice. **1.35**

The problem is illustrated very clearly in the case of *H.M. Advocate v. Martin*.[77] The charge there was of attempting to defeat the ends of justice, the facts that the three accused formed and carried out a plan to **1.36**

---

[75] At 80.
[75a] 1951 J.C. 76.
[75b] 1961 J.C. 79.
[76] *cf. H.M. Advocate v. Coutts* (1899) 3 Adam 50, Lord McLaren at 59.
[76a] 1961 J.C. 79.
[76b] 1951 J.C. 76.
[77] 1956 J.C. 1.

effect the escape of one of them who was serving a prison sentence, the escape to take place at a time when he was outside the prison walls in a working-party. This could easily have been dealt with as a new way of committing the old crime of prison-breaking resulting from the modern practice of allowing persons under sentence to work outside the prison under the charge of prison officers, by interpreting "prison" to include any place where a sentenced person was in lawful custody,[78] but for some reason neither the Crown nor the court took this course.[79] Lord Cameron, indeed, specifically rejected it. He noted that prison-breaking was not libelled and expressed the view that it was confined to walled prisons.[80] He pointed out that Hume and Alison both dealt with prison-breaking as a species of the genus of offences against the course of justice,[81] quoting Alison's description of the crime as "a violation of the order and course of justice, and a direct infringement of regulations essential to the peace and well-being of society."[82] His Lordship then held that, "What is libelled in this indictment is very plainly an attempt to hinder the course of justice and frustrate its ends by seeking to assist a sentenced criminal to escape or evade the penalty of his crime. That is an offence against public order and against the course of justice . . . what is libelled here is but one species of a well-recognised and undoubted genus of crime."[83]

To treat an act as a species of a genus of crime is not, it is submitted, the same as to treat it as a new way of committing an old crime. Hypnotising someone to drown himself would be a crime because it would be a new way of committing murder, not because it would be a species of the genus of crimes against the person: it is a sub-division of murder, not an independent species of crime like rape or assault. It is submitted that the correct approach in *Martin*[83a] would have been by way of the crime of prison-breaking which Alison regards as an independent crime and not just as a way of committing the crime of infringing the well-being of society,[84] and that Lord Cameron's argument misses a vital logical step in passing directly from offences against public order to the particular facts libelled.

To declare something criminal because it is an "infringement of regulations essential to the well-being of society", and at the same time to deny that one is exercising the declaratory power of "innovation or extension",[85] is contradictory. To treat the infringement of such regulations as *a* crime is to commit a type-fallacy — it is not a crime, it is rather a quality of actions which makes them proper subjects of punishment. Alison recognised this when, immediately after the passage quoted by Lord Cameron, he added, "It has, accordingly, always been

---

[78] *cf.* Prisons (Scotland) Act 1989, s.13(b), re-enacting s.12(b) of the Prisons (Scotland) Act 1952; see also *McAllister v. H.M. Advocate*, 1986 S.C.C.R. 688. The definition of 'legal custody' has been extended to cover 'privatised' prisons: Criminal Justice and Public Order Act 1994, s.110(4).

[79] In *Wm Hutton* (1837) 1 Swin. 497, a prisoner who escaped through a door which had been negligently left open pleaded guilty to prison-breaking without objection to the relevancy of the charge.

[80] 1956 J.C. at 2.

[81] Hume, i, 401; Alison, i, 555.

[82] Alison, *loc. cit.*.

[83] 1956 J.C. at 3.

[83a] 1956 J.C. 1.

[84] Alison, i, Chap. xxvii.

[85] *H.M. Advocate v. Martin, supra* at 4.

regarded as a point of dittay by our common law."[86] In other words, prison-breaking is a crime because it infringes the order of society, and the particular way in which it infringes this order is by interfering with the course of justice: it is not an example of the crime of infringing the order of society or of the crime of interfering with the course of justice.

WASTING THE TIME OF THE POLICE. Before leaving this branch of the subject it is necessary to consider *Kerr v. Hill*[87] which impinges on the development of attempt to pervert the course of justice because it deals with false statements to the police, although it was not charged as such an attempt.[88] The accused was charged that he falsely represented to police officers that an omnibus belonging to a particular company had knocked someone down, and "did cause officers . . . maintained at the public expense for the public benefit to devote their time and service in the investigation of said false story . . . and did temporarily deprive the public of the services of said officers and did render the lieges and particularly drivers [of the company] liable to suspicion and to accusation of driving recklessly." This was a charge the like of which had never been seen in a Scots court, and it is a rather sobering thought that a sheriff-substitute sitting in a summary court was prepared to deal with it and to impose a sentence of three months' imprisonment on it. The charge was lifted bodily from the English case of *R. v. Manley*[89] except for the omission of the concluding words of the English charge, its *nomen juris*, "and in so doing did unlawfully effect a public mischief".[90] This omission was necessary since there is no authority in Scotland (nor in England[91]) for a common law crime of effecting a public mischief. The Crown argued on appeal, *inter alia*, that the facts disclosed the crime of fraud, and the terms of the charge read more like fraud than anything else, but this point was not taken up by the court. Lord Morison treated the case as an example of the recognised crime of making false accusations,[92] although no individual was named by the accused, and indeed no accusation of crime was made, only a report that someone had been knocked down by an omnibus. Lord Justice-General Normand proceeded on a wider ground, in line with the approach of the English court in *Manley*[92a] where Lord Hewart C.J. had said that one of the ingredients of the mischief consisted in taking up the time of public servants.[93] Lord Normand said that, "Great injury and damage may be caused to the public interest, which is mainly to be regarded, by a false accusation",[94] and that the essence of the crime was "that the criminal authorities were deliberately set in motion by a malicious person by means of an invented story."[95] **1.37**

[86] Alison, i, 555.

[87] 1936 J.C. 71.

[88] It is so regarded in Northern Ireland: see *R. v. Bailey* [1956] N.I. 15. The English position is discussed in *R. v. Withers* [1975] A.C. 842. For the view that the type of development criticised is typical of the development of a mature legal system, see *R. v. Knuller (Publishing, etc.) Ltd* [1973] A.C. 435, Lord Simon of Glaisdale at 492–493, and the same judge, more cautiously, in *R. v. Withers, supra*, at 867–868.

[89] [1933] 1 K.B. 529.

[90] Which should not have formed part of the English charge anyway: see *R. v. Withers, supra.*

[91] *R. v. Withers, supra.*

[92] See *e.g., Elliott Millar* (1847) Ark. 355.

[92a] [1933] 1 K.B. 529.

[93] At 534–535: the other ingredient was the placing of the public in peril of accusation.

[94] 1936 J.C. at 75.

[95] *ibid.*, at 76.

Lord Fleming said that the case could have been charged as false accusation, but that it was immaterial that it had been charged under a different name, and that the malicious making of false statement to the police with the intention and effect of causing them to make inquiries was a crime, although no particular person was pointed at. Lord Fleming's opinion is very short and combines elements of both the other opinions, but it is reasonable to conclude that he regarded the case as an extension of the principle involved in false accusation.

1.38 Lord Normand's *ratio* was adopted in *Gray v. Morrison,*[96] a case wholly lacking in malice, and perhaps the least heinous in the whole history of the common law. Gray was visiting a friend, and to save the friend the trouble of driving him home said falsely that he had a cycle with him which he had left outside. His friend insisted on accompanying him to the cycle, and on discovering its absence suggested that they should report the matter to the police. Gray was caught in his own toils and agreed to report it. He accused no one, and said he did not wish any action to be taken or investigations made. As a result of his social *faux pas* Gray was charged that he did "cause officers . . . maintained at the public expense for the public benefit, to devote their time and service in the investigation of said false story told by you and did temporarily deprive the public of the services of said officers, and did render the lieges liable to suspicion and to accusations of theft." Gray pleaded guilty and appealed only against his sentence of 14 days' imprisonment, which was reduced to a fine. In disposing of the appeal Lord Justice-General Cooper said, "I have no doubt that . . . an offence within the sense of *Kerr v. Hill*[96a] was committed", and he went on to explain that "the gravamen of the charge is . . . the deliberate setting in motion of the police authorities by an invented story."[97] Lord Cooper, it is true, was anxious to emphasise that the story must be told in knowledge of its falsity, but it is perhaps unfortunate that instead of going on to say that *Kerr*[97a] and *Gray*[97b] were truly examples of common law fraud, he treated *Gray* as an example of "an offence within the sense of *Kerr v. Hill,*" which is the offence of wasting the time of the police by a false story. Now that is a specific crime, and one which was unknown to the common law before *Kerr.*[98] But the manner of its creation is if anything more unsatisfactory than the nature of the crime itself. The court in *Gray*[98a] accepted that the crime had been created in *Kerr,*[98b] but no one concerned in *Kerr* mentioned the declaratory power, and Lord Morison and probably also Lord Fleming thought that they were dealing only with a form of the recognised crime of false accusation. As a result the High Court has never faced up to the implications of saying that the principles of the common law require them to treat wasting the time of the police by lies as more heinous than wasting the time of the fire brigade or of a doctor. Sending the police on a fool's errand is the sort of thing which, if it is to be criminal at all, is eminently suitable for creation as a statutory

[96] 1954 J.C. 31.
[96a] 1936 J.C. 71.
[97] 1954 J.C. at 34.
[97a] 1936 J.C. 71.
[97b] 1954 J.C. 31.
[98] 1936 J.C. 71.
[98a] 1954 J.C. 31.
[98b] 1936 J.C. 71.

offence carrying some small penalty on summary conviction[99]: it is eminently unsuitable to be a common law crime.[99a]

Breach of the Peace. The scope of the crime of breach of the peace has **1.39**
been much extended in recent years[1] and in its present state it is capable of being used to punish almost any form of conduct regarded by the court as undesirable without the necessity of any reference to the declaratory power.[2] It is, in a sense, the equivalent of the now discredited English public mischief,[3] and also has something of the same position in Scots criminal law as conduct to the prejudice of good order and discipline has in military law: it is a blanket offence which is useful for catching conduct which cannot easily be brought under any other heading.[4]

Malicious mischief. In *H.M. Advocate v. Wilson*[5] it was held (Lord **1.40**
Stewart dissenting) that the crime of malicious mischief was not limited to causing physical damage to corporeal property, but extended to cases where loss was caused without any such damage. In that case a generator had been stopped by the pressing of a switch, causing a loss of electricity which cost well over £100,000 to replace. Notwithstanding that such an extension of a well-settled crime to pure economic loss was completely

---

[99] Wasting the time of the police by making a false report which tends to show that an offence has been committed, or to give rise to apprehension for the safety of persons or property, or to suggest that one has information material to a police inquiry is a summary offence in England under s.5(2) of the Criminal Law Act 1967. In Scotland, the common law offence now extends to any false report to the police, whether or not it involves an accusation of any kind: *Bowers v. Tudhope*, 1987 S.L.T. 748; *Robertson v. Hamilton*, 1988 S.L.T. 7. See Vol. II, Chap. 47.

[99a] Failing to give information to the police as to the insurance status or the identity of a driver in certain circumstances are offences under s.171 and s.172 (as substituted by the Road Traffic Act 1991, s.21) of the Road Traffic Act 1988, and giving false information would presumably be a contravention of these sections: see Vol. II, Chap. 47. Giving false alarm of a fire is also a statutory offence: Fire Services Act 1947, s.31(1). See also Telecommunications Act 1984, s.43(1)(b) as amended by the Criminal Justice and Public Order Act 1994, s.92 (as to penalty).

[1] See *Young v. Heatly*, 1959 J.C. 66; "Breach of the Peace," 1959 S.L.T. (News) 229; T.B. Smith, 130. See also, *e.g.*, *Turner v. Kennedy* (1972) S.C.C.R. Supp.30; *Stewart v. Lockhart*, 1990 S.C.C.R. 390; *McKenzie v. Normand*, 1992 S.C.C.R. 14; *MacDougall v. Dochree*, 1992 S.C.C.R. 331; *Wyness v. Lockhart*, 1992 S.C.C.R. 808; *Huges v. Crowe*, 1993 S.C.C.R. 320; *H.M. Advocate v. Forbes*, 1994 S.C.C.R. 163. *Cf., e.g., Fisher v. Keane*, 1981 J.C. 50; *Farrell v. Normand*, 1992 S.C.C.R. 866; *Cardle v. Murray*, 1993 S.C.C.R. 170; *Donaldson v. Vannet*, 1998 S.C.C.R. 422. See Vol. II, Chap. 41. It may be that the number of fairly recently reported cases on breach of the peace would lead the European Court of Human Rights to consider that the offence was sufficiently precise to "allow the citizen — if need be, with appropriate advice — to foresee, to a degree that is reasonable in the circumstances, the consequences which a given action may entail": see *Steel and Ors v. United Kingdom,* September 23, 1998, ECtHR, Applic. No. 00024838/94, where the English concept of Breach of the Peace was considered to have become sufficiently precise, as a result of case decisions over the past 20 years, for the purposes of Art. 5 of the European Convention on Human Rights. See also *McLeod v. United Kingdom,* September 23, 1998, ECtHR, Applic. No. 00024755/94, where the same English concept was found sufficient for the purposes of Art. 8.

[2] Similar observations may be made with reference to contempt of court, but it has always been regarded as something highly special.

[3] See *R. v. Withers, supra,* and Lord Simon of Glaisdale's comment that "the recognition of a generic offence of conspiracy to effect a public mischief would give an uncontrollable dynamism to this branch of the law" [1975] A.C. 842 at 872B.

[4] The development of breach of the peace is discussed in Vol. II, Chap. 41.

[5] 1984 S.L.T. 117; see commentary at 1983 S.C.C.R. 420, at 428 *et seq.*

novel, Lord Justice-Clerk Ross did not consider that this was "in effect introducing a new crime into the law of Scotland."[6]

1.41 *Supplying solvents for sniffing.* Although the crimes in *Khaliq v. H.M. Advocate*[7] and *Ulhaq v. H.M. Advocate*,[8] in which the accused were charged with supplying other persons with solvents, knowing they were to be used for inhalation to the danger of their health and lives, are examples of administering drugs[9] and/or culpably and recklessly endangering life and health, they might be seen from a pragmatic point of view as an extension of the law in order to control the undesirable but not illegal practice of glue sniffing.[10]

1.42 *Dishonest exploitation of confidential information.* In *Grant v. Allan*[11] the High Court held that to copy confidential information obtained as a result of one's employment and offer to sell it was not so obviously criminal in nature as to justify the intervention of the declaratory power.

The Effect of Art 7 of the European Convention on Human Rights

1.43 It is now unlawful for any court in Scotland to act in a way which is incompatible with a "Convention Right".[12] In particular, the High Court of Justiciary is obliged to act in accordance with Article 7 of the European Convention on Human Rights. The text of Article 7 is as follows:

No punishment without law

> "1. No one shall be held guilty of any criminal offence on account of any act or omission which did not constitute a criminal offence under national or international law at the time when it was committed. Nor shall a heavier penalty be imposed than the one that was applicable at the time the criminal offence was committed.[13]
>
> 2. This Article shall not prejudice the trial and punishment of any person for any act or omission which, at the time when it was committed, was criminal according to the general principles of law recognised by civilised nations."

---

[6] 1984 S.L.T. at 120. On malicious mischief generally, see Vol. II, Chap. 22.

[7] 1984 J.C. 23.

[8] 1991 S.L.T. 614.

[9] See Vol. II, Chap. 29.

[10] *cf.*, T.H. Jones, "Common Law and Criminal Law; The Scottish Example," [1990] Crim. L.R. 292.

[11] 1987 J.C. 71.

[12] *i.e.*, rights under the European Convention on Human Rights, as these are made applicable to the United Kingdom by the Human Rights Act 1998, ss.1(1); 6(1),(2)(a).

[13] The contents of the second sentence here are not particularly relevant to the present discussion; but this provision would apply where, *e.g.*, A in June 2000 commits a statutory offence for which a heavier maximum punishment is appointed by another statutory provision taking effect in October of that year. The original, lesser maximum penalty must be applied if A is convicted: see *Jamil v. France* (1995) 21 E.H.R.R. 65; *Welch v. United Kingdom* (1995) 20 E.H.R.R. 247. On the other hand, if a later provision appoints a lesser maximum penalty than previously was the case, that lesser penalty must be applied, since it is to A's advantage: see *G. v. France* (1995) 21 E.H.R.R. 288, at 300 para. 24.

This Article gives effect to the principle of legality,[14] in that a person can be convicted for his acts and omissions only if what he did or failed to do constituted an offence under Scots law at the time when that act or omission was committed.[15] This might suggest that once an offence had been defined, it could not thereafter be subject to interpretation by the courts in actual cases, if such interpretation in any way were to change the original conception of that offence. But the European Court of Human Rights has taken no such narrow view of Article 7(1). Indeed that Court has stated the position as follows:

> "However clearly drafted a legal provision may be, in any system of law, including criminal law, there is an inevitable element of judicial interpretation.
>
> There will always be a need for elucidation of doubtful points and for adaptation to changing circumstances. Indeed, in the United Kingdom, as in other Convention States, the progressive development of the criminal law through judicial law-making is a well entrenched and necessary part of legal tradition. Article 7 of the Convention cannot be read as outlawing the gradual clarification of the rules of criminal liability through their judicial interpretation from case to case, provided that the resultant development is consistent with the essence of the offence and could reasonably be foreseen."[16]

The important point which emerges is that development of an offence by the courts should not alter the essential elements of that offence, such that a different offence is in fact created. Provided the emphasis is upon progressive development for clarification or for adaptation to changed circumstances, and provided that such development is reasonably foreseeable, then there will be no violation of Article 7(1), notwithstanding that there may be created some retrospective effect. The reference to the "drafting" of a legal provision might suggest that the Court was thinking purely in terms of statutory or code-based offences; but this is not so, and it may be worthwhile to set out the paragraphs, from the same judgment, which make this plain:

> "46. In a common law system, not only written statutes but also rules of common or other customary law may provide sufficient legal basis for the criminal convictions envisaged in Article 7 of the Convention.
>
> 47. Where law is developed by application and interpretation of courts in a common law system, their law-making function must remain within reasonable limits. Article 7(1) excludes that any acts

---

[14] *nullum crimen sine lege; nulla poena sine lege*; see para. 1.16, *supra*.

[15] Article 7(1) also refers to what was criminal at the time under "international law". It is not entirely certain what this means, but a leading text takes the view that it is designed to apply to those contracting States which, as a matter of constitutional law, give effect to international law directly without the need for confirmatory domestic legislation, so that when a crime under international law is prosecuted there, the principle of legality will apply to it. See P. van Dijk and G.J.H. van Hoof, *Theory and Practice of the European Convention on Human Rights* (3rd ed., The Hague, 1998), p.486. The United Kingdom is not, of course, such a State.

[16] *SW v. United Kingdom*; *CR v. United Kingdom* (1996) 21 E.H.R.R. 363, at 399 para. 36/34. For the position in other Convention States, see A. Cadoppi, "*Nulla Poena Sine Lege* and Scots Criminal Law: A Continental Perspective", 1998 J.R. 73.

not previously punishable should be held by the courts to entail criminal liability or that existing offences should be extended to cover facts which previously did not clearly constitute a criminal offence.

48. It is however compatible with the requirements of Article 7(1) for the existing elements of an offence to be clarified or adapted to new circumstances or developments in society in so far as this can reasonably be brought under the original concept of the offence. The constituent elements of an offence may not however be essentially changed to the detriment of an accused and any progressive development by way of interpretation must be reasonably foreseeable to him with the assistance of appropriate legal advice if necessary.

49. In a common law system therefore, the courts may exercise their customary role of developing the law through cases but in doing so may not exceed the bounds of reasonably foreseeable change."[17]

Provided, therefore, that the High Court in Scotland does not invent a totally new crime, and provided that Scottish courts confine themselves to clarifying, or adapting to new circumstances, the existing elements of known offences, there will be *prima facie* compliance with Article 7, provided also that judicial development of such offences is confined to what an accused person might reasonably foresee — with legal assistance if required. But how would such foresight (not to the degree of absolute, but rather reasonable, certainty[18]) be demonstrated? In *SW v. United Kingdom; CR v. United Kingdom*,[19] the question lay whether a married man should have been convicted of raping, or attempting to rape, his wife prior to the authoritative decision of the House of Lords in *R. v. R.*[20] which removed the common law marital immunity in such cases. The view of both the Commission and the Court was that there had been no violation of Article 7(1) since it was reasonably foreseeable that the marital immunity rule would be abandoned; as the Commission put it: "It is apparent from the case law of the courts, legal text books and the Law Commission's examination of the state of the law that by 1990 the

---

[17] *SW v. United Kingdom*; *CR v. United Kingdom* (1996) 21 E.H.R.R. 363, at 375 (SW.'s case; with respect to CR.'s case, these paragraphs are repeated on p.390, as paras 47–50).

[18] See *The Sunday Times v. United Kingdom* (1979) 2 E.H.R.R. 245, at 271 para. 49: "[A] norm cannot be regarded as a 'law' unless it is formulated with sufficient precision to enable the citizen to regulate his conduct: he must be able — if need be with appropriate advice — to foresee, to a degree that is reasonable in the circumstances, the consequences which a given action may entail. These consequences need not be foreseeable with absolute certainty: experience shows this to be unattainable. Again, whilst certainty is highly desirable, it may bring in its train excessive rigidity and the law must be able to keep pace with changing circumstances. Accordingly, many laws are inevitably couched in terms which, to a greater or lesser extent, are vague and where interpretation and application are questions of practice." This case concerned Article 10 of the Convention, but what was said in the above passage by the Court was quoted with approval in *SW v. United Kingdom*; *CR v. United Kingdom* (1996) 21 E.H.R.R. 363, at 374 para. 45, and at 390 para. 46 respectively — as demonstrative also of the required degree of certainty for the purposes of Article 7(1).

[19] (1996) 21 E.H.R.R. 363.

[20] [1992] 1 A.C. 599.

general immunity afforded to a husband in respect of prosecution for rape of his wife had already been subject to a number of exceptions".[21]

Article 7(2) has caused concern to some authors since it seems at first glance to go far towards defeating the guarantee provided by Article 7(1). Provided that a Scottish court takes the view that the act or omission it proposes to treat as criminal is regarded as criminal by a significant number of "civilised nations", it might be argued that it matters not that that act or omission could not be brought within the definition of any previously known Scottish offence.[22] If that is truly the effect of Article 7(2), then the first part of the Article is rendered virtually worthless. It is submitted, therefore, that van Dijk and van Hoof are correct when they write: "In our opinion the concept of general principles of law as here referred to requires that the facts concerned are not only made punishable in the legal systems of nearly all countries and/or under international law, but that their punishable character ensues from a fundamental principle."[23] They have in mind, for example, war crimes and the principles which informed the tribunals at Nuremberg and Tokyo following the end of the Second World War,[24] as also crimes against humanity and peace in the context of "fundamental principles of human rights" such as the right to life and the right not to be subjected to torture or slavery.[25] If this view is correct, and the authors do express reservations, then it would be a very rare occurence indeed for Article 7(2) to be successfully invoked; more importantly, Article 7(2) would then provide no support for the Declaratory Power as understood and practised by the High Court during the 19th and 20th centuries.

Conclusion. There are three orders of proposition which can be **1.44**
adduced as grounds for treating any form of conduct as criminal. The first contains propositions of the kind, "This conduct is criminal because it is contrary to the good order of society" or "This conduct is criminal because it is *malum in se,* contrary to the laws of God and morality": the second contains propositions of the kind "This conduct is criminal because it is dishonest" or "This conduct is criminal because it involves the frustration of the course of justice": while the third contains propositions of the kind "This conduct is criminal because it constitutes theft," or "This conduct is criminal because it is a way of committing rape."

The last example of declaring conduct criminal on the broad ground that it was contrary to morality and social order was *Bernard Greenhuff*[26] in 1838. *Stante* Article 7(1) of the European Convention on Human

---

[21] (1996) 21 E.H.R.R. 363, at 376 para. 55. The case law referred to pointed to an evolutionary process of which the logical conclusion was the abandonment of the married man's immunity. At para. 51, the Commission also took note that the High Court in Scotland had dispensed with a similar alleged immunity by 1989 (see *S. v. H.M. Advocate*, 1989 S.L.T. 469, which, it may be added, itself followed case decisions which provided exceptions to the alleged immunity — see, *e.g.*, *H.M. Advocate v. Duffy*, 1983 S.L.T. 7; *H.M. Advocate v. Paxton*, 1984 J.C. 105).

[22] See, *e.g.*, S.C. Styles, "Something to Declare" in *Justice and Crime*, R.F. Hunter (ed.) (Edinburgh, 1993), 221, at 224. *Cf.*, I.D. Willock, "The Declaratory Power — Still Indefensible", 1996 J.R. 97, at 106–107.

[23] P. van Dijk and G.J.H. van Hoof, *Theory and Practice of the European Convention on Human Rights* (3rd ed., The Hague, 1998), at p.487.

[24] *ibid.*, pp.486–487.

[25] *ibid.*, p.488.

[26] (1838) 2 Swin. 236.

Rights, it is unthinkable that the Scots courts today would attempt to declare any act criminal on such a ground: it would be in clear breach of the Article's provisions.[27] It is equally unthinkable, and for the same reason, that the courts would now attempt to introduce new crimes on the basis of the second order propositions outlined above. This leaves to the courts the gradual extension or development of existing crimes, subject to the limitations declared in the jurisprudence of the European Court of Human Rights.[28] The Scots courts, however, have been reluctant to extend the scope of particular crimes, even where such extension would have been minimal, for example by extending rape to include intercourse with a sleeping woman[29] or by making it a crime to supply abortifacients to non-pregnant women with intent to cause them to abort.[30] On the other hand the courts did extend the crime of theft to cover clandestine taking and using,[31] and the crime of false accusation to cover a false report of a road accident,[32] but in both cases the judges seem to have been unaware of the full implications of what they were doing.[33]

1.45 The fruits of the Scottish courts' readiness in the past to rely on second order propositions,[34] particularly by characterising conduct as criminal because it involved indecency or perversion of the course of justice, remain, of course, as part of the existing catalogue of criminal law. Provided the courts are not tempted to add to the particular instances "discovered" by them under such propositions,[35] those particular instances may *ex facie* comply with Article 7(1) since no retrospectivity issue should arise: but there is another dimension to the right guaranteed by the Article — that the definitions of crimes should be sufficiently certain for persons to regulate their conduct in the knowledge of the consequences.[36] From this point of view, it might well be argued that Breach of the Peace, for example, is at its limits not sufficiently clearly defined to pass the Convention's test; and the same can probably be said for 'attempting to pervert the course of justice' and 'shameless indecency' — on the dubious assumption that these, limited to their existing manifestations, are truly crimes in their own right.

---

[27] See para. 1.43, *supra*.

[28] *ibid*.

[29] *Chas Sweenie* (1858) 3 Irv. 109.

[30] *H.M. Advocate v. Semple*, 1937 J.C. 41. *Cf. Forbes v. H.M. Advocate*, 1994 S.L.T. 861, where the court declined to recognise the crime of housebreaking with intent to commit rape — perhaps a rather more than minimal extension of housebreaking with intent to commit theft.

[31] *Strathern v. Seaforth*, 1926 J.C. 100, *supra*, para. 1.29.

[32] *Kerr v. Hill*, 1936 J.C. 71, *supra*, para. 1.37.

[33] *H.M. Advocate v. Martin* was in fact an example of this form of extension, but it was dealt with as a second or even a first order case, *supra*, para. 1.36.

[34] See para. 1.44, *supra*.

[35] And recent cases such as *Paterson v. Lees*, 1999 S.C.C.R. 231, and *H.M. Advocate v. Roose*, 1999 S.C.C.R. 259, suggest that the High Court is aware of the problem.

[36] See, *e.g.*, *Kokkinakis v. Greece* (1993) 17 E.H.R.R. 397, at 432, para. 52: "[T]he criminal law must not be extensively construed to an accused's detriment, for instance by analogy; it follows from this that an offence must be clearly defined in law. This condition is satisfied where the individual can know from the wording of the relevant provision and, if need be, with the assistance of the courts' interpretation of it, what acts and omissions will make him liable." See also *SW v. United Kingdom; CR v. United Kingdom* (1996) 21 E.H.H.R. 363, Judgment of the Court at 398–399, para. 34/32.

CHAPTER 2

THE CONCEPT OF RESPONSIBILITY[1]

This chapter deals in a general way with the more important of the concepts which are employed in discussions of criminal responsibility. It does not present a philosophy of responsibility, nor does it discuss all the difficulties involved in the use of words like "responsible", "voluntary" and so on. It is only a brief and rather superficial introduction in order to clear the ground for the analysis of the law which follows. It is important that lawyers should appreciate the philosophical and linguistic difficulties and backgrounds of the words they use, and this chapter is an attempt to sketch these in. **2.01**

LEGAL AND MORAL RESPONSIBILITY

The ascription of responsibility

The concept of responsibility, as used in the law, is not a simple characteristic of persons as, for example, are skin-colour, height or even drunkenness. Its use in sentences like "He is a responsible person", "He is a man in a position of responsibility", or "The judgment of responsible men" is from the lawyer's point of view a secondary one. When a man is referred to as responsible in that way he is being pointed out as the sort of man who is capable of weighing up the various factors in a situation, of sizing up alternatives, of acting dispassionately and with a proper appreciation of all the complexities and consequences of the situation. In this sense "responsible" is a word of praise, and refers to a quality of character. A responsible man is one who is not irresponsible, flighty, prejudiced or mad. This use is clearly distinct from the use of the word in sentences like, "Who is responsible for this accident?" Being a responsible person in the secondary sense is like being wise, or careful, or hot-tempered, it involves having a particular disposition, being a certain type of man; being responsible for an accident is something quite different. **2.02**

The responsibility of A for a situation S can only be decided by a consideration of the characteristics of S — which may include A's actions and state of mind — and is quite independent of his responsibility for S1, unless S and S1 are causally connected. The man who is responsible for setting a house on fire may be responsible for the consequent death of its inhabitants, but this responsibility is quite separate from his responsibility for, say, a motor theft committed by him some years earlier. Responsibility refers to a particular situation. "In this situation,

[1] For a discussion of the various uses of "responsibility", see H.L.A. Hart, *Punishment and Responsibility* (Oxford, 1968), Chap. IX.

seeing that the car was going too quickly, and the lorry was on the wrong side of the road, both drivers are responsible for the accident" is a typical responsibility statement.

Responsibility for an accident is not, however, a characteristic of the situation in the same way as is driving at 40 miles an hour in a 30 m.p.h. limit area, or failing to keep a proper look-out. Two observers can agree about all the factual characteristics of a situation, including the state of mind of the actors, and can agree that their review of the facts is exhaustive, and yet disagree about the responsibility for the situation, without either feeling that he is contradicting himself.[2] For responsibility is something additional to the facts of the situation; it is not one of them, nor is it something logically deducible from them. To say "A is responsible for S" is not to describe A or S, or any part of S; it is to ascribe *to* A responsibility *for* S. This ascription is made after reviewing the facts of S, but A's responsibility is not one of these facts.[3]

The amorality of legal responsibility

2.03 The principles of responsibility may be such that responsibility for a given situation can be decided in advance. If a teacher singles out one boy in his class and says, "I am going out of the room and I shall hold you responsible for any noise there may be in my absence", he is making known his decision to ascribe responsibility to that boy for any noise, whatever the circumstances of the noisy situation, and however little that boy had to do with it, or however unable he was to prevent it. It is not meaningless or contradictory to say to someone, "I know you are in no way to blame for this situation, but I am going to hold you responsible for it nonetheless", however morally reprehensible such an attitude may be. And a person can himself assume responsibility in advance, as Judah did for the safety of Benjamin.[4] Ascriptions of responsibility can be made into rules. The rules of a school may say that in any disturbance the senior boy present will be held responsible, the rules of an army may say that a particular officer is responsible for the cleanliness of a particular barrack room. If, then, there is a disturbance, or if the barrack room is dirty, the headmaster, or commanding officer, may mete out the appropriate punishment to the person declared by the rules to be responsible, however lacking that person may have been in moral blame for the situation.

Legal responsibility rests in the last resort on the same basis as that of the senior boy or the officer in charge of the barrack room in the above examples. Whether or not it is a good thing for a legal system to hold a man responsible for his wife's debts, his partner's contracts or his employee's carelessness, there is no logical objection to its doing so. Statements of responsibility are not statements of fact, and are not true or false. "The senior boy in any class is responsible for all noise made by the class" is a statement of intention, of the rule-maker's intention to hold the senior boy responsible for any noisy situation. Particular applications of the rule such as "A is responsible for the noise made last Tuesday", are true or false only in the sense that if A was the senior boy

---

[2] *cf.* A.J. Ayer, "On the Analysis of Moral Judgements" in *Philosophical Essays* (London, 1954), 231.

[3] *cf.* H.L.A. Hart, "The Ascription of Responsibility and Rights", *Proceedings of Aristotelian Society*, 1948–49, 171.

[4] Gen. 43, 8–9.

in the class which made the noise the rule is being properly applied, while if he was not, it is being improperly applied. What is true is that the school rules make the senior boy responsible, and one cannot go on to ask if he is "truly responsible". He may not be legally or morally responsible, but he will be responsible under the school rules. In the same way a person will be legally responsible for a particular situation if the appropriate legal rule properly applied to the situation results in his being regarded as responsible, and this will be so whether or not the rules of morality, or religion, or any other principles or rules, also regard him as responsible in the given situation.

RESPONSIBILITY AND LIABILITY. Despite the above it remains true **2.04** that "responsibility" is often used to mean moral responsibility, and also that legal responsibility often coincides with moral responsibility: but it does not always do so, and as a result the use of the term "responsibility" in the context of the criminal law often leads to confusion. It would probably, therefore, be advantageous not to use the term "responsibility" at all in a legal context, but to talk instead of liability or amenability to law, or of punishability, or to use some other concept which does not possess the moral overtones of "responsibility". The most suitable word is "liability" so that "criminal responsibility" would be replaced by "liability to legal punishment".

Such a usage would clarify the discussion of certain problems, such as those of the relationship between insanity and criminal responsibility, and of the problem of responsibility for certain statutory offences which may be committed quite independently of any moral culpability.

There are, however, two reasons for not adopting the proposed usage, and for continuing to talk of responsibility in legal contexts. The first is that "responsibility" is syntactically more convenient than "liability". A person who is "liable" must always be liable to something, such as a penalty. One can say that "A is responsible for S", but one cannot say that "A is liable for S" without adding to what it is that he is liable. "Responsible" is a shorthand way of saying "liable to be called to account".[5] There is also a sense in which "liability" can be used to mean something secondary to "responsibility". If A kills X out of premeditated malice, and B kills Y as the result of gross provocation, each is responsible for the death of his victim, but A is liable to more severe punishment than B. This usage may or may not be logically impeccable but, again, it is syntactically convenient.

The second reason is simply a matter of convention. There is no fixed usage, but "responsibility" seems more common, especially among judges, and it is enshrined in the phrase "diminished responsibility", although an abnormality of mind resulting in mitigation of punishment would be more accurately described as "diminished liability to punishment".[6]

---

[5] O.E.D.

[6] Mr. J.W.C. Turner talks of "responsibility" in his 1964 edition of *Russell on Crime*, and of "liability" in his 1958 and 1962 editions of Kenny. Professor Glanville Williams talks of "criminal responsibility": Gl. Williams, p.17, and "strict responsibility": *ibid*. Chap. 6. Professor Smith on the other hand, uses "liability": T.B. Smith, p.132. The Homicide Act 1957 adopts the term as well as the concept of "diminished responsibility," and talks also about "mental responsibility." *Smith and Hogan* tends to use the term "criminal liability"; and the English *Draft Code* uses "liability" rather than "responsibility", but does so sparingly, *e.g.* in clause 21 (Vol. 1 at p.52), and in Pt. 8 of the Commentary (Vol. 2 at p.190) — *cf.* clause 56, side-note only (Vol. 1 at p.67).

Accordingly, while emphasising that the ascription of responsibility by the criminal law is logically independent of moral responsibility or blameworthiness, it is proposed to use the word "responsible" instead of "liable to punishment" or "liable to be called to account by the criminal law."

2.05 *The moral content of the criminal law.* The rules regarding responsibility in the common law of crimes in fact rest almost entirely on moral ideas of praise and blame. The general rule in criminal law is that the person who is legally responsible for any situation is the person who is to blame for it. Thus while at common law the civil law ascribes responsibility to an employer for all his servant's actings in the course of his employment, even if they are criminal, unknown to the employer, and contrary to his interest,[7] the criminal law makes the employer responsible at common law only where he can be said to be morally responsible, for example because of his failure to deal with a situation whose dangerous potentiality was known to him.[8] Accordingly, at common law "Who was criminally responsible?" usually means "Who was to blame?": the general rule is that there is "no idea of a crime without guilt in the mind of the criminal."[9]

The moral nature of the common law of crimes is not a matter of logical necessity or of the definition of crime, but is a matter of fact, and of social policy. The common law has this moral quality because one of its functions is to represent the moral outlook of the community, and to inflict punishment where that moral outlook considers punishment to be appropriate. This does not mean that the law cannot ascribe criminal responsibility quite independently of moral guilt; such ascriptions are often made in statutory crimes, and are sometimes made by the common law itself. But because of the close connection between the common law of crime and ordinary moral judgments it is justifiable to ask in such cases not, of course, whether the person held responsible is "truly" so, or has "really" been guilty of a crime, but whether the criminal law ought to depart from ordinary moral standards; and it is also justifiable to criticise any rule of the criminal law from the standpoint of ordinary morality in order to determine if the rule is good, while conceding that it is in fact a rule of law.[10]

Subjective and objective right

2.06 *Utilitarianism and deontology.* One of the basic conflicts in moral philosophy is that between those who consider that the moral value of an action is to be determined by reference to its consequences, so that a man's duty is to produce the greatest possible good in a given situation, and those who consider that the moral value of an action is to be determined by reference to the motive of the agent, to whether it is done from a sense of duty or some other good motive, or from a bad motive.

---

[7] *e.g. Lloyd v. Grace, Smith and Co.* [1912] A.C. 716.
[8] *cf. Paton and McNab* (1845) 2 Broun 525, L.J.-C. Hope at 534.
[9] *John Grant and Ors.* (1848) J. Shaw 17, Lord Cockburn at 111.
[10] There may of course be forms of behaviour which a society considers morally wrong but for which, for one reason or another, punishment, or at least legal punishment, is inappropriate: see Report of Departmental Committee in Homosexual Offences and Prostitution, 1957, Cmd. 247, paras 12.15. The argument in the text, however, is directed rather to the concept of responsibility for what is *ex hypothesi* a crime than to the problem of what objective facts should be characterised as crimes.

Philosophers who hold the first view are often called Utilitarians, and those who hold the second Deontologists.

The law, which is concerned with the ordering of society, is naturally mainly utilitarian in outlook. It is more interested in the results of an action than in the motives which prompted it. The man who pays his debts out of a fear of the consequences has performed his legal duty just as much as the man who pays them out of a belief that it is right to do so. It follows that to fail in one's intentions is to fail in one's duty. If A has a legal duty to return a book to a friend this duty is not normally fulfilled merely by posting the book, if in fact it does not arrive at the friend's house. If a carelessly dispatched book arrives there is no duty to send another, but if a carefully dispatched book fails to arrive, through no fault of the sender, there may still be a duty to provide a replacement.[11]

But although the law is generally utilitarian, the criminal law is so closely bound up with ordinary morality that it contains many deontological features which also exist in ordinary moral thinking. The criminal law is concerned with apportioning blame and inflicting punishment, and in doing this ordinary people look not only to the results of actions but also to their motives. The man who has done his best, it is felt, should not be blamed because his efforts have been frustrated; and the man who meant no ill is not to be blamed because his actions turned out badly. For the Deontologist it is the road to Heaven, and not to Hell, which is paved with good intentions. This emphasis on motive leads to the view that actions performed from a good motive are of greater value than actions performed from a bad one, even though the results are the same. To do "the right act for the wrong reason"[12] is not, on this view, to have done one's duty; but, and this is more important, to do the wrong deed for the right reason may be regarded as praiseworthy because it exemplifies the good motive involved.

Subjective and objective right. To treat motive as all-important leads, **2.07**
however, to very peculiar results. It can lead to the view that the fanatic who puts his children through the fire to Moloch not from a desire to hurt them but because he considers it his religious duty to do so is a morally good man who has performed an unpleasant act conscientiously, and who therefore cannot be treated as blameworthy or punishable however wrong the action may be when judged objectively. The objectively right act is that act which the omniscient observer would judge to be right. It cannot, however, be a man's duty to do what is objectively right, because, since he is not omniscient, he cannot know what is objectively right. And it is axiomatic that there is no duty to do the impossible. Therefore, it is argued, a man's duty is merely to do what is subjectively right, what he thinks right; and so long as he does that, he cannot be blamed.

The strength of this argument lies in the fact that conscientiousness is admittedly regarded as a virtue. To do what one thinks right is generally to acquit oneself well; other people may feel they would have done otherwise, but will not blame one for what one did. "He acted properly, according to his lights" is a judgment of praise. Despite this, the argument leads to such gross paradoxes that it must be rejected, at least

---

[11] *cf.* W.D. Ross, *The Right and the Good* (Oxford, 1930), Chap. 2, esp. pp.45–46.
[12] T.S. Eliot, *Murder in the Cathedral*, Pt. 1.

in the mundane sphere of the criminal law. For it involves saying that the concentration-camp guards, the medieval heresy-hunters, the ancient Moloch worshippers, are praiseworthy if they performed their abominations in the sane belief that it was right to do so. It is at least as likely that one's judgment on such people will be that their belief that they were doing right makes them more and not less wicked than those who did the same things out of fear of the consequences of refusing them.

2.08 *Errors of fact and of morals.* The paradoxes are at least partly the result of a failure to distinguish between the factual and moral elements in a situation. If this distinction is made it can be said that a man's duty is to do what would be objectively right if the situation were as he believed it to be. If a man cuts off another's head in the belief that it is a block of wood, he is not to be blamed for killing him. In the same way, a man who mistakenly believes that he is being attacked is entitled to retaliate in self-defence,[13] although the act of retaliation would remain objectively wrong, and the victim would be entitled to defend himself against it in turn. What the retaliator does is wrong and unjustified, but he is excusable and not blameable for doing it.[14] But a mistake regarding moral values is irrelevant. If a man believes that it is right to kill all red-headed women, it is still his duty not to kill them, and he will be blameworthy if he does kill any of them. The man who acts under an error of fact cannot be blamed for the results of his error, unless of course the mistake is itself blameworthy, for his act was done in error, and therefore unintentionally. But the man who deliberately does what is wrong is blameworthy, even if he thought he was doing right, because he intended to do what he did. "If a man does something because he does not think it wrong he cannot plead that he did not choose to do it, and it is for choosing to do what is *in fact* wrong, whether he knows it or not, that a man is blamed."[15]

Whether or not this argument is conclusive in the field of moral philosophy, it is submitted that it is one the law must recognise as sound for its own purposes. It is clear that,

> " 'obligations of social morality' need not depend on the agent's thought about the situation . . .
> . . . the obligation arises, not from any completely 'objective' facts, *i.e.* facts which need be not cognized by anyone, but from the thoughts of society, *i.e.*, of most people in the society concerned . . .
> . . . If I told a creditor that his moral claim to have his bill paid was overborne because, in my opinion, my child's claim to a new coat was stronger, he would not agree that my judgment determined the status of his claim."[16]

Any other attitude would lead to anarchy, to a state in which every man was his own lawmaker, who could disobey any law he thought wrong, and do any illegal act he thought right.

---

[13] *cf. Owens v. H.M. Advocate,* 1946 J.C. 119.
[14] See *infra*, para. 13.13.
[15] P.H. Nowell-Smith, *Ethics* (Harmondsworth, 1954), p.294.
[16] D.D. Raphael, *Moral Judgement* (London, 1955), pp.135–139.

In *Reynolds v. U.S.*[17] a Mormon who was charged with bigamy pleaded in defence that it was his religious duty to marry more than one wife. In rejecting the plea Waite C.J. said:

> "If the defendant, under the influence of a religious belief that it was right, . . . deliberately married a second time, having a first wife living, the want of conscious evil intent — the want of understanding on his part that he was committing a crime — did not excuse him . . .[18]
>
> Every act necessary to constitute the crime was knowingly done and the crime was, therefore, knowingly committed. Ignorance of a fact may sometimes be taken as evidence of a want of criminal intent, but not ignorance of the law. The only defense of the accused in this case is his belief that the law ought not to have been enacted."[19]

PUNISHMENT AND RESPONSIBILITY

Theories of Punishment

Theories of punishment[20] fall into two main groups — retributive, and the rest — corresponding to the deontological and utilitarian groups of moral theories. The retributive theory finds the justification for punishment in a past act, a wrong which requires punishment or expiation. Its "object all sublime . . . [is to] let the punishment fit the crime." The other theories, reformative, preventive and deterrent, all find their justification in the future, in the good that will be produced as a result of the punishment. If it will do no good to punish someone, then on utilitarian principles there is neither right nor duty to punish him, however terrible his crimes. **2.09**

Utilitarian theories. The weakness of utilitarian theories lies in their failure to distinguish punishment from any other example of the infliction of pain. If the only justification for punishment is future good, then the lunatic who is put in an asylum is being punished as much as the prisoner in gaol, and his punishment is more justifiable than that of the prisoner, since the consequent good is probably greater, and is certainly more apparent. Again, on the deterrent theory, it would be proper to punish an innocent man who appeared to be guilty since failure to punish the apparently guilty has a deleterious effect on a policy of deterrence, because it makes it look as if crimes can be committed with impunity. **2.10**

"The utilitarian theory, taken alone, requires us to say, with Samuel Butler's Erewhonians, that sickness is a crime which deserves the

[17] 98 U.S. 145 (1878).

[18] At 162, quoting the trial judge.

[19] At 167.

[20] See A. Ashworth, *Sentencing and Penal Policy* (London, 1983) for a general review of sentencing theory and practice. For two interesting treatments of the problem of punishment, see R.A. Duff, *Trials and Punishment* (C.U.P., 1986) and N. Lacey, *State Punishment* (London and New York, 1988).

punishment of medicine. It also requires us to say, when 'it is expedient that one man should die for the people,' that he deserves this as a punishment."[21] It was this disregard for the right of the individual against the community that led to Kant's vehement opposition to any form of utilitarian theory of punishment. "Juridical punishment", he said, "can never be administered merely as a means for promoting another Good either with regard to the Criminal himself or to Civil Society, but must in all cases be imposed only because the individual on whom it is inflicted *has committed a Crime*. For one man ought never to be dealt with merely as a means subservient to the purpose of another."[22]

2.11 *The retributive theory.* The retributive theory also faces serious difficulties. Punishment involves the infliction of pain, and pain, in itself, is evil. Its infliction requires justification, and to justify it solely by reference to a prior infliction of evil by the person punished is rather like trying to make a white out of two blacks. What good, it may be asked, does it do to hang a murderer? It only leaves two dead men instead of one. "The suffering caused by the punishment is, considered by itself, an evil, and ought to be inflicted only for the sake of some prepondering good."[23] There is perhaps one positive good provided on the retributive theory, but it is of a rather vague kind. It is that punishment expresses and canalises the moral indignation of the community; and that it thus operates as a reassertion of the law that has been broken.[24] To leave an act unpunished may be regarded as equivalent to condoning it, for the connection between crime and punishment is a very close and fundamental one in the ordinary man's moral thinking. It is just because the utilitarian theories ignore this, and so ignore the factor of desert, that they are unsatisfactory. And it is because it clings so strongly to the concept of desert that the retributive theory retains its strength and its popular appeal.[25]

2.12 *A compromise theory.* It is possible to adopt a theory which stands midway between retribution and utility and combines the best features of both. One can accept the view that a man "must first be found guilty and *punishable*, before there can be any thought of drawing from his Punishment any benefit for himself or his fellow-citizens",[26] and at the same time decline to punish him unless some good will result. Thus, punishment of someone who has done no wrong can never be justified, and the connection between punishment and desert is maintained; but punishment of someone who deserves punishment can be justified only on the utilitarian ground that some good will come of the punishment and the form of punishment must therefore be chosen by reference to the possible production of good.[27]

Another approach is to argue that while the justification or general justifying aim of any system of punishment must be the utilitarian aim of

---

[21] D.D. Raphael, *op.cit.*, 70.

[22] Kant, *Philosophy of Law*, trans. W. Hastie (Edinburgh, 1887), p.195.

[23] Macaulay, p.455.

[24] See *e.g.* J. Andenaes, *Punishment and Deterrence* (Ann Arbor, 1974).

[25] See D.J. Calligan, "The Return to Retribution in Penal Theory," in *Crime, Proof and Punishment*, ed. Tapper (London, 1981), p.144.

[26] Kant, *op.cit., loc. cit.*

[27] See W.G. Maclagan, "Punishment and Retribution," *Philosophy,* Vol. XIV (1939), p.281.

crime prevention, the imposition of punishment on individuals must be justified by their having voluntarily broken a legal rule.[28]

The law in practice tends to combine retribution and deterrence. It takes the view that wrongdoers "ought to be punished with the pains of law, to deter others from committing the like crimes in all time coming", as the old indictments used to say, and it assumes that punishment has this effect; but it punishes only people whom it regards as guilty of a crime, and it moderates its punishment when there are factors present which diminish the criminal's guilt.[29] Even where the purpose of legal punishment is mainly preventive as it was in the now abandoned sentence of preventive detention, or reformative as it was in the now abandoned sentence of corrective training, the law still requires the commission of a criminal act as a necessary preliminary to punishment, and generally requires that the punishment be commensurate with the act. It required, indeed, for preventive detention, not merely a criminal act on the occasion of the punishment but a series of prior convictions followed by more usual forms of punishment. It is true that a man could be sentenced to eight years preventive detention for stealing a bundle of laundry, but he had to have stolen the bundle, and in addition he had to have been previously convicted on the statutory number of occasions.[30]

Punishment and treatment

A more radical approach to the whole question of criminal responsibility which enjoyed considerable acceptance amongst penologists and criminologists until recently, and which is reflected also in legislation such as the Social Work (Scotland) Act 1968 and the Children (Scotland) Act 1995 (Chapter 3),[31] is to abandon notions of crime and punishment in favour of notions of disease and treatment. Since on this view the delinquent is not being punished for the good of society but treated for his own good, there is no need for that treatment to be restricted by considerations of justice, of due process, or in particular by any need to limit the amount of treatment imposed by reference to the gravity of the actual offence.[32] Although this approach has been applied to children in Scotland, it has recently fallen out of favour.[33] The so-called "rehabilitative ideal" which it enshrines has been attacked as being dangerous to individual liberty,[34] and as being based on an untenable analogy between crime and disease.[35] It has also lost ground because of the absence of any **2.13**

[28] See *e.g.* H.L.A. Hart, *op.cit.*, esp. Chap. 1; J. Rawls, "Two Concepts of Rules" (1955) 64 *Philosophical Review* 3. There are collections of papers on theories of punishment in H.B. Acton (ed.) *Theories of Punishment* (London, 1969), and in A. von Hirsch and A. Ashworth (eds.) *Principled Sentencing* (Edinburgh, 1992).

[29] *cf. Kirkwood v. H.M. Advocate*, 1939 J.C. 36; *John McLean* (1876) 3 Couper 334.

[30] *e.g. H.M. Advocate v. Churchill*, 1953 J.C. 6 — the accused in fact had forty previous convictions.

[31] See Report of Committee on Children and Young Persons (The Kilbrandon Report), Cmnd. 2306/1964; A. Morris, "Scottish Juvenile Justice: A Critique" in *Crime, Criminology and Public Policy*, ed. Hood (London, 1974), p.347.

[32] See, esp., Kilbrandon Report, *supra*, para. 54.

[33] It had in fact already been subject to considerable attack in the United States — *re Gault*, 387 U.S. 1 (1967) — before its adoption in Scotland.

[34] See *e.g.* F.A. Allen, "Criminal Justice, Legal Values and the Rehabilitative Ideal" (1959) 50 J.Cr.L. Cry. and P.S. 226; N.H. Kittrie, *The Right to be Different* (Baltimore and London, 1971), and C.S. Lewis' *tour de force*, "The Humanitarian Theory of Punishment" (1953) 6 *Res Judicata*, 224.

[35] See *e.g.* A. Flew, *Crime or Disease?* (London, 1973).

evidence that there are any known effective means of treating delinquents: even psychiatrists seem now to accept that there is little they can do except in the small number of cases where the offender suffers from one of the recognised forms of mental diseases.[36]

The treatment approach also suggests that preventive measures should be available so that a person who has committed only a minor offence but is found to be dangerous can be dealt with for his dangerousness even if the "treatment" involves a long period of detention out of all proportion to the gravity of his actual offence.[37] Indeed, in theory, there is no need for any offence to be committed at all; what matters is the dangerousness and not whether any offence has been committed. Although the law does create preventive offences and punishes attempted crimes,[38] these are fairly clearly defined so that the individual knows what he must not do if he wants to keep out of the hands of the law. To allow the state to interfere with someone who has committed no offence or no serious offence would be to sacrifice individual choice to the protection of society: our society at present prefers to sacrifice some element of protection by waiting, so to speak, until the horse has actually bolted before it shuts the stable door.[39] Or rather this is its basic philosophy; the existence of attempted crimes represents an uneasy compromise. In any event any attempt to provide for the treatment of dangerous offenders who have not yet committed serious offences will founder on the absence of any reliable means of diagnosing dangerousness, far less of curing it or recognising that it has been cured. There are provisions in relation to psychopaths which do in effect provide for the treatment of dangerous offenders, but they are in practice usually invoked only in the case of persons who have committed serious offences.[39a]

---

[36] Compare the attitude of the psychiatrists at the time of the Royal Commission on Capital Punishment with their attitude at the time of the Butler Report on Mentally Abnormal Offenders, Cmnd. 6244/1975.

[37] See *e.g.* the current powers of children's hearings under the Children (Scotland) Act 1995; B. Wooton, *Crime and the Criminal Law*; Report of Butler Committee on Mentally Abnormal Offenders; Report of Scottish Council on Crime, 1974.

[38] *cf.* N. Walker, *Sentencing in a Rational Society,* Chap. 1.

[39] See H.L.A. Hart, *Punishment and Responsibility*, esp.Chap. 1.

[39a] Under Art. 5(1) of the European Convention on Human Rights, of course, "no one shall be deprived of his liberty save in the following cases and in accordance with a procedure prescribed by law: (a) the lawful detention of a person after conviction by a competent court; . . . (e) the lawful detention . . . of persons of unsound mind, alcoholics or drug addicts or vagrants." (See the Human Rights Act 1998, Sched. 1, Pt. I.) Recently, the 1st Div. of the Court of Session found legislation enacted by the Scottish Parliament (the Mental Health (Public Safety and Appeals) (Scotland) Act 1999), under which the existing conditions for the absolute discharge (by the Scottish Ministers or sheriffs on appeal from the Ministers) of patients detained under hospital orders and subject to restriction on discharge, were made secondary to a new requirement that discharge be refused if continued detention was considered to be "necessary, in order to protect the public from serious harm", to be in conformity with Art. 5(1)(e). The legislation did, however, insist that such patients be found to continue to suffer from a mental disorder; but there was no requirement that that should be the same mental disorder which had originally secured their admission to hospital, and no requirement that the current disorder should be treatable — although amenability to treatment had been an essential requirement of hospital admission at the outset, when the patients discussed in the case had been convicted of, or pled guilty to, serious crimes of violence (culpable homicide or manslaughter, on the basis of diminished responsibility). Within the criteria and principles established by the European Court of Human Rights, there was a balance to be struck, as L.P. Rodger put it, "between the interest of the community in protecting the lives and health of the members of the public and the protection of the individual rights of the restricted patient in question": see *A. v. The Scottish Ministers,* 2000 S.L.T. 873, at 885I.

Deterrence. The penological pessimism[40] which has led to the decline of the rehabilitative ideal has also led to a decline in belief in the proved efficacy of deterrence.[41] General deterrence, if effective at all, is thought to be effective only in the very general sense of reasserting the values of the community.[42] The result of applying a theory of this kind is to treat sentencing as primarily an exercise in denunciation, designed to reinforce the values supported by the law.[43] And this in turn means that the actual sentences imposed will be very similar to those which would be imposed on a retributive theory, unless some of the weight such a theory would give to mitigating factors has to be reduced for the sake of enforcing respect or fear of the law. **2.14**

It is impossible to form any conclusion on these difficult matters: there probably is no one theory of punishment which explains all the different punishments which are thought appropriate for all the different kinds of offence which a summary court in a large town will deal with in the course of a morning. Perhaps the best one can do is to recognise that in almost every case the sentence will be harmful to the offender, but that the protection of society does require the infliction of such harm, and try to do as little harm as is necessary. This form of justice tempered with mercy is at least preferable to the eagerness of the rehabilitative ideal to do as much "good" as possible to the delinquent in the name of a hypocritical belief that what is necessary for the protection of society is also for his own good.[44]

Punishment and freewill

So long as punishment is considered retributive to any extent, so long as it is bound up with the concept of desert, it can be inflicted only for an act freely done: in the classic Kantian phrase, "I ought implies I can"; a man cannot be blamed for something he could not help doing, or for failing to do the impossible. **2.15**

The problem of freewill is probably insoluble on the metaphysical level, and its application in every-day judgments involves many paradoxes. A man is punished only when he could have done otherwise than he in fact did, when his action stemmed from his free choice; but he is punished in the hope that his punishment will influence his future actions and those of other free agents. Fortunately the legal problem is simpler than this.

> "The truth is that the ethical question is not the metaphysical one, whether the human will as such is or is not absolutely uncaused, but

---

[40] See R. Cross, *Punishment, Prison and the Public* (London, 1971).

[41] See F. Zimring and G. Hawkins, *Deterrence: The Legal Threat in Crime Control* (Chicago, 1973). See also N.D. Walker, "The Efficiency and Morality of Deterrents" [1979] Crim.L.R. 129; "Punishing, Denouncing or Reducing Crime", in *Reshaping the Criminal Law*, ed. Glazebrook (London, 1978), p.391; "The Ultimate Justification: Varieties of the Expressive Theory of Punishment", in *Crime, Proof and Punishment*, ed. Tapper (London, 1981), p.109.

[42] See especially J. Andenaes, *op.cit.*, n.24. For an interesting variation on this approach, see N. Lacey, *State Punishment* (London and New York, 1988).

[43] See *e.g.* J. Fitzjames Stephen, *History of the Criminal Law of England* (London, 1883), Vol. II, Chap. 17; (1864) *Fraser's Magazine* 761. Denunciation is criticised by Hart in *Law, Liberty and Morality* (London, 1963), pp.60–69, and *Punishment and Responsibility*, Chap. VII.

[44] Some of the above arguments are developed in my review article on A. Ross, *On Guilt, Responsibility and Punishment*, in (1976) 26 U. of Toronto Law Journal 214.

> rather how to discriminate properly between those who should and those who should not be held accountable for legally prohibited acts. And here the prevailing ethical conscience today seems to recognise a commonsense distinction between voluntary and involuntary acts, and generally holds that no one should be punished for any act in which his will did not enter."[45]

The question, of course, is what acts are recognised as voluntary, as "free". "Freedom" is a vague word and can mean free from anything, but for legal purposes it means free from any influence which cannot be affected by punishment. The thief who steals from greed acts freely because his tendency to give way to the influence of his greed can be countered by the threat of punishment which will provide him with a motive of fear to set against his greed. But the kleptomaniac who steals because he is diseased does not act freely, since punishment cannot affect the mania which causes him to steal. Whatever the metaphysical or even ethical difficulties, it seems that the law can and indeed must accept Nowell-Smith's view that "A man is not punishable because he is guilty; he is guilty because he is punishable, that is to say, because some useful result is supposed to accrue from punishing him",[46] provided, of course, that it is remembered that he must also he guilty in the sense of having committed a criminal act. The result is that punishment can be inflicted only for a free and blameworthy act, but that an act is considered to be free and blameworthy only if it is capable of being affected by the threat of punishment.

2.16 *Self-determinism.* This view of guilt and freedom must be considered in the light of the theory of self-determinism. This is the theory that a man's actions are all ultimately determined by his character and are therefore not free. A man is not responsible for his character, it is argued, because it is something with which he is born, or at any rate which depends on hereditary, environmental and other factors beyond his control. A man acts as he does because he is the sort of person he is, and he cannot help being the sort of person he is. It may be that some facets of his character are corrigible while others are not, but the very corrigibility of any facet depends itself on the sort of man he is: some people are so made that they can be cured of a tendency to steal or drink, others are so made that they cannot be cured of such tendencies. And of course the man who is constitutionally incapable of being cured of a vicious tendency does not act freely when he succumbs to the promptings of that vice.[47]

This theory cannot, it is submitted, be adopted, though it emphasises an important aspect of certain problems, particularly that of addiction. It depends on a peculiar use of language, which distinguishes between a man on the one hand, and on the other his "character", which is sometimes referred to as his "universe of desires" because it is the result of a balance of all his inborn desires. It sees men spending their lives fighting a hopeless battle against their desires. The man born with only a weak desire to do his duty or to be kind and a strong desire to be selfish

---

[45] M.R. Cohen, *Reason and Law* (Glencoe, Ill., 1950), p.29.

[46] P.H. Nowell-Smith, "Freewill and Moral Responsibility," (1948) 57 *Mind* 45, 58.

[47] The theory is fully expounded in W.D. Ross, *Foundations of Ethics* (Oxford, 1939), Chap. 10.

or cruel will always choose to perform the more selfish or cruel of two possible actions: and since he cannot help being selfish or cruel he cannot be blamed for his choice. But this dichotomy between a person and his character is a surprising one, and contrary to ordinary usage. For a man *is* his character, the sum of his conflicting desires, and when one judges the man, it is his character that is being judged. It may sound meaningful to say "Is a man to be blamed for his dispositions?", but this apparent meaningfulness begins to disappear if one asks "Can he be blamed for his desires?", and disappears completely when one asks "Can he be blamed for his character, for being himself?" One does in fact praise a man for being kind, blame him for being selfish. It is just when an action is "in character" that one feels happiest about judging it. Where an action is "out of character" it is not hailed as an example of free choice, on the contrary a search is made for the external circumstances which caused the man to act in such an uncharacteristic way.

But though it does not make sense to say " 'Twas not Hamlet wronged you, but his character", it does make sense to say " 'Twas not Hamlet wronged you, but his madness."[48] This is because of the distinction between moral and non-moral characteristics, which is the distinction between what is corrigible and punishable, and what is not; and it is a distinction which ultimately the self-determinist cannot make. The stupid are not blamed, the wicked are; punishment may curb wickedness, it will not increase knowledge. "We might therefore say that moral traits of character are just those traits that are known to be amenable to praise or blame; and this would explain why we punish idle boys but not stupid ones, thieves but not kleptomaniacs, the sane but not the insane."[49]

The problem of addiction. Actions which spring from a diseased state of **2.17**
mind would thus be regarded as punishable only if (a) the agent could be considered responsible for his condition — the requirement of desert; and (b) the disease was amenable to punishment — the requirement of utility. These are probably two sides of the same coin: an action would not be attributed to disease if the agent was thought of as responsible. But the phenomenon of addiction presents awkward problems from whatever side of the question it is approached. The addict is by definition unable to control his craving, and so might be said not to be responsible for anything he does as a result of the craving, or of the effects of any drug for which he craves. Nor will punishment cure his addiction. But his condition may be the result of his own earlier actings, so that he can be said to have made himself an addict. His addiction was at one stage a habit, and it may be said that persons are responsible for their habits. Aristotle defined the good man as a man addicted to goodness. "Moral goodness", he said, "Is the child of habit . . . the moral virtues we acquire by first exercising them . . . we become just by performing just actions, temperate by performing temperate actions, brave by performing brave actions . . . We find legislators seeking to make good men of their fellows by making good behaviour habitual with them."[50] So the habit of doing good acts is something praiseworthy and

---

[48] *cf. Hamlet*, V.2.

[49] P.H. Nowell-Smith, *Ethics* (Harmondsworth, 1954), p.304. There may of course be individual cases where it is difficult to determine into which category an agent falls. On the problem of the psychopath in this connection see V. Haksar, "Aristotle and the Punishment of Psychopaths" (1964) 39 *Philosophy* 323.

[50] *Nichomachean Ethics,* II, 1, trans. J.A.K. Thomson (Harmondsworth, 1955), pp.55–56.

to be encouraged, the habit of doing evil something to be blamed and discouraged. But there comes a stage, at any rate in the case of the drug addict, when punishment is unable to discourage the habit.

At that stage there are two ways of judging the situation. On the one hand the addict can be thought of as being himself to blame for his addiction. "There was a time when he need not have been ill; but once he let himself go, the opportunity was lost."[51] He is therefore to blame for his addiction, and punishable, if only in order to deter others from allowing themselves to degenerate into a comparable state. But on the other hand, once a person has become an addict he is no longer capable of controlling his addiction; he is not to blame for taking the drink or drugs he now takes because he cannot help taking them. And punishment will not help or deter him or anyone else in his kind of state. "Addiction to opium is a vice, as is also any bad habit that a man cannot break however hard he tries. But these are not culpable states simply because, whatever may have been the case in the past, he cannot now avoid them."[52] To punish him now for those earlier indulgences from which he could have refrained seems futile, and suggests a failure to cope with or recognise the true situation. Another objection to punishing the fifty-year-old alcoholic for the drinks he took at the age of thirty is that when he drank at thirty he had no intention of becoming an alcoholic, and probably did not foresee the possibility of his becoming one. It is very difficult to find the occasions when he was not yet an alcoholic but should have realised that unless he stopped drinking he would soon become one. The nearer he comes to the state of addiction, the clearer it is that he may become an alcoholic — and the more difficult for him to stop the habit.

Addiction is the type case for those situations in which a man voluntarily puts himself into a condition in which he is incapable of free action, and then does something criminal. The problem is always, can the subsequent crime be punished because the agent himself created the situation in which he lost his freedom, because he was, so to speak, responsible for his own irresponsibility, or is he to be treated as the irresponsible person he has become?[53] If punishment is to be directed only to the original free act which made him irresponsible, there arises the further question whether he can be treated as responsible for the later acts as consequences of his free act, and the answer to this depends on the causal criterion adopted by the system under which he is judged.[54]

---

[51] *ibid.*, III, 5.

[52] P.H. Nowell-Smith, *op.cit.*, p.265. *Cf. Kiely v. Lunn*, 1983 J.C. 4.

[53] *cf. Brennan v. H.M. Advocate,* 1977 J.C. 38, *infra*, para. 12.12.

[54] See *infra*, Chap. 4.

PART II

THE CRIMINAL ACT
AND
THE CRIMINAL MIND

CHAPTER 3

THE CRIMINAL ACT

THE ACTUS REUS

It is axiomatic that before there can be a conviction for crime there must have been created a situation forbidden by the criminal law — and for each crime there is an appropriate forbidden situation. The forbidden situation is known as the *actus reus*. What constitutes the *actus reus* of any particular crime can be discovered only by reference to the definition of that crime. A criminal charge must set out facts which amount to a situation forbidden by law, and if it fails to do so because of the omission of an essential factor, it is *funditus* null, since it lacks the minimum requirement for conviction. However wicked a man's intentions may be he is guilty of no completed crime if he has brought about no *actus reus*, although he may be guilty of a criminal attempt. **3.01**

The concept of the actus reus

The *actus reus* of any crime can be positively defined, at least to some extent. There must, for example be the killing of a human being before there can be homicide. This positive definition may include certain attendant circumstances, so that the crime is constituted by S in circumstances C, and not merely by S. For example, the infliction of "cruel and barbarous usages" is not *per se* a crime,[1] not is it a crime merely to make threats[2]; but in the appropriate circumstances these things may be an essential part of an *actus reus*. **3.02**

The case of *McKenzie v. Whyte*[3] is an example of an act, neutral in itself, which may or may not be criminal depending on circumstances. The charge was that the accused "did . . . wickedly and feloniously, expose their persons in an indecent and unbecoming manner, and did take off their clothes and expose themselves . . . in a state of nudity, to the annoyance of the lieges", without further specification of circumstances, and it was held to be a bad charge. Lord Neaves pointed out that "A woman may be suckling her child by the roadside under circumstances which to some may constitute indecent exposure of her person. A female at a ball or in a ballet may be so dressed as to fall under a similar imputation",[4] but in these cases there is no crime. Indecent exposure in itself may be "for laudable and innocent objects",[5] and is only criminal if it happens in a situation calculated to outrage public decency.[6] This circumstance is therefore part of the positive definition of the *actus reus* of indecent exposure.

---

[1] *Watt and Kerr* (1868) 1 Couper 123.

[2] *Kenny v. H.M. Advocate,* 1951 J.C. 104.

[3] (1864) 4 Irv. 570.

[4] At 573.

[5] L.J.-C. Inglis at 576.

[6] In *Niven v. Tudhope*, 1982 S.C.C.R. 365, the conviction of a sunbather, whose loose clothing enabled his private parts to be seen, was quashed because of the absence of any finding of "wilful conduct".

3.03 The concept of *actus reus* is also a "defeasible" one, and the *actus reus* can be described as a "prima facie crime".[7] That is to say, the *actus reus* of a crime may be described by a sentence of the kind "bringing about (or doing) S unless in circumstances C1 or C2 or . . . ". The situation prohibited by law must occur in the absence of circumstances which would constitute legal justification. The killing of a human being is the "type situation" for homicide,[8] but killing a human being is not homicide if done in certain privileged circumstances, such as those surrounding a judicial execution or those of self-defence. The difference between a "defeasing" circumstance like this and a positive requirement such as one that indecent exposure to be criminal must occur in circumstances calculated to outrage decency, is this: indecent exposure is not criminal if certain other circumstances are absent; killing a human being is criminal unless certain other circumstances are present. For an indictment to be good it must set forth an *actus reus*, a prima facie crime. It is irrelevant merely to libel exposure because this is not prima facie a crime; it is necessary to libel also the circumstances which make it criminal. It is relevant to libel the killing of a human being, since this is prima facie a crime, and it is, as a matter of procedure,[9] unnecessary to set out the absence of any "defeasing" circumstances. Similarly the Prevention of Crimes Act 1871, section 3, made it an offence for "any dealer in old metals" to buy metals in less than specified quantities. In *Adams v. Mackenna*[10] a charge brought under this section was held to disclose no crime because it failed to narrate that the accused was a dealer in old metals, and so omitted an essential element of the offence.

3.04 *Actus reus and mens rea.* The most important "defeasing" circumstance is the absence of a criminal state of mind, of *mens rea*[11]: the maxim *actus non facit reum nisi mens sit rea* is proverbial. Strictly speaking, and leaving aside offences of strict responsibility, it is improper to call any situation an *actus reus* unless it was created with *mens rea*, but it is possible and convenient to treat the lack of *mens rea* as different from any other "defeasing" factor. The term "*actus reus*" can then be used for situations which would be criminal were they accompanied by *mens rea*; a term is necessary for all the objective or external ingredients of a crime, and "*actus reus*" is the obvious one to use.[12]

---

[7] On defeasible concepts see H.L.A. Hart, "The Ascription of Responsibility and Rights", *Proceedings of Aristotelian Society*, 1948–49, p.171, reprinted in *Essays on Logic and Language*, ed. Flew (Oxford, 1951) p.145. The criticisms in P.T. Geach, "Ascriptivism" (1960) 69 Phil. Rev. 221, and G. Pitcher, "Hart on Action and Responsibility", *ibid.*, p.226, do not affect the application of Hart's approach to the use of terms implying legal responsibility.

[8] See G.L. Radbruch, "Jurisprudence in the Criminal Law" (1936) 18 J. Comp.Leg. and Int. Law, 212, 220.

[9] *cf.* 1995 Act, Sched.3, para. 16; *Nimmo v. Alexander Cowan and Sons* 1967 S.C. (H.L.) 79.

[10] (1906) 5 Adam 106.

[11] For the concept of *mens rea*, see *infra*, paras 7.01 to 7.12.

[12] *cf.* Gl. Williams, p.18.

Although the absence of *mens rea* will usually prevent the conviction of the creator of the *actus reus*, it does not necessarily prevent the objective act or result being regarded as criminal for other purposes; it may still be a crime, albeit an "unenforceable crime" so far as the person who lacks *mens rea* is concerned. A man who forces someone else to commit a crime or tricks him into committing it cannot plead in answer to a charge of instigation that no crime was committed because the other party acted under duress or mistake.[13] If A mistakenly attacks B in self-defence, B is entitled to retaliate since, although A lacks *mens rea*, his attack on B is in fact unjustified.

There are some crimes which have a mental element as part of their definition.[14] The best example of such a crime is theft, which normally requires an intention to deprive B of his property. If this intent is absent there is no theft, just as if the physical act of taking is absent there can be no theft by taking. It is arguable, therefore, that where goods are taken by an infant or a lunatic, who is deemed to be incapable of forming the necessary intent, there is no *actus reus*, and someone who receives property "stolen" by such persons is not guilty of reset, although he may be guilty of theft.[15]

Result-crimes and conduct-crimes

There are a number of crimes in which the *actus reus*, the situation forbidden by law, is separable in time and/or place from the criminal conduct forbidding it, where the law is interested only in the result and not in the conduct bringing about the result. The typical example of such a crime is murder: murder is committed when a live human being is killed with *mens rea*, and the crime is the same whatever method is used to bring about the result. Crimes of this kind are called "result-crimes". There are other crimes in which the conduct and the *actus reus* are inseparable in time and place although they may be logically distinguishable, in which the nature of the conduct is the essential element of the *actus reus*. Perjury, for example, is just the giving of false evidence on oath, not the bringing about of any particular result or any result at all by so doing: uttering is completed when the false article is made public with the necessary *mens rea* whether or not any result follows. Crimes of this kind are called "conduct-crimes".[16] **3.05**

There are some crimes which do not fall neatly into either category, but are essentially result-crimes. Fraud, for example, consists in bringing about a result: inducing the dupe to behave in a certain way, by means of a certain form of conduct: the making of false representations. Capital murder was bringing about death in one of a number of ways.[17] In such cases the conduct is part of the *actus reus*, but the crime is not complete until the result is achieved.

---

[13] *R. v. Bourne* (1952) Cr.App.R 125; *Cf. D.P.P. v. Lynch* [1975] A.C. 653; *R. v. Cogan* [1976] Q.B. 217.

[14] This is in a sense true of all attempts, but the concept of *actus reus* cannot be fully applied to attempted crimes: see *infra*, para. 6.03.

[15] See Vol. II, Chap. 14.

[16] For a criticism of this terminology see *R. v. Treacy* [1971] A.C. 537, Lord Diplock at 560; J.C. Smith and B. Hogan, *Criminal Law* (9th ed., by Sir. John Smith, 1999), pp.29–30. Lord Diplock nevertheless made use of the distinction elsewhere: see, *e.g.*, *R. v. Miller* [1983] 2 A.C. 161, at 174–175.

[17] Homicide Act 1957.

The elements of the actus reus

3.06 The positive definition of most crimes is complex and includes a number of elements. Rape, for example, is forcible intercourse with a female against her will, bigamy is going through a valid form of marriage while one's spouse is alive, theft is taking or appropriating property which belongs to someone else without lawful authority. It is sometimes useful to divide the elements of a crime into a central element on the one hand, and attendant circumstances in the other.[18] No such distinction will be logically perfect, nor is it possible to fix any rules *a priori* for determining the central element of any crime. The most that can be said is that it should be defined narrowly rather than widely and that it is not co-extensive with the circumstances which make the act criminal. The central element of rape, for example, is forcible intercourse, of bigamy the going through a valid form of marriage. The distinction is important in connection with *mens rea*, especially in statutory crimes. For while a crime of intention always requires the *mens rea* of intention for its central element, it may not do so for its attendant circumstances. That is why it is posssible to say that a statutory offence like selling goods of a certain kind requires *mens rea*, an intention to do the act forbidden, and to hold at the same time that the crime is committed provided A means to sell the particular goods even if he is unaware of their character, the central element being taken as the act of selling, and the nature of the goods as an attendant circumstance.[19]

3.07 *The mental element in the actus reus.* Apart from the case of those crimes like theft whose definition contains a mental element, there is a sense in which the *actus reus* of almost[20] all crimes contains a mental element — the mental element necesary to constitute criminal conduct, that is to say, the element of volition.[21]

CRIMINAL CONDUCT

Voluntary conduct

3.08 The minimum requirement of moral responsibility is that a man can be held responsible for a situation only where it has been caused or contributed to by his acts or omissions. This is not a sufficient requirement but without it there can be no question of moral responsibility at all: and the term "act" is usually restricted to "voluntary" acts, so that a man is responsible only for his voluntary acts.

Unfortunately the two concepts, of voluntariness and of "an act", are both difficult ones.

3.09 There is a dispute as to whether voluntariness itself is a positive or a negative quality. On the one hand, it is said that to characterise an act as voluntary is merely to deny the presence of any of the factors recognised

---

[18] *cf.* Model Penal Code, T.D.4, 123 *et seq.*

[19] *cf. ibid.* and Lord Devlin, "Statutory Offences" (1958) 4 *J. Soc. of Public Teachers of Law* 206, 213. See *infra*, para. 8.01.

[20] The qualification is necessary in order to take account of situations like that in *R. v. Larsonneur* (1933) 97 J.P. 206, and of any difficulties created by crimes of omission or of possession.

[21] *cf.* Gl. Williams, para. 8.

as excluding voluntariness. "To say that a man acted voluntarily is in effect to say that he did something when he was not in one of the conditions specified on the list of conditions which preclude responsibility."[22] "The word 'voluntary' in fact serves to exclude a heterogeneous range of cases such as physical compulsion, coercion by threats, accidents, mistakes, etc., and not to designate a mental element or state, nor does 'involuntariness' signify the absence of this element or state.[23] On the other hand, it is argued that concepts like mistake and accident can be defined only by reference to the absence of some mental element in the agent, and the same can no doubt be said of compulsion or automatism. "There is little point in a theory that seeks to explain concept X by reference to another concept which in analysis is merely non-X. Definition should be in terms of the positive."[24]

In practice, it is for the accused to raise the issue of lack of voluntariness, and to point to the presence of some factor which is accepted by the law as excluding voluntariness, such as unconsciousness or overpowering compulsion. Nor is it clear what would constitute positive proof of voluntariness. The simple picture of a voluntary act as an external physical movement preceded by an internal act of willing, the picture of the "ghost in the machine", cannot survive the attacks of Gilbert Ryle[25] and other modern philosophers. Moreover, careless conduct cannot be comfortably described in terms of acts of will, and careless omissions cannot be so described at all. This is not to deny that physical behaviour can be controlled or affected by mental activity, but the mental activity and its relationship to action are much more complicated than in the traditional picture.

The classical definition of a "voluntary act" is "a willed muscular **3.10**
movement", but this is unhelpful, apart altogether from the problem of identifying acts of will. Persons do not commit crimes by making muscular movements, and most of us are wholly ignorant of what muscles we move when, for example, we lift our arms, or walk across a room. And even if we walk across a room after having deliberately formed an intention to do so, the object of our intention is walking across the room, and not moving the requisite muscles.

The most significant feature of the concept of an act is what Joel Feinberg has called its "accordion effect".[26] Take, for example, the facts of *Ryan v. The Queen*,[27] where the accused went armed to rob a garage, pointed his cocked sawn-off rifle without a safety-catch at the attendant, grappled with the attendant in order to tie him up, and in the struggle "pressed" the trigger, shot and killed the attendant. A system which has as its basic rule of responsibility a provision that a person is not responsible for "an act or omission which occurs independently of his

---

[22] P. Nowell-Smith, *Ethics* (Harmondsworth, 1954), p.292.

[23] H.L.A. Hart, "The Ascription of Responsibility and Rights", *Essays on Logic and Language*, ed. Flew (Oxford, 1951) pp.145, 153. The legal use of "involuntary" is in fact narrower than Hart's list of excuses suggests.

[24] Gl. Williams, *The Mental Element in Crime* (Jerusalem, 1965), p.16, talking of intention. See also G.E.M. Anscombe, *Intention* (2nd ed., Oxford, 1963), para. 7.

[25] *The Concept of Mind* (London, 1950).

[26] J Feinberg, "Action and Responsibility", *The Philosophy of Action*, ed. A.R. White (Oxford, 1968), pp.95, 106.

[27] (1967) 121 C.L.R. 205.

will, or for an event which occurs by accident",[28] has, when faced with a defence that the trigger was pressed involuntarily, to determine whether the relevent "act" is indeed the pressing of the trigger, or whether it is the pointing of the gun, or the carrying out of the robbery, or simply the killing of the deceased. Or take the case where the accused aims a blow at his wife in the dark and hits and kills the child she is carrying. Is the accused's "act" the wielding of the stick, the striking of the child, or the killing of the child?[29] This problem has forced the Australian courts into some very interesting but rather unrealistic semantic analyses of behaviour in order to determine whether or not an accused should be held responsible.[30]

Questions such as those raised in *Ryan* seem more suited to the study than to the forum, and there is something artificial in resting a man's guilt on such logical subtleties. This, together with the difficulties of the concept of "willed" acts, suggests that it would be better not to talk of voluntary acts at all. It is tempting to argue that the baseline, so to speak, should just be "something done" by the accused, and that in appropriate cases we can then go on to ask if what was done was done intentionally, or recklessly, or carelessly, or accidentally, and so on, but there is an understandable reluctance to count as acts *e.g.* things done while asleep, or to refuse to distinguish between falling and being pushed.

3.11 Professor Hart has suggested that the criterion should be whether what happens occurred as "part of anything the agent takes himself to be doing".[31] This would enable us to treat the tennis player's instinctive shot as voluntary and not as a mere reflex,[32] and would force us to treat Ryan's pressing of the trigger similarly, if what he took himself to be doing was armed robbery, but perhaps not if it was tying up the attendant. Professor P.J. Fitzgerald suggests that what distinguishes voluntary action is the accused's "ability to control his movements".[33] This seems to select the most important feature of voluntary behaviour, although the use of a term like "movements" is reminiscent of the old definition of act in terms of a willed movement. Ability to control one's movements may be affected by external compulsion or by unconsciousness,[34] and "unwilling" behaviour may be regarded by the law as voluntary providing the "agent" is conscious and not being totally and irresistibly manipulated by someone else. There remains the difficult problem of reflex actions, but they are perhaps best treated as a separate group.

---

[28] Queensland and Western Australian Codes, s.23; *cf.* Tasmanian Code, s.13: "No person shall be criminally responsible for an act, unless it is voluntary and intentional; nor for an event which occurs by accident." *Ryan* occurred in New South Wales, but the requirement of a voluntary act was regarded as fundamental; see also *The Queen v. O'Connor* (1980) 54 A.L.J.R. 349.

[29] *Timbu Kolian v. The Queen* (1968) 119 C.L.R. 473; *cf. R. v. Jarmain* [1946] K.B. 74.

[30] See also *Mamote-Kulang of Tamagot v. The Queen* (1964) 111 C.L.R. 62; *Kaporonowski v. The Queen* [1973] 1 A.L.R. 296.

[31] *Punishment and Responsibility* (Oxford, 1968), p.62.

[32] See I.D. Elliott, "Responsibility for Involuntary Acts: *Ryan v. R.*" (1968) 41 A.L.J. 497, 500.

[33] P.J. Fitzgerald , "Voluntary and Involuntary Acts," *The Philosophy of Action*, ed. A.R. White (Oxford, 1968), pp.120, 134; *Oxford Essays in Jurisprudence*, ed. A.G. Guest (Oxford, 1961) p.1.

[34] P.J. Fitzgerald, *op.cit.*, at p.130.

3.12 In practice, voluntariness is important only in two types of case. The first are cases of strict responsibility, since it seems to be accepted that even such cases require voluntary conduct.[35] The second are cases of crimes which require *mens rea*, "committed" where an accused is unconscious, or in a state of automatism which is not the result of insanity, and it is the latter which have caused much discussion and have also produced much case law on the definition of insanity.

Since, however, both "sane automatism" and "insane automatism" lead to acquittal, the adoption of a system which did not require the automatic detention of persons acquitted on the ground of insanity would make the distinction unimportant.[36]

Involuntary conduct

3.13 Voluntariness may be negatived in a number of different ways, only some of which involve unconsciousness on the part of the agent.[37]

Conscious behaviour. PHYSICAL COMPULSION. The simplest example of involuntary conduct is conduct under the compulsion of a physical force. If A's hand is gripped by a person stronger than he, placed on a trigger and moved so as to fire a gun, and A is physically unable to resist what is happening, the firing of the gun is not A's voluntary act, and he is not responsible for it. Indeed, the shooting is not in any important sense A's act at all, it is the act of the person who placed A's finger on the trigger: A is only an innocent agent, no more involved in the crime than is a postman who delivers a parcel containing a time-bomb. If A attacks B who is carrying a child and makes her squeeze and kill the child, it is A and not B who is responsible for the death.[38] Similarly, A is not responsible for failing to take up his salmon nets at the weekend if he is prevented from doing so by a violent storm which makes it impossible to lift them.[39] Again, if A is driving a car which is blown into and damages a lamp post because of a high gale, and without any negligence on A's part, A has not damaged the lamp post either negligently or accidentally.[40] Compulsion of this kind has, since at least the time of Aristotle,[41] been distinguished from situations of duress where the agent chooses to

---

[35] *Hill v. Baxter* [1958] 1 Q.B. 277; J.C. Smith and B. Hogan, *Criminal Law* (9th ed., 1999, by Sir John Smith) 37. See also *Finegan v. Heywood*, 2000 S.C.C.R. 460.

[36] As is now the case in Scotland (except in murder) — 1995 Act, s.57. English law is similar — see the Criminal Procedure (Insanity and Unfitness to Plead) Act 1991. *Cf.* Second Report of Committee on Criminal Procedure in Scotland (Thomson Committee), Cmnd. 6218/1975, Chap. 53.

[37] *cf.* "A Criminal Code for England and Wales" (Law Commission No. 177), Vol. 1, draft code, cl. 33(1), which treats as automatic actions which are reflexes, spasms or convulsions, or which occur while the actor is in certain conditions (of sleep, unconsciousness, impaired consciousness or otherwise) which deprive him of effective control of his acts, and which actions or conditions are not the result either of voluntary intoxication or "of anything done or omitted with the fault [as defined] required for the offence" in question. See the commentary (Vol. 2) to cl. 33, particularly at para. 11.2.

[38] *Hugh Mitchell* (1856) 2 Irv. 488.

[39] *Middleton v. Tough* (1908) 5 Adam 485.

[40] *Hogg v. Macpherson*, 1928 J.C. 15. *Cf.* Aristotle, *Nichomachean Ethics*, III, I, trans. J.A.K. Thomson (Harmondsworth, 1955), p.77: "An act, it is thought, is done under compulsion when it originates in some external cause of such a nature that the agent or person subject to the compulsion contributes nothing to it. Such a situation is created, for example, when a sea captain is carried out of his course by a contrary wind or by men who have got him in their power."

[41] *op. cit. loc. cit.*

act in a certain way "through fear of something worse to follow" as where A kills B in order to save his own life or that of others.

3.14 REFLEX ACTIONS. These are sometimes classed as involuntary because they are unconscious, but as they can happen while the "agent" is conscious they are perhaps better dealt with as comparable to acts under physical compulsion. An example of a reflex action would be the behaviour of a driver who jerked his body and swerved his car because he had been stung by a bee.[42] The reflex action must be one which is purely an unconscious reaction to an external stimulus, and not something which the agent should have been able to control. In *Johnston v. National Coal Board*[43] Lord Kilbrandon rejected a plea by a defender driver in a civil action that he had lost control and swerved because a fly got into his eye, on the ground that a skilled driver could have reacted in such a way as to avoid an accident.

Not all acting without thinking is reflex behaviour. In *McCann v. J.R. McKellar (Alloys) Ltd*[44] the jury in a reparation action had to determine whether a man who dropped an ingot on the pursuer and who explained that he had done so because a spike on the ingot penetrated his finger, had acted negligently. Lord Guest said, "For [the man] to say that his action was instinctive and automatic is no more than saying that he jerked his hand away without thinking".[45] Lord Upjohn said, "No one doubts that, if a workman receives a sudden and entirely unexpected injury, he may automatically and quite involuntarily drop what he is holding and cannot be held to blame . . . it all depends on the degree of pain and the place and unexpectedness of the injury."[46] On the other hand, it was held in *Devine v. Colvilles Ltd*[47] that no blame attached to a workman who injured himself by jumping from a platform in the general panic following an explosion. Neither of these civil cases deals with the question whether there was "an act" at all, but they do show the difficulty of defining reflex action.[48]

---

[42] *cf. Hill v. Baxter* [1958] 1 Q.B. 277; Holmes *The Common Law*, ed. Howe, (Cambridge, Mass. 1963) pp.45–46: "A spasm is not an act".

[43] 1960 S.L.T. (Notes) 84.

[44] 1969 S.C. (H.L.) 1.

[45] At 7.

[46] At 9. In this case the jury and the House of Lords, allowing an appeal from the First Division, held there was negligence.

[47] 1969 S.C. (H.L.) 67.

[48] *cf.* Windeyer J. in *Ryan v. The Queen* (1967) 121 C.L.R. 205, 245–246: "Such phrases as 'reflex action' and 'automatic reaction' can, if used imprecisely and unscientifically, be like 'blackout' mere excuses. They seem to me to have no real application to the case of a fully conscious man who has put himself in a situation in which he has his finger on the trigger of a loaded rifle levelled at another man. If he then presses the trigger in immediate response to a sudden threat or apprehension of danger, as is said to have occurred in this case, his doing so is, it seems to me, a consequence probable and foreseeable of a conscious apprehension of danger, and in that sense a voluntary act. The latent time is no doubt barely appreciable, and what was done might not have been done had the actor had time to think. But is an act to be called involuntary merely because the mind worked quickly and impulsively? I have misgivings in using any language descriptive of psychological processes and phenomena, especially as I doubt whether all those skilled in this field employ their descriptive terms uniformly. Guided however by what has been said in other cases and by writers on criminal law whose works I have read, and especially by the judgments in the House of Lords in *Bratty v. Attorney-General for Northern Ireland* [1963] A.C. 386, I have come to the conclusion that if the applicant, being conscious of the situation in which he had put himself, pressed the trigger as a result, however spontaneous, of the man whom he was threatening making some sudden movement, it could not be said

Smith and Hogan point out that the borderline between an immediate reaction to provocation and a reflex action "must be a fine one. The nature and effect of a reflex action is itself uncertain."[49] But there seems to be room for a rule which excludes simple bodily movements which are an almost instinctive and certainly unthinking reaction to an external stimulus. A jerk of the arm would not count as an act, but a blow directed at someone would.

HYPNOSIS. Actions committed under hypnotic influence are also usually regarded as forms of unconscious actings, analogous to actions while asleep, and hypnosis is certainly a mental condition of the agent, but a person under hyposis may not be unconscious, and the essential feature of the situation is that he is acting under the direction of someone else. That being so, hypnotic behaviour should be treated as analogous to behaviour under physical compulsion.[50] There is no law on the subject in Scotland.[51] It would, however, be reasonable for the law to adopt the view that where "the patient was entirely deprived of control over his actions it would seem consonant with principle to hold that the acts done by him were the acts rather of the hypnotiser than of himself."[52] This view is shared by French Law[53] although it approaches the matter from the standpoint of *mens rea*. The American Law Institute's Model Penal Code treats as involuntary actions[54] "conduct during hypnosis or resulting from hypnotic suggestion", along with reflexes and movements during sleep. **3.15**

The hypnosis must, of course, be itself involuntary. If A submits himself to hypnosis in order to enable him to carry out a crime he is guilty of the crime; if he submits himself to hypnosis without any criminal purpose, but as a result does commit a crime of negligence or recklessness, the defence of hypnosis may not always be open to him, in the same way as a man who knows he is liable to lose consciousness while driving may not be able to plead his unconsciousness in defence to a charge of dangerous or careless driving.[55]

---

that his action was involuntary so as to make the homicide guiltless. The act which caused the death was, it seems to me, using the language of s.18 of the statute, an act of the accused. The question for the jury was whether it was an act done by him in such a way as to make the resulting homicide murder."

[49] J.C. Smith and B. Hogan, *Criminal Law* (9th ed., 1999, by Sir John Smith) p.40. The authors speak of an "immediate and irresistible" reaction to provocation, but if truly irresistible there would, it is submitted, be no responsibility.

[50] *cf.* Gl. Williams, para. 250.

[51] Perhaps the nearest case is *Wm Ross and Robt Robertson* (1836) 1 Swin. 195 where Ross was an idiot who was induced by Robertson to commit murder — both men were charged but Ross was found unfit to plead. In a similar more modern case *Eliz. Thomson*, High Court at Stirling. Aug. 1939, unrep'd, the mentally weak agent was not prosecuted. But in these cases the mind was only "worked on" and not completely taken over as in hypnosis. *Cf.* the statement of Lord McCluskey to the jury in *H.M. Advocate v. Raiker* 1989 S.C.C.R. 149 at 154 C, *infra* at para. 12.17, n.8.

[52] W.F.S. Stallybrass. "A Comparison of the General Principles of Criminal Law in England with the 'Progetto Definitivo di un Nuovo Codice Penale' of Alfredo Rocco", in *Modern Approach*, 390, 403.

[53] *cf.* Donnedieu de Vabres, p.202.

[54] Model Penal Code, O.D., s.2.01(2) (a)-(c).

[55] See *MacLeod v. Mathieson*, 1993 S.C.C.R. 488 (Sh.Ct), a case of careless driving; and *cf. Hill v. Baxter* [1958] 1 Q.B. 277, *infra*, para. 3.28; *Waugh v. James K. Allan Ltd*, 1964 S.C. (H.L.) 102.

3.16 *Unconscious behaviour.* An act is not voluntary if the agent was unconscious at the time and did not know what he was doing.[56] If, then, the accused's mental state is such that he is unconscious of what he is doing, it should follow that he is not responsible for his actings, because they are not truly "acts" at all. Such "acting" is nowadays spoken of as automatic behaviour, and the defence of unconsciousness is referred to as a defence of automatism. To be classed as automatic, behaviour must be wholly unconscious, and a person who acts when his consciousness is reduced, impaired or merely clouded is not acting automatically.[57] Behaviour which is purposive cannot count as automatic behaviour, as in *R. v. Isitt* [58] where the accused drove off after an accident and engaged in manoeuvres designed to escape from pursuing police officers while he was in a fugue and his mind was shut to moral inhibitions.

3.17 INSANE AUTOMATISM. Logically, if A's conduct is involuntary it should not be necessary to consider his *mens rea* at all, since in the absence of any conduct there can be no criminal conduct. Where, therefore, A acts involuntarily as a result of insanity he should be acquitted by a simple verdict of not guilty, verdicts of not guilty by reason of insanity being confined to cases where A committed the act charged consciously but under the influence of insanity. Indeed, the form of insanity verdict includes a statement that A "committed the act charged", and is therefore strictly speaking inconsistent with a defence of automatism. But the courts have not adopted this approach, and the law is that where the automatism is caused by mental disease, as in the case of an epileptic fugue,[59] the appropriate verdict is one of not guilty by reason of insanity. The reason for this is practical: public safety may require that insane criminals be detained, and from the point of view of public safety it would be illogical to detain those who committed crimes consciously because of their insanity and not those who committed them unconsciously for the same reason. There are difficulties involved in the practice of treating as insane a person who is sane at the time of trial but was insane at an earlier time[60] but these difficulties are the same whether or not the insanity resulted in automatism. The best justification for the present situation is probably that a mental disease is an inherent condition which having once broken out in criminal activities may do so again until it is cured.[61]

---

[56] *cf. Bratty v. Attorney-General for Northern Ireland* [1963] A.C. 386, Lord Denning (obiter) at 409. The relevant part of his Lordship's observation is quoted by the Appeal Court in *Finegan v. Heywood*, 2000 S.C.C.R. 462, at 463E, and subsequently approved by them, it seems, at 464A.

[57] See *Roberts v. Ramsbottom* [1980] 1 W.L.R. 823; *Attorney-General's Reference (No. 2 of 1992)* [1994] Q.B. 91; *Cardle v. Mulrainey*, 1992 S.L.T. 1152.

[58] [1977] 67 Cr.App.R. 44. See also *Broome v. Perkins* [1987] R.T.R. 321.

[59] *H.M. Advocate v. Mitchell*, 1951 J.C. 53; *H.M. Advocate v. Cunningham*, 1963 J.C. 80; *Ross v. H.M. Advocate*, 1991 J.C. 210, L.J.-G. Hope at 213, 217.

[60] See *infra*, para. 10.04.

[61] *Hill v. Baxter* [1958] 1 Q.B. 277, Devlin J. at 285; *R. v. Sullivan* [1984] 1 A.C. 156, Lord Diplock at 172 E-F.

NON-INSANE AUTOMATISM. Where the cause of automatism is insanity, the disposal of the accused is governed by the provisions of the 1995 Act.[62] But there is no procedure for detaining or treating specially in any way non-insane persons who have been acquitted of criminal charges. In cases involving such persons who claim to have acted in a state of automatism three solutions are possible — acquittal followed by the discharge of the accused; a rule that all persons who have committed crimes in a state of automatism should be treated as insane; a rule that automatism is not a defence unless it results from insanity, although it may operate as a mitigating factor. Of these, the first is the logical solution[63] but it may be undesirable in certain cases because of the requirements of public safety[64]; the second is unsatisfactory because it involves a very extended definition of insanity in certain cases; the third is objectionable because it means saying that in certain cases a man is responsible for his unconscious actings.[65] **3.18**

Unconsciousness itself may of course be the result of an external cause, as where it is caused by a blow on the head or the taking of a drug. The argument for treating such cases as non-insane is stronger than it is in relation to unconsciousness caused by some chronic condition such as diabetes or arteriosclerosis, and that argument has found favour with Scottish and English courts. In both jurisdictions non-insane automatism is permitted as a defence leading to acquittal if the accused's unconscious condition was caused by an external factor,[66] provided certain criteria can be met. The effect of these criteria, in Scotland at least, is to emphasise that the defence is treated as one which shows an absence of *mens rea* rather than a lack of voluntariness in the accused's conduct.

The law accordingly is that where an accused is incapable of forming the necessary *mens rea* by reason of some external factor (and not by some disorder of the mind which is liable to recur) which was not self-induced, and was not a situation which he was bound to foresee, and which resulted in a total alienation of reason amounting to a complete loss of self-control, he is entitled to a simple acquittal.[67] The leading case is *Ross v. H.M. Advocate*,[68] which was decided on appeal by a full bench. A five-judge court was convened in order to reconsider the earlier law as

---

[62] s.57(2). A mandatory order confining the person acquitted on the ground of insanity to a hospital, and subjecting him to special restrictions without limit of time, applies only where that person had been charged with murder. Consequently the view that the "consequences of [such an acquittal] are severe" is less compelling than once was the case: see *Ross v. H.M. Advocate* 1991 J.C. 210, *per* L.J.-G. Hope at 213.

[63] And is the law in Scotland, England and Northern Ireland — *Ross v. H.M. Advocate*, 1991 J.C. 210; *Bratty v. Attorney-General for Northern Ireland* [1963] A.C. 386; *R. v. Quick* [1973] Q.B. 910; *R. v. Thornton* (1968) 19 N.I.L.Q. 60; in Canada — *R. v. Bleta* [1964] S.C.R. 561; *R. v. Minor* (1955) 112 C.C.C. 29; in Australia *R. v. Foy* [1960] Qd.R. 225; *R. v. Carter* [1959] V.R. 105; in New Zealand — *R. v. Cottle* [1958] N.Z.L.R. 999; and in South Africa — see E. M. Burchell and P.M.A. Hunt, *South African Criminal Law and Procedure* (3rd ed., 1997), Vol. 1, *General Principles of Criminal Law* (by J.M. Burchell), Chap. 4.

[64] See, *e.g.*, the concerns of Lamer C.J. in *R. v. Parks* [1992] 1 S.C.R. 871, at 892a-894f.

[65] Such responsibility may arise by reason of carelessness: *infra*, para. 3.28, but what is at issue here is direct responsibility for crimes of intent.

[66] See *Ross v. H.M. Advocate*, 1991 J.C. 210; *R. v. Quick* [1973] Q.B. 910; *R. v. Sullivan* [1984] 1 A.C. 156, Lord Diplock at 172H.

[67] *Ross v. H.M. Advocate,* 1991 J.C. 210, L.J.-G. Hope at 218, Lord Weir at 232; *Sorley v. H.M. Advocate,* 1992 J.C. 102, Opinion of the Court at 105. *Cf. Finegan v. Heywood*, 2000 S.C.C.R. 460.

[68] 1991 J.C. 210.

set out in *H.M. Advocate v. Cunningham*,[69] where the accused had been charged with a number of serious driving offences under the Road Traffic Act 1960. He lodged a special defence to the effect that at the relevant time "he was not responsible for his actings on account of the incidence of temporary dissociation[70] due to an epileptic fugue or other pathological condition." This defence was rejected by the High Court as incompetent, and as setting forth a hypothetical state of affairs which, if proved, would not entitle the accused to a verdict of not guilty. Lord Justice-General Clyde (with whom Lord Justice-Clerk Grant and Lord Carmont concurred) implied that the ranks of special defences in Scotland were closed, and opined that this attempt to create a new one "namely, something short of insanity which would lead to acquittal" was "a startling innovation which could lead to serious consequences so far as the safety of the public is concerned."[71] He then concluded:

> "It follows that if this present so-called special defence is to be made into a true special defence, as understood in the law of Scotland, it would require to include an averment of insanity at the time the offence was committed. . . . Any mental or pathological condition short of insanity — any question of diminished responsibility owing to any cause, which does not involve insanity — is relevant only to the question of mitigating circumstances and sentence."[72]

Cunningham was overruled by *Ross*,[72a] and it is no longer the case that *any* mental or pathological condition short of insanity goes only to mitigation. *Ross* in effect gives the authority of a full bench to the earlier case of *H.M. Advocate v. Ritchie*.[73] The accused in *Ritchie* was charged with culpable homicide by killing a pedestrian by reckless driving, and he lodged a special defence that "by the incidence of temporary mental dissociation due to toxic exhaustive factors he was unaware of the presence of the deceased . . . and was incapable of appreciating his immediately previous or subsequent actions." He was acquitted. *Ritchie* was specifically overruled in *Cunningham*, but was approved in *Ross*, except that *Ross* holds that while the evidential burden of raising the issue of non-insane automatism rests on the accused,[74] the persuasive burden of establishing *mens rea* remains on the Crown.[75] It seems that the defence of non-insane automatism is not technically a special

---

[69] 1963 J.C. 80. The decision in this case had been subjected to much criticism and speculation: see, *e.g.*, W.M. Reid, "Three Steps Back", 1963 S.L.T. (News) 166; J.W.R. Gray, "A Purely Temporary Disturbance", 1974 J.R. 227; G.H. Gordon, "Automatism, Insanity and Intoxication" (1976) J.L.S. 310; and the Second Edition of this book at para. 3.18.

[70] This is the term used for automatic behaviour of the kind typified by the epileptic fugue — see *H.M. Advocate v. Ritchie*, 1926 J.C. 45, at 47–48. A person in such a fugue would clearly be "legally insane", since he would be unaware of the nature of his acts by reason of mental disease: see *infra*, para. 10.38.

[71] 1963 J.C. 80, at 83.

[72] *ibid.*

[72a] 1991 J.C. 210.

[73] 1926 J.C. 45.

[74] 1991 J.C. 210, L.J.-G. Hope at 222. See also *Sorley v. H.M. Advocate*, 1992 J.C. 102, Opinion of the Court at 107; *MacLeod v. Napier*, 1993 S.C.C.R. 303, Opinion of the Court at 307.

[75] *Ross v. H.M. Advocate*, 1991 J.C. 210, L.J.-G. Hope at 218. *Cf. H.M. Advocate v. Ritchie*, 1926 J.C. 45, Lord Murray (directions to the jury) at 48.

defence,[76] but is now by statutory rule to be treated as such for the purpose of requiring the accused to give notice to the Crown of his intention to raise it.[77]

The criteria in Ross. Although the existence of the defence of non-insane automatism is recognised in *Ross*,[78] the requirements of the defence are stringent. The automatism, for example, must be caused by an external factor. If it is caused by an "internal factor"[79] which is likely to recur, then it is either irrelevant (except in mitigation[80]), or leads to an acquittal by reason of insanity.[81] The defence is also confined to demonstrating an absence of *mens rea* rather than *actus reus*, which means that, strictly speaking, it will not be applicable in any situation where *mens rea* is not required.[82] In strict liability driving offences, however, it has been accepted in sheriff courts that the accused may have to be shown to have been "driving" at the relevant time, in the sense of controlling the vehicle by conscious effort of will (as opposed to being merely seated at the controls, making unconscious movements of the limbs), provided he was not at fault for having undertaken that activity at all.[83] **3.19**

External factors. If English authority is to be followed (and *Ross*[84] goes far to equate Scots law with that of England as laid down by the House of Lords in *R. v. Sullivan*[85]), external factors are confined to external physical ones.[86] These would include violence (*e.g.*, blows on the head severe enough to cause concussion),[87] toxic gases from vehicle exhausts[88] or volatile substances,[89] and drugs (including alcohol) ingested or **3.20**

---

[76] For an account of special defences, see *Lambie v. H.M. Advocate*, 1973 J.C. 53. Of these defences, only insanity places a persuasive burden of proof (on the balance of probabilities) on the accused, and that solely by virtue of there being a presumption of sanity which the accused must overcome.

[77] Criminal Procedure (Scotland) Act 1995, s.78(2).

[78] 1991 J.C. 210.

[79] See *infra*, para. 3.22.

[80] See, *e.g.*, *Finegan v. Heywood*, 2000 S.C.C.R. 460, where parasomnia, induced by the voluntary and deliberate consumption of alcohol for its intoxicating effects, was discounted for the purposes of automatism but allowed as a special reason for not disqualifying the appellant from driving.

[81] Disposal is then governed by the Criminal Procedure (Scotland) Act 1995, s.57(2).

[82] See, *e.g.*, *Clark v. H.M. Advocate*, 1968 J.C. 53. Although the decision in this case was governed by the now overruled *H.M. Advocate v. Cunningham*, 1963 J.C. 80, it is difficult to see that the result could have been different after *Ross*. The accused submitted that their reason for not appreciating the effect of their admitted neglect of their child was incompetence and fecklessness — for which no external causal factor was revealed. In any event, it was declared that s.12(1) of the Children and Young Persons (Scotland) Act 1937 was divided into two parts, that the second part did not require *mens rea*, and that the accused's defence was directed only to that second part.

[83] See *Farrell v. Stirling*, 1975 S.L.T. (Sh.Ct.) 71; *MacLeod v. Mathieson*, 1993 S.C.C.R. 488, Sh.Ct. In each case, however, the accused was suffering from diabetes — which is an internal pathological disease, and which therefore introduces additional complications. *Cf. Finegan v. Heywood*, 2000 S.C.C.R. 460. See *infra*, para. 3.22.

[84] 1991 J.C. 210.

[85] [1984] 1 A.C. 156.

[86] See *R. v. Hennessy* [1989] 1 W.L.R. 287, Lord Lane C.J. at 294 D-E.

[87] See *Ross v. H.M. Advocate*, 1991 J.C. 210, L.J.-G. Hope at 216 (quoting Lord Diplock's opinion in *R. v. Sullivan* [1984] 1 A.C. 156, at 172 H.

[88] See *H.M. Advocate v. Ritchie*, 1926 J.C. 45.

[89] See *H.M. Advocate v. Murray*, 1969 S.L.T. (Notes) 85, where the accused claimed that he had been overcome by the fumes from tetrachlorethylene used in the dry-cleaning establishment where he had been shortly before he commenced driving. The opinion there must now be read in the light of *Ross*'s rejection of *Cunningham*.

absorbed. In each case, of course, the external factor must cause a total alienation of reason amounting to a complete loss of control in relation to the offence charged. A partial alienation will not suffice. Thus in *Cardle v. Mulrainey*,[90] the accused claimed that his unwitting consumption of amphetamines had made him unable to control his actions, of which he was nevertheless aware. According to the opinion of the court: "Where . . . the accused knew what he was doing and was aware of the nature and quality of his act and that what he was doing was wrong, he cannot be said to be suffering from some total alienation of reason in regard to the crime with which he is charged which the defence requires."[91] Loss of self-control is not, therefore, of itself conclusive unless it is caused by a total alienation of reason: loss of control accompanied by partial alienation of reason will at best lead to mitigation of sentence.[92]

The limiting criteria must also be borne in mind. Whilst an external factor may well effect the requisite alienation, this will not suffice if that factor was self-induced. This does not necessarily mean that the accused must have been unaware of his exposure to the factor. In *Ross*,[93] for example, the accused was unaware that quantities of drugs (temazepam and LSD) had been added to the can of lager from which he had been imbibing[94]; but in *Ebsworth v. H.M. Advocate*,[95] the accused voluntarily took quantities of the proprietary drug paracetamol together with some diamorphine[96] to ease the pain of a broken leg. On the assumption that these caused a total alienation of reason in relation to the crimes charged, his defence was rejected, but not on the basis that he had known he was taking the drugs; rather the defence was denied because the quantity and type of drugs taken (in defiance of, or without taking, medical advice) showed him to have been reckless.[97] As it is put in the Opinion of the Court: "Had it not been for the grossly excessive quantity which he consumed and the combination of the drugs which he took without medical advice, this would have raised a question of fact which could properly have been left to the jury. This is because, unless the accused's conduct was reckless, the fact that he had a legitimate purpose in consuming the drugs ought not to deprive him of the defence on the ground that, since he consumed them deliberately, the condition was self-induced."[98] The state of common (or even the accused's own) knowledge may also be significant in deciding whether he was reckless in exposing himself to the external factor. In relation to alcohol and halucinatory drugs such as LSD, this issue is not in doubt. Deliberate

---

[90] 1992 S.L.T. 1152.

[91] *ibid.*, at 1160 D.

[92] *ibid.*, at 1160 E-F. *Cf. Attorney-General's Reference (No. 2 of 1992)* [1994] Q.B. 91, Lord Taylor of Gosforth, giving the opinion of the Court, at 105C, *viz.*: "the defence of automatism requires that there was a total alienation of voluntary control on the defendant's part. Impaired, reduced or partial control is not enough."

[93] 1991 J.C. 210.

[94] This was also maintained in *Sorley v. H.M. Advocate*, 1992 J.C. 102; *Cardle v. Mulrainey*, 1992 S.L.T. 1152; and *MacLeod v. Napier*, 1993 S.C.C.R. 303. See also the pre-*Ross* case of *McGregor v. H.M. Advocate*, 1973 S.C.C.R. (Supp.) 54.

[95] 1992 S.L.T. 1161.

[96] This was unfavourable to his defence, since diamorphine is a controlled drug with unpredictable effects.

[97] This apparently supplies whatever *mens rea* the offence charged requires, since his conviction for assault was confirmed by the Appeal Court — and assault requires intention (see *Lord Advocate's Reference (No. 2 of 1992)*, 1993 J.C. 43, L.J.-C. Ross at 48 C-D).

[98] *Ebsworth v. H.M. Advocate*, 1992 S.L.T. 1161, at 1166 I-J.

consumption of such substances (perhaps limited to excessive consumption in the case of alcohol) for their intoxicating and unpredictable effects is taken as evidence of recklessness,[99] and it seems even evidence of intention.[1] Such an accused has no defence based on lack of *mens rea* by virtue of insanity or diminished responsibility[2] or non-insane automatism.[3] But the person who voluntarily takes prescribed or proprietary drugs or medicines in reasonable or prescribed quantities[4] and who suffers an unexpected alienation of reason in consequence, may well have a defence of non-insane automatism which the court or jury should consider on its merits.[5] A difficult case, however, concerns the taking of a drug which is prescribed for some enduring pathological condition. Thus a diabetic who takes insulin as prescribed for him may become hypoglycaemic and suffer a total alienation of reason as a result of the insulin itself, *or* for some other reason — such as a failure to follow a medically required regime of self-management, or because of the underlying condition of diabetes. If the reason is considered to be the disease, then the efficient cause is an internal one and must be dealt with in the manner appropriate to internally caused conditions of automatism. But if the cause is the insulin or a self-management failure, it seems that a defence of non-insane automatism is open for consideration[6] — unless the accused is regarded as being sufficiently at fault to enable the want of *mens rea* to be overcome. In *Carmichael v. Boyle*,[7] for example, the accused suffered from an unstable form of diabetes, which was tackled with regular injections of insulin and a management regime which required the regular ingestion of food and the avoidance of alcohol. The accused undoubtedly on the evidence became hypoglycaemic, since the insulin which he took was not followed by the food he required. He also drank beer in apparent defiance of his doctor's orders. But the personal fault inference which would normally have been drawn[8] posed difficulties in his case since he was also afflicted by unusually low intelligence. The case was disposed of at the time by the Appeal Court's invoking the now-discredited rule in *Cunningham*.[9]

---

[99] *Brennan v. H.M. Advocate*, 1977 J.C. 38. *Cf. Finegan v. Heywood*, 2000 S.C.C.R. 460.

[1] *Ross v. H.M. Advocate*, 1991 J.C. 210, *per* L.J.-G. Hope at 214, *viz.*: "In all such cases [*i.e.* those within the exception on public policy grounds where a self-induced condition, such as in *Brennan*, has resulted in an absence of *mens rea* but does not excuse] the accused must be assumed to have intended the natural consequences of his act." Such assumptions are not necessarily made in other jurisdictions, where the effect of voluntary consumption of drugs is simply weighed with all other factors in arriving at a decision whether or not the prosecutor has proved the fundamental elements of the crime — both *actus reus* and *mens rea*: see, *e.g.*, *R. v. O'Connor* (1980) 54 A.L.J.R. 349 (Australia); *R. v. Daviault* (1995) 118 D.L.R. (4th) 469 (Canada); *R. v. Chretien*, 1981 (1) S.A. 201 (A) (South Africa); *R. v. Kamipeli* [1975] 2 N.Z.L.R. 610 (New Zealand). *Cf.*, the approach of English law in *D.P.P. v. Majewski* [1977] A.C. 443.

[2] *Brennan v. H.M. Advocate*, 1977 J.C. 38, Opinion of the Court at 46.

[3] *Ross v. H.M. Advocate*, 1991 J.C. 210.

[4] *cf. Walker v. MacGillivray*, 1980 S.C.C.R. (Supp.) 244; *R. v. Hardie* [1984] 3 All E.R. 848.

[5] See *R. v. Hardie* [1984] 3 All E.R. 848. *Cf. Carrington v. H.M. Advocate,* 1994 S.C.C.R. 567, where it was claimed that the side effects of a particular, medically prescribed drug were unknown both by the accused and by medical science at the time of the offence. The appeal against conviction failed, however, on other grounds.

[6] See *R. v. Quick* [1973] 1 Q.B. 910.

[7] 1985 S.L.T. 399.

[8] *cf., R. v. Bailey* [1983] 1 W.L.R. 760, where the English Court of Appeal considered that it would not be commonly known — even to diabetics — that a failure to take food after insulin could have untoward effects on one's mental condition.

[9] *H.M. Advocate v. Cunningham*, 1963 J.C. 80.

Stante the opinions in *Ross v. H.M. Advocate*,[10] it is submitted that *Carmichael* should have resulted in a simple acquittal on the basis that the accused lacked *mens rea* owing to non-insane automatism. Unchecked diabetes results normally in hyperglycaemia[11]: the hypoglycaemia which Carmichael suffered was almost certainly due to insulin — an external factor. It was taken voluntarily, but for a therapeutic reason; and it could not be said that *he* was "bound to foresee" the alienation of reason which occurred. The circumstances were very different from those where a person voluntarily takes drugs or drink for their intoxicating and/or unpredictable effects.[12]

3.21 *Alienation of Reason.* As stated above, non-insane automatism requires a total "alienation of reason". This element of the defence is shared with the defence of insanity, but by hypothesis is not sufficient for insanity which requires the causative element to be mental disorder.[13] As Hume puts the matter: "To serve the purpose of a defence in law, the disorder must therefore amount to an absolute alienation of reason, 'ut continua mentis alienatione, omni intellectu careat',[14] — such a disease as deprives the patient of the *knowledge* of the true aspect and position of things about him".[15] In automatism, it would seem that what is required is a temporary[16] but total lack of understanding and reason in relation to the crime charged. In *Cardle v. Mulrainey*,[17] the matter was put thus: "[an] inability to exert self-control, which the sheriff has described as an inability to complete the reasoning process, must be distinguished from the essential requirement that there should be total alienation of the accused's mental faculties of reasoning and of understanding what he is doing." This seems borrowed from the appropriate element of the English M'Naghten rules for insanity,[18] as interpreted by Lord Diplock in *R. v. Sullivan*, *viz.*: "that 'mind' in the M'Naghten rules is used in the ordinary sense of the mental faculties of reason, memory and understanding."[19] Accordingly, non-insane automatism occurs where in relation to the act charged a total aberration of reasoning, memory and understanding, which would be sufficient for the defence of insanity, is caused not by mental illness, mental disease or defect or unsoundness of mind, but by an external factor.[20] There seems no reason why stress and

---

[10] 1991 J.C. 210.

[11] See *R. v. Hennessy* [1989] 1 W.L.R. 287.

[12] See *Brennan v. H.M. Advocate*, 1977 J.C. 38; *Ebsworth v. H.M. Advocate*, 1992 S.L.T. 1161, Opinion of the Court at 1166F: "The element of guilt or moral turpitude lies in the taking of drink or drugs voluntarily and reckless of their possible consequences."

[13] See *Brennan v. H.M. Advocate*, 1977 J.C. 38, Opinion of the Court at 45, *viz.*: "[I]nsanity in our law requires proof of total alienation of reason in relation to the act charged as the result of mental illness, mental disease or defect or unsoundness of mind".

[14] *i.e.*, so that by an uninterrupted aberration of the mind, he lacks all understanding.

[15] Hume, i, 37.

[16] See *Ross v. H.M. Advocate*, 1991 J.C. 210, L.J.-G. Hope at 213: "We are concerned here only with a mental condition of a temporary nature which was the result of an external factor and not of some disorder of the mind itself which was liable to recur"; and again at 221: "But no issue was taken in this case about the sanity of the appellant. It was not his contention . . . that he was 'abnormal and irresponsible' — that is to say, that he was irresponsible due to some underlying and continuing state of abnormality which affected his behaviour."

[17] 1992 S.L.T. 1152, Opinion of the Court at 1106G.

[18] *M'Naghten's Case* (1843) 10 Cl. & Fin. 200.

[19] [1984] 1 A.C. 156, at 172 D.

[20] See para. 3.20, *supra*.

anxiety or depression, if externally caused, should not fall within the ambit of such a total aberration.[21]

Automatism caused by non-external factors. In *Ross*[22] the earlier decision in *Cunningham*[23] was overruled "insofar as it held that *any* mental or pathological condition short of insanity is relevant only to the question of mitigating circumstances and sentence."[24] It follows that mental or pathological conditions falling short of the requirements of non-insane automatism but negating the accused's ability to form *mens rea* may not result in simple acquittals, in spite of the principle that those who lack *mens rea* should be acquitted.[25] Departure from principle here is justified on public policy grounds, *viz.*, that public safety is an overarching consideration.[26] In English law, the view is taken that 'criminal' conduct which is unconsciously done, by reason of non-externally caused mental conditions which are likely to recur, and which fall within the M'Naghten Rules,[27] will merit an acquittal — but only on the ground of insanity. These Rules lay down the test for insanity, *viz.*: "[that] at the time of the committing of the act, the party accused was labouring under such a defect of reason, from disease of the mind, as not to know the nature and quality of the act he was doing; or if he did know it, that he did not know he was doing what was wrong." Scots law has not generally followed such a narrow formularistic test for insanity[28]; but the reference to English authority in *Ross*,[29] the mention there with apparent approval of the virtual M'Naghten test as delivered by Lord Murray to the jury in *H.M. Advocate v. Ritchie*,[30] and the use there of phrases such as 'disease' or 'disorder' of the mind[31] strongly suggest that the English approach to automatism is now accepted in Scotland. Whilst it is true that the Lord Justice-General said that *Ross's* case was not concerned with a mental condition which was the result "of some disorder of the mind itself which was liable to recur"[32] or with a "continuing disorder of the mind or body which might lead to the recurrence of the disturbance of the appellant's mental faculties"[33], it seems reasonably clear that Scots law will follow English authority when cases involving such situations are encountered. The result will be that principle will be preserved — by acquitting the accused. But the fact that such acquittal will be on the ground of insanity will enable such measures to be taken as are deemed necessary for 3.22

---

[21] In *Walker v. MacGillivray*, 1980 S.C.C.R. (Supp.) 244, *e.g.* the accused's anxiety and depressive state were said to have been caused by the pressure of her responsibilities at work; but she had also been taking medically prescribed drugs for her condition. *Cf.*, *R. v. Hennessy* [1989] 1 W.L.R. 287, where there was medical evidence that anxiety and depression could increase blood sugar levels and lead to hyperglycaemia in a diabetic; but the defendant, an insulin dependent diabetic, had failed to take insulin for two or three days prior to the acts charged.

[22] *Ross v. H.M. Advocate*, 1991 J.C. 210.

[23] *H.M. Advocate v. Cunningham*, 1963 J.C. 80.

[24] *H.M. Advocate v. Ross*, 1991 J.C. 210, L.J.-G. Hope at 222.

[25] *ibid.*, L.J.-G. Hope at 213.

[26] See *R. v. Parks* (1992) 1 S.C.R. 871, LaForest J. at 896c, *et seq.*

[27] *M'Naghten's Case* (1843) 10 Cl. & Fin. 200, at 210.

[28] See *H.M. Advocate v. Kidd*, 1960 J.C. 61; *Brennan v. H.M. Advocate*, 1977 J.C. 38.

[29] Especially *R. v. Sullivan* [1984] 1 A.C. 156 — see *Ross v. H.M. Advocate*, 1991 J.C. 210, L.J.-G. Hope at 216.

[30] 1926 J.C. 45, at 48–49, quoted by L.J.-G. Hope in *Ross* at 215.

[31] See in *Ross*, L.J.-G. Hope at 213 and 214. See also *Sorley v. H.M. Advocate*, 1992 J.C. 102, Opinion of the Court at 105.

[32] *Ross v. H.M. Advocate*, 1991 J.C. 210 at 213.

[33] *ibid.*, at 214.

safeguarding public safety.[34] Where non-externally caused mental or pathological conditions are truly short of what the law counts as insanity, then convictions will have to follow (in the absence of any other defence).[35] These conclusions will affect a number of specific situations which may be considered separately.

3.23 (a) *Brain and nerve diseases.* The English courts at first experienced some difficulty in dealing with physical conditions such as brain tumours or arterio-sclerosis which led to mental deterioration.[36] But the matter now seems settled by the decision of the House of Lords in *R. v. Sullivan*,[37] where Lord Diplock said: "If the effect of a disease is to impair those faculties [of reason, memory and understanding] so severely as to have either of the consequences referred to in the latter part of the [McNaghten] rules, it matters not whether the aetiology of the impairment is organic, as in epilepsy, or functional, or whether the impairment itself is permanent or is transient and intermittent, provided that it subsisted at the time of commission of the act. The purpose of the defence of insanity . . . has been to protect society against recurrence of the dangerous conduct."[38] Whether a recurrent condition of unconsciousness is due to physical disease or internal mental disfunction is therefore irrelevant. It will be regarded in England as a defect of reason through disease of the mind and treated as insanity. It is submitted that the same result would now follow in Scotland, and that persons in the positions of the accused in *Cunningham*,[39] *Mitchell*,[40] and *Hayes*,[41] would now be acquitted on the ground of insanity, since automatism resulting from epilepsy cannot be regarded as non-insane.[42] The same will apply to cerebral tumours, arterio-sclerosis, or similar conditions of disease which result in automatic, criminal behaviour.[43]

3.24 (b) *Sleep.* One of the most famous cases in Scots law is *Simon Fraser*,[44] in which Fraser killed his son while in a state of somnambulism in which he believed him to be a wild beast attacking him. There was evidence

---

[34] See the Criminal Procedure (Scotland) Act 1995, s.57(2), for the range of disposals now available following such a verdict.

[35] For a modern discussion of the issues, see G.T. Laurie, "Automatism and Insanity in the Law of England and Scotland", 1995 J.R. 253. In *R. v. Parks* [1992] 1 S.C.R. 871, Lamer C.J. thought that simple acquittals (*i.e.*, not on the ground of insanity) could be coupled with an undertaking to keep the peace, thus preserving the principle that those who lacked *mens rea* should be acquitted whilst making provision for future public safety where required. This, however, would be impossible in Scotland, and was regarded as neither practicable nor lawful in Canada by the majority of the Supreme Court.

[36] Contrast *R. v. Charlson* [1955] 1 W.L.R. 317 (cerebral tumour) and *R. v. Kemp* [1957] 1 Q.B. 339 (arterio-sclerosis).

[37] [1984] 1 A.C. 156.

[38] *ibid.*, at 172 D-F.

[39] *H.M. Advocate v. Cunningham*, 1963 J.C. 80.

[40] *H.M. Advocate v. Mitchell*, 1951 J.C. 53.

[41] *H.M. Advocate v. Hayes*, High Court, November 1949, unreported (see C.H.W. Gane & C.N. Stoddart, *A Casebook on Scottish Criminal Law* (2nd ed., Edinburgh, 1988), at p.70).

[42] See *Ross v. H.M. Advocate*, 1991 J.C. 210, L.J.-G. Hope at 213, where he refers with apparent approval to *R. v. Sullivan* [1984] 1 A.C. 156, an epilepsy case favouring acquittal on the ground of insanity.

[43] In *Bratty v. Attorney-General for Northern Ireland* [1963] A.C. 386, Lord Denning at 412 seemed to confine 'criminal behaviour' to violence: but there seems no reason to so confine it — see, *e.g.*, *R. v. Bell* [1984] 3 All E.R. 842.

[44] (1878) 4 Couper 70.

that he was in the habit of getting up in his sleep and that he had in the past committed acts of violence in his somnambulistic states. The case is complicated by the presence of a delusion, but no plea of mistake was put forward by the defence, and the question of insanity was side-stepped by Lord Justice-Clerk Moncreiff, who said to the jury: "The question whether a state of somnambulism such as this is to be considered a state of insanity or not is a matter with which I think you should not trouble yourselves. It is a question on which medical authority is not agreed." His Lordship went on to tell the jury that their best course would be to "find the panel killed his child, but that he was in a state in which he was unconscious of the act which he was committing by reason of the condition of somnambulism, and that he was not responsible."[45]

The jury found as directed and the case was adjourned. Fraser then gave an undertaking to sleep alone in future, and at the resumed diet the case was dealt with by the following interlocutor: "In respect the Counsel for the Crown does not move for sentence, and in respect the panel has come under certain obligations satisfactory to Crown Counsel, the Court deserted the diet *simpliciter* against the panel, and dismissed him from the Bar."

This result is something of a compromise. Fraser was certainly not treated as insane, but the court was clearly concerned with the question of preventing a recurrence of his behaviour. The problem was solved by Fraser's agreeing to give the undertaking referred to. It is difficult to say what course would then have been adopted had the undertaking not been given, but it seems likely that the court may at that time have had no option but simply to discharge Fraser.[46] The court could perhaps have held that Fraser's condition amounted to a mental disease and treated him as insane, but, as has been seen, Lord Moncreiff declined to do this. *Fraser*[46a] may be authority for the view that actings in sleep do not constitute criminal conduct, and for the adoption in Scotland of Stephen's view that "no involuntary action whatever effects it may produce, amounts to a crime . . . I do not know indeed that it has ever been suggested that a person who in his sleep set fire to a house or caused the death of another would be guilty of arson or murder."[47]

This approach is certainly favoured by the Canadian Courts. In *R. v. Parks*[48] the accused drove for some 23 kilometres in his sleep. Whilst still asleep, he stopped his car outside the house of his parents-in-law and set

---

[45] At 75–76.

[46] In *John Andrew Hayes*, High Court, Oct. and Nov. 1949, unrept'd, the jury held a charge of "road traffic" culpable homicide proved, and also held proved a special defence of temporary dissociation due to masked epilepsy or other pathological condition by reason of which the accused was unaware of the presence of the stationary motor vehicle with which the motor omnibus driven by him collided. The trial judge certified the case to the High Court who advised him to discharge the panel on his giving an undertaking to surrender his driving licence and his public service vehicle driver's licence, and not to drive any motor or public service vehicle, including a tramcar, again.

[46a] (1878) 4 Couper 70.

[47] Sir J.F. Stephen, *History of the Criminal Law* (London, 1883), Vol. II, p.100. Lord McLaren in *Margt Robertson or Brown* (1886) 1 White 93, 102 seems to have accepted that somnambulism could be a defence, and indeed Mackenzie had recognised that "Such as commit any crime, whilst they sleep, are compared to infants . . . and therefore they are not punisht": Mackenzie, I, 1, 6. The most recent opinions of the Appeal Court suggest, however, that little guidance can be obtained from *Fraser*: see, *e.g.*, *Finegan v. Heywood*, 2000 S.C.C.R. 460, at 463B.

[48] [1992] 1 S.C.R. 871.

about them with a knife. One was killed and the other severely injured. He then drove to a police station and stated that he thought he might have killed two people. He was charged with murder and attempted murder. The Supreme Court of Canada upheld his acquittal on the basis of non-insane automatism.[49] The medical evidence at the trial had shown that there was no mental illness involved, that the accused was "sleep-walking" at the time and that he would have been unaware of his actions and unable to control them. Although Lamer C.J. and Cory J. expressed some concern over allowing an unfettered acquittal in such a case since future public safety should be catered for,[50] they joined the remainder of the Court in rejecting an insanity-type acquittal. The decision of the Court is firmly grounded upon the involuntariness of the accused's behaviour rather than on any lack of *mens rea*[51]; and although it was accepted that, in Canadian law, automatism based on internal factors would probably be treated as insanity,[52] sleepwalking could not easily in this case be said to stem from internal rather than external causes, and thus that an approach based on the internal-external dichotomy was not appropriate. A straightforward simple acquittal was, therefore, the preferred solution. The English case of *R. v. Burgess*[53] was considered, but in effect distinguished: it was held that evidence of possible recurrence of the condition (and thus of violence) was given in *Burgess*, where there also had been evidence that the accused suffered from a pathological condition. It may be doubted whether *Burgess* could so easily have been distinguished; and it is clear that the Canadian Courts would be prepared to reject non-insane automatism in favour of insanity where the medical evidence raised an issue of mental illness, with or without the danger of recurrence.[54] Nevertheless, it is clear that criminal behaviour during sleepwalking is not to be regarded as insane behaviour just because there was violence displayed and some possibility of recurrence.[55]

The current position in English law is that insanity is thought to be a proper defence where violent acts have been committed during sleep. In the leading case of *Burgess*,[55a] Lord Lane C.J. said: "We accept of course that sleep is a normal condition, but the evidence in the instant case indicates that sleep walking, and particularly violence in sleep is not normal".[56] He also accepted Lord Denning's well-known statement in

---

[49] The certified question from the Ontario Court of Appeal had been whether the defence should have been one of insane rather than non-insane automatism — as is pointed out by the Appeal Court in *Finegan v. Heywood*, 2000 S.C.C.R. 460, at 463D.

[50] They suggested that the acquittal should be combined with an order upon the accused to keep the peace: *ibid.*, 892a-894f.

[51] See, *e.g.*, Opinion of LaForest J., *ibid.*, at 896d-e.

[52] See LaForest J., *ibid.*, at 901c-f.

[53] [1991] 2 Q.B. 92, CA.

[54] See LaForest J., *ibid.*, at 907–909.

[55] See *The Queen v. Cottle* [1958] N.Z.L.R. 999, Gresson P. at 1007: "Automatism, which strictly means action without conscious volition, has been adopted in criminal law as a term to denote conduct of which the doer is not conscious...This may be due to some 'disease of the mind' or it may not; it may happen with a perfectly healthy mind (*e.g.*, in somnambulism which may be unaccompanied by any abnormality of mind)". See also North J., *ibid.*, at 1026: "There is also the rare case of the sleepwalker and no one has doubted that that, if evidence is given that the prisoner committed the crime while walking in his sleep, he is entitled to be acquitted."

[55a] [1991] 5 Q.B. 92, CA.

[56] At 100 F. The accused attacked the victim with a bottle and a video-recorder, causing her serious injury.

Bratty v. Attorney-General for Northern Ireland[57] that "any mental disorder which has manifested itself in violence and is prone to recur is a disease of the mind." Where a person, therefore, commits violent acts against another in his sleep, and there is no obvious external cause for his condition, it seems proper in English law to regard that condition as a mental defect due to a disease of the mind, even where there is no particular risk of recurrence of the violence.[58] In fact, the extensive medical evidence led in the case suggested that recurrence of serious violence was unlikely though the likelihood of fresh sleepwalking was high. It seems that there will be an assumption, subject to evidence to the contrary, that violent acts done during sleep will merit acquittal — but on the ground of insanity.

The present position in Scotland is somewhat unclear, but it would appear that *Simon Fraser*[59] is unlikely now to be followed, especially since Lord Justice-General Hope stated that he did not think that the case could "be regarded as anything other than a very special one".[60] Sleepwalking (or parasomnia) was advanced as automatism in the recent case of *Finegan v. Heywood*.[61] There, the accused had drunk at least six pints of beer before falling asleep. Whilst still asleep (in a parasomniac state) he had taken the keys to a car parked outside his home, and driven that car for some one and half miles in Dundee. He was convicted of taking and driving away a motor vehicle without the consent of the owner, driving with excess alcohol in his body, and driving without insurance.[62] On appeal, these convictions were upheld on the basis that the sheriff had found that the voluntary consumption of alcohol by the appellant had induced the state of parasomnia; thus, following *Brennan v. H.M. Advocate*,[63] "the defence of automatism . . . cannot be established upon proof that the appellant was in a transitory state of parasomnia which was the result of, and indeed induced by, deliberate and self-induced intoxication."[64] The Appeal Court's view was that this was in principle indistinguishable from the decision in *Brennan*[64a] that temporary malfunctioning of the mind due to self-induced intoxication amounted neither to insanity nor diminished responsibility. Where parasomnia had not been so induced, and assuming that the appellant had not been otherwise at fault[65] in relation to the state of somnambulism, it seems that the Appeal Court would have been prepared to find that he had had no criminal responsibility; but it is not clear whether the

[57] [1963] A.C. 386, at 412.

[58] *R. v. Burgess* [1991] 2 Q.B. 92. See Lord Lane C.J., *ibid.*, at 99 H: "It seems to me that if there is a danger of recurrence that may be an added reason for categorising the condition as a disease of the mind. On the other hand, the absence of the danger of recurrence is not a reason for saying that it cannot be a disease of the mind."

[59] (1878) 4 Coup.70.

[60] *Ross v. H.M. Advocate*, 1991 J.C. 210, at 217. See also the opinion of the Appeal Court in *Finegan v. Heywood*, 2000 S.C.C.R. 460, at 463B.

[61] 2000 S.C.C.R. 460.

[62] Contrary to ss.178(1)(a), 5(1)(a), and 143 respectively of the Road Traffic Act 1988: at least the latter two of these offences would normally be regarded as being of strict liability.

[63] 1977 J.C. 38.

[64] 2000 S.C.C.R. 460, at 464G.

[64a] 1977 J.C. 38.

[65] The issue of fault clearly arose in the case since the appellant had had previous episodes of parasomnia following the voluntary consumption of alcohol: the accused's recklessness or negligence was not, however, explored by the Court — presumably since the relevance of recklessness or negligence to the offences charged was questionable.

Court would have considered such a situation as one of non-insane automatism: this was simply an issue which the Court did not find it necessary to explore.[66] By way of contrast, however, the case of *Ross v. H.M. Advocate*[67] was distinguished "since it dealt only with those cases where there was no disease of the mind"[68] and where the external factor involved was not self-induced. It is probable, therefore, that Scots law would follow the approach in *R. v. Burgess*[69] in a suitable case. It remains to be seen, however, if the Crown will continue to exercise a discretion of the kind they exercised in one pre-*Ross* case. In that case involving a 14-year-old boy charged with assaulting his five-year-old cousin in which the accused had pled guilty, the Crown agreed to the plea being withdrawn and deserted the diet on receipt of two psychiatric reports expressing the opinion that the boy had been sleepwalking at the relevant time.[70]

Where the "sleep behaviour" is not the result of a neurotic or other abnormal condition of the sleeper, but is merely a reflex action, the result may still be a simple acquittal. If A throws his arms about in his sleep and inflicts a fatal injury on his wife who is lying beside him, he should be acquitted and discharged on the ground that his behaviour was purely reflexive. There is a difference between this situation and that where A gets up and walks about and attacks someone in what looks to the outsider like a course of deliberate conduct. In the one case there is no conduct at all, in the other there is what might be called "unconscious conduct".[71]

3.25 (c) *Diabetic coma.* Diabetes is presumably a pathological condition, and a condition of coma due to that disease itself will most likely be treated as insanity following English authority.[72] This will enable a judge to choose an appropriate disposal following upon an acquittal on that basis. Actual detention in a mental hospital need not, and probably should not follow — unless the charge had been one of murder.[73] Despite the fact that a hospital order need not now be made in such a case, it seems objectionable on common sense grounds to label a diabetic as "insane", although it is difficult to see how else public protection, if required, might be safeguarded.

3.26 (d) *Voluntary intoxication.* Automatism brought on by voluntary intoxication is treated as intoxication and not as automatism or insanity.[74]

---

[66] 2000 S.C.C.R. 460, at 463D.

[67] 1991 J.C. 210.

[68] 2000 S.C.C.R. 460, at 465A.

[69] [1991] 2 Q.B. 92.

[70] *H.M. Advocate v. X.*, High Court at Edinburgh, Dec. 1983, unrept'd; see the *Scotsman*, December 17, 1983.

[71] There are, of course, situations which cannot easily be placed into one or other of these categories. In *R. v. Dhlamini*, 1955 (1) S.A. 120 (T.P.D.) the accused had been dreaming that he was defending himself from an assault when he half awoke, and mechanically, without volition, stabbed a man kneeling beside him. He was acquitted and discharged.

[72] *R. v. Hennessy* [1989] 1 W.L.R. 287; *cf. R. v. Quick* [1973] 1 Q.B. 910, *R. v. Bailey* [1983] 2 All E.R. 503.

[73] 1995 Act, s.57(2), (3).

[74] *Brennan v. H.M. Advocate*, 1977 J.C. 38, disapproving *H.M. Advocate v. Aitken,* 1976 S.L.T. (Notes) 56; *Finegan v. Heywood*, 2000 S.C.C.R. 460; J.C. Smith and B. Hogan, *Criminal Law* (9th ed., 1999, by Sir J. Smith), 36–37; *R. v. Majewski* [1976] A.C. 443; *R. v. Lipman* [1970] 1 Q.B. 152; *contra* — *R.v. Kamipeli* [1975] 2 N.Z.L.R. 610; *S. v. Chretien* 1981 (1) S.A. 201 (A); *R. v. Daviault* (1995) 118 D.L.R. (4th) 469. Intoxication is treated above at para. 3.20, and in Chap. 12, below.

(f) *Reflex actions.* Although few cases in Scotland have touched upon reflex actions at all,[75] it is thought that such actings should not lead either to conviction or to acquittal on the ground of insanity — at least where an involuntary jerk or other movement of a purely reflexive kind is made in response to an external stimulus, such as the attack of a swarm of bees. This is probably not covered by the decision in *Ross v. H.M. Advocate*,[76] where acquittal depends on there being a total alienation of reason; nor, it is submitted, should it be covered by whatever residual authority is now accorded to *Cunningham*.[77] Where external stimulus was involved, or even an isolated movement made during normal sleep, the result should on principle be one of simple acquittal. 3.27

Forseeable automatism.[78] *Ross*[79] forbids the defence of automatism to an accused who is himself responsible for his recklessness or negligence. This result can be achieved by treating the accused's "act" as his whole conduct from the time at which he allowed himself to become unconscious until the time of the offence charged.[80] So, if A has an accident while driving and pleads in defence to a charge of careless driving that he had fallen asleep at the wheel and was asleep when the accident occurred, he will almost certainly be convicted.[81] This is usually said to be because although he was not responsible for his actings at the time of the accident he was careless in allowing himself to fall asleep at the wheel instead of stopping.[82] In *R. v. Scarth*[83] the defence of sleep was raised in answer to a charge of road traffic manslaughter. The trial judge held it to be irrelevant, but the conviction was quashed on appeal. Macrossan S.P.J. said: 3.28

> "It would appear from the earlier part of the learned judge's direction, which I have quoted, that he directed the jury that as a matter of law it could in no circumstances be an excuse available to the appellant that he had fallen asleep. In the latter part of the summing-up, however, the learned judge put the matter differently, when he said: 'I am directing you as a matter of law that, if this man was actually asleep at the time that he ran into these people, that in itself does not constitute a defence at all.' This statement in my opinion is correct. When a *prima facie* case of criminal negligence has been proved against the driver of a motor vehicle, evidence which showed that the driver of the motor vehicle was asleep at the relevant time, but showed nothing more than this, would not, in my opinion, destroy or weaken the *prima facie* case against him. On the contrary, it would strengthen it. But if a driver of a motor car fell asleep at the wheel without any prior warning of his inability to

---

[75] *cf. Jessop v. Johnstone* 1991 S.C.C.R. 238.

[76] 1991 J.C. 210.

[77] 1963 J.C. 80.

[78] See H.L.A Hart, "Acts of Will and Responsibility" in *Punishment and Responsibility* (Oxford, 1968), p.90; A.J. Ashworth, "Reason, Logic and Criminal Liability" (1975) 91 L.Q.R. 102.

[79] 1991 J.C. 210.

[80] *cf.* Ian D. Elliott, "Responsibility for Involuntary Acts: *Ryan v. The Queen*" (1967) 121 C.L.R. 205; *cf. Higgins v. Bernard* [1972] 1 W.L.R. 455.

[81] *Hill v. Baxter* [1958] 1 Q.B, 277; *Kay v. Butterworth* (1945) 173 L.T. 191.

[82] *ibid. cf.* P.J. Fitzgerald, "Voluntary and Involuntary Acts" in *Oxford Essays in Jurisprudence*, ed. A.G. Guest (O.U.P., 1961), pp.1, 19; Gl. Williams, pp.118, 485.

[83] [1945] St.R.Qd. 38.

> keep awake, and in circumstances where a reasonably careful driver would not have been aware that he was likely to fall asleep, and as a result of his so falling asleep personal injury or death was caused to some other person, no criminal liability would, in my opinion, attach to the driver of the motor car".[84]

But this is not an altogether satisfactory approach to the question. The carelessness with which A is charged is carelessness at the time of the accident, and not at an earlier stage. Suppose A did not fall asleep but went into a coma, and had had such comas on earlier occasions while driving — here his carelessness occurs when he decides to drive,[85] and so is not careless driving at all.[86] Again, he will not in practice be charged unless he drives in an objectively careless way, and if he does he may be charged only with careless driving whether or not his earlier carelessness amounted to recklessness. Speaking more generally, legally relevant carelessness must relate to a fairly specific risk — the man who is liable to go into a coma is liable to do anything and it is not really plausible to say, for example, that a diabetic who sets fire while in a coma should be convicted of reckless fire-raising because he knew that he was liable to blackouts.

The difficulty of this approach is even clearer in the case of an offence of strict responsibility such as failing to obey a traffic sign.[87]

Where what is involved is a crime that can be committed only intentionally, the defence of automatism can be excluded only by a policy decision limiting the scope of the defence to situations where the accused is in no way to blame for his condition. This seems to be the law in Scotland and in England where "acquittal on grounds of automatism is now limited to those cases in which the incapacitating condition was neither the foreseeable consequence of the accused's own behaviour nor capable of prevention by taking a precaution which the accused could and should have taken."[88]

The policy decision rests on the need to require persons who are liable to blackouts to refrain from driving, or persons like Simon Fraser[89] to sleep alone, and equally to provide some sanction for people who put themselves into a state in which they are unable to control their criminal conduct. When they disregard their weakness in circumstances involving crime they should probably be convicted of a specific offence of, for example, driving while subject to epileptic fits, or, in the case of the man who falls asleep, falling asleep at the wheel.[90] What the law does at present, however, is to treat the defence of automatism as irrelevant where the automatism is foreseeable,[91] and to justify this by way of the argument criticised above. It remains to be seen what will happen when

---

[84] At 42.

[85] See *McLeod v. Mathieson*, 1993 S.C.C.R. 488, Sh.Ct ; *cf. Farrell v. Stirling*, 1975 S.L.T. (Sh.Ct.) 71.

[86] Although it may, of course, constitute negligence entitling an injured party to reparation: see *Waugh v. James K. Allan Ltd*, 1964 S.C. (H.L.) 162.

[87] *Hill v. Baxter, supra*; Ashworth, *op.cit.*, p.107.

[88] Ashworth, *op.cit.* at p.109; *R. v. Quick* [1973] Q.B. 910.

[89] See *supra*, para. 3.24.

[90] See Ashworth, *op.cit.*, 130. *Cf.* the proposed crime of becoming drunk and committing an offence, *infra*, para. 12.29; and the power to refuse a driving licence on the ground of medical unfitness under s.92 of the Road Traffic Act 1988.

[91] *Ross v. H.M. Advocate*, 1991 J.C. 210. *Cf. H.M. Advocate v. Ritchie, supra,* Lord Murray at 49.

the question arises in Scotland in connection with a crime of intent — the result may be that if there is no analogous crime of recklessness or negligence the defence will simply be rejected and the accused convicted, but that where, as in homicide, there is an analogous crime of recklessness or negligence the accused will be convicted of that crime.[92]

The type of act necessary

There is no precise limitation on the type of act necessary or sufficient to constitute criminal conduct: any voluntary human action may be enough in the particular circumstances of a given case. Perhaps the only general requirement is that there must be a fairly specific act or course of action. Such a requirement is necessary because the *actus reus* must be seen to be causally connected with the conduct, and so to have been caused by an act of the accused. For this reason "we . . . leave unpunished those various modes of unkindness, ingratitude, treachery, and oppression, by which, in too many instances, the heart and health are broken, and the sufferer is conducted to the grave, by a longer and more painful passage."[93] But any type of act is sufficient, provided it is sufficiently specific. Words, for example, are as much acts as are deeds, and indeed some crimes, like fraud or blackmail, are usually committed almost entirely by the medium of words. To kill a person with a weak heart by deliberately sending him a telegram containing the false news of a dreadful occurrence would surely be murder if the shock in fact killed him. Hume[94] and Macdonald[95] both consider that it is murder to give material perjured evidence which leads to conviction and execution for a capital crime, although both stress the difficulty of proving such a charge. There seems no reason why this should not be so, although there is English authority to the contrary[96]; Biblical law specifically makes such conduct criminal.[97] In such cases intention, act, and causal connection with the *actus reus* are all present; the intervening actors such as the judge, jury and hangman are merely innocent agents of the perjurer. **3.29**

Omissions

Crimes of omission and crimes of commission by omission. A distinction must be drawn between crimes of omission on the one hand, and crimes of commission committed by means of omissions on the other.[98] The first class covers all those conduct-crimes which consist of a failure to do something, such as failing to register the birth of a child, or failing to have lights on a motor-car at night, where the omission itself constitutes the crime, and is the equivalent of an *actus reus*. Crimes of this class are **3.30**

---

[92] *cf. Stirling v. Annan*, 1984 S.L.T. (Notes) 88, where the Crown mysteriously conceded that a conviction for theft, where the accused was apparently suffering from spontaneous hypoglycaemia, might have involved a miscarriage of justice, and the conviction was quashed. The approach in *Scarth, supra*, is, however, in line with the law on voluntary intoxication: *infra*, para. 12.12.

[93] Hume, i, 189.

[94] *ibid*. pp.190–191.

[95] Macdonald, pp.92–93.

[96] See Kenny, para. 13.

[97] Deut. 19, 16–20.

[98] The distinction is known in French law as that between *délits d'omission* and *délits de commission par omission*: G. Stefani, G. Levasseur, B. Bouloc, *Droit Pénal Général*, (15th ed., 1995, Dalloz, Paris), pp.184–186.

almost wholly statutory.[99] The second class comprises result-crimes where it is not the omission itself but its consequence which constitutes the *actus reus*. To commit homicide by refraining from feeding a child is to commit a crime of commission by means of an omission: the omission is the criminal conduct which leads to the *actus reus* of homicide.

3.31 *Voluntary and involuntary omissions.* It is not easy to apply the concepts "voluntary" and "involuntary" to omissions.[1] The problem does not appear to have been discussed in Scotland in relation to common law offences. The best approach is probably to regard an omission as voluntary where it consists in a failure to do something which it was physically possible for the accused to have done, that is to say, something he was not prevented from doing by some physical inability or by external force of a kind amounting to duress or rendering performance of the act physically impossible.[2] Whether a voluntary omission is to be regarded as intentional, reckless or negligent, or as non-culpable because of error or ignorance, or for any other reason, will depend on the same principles as apply to acts.

3.32 *Negligent conduct.* A negligent failure to carry out an act is a negligent omission. But to do something carelessly by reason of a failure to carry out the appropriate precautions in its performance is better regarded as the commission of an act carelessly than as an omission, and conduct of this kind belongs to the category of negligent behaviour rather than to that of omissions.[3]

3.33 *When omissions are criminal.* It is only in certain restricted circumstances that an omission is regarded as criminal conduct. "Not to prevent an event, which it is obligatory to prevent, is equivalent to causing it",[4] but where there is no such obligation, there is no criminal responsibility for failure to prevent the event.[5] This is tautologous: there is a duty to prevent something only if there is an obligation to prevent it. And the law can have regard only to legal obligations: it does not enforce the obligations of morality unless these have been adopted as

---

[99] Although one of them — concealment of pregnancy — is perhaps old enough to be treated as a quasi-common law crime, but it is in part a result-crime (see Vol. II, Chap. 27). It has been suggested that the common law crime of "wilful neglect of duty by a public official" (see Vol. II, Chap. 44) may be of this nature: see A. Brown, "Wilful Neglect of Duty by Public Officials" (1996) 64 Sc. Law Gaz. 130, where the author narrates the sheriff court case of *Wilson v. Smith* (Stornoway Sheriff Court, January 9, 1996, unreported) which seems to have revived this offence.

[1] *cf.* Gl. Williams, pp.44–45.

[2] See A. Ashworth, *Principles of Criminal Law* (3rd ed., 1999), pp.115–116. *Cf. Middleton v. Tough* (1908) 5 Adam 485, which dealt with a statutory offence; Model Penal Code, O.D., s.2.01; G. Hughes, "Criminal Omissions" (1958) 67 Y.L.J. 590, 607. Where, however, the impossibility is itself the fault of the accused it will normally not be a defence. It may not, for example, be a defence to a statutory charge of failing to produce a document that the accused did not possess the document if his lack of possession was due to his own fault: see J.T. Gibney, "The Rare Defence: Impossibility" [1963] Crim.L.R. 490.

[3] *cf.* Gl. Williams, p.16.

[4] See W.T.S. Stallybrass, *op.cit.*, 397; Model Penal Code O.D., s.2.01 (3). For a review of English law, see P.R. Glazebrook, "Criminal Omissions" (1960) 76 L.Q.R. 386.

[5] *cf. Fishmongers' Company v. Bruce*, 1980 S.L.T. (Notes) 35, 36: "[N]o one can be held guilty of contravening a bye-law which requires that a certain result shall be secured unless he is a person who is charged by the bye-law or by statute with a duty to secure that result."

legal obligations. In law, a man is not his brother's keeper and is not obliged to act like the good Samaritan.[6]

There is not even a legal duty to prevent the commission of a crime, and to stand by and watch one's friends committing a theft is neither in itself theft nor a separate crime of omission.[7] In *Geo. Kerr and Ors.*[8] a number of men were engaged in the rape of a woman; one of their friends stood by and watched the crime but took no part in it; he was acquitted. Lord Ardmillan declined to "attempt to decide the general question . . . whether a man is a *particeps criminis* who sees a crime committed and passes by or looks on without doing anything",[9] but the law seems to be that he is not, and there is no ground for holding that he is guilty of a separate crime of his own.[10] *Kerr*[10a] is supported by the older case of *Taylor and Smith*[11] where a surgeon's apprentice who watched his friend kill a child, and then himself took the body to his master, was acquitted of homicide. If watching one's friends commit a crime is not criminal, it must follow that merely to pass by strangers who are committing a crime is not criminal either.

There are four types of case in which there may be a legal duty to prevent a situation, so that failure to do so is equivalent to bringing it about by an act. These are: **3.34**

(1) *Where the omission follows on a prior dangerous act.* Where a person by his actings has created a situation of danger, he has a duty to do what he can to avert the danger he has created.[12] Once a surgeon has started to operate upon a patient he cannot just stop halfway leaving the patient open on the table: if he does so and the patient dies as a result, the surgeon will be responsible for the death. This will be so whether the

---

[6] It is not clear how far this kind of criminal responsibility for omissions goes, but in theory it should be commensurate with liability under the civil law, although it may be specifically extended beyond this. The criminal law duty to prevent cannot be based on the criminal law, but it must be based on a legal duty; accordingly it must be co-extensive with the duties imposed by the civil law. Where therefore there is a civil law duty to do something, any failure in that duty which results in the creation of an *actus reus* should be treated as if it were an act.

[7] *cf. infra*. para. 5.36.

[8] (1871) 2 Couper 334.

[9] At 337. The indictment averred that the spectator had aided and abetted the crime "by looking on and failing to interfere in [the victim's] behalf, or to call for assistance." *Cf. R.v. Allan* [1965] 1 Q.B. 130; *R. v. Clarkson* [1971] 1 W.L.R. 1402.

[10] Although, of course, the circumstances of an accused's presence at the scene of a crime may lead to the inference that he was "in it" along with his co-accused, and so to art and part guilt: see Burnett, pp.269–270.

[10a] (1871) 2 Couper 334.

[11] (1807) Burnett, p.270.

[12] This was Lord Diplock's preferred approach in *R. v. Miller* [1983] 2 A.C. 161, where a vagrant squatting in an unoccupied house fell asleep whilst smoking a cigarette. The cigarette fell and set fire to the mattress on which he was sleeping. When he woke and appreciated what had happened, he failed to take any steps to put out the fire but transferred to another room to resume his slumbers. Damage was done to the building by fire and the accused was charged with arson. The Court of Appeal, however, had taken a different view, *viz.* that the whole train of events from the moment the defendant fell asleep and dropped the cigarette until the damage to the building was complete was one continuous act, the initial unintended act being adopted by the defendant when he chose to do nothing to extinguish the fire. Since both the "continuous act" theory and the "duty" theory led in this case to the same conclusion, it was unnecessary to decide which in fact represented the law. See A. Ashworth, *Principles of Criminal Law* (3rd ed., 1999), pp.113–114.

operation was conducted in pursuance of a contract, or out of mere benevolence, since in either case the surgeon has started something which it is dangerous to leave unfinished, and has in fact left it unfinished.[13]

Similarly, it is criminal to assault a man and leave him unconscious in a room filled with coal gas,[14] to place a man in a cell with a homicidal lunatic and leave him there to be killed, to expose a child with fatal results,[15] to put one's wife into a closet and leave her there without food and water until she dies.[16]

In *McManimy and Higgans*[17] a lodging-house keeper in Stirling discovered that one of his guests had typhoid. In order to prevent the spread of the infection the keeper and a friend carried the invalid out of the house without his consent, took him to Glasgow, and left him in the street where he lay until a policeman took him to hospital where he died. In these circumstances the accused were charged with culpable homicide, but this charge was dropped because it was thought that the deceased might have died of the typhoid in any event, and the accused pleaded guilty to an alternative charge of removing the deceased from his bed and cruelly treating and deserting him. They were charged specifically as persons entrusted with the custody of the victim, but it is submitted that this qualification was unnecessary. To *put* someone in the street and leave him there is quite different from refusing to render aid to someone one happens to pass by while he is lying ill in the street.

The fact that the deceased was a lodger with the accused is either too narrow or too wide a *ratio decidendi*. It is too narrow if it means that only a lodging-house keeper is guilty of a crime if he removes a sick person from a sheltered to an exposed place and leaves him there; it is too wide if it means that a landlord has a duty to look after the health of his lodgers. It is submitted that it is not the law that a hotel manager who allows a sick guest to linger in his room and die is guilty of homicide because of his failure to provide the deceased with medical assistance. It is true that in passing sentence Lord Justice-Clerk Hope referred to the fact that the principal accused was in the business of keeping a lodging-house for profit, but however relevant that may have been to the accused's moral duty, or to the question of sentence, it was irrelevant to his legal responsibility.

In *H.M. Advocate v. McPhee*[18] the accused was charged with punching and kicking a woman, and thereafter exposing her "while in an injured and unconscious condition to the inclemency of the weather." This was

---

[13] *cf.* Holmes, *The Common Law*, ed. Howe (Cambridge, Mass., 1963), pp.218–219.

[14] *Wm O'Neill*, High Court at Glasgow, Sept. 1961, unrep'd; a charge of assaulting D, wrenching a gas meter from its place and breaking its inlet pipe, forcing open its lockfast money box "and knowing that coal gas was escaping from said inlet pipe you did leave [D] lying unconscious and he inhaled said coal gas and was asphyxiated and you did murder him." A plea of guilty to culpable homicide was accepted.

[15] Hume, i, 190.

[16] *Geo. Fay* (1847) Ark. 397. See also *Robert Watt and Jas. Kerr* (1868) 1 Couper 123; *John Nicol* (1835) 1 Couper 128n. In *Wm Gray* (1836) 1 Swin. 328 the accused was an engine driver who was charged with culpable homicide following on the death of someone he had allowed, contrary to the regulations of the company, to travel on the tender of his engine. The indictment was challenged because it did not libel any act committed by the accused. It was also argued that as railway employees were allowed to travel on the tender, what the accused had allowed was not dangerous and that his duty to members of the public was the same as that to his fellow-employees. The case was dropped by the Crown before the court gave any judgment on relevancy.

[17] (1847) Ark. 321.

[18] 1935 J.C. 46.

held to be a relevant charge of murder, but the accused was convicted only of culpable homicide because he had no deliberate intention of killing her by exposure. Again, the exposure was criminal because it was the creation by the accused of a situation of danger, followed by a "washing of his hands" of the consequences. The accused was responsible for the death, not just because it was a consequence of his initial assault, but because having assaulted the deceased he left her in a dangerous condition, a condition he had himself created.[19]

In both these cases the accused's prior dangerous act was a criminal one, but, as the example of the surgeon shows, this is not necessary; it is enough that it should be dangerous.[20] In *MacPhail v. Clarke*,[21] for example, a farmer was burning straw in a field, but the fire spread to the verge of an adjacent road where smoke gathered, obscured the carriageway and caused a traffic accident in which persons were injured. He was charged, however, only with culpably and recklessly endangering the road users and not with culpably and recklessly injuring them.

(2) *Where there is a personal relationship involved.* The most obvious example of such a duty is that of a parent towards his children.[22] A father who stands by and watches someone kill his children may be guilty **3.35**

---

[19] Where A assaults B and leaves him to die from the blow, no question of omission arises and the case is simply one of causing death by violence whether it occurs in a warm room or on a cold mountain. Where, however, death is caused, not by the blow, but by the weather acting on B's weakened condition, A's responsibility rests both on his active blow and his passive failure to remove B from a place of danger. If removal is not practicable, then at the very least A should have obtained assistance, such as medical assistance, for B — as in *Jas. Paterson Duff*, Criminal Appeal Court, May 1979, unrept'd, where the charge was one of culpable homicide by assaulting the victim to her severe injury and thereafter failing to obtain medical assistance for her, whereby she died owing to her injuries and the lack of medical attention. *Cf. Sutherland v. H.M. Advocate (No. 1)* 1994 S.C.C.R. 80, where the accused and the deceased set fire to the accused's house in order to defraud insurers. As a result of the reckless way in which the fire raising was achieved, the deceased was trapped in the blazing building whilst the accused escaped. He was charged with the culpable homicide of the deceased in terms which included: "and you did thereafter pretend to members of the emergency services that there was no one in [your] house the truth being as you well knew that the [deceased] was trapped [there]". Part of the crown's case was that the accused had had a legal duty to tell the truth and thus assist the emergency services to rescue the deceased, since the accused was art and part guilty of creating the dangerous situation. In the event, however, the evidence did not support the argument that there was a causal connection between the accused's failure to tell the truth and the death. The jury deleted the words quoted above, but were able to convict the accused of culpable homicide on the basis that the accused had shown criminal negligence in the way in which the joint enterprise had been conducted.

[20] A South African civil case is of interest in this connection. A fishing boat broke down and after drifting for some days foundered, and the crew were killed. The widow of one of the fishermen sued the owner of the boat who was the owner of a fishing fleet, for damages for the death of her husband, and she succeeded in her action. One of the grounds of judgment was that in providing the fishermen with a boat for fishing the owner had engaged in an activity which was potentially noxious to others, and that accordingly he had a duty to try to prevent the danger which occurred by taking steps to rescue the crew, so that his omission to initiate rescue operations amounted to an act of negligence: *Silva's Fishing Corporation (Pty) Ltd v. Maweza*, 1957 (2) S.A. 256 (A.D.). The case is complicated by the fact that although the plaintiff was not employed by the owners he was regarded by the court as engaged on a joint enterprise with them, but it does seem to provide authority for the view that the creator of a danger is liable for omitting to take precautions to prevent it.

[21] 1983 S.L.T. (Sh.Ct.) 37.

[22] *e.g., R. v. Senior* [1899] 1 Q.B. 283; *R. v. Watson and Watson* (1959) 43 Cr.App.R. 111, both cases of failure to provide medical attention for a child resulting in a charge of manslaughter.

of their homicide because of his failure to prevent their death, while a stranger who stood by would be free of guilt. In the Australian case of *R. v. Russell*[23] it was alleged that a father had pushed his wife and children into a pond and murdered them. The accused said that after a quarrel with him his wife had thrown the children and herself into the water. A direction by the trial judge that the father could be convicted of the manslaughter of the children even if he had not in any way encouraged his wife to kill them, but had merely stood by, was upheld by the Full Court of the Supreme Court of Victoria. A distinction was made between an omission to intervene due to gross and culpable neglect which would amount to manslaughter, and a deliberate and intentional omission which would amount to murder. The father was also convicted of killing his wife, but this conviction was sustained partly on the ground that the jury were entitled to find that he had participated in his wife's death. McArthur J. distinguished between the position with regard to the wife who was capable of protecting herself and that with regard to the helpless children, and would have quashed the conviction for killing the wife.[24]

The essence of the matter in this type of omission lies in the legal relationship between the accused and the deceased. As the Commission appointed to consider English criminal law in 1839 said: "where death has been occasioned by the omission to discharge the legal obligation imposed by some civil relation existing between the deceased and some other person . . . the particulars of the civil rights and liabilities of parties so circumstanced become absolutely essential to the determination of the criminal responsibility of the accused."[25] The importance of the legal relationship was stressed in the American case of *People v. Beardsley*[26] where a man was charged with killing his mistress by allowing her to take poison tablets when he was in a position to stop her doing so by taking the tablets away from her. It was said there that, "Seeking for a proper determination of the case . . . by the application of the legal principles involved, we must eliminate from the case all consideration of mere moral obligation, and discover whether respondent was under a legal duty towards [the deceased] at the time of her death . . . which required him to make all reasonable and proper effort to save her; the omission to perform which duty would make him responsible for her death."[27] As the deceased was the accused's mistress only and not his wife, the court held that there was no such duty, and that he was

---

[23] (1933) 39 Argus Law Rep.76.

[24] The question in *Russell* was not considered in *H.M. Advocate v. Robertson* (1896) 2 Adam 92. In that case the parents of a child were charged with killing it by violence. There was no evidence to show which of them had inflicted the fatal blows, and the jury were directed to acquit both, as there was likewise no evidence of any concert between them, or even that the blows were inflicted by one in the presence of the other. The directions given to the jury by L.J.-C. Macdonald are the standard ones in this type of case — see *infra*, para. 5.44 — and make no mention of the special relationships of the accused to the victim. They indicate that presence at the time of the assault must be proved by the Crown, but do not mean that such presence necessarily involves guilt either by reason of an omission to prevent the crime, or as evidence of active participation.

[25] Fourth Report of Her Majesty's Commissioners on Criminal Law, p.vii, Parl. Papers, 1839, xix, 241.

[26] (1907) 150 Mich. 206; Hall and Glueck (1st ed.), p.159.

[27] Hall and Glueck (1st ed.), p.164.

therefore not guilty of homicide.[28] *Beardsley*[28a] suggests that there would have been a "duty of care" had the parties been married, while *Russell*[28b] suggests that the duty does not extend to spouses; but this is only a difference as to the civil rights involved, and not a difference in approach to the problem of criminal liability for omissions. The question has arisen in Scotland only in relation to the failure of a mother to call for help at the birth of her child, as a result of which the child dies, and this is accepted as constituting homicide, provided the necessary *mens rea* is present.[29]

(3) *Where there is an express contract.* The position in such cases is that, **3.36** in the words of the English Draft Code of 1879, "Every one who undertakes to do any act the omission to do which is or may be dangerous to life, is under a legal duty to do that act, and is criminally responsible for the consequences of omitting without lawful excuse to discharge that duty."[30] The obvious case of a breach of contract which would be regarded as criminal is the failure by persons in charge of the sick to fulfil their duties. A surgeon cannot be convicted of homicide for refusing to operate on someone, but a surgeon who enters into a contract to perform a necessary operation and then fails to do so, may be guilty of homicide if the patient dies as a result of his failure.[31] Similarly, a person who undertakes to look after a child may be guilty of cruel treatment or even of killing the child if she fails to provide it with the necessities of life.[32]

The contractual obligation may arise either from a contract with the victim, or from a contract with a third party, such as a sick person's relative, a charitable organisation, or the state itself. Macaulay gives the following example of an "official" duty failure to perform which may be criminal:

> "A omits to tell Z that a river is swollen so high that Z cannot safely attempt to ford it, and by this omission voluntarily causes Z's death. This is murder, if A is a person stationed by authority to warn travellers from attempting to ford the river. It is murder if A is a guide who had contracted to conduct Z. It is not murder if A is a person on whom Z has no other claim than that of humanity."[33]

In *Thos. Mitchell*[34] a magistrate who declined to assist a messenger-at-arms who had been attacked by a crowd and deprived of his prisoner,

---

28 This decision is severely criticised by G. Hughes, "Criminal Omissions" (1958) 67 Y.L.J. 590, as "smug, ignorant and vindictive". Mr Hughes argues that there is a duty to aid a helpless sick companion who has no other source of aid. This might be so on the principle of *R. v. Instan, infra,* but if the circumstances cannot be brought under that principle the approach of the court in *Beardsley* will be adopted.

28a (1907) 150 Mich. 206.

28b (1933) 39 Argus Law Rep. 76.

29 *Isabella Martin* (1877) 3 Couper 379; *H.M. Advocate v. Scott* (1892) 3 White 240.

30 Report of Royal Commission on Draft Code, 1879, C. 2345, Draft Code s.164. This section of the Code is concerned with the preservation of life and most of the cases deal with homicide, but there is no reason in principle to confine the law of omissions to homicide. The passive acquiescence by a nurse in the theft of a child in her charge might in certain circumstances amount to art and part theft.

31 *cf.* Macaulay, p.494.

32 *cf. Barbara Gray or McIntosh* (1880) 4 Couper 389.

33 Macaulay, p.495. *Cf. R. v. Smith* (1869) 11 Cox C.C. 210; *R. v. Pittwood* (1902) 19 T.L.R. 37.

34 (1698) Hume, i, 397.

was convicted of being art and part in the crowd's deforcement of the messenger. Hume points out that "this sort of tacit encouragement would not, however, be reputed an accession in the case of any ordinary person" and cites the case of *Francis Duguid*[35] in which a charge of deforcement against a father who did not stop his sons from rescuing his son-in-law from a messenger was held to be irrelevant.

In *Wm Hardie*[36] the accused was an Inspector of Poor who was charged with the culpable homicide of a woman whose application for poor relief he had ignored, and who had died of want as a result. The charge was held relevant, but was not proceeded with.

3.37 (4) *Duties arising from the imposition of a legal obligation.* In certain circumstances — other than those where there is a permanent legal relationship such as that of parent and child — the law imposes an obligation because of the relationship of the accused to the victim. The classic example of this is the English case of *R. v. Instan.*[37] There the accused lived alone with her bedridden aunt; for ten days she gave her aunt no food and called for no medical attention; the aunt died as a result. The accused was convicted of manslaughter. Lord Coleridge C.J. purported to decide the case on the ground that the accused had failed in a moral duty to take care of her aunt, and said: "A legal common law duty is nothing else than the enforcing by law of that which is a moral obligation without legal enforcement."[38] This, however, is unnecessarily wide, and confuses law and morality.[39] A better *ratio* for *Instan*[39a] is that where people related as were the accused and the deceased live in the circumstances in which they lived, the law imposes an obligation — perhaps because it implies an undertaking — on the healthy person to look after the invalid.[40]

Hall, who is himself a staunch upholder of the moral nature of the criminal law, points out that Lord Coleridge's equation of law and morality does not represent the law properly. Hall says:

> "Although this hypothesis seems persuasive, it is also evident that it is not a sufficient explanation of the case-law. For example, an expert swimmer might be the only person to see a child drowning. He would know that he was the only one who could rescue the child, and he should certainly feel obliged to save him. How can such a situation be differentiated from one identical with it — except that the by-stander is the child's father? . . . The essential difference, it is suggested, inheres not in moral obligation, but in the

---

35 (1673) *ibid.*

36 (1847) Ark. 247.

37 [1893] 1 Q.B. 450. See also *R. v. Stone* [1977] Q.B. 354.

38 At 453.

39 Or else it is tautologous and only says that any moral duty which has been made a legal duty as well is a legal duty.

39a [1893] 1 Q.B. 450.

40 *cf.* New Zealand Crimes Act 1966, s.141: "Every one who has charge of any other person unable, by reason of detention, age, sickness, insanity, or any other cause, to withdraw himself from such charge, and unable to provide himself with the necessaries of life, is (whether such charge is undertaken by him under any contract or is imposed on him by law or by reason of his unlawful act or otherwise howsoever) under a legal duty to supply that person with the necessaries of life, and is criminally responsible for omitting without lawful excuse to perform such a duty if the death of that person is caused, or if his life is endangered or his health permanently injured, by such neglect."

mores, in the public attitudes regarding the respective parties; and these, in turn, are influenced by the relationship of the parties to the child."[41]

The reference to public mores may seem at first sight to be out of place in a discussion of legal obligation. But once it is conceded that the obligation may be implied from, or imposed in, the circumstances of the case, the question arises, "In what circumstances does the law impose such a duty?" — and this may depend on public attitudes, since the decision whether or not to impose a duty in any given case will be influenced by the normal reaction of society to the circumstances of the case.

The answer to the question is by no means clear, but it can be said with some confidence that the criminal law does not recognise a duty to take steps to prevent harm to anyone "who is in law my neighbour", in the sense that he is "so closely and directly affected by my act that I ought reasonably to have [him] in contemplation as being so affected when I am directing my mind to the acts or omissions which are called in question."[42] Of course, the civil law does not go as far as this either: it is not an actionable wrong to fail to render assistance to a stranger in need. As Hall puts it, "we have not reached the point of really believing that everyone is morally obliged to be his brother's keeper; or, at least, that is not believed sufficiently to be given implementation by the criminal law."[43]

The law, as it stands, is generally regarded as unsatisfactory, since it **3.38** refuses to punish people who are morally guilty of great callousness. There is much to be said for Bentham's view that, "The limits of the law on this head seem, however, to be capable of being extended a good deal farther than they seem ever to have been extended hitherto."[44] This contention gains force from the examples Bentham gives, which are as follows:

> "A woman's head-dress catches fire: water is at hand: a man, instead of assisting to quench the fire, looks on, and laughs at it. A drunken man, falling with his face downwards into a puddle, is in danger of suffocation: lifting his head a little on one side would save him: another man ses this and lets him lie. A quantity of gunpowder lies scattered about a room: a man is going into it with a lighted candle: another, knowing this, lets him go in without warning. Who is there that in any of these cases would think punishment misapplied?"[45]

On the other hand, there is difficulty in extending the law, firstly because of the principle that the criminal law should be construed narrowly, and secondly because of the difficulty of setting limits to the duty to protect others, although they might be set by reference to the concept of reasonableness if the proposed offence were treated as one of

---

[41] Hall, p.210.
[42] *Donoghue v. Stevenson*, 1932 S.C. (H.L.) 31. Lord Atkin at 44.
[43] Hall, p.210.
[44] Bentham, *Principles*, XVII, p.19.
[45] *ibid.*

criminal negligence.[46] Bentham suggests that "where the person is in danger" it should be "made the duty of every man to save another from mischief, when it can be done without prejudicing himself".[46a] His examples concern cases where the victim can be saved easily without exertion by, or danger to, the rescuer, and where it is clear that a slight intervention will be sufficient. And any extension of the criminal law would probably have to be limited by these considerations: "La loi pénale n'impose pas l'héroisme".[47] But in fact the law has not even gone the length of constructing a system of obligations within these requirements — indeed there seems to be no law at all on the matter in Scotland, although *Instan*[48] would probably be followed. It seems clear that if Bentham's views were to be acccepted at all the duty would be restricted to situations in which only two persons were involved — that is, to cases where the accused should have saved the victim from some natural danger — and would not extend to cases of preventing someone else from harming the victim. But even so the law would be very vague, and it would be an objection to it that it would be very difficult for the potential rescuer to know whether or not his failure to rescue would lay him open to a charge of homicide. It would be unfair to ask him to weigh up the situation and decide on his legal duty under the same penalty for failure as is imposed on an assailant for the foreseeable consequences of his assault: conviction for culpable homicide. In order, therefore, to achieve certainty the law may have to forbear from punishment in certain cases in which punishment would be morally unexceptionable. The position is summed up by Macaulay, who apologises in his Notes on the Indian Penal Code for the leniency of the law, and explains:

> "[W]e do not think that it can be made more severe without disturbing the whole order of society. It is true that the man who, having abundance of wealth, suffers a fellow creature to die of hunger at his feet is a bad man, a worse man, probably, than many of those for whom we have provided very severe punishment. But we are unable to see where, if we make such a man legally punishable, we can draw the line. If the rich man who refuses to save a beggar's life at the cost of a little copper is a murderer, is the poor man just one degree above beggary also to be a murderer if he omits to invite the beggar to partake his hard-earned rice?
>
> . . . The distinction between a legal and an illegal omission is perfectly plain and intelligible; but the distinction between a large and a small sum of money is very far from being so, not to say that a sum which is small to one man is large to another."[49]

Instan[49a] suggests that the law is prepared to go further than Macaulay, but it is doubtful if it will go much further; it should also be remembered that the position in *Instan*[49b] was very like that between nurse and patient, and that the actual relationship of aunt and niece made the

---

[46] *cf. Goldman v. Hargrave* [1967] 1 A.C. 645, 663 (P.C.).

[46a] Bentham, *Principles,* XVII, p.19.

[47] H. Donnedieu de Vabres, *Traité de Droit Criminal et de Législation Pénale Comparée* (3rd. ed., Paris, 1947), p.74.

[48] (1893) 1 Q.B. 450.

[49] Macaulay, p.496.

[49a] (1893) 1 Q.B. 450.

[49b] *ibid.*

accused's conduct appear even more heinous than if it had been that of nurse and patient.[50]

Possession

It is even more difficult to apply ideas of voluntariness to possession than to omission, since the former refers to a state rather than to a form of behaviour, and at the same time contains in itself the notion of some mental element distinguishing it from mere custody.[51] Common law crimes such as theft and reset are usually concerned with taking possession of a thing rather than with just possessing it, but there may be cases where the only element of *actus reus* present is that of being in possession of a thing, as where A decides to appropriate goods of which he is lawful possessor, and there are also certain statutory offences constituted by being in possession of certain articles. **3.39**

The minimum requirement for an *actus reus* of possession was the subject of discussion and dissension in the House of Lords in the English case of *R. v. Warner.*[52]

There seem to be three possible ways of answering the question, "When is a person in possession of goods over which he has actual control?"

(1) He is always in possession of such goods whether or not he is aware of the fact. On this view, if a drug peddler who sees an approaching detective slips a packet of drugs into the shopping bag of a woman beside him she is in possession of the drugs from the moment they enter her bag. Similarly, if a vindictive miner slips a packet of matches into the deputy's pocket when they are underground, the latter is in possession of them. Consistency in the application of the distinction between the objective and the mental elements of an offence might lead to this answer: that it leads to injustice in cases like those just mentioned is an argument against the creation of strict responsibility offences of

---

[50] Some European codes have adopted a compromise solution which allows them to take into account situations like those posited by Bentham without relaxing their attitude to crimes of commission by omission. They do this by creating a new crime of omission — the crime of failing to render help to someone in peril or prevent a "crime" or a "délit contre l'integrité corporelle de la personne" where this can be done "par son action immédiate, sans risque pour lui ou des tiers": French Penal Code Art. 63, Ordonnance de 25 Juin 1945 (see now Nouveau Code Pénal, Arts 223–6). This applies both to the prevention of crime and to giving assistance to someone in danger caused other than by criminal conduct — it would apply, for example, to a doctor refusing to treat a dangerously sick man. Gaston Dominici was sentenced to two months' imprisonment for a breach of this provision in failing to succour the wounded Elizabeth Drummond: see [1955] Crim.L.R. 5. Article 330c of the German Penal Code imposes a similar duty. Failure to obtemper these provisions is not by itself equivalent to an act of commission should the person in danger die. See also G. Hughes, "Failure to Rescue" (1952) 52 Col.L.Rev. 631, and "Criminal Omissions" (1958) 67 Y.L.J. 590. For a review of various provisions and a discussion of some of their problems see F.J.M. Feldbrugge, "Good and Bad Samaritans" (1966) 14 A.J.Comp.L. 630. For arguments for and against extending the scope of criminal omissions, see A.Ashworth, "The Scope of Criminal Liability for Omissions" (1989) 105 L.Q.R. 424; Gl. Williams, "Criminal Omissions — The Conventional View" (1991) 107 L.Q.R. 86..

[51] T.B. Smith, p.462.

[52] [1969] 2 A.C. 256; adopted in *McKenzie v. Skeen*, 1983 S.L.T. 121. The ratio of *McKenzie v. Skeen* was clarified in *Salmon v. H.M. Advocate; Moore v. H.M. Advocate*, 1998 S.C.C.R. 740.

possession. This answer has, however, been decisively rejected in England.[53]

(2) He is in possession only of goods of whose existence he is aware, even if he is unaware of their nature. In particular, possession of a box or parcel involves possession of its contents, even if the agent believes the box or parcel to be empty. This was the answer given by Lord Morris of Borth-y-gest in *R. v. Warner* where he said:

> "In my view, in order to establish possession the prosecution must prove that an accused was knowingly in control of something in circumstances which showed that he was assenting to being in control of it: they need not prove that in fact he had actual knowledge of the nature of that which he had. In *Lockyer v. Gibb* Lord Parker, at p.248, gave the illustration of something being slipped into a person's basket. While the person was unaware of what had happened there would be no possession. But in such circumstances, on becoming aware of the presence of the newly discovered article, there would be opportunity to see what the article was: whether the opportunity was availed of or not, if the article was deliberately retained there would be possession of it . . . If there is some momentary custody of a thing without any knowledge or means of knowledge of what the thing is or contains — then, ordinarily, I would suppose that there would not be possession. If, however, someone deliberately assumes control of some package or container, then I would think that he is in possession of it. If he deliberately so assumes control knowing that it has contents he would also be in possession of the contents. I cannot think that it would be rational to hold that someone who is in possession of a box which he knows to have things in it is in possession of the box, but not in possession of the things in it. If he had been misinformed or misled as to the nature of the contents or if he had made a wrong surmise as to them it seems to me that he would nevertheless be in possession of them. Similarly, if he wrongly surmised that a box was empty which in fact had things in it, possession of the box (if established in the way which I have outlined) would involve possession of the contents."[54]

This may be thought to offer a reasonable compromise since, while it requires some mental element, it still retains a fairly clear distinction between *actus reus* and *mens rea*, and so between offences of strict responsibility and other offences.[55]

(3) He is in possession only of goods of whose existence and, in general terms, of whose quality he is aware. A person knowingly in possession of a bottle of pills which are in fact but unknown to him prohibited drugs is then in possession of the drugs.[56] In addition, he is in possession of goods of whose existence he is aware if he takes no steps to

---

[53] *R. v. Warner, supra; R. v. Woodrow* (1846) 15 M. & W. 404: "a man can hardly be said to be in possession of something without knowing it", Pollock C.B, at 415; *Lockyer v. Gibb* [1967] 2 Q.B. 243; *R. v. Irving* [1970] Crim.L.R. 642; *cf. Baender v. Barnett,* 255 U.S. 224 (1921). For the present Scottish position, see para. 3.40, *infra*.

[54] *R. v. Warner, supra* at 289–290.

[55] Although the sentence about "momentary custody" betrays a certain uncertainty.

[56] But not if the prohibited drug is a pill which has been placed in his aspirin bottle by someone else without his knowledge: *R. v. Irving, supra; cf. R. v. Warner, supra*, Lord Reid at 280–281.

ascertain their quality. But if he reasonably believes them to be quite other than they are (*e.g.* scent and not L.S.D.) he is not in possession of them, unless perhaps he has failed to take reasonable steps to discover their true character. This is the answer given by Lord Pearce and Lord Wilberforce in *Warner*,[56a] but it is open to the objection (a) that the proposed difference between *e.g.* believing a parcel of L.S.D. pills to be a parcel of sweets and believing it to be a parcel of scent is difficult to state precisely or apply consistently, and (b) that it confuses the *actus reus* of possession with the elements of *negligent* possession and the requirements of fairness.[57] Lord Pearce said:

> "I think that the term 'possession' is satisfied by a knowledge only of the existence of the thing itself and not its qualities, and that ignorance or mistake as to its qualities is not an excuse. This would comply with the general understanding of the word 'possess'. Though I reasonably believe the tablets which I possess to be aspirin, yet if they turn out to be heroin I am in possession of heroin tablets. This would be so I think even if I believed them to be sweets. It would be otherwise if I believed them to be something of a wholly different nature. At this point a question of degree arises as to when a difference in qualities amounts to a difference in kind. That is a matter for a jury who would probably decide it sensibly in favour of the genuinely innocent but against the guilty . . . For a man takes over a package or suitcase at risk as to its contents being unlawful if he does not immediately examine it (if he is entitled to do so). As soon as may be he should examine it and if he finds the contents suspicious reject possession by either throwing them away or by taking immediate sensible steps for their disposal."[58]

The current position in Scotland accords in general terms with the **3.40** second of the three answers set out in the foregoing paragraph. This is strikingly shown in *McKenzie v. Skeen*.[59] There, the Crown argued that in terms of the offence of possessing controlled drugs,[60] it was unnecessary to establish anything beyond the mere fact of physical possession of the drugs in question by the accused.[61] As Lord Cameron put the argument: "This would mean that if unknown to the appellant in this case, the other accused had put this jar in her suitcase she was guilty of the offence created by s.5(2) and, on construction of s.28(2)[62] it would not be open to her to exculpate herself by proving she did not know of the presence of the article because proof of an accused's possession of the article was not necessary to establish the offence."[63] The Court rejected the Crown's contention, holding instead that the interpretation to be

---

56a [1969] 2 A.C. 256.

57 See especially Lord Wilberforce at 308–309, 310 E-F.

58 At 305 F–G, 306 B.

59 1983 S.L.T. (Notes)121. The decision here was actually made by the High Court on Appeal on April 2, 1977.

60 Misuse of Drugs Act 1971, s.5(2).

61 The cannabis in question was in fact found in a semi-opaque closed glass jar within a suitcase in the accused's apartment.

62 This subsection allows the defence that the accused "neither knew of nor had reason to suspect the existence of some fact alleged by the prosecution which it is necessary for the prosecution to prove if [the accused] is to be convicted of the offence charged." Both subss. 28(2) and 28(3) were authoritatively interpreted by L.J.-G. Rodger in *Salmon v. H.M. Advocate; Moore v. H.M. Advocate*, 1998 S.C.C.R. 740, at 746F to 759D.

63 1983 S.L.T. 121, at 122.

placed on the word 'possession' was that laid down in *R. v. Warner*,[64] or at least the particular interpretation given out in that case "in a sentence[65] by Lord Pearce at p. 307: 'If a man has physical control or possession of a thing that is sufficient possession under the Act provided he knows he has the thing. But you do not (within the meaning of the Act) possess things of whose existence you are unaware.' "[66] This would leave open the issue of whether the accused should also be shown to have been aware of the general quality of the article in question; but Lord Cameron concluded that in his opinion "proof of knowledge of possession of the article itself though not of its nature or quality is essential proof of the offence created by s.5(2) of the Act of 1971."[67] It has subsequently been confirmed in several cases that both knowledge and control are essential for possession to be established[68]; and it is now clearly accepted that knowledge of the nature of what is within one's control is not required.[69] Proof of the requisite knowledge and control is a matter of fact and circumstances[70]; but control means the ability to exercise practical control,[71] involving *inter alia* the ability to use, dispose of or decide the location of the article in question. It seems, however, that if A gives permission to B to leave drugs in A's room while he is on holiday and B does so, then A is in possession of the drugs, even though he did not know these particular drugs were there or that B had taken advantage of the permission given to him, and even perhaps if he expected B to have removed the drugs before his return from holiday.[72] It has also been decided that once a person is knowingly in possession of an article he continues to be knowingly in possession of it even during periods of time in which he has forgotten that he has it.[73]

---

[64] [1969] 2 A.C. 256.

[65] Or, rather, in two sentences.

[66] *Per* Lord Cameron at 122.

[67] *ibid*. See also the opinion of L.J.-G. Emslie at 121.

[68] *Mingay v. Mackinnon*, 1980 J.C. 33; *Crowe v. MacPhail*, 1987 S.L.T. 316; *Hughes v. Guild*, 1990 J.C. 359; *Murray v. MacPhail*, 1991 S.C.C.R. 245; *Feeney v. Jessop*, 1991 S.L.T. 409; *Davis v. Buchanan*, 1994 S.C.C.R. 369 (relative to the Firearms Act 1968, s.21); *Salmon v. H.M. Advocate; Moore v. H.M. Advocate*, 1998 S.C.C.R. 740, L.J.-G. Rodger at 751C and 754B-D.

[69] *Salmon v. H.M. Advocate; Moore v. H.M. Advocate*, 1998 S.C.C.R. 740, L.J.-G. Rodger (with whom Lord Johnston expressed agreement) at 752F to 754D, where the earlier opinions in *McKenzie v. Skeen*, 1983 S.L.T. 121, and *Sim v. H.M. Advocate*, 1996 S.C.C.R. 77, are clarified: *cf. R. v. McNamara* (1987) 87 Cr.App.R. 246; *R. v. Leeson* (2000) 1 Cr.App.R. 233; see also *Smith v. H.M. Advocate*, 1996 S.L.T. 1338 (relating to s.1(1)(a) and (b) of the Firearms Act 1968), following English authority — *viz., R. v. Hussain* [1981] 1 W.L.R. 416; *R. v. Steele* [1993] Crim L.R. 298; *R. v. Bradish* (1990) 90 Crim.App.R. 271; *R. v. Waller* [1991] Crim.L.R. 381. *Cf., Black v. H.M. Advocate*, 1974 S.L.T. 247, opinion of the court at 252, where in relation to offences under ss.3(b) and 4(1) of the Explosive Substances Act 1883, it is stated: "Even if a man is knowingly in possession of a box or parcel containing explosives that knowledge by itself is insufficient to establish the quality of knowledge necessary to constitute the knowledge which is of the essence of the offence, that knowledge must include knowledge of the fact that the substance or substances are explosives." It is submitted that this statement is confined to the particularly worded statutory offences to which the case related.

[70] *Bain v. H.M. Advocate*, 1992 S.C.C.R. 705; *Hughes v. Guild*, 1990 J.C. 359.

[71] *Hughes v. Guild*, 1990 J.C. 359; *Black v. H.M. Advocate*, 1974 S.L.T. 247.

[72] *Murray v. MacPhail*, 1991 S.C.C.R. 245.

[73] *Gill v. Lockhart*, 1988 S.L.T. 189; *R. v. Martindale* [1986] 1 W.L.R. 1042. *Cf., McKee v. MacDonald*, 1995 S.L.T. 1342, Lord Sutherland at 1344 B.

The Place of the Crime

At common law in Scotland, a version of the 'territorial principle' applies for jurisdictional purposes. The view, expressed in a previous edition of this book[74] that in the absence of any legislation to the contrary the jurisdiction of the Scottish criminal courts is limited to crimes committed in Scotland, has been upheld as generally correct[75] (although this begs the question as to what 'committed in Scotland' actually means). Mackenzie discussed three possible locational principles under which the courts of his time might assume jurisdiction — the *forum originis* (the place of the culprit's birth), the *forum domicilii* (the place where he dwells), and the *forum delicti commissi* (the place where the crime was committed); but the last was regarded by him as the most competent of the three, since it ensured maximum local deterrence, increased victim satisfaction, and was convenient for witnesses.[76] It might also be said that the *forum delicti* will usually have more interest than any other in the prosecution of the crime.[77] Mackenzie's first two possibilities are reflections of the 'nationality' principle of jurisdiction, under which a state would be prepared to exercise jurisdiction over its own crimes committed wholly outside its territory by its own nationals.[78] This principle appears only exceptionally in modern Scots law — either in relation to offences where nationality is of the essence, as in Treason,[79] or where statute dictates.[80] Where it does so appear, of course, it is British Nationality which is at stake, since Scotland, notwithstanding that it has its own parliament, remains part of the United Kingdom and is not a nation-state in its own right.[81] But as it has its own, separate system of criminal law, it is entitled to have its own common law rules for determining when its courts may have jurisdiction over offenders. Of all the principles which international law recognises as 3.41

---

[74] 2nd ed., para. 3.39.

[75] *Clements v. H.M. Advocate*, 1991 J.C. 62, L.J.-G. Hope at 68, Lord Coulsfield at 73. For instances of contrary legislation, see Renton & Brown, para. 1.22 *et seq*; *Mortensen v. Peters* (1906) 5 Adam 121; *H.M. Advocate v. Hetherington & Wilson* (1915) 7 Adam 663: *cf.* Criminal Jurisdiction Act 1975.

[76] Pt. II, tit. ii, §.1, 355–356 (1678 ed.).

[77] See I. Brownlie, *Principles of International Law* (4th ed., Oxford, 1990) 300. See also *H.M. Advocate v. Al Megrahi*, 2000 S.C.C.R. 177.

[78] In France, for example, the courts can deal with "crimes", the most serious offences under the criminal code, committed by French nationals outside the territory of the Republic, and with "délits" so committed if the conduct in question is also punishable under the law of the *forum delicti* (Nouveau Code Pénal, 1994, Bk. I, Tit. I, ch. III, §.2, Art. 113–6). On this principle generally, see I. Brownlie, *op.cit.*, 303.

[79] See Hume, ii, 50.

[80] See, *e.g.*, the Criminal Law (Consolidation) (Scotland) Act 1995, s.16B (inserted by the Sex Offenders Act 1997, s.8) which provides that British citizens or those resident in the United Kingdom who have committed certain sexual offences outwith the U.K. may be prosecuted in Scotland, provided what they did was criminal under both Scots law and the law of the place where it was done. See also the Criminal Procedure (Scotland) Act 1995, s.11(1): "Any British citizen or British subject who in a country outside the United Kingdom does any act or makes any omission which if done or made in Scotland would constitute the crime of murder or of culpable homicide shall be guilty of the same crime and subject to the same punishment as if the act or omission had been done or made in Scotland." *Cf.* the English provisions in the Offences Against the Person Act 1861, ss.9 and 10. Curiously, intra United Kingdom homicides (and the listed sexual offences mentioned in s.16B, above) are not covered by the legislation: see Michael Hirst, "Murder in England or Murder in Scotland?" [1995] C.L.J. 488.

[81] See the Scotland Act 1998, ss.29 and 30; Sched. 5, Pt. I, para. 1(b), and Pt. II, s.B6.

appropriate for states to use in the matter of criminal jurisdiction,[82] Scots law favours the one which links the *actus reus* of the offence to Scottish territory.[83] It seems that if an appropriate link is shown to exist, then the crime can be deemed to be committed in Scotland.

3.42 *The principle of territorial jurisdiction.* In its most general form, this principle asserts that a state (including part of a state having an independent criminal law system) has jurisdiction over crimes which are committed within its territory.[84] This could mean that the whole of the *actus reus* of the crime must occur within, for example, Scottish territory. Such a restrictive rule may be practicable for some conduct crimes such as perjury: but where the implementation of a crime occupies a greater time-span than is involved in, for example, telling lies under oath in particular court proceedings, and more especially in relation to a result crime,[85] the *actus reus* may be fragmented over the territory of more than one country. Thus, a fraudulent scheme may be planned in one state and executed in another: and the situation is proverbial where a person on the English side of the border shoots at and kills another on the Scottish side. To cater for these well-known eventualities, without surrendering the territorial principle, international law recognises two applications of that principle. The first is the objective application,[86] under which jurisdiction lies with the state where the *actus reus* is completed. This makes it necessary to identify which element in the definition of the crime is the vital one which signifies completion: in a result crime, for example, it may be thought of as the result itself. But this is not necessarily so. In homicide, for instance, the result is the death of the victim consequent upon the conduct of the accused — which will give a clear rule to follow if X in England shoots Y in Scotland, killing Y instantly there.[87] The position will not be so clear, however, if X shoots Y whilst they are both on the English side of the border, and Y staggers into Scottish territory only to die of his wounds in a Scottish hospital at a later date. To deny jurisdiction for murder to the English courts in such a scenario has been described as "absurd", and it may be preferable, therefore, to regard the essential completion ingredient as the infliction of the fatal injury, although that is not quite the "result" as usually understood in a homicide case.[88] This application of the principle may

---

[82] See *Oppenheim's International Law* (9th ed., 1992, edited by Sir R. Jennings and Sir A. Watts), 458 *et seq.*; I. Brownlie, *op.cit.*, 300 *et seq.*; Draft Convention on Jurisdiction with respect to Crime (Supplement to 29 Am.J.Int.Law (1935), 439 *et seq.*) which includes introductory comment and commentary on the Draft Code itself.

[83] See *Clements v. H.M. Advocate*, 1991 J.C. 62; *Laird v. H.M. Advocate*, 1985 J.C. 37. Both are discussed *infra* at para. 3.47.

[84] It has been stated that this principle is so well established in international law as not to require any particular recitation of authority: Supplement to 29 Am.J.Int.Law (1935) pp. 480–481, where it is also said to be the basic principle in Anglo-American jurisprudence.

[85] For conduct and result crimes, see para. 3.05, *supra*.

[86] I. Brownlee *op.cit.* at 300. Williams calls this the "terminatory theory" of territorial jurisdiction: see Gl. Williams, "Venue and the Ambit of Criminal Law" (Pt. 3) (1965) 81 L.Q.R. 518 at 518.

[87] See *State v. Hall* 114 N.C. 909, 19 S.E. 602 (1894), where the defendant in North Carolina shot across the border at the victim in Tennessee, killing him there. The Supreme Court of North Carolina ruled that the courts of the State of Tennessee alone had jurisdiction.

[88] See M. Hirst, "Jurisdiction over Cross-Frontier Offences" (1981) 97 L.Q.R. 80 at 100. See also W. R. LaFave and A.W. Scott, *Criminal Law* (2nd ed., St. Paul, Minn., 1986) at p.129.

not, therefore, be entirely consistent with the view that the crime is committed where the result occurs — but, in so far as it specifies a particular part of the result, should still be capable of identifying the *one* state or country whose courts have the greatest or greater claim to jurisdiction.[89]

The second application is referred to as "subjective"[90] in that jurisdiction lies in the place where the accused performed his criminal conduct, irrespective of the place where that conduct had its result or effect. Thus, on this theory, a person who shoots from state A across the border at his victim in state B is triable in the courts of state A for the homicide, even though the consequent death of the victim does not occur in that state.[91] Once again the intention of this application is to identify clearly the one state with the best or better claim to jurisdiction where the *actus reus* flows across more than one country. But once again it involves the identification of the essential element or elements in the *actus reus* of the crime which will enable the theory to operate successfully. Whether or not, for example, the initial steps taken in state A in a complex international fraud are sufficient to establish jurisdiction for the whole fraud in the courts of that state is not necessarily easy to decide.[92]

In view of the practical problems and limitations attendant on these two applications of the principle, the 1935 Draft Convention on Jurisdiction with Respect to Crimes followed the lead set by some states and combined the two into a much more general account of territoriality, namely that "a state has jurisdiction with respect to any crime committed in whole or in part within its territory."[93] It was made plain, however, that "in whole" should be taken to mean that all constituent elements of the offence occurred within the state in question, and that "in part" should mean that any constituent element occurred there.[94] At basis, then, on this theory it does not matter where the result of conduct occurred, nor where all of the conduct involved in the offence took place, nor whether the conduct that occurred in state A was 'sufficient' *aliunde* to establish jurisdiction: what matters is that one definite element (conduct or consequence) of the *actus reus* took place in the

---

[89] Mackenzie appears to consider the further case where the victim is shot on the border between two states — where the body falls partly in one and partly in the other. Rejecting the opinion of some, that jurisdiction lies with the state where the head of the body happens to be, he suggests that the state with the greater number of satisfied jurisdictional criteria should try the case (see Pt. II, tit. ii, § 1, 357, 1678 ed.). This seems unnecessarily complex, however, and dual jurisdiction, as accepted by him elsewhere (see, *e.g.*, 356) may be the most appropriate response in such circumstances. The non-exclusivity of jurisdiction is in practice a feature of the modern law (see para. 3.44, *infra*).

[90] See I. Brownlie, *op.cit.*, p.300. Gl. Williams (see n.86, *supra*) refers to this as the "initiatory theory" of territorial jurisdiction.

[91] *cf. People v. Botkin* 132 Cal. 231, 64 P. 286 (1901) where it was decided that the Californian courts had jurisdiction over a defendant who sent poisoned confectionery to his victim in Delaware. The victim ate the sweetmeats and died — in Delaware; but the decision that the murder was justiciable in California was based on the precise terms of the then California Penal Code, s.27–1, *viz.* that jurisdiction existed over all persons who committed in whole *or in part* any crimes within the state.

[92] *cf.* the complex facts in *Laird v. H.M. Advocate*, 1985 J.C. 37 (see para. 3.47, *infra*).

[93] Article 3. See Supplement to the Am.J. of Int. Law (1935) Vol. 29, "Codification of International Law", at 439. *Cf.* Model Penal Code (Proposed Official Draft, 1962), s.1.03(1)(a).

[94] At 495.

territory of that state.[95] That will then be enough to furnish a 'territorial nexus'[96] between the crime and the state claiming jurisdiction over the perpetrator. Modern Scots law appears to have moved a long way towards such a general account of territoriality — without the aid of any general legislative intervention.

3.43 *Territorial Jurisdiction in Scots law.* Where conduct, which would be criminal under statute or at common law if committed within Scottish territory, is in fact wholly committed outwith that territory, the Scottish courts will have no jurisdiction over it, unless exceptionally there is legislation to the contrary.[97] This follows from the principle of international comity under which a state (or country with an independent criminal law system) should not interfere in the internal affairs of other states.[98] Thus, that which would amount to the *actus reus* of a crime if committed in Scotland under Scots law is not necessarily criminal at all if committed in France or Germany under the law which pertains there. For this reason, a criminal charge brought in Scotland will generally be incompetent if it fails to state any *locus* at all; to take any other view would be to sanction Scottish criminal proceedings for conduct which would have been criminal if committed in Scotland but which *ex facie* may have been committed anywhere in the world.[99] There is, of course, a recognised principle in international law which permits a state (or country) to take jurisdiction over criminal acts (as defined by that state)

---

[95] *cf.* the 1980 Criminal Code of the People's Republic of China, art. 3: "A crime of which one element or its consequence occurs within the territory of the People's Republic of China shall be considered committed within the territory of the People's Republic of China." (American Series of Foreign Penal Codes, No. 25, transl. Chin Kim, 1982, Sweet & Maxwell, London).

[96] This term is used in the amended South Australia and New South Wales Criminal Codes — see Criminal Law Consolidation Act 1935, s.5c (South Australia) and Crimes Act 1900, s.3A (New South Wales). These codes go further than the 1935 Draft referred to in the text, in that jurisdiction is established if any event (*i.e.* an act, omission, occurrence, circumstance or state of affairs) forming at least part of one element of the offence occurs within the state. *Cf.* the New Zealand Crimes Act 1961, s.7: "For the purpose of jurisdiction, where any act or omission forming part of any offence, or any event necessary to the completion of any offence, occurs in New Zealand, the offence shall be deemed to be completed in New Zealand, whether the person charged with the offence was in New Zealand or not at the time of the act, omission or event." This New Zealand solution has commended itself to Gl. Williams (81 L.Q.R. 518, at 527) and the English Law Commission (L.C. No. 180, H. of C. No. 318, 1988/89, para. 2.26; *cf.* M. Hirst, "Jurisdiction over Cross-Frontier Offences", (1981) 97 L.Q.R. 80, at 101. See also the French Nouveau Code Pénal (1994), Bk. 1, Tit. 1, ch. III, § 2, Art. 113–2.

[97] See, *e.g.*, the Criminal Procedure (Scotland) Act 1995, s.11(1), quoted at n.80 *supra*. Similarly, s.11(2) provides that any British citizen or British subject who, while acting or purporting to act in the course of employment as a Crown servant abroad "does any act or makes any omission which if done or made in Scotland would constitute an offence punishable on indictment shall be guilty of the same offence and subject to the same punishment, as if the act or omission had been done or made in Scotland." See also the Criminal Law (Consolidation) (Scotland) Act 1995, s.16B (inserted by the Sex Offenders Act 1997, s.8). It seems to be accepted in England that statutory crimes in general should have no extra-territorial effect — see *Somchai Liangsiriprasert v. The Government of the U.S.A.* [1991] 1 A.C. 225, Lord Griffiths at 252E (Privy Council) — and some Scottish support for the same general rule has been shown in *Clements v. H.M. Advocate*, 1991 J.C. 62, by L.J.-G. Hope at 71, and Lord Coulsfield at 73.

[98] See I. Brownlie, *op.cit.*, at p.310.

[99] See, *e.g.*, *Thomson, Petitioner* 1997 S.L.T. 322. *Cf. H.M. Advocate v. Semple*, 1937 J.C. 4, which appeared to sanction jurisdiction over an attempt to procure abortion although no *locus* for the actual attempt had been stated in the indictment. For the approach taken to inchoate crimes, see para. 3.48, *infra*.

performed by foreigners abroad if these threaten the internal government or security of that state[1]: but the principle is very vague in its operation, and it may be difficult to see how it could be applied specifically in Scotland which is but one part of a larger state. There is no reason in principle to suppose that a foreigner, for what he does abroad in relation to a completed crime committed by another in Scotland, could not be prosecuted in this country on an 'art and part' liability basis[2]: there would clearly be a territorial connection between his acts and a Scottish *actus reus*.[3] But inchoate offences (attempts, conspiracies and incitements — where the object of conduct wholly performed abroad is ultimately the commission of a crime in Scotland) *may* be subject to different considerations, depending upon whether or not the Scottish courts choose to follow modern English authority.[4] For this reason, inchoate crimes will be dealt with separately.[5]

When a territorial connection exists. For a crime under Scots law to be 'committed in Scotland',[6] some part of the *actus reus* must occur in Scotland so that a suitable territorial connection can be established. If the whole of the conduct or, where appropriate, the result of it occurs in this country, no difficulties will be encountered. As Lord Coulsfield stated in *Clements v. H.M. Advocate*: **3.44**

> "In the ordinary case, a crime may be held to have been committed in Scotland either if there has been conduct in Scotland which amounts to a crime there, or there has been conduct abroad which has had as its result an *actus reus* in Scotland. In considering questions of jurisdiction, therefore, crimes may be classified as 'conduct crimes' and 'result crimes' although, as has been pointed out, it must not be forgotten that conduct on the part of the accused is an essential element in both types of crime (see Gordon, p. 93 [2nd edn., para 3-39], *R. v. Treacy* [1971] A.C. 537, *per* Lord Diplock at p. 560)."[7]

Whilst from the point of view of jurisdiction it is undoubtedly sufficient to establish that the whole conduct in a 'conduct crime' or the entire result in a 'result crime' occurred in Scotland, it is not necessary to show such an extensive territorial connection.[8] And since it is not so necessary, it must be accepted that the modern rule does not create exclusive jurisdiction in the Scottish courts: where the *actus reus* of a crime under Scots law is partly committed outside Scotland, there may also be jurisdiction in a foreign country, depending on the precise state of the criminal law in that country. Such a view has appeared in early text

---

[1] This is known as the protective or security principle. See I. Brownlie, *op.cit.*, at p.304. *Cf.* the Criminal Code Act 1983 of the Northern Territory of Australia, s.15: "If a person is guilty of the conduct proscribed by any offence it is immaterial that that conduct or some part of it did not occur in the Territory if that conduct affected or was intended to affect the peace, order or good government of the Territory."

[2] See Chap. 5, *infra*.

[3] The matter was raised, but not decided, in *Clements v. H.M. Advocate*, 1991 J.C. 62.

[4] See *Somchai Liangsiriprasert v. The Government of the U.S.A.* [1991] 1 A.C. 225, PC; *R. v. Sansom* [1991] 2 Q.B. 130, CA.

[5] See para. 3.48, *infra*.

[6] See para. 3.41, *supra*.

[7] 1991 J.C. 62, at 73.

[8] See *Laird v. H.M. Advocate*, 1985 J.C. 37, dealt with in para. 3.47, *infra*.

writings[9] and in judicial *obiter dicta*,[10] but has also been more recently endorsed by the High Court.[11] Where jurisdiction also exists in such a foreign country and has been exercised there, the principle against double jeopardy should, however, prevent the culprit from being prosecuted again in this country.[12]

3.45 *Objective territoriality in Scotland.* The Scottish cases dealing with jurisdiction relative to 'result crimes'[13] have mainly been concerned with fraud at common law. It has been clear since at least 1925 that the essence of the crime of fraud is inducing B to do something which he would not have done but for a false pretence,[14] so that the crime is completed where B dispatches goods to A on the strength of (*e.g.*) a fraudulent letter, irrespective of whether the Post Office or the carriers of the goods are regarded as agents of the rogue or of the dupe. But in the nineteenth century, the typical fraud involved obtaining something by false pretences (although the law did recognise other forms of fraud),[15] and where goods were obtained by fraud the crime was thought of as being a form of dishonest appropriation, a sort of non-capital theft or "theft by fraud".[16] The *actus reus* of fraud was therefore naturally thought of as being the obtaining of goods, and not the inducing of their dispatch.[17] In the older cases, therefore, the crime was completed where the goods were obtained; but where public carriers were used to convey the goods, the rule of Scots law was (and is) that "where something is going on by the medium of the post, the offence is really committed, if I may use the expression, at both ends of transmission by the Post Office",[18] and the same applied to other common carriers such as the railways.[19] This explains and reconciles the earlier fraud cases when jurisdiction was taken in Scotland both where the goods were sent by the dupe from England to the rogue in Scotland (and received there by him)[20] and where the goods were sent by the Scottish dupe to the rogue across the border.[21] All such cases, therefore, are consistent with the objective application of the territorial principle of jurisdiction,[22] although

---

[9] See Mackenzie, Pt. II, tit. ii, § 1, 356–357 (1678 ed.).

[10] See, *e.g.*, *Wm Bradbury* (1872) 2 Coup. 311, *per* Lord Neaves at 318; *Wm Allan* (1873) 2 Coup. 402, *per* Lord Ardmillan at 407 and L.J.-C. Moncreiff at 408.

[11] *Laird v. H.M. Advocate*, 1985 J.C. 37, *per* L.J.-C. Wheatley at 40; *Clements v. H.M. Advocate*, 1991 J.C. 62, *per* L.J.-G. Hope at 71, Lord Coulsfield at 73.

[12] See, *e.g.*, *Thos. MacGregor & Geo. Inglis* (1846) Ark. 49, L.J.-C. Inglis at 60; *Clements v. H.M. Advocate*, 1991 J.C. 62, L.J.-G. Hope at 71, Lord Coulsfield at 73.

[13] See para. 3.05, *supra*.

[14] See *Adcock v. Archibald*, 1925 J.C. 58.

[15] See Vol. II, Chap. 18.

[16] See, *e.g.*, *Samuel Michael* (1842) 1 Broun 472.

[17] In this respect, there are similarities with the English offence of "obtaining property by deception" under section 15 of the Theft Act 1968.

[18] *Lipsey v. Mackintosh* (1913) 7 Adam 182, L.J.-G. Dunedin at 187. The charge was of sending invitations to bet, the invitations being sent from Glasgow to Dundee, and it was held that the sheriff court at Dundee had jurisdiction to try the case.

[19] The effect is to give jurisdiction "at both ends" — as if the rogue and the dupe stood face to face at either end of the communicating agency. It is probable that this rule will now apply to electronic means of transfer, such as where money is transferred from one bank account to another: see *R. v. Smith (Wallace Duncan)* [1996] Crim.L.R. 329, CA.

[20] See *Thos. MacGregor & Geo. Inglis* (1846) Ark. 49.

[21] See *Wm Bradbury* (1872) 2 Coup. 311; *Wm Allan* (1873) 2 Coup. 402; *John Thos. Witherington* (1881) 5 Coup. 475.

[22] See para. 3.42, *supra*. See also the opinion of Lord Keith in *D.P.P. v. Stonehouse* [1978] A.C. 55, HL, at 93, although his *dictum* was not followed in the later case of *Somchai Liangsiriprasert v. the Government of the U.S.A.* [1991] 1 A.C. 225, PC — a conspiracy case.

the opinions in them also refer more obliquely to the importance of the place where the person injured suffers,[23] the place where success is realised,[24] or to the offence being a "continuous" one[25] — all issues which have figured again in the more modern decisions.[26] There is ample authority, therefore, to support the conclusion that if the result, as required by the definition of a crime under Scots law, occurs in Scotland, the Scottish courts have jurisdiction. Where the conduct leading to that result took place is not material for this purpose.[27]

With respect to a 'conduct crime'[28] under Scots law, if all conduct specified by the definition of that crime occurs in Scotland, then the Scottish courts will have jurisdiction in Scotland without doubt. The paradigm referred to in most cases is "uttering as genuine"[29] (or "forgery" in older terminology) since all that is required is for the accused to present a false document (which he knows to be false) to another with the intention of deceiving him.[30] It is not necessary for that other person to be deceived at all. Thus, if A in Scotland presents such a false document to B, the crime is complete — and this will be so even if B is not in Scotland at the material time, provided that A used the Post Office or other public carrier to convey that document to him.[31] The argument would be the same in this instance as in result crimes, namely that the uttering is achieved at both ends of the line of transmission. This again is essentially an exercise of the objective application of territoriality, since the conduct, by hypothesis occurring wholly in Scotland, completes the crime there. Where only part of the required conduct or result occurs in Scotland, however, the position is more difficult.

Possible jurisdictional solutions where part of the actus reus occurs in Scotland. Where part of the *actus reus* of a crime under Scots law occurs in Scotland, the Scottish courts *may* have jurisdiction. According to Mackenzie: "Not only where the crime itself was fully committed, may it be tryed, but where *any part* of it was committed."[32] It is clear, however, that this goes further than the modern common law.[33] It may be that Mackenzie was addressing himself to a particular type of crime, since he immediately follows with an illustration involving theft. In his view, a thief may be judged not only where he committed a housebreaking but also where he is arrested with the spoils. Alison regards **3.46**

---

[23] See *Wm Bradbury* (1872) 2 Coup. 311, *per* Lord Neaves at 319. His Lordship also refers to the crime having been directed to or against Scotland.

[24] See *John Thos. Witherington* (1881) 5 Coup. 475, L.J.-C. Inglis at 489.

[25] *Wm Allan* (1873) 2 Coup. 402, L.J.-C. Moncreiff at 408.

[26] *Laird v. H.M. Advocate* 1985 J.C. 37; *Clements v. H.M. Advocate* 1991 J.C. 62: see para. 3.47, *infra*.

[27] The same has been said to be true at common law in England — *D.P.P. v. Stonehouse* [1978] A.C. 55, HL, Lord Diplock at 65C. The English Law Commission, however, has stated that no universal rule of jurisdiction is possible, and that it is necessary to consider particular rules in the context of individual offences: see L.C. No. 180: "Jurisdiction over Offences of Fraud and Dishonesty with a Foreign Element" (H. of C. No. 318, Session 1988/89), at para. 1.2. In accordance with such thinking, the Criminal Justice Act 1993, Part I, establishes particular rules for certain English offences of dishonesty and related inchoate offences.

[28] See para. 3.05, *supra*.

[29] See *Wm Bradbury* (1872) 2 Coup. 311, *per* Lord Neaves at 319; *John Thos. Witherington* (1881) 5 Coup. 475, *per* L.J.-C. Inglis at 489.

[30] See Vol. II, Chap. 18. See in particular *Michael Hinchy* (1864) 4 Irv. 561, Lord Neaves at 565–566; *John Smith* (1871) 2 Coup. 1, L.J.-G. Inglis at 8–10.

[31] See *William Jeffrey* (1842) 1 Broun 337.

[32] Mackenzie, Pt. II, tit. ii, § 1, at 356 (emphasis added), 1678 ed.

[33] See para. 3.47, *infra*.

Mackenzie as having confined himself here to the *exceptional* case of theft rather than having expressed any general rule,[34] and indeed there is some authority to suggest that theft may be exceptional in that it constitutes a continuing offence for jurisdictional purposes.[35]

Hume, on the other hand, refers to jurisdiction lying where the "main act" takes place, but tempers this by adding that such an act is the one "which completes the crime".[36] His illustrations relate to forgeries (*i.e.* utterings as genuine) where the utterings take place in Scotland, an incendiary letter received in Scotland from England, and the forcible abduction and marriage of a woman. With the exception of the last (which is clearly a continuing crime, at least *quoad* the woman's confinement by the accused), these illustrations are explicable in terms of the objective application of territoriality.[37]

Macdonald, however, espouses the "main act" test as if it were a separate principle of its own justified by reference to the authorities which he cites[38]: his authorities concern utterings as genuine (where the uttering occurred in Scotland),[39] and the fraudulent obtaining of goods (where the obtaining occurred or was deemed to occur, by virtue of the agency employed, in Scotland).[40] The one unusual case to which he refers is that of *John McKay or McKey*,[41] where a bankrupt was charged with the fraudulent concealment of his property and fraudulent putting away of assets. It appears that the accused, knowing that sequestration was inevitable, had deposited two sums of money with a bank in Liverpool. He then, after sequestration, uplifted the balances from that bank — all without disclosing that such assets existed at all. If the "main act" test was to be applied, as Macdonald suggests, then it would seem to follow that the main act took place in England rather than Scotland; but in truth, of course, the decision is predicated on the accused's failure to obtemper his legal duty of full disclosure of his assets — a duty which fell to be discharged in Scotland where sequestration had been awarded. This, therefore, accords with the general rule relating to the place of an omission — namely, the place where the obligation is due to be carried out.[42] It follows then that a "main act" test, distinct from the objective territoriality test, receives little support from these Scottish authorities.[43]

---

[34] Alison, ii, 78.

[35] See *Jas. Taylor* (1767) Maclaurin's Cases, No. 76, where a person, who had stolen horses near Carlisle and taken them to Scotland, unsuccessfully objected to his being prosecuted for that theft before the High Court. The reasoning of the Court is not recorded by Maclaurin, but Hume (at ii, 54–55) considers that the decision may be based upon the continuing nature of theft or on grounds of pure expediency. See para. 3.50, *infra*.

[36] Hume, ii, 54.

[37] See para. 3.42, *supra*.

[38] Macdonald (5th ed., 1948) at p.191.

[39] *Alexander Humphreys* (1839) Bell's Notes 148; *William Jeffrey* (1842) 1 Broun 337.

[40] *Samuel Michael* (1842) 1 Broun 472; *Thos. MacGregor & Geo. Inglis* (1846) Ark. 49; *John Thos. Witherington* (1881) 4 Coup. 475; *Wm Bradbury* (1872) 2 Coup. 311; *Wm Allan* (1873) 2 Coup. 402.

[41] (1866) 5 Irv. 329.

[42] See *Smith v. Inglis*, 1982 S.C.C.R. 403, and the decision in *John McKay or McKey* itself.

[43] In the leading case of *Laird v. H.M. Advocate* 1985 J.C. 37, the trial judge (Lord Kincraig) did dispose of the objections to jurisdiction on the ground that the "main actings" occurred in Scotland; but "main actings" are not quite the same thing as the "main act", and, in any event, this formula was not endorsed by the Appeal Court. (Lord Kincraig's decision can be seen at 1984 S.C.C.R. 469, at 470.).

Indeed it would be a difficult rule to follow in many cases, since it might either require detailed case-by-case consideration of what constituted the principal act in relation to any particular offence or be subject to arbitrary application.

Macdonald also, however, suggests that there "may even be jurisdiction if an act done out of Scotland take practical effect in Scotland"[44]; but he appears to mean by this that there will be jurisdiction where the intended victim suffers[45] — which suggests straightforward involvement of the objective application of the territorial principle.[46] Finally he mentions two decisions on jurisdiction which seem unrelated to any particular test or principle — namely *H.M. Advocate v. Hetherington and Wilson*[47] and *H.M. Advocate v. Semple*.[48] In the former, the accused was charged with supplying goods to the enemy in contravention of the Trading with the Enemy Act 1914. The goods in question (a quantity of iron ore) were already on the quayside at Rotterdam, and it was alleged that a contract for the supply of them had been made abroad with an enemy during the First World War. It was held that as long as the accused were resident in Scotland it did not matter where the goods happened to be or where the supply had occurred — there would still be jurisdiction in the Scottish courts. This goes further than any principle suggested by Macdonald, since the decision did not require any criminal conduct to occur in Scotland at all. It breaches any view of the territorial principle. But the case dealt with wartime legislation, and the ground of jurisdiction asserted was similar to that which exists relative to the statutory crime of treason, and it is submitted that the case has no application to ordinary common law crimes. *Semple*, on the other hand, deals with an attempted crime — an attempt to procure an abortion following upon the supply of abortifacients in Glasgow. Although the *locus* of the supply was thus stated, there was no indication of where the abortifacients were to be used. The indictment did aver supplying drugs with intent to cause abortion and instigating and causing a woman to take them. But the crime charged was not supplying drugs with intent to cause abortion nor incitement to abortion, but simply attempted abortion. That being so, it would appear that if any place was relevant it was the place of the proposed abortion — which might be anywhere in the world — including a country where abortion might not be criminal. The High Court dismissed the objection to jurisdiction on the ground that "the attempt to procure abortion began with the supply of the drug with the intention that it should be used [and that was] in Glasgow." The contemporary correctness of this decision would, however, have been open to doubt. There was no evidence at the time that the subjective application of the territorial principle[49] (or any version of it) was accepted in Scotland; and even if it had been, the question would have arisen as to whether the mere supplying of abortifacients was sufficient conduct on the part of the accused in relation to what was in fact charged. In any event, whatever the principles pertaining to completed

---

[44] At 191.

[45] His example of a person in England sending explosives to a person in Scotland, so that that latter person will be injured by them in this country, is reminiscent of Lord Neave's account of the "*locus delicti*" in *Wm Bradbury* (1872) 2 Coup. 311 at 319.

[46] See para. 3.42, *supra*.

[47] (1915) 6 Adam 663.

[48] 1937 J.C. 41.

[49] See para. 3.42, *supra*.

crimes, inchoate offences may be subject to separate rules of jurisdiction.[50]

3.47 *The modern Scots approach.* It is now clear that it is not necessary (though sufficient) for the result (in a result crime) or all of the conduct (in a conduct crime) to occur in Scotland for the Scottish courts legitimately to take jurisdiction in relation to an offence under Scots law. What is important relative to completed crimes (as these are defined by Scots law) is that the events or conduct occurring in Scotland should play a material part in the fulfilment of a criminal scheme. It would seem to go too far to assert that the 'main act' must take place in Scotland[51] for that was not held to be so in the leading case of *Laird v. H.M. Advocate*.[52] There the accused directors of a Glasgow-based company formed a plan to obtain money by fraud from a company registered in London. The plan was hatched in Glasgow, and various letters and phone calls emanated from Glasgow and were received in England as part of the fraudulent scheme. In brief, the accused directors fraudulently convinced the English company of their ability to supply steel of high quality in return for an agreed price. The contract for supply of the steel was arguably concluded in England. Further, the directors forged certificates as to the quality of the steel in Glasgow, but personally took these to an English steel yard where they were adhibited to a quantity of low-grade steel. In this way, the English company were deceived in England into believing that the goods were of the quality they required. They then handed over the purchase price to the accused — again in England. Whilst it is true that the accused thereafter proceeded to have the inferior steel delivered to a fabrication yard near Inverness,[53] such delivery could not count as part of the *actus reus* of the crime charged.[54] Had the 'main act' test been applied, the Scottish courts would probably not have had jurisdiction since the principal parts of the crime of fraud (the deception and the handing over of the money) took place in England. But that did not necessarily make the Scottish actings merely ancilliary to the crime; the formation of the fraudulent scheme itself, the initial overtures and communications, and the forging of the certificates were all soundly based in Scotland. As Lord Justice-Clerk Wheatley put it:

> "[W]here a crime is of such a nature that it has to originate with the forming of a fraudulent plan, and that thereafter various steps have to be taken to bring that fraudulent plan to fruition, if some of these subsequent steps take place in one jurisdiction and some in another, then if the totality of the events[55] in one country plays a material

---

[50] See para. 3.48, *infra*.

[51] *cf.* Renton & Brown, 6th ed., at para. 1.20.

[52] 1985 J.C. 37.

[53] In *Laird* at 41, L.J.-C. Wheatley thought this important since it concluded the fraudulent scheme — and was in any event necessary to prevent the deception being found out sooner rather than later. Lord Robertson agreed *de plano* with what the Lord Justice-Clerk said, but Lord Dunpark, correctly it is submitted, did not include the delivery of the steel as one of his Scottish connecting-links *quoad* the crime of fraud actually charged.

[54] The crime was one of obtaining money by fraud — and that object had been achieved before the delivery of the goods to Scotland took place.

[55] *cf.* the definition of 'event' in the Criminal Law Consolidation Act 1935 (South Australia) s.5(c)(10), *viz.* "any act, omission, occurrence, circumstance or state of affairs (not including intention, knowledge or any other state of mind)." The Crimes Act 1900 (New South Wales) s.3A(10) is in identical terms.

part in the operation and fulfilment of the fraudulent scheme as a whole there should be jurisdiction in that country."[56]

It was accepted that jurisdiction might also exist in England,[57] in relation to what had been done there — provided, of course, that English law would have recognised as criminal what had been done.[58] Of course, the rule in *Laird* is *ex facie* tied to a fraudulent scheme, where both a plan and its execution are involved. It would seem, however, that that rule must be applicable to any crime where the "totality of the events" in Scotland "plays a material part" in the bringing of a criminal plan to fruition.[59] As this requires a definite connection between at least part of the *actus reus* of the crime and Scotland, but without requiring all of the criminal conduct to be located there, a situation close to the combined applications of the territorial principle has been attained.[60]

But the Scottish courts have also recognised that conduct by persons in another part of the United Kingdom which is materially linked to a "practical effect"[61] in Scotland may be sufficient to found criminal jurisdiction in this country — although again not necessarily on any exclusive basis. This was decided in *Clements v. H.M. Advocate*.[62] There, the statutory crime in question was that of being concerned in the supplying of controlled drugs to another (in contravention of the declaration that it is unlawful to supply such a drug to another).[63] What happened was that Dunn travelled by train from Edinburgh, and met Clements in London. Clements received a bag from Dunn and, in Dunn's absence and with Gouner's assistance, obtained some seven kilogrammes of cannabis resin.[64] This was placed in the bag which was then returned to Dunn. Dunn proceeded to take the train from London to Scotland, and was arrested in Edinburgh with the drugs still in his possession some hours later. The case was concerned with the prosecution of Clements and Gouner in Scotland for having committed that statutory crime. Both of them argued that the High Court in Scotland had no jurisdiction over them, since what they were alleged to have done had been performed entirely in England and although it might he said, following Macdonald, that their conduct had had a practical effect in Scotland, that such a jurisdictional "rule" did not apply to statutory offences. The arguments for Gouner were said to be all the more cogent

---

[56] *Laird v. H.M. Advocate*, 1985 J.C. 37, at 40.

[57] *ibid., per* L.J.-C. Wheatley at 40, where the judgments of the majority in *John Thos. Witherington* (1881) 5 Coup. 475 were taken to include the recognition of multi-country jurisdiction in the two earlier cases of *Wm Bradbury* ((1872) 2 Coup. 311, see Lord Neaves at 318) and *Wm Allan* ((1873) 2 Coup. 402, see Lord Ardmillan at 407 and L.J.-C. Moncreiff at 408). Neither Lord Robertson, who concurred, nor Lord Dunpark disputed that assumption.

[58] It could probably have been charged as an offence contrary to s.15 of the Theft Act 1968, *i.e.* obtaining property by deception. There would certainly have been jurisdiction in England, either at common law (see *D.P.P. v. Stonehouse* [1978] A.C. 55, Lord Diplock at 65C; Law Commission No. 180, "Jurisdiction over Offences of Fraud and Dishonesty with a Foreign Element", H. of C. No. 318, 1988/89, paras 2.1 and 2.2) or now under the Criminal Justice Act 1993, ss.1, 2 and 4.

[59] *cf.* Alastair N. Brown, *Criminal Evidence and Procedure* (T.&T. Clark, 1996) at p.11.

[60] See para. 3.42, *supra*.

[61] To quote Macdonald at p.191.

[62] 1991 J.C. 62.

[63] Misuse of Drugs Act 1971, ss.4(1)(b) and 4(3)(b).

[64] This was clearly far more than could plausibly be required for personal use.

since, as the Crown conceded, he had not known the ultimate destination of the drugs.[65] The court's attention was thus focused on the stronger case: if jurisdiction could be taken in relation to one who did not know where the supplying was to take place, then it could be taken *a fortiori* in respect of Clements. The offence under section 4(3)(b) of the Misuse of Drugs Act 1971 is, of course, a rather peculiar one in that it has the shape of a conspiracy charge, and would appear to lend itself to the notion of art and part guilt: but the offence is nevertheless an independent, substantive one. If Clements and Gouner were to be convicted, they would be so not as participants in a crime in fact committed by Dunn but as principal offenders themselves.[66] Lord Coulsfield also noted that depending on the circumstances, the offence was of such width as to be capable of involving conduct in Scotland which was criminal there, or conduct outwith Scotland having a criminal result there, or a mixture of the two. In this case, he decided that there was such a mixture, since the total enterprise involved the supplying of drugs in Scotland, as also conduct in England designed to have that sort of criminal result in Scotland.[67] His conclusion, therefore, was that Gouner:

> "freely participated in a plan which, as he must have known,[68] would *inter alia* have a criminal result somewhere. That place was, in the event Scotland, and . . . that is sufficient to give rise to jurisdiction to try him in Scotland. This is a result which . . . follows from the application of the accepted rules governing questions of jurisdiction".[69]

But what were the "accepted rules" which had been applied here? It is submitted that Lord Coulsfield was in fact applying and thus approving Macdonald's "practical effect" test.[70] What Clements, and indeed Gouner, did in and around London was part of a chain of events which had an effect in Scotland and which was criminal there: their conduct was inextricably linked with what transpired in this country — and that provided the necessary territorial connection. Whether they knew precisely the destination of the drugs was not a material factor from the point of view of jurisdiction, bearing in mind that the English courts would also have been able to try them. On Lord Coulsfield's view, the same conclusion might[71] have been arrived at had the accused in the case obtained the drugs, for example, in France and handed them to Dunn in Paris — provided, perhaps, that their individual conduct would also have been criminal under French law.[72] Whether that view is correct or not, it

---

[65] There was evidence from which it could be inferred that Clements had been well aware that the drugs were to be taken to Edinburgh and supplied to persons there, so that he was, in Lord Coulsfield's words (at 72), "concerned in the supply of drugs to persons in Scotland in a quite direct and straightforward sense. He took an active part in a plan for supplying drugs there and that plan was put into effect. He was a party to the carrying out of the plan in Scotland as well as in England."

[66] See L.J.-G. Hope at 68 on this matter.

[67] Lord Coulsfield at 73.

[68] From, *e.g.*, the "elaborate and clandestine arrangements for obtaining the drugs and handing them over to Dunn" (Lord Coulsfield at 73–74).

[69] Lord Coulsfield, at 74. See also *H.M. Advocate v. Al Megrahi*, 2000 S.C.C.R. 177.

[70] See para. 3.46, *supra*. See also Lord Coulsfield's remarks relative to Macdonald's test at 73.

[71] Since he in fact reserved his opinion on this point.

[72] L.J.-G. Hope (at 69) and Lord Wylie (at 76) on the other hand stressed that the legislation under which the charges had been brought applied to the whole of the United Kingdom, and that everything that had been done had been so within the United Kingdom.

seems reasonably clear that all members of the court in *Clements* in effect subscribed to the same general rule,[73] which follows Macdonald and which is somewhat wider than the objective application of the territorial principle[74] in that the 'practical effect' in Scotland need not be one which is necessary to complete the *actus reus* of the offence.

The crime under section 4(3)(b), for example, does not require any actual supplying to occur for conviction to follow.[75]

It is submitted, therefore, that the present position in relation to completed crimes is as follows: where there has been conduct amounting to the *actus reus* of a crime under Scots law on the part of an accused person, the Scottish courts may try the case (but not necessarily on an exclusive basis) if the totality of that conduct occurring in Scotland plays a material part in the fulfilment of that accused's criminal plan, or, in relation to such conduct occurring outside Scotland, if that conduct is designed to have a practical effect somewhere and does have a practical effect in Scotland, provided perhaps that such foreign conduct is also criminal according to the law of the place where it was actually performed. These are admittedly fairly flexible rules; but they continue to stress the importance of a definite territorial link between Scotland and the conduct in question, respect the principle of international comity[76] and accord well with the modern sentiment that "crime has ceased to be largely local in origin and effect [but] is now established on an international scale and the common law must face this new reality."[77] These rules may not be adequate, however, to solve jurisdictional problems relative to inchoate offences.

Inchoate offences. The range of inchoate offences extends to attempts, **3.48**
conspiracies and incitements.[78] It is customary to regard such offences as substantive crimes in their own right.[79] They must have an *actus reus* element as also an appropriate mental element. When those elements are satisfied, they can to that extent be described as 'completed crimes', and it might then be argued that the modern jurisdictional rules which apply, for example, to a completed fraud should also apply to an attempt to commit fraud. But inchoate offences are peculiar substantive crimes. Williams, for example, has aptly described them as "auxiliary crimes".[80] There is no self-sustaining offence of 'attempt' or 'conspiracy' or 'incitement' in the way that there are independently definable offences such as murder or theft. As Fletcher remarks: "The punishability of specific behavior as an attempt is inferred from a defined offense-in-

---

[73] See, *e.g.*, L.J.-G. Hope at 71: "the underlying mischief at which these provisions [ss. 4(3)(b) and 4(1)(b)] are directed is the supply or offer to supply of a controlled drug to another, and to look to the place of the mischief as the place where jurisdiction can be established against all those involved would be consistent with the idea that the courts of the place where the harmful acts occur may exercise jurisdiction over those whose acts elsewhere have these consequences: see Lord Diplock's discussion of this point in *R. v. Treacy* [1971] A.C. 537 at p.562."

[74] See para. 3.42, *supra*.

[75] See, *e.g.*, *Kyle v. H.M. Advocate*, 1988 S.L.T. 601, L.J.-C. Ross at 603; *Kerr v. H.M. Advocate*, 1986 S.C.C.R. 81, L.J.-C. Ross at 89.

[76] See para 3.43, *supra*.

[77] *Somchai Liangsiriprasert v. the Government of the U.S.A.* [1991] 1 A.C. 225, PC, *per* Lord Griffiths at 251C. This sentence (*inter alia*) was quoted by L.J.-G. Hope in *Clements v. H.M. Advocate*, 1991 J.C. 62 at 70.

[78] See Chap 6, *infra*.

[79] See, *e.g.*, the 1995 Act, s.294, which deals with attempt.

[80] Gl. Williams, p.609.

chief, such as murder, robbery or rape."[81] Criminal liability in relation to inchoate offences is a "derivative" one[82]; liability depends on there being a specific crime which the accused was attempting, or conspiring with another, or inciting another to commit. If the object of the attempt, conspiracy or incitement was not the commission of a crime, then the basis of inchoate criminal liability simply disappears.[83]

In addition, inchoate offences obviously do not involve the completion of the harm which the crime aimed at would have entailed: thus, in attempted theft nothing is in fact stolen, and if there is but a mere agreement to commit murder no life is lost. But the imposition of criminal liability where the harm aimed at has not materialised can at least in part be justified by considering that the attempt or conspiracy or incitement has generated a harm of its own — a "second order harm", as Gross refers to it.[84] This entails a threat of harm from which the law of a particular state may legitimately wish to protect persons within that state. "The interest [of the law] is one in *security* from harm, and merely presenting a threat of harm violates that security interest. Still, it is only a second order harm. If what it now threatens were no harm it would itself be no harm, for then it would no longer pose a threat of harm and so no longer be a violation of an interest in security from harm."[85]

The above considerations suggest that inchoate offences are sufficiently different from other substantive crimes as to justify distinct treatment relative to jurisdictional problems: and in so far as *H.M. Advocate v. Semple*[86] implies that distinct treatment is not justified, it is submitted that it is wrongly decided.

3.49 *H.M. Advocate v. Semple.* In *Semple*[86a] one of the charges alleged that the accused supplied a pregnant woman with abortifacient drugs in Glasgow with intent to cause her to abort, instigated her to use them and "did attempt to cause her to abort". The judges agreed that the supply of the drugs coupled to instigation (and, it seems, actual use by another) was sufficient for the *actus reus* of an attempt to procure an abortion,[87] and that as the supply had taken place in Scotland, it did not matter that the indictment did not specify where the use of the drugs was to take place or had taken place. Lord Justice-Clerk Aitchison rejected the argument that attempted abortion began only when the drugs were used.[88] No jurisdictional problem was thus identified. It was also specifically held by Lords Fleming[89] and Moncreiff[90] that the accused could alternatively be art and part guilty of attempted abortion, the actor being the pregnant woman herself.

It is submitted, however, that the place where the drugs were to be used (or actually were used) was crucial in this case. What the accused

---

[81] G. Fletcher, *Rethinking Criminal Law* (Boston, 1978), p.132.

[82] *ibid*.

[83] This is at least the rule in Scots law; *cf.* conspiracies at common law in England — see J.C. Smith and B. Hogan, *Criminal Law* (9th ed., 1999, Sir J. Smith (ed.)), at p.272.

[84] H. Gross, *A Theory of Criminal Justice* (Oxford, 1979), at p.125.

[85] *ibid*.

[86] 1937 J.C. 41. See also para. 3.46, *supra*.

[86a] *ibid.*

[87] It may be doubted, however, if this is a correct view of the stage at which attempted abortion begins: see *H.M. Advocate v. Baxter* (1908) 5 Adam 609, *infra*, para. 6.36.

[88] 1937 J.C. 41, at 44–45.

[89] *ibid*., at 46.

[90] *ibid*., at 48.

did in Glasgow could have been relevant to a criminal attempt to commit an abortion only if abortion was criminal where the drugs were to be used. It is evident from the derivative nature of attempt that what mattered was the place of the intended abortion rather than the place of the supply. It should have followed that the supplying could be criminal only if the proposed abortion was criminal, and if that abortion was to take place in a country in which abortion was legal, the supply would not be criminal, or at least would not amount to attempted abortion.[91] If the drugs were supplied for the purpose of being used to procure a miscarriage in Ruritania, and were used there, the attempted crime would be an attempt to procure a miscarriage in Ruritánia: and if abortion were not a crime in Ruritania it is impossible to see how anyone could be convicted in Scotland of attempting to commit it. Or again, the supplier's guilt was accessory to the guilt of the person who actually tried to procure the miscarriage; now if that person committed no crime because he tried to procure the miscarriage in Ruritania where such actings are not criminal, how could the Scots supplier be guilty of being an accessory to that crime? And even if use of the drugs was made in a foreign state which shared exactly the views of Scots common law on the matter of abortion, it would still be objectionable for the courts of this country to presume to use Scots common law to protect persons in that foreign state from harms threatened there. No threat of harm would have existed in Scotland, and there would have been no violation of any interest in security from harm cognizable by Scottish courts. It is submitted, therefore, not only that *Semple* was wrongly decided but also that the proper approach to such problems relative to inchoate offences, where legislation does not dictate otherwise, is that of the common law in England.

English common law, for example, holds that a conspiracy formed in that country to commit abroad what would be criminal if performed in England is not justiciable before English courts since the offence of conspiracy is designed to prevent actual infraction of the Queen's peace; and the Queen's peace will not be affected by what is planned to take place entirely abroad. The test concerns whether the planned crime, if it were to be completed as planned, would be triable in England.[92] The same test seems to apply at common law to attempt,[93] and possibly also to incitement, although the position of incitement to commit a crime abroad at common law is less certain.[94] Although such an approach has

---

[91] If the mere supply of such substances to another had been itself criminal in Scotland, then that supply might have been prosecuted *per se*, without reference to the accused's ultimate intention.

[92] See *R. v. Cox* [1968] 1 W.L.R. 88 (conspiracy in England to defraud French shopkeepers in France), and J.C.Smith and B. Hogan, *Criminal Law* (9th ed., 1999, Sir J. Smith (ed.)), 286 at i). See also *Board of Trade v. Owen* [1957] A.C. 602, HL (conspiracy in England to defraud Germans in Germany — although it was also material there, no doubt, that the crime proposed was not one which was criminal in Germany in any event); *Attorney-General's Reference (No. 1 of 1982)* [1983] Q.B. 751 (conspiracy to defraud Lebanese purchasers in the Lebanon by affixing false labels to whisky due for export from Frankfurt to the Lebanon); and *R. v. Atakpu* [1994] Q.B. 69 (conspiracy to steal cars not justiciable in England since the cars were to be stolen in Europe — and indeed were stolen there) — but see the criticism of this decision in G.R. Sullivan and Colin Warbrick, "Territoriality, Theft and Atakpu" [1994] Crim.L.R. 650; jurisdiction could be taken, however, if the object of the conspiracy was something which might be done in England or Wales, as well as elsewhere — see, *e.g.*, *R. v. Naini* (1999) 2 Cr.App.R. 398.

[93] See J.C. Smith and B. Hogan, *Criminal Law* (9th ed., 1999, Sir J. Smith (ed.)), 318 at (a).

[94] See Law Commission, "Jurisdiction over Offences of Fraud and Dishonesty with a Foreign Element" (L.C. 180, 1989; H. of C. No. 318, 1988/89), at para. 4.12.

been criticised by the Law Commission[95] and altered to a significant extent by legislation,[96] it is submitted that Scots law, wherever statute does not dictate otherwise, should follow the English common law rules. Conduct in Scotland which is relative to a plan to commit a crime in another country or state should not be justiciable in Scotland as, for example, an attempt to commit that crime: the place of the proposed crime is clearly outwith Scottish territory and a Scottish inchoate crime should not be used to tackle a threat which is beyond the interests of Scots common law and outwith the protective competence of its courts. The same should in principle apply to conspiracies and incitements.[97]

The above submission may be thought to be somewhat undermined, however, by recent legislation which in particular governs Scottish based conspiracies relative to the commission outside the United Kingdom of any sort of crime,[98] as also Scottish based incitements in relation to certain sexual offences designed to be committed outside the United Kingdom.[99] The very application of such statutory provisions suggests, of course, that the United Kingdom Parliament thought the Scottish and English common law positions relative to jurisdictional issues concerning conspiracies and incitements to have been broadly similar, and, therefore, equally ripe for "reform". Nevertheless, the legislation in

---

[95] *ibid.*, Pt. V, paras 5.1 to 5.13.

[96] See, *e.g.*, the Criminal Justice Act 1993, Pt. I; the Sexual Offences (Conspiracy and Incitement) Act 1996, ss.1–5; the Sex Offenders Act 1997, s.7; and the Criminal Justice (Terrorism and Conspiracy) Act 1998, s.5.

[97] If the conduct in Scotland amounts to an offence there — such as obtaining a firearm in contravention of Scots law — that conduct can be prosecuted as such without reference to the ultimate aims of the persons concerned.

[98] See the Criminal Procedure (Scotland) Act 1995, s.11A (added by the Criminal Justice (Terrorism and Conspiracy) Act 1998, s.7), which (*inter alia*) provides:
"(1) This section applies to any act done by a person in Scotland which would amount to conspiracy to commit an offence but for the fact that the criminal purpose is intended to occur in a country or territory outside the United Kingdom.
(2) Where a person does an act to which this section applies, the criminal purpose shall be treated as the offence mentioned in subsection (1) above and he shall, accordingly be guilty of conspiracy to commit the offence.
(3) A person is guilty of an offence by virtue of this section only if the criminal purpose would involve at some stage—
(a) an act by him or another party to the conspiracy; or
(b) the happening of some other event, constituting an offence under the law in force in the country or territory where the act or other event was intended to take place; and conduct punishable under the law in force in the country or territory is an offence under that law for the purposes of this section however it is described in that law."

[99] See the Criminal Law (Consolidation) (Scotland) Act 1995, s.16A (originally added by the Sexual Offences (Conspiracy and Incitement) Act 1996, s.6, but now amended by the Criminal Justice (Terrorism and Conspiracy) Act 1998, Sched. 1, para. 80), which (inter alia) provides:
"(1) This section applies to any act done by a person in Scotland which would amount to the offence of incitement to commit a listed sexual offence [see subs. (9)] but for the fact that what he had in view is intended to occur in a country or territory outside the United Kingdom.
(2) Where a person does an act to which this section applies, what he had in view shall be treated as the listed sexual offence mentioned in subsection (1) above and he shall, accordingly, be guilty of . . . incitement to commit the listed sexual offence.
(3) A person is guilty of an offence by virtue of this section only if what he had in view would involve the commission of an offence under the law in force in the country or territory where the whole or any part of it was intended to take place, and conduct punishable under the law in force in the country or territory is an offence under that law for the purposes of this section however it is described in that law."

question[1] applies to Scotland the reverse of the English common law rule in relation to conspiracies, and harmonises with that the law relating to incitements — at least to the extent of certain sexual offences intended to be committed abroad. These statutory provisions leave untouched, however, the Scots law pertaining to attempts to commit crimes, as also incitements to commit non sexual offences, outwith the United Kingdom; and they also do not cover jurisdictional problems concerning inchoate offences within the United Kingdom itself. Where the relevant legislation does not run, therefore, it is submitted that the modern rules devised for settling jurisdiction in the case of completed crimes[2] should not be applied to inchoate offences.

The position may be different in the case of an attempt, conspiracy or incitement to commit in Scotland a crime as defined by Scots law, where the conduct involved in the inchoate offence all takes place abroad. Clearly there is then sufficient interest in Scotland to argue plausibly that the Scots courts should take jurisdiction over those concerned. This is now the rule at common law in England[3] and replaces the former English law that jurisdiction in such cases depended upon some effect of the planned crime being actually felt in England, or some overt act in furtherance thereof being committed there.[4] On the other hand, there is no territorial nexus other than a prospective one in such cases, and it may be that Scots law in practice would adhere to the older English position.[5]

Clearly, if persons normally resident in Scotland plan crimes abroad where these are to be committed abroad, or enter into conspiracies abroad to commit crimes outwith Scotland, or carry out incitements abroad such that there are no territorial Scottish links whatsoever, either

---

[1] See nn. 98 and 99, *supra*.

[2] See para. 3.47, *supra*.

[3] *Somchai Liangsiriprasert v. the Government of the U.S.A.* [1991] 1 A.C. 225, PC; *R. v. Sansom* [1991] 2 Q.B. 130, CA. Although these are conspiracy cases, there was no suggestion that the rule did not apply to all inchoate offences where the conduct was wholly performed abroad: see in particular Lord Griffiths in *Somchai* at 251C.

[4] See *R. v. Doot* [1973] A.C. 807, HL (conspiracy abroad to evade the prohibition against importing of dangerous drugs into England — overt acts done in England); *R. v. Baxter* [1972] 1 Q.B. 1 (attempt to obtain property by deception, by posting in Northern Ireland false claims to football pool winnings, the letters being addressed to promoters in Liverpool and received there). See also *D.P.P. v. Stonehouse* [1978] A.C. 55, HL where there was an attempt to obtain property by deception by a person in Florida pretending to have died by drowning there, so that his wife in England could — as an innocent party — claim certain insurance monies on policies placed with English companies. The "effect in England" was taken to be satisfied by media reports in England of that person's "death". Lord Diplock in this case (at 67C-F) opined that jurisdiction existed when the actings of the accused abroad amounted to an attempt to commit a crime in England — without the necessity of any effect being felt in England at all. He was also prepared to interpret *Baxter* in that way. Michael Hirst has regarded Lord Diplock's views as "unorthodox" and "frequently out of step" with the views of his fellow judges (*Jurisdiction over Cross-Frontier Offences*, (1981) 97 L.Q.R. 80, at 90), but such views have come to represent the modern law in that country. Similar views to those of Lord Diplock were expressed by Lord Salmon in *R. v. Doot* at 835B-C.

[5] *cf. H.M. Advocate v. Megrahi*, 2000 S.C.C.R. 177, Lord Sutherland at 187E-190A, where his Lordship considers the jurisdictional nicety of a foreign conspiracy to blow up a plane in flight where there was no necessary intention to do so over Scotland: see also *R. v. Naini* (1999) 2 Cr.App.R. 398, at 416G, where Bingham L.J. said: "[I]n our view the authorities establish that the courts of England and Wales do have . . . jurisdiction if the conspiracy wherever made is to do something here or to do something which may be done here, whether wholly or in part, even if no overt act pursuant to the conspiracy is done in England and Wales."

at that time or prospectively, the Scottish courts should have no jurisdiction over such inchoate offences at all. Exceptionally, of course, legislation may confer jurisdiction on a "nationality principle" basis; but unless such legislation specifies that attempts, conspiracies and incitements are covered by it in addition to completed crimes, there may be reasonable doubt as to whether inchoate offences were intended to be included.[6]

Continuing crimes

3.50 Continuing crimes, such as crimes of possession, are committed wherever the criminal goes. Reset, for example, is committed wherever the accused goes with the stolen goods.[7] But the thief himself cannot be guilty of reset,[8] and the question arises whether a person can be tried in Scotland for a theft committed abroad if he is found in Scotland with the stolen property in his possession. It may be true that "Possession in Scotland [is] evidence of stealing in England",[9] but the question is whether it is theft in Scotland. On principle a man's presence in Scotland in possession of the proceeds of an English theft should no more give the Scots courts jurisdiction to try him for theft, than his possession of the proceeds of an English housebreaking gives jurisdiction to try him for the offence, or rather aggravation, of breaking into the house.[10] But there is some common law authority in *Jas. Taylor*[11] that the Scots courts can try a person for an English theft if he is found in possession of the proceeds in Scotland. This decision must depend on the view that theft is a *crimen continuum*, committed wherever the thief goes with the stolen property, and not simply the taking of the property, which would be a once-for-all thing like housebreaking.[12] Whether that view of theft is correct depends on the law relating to the specific crime of theft, and not on any general principles regarding criminal jurisdiction.

Hume held that a kidnapper commits a crime wherever he goes with the abducted person, but this seems to be because the victim has a claim to the protection of the courts wherever he is[13]: which is probably

---

[6] *cf.* the Criminal Law (Consolidation) (Scotland) Act 1995, s.16B (inserted by the Sex Offenders Act 1997, s.8) which makes specific provision for conspiracy and incitement to commit specific sexual offences outwith the United Kingdom, and the Criminal Procedure (Scotland) Act 1995, s.11(1) which allows acts or omissions by British citizens or British subjects outwith the United Kingdom to be treated as if done or made in Scotland where these acts or omissions would amount to murder or culpable homicide if in fact done or made in Scotland — but the legislation is silent, for example, as to acts amounting to attempts to commit murder outwith the United Kingdom.

[7] *Gracie v. Stuart* (1884) 5 Coup. 379. Under the Criminal Procedure (Scotland) Act 1995, s.11(4)(b), a person who in Scotland receives property stolen in any other part of the United Kingdom may be dealt with as if he had stolen it in Scotland. But this cannot be correct, since it would make reset in these circumstances punishable as theft. The draftsman, with commendable but misplaced zeal for economy of words, has applied the provision "as if he had stolen it in Scotland" to both limbs of subs. (4), thus ignoring the clear wording of every prior encapsulation of the rule — see the Criminal Law Act 1772 (13 Geo. III, c.31), s.5; the Larceny Act 1916, s.39(3); the Criminal Procedure (Scotland) Act 1975, s.7(2). Relative to s.11(4)(b) of the 1995 Act, the provision should read — "as if it had been stolen in Scotland."

[8] *Wilson v. McFadyean*, 1945 J.C. 42.

[9] *Clement's Case* (1830) 1 Lewin C.C. 113, quoted in R.C. Megarry, *Miscellany-at-Law* (London 1955), p.289.

[10] Alison, ii, 78.

[11] (1767) *Maclaurin's Cases*, No 76.

[12] *cf. R. v. Atakpu* [1994] Q.B. 69, and the criticism of the decision there in G.R. Sullivan and Colin Warbrick, "Territoriality, Theft and Atakpu" [1994] Crim L.R. 650.

[13] Hume, ii, 54.

correct, because the kidnapper is continually depriving his victim of his liberty, and the protection of the liberty of everyone within their jurisdiction is one of the basic functions of courts of law. The picture with regard to the theft of property is by no means so clear. Hume himself seems to have regarded *Taylor*[14] as rather anomolous, and as perhaps simply based on "the high expediency of bringing the possessors of stolen goods to speedy justice, and at a moderate expense, upon either side of the Border",[15] a view which, as he remarks, is borne out by the fact that the matter as between Scotland and England was regulated by legislation[16] shortly after *Taylor's*[16a] case. It is now regulated by section 11(4)(a) of the 1995 Act, but so far as other countries are concerned, *Taylor* may still represent the law.[17]

On a more general point, it has not been uncommon for Scottish judges to regard particular offences as continuing ones, either as their sole ground or as a supplementary reason for assuming jurisdiction over offences which might seem to have been completed abroad.[18] This has been noticeable in English law too — especially in relation to inchoate offences which, plausibly, have been regarded as continuing until the plan or attempt succeeds, fails or is abandoned.[19]

---

[14] (1767) *Maclaurin's Cases*, No. 76.

[15] Hume, ii, 55.

[16] Criminal Law Act 1772.

[16a] (1767) *MacLaurin's Cases,* No. 76.

[17] For later examples of common law charges of theft as a *crimen continuum*, see *Robt Hay* (1877) 3 Coup. 491; *Jas. Stevenson* (1853) 1 Irv. 341.

[18] See *Wm Allan* (1873) 2 Coup. 311, Lord Ardmillan at 407 (relative to theft or fraud), L.J.-C. Moncreiff at 408 (relative to the fraud which was charged in the case); *John Thos. Witherington* (1881) 5 Coup. 475, Lord Mure at 497 (of the fraud charged in the case); *Clements v. H.M. Advocate*, 1991 J.C. 62, Lord Wylie at 76 (in relation to the statutory offence under s.4(3)(b) of the Misuse of Drugs Act 1971).

[19] See, *e.g., R. v. Doot* [1973] A.C. 807, HL, Viscount Dilhorne at 8232A, 823D-E, and 825B; Lord Pearson at 827D-E, and Lord Salmon at 835D: *R. v. Baxter* [1972] Q.B. 1, CA, Sachs L.J. at 12A-C.

CHAPTER 4

THE PROBLEM OF CAUSATION[1]

CAUSATION AND RESPONSIBILITY

The first condition that must be satisfied before A can be held legally responsible for a result R is that A must have caused R, in whatever sense the law uses the word "cause". The problem usually offers itself in the form: is R a relevant consequence of A's conduct? Logically the question of causation is necessarily prior to that of responsibility: one cannot ask whether A deserves to be punished for having brought about a particular situation until one is satisfied that he did bring it about; but in practice the law tends to answer the question, "Did A cause R?" by reference to the question, "Is A to be held responsible for R?" It is true, of course, that it may be held that A caused R but is not to be held responsible because he acted in error, or was insane, but in the absence of such "defeasing" circumstances "A caused R" will usually mean the same as "A is responsible for R". In *Weld-Blundell v. Stephens*[2] Lord Sumner said, "The object of a civil enquiry into cause and consequence is to fix liability on some responsible person . . . The trial of an action for damage is not a scientific inquest into a mixed sequence of phenomena . . . It is a practical enquiry," and the same is true of a criminal trial. **4.01**

It has often been said that the law is not interested in philosophical questions of causality, and indeed such questions are so difficult and complicated as to be insoluble. Instead, the law purports to adopt a common-sense approach[3]; as Lord Justice-Clerk Thomson said in his usual forthright manner in *Blaikie v. British Transport Commission*[4]:

> "The law has always had to come to some kind of compromise with the doctrine of causation. The problem is a practical rather than an intellectual one. It is easy and usual to bedevil it with subtleties, but the attitude of the law is that expediency and good sense dictate that for practical purposes a line has to be drawn somewhere, and that, in drawing it, the Court is to be guided by the practical experience of the reasonable man rather than by the theoretical speculations of the philosopher."

Similarly, in *Alphacell Ltd v. Woodward*,[5] Lord Salmon said:

---

[1] For a detailed study of causation in the law, see H.L.A. Hart and A.M. Honoré, *Causation in the Law* (2nd ed., Oxford, 1985). There is also a concise survey of American and Continental causal theories by G.O.W. Mueller, "Causing Criminal Harm" in *Essays in Criminal Science*, ed. Mueller (New York and London, 1961), p.169.

[2] [1920] A.C. 956, 986.

[3] *e.g. Stapley v. Gypsum Mines Ltd.* [1953] A.C. 663, Lord Reid at 681.

[4] 1961 S.C. 44, 49.

[5] [1972] A.C. 824, 847C.

"The nature of causation has been discussed by many eminent philosophers and also by a number of learned judges in the past. I consider, however, that what or who has caused a certain event to occur is essentially a practical question of fact which can best be answered by ordinary common sense rather than by abstract metaphysical theory."

What often happens in practice is that courts discuss causal theories learnedly and at length, and purport to reach a conclusion by reference to a logical appraisal of these theories; but in fact the causal criterion applied to the case is chosen, not because of its intrinsic logic and correctness, but because it is the one which leads most easily to the same answer as would be given to the question: "Should A bear the blame for this?" Although the decision of the court appears to be based on causal reasoning, it is really based on the views of the court as to the fittingness of punishing A for what has happened.[6] The best that can be said for the legal use of causal theories is, as Glanville Williams puts it, that — "In so far as [causation] is a question of law, it must be determined partly in accordance with certain rules but otherwise according to the intuitive reaction of the tribunal."[7]

The complexity of causal factors

4.02 This manner of dealing with causal questions is made easier by the complexity of the causal factors involved in any situation, as a result of which it is usually possible to find a plausible causal argument to use as a rationalisation of a responsibility decision. There is a multitude of causes for any given event and a multitude of effects follows on any given cause.

"One is but using a commonplace if one repeats that many causes have some place in the sequence of events which lead to a result, or follows Lord Shaw in saying that 'causation is not a chain, but a net'.[8] The question always is how far back is one justified in going or how wide a net must one envisage."[9]

4.03 Moreover, events exist on different planes and can be regarded from different points of view, in different "universes of discourse". Choice of the relevant cause or effect depends on the purposes of the person making the choice: different people give different causes for the same effect. An engineer may ascribe a collision at sea to a fault in the ship's engine structure, a Department of Trade and Industry official to a failure to make the proper routine inspection, a meteorologist to bad weather, a metallurgist to metal fatigue, an astrologer to the star under which the captain was born, and so on. The "legal cause", as Glanville Williams points out, is only the legally significant factual cause, and even the legal cause may vary from one branch of the law to another.[10] A may be regarded as having caused a particular injury for the purpose of determining that he is liable to pay damages in delict to the injured person, but it does not follow that he would be regarded as having caused the injury for the purpose of determining whether he is liable to criminal punishment in respect of the occurrence.

---

[6] *cf.* O.C. Jensen, *The Nature of Legal Argument* (Oxford, 1957), Part II.
[7] Gl. Williams, "Causation in Homicide" [1957] Crim.L.R. 429, 430.
[8] *Leyland Shipping Co. Ltd v. Norwich Union Fire Insurance Ltd.* [1918] A.C. 350, 369.
[9] *Stapley v. Gypsum Mines Ltd* [1953] A.C. 663, Lord Porter at 676.
[10] Gl. Williams, "Causation in the Law" [1961] C.L.J. 62, 63.

There is a strong tendency for people to ascribe effects to causes in which they have a special interest, and this is important from the point of view of responsibility, because it often results in the ascription of events to causes constituted by actions forbidden by the ascriber. Such situations are common in everyday life. For example: a father lends his son the family car to go to a party but stipulates that the son will return home directly and not drive any girls home first. The boy disobeys this stipulation and takes a girl home. On his own ultimate return homewards he is involved in a collision which is not due to his fault. The father may well insist that the accident was due to the boy's disobedience of his orders. If the boy points out the illogicality of this, it will be easy enough for the father to show that this was *a* cause of the accident, since if the son had come straight home he would not have been at the place of the accident when it happened, and so it would not have happened — and the father may consider this sufficient to enable him to hold the boy responsible for the accident as a consequence of his disobedience.

If the father is a lawyer he may try to reinforce his argument by saying that the boy's wrongful act of disobedience was a *sine qua non* of the accident. And so it was; but so also were many other factors in the situation such as, for example, that the father lent the boy the car, or indeed that the father ever begot his son, and so on in a regression which if not infinite can at least be taken back to the bounds of human history. The father stops at the son's disobedience, not because this has any special causal status, but because he is interested in enforcing his prohibition against the boy taking girls home in the car, and he hopes to do so and to prevent the infringement of any similar future prohibition by pointing to the accident and by whatever disciplinary measures he may take against the boy for getting involved in the accident "as a result of his disobedience".[11] **4.04**

The special position of human causes

Another important common tendency in the ascription of causes, and one which often leads to results similar to those reached by picking out prohibited acts, is the tendency to ascribe an event to a cause the ascriber can influence. As Professor Collingwood pointed out, the cause is "the thing I can put right." He gave the following example: **4.05**

> "If my car 'conks out' on a hill . . . If I had been a person who could flatten out hills by stamping on them, [a] passer-by would have been right to call my attention to the hill as the cause of the stoppage; not because the hill is a hill, but because I can flatten it out . . .
>
> If I find that I can get a result by certain means, I may be pretty sure that I should not be getting it unless a great many conditions were fulfilled; but so long as I get it I do not mind what these conditions are . . .
>
> For any given person, the cause of a given thing is that one of its conditions which he is able to produce or prevent."[12]

---

[11] If anyone were to take the view that this example is childish, and the father's attitude too stupid to merit consideration, he would be quite right. But the father's attitude is similar to that of the law of Scotland regarding certain forms of culpable homicide: see Vol. II, Chap. 26, as well as to the old English felony-murder rule.

[12] R.G. Collingwood, "On the So-Called Idea of Causation," *Proceedings of Aristotelian Society*, 1937–38, 85, 91–92.

Since the purpose of the criminal law is to influence human beings, human causes are of particular importance to it: they are what it can put right, or at any rate what it is supposed to be able to put right. Voluntary human actions are also of special importance as causal factors because they are regarded as themselves uncaused. This is a necessary inference from the doctrine of freewill; and without some form of that doctrine, however restricted, there can be no moral responsibility in the sense of praise or blame. "[I]n the common-sense notion of causation a deliberate human action has a special status as a cause and is not regarded in its turn as something which is caused."[13]

4.06 There is a tendency, therefore, to ignore remoter agencies, human or not, and to take *the* cause as the human agency nearest the event in question. Human actions are thus regarded as breaking any chain of causation, and as starting a new series, "caused" by the human intervention. An event which "breaks" a causal chain in this way is known in the law as a *novus actus interveniens*, and the typical *novus actus* is a human action. An example of this within very small compass is the typical case of a motor-car knocking down a careless pedestrian, who then sues the motorist for causing her injury. In *McLean v. Bell*,[14] which was such a case, it was said:

> "In one sense, but for the negligence of the pursuer (if she was negligent) in attempting to cross the road, she would not have been struck; and, as a matter simply of causation, her acts formed a necessary element in the final result, since without them no accident could have occurred. The decision, however, of the case must turn not simply on causation, but on responsibility. The pursuer's negligence may be what is often called *causa sine qua non*, yet, as regards responsibility, it becomes merely evidential or matter of narrative if the defender acting reasonably could and ought to have avoided the collision."[15]

The key phrase is "could and ought to have avoided". It is because he ought to have avoided the accident that the search for a cause can stop with the driver — someone has been found who ought to have done otherwise than he did, and who, in fact, had he done otherwise, could have prevented the accident; someone has been found who can be blamed, who is responsible for what happened.

There are, however, also cases where B's voluntary human action intervening between A's conduct and the *actus reus* is not treated as a *novus actus*. There are cases in which the courts wish to hold A responsible for the *actus reus* and to treat B as blameless[16], or sometimes even cases in which it is desired to hold both A and B responsible.[17]

---

[13] H.L.A. Hart and A.M. Honoré, "Causation in the Law" (1956) 72 L.Q.R. 58, 77.

[14] 1932 S.C. (H.L.) 21.

[15] Lord Wright at 29.

[16] It has been held in Scotland, for example, that where A sells to B substances capable of being used in a way which endangers or harms B, in the knowledge that B intends to use them in such a way, and B does use them in that way, A is to be treated as if he had administered the substance to B and so caused the resultant harm or danger: *Ulhaq v. H.M. Advocate,* 1991 S.L.T. 614 — supplying solvents and gas lighter fuel to adults in the knowledge that they intended to inhale the vapours. This case followed and extended that of *Khaliq v. H.M. Advocate,* 1984 J.C. 23 — a very special case, since children were the persons supplied by the accused; although it was observed that the youth of the victims was not central to the charge, it was easier to see there that the supplier's responsibility as an

"Caused" human actions

Certain types of human behaviour are treated only as effects, as events themselves caused by prior human behaviour, or at least as not breaking the causal chain of which they form a link. These types are: **4.07**

(1) *Reflex actings.* As has already been pointed out, reflex behaviour is not regarded by the law as involving an "act" at all.[18] If A frightens B and makes him jump and by an unthinking reflex pull the trigger of the gun he is carrying, B has not "fired" the gun, and the "cause" of the shot and any of its consequences is A's conduct.[19]

(2) *Coerced actings.* In the same way, if A takes B's hand and forces it to pull the trigger the only act involved is A's. Where the force applied by A is psychological, and is of a kind recognised by the law as sufficient to enable B to succeed in a defence of coercion,[20] B will not be held responsible for *e.g.* shooting C, although it may be accepted that the shooting was his act, and the subsequent injury caused by him, as well as by A. The important point here, however, is that B's behaviour will not break the causal link between A's behaviour and the criminal result. **4.08**

(3) *Innocent actings.* If A sends a time bomb to B by the hand of a postman or other messenger who is wholly ignorant of the situation, then, although it may be the messenger who places the bomb in B's hand at the fatal moment, he is only an innocent agent, and the only act which can count as a cause is A's. If A puts B into a cell with a homicidal lunatic, A's position is the same as if he had put him into a cell with a starved man-eating tiger: A's action is a legally relevant cause of B's death, whether or not the behaviour of the lunatic or animal is also regarded as a cause.[21] **4.09**

Inducement. It often seems reasonable to say that one person "made" another act in a particular way — for example that Lady Macbeth made her husband murder Duncan, or that Iago made Othello murder Desdemona. This use of causal language is unexceptionable, although it may raise difficulties for libertarian philosophers. It is recognised by the **4.10**

---

adult far outweighed any blame which could be attached to the victims. It has also been held that where A, at B's request, supplies potentially lethal drugs to B (an adult) who then ingests them and dies of the effect, A, if he knows that B intended to so consume them, causes that death and can, therefore, be guilty of culpable homicide: *Lord Advocate's Reference (No. 1 of 1994)* 1995 S.L.T. 248 (*cf. R. v. Dalby* [1982] 1 All E.R. 916 and *R. v. Armstrong* [1989] Crim. L.R. 149). This suggests that a foreseeable voluntary action by an adult does not count as a *novus actus*, a view which seems to be shared by the English Law Commission — see 1989 Draft Code, s.17(2) — but is contrary to what might be called the "classical" or "traditional" idea of *novus actus*. For a criticism of the Draft Code provision, see Gl. Williams, "*Finis* for *Novus Actus*" [1989] C.L.J. 391.

17 See *infra*, paras 4.24 *et seq.*; 4.32–4.33.

18 *supra*, para. 3.14.

19 *cf. McCann v. J.R. McKellar (Alloys) Ltd*, 1969 S.C. (H.L.) 1 and *Devine v. Colvilles Ltd*, 1969 S.C. (H.L.) 67.

20 *infra,* paras 13.28 *et seq.*

21 Hume, i, 189–190.

law for the purposes of crimes such as fraud and instigation to commit crime. But where A "induces" B to do something criminal, B is treated as having caused the *actus reus* unless he acted automatically or under superior force, or was so completely deceived as to be only an innocent agent of A; both Macbeth and Othello were guilty of homicide.[22]

4.11 *Statutory causing.* Many modern statutes make it an offence for A to cause someone else to commit a breach of the law. The statute may make it unlawful to cause the offence to occur, for example, to cause a vehicle to be used while it is in a certain condition,[23] or state in terms that it shall be an offence to cause any other person to use a vehicle unlawfully,[24] but the difference in phraseology is not important. In most cases of this kind the behaviour of the person who actually perpetrates the breach of the law is as voluntary as that of the person who causes it, and both are usually charged together.[25]

Causation in art and part guilt

4.12 Where a number of people form a common plan to commit a crime, they may all be responsible for the consequences of the carrying out of that plan. If, for example, a group of people set out to commit theft by housebreaking, and one of them assaults the householder who subsequently dies, they may all be guilty of homicide, including those who were never in the house but only kept watch outside. Their guilt will depend on two causal factors. The first is that the death must be the result of an act by one of the group, and this will be decided in the same way as if the actual assailant had been on his own. The second is that the act of the assailant must itself be a legally relevant consequence of the common purpose. This is usually decided by reference to the criterion of foreseeability. If, for example, the householder was shot, the liability of other members of the group will depend on whether it was foreseeable that a firearm would be used in the course of the housebreaking. In determining foreseeability the state of knowledge of the other members of the group is relevant. If they knew that one of their number carried a firearm, they will probably all be held responsible for its use, even though it was agreed that it would not be used, or would be used only to frighten.[26] If, however, all or some of the others did not know of the carrying of the gun, they will not be held responsible for its use: or, to put it another way, its use will not be in the course of or as a result of the plan to which they were party.

---

[22] So probably also were Iago and Lady Macbeth although their position is more complicated than that of the actual assailants.

[23] *e.g.* Road Traffic Act 1988, s.42(b), as substituted by the Road Traffic Act 1991, s.8(2).

[24] *ibid.*, s.143(b).

[25] For a discussion of statutory causing see *infra*, paras 8.73 *et seq.*

[26] Some of the above may now be too broadly stated in view of the opinion of the court in *Brown v. H.M. Advocate*, 1993 S.C.C.R. 382. In that case, one of two assailants must have stabbed and killed the victim but it was impossible to determine which one of them had had or wielded the knife. The court held that, in order to take the verdict against both of them beyond assault, it was necessary for there to have been evidence that both were aware that a knife was likely to be used in the attack. And to take the verdict beyond culpable homicide, it was further necessary for there to be evidence that both had in contemplation, as part of the joint purpose, an act of the necessary degree of wicked recklessness, such as that the deceased would be stabbed by plunging a knife into his heart (opinion of the court at 391 E-F). Since the court did not over-rule or refer to prior authorities which favour what is stated in the text above, the position is currently somewhat uncertain. For a fuller discussion of this matter see *infra*, paras 5.38 *et seq.*

The Causal Criteria

Before dealing with the case law on the subject it may be useful to look briefly at the principal criteria which the courts apply in causal questions. **4.13**

(1) *The objective standpoint: Directness*

From the objective point of view everything that follows from a given act is caused by that act. Other causes, of course, will also operate — there is no such thing as *the* cause of any event — but the act taken as the beginning of a series of events is *a* cause of everything in the series. Starting from a given act there can be traced a sequence that is never broken: it may gather into itself factors which themselves can be traced back to an act outside the series, but it is not broken by these factors, it is joined by them. The intervening factors are merely additional links in the final series, a series which is continually coming into being and expanding as it meets and joins other series, rather like a tributary running into a river and then being joined by later tributaries.[27] The series can be described only in so far as it has been completed at the time of description, and when so described it can always be described as unbroken.

The only distinction which can be made objectively in this series is that between direct and indirect consequences of the given act. Anything which can be traced back to an act may be said to be a consequence of it, but it may not be a direct consequence. Where the consequences of an act are sought, and there enters the sequence something not itself traceable to that act, whether it is a *novus actus interveniens* or merely an event, later events in the series may be described as indirect consequences of the act. If a man receives a wound which becomes septic, and leads to blood poisoning of which he dies, his death is a direct consequence of the wound.[28]

But if, while in hospital being treated for the wound, he catches typhoid from his neighbour and dies, his death is not a direct consequence of his wound. It is a consequence of it — what caused him to catch the typhoid was *inter alia* being in hospital, but it is not a direct consequence, because the typhoid was not caused by the wound but entered the sequence, so to speak, from the outside, with a causal history independent of the wound. This, again, is by no means logically impeccable — the existence of the hospital itself is an outside factor — but there is a rough distinction and it is a distinction which is used in legal reasoning about direct and indirect causation.

(2) *The objective standpoint: Remoteness*

Whatever the philosophical implications of using directness as an exclusive causal criterion, such a use would be clearly impractical. It is not feasible to treat A as having caused every consequence of all his acts, **4.14**

---

[27] Metaphors are of course inexact and misleading, but they are inevitable if this question is to be discussed in language and not in mathematical symbols.

[28] Of course, it could be said that even in the simplest and shortest series external factors enter the sequence, but for legal purposes it is possible and indeed necessary to deal in rather broad terms.

to the end of time. Somewhere along the line there comes a point at which the effect of A's act must be deemed to cease.[29] The criterion commonly used for determining when this point is reached is "remoteness". A is not treated as having caused any consequences of his act which are too "remote" to be attributed to him.

Remoteness is at once the most difficult and the most useful of the causal criteria, because it is the vaguest. It is accepted in Scots law that mere remoteness in time is irrelevant — the fact that the victim lingers a long time before dying from the wound inflicted by A does not affect A's responsibility for the death.[30] Some indirect cause must probably intervene before responsibility is affected. But remoteness in time makes it easier to regard a subsequent occurrence as breaking the causal series, since it can be said that the original cause had spent its effect at the time of the intervention, so that the latter must be regarded as the substantial or effective cause of the ultimate result.

4.15 *Operative cause.* Conversely, the idea of remoteness can be used to exclude what might otherwise be regarded as a *novus actus interveniens*, on the ground that it occurred when the effect of the accused's act was still operative. In *R. v. Smith*[31] S assaulted a fellow-soldier; it was found that the doctor had made a faulty diagnosis and applied an improper remedy, and the victim died. In upholding S's conviction for murder, and distinguishing the case from one in which the alleged improper treatment had followed on a stab wound from which the victim had recovered to a considerable extent at the time of the impropriety, and in which the accused had been acquitted,[32] Lord Parker C.J. said:

> "[I]f at the time of death the original wound is still an operating cause and a substantial cause, then the death can properly be said to be the result of the wound, albeit that some other cause of death is also operating. Only if it can be said that the original wounding is merely the setting in which another cause operates can it be said that the death does not result from the wound . . . only if the second cause is so overwhelming as to make the original wound merely part of the history can it be said that the death does not flow from the wound."[33]

Lord Parker's language is in the main untechnical, and his use of words like "substantial" and "overwhelming" suggests that in making causal judgments the courts do not apply logical concepts at all, but "weigh" the causes in some vague scale, and regard the "heaviest" as *the* cause. This is probably what people in fact do when they judge untrammeled by such pseudo-logical or pseudo-legal concepts as directness, *novus actus interveniens* and the rest. What is being sought is just the "most important" cause, and in such a search remoteness is of great importance. But remoteness in this sense means something other than place in a temporal sequence: if A shoots B and the operating surgeon's hand accidentally slips and causes B's death in the sense that B, who would probably have died anyway, dies immediately following the cut caused by the surgeon, it can be said that the important, or effective, or

---

[29] *cf. Blaikie v. British Transport Commission*, 1961 S.C. 44, L.J.-C. Thomson at 49.
[30] Hume, i, 185; and see *Tees v. H.M. Advocate*, 1994 J.C. 12.
[31] [1959] 2 Q.B. 35.
[32] *R. v. Jordan* (1959) 40 Cr.App.R. 152. See *infra*, n.2.
[33] [1959] 2 Q.B. at 42–43.

substantial, cause of death was A's act, and not the surgeon's "trivial" error. This way of thinking, of course, may lead to the view that the substantial cause is the most violent act in the series, and that only an "overwhelming" intervention can be a *novus actus interveniens*, and this in itself is unsatisfactory: it might mean that if B was killed by a bomb explosion on the way to hospital A would be acquitted, but if he were killed in an accident caused by a slight error of judgment on the part of the ambulance driver, A would be convicted.

(3) *The subjective standpoint: Intention*

It seems reasonable to blame A for all the intended results of his **4.16** actions, but in practice the law applies this as a sole criterion only in exceptional cases, such as the situation where A shoots B intending to kill him, and C then comes along and kills B while the latter is still languishing from A's shot. Intention can, in any event, be used as a criterion only where the result is a natural consequence of the act in question. If someone sticks pins in an effigy of his enemy intending to kill him, and the enemy does in fact die at that time, or soon afterwards, no system which disbelieved in sympathetic magic would regard the death as caused by such conduct.[34] The principal importance of intention in relation to causality is that the courts will be more ready to treat A as having caused a result he intended than a result he did not intend, but the criterion explicitly adopted will usually be something other than intention. It should also be noted that A will not be regarded as having caused an intended result which in fact comes about by reason of something outwith his plan of conduct, as where the victim is killed in an accident on the way to hospital,[35] or dies of heart failure while sipping the poison supplied by A.[36]

(4) *The standpoint of the reasonable man: Foreseeability*

Foresight and foreseeability. The difference between foresight and fore- **4.17** seeability is that the former relates to what A actually foresaw, and the latter to what the courts regard as foreseeable. In practice the subjective criterion of foresight is not used in making causal judgments: the courts do not seek to discover whether A foresaw R as a result of his behaviour, but whether R was a foreseeable result of that behaviour.

The reasonable man. In order to determine foreseeability the courts **4.18** have recourse to the reasonable man, a creature as unreal as the economic man or *l'homme moyen sensuel*. The reasonable man is sometimes spoken of as "the man on top of an omnibus" in the Clapham Road, or Princes Street, or the main street of whatever town the court sits in. But this is misleading. The reasonable man is not the average man of statistics: for one thing he is more careful and more law-abiding than the average man.[37] Nor is he a man of reason, guided only by logical considerations. "Reasonable" in this connection means "fair" or "moderate," and not "rational". The reasonable man is not so much the

---

[34] *cf.* Gl. Williams, para. 207(f).
[35] *infra*, para. 4.43.
[36] *R. v. White* [1910] 2 K.B. 124.
[37] *cf. Blaikie v. British Transport Commission*, 1961 S.C. 44, L.J.-C. Thomson at 49: "The reasonable man goes round in bogey because he plays the orthodox shots, is never in trouble, and is not called on to do the unexpected."

normal man, as an artifact used by the courts as a norm by reference to which the conduct of other, real, men is to be judged. He is, indeed, when all is said and done, neither more nor less than a device used by the law to achieve objectivity and uniformity, and to avoid having to inquire into the state of mind of the particular agent in every case. And as a norm, his standards are those of his creators — the law and the judges.[38]

The Case Law

4.19 The situations in which difficult causal judgments have to be made can be classified as follows:

(1) Those where the result depends on A's act taken in conjunction with a pre-existing circumstance.
(2) Those where two independent acts lead to the same result.
(3) Those where a subsequent event or act intervenes between A's act and the result.

Subsequent acts are divided into acts of the victim, and acts of a third party.

(1) *Pre-existing conditions*

4.20 Hart and Honoré state: "An abnormal *condition* existing at the time of a human intervention is distinguished both by ordinary thought and, with a striking consistency, by most legal systems from an abnormal event or conjunction of events subsequent to that intervention."[39] The pre-existing condition may occur in the state of the victim, or be part of the surrounding circumstances.

4.21 *Pre-existing conditions of the victim: taking your victim as you find him.* The most generally accepted rule in the whole field of causation is the rule that an assailant must take his victim as he finds him.[40] If A inflicts a minor wound on B who dies because he suffers from haemophilia or has a weak heart, his death is always regarded as caused by A's blow, whether or not A knew of his condition, or the condition

---

[38] *cf.* Lord Devlin, *The Enforcement of Morals* (London, 1965), p.15: "He is not to be confused with the rational man. He is not expected to reason about anything and his judgment may be largely a matter of feeling. It is the viewpoint of the man in the street — or to use an archaism familiar to all lawyers — the man on the Clapham omnibus. He might also be called the right-minded man. For my purpose I should like to call him the man in the jury box, for the moral judgement of society must be something about which any twelve men or women drawn at random might after discussion be expected to be unanimous." But in practice the standards are often set not by juries but by judges who even collectively do not make up the microcosm of society which is ideally present in a jury box. This is particularly noticeable in relation to negligence, which is *par excellence* the province of the reasonable man, but which is often treated as a question of law for the judge and not a question of fact for the jury: see *e.g. Malcolm v. Dickson*, 1951 S.C. 542; *H.M. Advocate v. Miller and Denovan*, High Court at Glasgow, November 1960, noted at 1991 S.L.T. 211; See Vol. II, Chap. 23.

[39] H.L.A. Hart and A.M. Honoré, *Causation in the Law* (2nd ed., Oxford, 1985), 79–80.

[40] *H.M. Advocate v. Rutherford*, 1947 J.C. 1; *Robertson and Donoghue*, High Court at Edinburgh, Aug. 1945, unrep'd; *Jas. Williamson* (1866) 5 Irv. 326. *Cf. Chas Donaldson* (1836) 1 Swin. 108, L.J.-C. Boyle at 121; *Thos. Breckinridge* (1836) 1 Swin. 153.

was reasonably foreseeable. In the civil case of *McDonald v. Smellie*[41] it was held that if a dog bites a boy who is predisposed to meningitis so that the boy contracts the disease as a result of the bite, his death is to be regarded as having been caused by the dog.[42]

Similarly it is homicide to accelerate death by however short a period, and it is equally homicide to kill a person who is on his death bed as to kill someone in the best of health.[43] If, therefore, A inflicts a mortal wound on B, and C kills B when he has but a short time to live, C is clearly guilty of homicide whether or not A is also guilty. From the point of view of C's guilt the earlier injury inflicted by A is irrelevant.[44] **4.22**

Other circumstances. It is equally clear that if A inflicts a minor injury on B, for example, by punching or pushing him, and B falls and strikes his head on the pavement or a piece of furniture and cracks his skull, or falls into the sea and drowns, A's blow will be accounted the cause of death.[45] **4.23**

(2) *Concurrent causation*

The only Scots cases which deal with the situation where two separate causes operate simultaneously to produce one result concern negligent acts. Although the factual situations involved are not easy to categorise, the cases in the main fall into three groups. **4.24**

(a) *Art and part guilt.* Where A and B agree to do something which is negligent, and which in fact injures someone, the situation is the same as if they agree to commit a crime: the result is caused by their concerted action for which both are responsible. The clearest example of this kind of situation is *Geo. Barbier and Ors*[46] where three men went shooting on a range; they did not put up the customary warning flags, or take any other precautions; they then shot in the direction of a public beach and a girl was killed, having been shot by only one bullet. In that situation all are responsible for the girl's death, the cause of which is taken to be the dangerous way in which they agreed to carry out their shooting expedition.[47] The cases which deal with racing by vehicles in the street are best considered as falling into this group. If two drivers agree to race each other and drive so recklessly that someone is knocked down by one of them, both may be treated as having caused the accident.[48] Should one of the drivers himself be killed, the fact that the two of them were **4.25**

---

41 (1903) 5 F. 955.

42 *cf.* Donnedieu de Vabres, "Un chien, mal surveillé par son propriétaire, mord à la jambe un passant. Ce passant, qui portait un pantalon sale, meurt du tétanus, à la suite de la morsure. Le propriétaire du chien est condamné pour homicide par imprudence": at p.82. See also Gl. Williams, "The Risk Principle" (1961) 77 L.Q.R. 179, 193–197, where he calls this rule "The 'Thin Skull' Rule"; *R. v. Blaue* [1975] 1 W.L.R. 1411; *infra*, para. 4.51.

43 Hume, i, 183; Alison, i, 71, 149.

44 Hume, i, 181–182; Macdonald, pp.87–88.

45 Hume, i, 234; Alison, i, 94–100; *Geo. Broadley* (1884) 5 Couper 490.

46 (1876) 5 Irv. 482; see also *Gizzi v. Tudhope*, 1983 S.L.T. 214.

47 See *infra*, para. 5.47.

48 *Andrew and Adam Scott* (1805) Hume, i, 192; *Thos. Crichton and Thos. Morrison* (1822) Hume, i, 193; *J. Bartholomew and Ors* (1825) *ibid.; John Ross and Ors* (1847) Ark. 258; *cf. Skipper v. Hartley*, 242 S.C. 221 (1963); 13 A.L.R. (3d.) 426.

acting in concert may not prevent the survivor from being regarded as the cause of the other's death.[49]

4.26 (b) *Combined negligence.* There are a number of nineteenth-century cases in which negligence by A is followed by negligence by B, and both combine to create one result. Although the two acts are consecutive in such cases, they can be distinguished from cases where A inflicts an injury on C which is followed by an injury inflicted by B, because in the negligence cases there is only one injury. Cases of combined negligence have been concerned mainly with two kinds of factual situation. One is exemplified by *Robert Henderson and Wm Lawson*[50] in which a druggist left an inexperienced servant in charge of his shop without instructing him in the proper administration of drugs, and the latter carelessly dispensed a fatal dose to a customer. Both were charged with culpable homicide, and the indictment held relevant.[51] The other is exemplified by the railway cases in which two or more railway employees were charged together with culpable homicide where their successive negligence resulted in death, as in *Wm Baillie and Jas. McCurrach*[52] where two stationmasters were charged with culpable homicide, one for permitting a train to leave without giving due warning to other traffic, and the other for leaving his station in charge of an inexperienced porter who did not appreciate the situation which had developed or the necessity to take steps to avoid a collision, and *Geo. Little and Ors*[53] where a stationmaster who instructed a train to start when it was unsafe and the two drivers of the train[54] who failed to take proper precautions in the course of their journey were all charged with culpable homicide.[55]

4.27 The basic principle on which all the negligent acts are treated as causing the result in cases of this kind does not appear to have been fully explored by the courts. The facts of some of the cases can be read as involving art and part guilt,[56] but this is not always or necessarily so. In the employer-workmen cases the best reason for holding the employer responsible may be that the result was foreseeable as a result of the system of working, but that would make these cases an exception to the general rule that a blameworthy intervention, in this case the workman's culpable carelessness, is treated as an unforeseeable *novus actus*.[57] In any

---

[49] See *Sutherland v. H.M. Advocate (No. 1)*, 1994 S.C.C.R. 80, a case of concerted fire-raising where one of the two accused was killed because of the reckless way in which the fire had been set. There may be a greater number of risk-variables in a road race, however, than were involved in the factual situation disclosed in *Sutherland*, and it may consequently be more difficult to establish the causal connection. *Cf. Cmwth. v. Root*, 403 Pa 571; 170 A 2d 310 (1961).

[50] (1842) 1 Broun 360.

[51] See also *e.g. Wm Paton and Richard McNab* (1845) 2 Broun 525, L.J.-C. Hope at 534; *John Drysdale and Ors* (1848) Ark. 440; *Jas. Kirkpatrick and Robt Stewart* (1840) Bell's Notes 71; *Thos. K. Rowbotham and Ors* (1855) 2 Irv. 89.

[52] (1870) 1 Couper 442.

[53] (1883) 5 Couper 259.

[54] It was pulled by two engines with a driver in each.

[55] See also *e.g. John McDonald and Ors* (1853) 1 Irv. 164; *Hugh McLure and Ors* (1848) Ark. 448.

[56] *e.g. Wm Paton and Richard McNab, supra,* and the cases involving negligence by various members of a ship's crew: *e.g. Thos. Henderson and Ors* (1850) J. Shaw 394; *Wm Drever and Wm Tyre* (1885) 5 Couper 680.

[57] *cf.* the argument for the defence in *Robt Henderson and Wm Lawson* (1842) 1 Broun 360, 365, that the case could not be distinguished from that where A leaves a loaded gun lying and B picks it up and shoots someone, in which case B is alone responsible, an argument which was rejected.

event, this reasoning would not apply to the railway cases. It seems that cases of combined negligence have been treated as analogous to cases involving art and part guilt, whether or not the facts came up to art and part, with little or no attempt being made to challenge the practice. Apart from *Henderson and Lawson,*[58] the only serious challenge was in *Geo. Little and Ors*[58a] where the Crown argued successfully that "where a loss of life has been caused by the negligence of two separate officials, each in his own department of one system, and where it could not have resulted without the concurrence of failure of duty on the part of both, both are relevantly charged with culpable homicide."[59]

The cases on combined negligence all belong to a type of culpable homicide which is rarely prosecuted in modern times[60] and in which, even in the nineteenth century, the Crown were often unsuccessful. As a result, however, of at least one successful prosecution in England, there has been renewed interest in the criminal responsibility of an employer for culpable homicide in respect of a death caused by the carelessness of an incompetent employee, or for operating an unsafe system of work.[61] And it is not now as unlikely as once might have been thought for a person to be held responsible for a result which would not have occurred had his own negligence not been added to by a subsequent careless act on the part of someone else.

(c) *Concurrent independent negligence.* There are also a few cases of negligence in which there is clearly no question of art and part guilt. In *John Ross and Ors*[62] R was a driver who had left his horse and cart unattended; A and W, the two other accused, were also cart drivers, each of whom drove his cart recklessly into R's cart, whereupon R's horse bolted and threw its passenger out of the cart. All three were charged with culpable homicide, and the indictment against R was held to be relevant, although the Crown subsequently abandoned the case against him. So far as A and W were concerned, they were probably acting in concert as they appear to have been racing, and their negligences were in any event simultaneous in their occurrence as well as in their result. But it is difficult to see how the charge against R was held relevant. By the time A and W ran into his cart it had become a static factor, a pre-existing condition on which their behaviour operated, and it would be **4.28**

---

[58] *supra.*

[58a] (1883) 5 Couper 259.

[59] (1883) 5 Couper at 263.

[60] See Vol. II, Chap. 26.

[61] At Winchester Crown Court in 1994, OLL Ltd and their managing director were convicted of manslaughter in respect of the deaths of four schoolchildren. The company ran an outdoor activity centre from which on March 22, 1993 an expedition was organised involving a canoe voyage across open sea. The fatalities were caused by a combination of bad weather, inexperience and the company's system of work. In particular, the company had not ensured that the instructors it employed had sufficient qualifications or experience, nor had it provided basic safety equipment such as distress flares, spray-decks (to prevent sea water swamping canoes), or a safety boat. There was also a poor communication system between management and staff, and a lack of procedures for coping with emergencies. All of this was compounded by the acts and omissions of the instructors themselves — none of them (for example) having sought weather forecasts before undertaking the sea trip, and one of them having informed the canoeists that they should not inflate their life-jackets whilst at sea. The company was fined £60,000 and the managing director was imprisoned for three years. The manager of the outdoor centre was also indicted but acquitted of manslaughter. See "The Times" newspaper for December 9, 1994, and G. Slapper, "A Corporate Killing" (1994) 144 N.L.J. 1735.

[62] (1847) Ark. 258.

difficult to say that their reckless and culpable behaviour was foreseeable. The only reason given for the decision was that R's horse was frightened because he was not with it, and the case can probably be discarded as authority.

4.29 The later case of *H.M. Advocate v. Parker and Barrie*[63] is of more importance. In that case the pilots of two ships which were approaching each other were charged with failing to take the precautions required by the regulations under the Merchant Shipping Amendment Act 1862, causing a collision, and thus killing a number of passengers. The objection taken to the indictment seems unfortunately to have been mainly procedural, namely that the two accused should have had separate trials, rather than that they could not both be guilty of the charge. In repelling the objection Lord Justice-Clerk Macdonald simply referred to the practice of trying all the accused together where the offences committed occurred simultaneously and led to one result.[64] No attempt seems to have been made to distinguish between the case where all the accused are on one side of the fence, so to speak, all part of one enterprise, and the case where, as in *Parker and Barrie*[64a] they are on opposite sides of the fence, engaged in independent enterprises. The procedural nature of the argument also shows a failure to distinguish two quite different situations. In the common modern case in which two drivers are charged with the statutory offence of careless driving, each is charged with the separate offence constituted by his own carelessness; the normal reference to the consequent injury or damage is present only as matter of narrative and fair notice; there is no question of both, or either, being charged with the crime of causing such injury or damage. In such a case, whether they should be tried together or separately is just a question of procedural and administrative convenience.[65] But in *Parker and Barrie*[65a] it was the reference to statutory carelessness which was narrative, the charge being one of culpable homicide. *Parker and Barrie*[65b] does not appear to have been followed, and in view of the current tendency to restrict "lawful act" culpable homicide[66] it is unlikely that it ever will be followed. On the other hand, consider the case of two obstinate drivers, each determinedly asserting his "right of way"; as a result the cars collide and a passenger in one of them is killed. It seems reasonable to treat both as to blame for causing the death. In such cases, however, the drivers are in a perverse way almost art and part with each other; the situation is like a competition or race.

4.30 (d) *Concurrent deliberate acts.* If A and B simultaneously shoot at C and each bullet inflicts a fatal wound, the only alternatives appear to be to acquit both or to convict both. As the latter is clearly just, and the former unjust, it is likely that the law will ignore any causal questions in such a situation and convict both, although such a course is contrary to the general rule that two people cannot be guilty of one crime unless

---

[63] (1888) 2 White 79.
[64] At 86.
[64a] See n.63, *supra.*
[65] See *Mathewson v. Ramsey*, 1936 J.C. 5, which, like *Parker and Barrie* itself, distinguishes and virtually overrules *Clelland v. Sinclair* (1887) 1 White 359.
[65a] See n.63, *supra.*
[65b] *ibid.*
[66] See Vol. II, Chap. 26.

they are art and part,[67] and is unsupported by any Scottish authority other than *H.M. Advocate v. Parker and Barrie.*[68]

(3) *Subsequent occurrences*

Generally speaking, A's act is regarded as the cause of a result R only where R is a direct consequence of that act, but this is not always so, and the criterion of foreseeability is sometimes called in aid in order to hold that A has caused results which are not direct consequences of his acts, and to disregard subsequent actings by other persons which would normally be classed as *novi actus interveniententes*. As Lord Wright said in *The Oropesa*,[69] "To break the chain of causation it must be shown that there is something which I will call ultroneous, something unwarrantable, a new cause which disturbs the sequence of events, something which can be described as either unreasonable or extraneous or extrinsic." **4.31**

(a) *Subsequent intentional acts.* Macdonald states in relation to homicide: **4.32**

> "Death must result directly from the injury. If, after the injury some other person has done an act which causes death, the person who did the first injury cannot be held guilty of homicide. Thus, if A mortally stab B, but C administer poison to B and kill him, A cannot be found guilty of homicide, the direct cause of death being the poison."[70]

Macdonald's authorities are a passage in Hume which does not go quite so far as this, since it deals with the case where the initial wound is not necessarily mortal, but is "of that sort which either may or may not prove mortal",[71] and a passage in More's Lectures which may support his view but itself refers to no authority.[72] There is no case law dealing with this sort of situation in Scotland. The argument in favour of Macdonald's view is, however, clear, if it is accepted that the appropriate criterion is directness. The objective break in the causal series occurs irrespectively of whether A intended to cause B's death by his act, and equally irrespectively of whether C intended to cause death. The only relevance C's intention has is that it makes his act criminal and therefore clearly a *novus actus*.

Nonetheless, it is quite possible that the courts would wish to treat both A and C as responsible for the death, since both intended to kill B and B died. According to Glanville Williams:

> "[I]f D and E independently stab P, and the wound inflicted by each is enough to cause the death of P, each is guilty of murder when P

---

[67] *Greig v. Muir*, 1955 J.C. 20, L.J.-C. Thomson at 23.

[68] See n.63, *supra.* The conviction of both is supported by Hall, p.268; Smith and Hogan, p.335n.; Gl. Williams "Causation in the Law" [1957] Crim.L.R. 429, 436; *cf. Baker v. Willoughby* [1970] A.C. 467, Lord Reid at 492 B-C. In *Attorney-General's Reference (No. 4 of 1980)* [1981] 1 W.L.R. 705, where any one of three intentional acts of the defendant might have caused the death of the victim, it was held unnecessary to establish which of the three had actually produced the fatality in order to convict of manslaughter; although matters were simplified there since the acts had but one author, it seems reasonably clear that where the acts had been committed by separate defendants, then a properly directed jury could legitimately have found both or all three guilty of manslaughter.

[69] [1943] P. 32, 39. This passage was applied in *Finlayson v. H.M. Advocate*, 1979 J.C. 33, *infra*, para. 4.34.

[70] Macdonald, p.87.

[71] Hume, i, 181.

[72] J.S. More, *Lectures on the Law of Scotland* (Edinburgh, 1864), Vol. 2, p.361.

dies as a result of the weakness induced by the two wounds. D is not excused of responsibility merely because E's act was later in time, his own act having contributed to the death at the moment when it occurred. E also is responsible, since it is a well-settled principle that homicide can be committed merely by hastening death. In fact that is all that any killer ever does."[73]

4.33 In the American case of *People v. Lewis*,[74] L. inflicted a fatal wound on the deceased who cut his own throat a few minutes later, and died after another five minutes. It was assumed that the deceased was guilty of suicide, and that his suicide was a voluntary act for which he was responsible, and the only question was whether L. could be regarded as having also been responsible for the death. The defence, as described by Temple J. in L.'s appeal, was, "that this is a case where one languishing from a mortal wound is killed by an intervening cause, and, therefore, the deceased was not killed by Lewis . . . He was as effectually prevented from killing as he would have been if some obstacle had turned aside the bullet from its course and left [him] unwounded."[75]

The judge then rejected the argument that the suicide had been caused by the wound, saying, "The wound induced the suicide, but the wound was not, in the usual course of things, the cause of the suicide." He nonetheless took the view that Lewis was guilty of murder, and said:

"The test is — or at least one test — whether, when the death occurred, the wound inflicted by the defendant did contribute to the event. If it did, although other independent causes also contributed, the causal relation between the unlawful acts of the deceased and the death has been made out. Here, when the throat was cut, [the deceased] was not merely languishing from a mortal wound. He was actually dying — and after the throat was cut he continued to languish from both wounds. If the throat cutting had been by a third person, unconnected with the defendant, he might be guilty; for, although a man cannot be killed twice, two persons, acting independently, may contribute to his death and each be guilty of a homicide. A person dying is still in life, and may be killed, but if he is dying from a wound given by another both may properly be said to have contributed to his death."[76]

In its approach to causality this decision is in line with the approach of the court in *R v. Smith*[77]: so long as the original wound remains an operating and substantial cause, the person who inflicted it is guilty of homicide (although the English courts might have regarded the deceased's suicide as an overwhelming event breaking the causal link).

Lewis[77a] has been strongly criticised,[78] and from the objective causal point of view it may well be indefensible. From that point of view, however, it does not matter whether B's conduct is deliberate, negligent, or merely accidental, but the law does distinguish between blameworthy and non-blameworthy behaviour by B, as the medical cases show.[79] If,

---

[73] "Causation in Homicide" [1957] Crim.L.R. 429, 436.

[74] (1899) 124 Cal. 551; Sayre, p.189.

[75] Sayre, p.190.

[76] *ibid*. pp.191–192.

[77] [1959] 2 Q.B. 35, *supra*, para. 4.15; *cf. S. v. Mabole*, 1968 (4) S.A. 811 (R.).

[77a] (1899) 124 Col. 551; Sayre, p.189.

[78] *e.g.* Hall, p.266. For a contrary American decision see *State v. Angelina* (1913) 73 W.Va. 146; 80 S.E. 141.

[79] *infra*, paras 4.35 to 4.41. See also *People v. Fowler* (1918) 178 Cal. 657; 174 Pac. 892; Sayre, 183.

then, the law has recourse to B's moral responsibility, it may be proper that it should also consider A's moral responsibility as more important than purely causal considerations, and treat A as having caused death provided he intended to cause death and the injury inflicted by him was still operative at the time of death and could therefore be regarded as having contributed to the death.

Life support machines. In *Finlayson v. H.M. Advocate*,[80] an injection of a controlled drug caused brain death, but the victim's heart was kept going on a life-support machine. Thereafter it was decided that because there had been brain death the machine should be turned off. At the subsequent trial for culpable homicide of the person who had administered the drug, it was argued that death had been caused by the stopping of the machine. It was held that the effects of the injected drug were "a substantial and operating and continuing cause of the death which occurred",[81] that that had not been affected by the decision to turn off the machine, and that (as had been conceded) that decision had been a reasonable one. "It follows accordingly that the act of disconnecting the machine can hardly be described as an extraneous or extrinsic act within the meaning of those words as they were used by Lord Wright in their context. Far less can it be said that [it] was either unforeseeable or unforeseen, and it certainly cannot be said that [it] was an unwarrantable act."[82] No special point was made of the fact that the victim was, in one sense at least, already dead before he was put on the machine.[83] **4.34**

(b) *Subsequent unintentional acts.* Most of the cases in this group are concerned with the problem of *malregimen,* of the effect of negligent medical treatment on the wounds originally inflicted by the assailant, and the general rule is that reasonable medical treatment is considered to have been foreseeable, while grossly improper treatment is regarded as something which interrupts the causal series and so prevents the victim's ultimate condition from being regarded as a consequence of the original injury. **4.35**

THE CREATION OF A NEW INJURY. In the American case of *Purchase v. Seelye*[84] a railway employee was injured through the negligence of his employers. He was taken to hospital where he was operated on by a surgeon who mistook him for another patient, and instead of operating on his wound operated on the other side of his body. The question raised in the case was whether the employee was entitled to damages from his employers for the additional injuries caused by the surgeon. It was held that he was not. The court pointed out: **4.36**

> "The question is whether the act of the [surgeon] in operating by mistake upon the . . . left side was a natural and probable result of

[80] 1979 J.C. 33.

[81] *ibid.*, L.J.-G. Emslie at 35.

[82] *ibid.*, L.J.-G. Emslie at 36. For Lord Wright's words, see the reference to *The Oropesa* in para. 4.31, *supra*.

[83] See also *R. v. Malcherek* [1981] 1 W.L.R. 690; Wilson, Harland and MacLean, "Brain Stem Death" (1978) 23 J.L.S. 433; P.D.G. Skegg, "Termination of Life-Support Measures and the Law of Murder" (1978) 41 M.L.R. 423. *Cf.* the different but related issue in the civil case of *Law Hospital N.H.S. Trust v. The Lord Advocate* 1996 S.C. 301, where it was not settled whether the cause of death would be the deliberate removal of feeding and hydration (classified as treatment since they were artificially supplied) or the original injury — in this case, the taking of an overdose of drugs by the patient herself.

[84] (1918) 231 Mass. 434; 8 A.L.R. 503.

> the negligence of the railroad company . . . The reason why a wrongdoer is held liable for the negligence of such a physician whose unskilful treatment aggravates an injury is that such unskilful treatment is a result which reasonably ought to have been anticipated by him.
>
> The railroad company could not be held liable because of the [surgeon's] mistaken belief . . . The fact that the mistake . . . might possibly occur is not enough to charge the railroad company with liability; the unskilful or improper treatment must have been legally and constructively anticipated by the original wrongdoer as a rational and probable result of the first injury."[85]

Although the court applied the criterion of foreseeability, it should be noted that the additional injuries were not merely unforeseeable but would also have been regarded as breaking the chain of direct causation.

By way of contrast, in the English case of *R. v. Cheshire*,[86] the victim was taken to hospital after he had been shot in the thigh and stomach by the defendant. Surgery was performed, but the victim experienced difficulty in breathing with the result that a tracheotomy had to be carried out. The tracheotomy tube had to be left in place for four weeks. Not long after it was removed, and about two months after he sustained the original injuries, the victim asphyxiated, since his windpipe had narrowed to the point that a very small amount of mucous was sufficient to block it completely. This was a rare but not unknown side effect of the procedure. It went undiagnosed, however, until too late. The argument that this constituted sufficient negligence to break the chain of causation stemming from the original shooting was dealt with as follows by the Court of Appeal:

> "Whilst medical treatment unsuccessfully given to prevent the death of a victim with the care and skill of a competent medical practitioner will not amount to an intervening cause, it does not follow that treatment which falls below that standard of care and skill will amount to such a cause. As Professors Hart and Honoré comment,[87] treatment which falls short of the standard expected of the competent medical practitioner is unfortunately only too frequent in human experience for it to be considered abnormal in the sense of extraordinary. Acts or omissions of a doctor treating the victim for injuries he has received at the hands of a defendant may conceivably be so extraordinary as to be capable of being regarded as acts independent of the conduct of the defendant but it is most unlikely that they will be."[88]

Thus in England, it would be a matter for a jury to decide whether, for example, a mistake leading to the performing of the wrong operation on an injured patient was so extraordinary as to break the causal chain: and a jury should be reminded in such cases that:

> "the defendant's act need not be the sole cause or even the main cause of death it being sufficient that his acts contributed significantly to that result. Even though negligence in the treatment of the

---

[85] 8 A.L.R. 505–506, Crosby J.

[86] [1991] 1 W.L.R. 844.

[87] H.L.A. Hart and T. Honoré, *Causation in the Law* (2nd ed., Oxford, 1985), at pp.355–6.

[88] [1991] 1 W.L.R. 844, *per* Beldam L.J. at 849D–F.

> victim was the immediate cause of his death, the jury should not regard it as excluding the responsibility of the defendant unless the negligent treatment was so independent of his acts, and in itself so potent in causing death, that they regard the contribution made by his acts as insignificant."[89]

In that jurisdiction then, it seems that even the creation and misdiagnosis of a potentially fatal condition (which in fact proves fatal) will not easily be regarded as relieving the assailant of his liability for the result — so long as his original acts can "fairly be said to have made a significant contribution to the victim's death."[90] This appears to represent a hardening of judicial attitude since the case of *R. v. Jordan*[91] was decided, but probably, though not ex facie, again shows an application of the foreseeability criterion. It seems, however, that only the most crass and extraordinary lapse from good medical practice can now be regarded as unforeseeable in English law.[92]

The only Scots case on this point is not altogether conclusive. It is **4.37** *Hugh and Euphemia McMillan*.[93] The accused threw acid at the victim; she received injuries to her face; as part of the medical treatment given her she was subjected to blood-letting, and a cut was made in her arm for that purpose; this cut became inflamed and caused her death. In these circumstances the Lord Advocate dropped the charge of murder, and proceeded on a statutory capital charge of assault by acid-throwing, but in doing so he commented that it might be a nice question whether the accused were guilty of murder since blood-letting was the normal remedy for the deceased's injuries.[94] It remains a nice question. The case seems to have proceeded on the criterion of direct causation; it is likely, however, that if a similar situation were to arise today, it would be decided by way of the criterion of foreseeability in which case, since blood-letting is *ex hypothesi* the normal treatment, and so is to be regarded as foreseeable, the accused would be convicted of homicide.

AGGRAVATION OF THE ORIGINAL INJURY. This is a more difficult **4.38** case, but the approach in Scotland is probably fairly simple, although not altogether logical. The general rule is that negligent treatment is irrelevant, since the accused must "stand the peril of the consequences of his act."[95] Where, however, "it could be clearly proved that the wound would not naturally have led to a mortal issue, and that this result has been produced, not by the wound, but by bad treatment . . . it will be difficult to sustain a charge of murder."[96] A distinction is thus drawn between injuries which are foreseeably fatal, and those which are not. When the wound is foreseeably fatal the law seems to be that

---

89 *ibid.*, 851H–852A.

90 *ibid.*, 852B.

91 (1956) 40 Cr.App.R. 152.

92 See J.E. Stannard, "Criminal Causation and the Careless Doctor" (1992) 55 M.L.R. 577, esp. 582–3.

93 (1827) Syme 288.

94 At 293.

95 *Jas. Wilson* (1838) 2 Swin. 16, Lord Cockburn at 18. See also Hume, i, 184; *Francis Johnstone* (1831) Bell's Notes 69; *cf. Alex. Dingwall* (1867) 5 Irv. 466, Lord Deas at 474.

96 J.S. More, *Lectures on the Law of Scotland* (Edinburgh, 1864), Vol. 2, p.364.

subsequent aggravation is irrelevant; where it is not it may be that the subsequent aggravation will be taken as the cause of death. In *Jas. Williamson*[97] Lord Justice-Clerk Inglis said:

> "If a person receives a wound from the hand of another which is not fatal in itself — it may be a simple and easily cured wound — and then afterwards by unskilful and injudicious treatment this wound assumes a more serious aspect, and finally terminates in death, it is possible to say, and to say with perfect truth, that the wound inflicted by the hand of the prisoner is not the cause of death, because it would not by itself have caused death but for the bad treatment which followed on it. But it will never do, on the other hand, if a wound calculated to prove mortal in itself is afterwards followed by death, to say that every criticism that can be made on the treatment of the patient . . . is to furnish a ground for acquitting the person who inflicted the wound"

4.39 The position was put more grudgingly by Lord Moncreiff in *Heinrich Heidmeisser*[98] where he was not prepared to go further than to say that if improper treatment followed on a wound which was not in itself foreseeably fatal, it did not *necessarily* follow that the wound would be regarded as the cause of death. It appears, therefore, that there may be cases where subsequent maltreatment will not be regarded as the sole cause of death even where the original wound was not in itself mortal.

4.40 There is authority that where the wound is foreseeably fatal, then even if the victim might have recovered had the best attention been available the absence of such attention does not prevent the wound being regarded as the cause of death.[99] Again, where the wound might have been cured by ordinary treatment but no treatment at all was given, the wound is the cause of death.[1]

It does not, however, follow from the above that where a foreseeably fatal injury is followed and aggravated by improper treatment the assailant must always be regarded as having caused the death. There is a difference between the absence of treatment, which means that the injury is left to take its course, or the presence of improper treatment of a kind which fails to prevent the injury taking its course, on the one hand, and on the other hand improper treatment which itself operates on the injury or on the weak condition produced by the injury to aggravate it and so to cause death. In the first case it can be said that death was a direct consequence of the injury, in the second the improper treatment has been added to the causal series, and has in fact altered the "natural" progress of the injury by aggravating its seriousness, so that it becomes necessary to ask if the introduction of this new causal factor is to be regarded as interrupting the series.

It is submitted that the foreseeability of the original injury being fatal is not a sufficient condition for treating it as the cause of death (nor indeed, from the causal point of view, whatever the requirements of morality, is it a necessary condition, a fact which is recognised in the "take your victim as you find him" cases); the wound must be shown to

---

[97] (1866) 5 Irv. 326, 328.
[98] (1879) 17 S.L.R. 266, 267.
[99] *ibid*. See also Hume, i, 184; Alison, i, 149.
[1] *John Macglashan*, Bell's Notes 69; *Margt Shearer* (1851) J. Shaw 468.

have caused death. Suppose A injures two people, X and Y; X's wound is foreseeably fatal, Y's is not. X and Y are both taken to hospital and both die because they both happen to be allergic to a drug they are given as an anaesthetic. Is A guilty of killing X and not Y? This cannot be the case, but it is the result of concentrating on the likelihood of the original wound proving fatal, a concentration which can be explained by the fact that the more likely the original wound was to be fatal, the more likely was serious injury intended, and the more wicked the accused must have been.

The proper causal approach is by way of the foreseeability, not of the original wound proving fatal, but of the subsequent events. Whether or not medical negligence operates as a *novus actus interveniens* should depend on the foreseeability of the particular intervention, of the particular mistake, or at any rate on the foreseeability of an intervention or mistake of that kind. If this approach is adopted it can be said that "death resulting from any normal treatment employed to deal with a felonious injury may be regarded as caused by the felonious injury", but that death resulting from abnormal treatment may be regarded as caused by the treatment.[2] Abnormal treatment is usually grossly improper treatment, but this need not be so. A surgeon may use a new, unusual, experimental treatment without impropriety, but the treatment may be so unusual — and so risky — as to rank as a *novus actus interveniens*. **4.41**

The insistance on impropriety is the result of adopting the view that what the doctor does can operate as a *novus actus interveniens* only if the doctor is to blame for it, so that he can be substituted for the accused as an object of punishment. The question whether the doctor is guilty of homicide and the question whether the doctor's behaviour operates as a *novus actus* are two separate questions. The doctor's behaviour may be the "legal cause" of death, operating on the patient's "static condition," and at the same time it may not be proper to punish the doctor.[3]

OTHER CASES. There is little or no Scots authority on cases not involving medical treatment of the victim. Whether or not A is held responsible for a result despite a subsequent intervention by B depends on the circumstances of the particular case. Generally speaking, the criteria adopted would be those of directness and remoteness, but resort might be had to foreseeability if the result of applying the other criteria would clearly not be in accord with the requirements of moral fitness. In *People v. Fowler*[4] F. struck the deceased on the head and left him lying at the roadside where he was subsequently run over by a vehicle. It was held that as there was no suggestion that the driver of the vehicle had purposely driven over the body his actions did not affect F.'s guilt. Leaving a man on a road is very much like leaving a child exposed to the **4.42**

---

[2] *R. v. Jordan* (1956) 40 Cr.App.R. 152, 157. This case was said in *R. v. Smith* [1959] 2 Q.B. 35, 43, to be "a very particular case depending on its exact facts." See also *R. v. Cheshire* [1991] 1 W.L.R. 844, considered in para. 4.36, *supra*.

[3] Gl. Williams suggests that "any positive act of negligence" of the degree recognised in the civil courts would exclude a charge of homicide against the original assailant and that "gross negligence" is not necessary: Glanville Williams "Causation in Homicide" [1957] Crim.L.R. 429, 513. But the civil standard of negligence applied to doctors is itself a high one: *Hunter v. Hanley*, 1955 S.C. 200. In any event, the opinion in *R. v. Cheshire* [1991] 1 W.L.R. 844, suggests that Williams's view is incorrect.

[4] (1918) 178 Cal. 657; 174 Pac. 892; Sayre, p.183.

elements[5]: the likelihood of further injury whether caused accidentally or negligently is very great, and would be regarded as a risk that an assailant must take as one of the natural and probable consequences of his act.[6] The subsequent act is equivalent to a non-human event, and being foreseeable it is not treated as breaking the causal series.

4.43 On the other hand if the victim is killed while being taken to hospital in an ambulance because of the negligence of the ambulance driver, or of another driver, this would probably be accepted as breaking the causal series although such an occurrence is by no means unforeseeable.[7] The authors of the American Law Institute's proposed Model Penal Code suggest that if A leaves his car keys with someone who is known to him as a "mad driver" and he kills someone with the car, A should be guilty of homicide, and also that if A provokes his victim B to shoot in self-defence and B's shot kills C, A is the cause of C's death[8] but this should not be the case in Scotland.[9] 'Moral fitness' may suggest, however, that the reasoning adopted by the Court of Appeal in *R. v. Pagett*[10] might be preferred in a like case. There the defendant, holding a girl in front of him as a shield, opened fire on armed police officers who were trying to arrest him. They fired back and fatally wounded the girl. The defendant was convicted of the manslaughter of the deceased. In affirming the conviction, the Court of Appeal held that the action of the police in returning fire was an involuntary and reasonable act of self-defence caused by the act of the defendant in firing at them, and also that that action was done in the execution of their duty to apprehend the defendant. On those bases, the action of the police could not "be regarded as a voluntary act independent of the wrongful act of the accused."[11] On neither of those rationales, therefore, could the shots fired by the police be regarded as *novi actus intervenientes*. The opinion of the court there has been subject to criticism, however;[12] and, if not effectively grounded on the foreseeability of the police response, the decision must have been much influenced by the unacceptability in the circumstances of attributing the cause of the victim's death to the police rather than the morally culpable defendant.

4.44 It has been held in a civil case that if A negligently creates a situation of danger and B is injured while trying to prevent injury or damage actually occurring, A is the cause of B's injury if B's rescue operation is a foreseeable result of A's conduct.[13] But it does not follow that the

---

[5] *ibid.*; Sayre, 185, Shaw J.
[6] *cf. Jas. Wilson, supra,* n. 93.
[7] T.B. Smith, p.711. *Cf.* H.L.A. Hart and A.M. Honoré, *Causation in The Law* (2nd ed., Oxford, 1985), pp.77–8, 391.
[8] Model Penal Code, T.D. 1, 17. But see now *Cmwth v. Redline*, 391 Pa. 486, 137 A.2d 472 (1958) holding a robber not guilty of the death of his fellow-robber justifiably killed by an arresting policeman. *Cf.* H.L.A. Hart and Tony Honoré, *Causation in the Law* (2nd ed., Oxford 1985), at pp.330–333.
[9] *cf.* G.O.W. Mueller, "Causing Criminal Harm" in *Essays in Criminal Science*, Mueller (ed.) (N.Y. and London, 1961), pp.169, 178.
[10] (1983) 76 Cr.App.R. 279.
[11] *ibid., per* Goff L.J. at 290. It seems that the Court of Appeal would have applied the view it reached on causation even if the defendant had done no more than use the girl as a shield and had not himself shot at the police — provided that the subsequent conduct of the police was within the reasonable execution of their duty.
[12] See A. Ashworth, *Principles of Criminal Law* (3rd ed., Oxford, 1999), at pp.130–131.
[13] *Steel v. Glasgow Iron and Steel Co.*, 1944 S.C. 237, see *infra*, para. 4.52.

criminal law would take the same view, particularly if the intervention was by a third party and not the victim.

(c) *Subsequent events.* (i) DISEASE. The reported Scots cases on subsequent events concern the incidence of disease supervening on an injury. The basic criterion is that of direct causation, allied to the idea of remoteness. So Hume says that if "A person of a weakly habit receives a wound, of which, after some space of time, he is cured; but owing to the long confinement, he is taken ill of a consumption, or some other malady incident to such a state of weakness; and of this he dies", the assailant is not responsible for the death, since "Inferences of this kind are far too remote, and too uncertain, to serve as the grounds of judgment in human tribunals."[14] **4.45**

At the other extreme is the case of *Heinrich Heidmeisser.*[15] There the victim was in hospital recovering from a wound inflicted by the accused. He died of a chill caught when "He had been brought through the danger, and nothing more was required but ordinary skill and care, — but he had not recovered, and if a chill was sufficient to carry him off, as in point of fact it seems to have done, the man who put his fellow-man in a position where a chill would carry him off is responsible."[16] Now, although the deceased had not entirely recovered from his wound, the general tenor of the case seems to conflict with Hume's statement of the law. And the *ratio* of the case — that the accused put the deceased into a position in which a chill might carry him off — is capable of much wider application. Indeed, it is very like the unsatisfactory criterion of the *causa sine qua non.*[17] If Heidmeisser's victim had caught a disease which might have been fatal to a healthy man and which was endemic in the hospital in which he was recovering from his wound it could still have been said that Heidmeisser had "put him in a position" where this disease would carry him off. **4.46**

It is submitted that *Heidmeisser*[17a] is wrong, and that the proper criterion is that of directness, subject to an exception in the case of direct consequences which appear too remote to make it reasonable to attribute them to the accused's act. The law is probably contained in Lord Cockburn's summing-up in *Jas. Wilson.*[18] In that case the wound developed into lockjaw, and the victim then contracted erysipelas, but there was dispute as to whether he had caught erysipelas from a patient in the bed next to him or whether it was a direct complication of his original injury. Lord Cockburn directed the jury, that provided the disease was "not altogether new, but a natural consequence of the injury" the injury was the cause of death: if, on the other hand, "the disease was an entirely new disease — not produced by the wounds, but **4.47**

---

[14] Hume, i, 182. Hume also quotes a case in which the accused broke into a house in order to beat the owner, and their "roaring and raging" caused his wife, who was in childbed, to contract a fever of which she died, and in which a charge of murder was held to be irrelevant: *Duff of Braco* (1707) Hume, i, 182; see also *Patrick Kinninmonth* (1697) *ibid.*, p.183.

[15] (1879) 17 S.L.R. 266.

[16] L.J.-C. Moncreiff at 267.

[17] *cf. supra*, para. 4.04.

[17a] (1879) 17 S.L.R. 266.

[18] (1838) 2 Swin. 16, 19.

by infection, or some other external cause" death was caused by the infection and not by the wound.[19]

4.48 (ii) OTHER EVENTS. There is very little Scots authority on this. Where the subsequent event is foreseeable and the whole course of events follows naturally on A's actings, A is treated as having caused the ultimate *actus reus*. So, for example, if the victim is exposed to the elements and dies of cold, or even from the effects of a storm of rain, the person who exposed him has caused his death. If he is exposed in winter and is buried in a snowstorm or an avalanche, the position will be the same, but if the snowstorm occurred in summer on low ground it might be treated as sufficiently exceptional to break the causal series. Again, if the victim is left with a dangerous lunatic or animal the person who left him will be treated as having caused any injuries inflicted by the lunatic or animal.[20]

But where the subsequent event is not reasonably foreseeable, and perhaps even where although foreseeable it is overwhelming in its effect, it breaks the series. If A "intending to kill his victim, poisoned his food and the victim, while on the way to hospital for treatment, was struck by a falling tree and died, [A] would not presumably be convicted of murder although he intended the victim's death and it would not have occurred but for his act."[21] In such cases, the law is concerned with what in fact happened and not with what might have happened, and in fact A did not kill the victim.[22]

4.49 (d) *Acts of the victim.* In this branch of the problem, more than in any other, the idea of responsibility takes precedence over concepts of causality. If it appears fair to say that the victim had only himself to blame, his death or other eventual injury will probably not be attributed to the original assailant: while if his subsequent acts appear excusable, or excite sympathy, or have been "induced" by the original injury, the courts will often exert themselves to avoid treating them as *novi actus.*

In the civil case of *McKew v. Holland and Hannen and Cubbitts (Scotland) Ltd*,[23] Lord Reid said:

> "But if the injured man acts unreasonably, he cannot hold the defender liable for injury caused by his own unreasonable conduct. His unreasonable conduct is *novus actus interveniens*. The chain of causation has been broken and what follows must be regarded as caused by his own conduct and not by the defender's fault or the disability caused by it. Or one may say that unreasonable conduct of the pursuer and what follows from it is not the natural and probable

---

[19] See also *Mary Wilkie or Finlay* (1836) 1 Swin. 179; *J. Campbell* (1819) Alison, i, 147; Macdonald, p.88, n.7. Cases where a wound results directly in a disease or leads to a general weakness are cases in which the wound keeps "a regular progression from bad to worse", Hume, i, 185, and there is no difficulty in treating the original injury as the cause of whatever develops. See *e.g. John Jones and Edward Malone* (1840) 2 Swin. 509; *Carl Johan Peterson and Anr* (1874) 2 Couper 557; *Jas. Stewart* (1858) 3 Irv. 206; *A. McKenzie* (1827) Syme 158; *Chas Rae* (1888) 2 White 62.

[20] Hume, i, 190; *Geo. Fay* (1847) Ark. 397.

[21] H.L.A. Hart and A.M. Honoré, "Causation in the Law" (1956) 72 L.Q.R. 58, 404. *Cf.* the book of the same name by the same authors (2nd ed., Oxford, 1985), pp.77–8; 391; D. 9.2.15 (1); T.B. Smith, p.711.

[22] *cf.* Hall, p.266.

[23] 1970 S.C. (H.L.) 20, 25.

> result of the original fault of the defender or of the ensuing disability. I do not think that foreseeability comes into this. A defender is not liable for a consequence of a kind which is not foreseeable. But it does not follow that he is liable for every consequence which a reasonable man could foresee. What can be foreseen depends almost entirely on the facts of the case, and it is often easy to foresee unreasonable conduct or some other *novus actus interveniens* as being quite likely. But that does not mean that the defender must pay for damage caused by the *novus actus*. It only leads to trouble if one tries to graft on to the concept of foreseeability some rule of law to the effect that a wrongdoer is not bound to foresee something which in fact he could readily foresee as quite likely to happen. For it is not at all unlikely or unforeseeable that an active man who has suffered such a disability will take some quite unreasonable risk. But if he does, he cannot hold the defender liable for the consequences."

There may, however, be cases of "unreasonable" behaviour such as suicide, for which the original wrongdoer is responsible.[24]

(i) IMPRUDENT TREATMENT OF THE INJURY. As Hume says, "If a person receive some slight injury, in itself nowise dangerous or difficult to be cured, but which, owing to his obstinacy and intemperance, or to rash and hurtful applications, degenerates in the end into a mortal sore", he is regarded as having "killed himself".[25] **4.50**

In *Jos. and Mary Norris*[26] the wound was trivial, but the victim went drinking, exposed himself to the cold, and took off his bandages, so that he contracted tetanus and died. Lord Craighill told the jury that the question for them to consider was whether the tetanus would have developed whether or not the victim had behaved as imprudently as he did.[27] These cases are perhaps comparable to cases where improper treatment makes a trivial wound fatal, but the reference to "obstinacy and intemperance" suggests that the courts were influenced by the generally unfavourable view which the law takes of alcoholic indulgence.

There may also be cases even where the wound is foreseeably fatal in which the victim's own behaviour will be regarded as the cause of death. To take an extreme example, if a spiteful victim deliberately disobeyed his doctor in order to ensure the conviction of his assailant for murder, this would surely rank as the cause of death, rather than the original injury. If, however, the victim refused medical care on conscientious grounds, or out of inertia, the assailant would probably be liable for whatever injury resulted from his original attack. In one case, *Daniel Houston*,[28] the court expressed doubts whether the rejection of medical advice was on a different footing from improper treatment, but the point was left undecided.

Conversely, there may be cases in which the victim's conduct, though imprudent, would not operate as a *novus actus*. If A inflicts an injury on

---

[24] *infra*, para. 4.53.

[25] Hume, i, 182.

[26] (1886) 1 White 292.

[27] At 295. See also *Christian Paterson* (1823) Alison, i. 147; and *Jas. Finn and Margt Brennan* (1848) J. Shaw 9. In both cases the victim was struck on the head and then drank whisky and died, and the Crown dropped the charge of homicide.

[28] (1833) Bell's Notes 70.

B which induces a strong thirst in B and at the same time makes it dangerous for him to drink, and both results are foreseeable, B's conduct in drinking, even although done in the knowledge of the danger involved and so showing a lack of self-control, would not constitute a *novus actus. A fortiori*, if B was unaware of the danger and drank only water or other innocuous liquids, or even perhaps drank alcohol temperately, this would not be a *novus actus* but only part of the normal course of events for which A would have to take responsibility.

4.51 In *R. v. Blaue,*[29] it was held that the refusal by a Jehova's Witness to have a blood transfusion did not operate as a *novus actus*, on the rather unusual ground that the rule that an assailant takes his victim as he finds him extends to the whole man and not merely to his physical condition. It was held that it did not lie in the assailant's mouth to say that the victim's religious beliefs were unreasonable.

4.52 (ii) RESCUE CASES. In *Steel v. Glasgow Iron and Steel Co.*[30] the defenders negligently allowed one of their wagons to run down a slope; B, an employee, saw the wagon and tried to stop it; in doing so he was injured. He sued the defenders who pleaded that his intervention constituted a *novus actus*, but the court held that his action was foreseeable and that his injuries had been caused by the defenders' negligence.[31] Similarly, in *Haynes v. Harwood*[32] a policeman who rushed out of a police station in an endeavour to stop a runaway horse van in the street outside and was injured by the van recovered damages from the person responsible for the horse bolting. There are no reported Scots criminal cases of this kind, but a similar decision might be arrived at in a criminal case if the conduct of the victim was foreseeable and commendable, and was "induced" or "inspired" by a blameworthy act of the accused, although it would probably be only in very special and extreme circumstances that this course would be adopted.[33]

---

[29] [1975] 1 W.L.R. 1411.

[30] 1944 S.C. 237.

[31] See also *Malcolm v. Dickson*, 1951 S.C. 542; *Macdonald v. David Macbrayne Ltd,* 1915 S.C. 716.

[32] [1935] 1 K.B. 146.

[33] In the American case of *State v. Glover* (1932) 330 Mo. 709, 50 S.W. 2d 1049; Hall and Gluek, p.61, a man who set fire to his property in order to defraud insurers was held to have caused the death of a fireman who was killed while trying to put out the fire. The reaction of the victim to an emergency created by A may or may not break the link between A and the injury; *Devine v. Colvilles Ltd*, 1969 S.C. (H.L.) 67, Lord Avonside at 79; *McCann v. J.R. McKellar (Alloys) Ltd*, 1968 S.C. 174. *Cf. Cmwth v. Rhoades*, 401 N.E.2d 342 (1980), where the Supreme Court of Massachusetts reversed the conviction of a fire-raiser for the second degree murder of a fireman who had responded to the fire-alarm — but on the basis that the trial judge had directed that any contributory link no matter how remote between the defendant's acts and the fatality would suffice: more than that was required, namely that the defendant's acts must be found to be the proximate or efficient cause of the fatality, which would have been a possible inference in the circumstances had the jury been properly directed (see Kaplan J. and Weisberg R., *Criminal Law: Cases and Materials*, Boston, 1986, at p.483). At Exeter Crown Court on June 13, 1997, Martin Cody was convicted of the manslaughter of a firefighter, Fleur Lombard, who had died whilst checking for trapped persons in a store which Cody had deliberately set on fire, which suggests at least that causal problems are not insurmountable (see The *Scotsman*, June 14, 1997). Thus, in *Sutherland v. H.M. Advocate (No. 1),* 1994 S.C.C.R. 80, had a member of the emergency services been killed in a search for the accused's trapped companion in crime, the accused might well have been convicted of the culpable homicide of that person in addition to the homicide of his said companion.

4.53 (iii) INDUCED SUICIDE. Difficult problems arise where the victim causes his own death under stress of a situation caused by A's wrongful act. Strictly speaking the suicide, so long as it is voluntary and occurs while the victim is not rendered irresponsible from insanity or coercion, is a voluntary act and constitutes a *novus actus*. Where A merely encourages B to commit suicide there can be little doubt that A is not the cause of death.[34]

In *People v. Lewis*[35] it was accepted that where B committed suicide after being mortally wounded by A, A was guilty of murder although B was also guilty of suicide.

Another American case in which suicide was not treated as a *novus actus* is *Stephenson v. State*.[36] In that case the accused captured and raped a girl, and in doing so inflicted a wound on her breast. The wound caused an abscess and the girl took poison a few days after the rape while still a captive and with the intention of killing herself. The poison itself would not have caused death but it did so in combination with a complication of the abscess which itself had partly healed at the time the poison was taken. The appeal court upheld the accused's conviction of homicide, holding that the abscess had actively contributed to death, that the suicide was not a responsible act, and that in any event the girl was compelled to commit suicide to escape the accused's violence. As was pointed out in a note in the *Michigan Law Review*[37] none of these grounds was sufficient according to the letter of the law — the abscess was not foreseeably fatal, there was no precedent for treating the suicide, on the evidence adduced, as involuntary or irresponsible, and the evidence showed that the girl took the poison not to escape violence but to escape shame. The accused was convicted because "Assuming that his act has caused a death in fact, its punishability as a homicide should be determined, not so much by the more or less fortuitous course of events subsequent to the acting, as by the social menace of the act and the viciousness of the actor's intent."[38]

It was said in *Ex p. Minister of Justice, Re S. v. Grotjohn*[39] that whether or not there is homicide is a question of fact. The court declined to approve a general doctrine that a final voluntary act by the victim would always lead to the acquittal of the accused "without some reservation in

---

[34] *cf. R. v. Nbakwa*, 1956 (2) S.A. 557 (S.R.) in which the accused provided the victim with the means for killing herself and to some extent persuaded her to do so, but she herself put her head in the noose and kicked away the block supporting her, and it was held that the most the accused had done was to incite her to commit suicide, which was not criminal since suicide was not a crime. The earlier case of *R. v. Peverett*, 1940 A.D. 213 where the accused and the deceased sat in a closed car and the accused who started the engine was convicted of attempted murder, can be distinguished on the ground that the starting of the engine was there the final act preceding the intended fatal result: see *S. v. Gordon*, 1962 (4) S.A. 727 (N.P.D.).

[35] *supra*, para. 4.33.

[36] (1933) 205 Ind. 141; 179 N.E. 633; see G.C.T., "A Note on *Stephenson v. State*" (1932–33) 31 Mich.L.R. 659.

[37] *supra*.

[38] 31 Mich.L.R. at 663. Hall treats *Stephenson* as an example of a general principle of "causation by motivation", Hall, pp.273–274, but there is no ground for accepting any such general principle in Scots law. If the Scots courts were faced by a situation like *Stephenson* they would doubtless approach it in the same theoretically unsatisfactory way as did the court in Indiana, but it is unlikely that the Crown would bring a charge of homicide in such circumstances: they would charge rape and assault and expect the subsequent events to be reflected in the sentence.

[39] 1970 (2) S.A. 355 (A.D.).

regard to the independence of the act". Where the two acts were not totally unconnected, and especially where the result was an eventuality which the perpetrator foresaw as a possibility which he wanted to employ to attain his object (the death of the suicide), or as something on which he could depend to bring about the desired result, "it would be contrary to accepted principles of law and to all sense of justice to allow him to take shelter behind the act as a *novus actus interveniens*." In *Grotjohn* the accused had had a row with his wife who threatened to shoot herself, whereupon he had loaded a rifle and given it to her, saying, "Shoot yourself if you want to, because you're a nuisance", and had been acquitted. The Minister of Justice then referred the case to the court.

In *S. v. Hibbert*,[40] the facts were much the same, and the accused was convicted on the ground that he must have appreciated the possibility of serious injury and death, and therefore had the necessary intention to murder, and so was reckless as to the consequences of his conduct. Shearer J. said, "the act of pulling the trigger to which all the other conduct conduced, cannot in any sense be described as independent of the course of conduct", so that there was no *novus actus*.[41]

4.54 The only reported Scots case in which the problem was raised is *John Robertson*[42] where the charge was one of assault, and the indictment concluded by narrating that the victim, having been terrified by the violence used towards her, drowned herself. This part of the indictment was held to be irrelevant since it was not covered by the charge of assault and was not libeled as an aggravation. Lord Handyside reserved his opinion on whether it would have been a competent aggravation, and also said, "If the act of suicide was the immediate consequence of the violence, I am not prepared to say what such a state of facts might warrant. I do not say that it would amount to culpable homicide, although it would certainly come very near to it."[43] *Patrick Slaven and Ors*[44] is rather different. There the accused assaulted a woman with intent to ravish her, and when she tried to escape they ran after her, and she fell over a cliff and died. In that case there was no question of any suicidal intent on the part of the victim, nor can her fall be treated as voluntary: to chase someone over a cliff is only a more subtle way of pushing her over, and there can be little doubt that Lord Young was correct in summarily dismissing the objection to the relevance of the charge by saying that death was a consequence of the violent conduct of the accused.

4.55 In the English civil case of *Pigney v. Pointers Transport Services Ltd*[45] a man who sustained a head injury in an accident developed an anxiety neurosis and committed suicide eighteen months later. Pilcher J. held that he was not insane but, applying the now discredited *Polemis*[46] rule,

---

[40] 1979 (4) S.A. 717 (D. and C.L.D.).

[41] For discussion of a number of relevant situations, see D.J. Lanham, "Murder by Instigating Suicide" [1980] Crim. L.R. 215.

[42] (1854) 1 Irv. 469.

[43] *ibid.* at 470.

[44] (1885) 5 Couper 694.

[45] [1957] 1 W.L.R. 1121.

[46] *Re Polemis and Furness, Withy and Co. Ltd.* [1921] 3 K.B. 560.

found that the suicide was the result of the accident, although it was unforeseeable. This decision would not be followed by a criminal court, quite apart from any question of *Polemis.*[47]

Omissions

There is very little authority on the position of omissions as causal factors. In *Isabella Martin*[48] the accused was charged with culpable homicide by failing to obtain assistance at the birth of her child. Lord Justice-Clerk Moncreiff told the jury that in order to convict they must be satisfied that: **4.56**

> "If the panel had obtained assistance at its birth it would have lived. Not merely that it would, on that account, have had a chance of survivance; but that the neglect on the part of the panel to call for assistance at its birth was the direct cause of its death.
>
> . . . that but for the panel's neglect her child must have lived".[49]

In the English case of *R. v. Morby*[50] a father was charged with manslaughter by failing to provide proper medical aid for his child. There was evidence that a doctor might have saved or prolonged life and would have increased the chances of recovery, but that on the other hand his efforts might have been of no avail. In these circumstances the father's conviction was quashed on appeal, and it was held that the Crown could not succeed unless they showed that the father's behaviour had caused or accelerated death. The position probably is that a result is not caused by an omission unless it can be shown that but for the omission the result would have been different. This recourse to "but for" causation is not very satisfactory but it is probably the best that can be done.

---

[47] See also *Cowan and Ors v. National Coal Board*, 1958 S.L.T. (Notes) 19. The "rule in *Polemis*" of responsibility for all direct consequences was overruled in effect in *The Wagon Mound* [1961] A.C. 388.

[48] (1877) 3 Couper 379.

[49] At 381.

[50] (1882) 8 Q.B.D. 571.

CHAPTER 5

ART AND PART

THE BASIS AND SCOPE OF ART AND PART GUILT

It is a basic principle of Scots law that all persons who are concerned in the commission of a crime are equally guilty and that each is responsible for the whole of the ultimate *actus reus*, whatever his own part in the criminal conduct: the subordinate nature of the participation of any one of the persons involved is irrelevant to the question of his guilt, although it may, of course, influence his sentence.[1] The general position is well illustrated in a summing-up by Lord Patrick in a case where a number of persons were charged with organising and carrying out a bank robbery. Lord Patrick said: **5.01**

> "[I]f a number of men form a common plan whereby some are to commit the actual seizure of the property, and some according to the plan are to keep watch, and some according to the plan are to help to carry away the loot, and some according to the plan are to help to dispose of the loot, then, although the actual robbery may only have been committed by one or two of them, every one is guilty of the robbery, because they joined together in a common plan to commit the robbery. But such responsibility for the acts of others under the criminal law only arises if it has been proved affirmatively . . . that there was such a common plan and that the accused were parties to that common plan. If it has not been proved that there was such a common plan, or if it has not been proved that the accused were parties to this previously conceived common plan, then in law each is only responsible for what he himself did, and bears no responsibility whatever for what any of the other accused or any other person actually did."[2]

Normally, a man is responsible only for his own actings, but a group is responsible for the actings of the group, and therefore each member of the group is responsible for the acts of all the other members, excluding acts done before his accession to the plot.[3] The group is defined by

---

[1] Macdonald, p.2; Hume, ii, 181, 225, 441. Although not as close to the Scottish position as once might have been the case, South African Law still provides some useful comparative material: see J. Burchell and J. Milton, *Principles of Criminal Law* (2nd ed., Cape Town, 1997), Chap. 44. For a comprehensive account of the theory and (English) practice relating to this method of acquiring criminal liability, see K.J.M. Smith, *A Modern Treatise on the Law of Criminal Complicity* (Oxford, 1991).

[2] *H.M. Advocate v. Lappen*, 1956 S.L.T. 109, 110.

[3] *McLaughlan v. H.M. Advocate,* 1991 S.C.C.R. 733. *Cf. Kabula v. H.M. Advocate*, 1999 S.C.C.R. 348, where the Appeal Court proceeded on the assumption that a person who joins in an assault after he witnessed (or must have witnessed) the degree of violence which caused the victim's death may be held to have accepted that degree of violence and thus be guilty of murder; but it was conceded in that case that the appellant had been a party to a prior plan to assault, though not to kill, the victim.

reference to its common purpose, and so each member of the group is responsible for what any of them does in furtherance of that common purpose.

Art and part guilt requires involvement in a specific crime, of which each plotter is guilty. It may be, however, that where A is a member of a gang and is sent out to do "a job" without being told specifically what that job involves, he will be guilty of whatever crime is actually committed, provided it is within the range of activities which could reasonably be expected to be carried out by the gang in the circumstances. So, where a terrorist assists in an attack on a target without knowing whether guns or explosives are to be used and in fact explosives are used, he may be guilty art and part of possessing and using explosives, although his own involvement was only to guide the bombers to the scene of the crime and he drove off without seeing any explosives.[4]

5.02 *Where A cannot be guilty as principal.* This principle applies even where it is impossible for a particular accused to have committed the crime himself. Thus, for example, a person who is not himself related to the parties may be art and part guilty of incest.[5] In a similar way a woman who assists a man to rape another woman is guilty of rape.[6] Hume defines bigamy as "the contracting of a second marriage during the subsistence of a former",[7] but has no doubt that the other party to the marriage is guilty even if himself or herself unmarried, as also are any witnesses, officiants or other persons who assist in the crime, provided, of course, that they knew that one of the parties was already married.[8] A person who is not bankrupt can be guilty of concealment by assisting a bankrupt to cheat his creditors,[9] and a person who is not in a position of trust can be guilty of breach of trust by assisting the entrusted party.[10] It may also be the law that a person can be guilty of perjury in respect of evidence given by another, although the more usual charge would be of conspiracy or of subornation of perjury.[11]

---

[4] See *R. v. Maxwell* [1978] 1 W.L.R. 1350.

[5] See *Vaughan v. H.M. Advocate*, 1979 S.L.T. 49.

[6] *Chas Matthews and Margaret Galbraith*, High Court at Glasgow, Dec. 1910, unrep'd; *Walker and McPherson*, High Court at Dundee, March 1976, unrep'd. Both cases are referred to in the Scottish Law Commission's Report on "Art and Part Guilt of Statutory Offences", Cmnd. 9551 (1985), para 15, fn. 2. The same rule applies in statutory offences: see the Criminal Procedure (Scotland) Act 1995, s.293(1), and *Reid v. H.M. Advocate*, 1999 S.C.C.R. 19 (where it was held that a woman might be guilty art and part of a contravention of s.11(1)(a) of the Criminal Law (Consolidation) (Scotland) Act 1995, *viz.*: "Every male person who knowingly lives wholly or partly on the earnings of prostitution . . . shall be [guilty of an offence]").

[7] Hume, i, 459.

[8] Hume, i, 462. See *Bell and Falconer* (1832) Bell's Notes, 113; *Catherine Potter and David Inglis* (1852) 1 Irv. 73. If bigamy is defined as contracting a bigamous marriage this particular issue does not arise at all since there is no difficulty in saying that the other party assists in the contracting of the marriage.

[9] *Richd F. Dick and Alex. Lawrie* (1832) 4 S.J. 594; *Robt and John Moir* (1842) 1 Broun 448.

[10] *Robt Smith and Jas. Wishart* (1842) 1 Broun 134. There is even a case in which a man was charged with being art and part in the forgery of his own signature, but its circumstances were very special: *Wm Duncan and Alex. Cumming* (1850) J. Shaw 334; see Vol. II, Chap. 18.

[11] *cf. Marr and Ors v. Stuart* (1881) 4 Couper 407 where, however, all the accused had given evidence, and were charged together with conspiracy and perjury and convicted of perjury. See also *Bole and Ors v. Stevenson* (1883) 5 Couper 350.

Innocent Accomplices. A may be convicted of an offence actually, *i.e.* physically, committed by B, even if B is acquitted of the offence for lack of *mens rea*, or because of some excuse personal to him, such as non-age or insanity. It is murder for A to employ a lunatic or a child to kill B, or to employ a postman to deliver a bomb to him. A is also guilty where he coerces B into committing the offence in circumstances in which B is entitled to an acquittal on the ground of coercion,[12] or where he induces B to believe that the circumstances are such that no offence is being committed. If A and B are charged with raping A's wife, and B (who was the only one of the two to have intercourse with her) is acquitted because he believed that the wife was a consenting party, A is nevertheless guilty of rape (assuming, of course, that he knew that in fact there was no consent).[13] In one such case it was said: **5.03**

> "Her ravishment had come about because Leak had wanted it to happen and had taken action to see that it did by persuading Cogan to use his body as the instrument for the necessary physical act. In the language of the law the act of sexual intercourse without the wife's consent was the actus reus: it had been procured by Leak who had the appropriate mens rea, namely, his intention that Cogan should have sexual intercourse with her without her consent. In our judgment it is irrelevant that the man whom Leak had procured to do the physical act himself did not intend to have sexual intercourse with the wife without her consent. Leak was using him as a means to procure a criminal purpose.[14]

It has also been held in England that to "lace" someone's drink in the knowledge that he is about to drive may amount to procuring his commission of the offence of driving with an excess of alcohol in his blood.[15]

---

[12] *R. v. Bourne* (1952) 36 Cr.App.R. 125; *cf. D.P.P. v. Lynch* [1975] A.C. 653.

[13] *R. v. D.* 1969 (2) S.A. 591 (R., A.D.); *R. v. Cogan* [1976] Q.B. 217; *cf. R. v. Morgan* [1976] A.C. 182.

[14] *R. v. Cogan, supra,* Lawton L.J. at 223 C-D. *Cf.* the criticism of Leak's conviction for rape in J.C. Smith and B. Hogan, *Criminal Law* (9th ed., 1999, Sir John Smith (ed.)), pp.153–154, based on the view that the husband (Leak) could not have been guilty as a principal, since he was not charged as having had any *relevant* sexual intercourse with his wife on the occasion in question (the law of England at that time being that a husband could not be guilty of raping his wife by any act of personal sexual intercourse with her; see now *R. v. R.* [1992] 1 A.C. 599; *SW v. U.K.; CR v. U.K.*, 1996 21 E.H.R.R. 363), nor as an accessory (based on the English concept of derivative liability), since Cogan's belief in consent negatived (in their view) any suggestion that Leak's wife had been "raped" in law: their opinion is that Leak had been guilty of procuring the *actus reus* of the offence, and that this had thus been recognised as a new crime in its own right. See Law Commission, Consultation Paper No. 131 (1993) "Assisting and Encouraging Crime", paras 2.43 to 2.44; *R. v. Millward* [1994] Crim. L.R. 527; *R. v. Wheelhouse* [1994] Crim. L.R. 756; *D.P.P. v. K. & B.* [1997] 1 Crim. App.R. 36; *cf. R. v. Loukes* [1976] R.T.R. 164, where it was held that a procurer cannot be guilty of a strict liability offence where the person procured had not committed the *actus reus* of the offence — see in particular the opinion of Auld L.J. at 172 J-K.

[15] *Attorney-General's Reference (No. 1 of 1975)* [1975] Q.B. 773. The offence here is one not requiring *mens rea*, but even if it did require *mens rea* and the driver was acquitted — *cf. R. v. King* [1962] S.C.R. 747 — there could, on the authority of *R. v. Cogan, supra*, be a conviction of the procurer.

5.04 The matter has been somewhat complicated in England by the distinction between principals and accessories, which leads to a distinction between acting as principal through an innocent agent, and abetting or procuring the commission of an offence by such an agent.[16]

The distinction creates a problem only if it is held that A cannot be guilty of procuring the commission of an offence by an innocent party[17] and cannot himself be guilty as a principal of *e.g.* a driving offence unless he is actually driving.[18] It has, however, been held that the husband who engineers the rape of his wife by an innocent third party may be convicted either of rape or of procuring the third party to commit rape, the distinction being regarded as a technicality.[19] And if someone who is not having intercourse can be guilty of rape it is difficult to see why someone who is not driving cannot be guilty of a driving offence[20]: but the matter in English law is in fact far from being settled or conceptually clear.[21] Modern Scots law has never distinguished between principals and accessories, nor has it any statutory definition of what constitutes common law guilt art and part: in particular the common law does not know any offence of procuring the commission of a completed offence.[22] It is, however, inconceivable that conduct as wicked as that exhibited in the situations discussed above should not be punishable at Scots common law, and in the absence of any separate offence of procuring, the only solution is to convict A of the full offence whether the "actual" offender's acquittal is due to lack of *mens rea* or to some excuse such as coercion: Scots law does not distinguish between parties to an offence, and therefore does not distinguish between persons who use innocent agents and persons who use guilty agents, nor between agents who lack *mens rea* and agents who are acquitted on some other ground such as coercion.

5.05 *Victims, etc.* Although there is no express decision on the matter, it cannot be doubted that the unwilling victim of a crime is not art and part guilty. For example, a person who pays ransom or blackmail is not guilty of kidnapping or extortion.[23]

The position is more difficult where the "victim" is a fully consenting party. So far as sexual offences are concerned the law probably is that where an offence is created in order to protect a particular class of persons a member of that class cannot be convicted of being art and part in its commission against herself. So a girl of fifteen who allows an older man to have intercourse with her is not guilty of a contravention of the Criminal Law (Consolidation) (Scotland) Act 1995,[24] and the same is

---

[16] See J.C. Smith and B. Hogan, *Criminal Law* (9th ed., 1999, Sir John Smith (ed.)), pp.123–124 and 153–154; Law Commission, Consultation Paper No. 131 (1993), "Assisting and Encouraging Crime", paras. 1.15 to 1.18.

[17] *R. v. Curr* [1968] 2 Q.B. 944.

[18] See *Thornton v. Mitchell* [1940] 1 All E.R. 339; *R. v. Loukes* [1996] R.T.R. 164; Law Commission Consultation Paper No. 131 (1993), "Assisting and Encouraging Crime", para 2.42.

[19] *R. v. Cogan, supra.*

[20] But see *infra*, para. 5.12.

[21] See Law Commission Consultation Paper No. 131 (1993), "Assisting and Encouraging Crime", paras 2.39 to 2.46; English Draft Code, cl.26 (1)(c) and (3)(a), (b).

[22] For the offence of incitement, see *infra*, paras 6.71 *et seq.*

[23] *cf.* Model Penal Code, T.D.1, 35, s.2.04 (5) (*a*); B. Hogan, "Victims as Parties to Crime" [1962] Crim.L.R. 683.

[24] Section 5(3), as amended by the Crime and Punishment (Scotland) Act 1997, s.14(1)(b). See also the English Draft Code, cl.27(2). *Cf. R.v. Tyrrell* [1894] 1 Q.B. 710; *R. v. Whitehouse* [1977] Q.B. 868.

probably the case where the girl herself instigates the offence by seducing the man, or even where a younger boy has intercourse with a girl under sixteen.[25] At common law the girl who is a party to an act of lewd conduct is not art and part in the offence, and the same may be true of a boy under or about the age of puberty in respect of whom an older man is charged with lewd practices.[26] But if a man is charged with committing sodomy with a consenting boy under the age of puberty the boy is probably art and part guilty (although he would not in practice be prosecuted), perhaps because common law sodomy can be committed by or "against" a male of any age. Under the Criminal Law (Consolidation) (Scotland) Act 1995, however, it is not possible to convict of sodomy (or gross indecency or shameless indecency)[27] if the parties to the act are at least eighteen years of age, and certain other conditions are met.[28] As it is a specific offence under the Act "to commit or to be party to the commission of, or to procure or attempt to procure the commission of a homosexual act with a person under the age of eighteen years",[29] it may be argued plausibly either for or against Parliament's having intended to protect the class of young males under that age. There are uncertainties, therefore. There are also paradoxical situations: if A is charged with incest[30] with a young person his partner is art and part guilty, but if the charge is laid as one of lewd practices or a contravention of the current legislation relating to girls[31] the partner is not guilty, although the facts are the same in each case. In practice where only one party is under age he or she will not be charged, but the question of his or her art and part guilt may still be of some importance at the trial of the older man in relation to the credibility[32] of the evidence tendered.[33]

Where Parliament provides expressly that one party to a transaction shall be guilty of an offence, it is at least a general rule that the other party cannot be guilty art and part merely because he is the other party. If, therefore, it is an offence to sell drugs, or show obscene pictures, or keep a brothel, the buyer or viewer or client is not art and part guilty if his involvement is limited to buying, viewing or using the facilities offered.[34] This is presumably because the specific penalisation of *e.g.* **5.06**

---

[25] Although she might conceivably be guilty of a common law crime of shameless indecency. The American Supreme Court has pointed to a distinction between the woman who merely consents and the woman who initiates the offence, but that was in relation to adult women in charges under the Mann Act and no such distinction is made under the Criminal Law (Consolidation) (Scotland) Act 1995; see *Gebardi v. U.S.*, 287 U.S. 112 (1932); *U.S. v. Holte*, 236 U.S. 140 (1914); *R. v. Tyrrell, supra.*

[26] But see Macdonald, p.150.

[27] All of these are referred to as homosexual acts under s.13(4) of the Act.

[28] See s.13(1).

[29] See s.13(5)(c).

[30] See the Criminal Law (Consolidation) (Scotland) Act 1995, s.1.

[31] *ibid.*, ss.5, 6.

[32] This issue is of no higher importance than that, however. Automatic *cum nota* warnings as to the evidence of a *socius criminis* were discarded following the decision in *Docherty v. H.M. Advocate,* 1987 J.C. 81.

[33] The problem narrated in the text does not arise in abortion which is a crime not against the mother but against the child, or perhaps just against religion, morals or society, and the mother is always guilty.

[34] *cf.* L.C.W.P. No. 43, "Codification of the Criminal Law: General Principles: Parties, Complicity and Liability for the Acts of Another" (1972), Proposition 8: "A person does not become an accessory to an offence if the offence is so defined that his conduct in it is inevitably incidental to its commission and such conduct is not expressly penalised", Model Code, O.D. s.2.06 (6); this formulation covers both victims and consumers. See also *Poitras v. The Queen* [1974] S.C.R. 649; *The Queen v. Greyeyes* [1997] 2 S.C.R. 825.

selling is taken to show that Parliament wished to restrict liability to sellers and not to penalise buyers.

5.07 *Special Offences.* There is at least one offence which can perhaps not be committed art and part, and that is concealment of pregnancy, but that would be because of the definition of the offence and not because of any general principles of the law of art and part.[35] Other crimes, such as mobbing and rioting, are so defined that the application to them of the law of art and part has its own specialities.[36] On the other hand, the statutory offence of 'being concerned in the supplying of a controlled drug to another'[37] has been considered to involve art and part guilt by necessary implication,[38] quite independently of any general implication of concert applicable to charges by operation of some rule of law[39]; but the general view seems to be that "the breadth of that statutory charge is such that there is . . . no place for an application of the common law doctrine of concert."[40]

5.08 *Statutory offences.* Although Hume held the view that the principles of art and part guilt applied equally to statutory and to common law offences[41] this remained a matter of some doubt for a considerable time.[42] In the Criminal Justice (Scotland) Act 1949 it was declared, specifically for the removal of doubt, that a person might be convicted of a statutory contravention notwithstanding that he was guilty art and part only[43] but, despite this, doubts continued to exist until comparatively recently with regard to two types of situation.

5.09 (i) SPECIAL CAPACITIES. Where a statute provides that certain conduct shall be an offence, or that "any person" behaving in a certain way shall be guilty of an offence, there is no difficulty in extending the provision to cover persons who are art and part with the principal offender. So, for example, the law of art and part applies to section 5 of the Criminal Law (Consolidation) (Scotland) Act 1995[44] in the same way as it applies to rape. It applies to section 4 of the Explosive Substances Act 1883[45] as it does to reset. In *Lawson v. Macgregor*[46] the owner of an omnibus, his driver and his conductress were all convicted of permitting standing

---

[35] See Vol. II, Chap. 27.

[36] See Vol. II, Chap. 40.

[37] Misuse of Drugs Act 1971, s.4(3)(b).

[38] *H.M. Advocate v. Hamill*, 1998 S.C.C.R. 164, Lord Marnoch (trial judge) at 167A. (This was not his Lordship's main reason, however, for deciding the objection to admissibility of evidence in that case in favour of the Crown.)

[39] See para. 5.14, *infra*.

[40] *H.M. Advocate v. Hammill*, 1998 S.C.C.R. 164, Lord Marnoch at 166A; *Salmon v. H.M. Advocate; Moore v. H.M. Advocate*, 1998 S.C.C.R. 740, L. J.-G. Rodger at 763B, Lord Bonomy at 771B: *cf., Duffin v. H.M. Advocate*, 2000 S.C.C.R. 224, at 227B where L.J.-C. Cullen expressed surprise that the Crown had conducted the prosecution of the appellant for a s.4(3)(b) offence on the basis of concert. ('Acting in concert' is a synonymous expression for 'art and part', see para. 5.16, *infra*.)

[41] Hume, ii, 239.

[42] *cf. Isabella Murray and Helen Carmichael or Bremner* (1841) 2 Swin. 559; *Colquhoun v. Liddell* (1876) 3 Couper 342; *Stoddart and Ors. v. Stevenson* (1880) 4 Couper 334; *Wood v. Collins* (1890) 2 White 497; W.J. Dobie, "Art and Part in Statutory Offences" (1944) 56 J.R. 89; W.P.M. Black, "Police Offences and Guilt by Association" (1896) 3 S.L.T. 271.

[43] s.31; now the Criminal Procedure (Scotland) Act 1995, s.293(1).

[44] See Vol. II, Chap. 36.

[45] See Vol. II, Chap. 15. See also, *e.g., R. v. McCarthy* [1964] 1 W.L.R. 196.

[46] 1924 J.C. 112.

passengers to be carried in contravention of a byelaw made under the Public Health (Scotland) Act 1897. Lord Justice-General Clyde said, "When there is a general prohibition against a particular act, it seems to me to be indisputable that anybody who is concerned in a contravention of the general rule is liable to the penalty attached to the general rule."[47]

Difficulties at one time arose where the statute appeared to restrict liability to members of a particular class such as licensees or owners (but probably not car drivers). *Robertsons v. Caird*[48] dealt with section 13 of the Debtors (Scotland) Act 1880[49] which provided that "the debtor in a process of sequestration . . . shall be deemed guilty of a crime" if he does certain things. The court held that someone other than the debtor could not be charged as being art and part guilty of an offence under the section. In *McIntyre v. Gallacher*[50] a charge was brought against a foreman for a contravention of section 188 of the then extant Burgh Police (Scotland) Act 1892, which provided that when any hole was made in the street "the person causing such . . . hole to be made, shall at his own expense" cause it to be adequately lit. His conviction was quashed on the ground (a) that it had not been proved that he was the person who had made the hole, and (b) that it was clear that the obligation was laid on the contractors and not on their workmen who could hardly be expected to provide lighting at their own expense. This case is of little value as authority, since it could have been decided on ground (a) alone, and since it did not deal expressly with the possibility of art and part guilt. **5.10**

In the above cases Parliament provided that persons of a certain class should be guilty of offences in certain circumstances, and it is submitted that, contrary to the view taken in these cases, it is not inconsistent with such a provision to hold that other persons can be art and part guilty with persons of the specified class. As a general principle, statutory offences should, it is submitted, be read subject to the general principles of art and part guilt whose application to statutory offences was confirmed by the Criminal Justice (Scotland) Act 1949.[51]

In cases of vicarious responsibility the restriction of art and part guilt to members of the specified class would work injustice. If a statute provides that a licensee shall be guilty of an offence if the conditions of his licence are broken, and they are broken unknown to him by one of his servants, it would be unfortunate if he could be convicted while the servant was free of all guilt: it may seem odd to say that in such a situation the servant who is the actual offender is art and part in the licensee's offence, but it is preferable to exculpating him altogether.[52]

---

[47] At 116. *Cf. Spires v. Smith* [1956] 1 W.L.R. 601 where the court held that a conductor could not be charged with "carrying" excess passengers since it was his employers who did the carrying, but that he could be charged with aiding and abetting the employers.

[48] (1885) 5 Couper 664.

[49] Now Bankruptcy (Scotland) Act 1985, s.67.

[50] 1962 J.C. 20.

[51] Section 31; now the Criminal Procedure (Scotland) Act 1995, s.293(1).

[52] *cf. Spires v. Smith, supra; Ross v. Moss* [1965] 2 Q.B. 396. Conversely, it now seems in English law that an employer who is aware of a defect which makes a vehicle dangerous will be guilty of aiding, abetting, counselling or procuring an offence of causing death by dangerous driving only where the actual driver-employee has committed the *actus reus* of that offence (see ss.1 and 2A, as substituted by s.1 of the Road Traffic Act 1991). Thus where the driver did not know of the defect, nor would it have been obvious to a

If these contentions are correct then *Robertsons v. Caird*[52a] is wrongly decided, and it was therefore submitted in the second edition of this book[53] that it should not be followed.[54] That submission has been considerably strengthened by three modern decisions, although *Robertsons v. Caird*[54a] was not overruled by any of them. In *Vaughan v. H.M. Advocate,*[55] it was decided that a person not related to the persons participating in the unlawful intercourse was nevertheless guilty of incest[56] art and part. Although the advocate-depute conceded that a statutory offence might be so framed that only a person in a special capacity could be charged and referred to *Robertsons v. Caird*[56a] as providing one example of such an offence, the court in fact ignored that earlier case and said: "In our opinion, the issue here can be determined simply by reference to s.216,[57] whatever the position may have been prior to the passing of s.31 of the Criminal Justice (Scotland) Act 1949 which was its predecessor." Again, in *Templeton v. H.M. Advocate*,[58] it was held that a bank manager and his wife (who was not an employee of the bank) could both be charged with contraventions of the Prevention of Corruption Act 1906 in that they corruptly accepted payments in respect of repayments on a loan arranged by them both, as inducements for the manager showing favour to the payer in relation to the bank's business. *Robertsons v. Caird*[58a] was said to depend on the particular provisions of the Debtors (Scotland) Act 1880, and to have in any event preceded section 31 of the Criminal Justice (Scotland) Act 1949, and the court preferred to follow *Vaughan v. H.M. Advocate*.[58b] Lord Clyde in particular said[59]: "it may be questioned whether in the absence of express provision any exception could now be founded merely on inference from the terms of a statute." Most recently, it was argued in *Reid v. H.M. Advocate*[60] that a woman could not be convicted art and part of the statutory offence of living on the earnings of prostitution, since the enactment in question[61] restricted those who could commit the offence to male persons and indeed provided a separate offence for female accused.[62] The Appeal Court, however, in rejecting the argument took

---

competent and careful driver, both the driver and employer had to be acquitted: *R. v. Loukes* [1996] R.T.R. 164.

[52a] (1885) 5 Couper 664.

[53] At para. 5.10.

[54] *Robertsons v. Caird* is itself objectionable on the ground that at common law a person other than the debtor who assists the debtor to do the same things as are forbidden by the provisions of the relevant section is art and part guilty: *Sangster and Ors. v. H.M. Advocate* (1896) 2 Adam 182.

[54a] (1885) 5 Couper 664.

[55] 1979 S.L.T. 49. See also *Skinner v. Patience and Crowe*, 1982 S.L.T. (Sh.Ct.) 81.

[56] Incest was then an offence framed by the Incest Act 1567. See now the Criminal Law (Consolidation) (Scotland) Act 1995, s.1.

[56a] (1885) 5 Couper 664.

[57] Under the Criminal Procedure (Scotland) Act 1975. See now s.293(1) of the Criminal Procedure (Scotland) Act 1995.

[58] 1988 J.C. 32.

[58a] (1885) 5 Couper 664.

[58b] 1975 S.L.T. 49.

[59] 1988 J.C. 32, at 41.

[60] 1999 S.C.C.R. 19.

[61] Criminal Law (Consolidation) (Scotland) Act 1995, s.11(1): "Every male person who (a) knowingly lives wholly or in part on the earnings of prostitution . . . shall be [guilty of an offence]."

[62] *ibid.*, s.11(4): "Every female person who is proved to have, for the purpose of gain, exercised control, direction or influence over the movements of a prostitute in such a manner as to show that she is aiding, abetting or compelling her prostitution with any other person, or generally, shall be liable to the penalties set out in subsection (1) above."

the view that section 293(1)[63] of the Criminal Procedure (Scotland) Act 1995 was general in its terms and was "not stated to be subject to a contrary intention appearing in the terms of any statutory offence."[64] Thus, the "submission that section 11 contains within it a structure which determines the gender of the person who can competently be convicted is attractive at first sight, but we do not consider that it has substance when regard is had to the terms of section 293(1)".[65] Although the Court did not consider the case of *Robertsons v. Caird*[66] at all, there could hardly be a clearer illustration that the decision in that case has ceased to carry any authoritative weight.

Notwithstanding what was said by the Court in *Reid v. H.M. Advocate*[67] it must be conceded that Parliament *can* restrict art and part guilt to members of a particular class, or to a particular person,[68] but it is contended that to achieve this result clear and express provisions should be necessary. It may be that where the penalty is expressly limited to a particular class art and part guilt is excluded, on the view that there is no provision for imposing a penalty on any other persons. Normally the penalty for art and part guilt is the penalty for the offence, so that if a statute provides that a licensee doing a certain thing shall be guilty of an offence with a penalty anyone who is art and part with him is liable to the same penalty. But if Parliament says merely that in certain circumstances a licensee shall be liable to a penalty, it is arguable that only the licensee can be penalised. The distinction between this type of provision and that dealt with in *Robertsons v. Caird*[69] is admittedly thin, and not a very satisfactory basis for imposing or excluding responsibility, but it does exist, and makes it possible to distinguish two cases which might otherwise be regarded as supporting *Robertsons v. Caird*[69a] against the views here contended for. *Phyn v. Kenyon*[70] dealt with the Salmon Fishery Act 1861, section 11 of which provided that any fixed engine placed in contravention of the section may be destroyed and "the owner of any engine . . . shall . . . incur a penalty", and held that fishermen employed by the tenant of the fishing could not be convicted under the section. Again in *Graham v. Strathern,*[71] where the facts were similar to those in *Lawson v. Macgregor*[72] and *Spires v. Smith,*[73] but the conductor was acquitted, the true ground of judgment was that the penalty clause in the statute under consideration applied only to the transport undertakers.[74] **5.11**

---

[63] "A person may be convicted of, and punished for, a contravention of any enactment, notwithstanding that he was guilty of such contravention as art and part only."

[64] 1999 S.C.C.R. 19, L.J.-C. Cullen at 22C.

[65] *ibid.*, L.J.-C. Cullen at 22D.

[66] (1885) 5 Couper 664: the Court did, however, refer to *Vaughan v. H.M. Advocate, supra.*

[67] 1999 S.C.C.R. 19; see para. 5.10, *supra*.

[68] Joint licensees are art and part guilty with each other even if guilt is restricted to licensees, but in some cases, like that of sequestration, there will only be one person who is debtor in any process of sequestration.

[69] (1885) 5 Couper 664; see para. 5.10, *supra*.

[69a] *ibid.*

[70] (1905) 4 Adam 528.

[71] 1927 J.C. 29.

[72] 1924 J.C. 112; see para. 5.09, *supra*.

[73] *supra*, n.47.

[74] In South Africa it has been held that a white person could be punished for aiding a coloured person to commit a statutory offence where the statute provided a penalty only for coloured persons: *R. v. Jackelson* [1920] A.D. 486. See generally *Mapolisa v. The Queen* [1965] A.C. 840.

It has been successfully argued that liability for a statutory omission may not extend beyond the class of persons specifically charged with the relevant duty.[75] The statutory provisions were, however, somewhat special. A bye-law in Schedule D of the Salmon Fisheries (Scotland) Act 1868 narrated that, during the weekly close time, the leaders of bag-nets must be taken out of the water. The bye-law itself did not indicate on whom the duty of removal lay; but section 24 of the Act charged "the proprietor, or where let the occupier" of any fishing station with the responsibility of doing relative to bag-nets all acts required under any bye-law, and further appointed a penalty for any such proprietor or occupier who omitted to carry out such acts. No other person was mentioned in the Act as having any like duty or as being subject to any penalty for failing to discharge it. In the case itself, the manager of a fishing station was prosecuted — the proprietor-occupier having already been convicted of a contravention of section 24. The complaint alleged a contravention of section 15(2), under which it was an offence for "every person" to fish for or take, or attempt to take, or aid or assist in fishing for, taking or attempting to take salmon during the weekly close time or "contravene in any way any bye-law in force regarding the observation thereof". The sheriff held that the two parts of the subsection were not disjunctive, that the first part was limited on its terms to positive acts of commission and thus coloured the way in which any bye-law might be contravened, and that the complaint must therefore be dismissed. The accused was alleged to have failed to remove the leaders of bag-nets from the water — an omission for which only proprietors or occupiers could be responsible in terms of the Act. The sheriff's decision was upheld on appeal, on the rather more general ground that "no one can be held guilty of contravening a bye-law which requires that a certain result shall be secured unless he is a person who is charged by the bye-law or by statute with a duty to secure that result."[76] The sheriff's view, that an act of commission in breach of the statutory bye-law could be committed by anyone, was not commented upon.

5.12 (ii) SPECIFIC PROVISION. Prior to 1987, some statutes specifically provided for a separate offence of aiding, abetting, counselling, procuring or inciting the offences contained within them whereas other statutes did not. Such a separate offence was normally construed as meaning the same as art and part guilt, and normally proceedings against persons who were art and part guilty would be taken in reliance on the statutory provisions rather than on the general law. The Road Traffic Acts prior to 1962 presented particular difficulties here in that aiding and abetting was punishable only in relation to some offences.[77] But lingering difficulties and inconsistencies were removed by the Criminal Justice (Scotland) Act 1987 which introduced a general 'separate offence' provision. In its present form[78] this reads:

> "Without prejudice to subsection (1) above [that a person may be convicted of, and punished for, a contravention of any enactment notwithstanding that he was guilty as art and part only] or to any express provision in any enactment having the like effect to this

[75] *Fishmongers Co. v. Bruce*, 1980 S.L.T. (Notes) 35.
[76] *ibid.*, L.J.-G. Emslie at 36.
[77] See, *e.g.*, Road Traffic Act 1960, s.240.
[78] See the Criminal Procedure (Scotland) Act 1995, s.293(2).

subsection, any person who aids, abets, counsels, procures or incites any other person to commit an offence against the provisions of any enactment shall be guilty of an offence and shall be liable on conviction, unless the enactment otherwise requires, to the same punishment as might be imposed on conviction of the first-mentioned offence."

At first glance, it would seem that a prosecutor is here offered an alternative without much substance — on the assumption that art and part liability on the one hand and an 'aiding and abetting' offence on the other are similar in scope, meaning and penalty. The Scottish Law Commission, however, whose report led to the 1987 change in the law, considered that an 'aiding and abetting' separate offence had conceptual advantages over, and was potentially more focused than the common law notion of art and part.[79] But there have been far too few reported decisions involving the 'aiding and abetting' separate offence to determine whether there are indeed classes of case where its use has any particular advantage over the traditional approach.[80]

The phrase "aid, abet, counsel, procure or incite" is adapted from section 8 of the English Accessories and Abettors Act 1861.[81] "Aid and abet", "counsel" and "incite" are familiar in Scots law, and would presumably be given their normal meaning. "Procuring" has been defined in England as follows: **5.13**

> "To procure means to produce by endeavour. You procure a thing by setting out to see that it happens and taking the appropriate steps to produce that happening. We think that there are plenty of instances in which a person may be said to procure the commission of a crime by another even though there is no sort of conspiracy between the two, even though there is no attempt at agreement or discussion as to the form which the offence should take. In our judgment the offence described in this reference is such a case."[82]

---

[79] Scottish Law Commission, Report No. 93, "Art and Part Guilt of Statutory Offences" (1985), Cmnd 9551. See especially paras 35–38, and 40. It may be noted that one of the Commission's perceived advantages was the resolution of 'special capacity' difficulties: but these were all but resolved in *Templeton v. H.M. Advocate* 1988 J.C. 32, which was decided under the general law — in a situation to which the 1987 legislation was not at that time applicable. See para. 5.10, *supra*.

[80] Under the Road Traffic Acts, which apply to the U.K. generally, there is certainly an argument in favour of consistency since the separate offence approach utilises much the same terminology as is used in English law: thus in *Valentine v. Mackie*, 1980 S.L.T. (Sh.Ct.) 122, where a passenger was convicted of aiding and abetting the driver to drive with an excess of alcohol in his blood, the sheriff was moved to follow the earlier English case of *Carter v. Richardson* [1974] R.T.R. 314. There are potential dangers, however, in thinking that similar terms have similar meanings in Scotland and in England: see para. 5.13, *infra*.

[81] "Incite" is not used in the English legislation. See also the Magistrates' Courts Act 1980, s.35.

[82] *Attorney-General's Reference (No. 1 of 1975)* [1975] Q.B. 773, Lord Widgery C.J. at 779F.

But there seems little agreement in English law whether all of these terms are to be given specific different meanings as technical terms[83] or whether they may be taken together and collapsed into something simpler such as the non-technical "assists or encourages".[84] Caution is, therefore, called for in using as persuasive authority English decisions which involve these terms.

As is implied in section 293(2) of the 1995 Act,[85] specific provision for 'aiding and abetting' continues to exist in certain statutes.[86] When that is so, and especially where the specific provision modifies the punishment for the offence assisted[87] or alters the general formula[88], it is clearly highly desirable, if not essential, that conviction for 'aiding and abetting' should be based on that statute's own provision and not on any general provision in the 1995 Act.

5.14 *Terminology.* ART AND PART. It is probably still the case that every charge now impliedly contains the words "actor or art and part",[89] so that if A is charged simply with stealing a watch or killing a man he can be convicted whether it is proved that he actually took the watch or struck the man, or only that he was accessory to the taking or striking.[90] It may be that "art" at one time applied to the principal actor, but in modern parlance "art and part" means simply "by accession".[91]

5.15 AIDING AND ABETTING. The phrase "aiding and abetting" is sometimes used in common law charges in order to avoid linguistic difficulties, but it has no special meaning and is only another way of describing art and part guilt. So, for example, where a woman is charged with rape, the part she actually played is narrated in detail in the

---

[83] *ibid.*, 779 E-F; *cf.* J.C. Smith and B. Hogan, *Criminal Law* (9th ed., 1999, Sir John Smith (ed.)), at p.125.

[84] See J.C. Smith, "Criminal Liability of Accessories: Law and Law Reform" (1997) 113 L.Q.R. 453, at 453; Law Commission Consultation Paper No. 131, "Assisting and Encouraging Crime" (1993) paras 4.9 to 4.11.

[85] See para. 5.12, *supra*, for text of s.293(2).

[86] See, *e.g.*, Road Traffic Regulation Act 1984, s.119. There is no longer any such provision in the Road Traffic Act 1988; *cf.*, the now superseded Road Traffic Act 1972, s.176.

[87] See, *e.g.*, Road Traffic Offenders Act 1988, s.34(5).

[88] See, *e.g.*, Criminal Law (Consolidation) (Scotland) Act 1995, s.45(1), (2).

[89] This was last expressly stated in the Criminal Procedure (Scotland) Act 1975, at ss.46 and 312(d). These provisions have been repealed and are not repeated in the Criminal Procedure (Scotland) Act 1995; but, as to their de facto continuation in effect, see the Criminal Procedure (Consequential Provisions) (Scotland) Act 1995, s.6(2), and Renton and Brown, paras 8–05 n.1, and 8–08. In *H.M. Advocate v. Hamill*, 1998 S.C.C.R. 164, Lord Marnoch appeared to have proceeded on the basis of defence submissions that the repeal of ss.46 and 312(d) made it impossible for concert to apply by general implication to all charges; but the Crown did not make a formal concession to that effect, and the meaning of s.6(2) of the last mentioned Act of 1995 was not examined. It is respectfully submitted, however, that the opinion of Lord Eassie in *H.M. Advocate v. Meikleham*, 1998 S.C.C.R. 621 at 624F to 625B, is to be preferred — *viz.* that consolidating Acts (such as the Criminal Procedure (Scotland) Act 1995 and the Criminal Procedure (Consequential Provisions) (Scotland) Act 1995) are not intended to alter the existing law or practice, and that the position as it was under the 1975 Act continues unchanged.

[90] See, *e.g.*, *Mitchell v. H.M. Advocate,* 1994 S.C.C.R. 440.

[91] According to Mackenzie, "By *art* is meant that the crime was contrived by their art or skill . . . By *part* that they were sharers in the crime committed when it was committed, *et quorum pars magna*": Mackenzie, I, 35, 1. Hume relates the phrase to *artifex et particeps*: Hume, ii, 225. The phrase is now just a way of expressing guilt by accession, and any share, however small, is sufficient.

indictment which then avers that she "aided and abetted" the man involved.[92] Similarly, where it is known that one of the accused actually raped a woman while others assisted him, the assisters may be charged with aiding and abetting the rapist.[93] The term "aid and abet" is also used from time to time for no particular reason except perhaps to provide specification of the acts to be proved against the accused.[94]

ACTING IN CONCERT. "Acting in concert" is just another way of **5.16** describing art and part guilt, and is the phrase more often used where a group of people are found engaged in an allegedly criminal activity, all at one time. Where A supplies B with instructions to carry out a crime and with the means of carrying it out, and B carries it out, one would normally speak of A as being guilty art and part, and of B as being the principal actor. But both are equally guilty, and they are acting in concert. Where there is a group of people, such as a gang of youths, engaged in a crime, such as breaking into a shop or attacking someone, they are spoken of as committing the crime while acting in concert. This phrase is normally used where there is no independent evidence of any prior group purpose, of any meeting at which it was decided to commit the crime. But persons "acting in concert" are art and part in the crime, since concerted action involves a plan, however spontaneously conceived, and therefore each is guilty of the whole crime. This concept is of great use in gang fights. For if it can be shown that a group of people acted in concert, and one or more of them delivered a fatal blow, all are guilty of the homicide. Moreover, because their guilt (subject to variations in individual *mens rea*[95]) is equal it is unnecessary to prove which of them actually delivered any blows — they may all be convicted of homicide even if no one saw a blow delivered, provided it is proved that they were acting in concert and that the fatal blow must have been delivered by one of them.[96]

The position of co-accused

Where A and B are tried together on a single charge which involves **5.17** the expression or implication that they committed a particular offence while acting in concert with one another, there may be insufficient evidence to establish any concert at all. In that situation, each accused can then be guilty of the crime only in terms of his own actings, and it follows that if the crime is such that it could not have been committed by

---

[92] *Chas Matthews and Margt Goldsmith*, High Court at Glasgow, Dec. 1910, unrep'd, where the charge was of aiding and abetting rape by closing the door and preventing the victim from escaping or calling for assistance; *Walker and McPherson*, High Court at Dundee, March 1976, unrep'd. See also *Vaughan v. H.M. Advocate,* 1979 S.L.T. 49, at 50, where, although the indictment is not set out in detail, the following appears in the opinion of the court: "The incestuous intercourse was with the mother, and the applicant's involvement was that he aided and abetted in securing that incestuous intercourse. The conviction against him had accordingly to proceed on the ground that he was art and part in the commission of the offence."

[93] *Jas. Hughes* (1842) 1 Broun 205; *John Rae and Robt Montgomery* (1856) 2 Irv. 355; *Geo. Kerr and Ors.* (1871) 2 Couper 334. *Cf. John Jamieson and Ors.* (1842) 1 Broun 466.

[94] *e.g., H.M. Advocate v. D.T. Colquhoun* (1899) 3 Adam 96; *H.M. Advocate v. Martin,* 1956 J.C. 1.

[95] See para. 5.39, n.55, *infra*.

[96] *cf. Crosbie and Ors*, High Court at Glasgow, December 1945, unrep'd, discussed *infra*, para. 5.53.

A acting on his own he must be acquitted.[97] Where concert can be established, however, the evidence of concert in relation to A and B must be considered separately. Thus, it is competent for A to be convicted of the offence on the ground of his concert with B, whilst B is acquitted of the charge; the evidence of A's having been in concert with B may not, for example, be matched by sufficient evidence of B's having been in concert with A.[98]

5.18 Where A is tried on an indictment which avers that he committed a particular crime in concert with B but B is not tried with him, A's conviction "as libelled" is not an evidential fact at any later trial of B on an indictment which, *mutatis mutandis*, is identical to that brought against A. Similarly, were A to have been acquitted at his trial, that acquittal will not prevent B's subsequent trial or conviction on the basis that he had been acting in concert with A. As Lord McCluskey, who delivered the Opinion of the Court in *Howitt v. H.M. Advocate; Duffy v. H.M. Advocate*,[99] put the matter: "[T]he character of an accused's involvement in the commission of an alleged crime charged in an indictment on which he goes to trial is a matter to be determined on the evidence adduced in that trial . . . [A] finding in one trial as to the character of the involvement of an accused person has no relevance to the determination of the guilt in other proceedings of any person not then on trial in the same indictment."[1] Clearly, then, it is not a bar to the raising of an indictment against B that that indictment alleges that B committed a crime whilst acting in concert with A — A having been previously acquitted of an identical charge involving the allegation that he acted in concert with B.[2]

The Forms of Art and Part Guilt

5.19 There are three ways in which a person may be art and part in a crime — by counsel or instigation; by supplying materials for the commission of the crime; by assisting at the time of the actual commission of the crime.

---

[97] See *Young v. H.M. Advocate*, 1932 J.C. 63. Young was charged along with the directors of a company of acting art and part with them in the allotting of shares in the company in pursuance of an alleged fraudulent scheme to deceive the public. The directors were acquitted, whereas Young was convicted; but his appeal succeeded on the bases that the offence was not one he could have committed on his own (since he was not himself a director), that the trial judge had directed the jury that there was no sufficient evidence to support Y's having been in concert with the directors, and also that the jury had negatived concert in terms of their verdict.

[98] See *Howitt v. H.M. Advocate*; *Duffy v. H.M. Advocate*, 2000 S.C.C.R. 195, Lord McCluskey (delivering the opinion of a Court of five judges) at 205B. See also *Capuano v. H.M. Advocate*, 1984 S.C.C.R. 415, where admittedly the group in question was larger than the three persons actually brought to trial for a serious assault; but the conviction of C. on an art and part basis despite the acquittal of his two co-accused (who had been thought to have been the principal offenders) was not necessarily predicated on there being other unknown persons with whom he could have been acting in concert: see the example given by L.J.-G. Emslie at 418, and the account of the case proferred in *Howitt* at 205D. See too *Low v. H.M. Advocate*, 1993 S.C.C.R. 497, L.J.-C. Ross at 505B-C.

[99] 2000 S.C.C.R. 195 (Court of five Judges).

[1] *ibid*., at 205A.

[2] *Howitt v. H.M. Advocate; Duffy v. H.M. Advocate*, 2000 S.C.C.R. 195. The decision of the Court overruled the earlier contrary opinion of L.J.-C. Cooper (with whom Lords McKay and Stevenson concurred) in *McAuley v. H.M. Advocate*, 1946 J.C. 8. The Court's decision also vindicates what was done by the Crown in *Hoy v. H.M. Advocate*, 1998 S.C.C.R. 8.

Counsel and instigation

The distinction between counsel and instigation is not of real importance in the context of art and part guilt. But where the intended crime is not in fact carried out the distinction may be important, since where there is only counsel and not instigation the plotters are all guilty of conspiring to commit the intended crime, even if no particular one can be convicted of inciting the others to commit it.[3] It may be, also, that a man should not be convicted of conspiring with a hired assassin but only of inciting him. There is no great practical importance in the distinction, but equally there is no great harm in retaining it. **5.20**

Counsel. The simplest form of concert is the case of a conspiracy to commit a crime, and in such a case none of the conspirators need incite any of the others, so long as there is mutual counsel among them. Where a group of people plan a crime and decide that one of them will hire a professional assassin to carry it out, they may all be said to have counselled together to instigate the assassin to commit the crime. They are all guilty of the instigation, and of the ultimate crime if it is carried out, not because they instigated one of their number to hire the assassin, but because they agreed that he should do so. The basic principle in such a case is probably *qui facit per alium facit per se.* **5.21**

Again, anyone who is in a position of authority such that the conspirators have to apply to him for his *fiat* before proceeding with the projected crime becomes art and part in the crime by giving his permission for it to be carried out.[4] From a slightly different perspective, a lawyer who advises his client to adopt a criminal course of action may be guilty art and part of the offence subsequently committed by that client. This point arose tangentially in *Martin v. Hamilton*[5] where it was alleged that a driver, who had not stopped at the scene of an accident involving his motor vehicle, had later telephoned his solicitor for advice. The advice allegedly tendered was that the driver should not report the accident to the police, contrary to the driver's clear duty under the Road Traffic Acts.[6] The solicitor was in fact charged with the general offence of aiding, abetting, counselling, procuring or inciting the driver to commit the statutory offence[7] rather than with art and part — although in this context the distinction may be regarded as insignificant.[8] In the event, however, the complaint was dismissed as irrelevant since the charge did not clearly exclude the possibility that the driver's crime might have been committed prior to the advice being tendered.

Another example of a concerted plot without the element of instigation occurs where two criminals decide independently to steal a particular article, and then on discovering each other's plans agree to pool their resources and do the job together. Here it is submitted that the ultimate crime is the result of a concerted plot, so that both will be guilty of theft

---

[3] See *infra*, paras 6.57 *et seq.*

[4] For an example of such situations see B. Turkus and S. Feder, *Murder Inc.* (London, 1953).

[5] 1989 S.L.T. 860.

[6] This was then an offence under the Road Traffic Act 1972, s.25. See now Road Traffic Act 1988, s.170.

[7] Then provided for by s.176 of the Road Traffic Act 1972. See now the Criminal Procedure (Scotland) Act 1995, s.293(2).

[8] *Pace* the Scottish Law Commission's views in their 1985 Report (No. 93), "Art and Part Guilt of Statutory Offences".

even if one of them merely supplies the other with information regarding the location of the article in return for a share of the proceeds.

5.22 *Instigation.* There is instigation where A hires or induces B to do something, even if A and B are not involved in any plot or pre-formed group at the time of the instigation, and even though there is no detailed discussion between them about the commission of the crime.[9] The instigation must be more than "a naked advice, which has no effect on him who receives it, further than as a coincidence of wishes",[10] but must be "very serious, earnest, and pointed".[11] Hume states that, "No proclaiming of it as a meritorious thing to destroy the hateful object; no words of mere permission or allowance to do the deed; no intimation of thanks or approbation if it shall be done; not the strongest expressions of enmity to the person, or the most earnest wishes for his death: None of these things amount to what the law requires on such an occasion."[12]

5.23 MODE OF INSTIGATION. Just what words will be treated as instigation depends on the circumstances of each case. The offer of a reward will probably be enough in any case, since it clearly shows interest and seriousness.[13] Short of that, it must be shown that the instigation was such as to be capable of influencing the perpetrator, and that it did in fact influence him. There must always be difficulty in making one man responsible for influencing the "free" actions of another, and the case of financial inducement is perhaps special because there the perpetrator becomes the agent of the instigator. Where there is only persuasion or suggestion the difficulty is greater, although it is as much a difficulty of proof as of anything else — how to prove that it was because of the suggestion that the crime was committed? If it was committed independently of the suggestion or inducement, there is no connection between the instigation and the crime, and so no art and part guilt. If A decides by himself to steal an object and lays all his plans to do so, and B then incites him to steal this same object, B would probably not be guilty of theft (although he would be guilty of attempted instigation[14]), because the theft would have been committed independently of the instigation: B's criminal conduct would not have caused the *actus reus*. This situation is different from that where two thieves pool their individual plans, since then the resultant theft is the result of their combined plan.

It is because of the evidential difficulty that Hume desiderates "a direct and a special counsel" which must be "relative, less or more, to

---

[9] For examples of instigation see *Malcolm McKinlay and David McDonald* (1836) 1 Swin. 304; *Wm Ross and Robt Robertson* (1836) *ibid.* 195; *Thos Hunter and Ors* (1838) 2 Swin. 1; *H.M. Advocate v. Coutts* (1899) 3 Adam 50; *Little v. H.M. Advocate,* 1983 J.C. 16.

[10] Hume, i, 278.

[11] *ibid.*

[12] *ibid.* These strict requirements may not, however, apply where the relationship of speaker to hearer is such that any expression of wish by the former is treated as command by the latter: *cf.* Burnett, 264. In *Archd Gowans* (1831) Bell's Notes 70 a coach driver and S were charged with homicide in that the driver gave the charge of driving the coach to S and did "suffer and permit" him to drive dangerously, which is perhaps an extreme case. In this sort of situation, in any event, the "inciter's" guilt, if it exists at all, should be regarded as guilt as a principal responsible for the result of his recklessness. Statutory causing or permitting is, of course, special: see *infra*, paras 8.72 *et seq.*

[13] See, *e.g.*, *Little v. H.M. Advocate,* 1983 J.C. 16. *Cf.*, *Baxter v. H.M. Advocate,* 1997 S.C.C.R. 437, a case of incitement to kill where L.J.-G. Rodger opined at 19 that "the general approach must be the same" as in art and part guilt.

[14] *infra*, paras 6.71; 6.77 *et seq.*

some near occasion of doing the deed, so as to excite *him* to an immediate course of action."[15] Mere general expressions of desire cannot amount to instigation, being "nothing more than the expression of the party's own distempered state of mind."[16] But where the evidence is clear Hume allows the possibility of treating a series of suggestions as an instigation, even where there is no specification as to how or when the crime is to be committed. He gives the example of a series of letters written by a man to a woman pregnant by him in which he gradually persuades her to have an abortion.[17] If the evidence shows that there was instigation — that the mind of the perpetrator was turned towards the crime because of the deliberate suggestions made to him by the instigator, there seems no need to require the instigator to say how the crime is to be committed, any more than there is such a need in the case where a hired assassin is told "Kill X and I will pay you £1,000 — I leave the details to you."

WITHDRAWAL OF INSTIGATION. Since the instigation is the conduct of which the *actus reus* is the consequence, the instigator will be guilty of the completed crime if it follows on the instigation, even although he had changed his mind in the meantime and no longer wished the crime to be committed. Such a change is no more significant than the repentance of a murderer after the death of his victim. In order to clear himself of guilt the instigator must interrupt the chain of events either by preventing the commission of the crime or, at least, by removing the influence of his instigation.[18] This he can perhaps do by telling the prospective perpetrator that he has changed his mind and no longer wishes him to commit the crime. If the perpetrator then carries on and commits the crime the instigator will be free of responsibility, not because he has given evidence of the sincerity of his repentance, but because it will no longer be true to say that the crime was committed under the influence of his instigation. **5.24**

That is the simple case, but there may be cases where even although the instigator has intimated his change of mind to the perpetrator the latter carries on as a result of the state of mind induced in him by the instigation. Suppose that in Hume's example of the young man who suggests that his mistress should have an abortion the man changed his mind and told the girl he would rather she had the child, but that the girl had by then become convinced by him that she should not have the child, an idea she would never have entertained but for his suggestions, and went on and did abort herself. It could be said that the young man had intentionally set in train a series of events calculated to lead to abortion, that they had in fact led to abortion, and that his ineffective change of mind is no more relevant than the ineffective attempts of a murderer to save his victim's life after he has shot him.[19] On the other hand, it can be said that by intimating his change of heart the young man broke the connection between his suggestions and the abortion, and that the latter must be regarded as the consequence of the girl's voluntary decision to have the abortion, and of that alone. There is a suggestion in **5.25**

---

[15] Hume, i, 279.
[16] Hume, i, 278.
[17] *ibid.* 279. *Cf. H.M. Advocate v. Baxter* (1908) 5 Adam 609.
[18] *cf.* Hume, i, 279–280.
[19] *cf.* Gl. Williams, p.383.

H.M. Advocate v. Baxter,[20] a case of supplying abortifacients, that the supplier if he changed his mind should write to the recipient "forbidding him to use them for the purpose for which he sent them, and saying that, if he did not get an undertaking at once that they would not be so used, he would himself inform the police of the matter."[21] If the police act and prevent the abortion, all will be well; but suppose the police fail — in strict logic is the instigator not guilty of being art and part in the abortion? Perhaps so, in strict logic, but in practice his having done all he could to avert the danger he has created will probably be treated as excusing him.[22]

5.26 *Dissociation.* There is no defence of dissociation in Scots law. The fact that one conspirator withdraws from the enterprise at some stage after the perpetration of the crime has begun does not relieve him of responsibility for the completed offence, unless, perhaps, he takes steps to prevent its completion.[23]

Supply of materials

5.27 Where the person who supplies the tools with which a crime is committed is also a conspirator or instigator his responsibility as an accessory can be dealt with under that head. Normally there will have been some element of concert beyond what is involved in the supply of materials, but it is possible to infer art and part guilt merely from the circumstances surrounding the supply of the materials; the supplier may bring himself into the plot just by supplying the materials with which the crime is carried out. "Whosoever, being in the knowledge of the mortal purpose, though contrived and imagined by another, shall lend immediate and material aid towards the execution, is thus involved in the guilt of murder."[24]

Knowledge of the criminal plot is of course essential — a man cannot be art and part in a crime of which he knows nothing, he cannot be in a plot without knowing of its existence. The gunsmith who sells a murderer

---

[20] (1908) 5 Adam 609.

[21] L.J.-C. Macdonald at 615.

[22] The Model Penal Code provides that a person is not an accomplice if "he terminates his complicity prior to the commission of the offense and (i) wholly deprives it of effectiveness in the commission of the offense; or (ii) gives timely warning to the law enforcement authorities or otherwise makes proper effort to prevent the commission of the offense": Model Penal Code, O.D. s.2.06(6)(c); *cf.* L.C.W.P. No. 43, "Codification of the Criminal Law: General Principles: Parties, Complicity and Liability for the Acts of Another" (1972), proposition 9: "A person who has incited or given help towards the commission of an offence is not guilty as an accessory if he genuinely withdraws from participation in time to make it possible for the offence not to be committed, and . . . communicates his withdrawal to the principal, or to one of them if there are more than one; or takes reasonable steps in an endeavour to prevent the offence being committed." This proposition was apparently not well received by consultees, and was replaced by a more restricted formula in the English Draft Code, clause 27(8), *viz.*: "A person who has encouraged the commission of an offence is not guilty as an accessory if before its commission — (a) he countermanded his encouragement with a view to preventing its commission; or (b) he took all reasonable steps to prevent its commission." See the Commentary to the Code, at paras 9.41 and 9.42. See also *R. v. Beccerra* (1976) 62 Cr.App.R. 212, approving *R. v. Whitehouse* (1941) 1 W.W.R. 112 (British Columbia); and *R. v. Whitefield* (1984) 79 Cr.App.R. 36.

[23] *MacNeil v. H.M. Advocate,* 1986 J.C. 146. *Cf.* the discussion of the issue of withdrawal in Law Commission Consultation Paper, No. 131, "Assisting and Encouraging Crime" (1993), paras 2.95 to 2.101.

[24] Hume, i, 274.

the fatal weapon in the normal course of his business and in ignorance of the latter's purpose cannot be art and part in the murder. But mere knowledge is probably not enough either. If he sells the gun in the ordinary way at the ordinary price, without any discussion regarding its proposed criminal use, the seller does not become art and part in the crime.[25] Similarly, "the generous host, with somewhat bibulous friends" is not art and part in the offences of driving with an excess of blood-alcohol committed by his friends when they drive home.[26] As Lord Widgery C.J. said: "That is a case in which the driver knows perfectly well how much he has to drink and where to a large extent it is perfectly right and proper to leave him to make his own decision."[27] In any event there is no element of conspiracy to commit a crime in such a situation. On the other hand, a member of a criminal organisation whose "job" is to supply the materials necessary for the carrying out of the organisation's criminal purpose, is clearly art and part in the ultimate crime; but he has been one of the counsellors of the crime, and so is in concert with the principal perpetrators.[28] And so is someone who hears that a crime is to be committed, and offers to help by supplying the necessary materials.

The situation which raises acutely the problem of whether mere supply **5.28**
of materials can make the supplier art and part is intermediate between that of the gunsmith and that of the member of the organisation. This is the situation of the tradesman who knows that his goods are being bought for a criminal purpose, and as a result charges more than their usual price, but who has no further interest in the crime. This situation is referred to by Hume, but he gives no answer to the problem.[29] The answer probably depends on the precise circumstances in which the materials were supplied. Consider the following situations:

(a) A man takes a fourteen-year-old girl to a hotel with the intention of seducing her. He asks the hotelier for a room. The latter knows that the reason A wants the room is to seduce the girl, but he says nothing of this and lets the room at the usual price. It is difficult to see how the hotelier can be said to have made himself party to any plan to seduce the girl, and so he is not art and part.

(b) The hotelier discloses his knowledge and tells A that since he wants the room for an immoral purpose he must pay extra. In such a case it can be said that the hotelier has pushed himself into the plot, and so made himself art and part in the seduction. Once the hotelier has disclosed his knowledge and demanded his reward, he becomes a conspirator.

---

[25] Hume, i, 157.

[26] *Attorney-General's Reference (No. 1 of 1975)* [1975] Q.B. 773.

[27] At 780F-G.

[28] Hume, i, 157.

[29] *ibid*. 158. In *R. v. Bainbridge* [1960] 1 Q.B. 129, B. bought equipment on behalf of thieves knowing it was to be used to break and enter into premises but not knowing of the particular crime for which it was used about a month later. He was convicted of being an accessory before the fact as he knew of the type of crime it was proposed to use the equipment for. Lord Parker C.J. said that it was not enough merely to show knowledge of an illegal venture, such as the disposal of stolen property, but unnecessary to show knowledge of the particular date and place of the crime. But Scots law may require more exact knowledge than this. See also *R. v. Maxwell* [1978] 1 W.L.R. 1350, where the accused's knowledge that one of a limited range of crimes was very likely to be carried out was sufficient to convict him of accessorial liability relative to a crime falling within that range. *Cf. People v. Egan* [1989] I.R. 681, where an agreement to assist in hiding the proceeds of what the accused thought was going to be a theft led to his conviction for armed robbery.

(c) A discloses his purpose to the hotelier and asks the latter to help him by providing a room. Here the hotelier, if he agrees, is clearly art and part, since he is acceding to a request for help from the principal criminal.

(d) The hotelier knows of A's purpose, but he says nothing, and doubles the price of the room, pretending that that is the normal price. This is the most difficult of all. There is here no concert, there is no officious attempt to "get into the plot" as there is in case (b), but the hotelier is making a profit out of the crime. It is submitted that in the absence of the essential element of concert, there can be no conviction of the hotelier as art and part in the seduction, but it must be admitted that the distinction between (b) and (d) is a difficult one to make.

5.29 The essential question in every case is one which is best expressed in the vernacular "Was the accused *in it* along with the others?" Or, in more elaborate terms, "Was the accused a party to the design or plot to commit the crime?"[30]

The importance of the element of concert, of participation in a plot with the principal perpetrator, can be seen by examining two cases. The first is *H.M. Advocate v. Johnstone*,[31] where J. gave another woman the name of an abortionist with whom J. had no connection herself, and whom she knew only by name; she was acquitted of being art and part in the subsequent abortion. Lord Moncrieff pointed out that it would be straining the law to hold that the mere giving of a name by a party who was not in actual communication with the party named amounted to participation in the crime. He told the jury that what they had to consider was whether there was any association between the accused and the abortionist.[32] Had the accused been employed by the abortionist as a canvasser, or received a commission on business introduced, the necessary connection would have been present and the supply of the abortionist's name would have been sufficient to make the accused art and part in the abortion. If a woman approaches X and asks, "Do you know a good man for abortions?" and X replies, "Yes, A.B.," he is not art and part with the woman, because he has done no more than impart information, or at most give a "naked advice"[33]; and he is not art and part with A.B. if he has no dealings with him.

5.30 In *H.M. Advocate v. Semple*,[34] on the other hand, there was ample evidence of complicity. The accused supplied a woman with abortifacients, told her how to use them, and advised her to make use of them. Lord Justice-Clerk Aitchison said, "supply by itself does not amount to a crime, but here it is coupled with use, and the distinction between supply and administration does not appear to me to be material in a case where the supply is closely related to the use by words of instigation or by some act of instigation".[35] It is submitted that it is not necessary for the supplier to be a moving spirit in the enterprise, or the equivalent of an instigator, but the law does require an element of complicity, and it is this which

---

30 *cf.* Burnett, pp.268–269.
31 1926 J.C. 89.
32 At 90.
33 Hume, i, 278.
34 1937 J.C. 41.
35 At 44.

distinguishes the mere supply of *Johnstone*[35a] from cases of art and part by supply in circumstances which make the supplier a conspirator.

The supply must be for an imminent crime. The material must be supplied for the commission of an imminent crime.[36] This requirement rests partly on evidential grounds, and partly on the rules regarding *mens rea*. Suppose A says to B, "I am on my way to kill C. If you lend me your car, I'll just catch him before he goes to work"; B lends A the car, and A goes off and kills C: B is art and part in the killing. Now suppose A says, "Lend me your car please. I want to catch C before he leaves for work; I've a bone to pick with him. In fact, I'm getting a bit fed up with him, and if he doesn't change his ways I'll kill him one of these days"; B lends him the car; A goes off and kills C: B is probably not art and part, because he did not supply his car for the purpose of helping A to kill C.[36a] The intention necessary to bring B into A's plot is lacking in the second case, and in any event a vague threat to kill someone in the future is hardly a plot. If A all along intended to kill C that day B cannot be art and part because he knew nothing of this; if he did not, but was only mouthing vague threats, there was no plot for B to join. Again, if A lends assistance at a time when the idea of the crime is only in embryo and no definite plans have been made, and is not consulted again nearer the time of the actual commission of the offence, his assistance will be treated as too remote to involve art and part guilt.[37] **5.31**

Assistance in the actual commission of the crime

(1) *Where there has in fact been a prior agreement.* Examples of this type of art and part guilt are very common. The man who keeps watch while his friend breaks into a house, the man who stands on the edge of a crowd and collects the property his friend has picked from the pockets of members of the crowd,[38] the man who holds a girl down while his friend rapes her; all these are art and part in the principal crime. Similarly if two people agree to go out on a joint pocket-picking expedition and arrange that one shall operate on one side of the street and one on the other, but that they will share the proceeds and be prepared to help each other should occasion arise, each will be guilty art and part of the thefts carried out by the other. **5.32**

In all these cases the assistance is tendered in consequence of a prior agreement, and is evidence of that agreement. Where there is independent evidence of the agreement, where, for example, someone has overheard the criminals arranging their crime, it does not matter what part each actually took in the crime. Where there is no such evidence then what each did will be important in the sense that it will constitute the facts from which the prior agreement is to be inferred; and the more active a man's part in the actual crime, the easier it will be to infer a prior agreement. It is easier to convict a person of art and part guilt where he has stood by and encouraged his friend to commit a crime than where he has just stood by and watched, since in the latter case there is probably not enough evidence to enable a jury to infer any prior

---

35a 1926 J.C. 89.

36 Hume, i, 276.

36a *ibid.*

37 Hume, i, 276; Burnett, p.269.

38 *cf.* Hume, i, 115.

agreement about the crime and, in the absence of independent evidence of such an agreement, mere presence is insufficient to make a person art and part.[39] Again, where two pickpockets are operating on opposite sides of the street it will be very difficult to convict one of being art and part in the other's crime in the absence of independent evidence of their agreement to "go into business" together; but if one of them does actually come to the assistance of the other it will be easy to infer such an agreement. In all such cases the difficulty is evidential, and the question always is: are there facts from which prior agreement can be inferred?

The agreement need not be of long standing, but may have been formed just before the crime was committed.

5.33 (2) *Where there is no prior agreement.* There may be art and part guilt even in cases where there has been no prior agreement, not even one formed more or less simultaneously with the commission of the crime. In such cases the assistance given is not evidence of a concerted plot, but constitutes the plot, which is created by the act of assistance. The plot, accordingly, can be defined only by reference to the intention of the assister. Suppose A sees his friend B attacking a girl and thinks he intends to rape her; the girl tries to escape; A, without any prior arrangement with B, intervenes and takes hold of the girl to prevent her escaping, and so enables B to rape her: A is art and part in the rape. But suppose in such a case B does not rape the girl but stabs her. A is then not art and part in the stabbing, because he did not enter into any agreement to stab the girl, but only to rape her. The "agreement" is, of course, of a peculiar nature, in that it is spontaneous and may be entered into without the knowledge of the principal criminal. But by lending his assistance A brings himself into a plot which at the same time he creates, a kind of spontaneous concert; and by doing so, he renders himself liable to be treated as if he had entered into a prior agreement with B to carry out the crime.

5.34 It is difficult to find illustrations of this type of art and part activity. The case of *Ryach*[40] did, however, proceed on the same principle. The accused there intervened in a fight which was going on between her husband and the deceased. She held the deceased by the hair while her husband stabbed him. But she did not know that her husband had a knife, and she was trying to stop the deceased attacking him, so she was acquitted of killing the deceased.

The more modern case of *Gallacher and Ors*[41] may also be an example of "spontaneous concert". In *Gallacher*[41a] three of the accused were part of a group which stood round the deceased and kicked him to death. There was no evidence of any prior agreement among these three or other persons to attack the deceased, but the three were all convicted of murder since they "were in a kicking crowd animated by a common purpose, joining in the attack, assisting and encouraging."[42]

---

[39] *cf. Geo. Kerr and Ors* (1871) 2 Couper 334. See also *Quinn v. H.M. Advocate,* 1990 S.L.T. 877; *Stillie v. H.M. Advocate,* 1990 S.C.C.R. 719; *Lawler v. Niezer,* 1993 S.C.C.R. 299; *R. v. Allan* [1965] 1 Q.B. 130; *R. v. Clarkson* [1971] 1 W.L.R. 1402; *supra* para. 3.33, *infra*, para. 5.36.

[40] (1721) Burnett, 277; Hume, i. 267.

[41] High Court at Glasgow, Oct. 1950, unrep'd — it is reported on another point in 1951 J.C. 38; see also *Ramnath Mohan v. The Queen* [1967] 2 A.C. 187, PC.

[41a] *supra.*

[42] Lord Keith, Transcript of Judge's Charge, 37.

5.35 The position is usually looked at from the point of view of the intervener. But what about the original criminal? He is not in any plot, and has not asked for help. Suppose A intends to steal a man's watch-chain; an officious friend sees him, helps him to steal the chain and, thinking A was going to steal the man's wallet, takes it as well. A is surely not guilty of stealing the wallet, since he did not intend to steal it, and entered into no agreement with his friend to steal it. There can only be a plot in so far as the intentions of the two criminals coincide,[43] and this rule must operate in favour of the original criminal as well as in favour of the intervener.

In *Gallacher*[43a] the matter was complicated by the rule that all the members of a concert, spontaneous or prearranged, are responsible for the consequences of the concerted action.[44] Suppose A starts to kick X with the intention of causing slight injury, and other persons come along and join in the kicking so that X is killed. If A retires as soon as the others join in he cannot, it is submitted, be guilty of homicide, unless his own acts would have been sufficient to cause death. But if he continues to kick X after the others have joined in and the assault has become foreseeably fatal, he will be guilty of homicide even although his own acts were not in themselves foreseeably fatal, because he will have made himself party to a spontaneous concert to kill X, or at any rate to inflict foreseeably fatal injuries on him.[45]

5.36 ART AND PART BY MERE PRESENCE. Presence at the scene of the crime coupled with a failure to prevent the crime does not of itself constitute art and part guilt. But the circumstances of A's presence may be such as to enable the court to infer that he was "in it" with the principal offenders.[46] Where, for example, A acts as a lookout, the court will infer that he was a party to a prior agreement to commit the crime. Where A remains at the scene of the crime, and does not merely watch its commission but offers encouragement to the perpetrators, or deliberately stations himself so as to deter others from interfering with the commission of the crime, or so that his presence adds to the terror of the victim, thus making the crime easier to commit, the court may infer either a prior concert, or that A has made himself party to the crime without any prior concert.[47] Where the accused's presence was wholly

---

[43] *Ryach, supra; Ross and Roberts* (1716) Hume, i, 267.

[43a] High Court at Glasgow, Oct. 1950, unrep'd — it is reported on another point in 195, J.C. 38; See also *Ramnath Mohan v. The Queen* [1967] 2 A.C. 187, PC.

[44] See *infra*, paras 5.38 *et seq.*

[45] *cf. S. v. Motaung* 1990 (4) S.A. 485 (A.D.), where the 'ratification' approach of Schreiner J.A. in *R. v. Mgxwiti*, 1954 (1) S.A. 370 (A.D.) was rejected in favour of the causal approach of Wessells J.A. in *S. v. Thomo,* 1969 (1) S.A. 385 (A.D.) at 382H to 383 A.

[46] See *Wilson Latta and Rooney*, High Court at Glasgow, Feb., 1968, unrep'd, L.J.-C.'s charge to jury, Transcript of Proceedings, 1315–1316; *Stillie v. H.M. Advocate,* 1990 S.C.C.R. 719; *White v. MacPhail*, 1990 S.C.C.R. 578; *Quinn v. H.M. Advocate,* 1990 S.C.C.R. 254; *cf. Jamieson v. Guild*, 1989 S.C.C.R. 583.

[47] See Hume, i, 267; *Geo. Kerr and Ors* (1871) 2 Couper 334. It has been held in England that presence coupled with an intention to assist or encourage is insufficient in the absence of actual encouragement: *R. v. Allan* [1965] 1 Q.B. 130; *R. v. Clarkson* [1971] 1 W.L.R. 1402; *R. v. Tait* [1993] Crim. L.R. 538. *Cf.* L.C.W.P. No. 43, "Codification of the Criminal Law: General Principles: Parties, Complicity and Liability for the Acts of Another" (1972), proposition 6(3)(b), including as "help": "conduct of a person which leads the principal to believe when committing the offence that he is being helped or will be helped if necessary by that person in its commission." Given the accessory's *mens rea* it would seem that the effect of his presence on the victim's state of mind is more important than its effect on the principal's.

passive and the Crown are therefore forced to rely on prior concert the jury must be specifically and forcefully directed on the point.[48]

If, of course, A is under a duty to prevent the crime, as where his child is being assaulted, his mere presence coupled with his non-interference could make him art and part.[49] Similarly, the owner of a vehicle or the supervisor of a learner-driver who fails to prevent speeding or dangerous driving may be art and part in the driver's offence.[50]

Responsibility for the Unintended Consequences of a Plot

Responsibility for consequences in the case of an individual

5.37 The criminal law sometimes holds a man responsible for the unintended consequences of his actions, and where a person unintentionally causes death he may be guilty of murder if his acts were so clearly dangerous that he must have realised they might well be fatal, *i.e.* if he acted with wicked recklessness.[51] A man who beats another to death with a crow-bar may be guilty of murder whether or not he intends to kill him. Where the act which caused death was so dangerous as to be foreseeably fatal, but not so dangerous as to be regarded as reckless, the agent may be guilty of culpable homicide. In addition, there is a rule of law that any death caused by an assault is culpable homicide, however unforeseeable the fatal consequence was. So if A punches B and B falls and cuts his head on a stone and dies, A is guilty of culpable homicide.[52]

Responsibility for the consequences of a plot

5.38 Where death is the unintended result of a plot the same rules apply, so that if the plot is, so to speak, reckless, each conspirator may be convicted of murder if death is caused in the course of carrying it out. In other words, the conspirators are regarded as one person, and the plot and its carrying out as their act, so that if someone is killed as a result of the carrying out of the plot, all the conspirators are guilty of homicide. The cases are mostly concerned with homicide, but the principles apply to any crime which can be committed unintentionally.

5.39 *Death as the consequence of a criminal purpose.* The simplest example of this principle is that of a concerted housebreaking in the course of which one of the housebreakers kills the householder. If the housebreakers had agreed to use whatever violence was necessary to effect

---

48 *Spiers v. H.M. Advocate*, 1980 J.C. 36.

49 The decision in *Bonar v. McLeod*, 1983 S.C.C.R. 161, indicates that a senior police officer who fails to interfere when a junior officer assaults a prisoner whom they are both escorting may be art and part guilty of the assault. See *supra*, paras 3.35–3.37. See also Law Commission No. 177, H. of C., No. 299, "A Criminal Code for England and Wales", cl.27(3): "Assistance or encouragement includes assistance or encouragement arising from a failure by a person to take reasonable steps to exercise any authority or to discharge any duty he has to control the relevant acts of the principal in order to prevent the commission of the offence."

50 *R. v. Kelbacke* (1965) 52 D.L.R. (2d) 283; *Du Cros v. Lambourne* [1907] 1 K.B. 40; *Rubie v. Faulkner* [1940] 1 K.B. 571. *Cf. Smith v. Baker* [1971] R.T.R. 350: passenger not guilty of aiding and abetting driving without insurance.

51 See *infra*, para. 7.60. See also Vol. II, Chap. 23.

52 These rules are discussed in detail in Vol. II, Chap. 26.

their purpose they are all guilty of homicide, unless the violence was employed for a private purpose and not to further the housebreaking.[53] So long as the violence used can be regarded as part of the plot all are guilty. If the agreement is to use only limited violence, say only hand blows, and the householder is killed by such a blow, all are guilty of homicide because of the rule that death caused by criminal violence is culpable homicide even where it is unforeseeable.[54] It is probably therefore the law that all parties to a robbery are guilty of homicide if the victim is killed, since an agreement to rob involves an agreement to use force.[55] And a person who arranges an illegal abortion will be guilty of culpable homicide if the abortionist kills the mother.[56]

The only exception to the above rule is that where the violence used is more serious than that agreed upon, it may be that only the persons who use the violence are guilty of its results.[57] In order to convict all the conspirators it is essential to show that the violence used was a result — intended or foreseeable[58] — of the plot, and if the violence used was so different from that contemplated that it could not be regarded as a **5.40**

---

[53] See, *e.g.*, *R. v. Slack* [1989] 1 Q.B. 775, Lord Lane C.J. at 780H to 781H, commenting on the correctness of the directions of the trial judge in the 1986 case of *R. v. Barr* (1989) 88 Cr. App.R. 362.

[54] See generally Hume, i, 268 *et seq.*; Alison, i, 65 *et seq.*

[55] *cf. H.M. Advocate v. Fraser and Rollins*, 1920 J.C. 60; *Wm and Helen Harkness*, High Court at Glasgow, Jan. 1922, unrep'd. Whether the guilt of any party is of murder or culpable homicide should depend on his *mens rea*. In *Melvin v. H.M. Advocate*, 1984 S.C.C.R. 113, A and B were charged with robbery and murder, and A was convicted of murder and B of culpable homicide. In dismissing A's appeal on the ground that the verdicts were inconsistent, Lord Cameron said at 117: "In determining the quality of the crime, *i.e.* as between culpable homicide and murder, a jury would be entitled, in a case where intent to kill was not suggested or established or indeed any antecedent concerted intention to carry out an assault and robbery on the deceased or any other person, to consider and assess the degree of recklessness displayed by each participant and return, if their judgment so required, a discriminating verdict in accordance with their assessment." (See also *Malone v. H.M. Advocate*, 1988 S.C.C.R. 498; *Johns v. The Queen* (1980) 54 A.L.J.R. 166, applied in *McAuliffe v. The Queen* (1995) 69 A.L.J.R. 621.) Thus, if A embarks on an expedition with B in which the use of force of a kind unlikely to result in death is contemplated and B in fact uses greater force and death ensues, A may be guilty of culpable homicide and B of murder; *cf. Cadona v. H.M. Advocate*, 1996 S.C.C.R. 300, where the appellant's liability for culpable homicide was not discussed owing to the lack of evidence to show that she had in fact participated in the fatal assault. In practice, however, it is likely that where A's guilt is appreciably less than B's he will not be charged with homicide at all, although in theory he might often be guilty of constructive culpable homicide as being responsible for a criminal enterprise which caused death. (On the matter of constructive guilt of homicide in such cases, see the exchange of letters between P.W. Ferguson and Prof. Sir J.C. Smith, [1998] Crim. L.R. 231–232.)
Where, on the other hand, violence of a kind contemplated by A is used by B and has fatal results it used to be reasonably clear that if B was guilty of murder A was also guilty of murder: *Crosbie and Ors*, High Court at Glasgow, Dec. 1954; *Harris and Ors*, High Court at Glasgow, Sept. 1950; *Miller and Denovan*, High Court at Glasgow, Nov. 1960, all unrep'd, see *infra*, paras 5.53–5.55. The position is less straightforward, however, following the case of *Brown v. H.M. Advocate*, 1993 S.C.C.R. 382, where in a situation of uncertainty as to which of two accused persons delivered the single fatal knife blow, L.J.-G. Hope declared that to find both of them guilty of murder the jury "had to be satisfied that they both had in contemplation, as part of their joint purpose, an act of the necessary degree of wicked recklessness such as that the deceased would be stabbed by plunging a knife into his heart."

[56] *R. v. Creamer* [1966] 1 Q.B. 72.

[57] *cf. Cadona v. H.M. Advocate*, 1996 S.C.C.R. 300.

[58] Probably, if murder is to be sustained, in the sense conveyed by the court in *Brown v. H.M. Advocate*, 1993 S.C.C.R. 382.

foreseeable development of the plot this essential requirement will not be satisfied. If the plotters agree to use their fists and one of them uses a fruit dish, or if they agree to use violence only to effect their escape and one of them attacks the housekeeper in order to effect entry, it will depend on the circumstances of the case whether or not the use of violence is regarded as a consequence of the original plot. An example of circumstances in which it would not be so regarded was given by Lord Justice-Clerk Thomson in *Harris and Ors*[59] where he said:

> "Suppose three men set out to perpetrate some act of minor violence on a fourth man and proceed to beat him up. Now, if quite unexpectedly one of the assailants produces a revolver, which none of the rest knew he had with him, and the man who produces the revolver shoots the victim . . . the unexpected character of that event could not be laid at the doors of those who had no just cause to expect such a thing to happen. That is to say, shooting would not be within the scope of the common purpose."[60]

What is important is not the unexpectedness of the death in relation to the violence actually used, but the unexpectedness of the violence actually used in relation to the violence agreed upon. Had the victim died as a result of the beating up, however unexpected such an event, all three men would be guilty of homicide — even if one of them only kept watch while the other two assaulted the victim.

5.41 The level of violence agreed to is a matter of evidence; but what had been agreed to may be implied rather than expressed. In *Cadona v. H.M. Advocate*,[61] the appellant had witnessed, but not participated in, two separate assaults and robberies carried out by various young men with whom she had been in company. The two victims had been punched, kicked and jumped on; they had also been attacked or threatened with weapons such as a knife or a bottle. Neither, however, had been injured to the extent of requiring medical attention. The Crown case against the appellant for murder was that she had confessed to participation in an attack by those young men on a third victim, who had been killed by repeated severe stamping on his head. Her alleged involvement went no further than one kick on the back of the victim's feet at the very outset of the assault, and that limited role (quite apart from the fact that her confession was eventually deemed inadmissible) might have been sufficient to convince the court that the should be acquitted of murder. The true reason, however, why her conviction for murder could not have been sustained was that she could not have foreseen from the earlier assaults the savage level of violence which was meted out to the third victim. Had there been evidence to support her participation, it would have been evidence of her tacit agreement to take part in an attack involving non-fatal violence. She knew or must have known, of course, that weapons capable of causing death or serious injury were being carried by her associates who were likely to use them. But such weapons need not be used to fatal effect — and were indeed not so used in *Cadona* itself. It is not the carrying of weapons capable of causing death nor the likelihood of their use which matters in a question whether a

---

[59] High Court at Glasgow, Sept. 1950, unrep'd, see *infra*, para. 5.54.
[60] Transcript of proceedings, 375.
[61] 1996 S.C.C.R. 300.

person is guilty art and part of murder, but rather whether that person contemplated that they were likely to be used specifically to kill the victim or at least with such a degree of wicked recklessness as to satisfy the *mens rea* requirement of that crime. Such contemplation requires to be part of the plan.[62]

Where there is no pre-awareness that a lethal weapon will be employed, there can be no such contemplation: but if such a weapon is unexpectedly produced and used to kill by one of one's co-assailants in a concerted attack, one may become liable for the homicide if one continues with one's role in the assault. Persistence after one has become aware that one's co-accused has produced and is using a lethal weapon will go far to elide the plea that the actual level of violence used by a co-accused exceeded what was contemplated. The principle seems one of adoption of the escalated level of violence.[63] Of course, if the actual weapon produced by a co-accused is of a similar nature to that which was or could have been contemplated,[64] then the level of actual violence is really no different from that anticipated, and art and part guilt will not be elided. In *O'Connell v. H.M. Advocate*,[65] for example, a group of men assaulted the deceased with sticks, and during the attack one of the accused struck the deceased the fatal blow with a hammer which had belonged to the deceased. It was held that whether a hammer was to be regarded as sufficiently similar to a stick for its use to be within the reasonable contemplation of all of the group was a jury question, and the jury were entitled to convict all the accused of culpable homicide.

Even if there is no agreement to use any violence at all the plotters **5.42**
may all be guilty of homicide (but not necessarily murder[66]) if fatal violence is used by one of them, provided that such violence was foreseeable. Suppose a group of housebreakers agree that they will not use force to effect their purpose, but one of the group carries a gun with him and this is known to the others. If he uses the gun in breach of the agreement the others may be guilty of homicide, since it is foreseeable that such a weapon may be used at the very least to menace[67] householders and others encountered in the execution of the plan. Whether he is guilty of murder or not will be determined by his own *mens rea* at the time of the causing of death; and this will apply also to

---

[62] *Brown v. H.M. Advocate*, 1993 S.C.C.R. 382. *Cf. Carrick v. H.M. Advocate*, 1990 S.C.C.R. 286. See also *Chan Wing-Siu v. The Queen* [1985] A.C. 168, PC; *Hiu Chi-Ming v. The Queen* [1991] 3 All E.R. 897, PC; *R. v. Hyde* [1991] 1 Q.B. 134; *R. v. Powell; R. v. English* [1997] 3 W.L.R. 959.

[63] See *Walker v. H.M. Advocate,* 1985 J.C. 53; *Mathieson v. H.M. Advocate*, 1996 S.C.C.R. 388. An accused's awareness that a weapon has been produced and is being used with wicked recklessness if not an intent to kill is, of course, a matter of evidence. But in *Mathieson, supra,* it was held that where direct evidence is awanting, knowledge can be inferred from, *e.g.*, the proximity of the accused to the person wielding the weapon and the nature (and number) of the blows struck with it: *cf. Collins v. H.M. Advocate*, 1991 S.C.C.R. 898. Participation at the time of use of the weapon is obviously important: *cf. Jamieson v. Guild*, 1989 S.C.C.R. 583 (a case of theft by shoplifting, which nevertheless emphasises the distinction between being present as a spectator and as a participant).

[64] It is not certain whether 'contemplation' is objectively or subjectively assessed. In England and elsewhere, subjectivity would apply: see *R. v. Powell; R. v. English* [1997] 3 W.L.R. 959; *McAuliffe v. The Queen* [1995] 69 A.L.J.R. 621. But this is not the tradition in Scotland. See Chap. 7, *infra*.

[65] 1987 S.C.C.R. 459. *Cf. R. v. Powell; R. v. English, supra,* especially relative to English's appeal, and the opinion of Lord Hutton at 981B.

[66] See *Brown v. H.M. Advocate*, 1993 S.C.C.R. 382.

[67] Which in Scots law is an assault: see Vol. II, Chap. 29.

the other members of the group. If the weapon was used in a wickedly reckless way to cause death, those others will be guilty of murder art and part only if they contemplated that such reckless use was likely to occur. At one time, prior to the decision in *Brown*,[67a] it would have been possible to say that if A became party to a criminal operation, he took the risk of any offence his colleagues in crime might commit in the furtherance of that operation, provided such an offence was reasonably foreseeable — in other words, that A might be convicted of an offence he neither desired nor contemplated.[68] Although the cases supporting such a view have not formally been overruled,[69] it now seems likely that a person cannot be convicted art and part of an offence he did not contemplate; at least, he cannot be convicted of murder art and part unless he contemplated that one of his co-accused might act with wicked recklessness. It would go too far to suggest that he must actually be shown to have had the *mens rea* for murder himself. But the Scots courts seem to have moved far towards the English position where the defendant must contemplate the possibility of the principal's killing someone with the *mens rea* which murder requires.[70]

Consequently, it cannot now be confidently stated that he who knows weapons are being carried and/or knows they are likely to be used is responsible for any use that may be made of them. As far as murder is concerned, art and part guilt will depend on the accused's preparedness to associate himself with a foreseen act of wicked recklessness which ends in death.

5.43 If there is an agreement to use minor force, or minor force is foreseeable, and unintended and unforeseeable major "murderous", force is used, only the actual user of such force should be guilty of homicide.[71] But there is English authority for the view that where the death was caused by the murderous use of a weapon whose use for minor violence was expected, the actual user is guilty of murder and the other members of the group of manslaughter on the basis that death was the result of their criminal enterprise.[72] Conversely, it has been held that if A employs B to inflict grievous bodily harm on the victim, and he in

---

67a 1993 S.C.C.R. 382.

68 This would be a harsh rule — see J.A. Andrews, "Reform in the Law of Complicity" [1972] Crim. L.R. 764.

69 See paras 5.53 to 5.55, *infra*.

70 *R. v. Powell; R. v. English* [1997] 3 W.L.R. 959; *McAuliffe v. The Queen* (1995) 69 A.L.J.R. 621. See also the New Zealand Crimes Act 1961, s.66(2): "Where two or more persons form a common intention to prosecute any unlawful purpose, and to assist each other therein, each of them is a party to every offence committed by any one of them in the prosecution of the common purpose if the commission of that offence was known to be a probable consequence of the prosecution of the common purpose." *Cf.* Canadian Criminal Code, s.21(2): "Where two or more persons form an intention in common to carry out an unlawful purpose and to assist each other therein and any one of them, in carrying out the common purpose, commits an offence, each of them who knew or ought to have known that the commission of the offence would be a probable consequence of carrying out the common purpose is a party to that offence." The variations as to whether knowledge is to be treated subjectively or objectively, and as to the probability or just possibility (English and Australian law) of the criminal consequence, are noteworthy.

71 *cf. Cadona v. H.M. Advocate,* 1996 S.C.C.R. 300.

72 *R. v. Betty* (1964) 48 Cr.App.R. 6; *R. v. Smith (Wesley)* [1963] 1 W.L.R. 1200; *R. v. Stewart and Schofield* (1995) 1 Cr.App.R. 441, approving dicta of Lord Lane C.J. in *R. v. Reid* (1976) 63 Cr.App.R. 109, at 112. *Stewart and Schofield* has been subjected to criticism — see Smith and Hogan, p.147 *et seq*. It was not overruled, however, by the House of Lords in *R. v. Powell; R. v. English* [1997] 3 W.L.R. 959. *Cf. R. v. Mahmood* [1995] R.T.R. 48.

fact inflicts only minor injuries and is convicted only of unlawful wounding A cannot be convicted of assault with intent to cause grievous bodily harm, since no such offence occurred.[73]

The type of situation in which only the person who uses the violence is responsible for its consequences may be illustrated by *H.M. Advocate v. Welsh and McLachlan*[74] in which it was alleged that two men had broken into a house and that one of them had beaten the owner to death with a crowbar. It was not known which accused had struck the blows, and indeed there seems to have been no evidence at all about what happened in the house. In these circumstances Lord Young told the jury that in view of the sudden and unexpected nature of the violence, and the absence of any agreement between the accused to use violence, each could be held responsible only for his own part in the affair. Accordingly, since it was not known who had struck the blows, both must be acquitted of homicide.[75] **5.44**

Even where there is no prior agreement to use violence there may, of course, be art and part guilt by reason of concert, a concert which would require to be established by evidence of what happened at the time of the assault, evidence which was lacking in *Welsh and McLachlan.*[75a] Such a concert to do violence would be quite independent of the original plan to break in. The case of *McCudden and Cameron*[76] may be regarded as an example of this type of situation. The two accused agreed to break into a shop, expecting the caretaker to be absent. They asked a friend to keep watch for them, and assured him that no violence would be used. In fact the caretaker was present and disturbed the accused who killed her, one of them apparently striking her after the other had bound and gagged her. It was accepted that neither had intended to kill her. Lord Blackburn directed the jury that both were responsible for the death. His Lordship also referred to the position of the man who was supposed to keep watch for them — it seems that in fact he did not do so — and said, "As a matter of law, if [he] had been keeping cop outside as part of the general scheme to rob the shop, he might quite well have been sitting here today in court on the charge of art and part in the murder, although he may have had a different defence that he was only keeping cop to enable the two accused to escape detection when burgling the safe and that defence might have been good, but he would just as likely have been charged with murder".[77] It is submitted that he would have been guilty of murder only if he had known that serious violence involving wicked recklessness was contemplated. If he had been charged with murder and **5.45**

---

[73] *R. v. Richards* [1974] Q.B. 776. But A would be guilty of inciting B to cause grievous bodily harm.

[74] (1897) 5 S.L.T. 137.

[75] In fact both were acquitted of housebreaking as well, but that does not affect the argument. In *Webster v. Wishart*, 1955 S.L.T. 243 the accused were two thieves who used a car to make their getaway. The car was driven recklessly and both were convicted of reckless driving. On appeal the convictions were quashed since there was no evidence to show which had driven the car, and no evidence of the circumstances of the reckless driving — *i.e.* no evidence of a concert to drive recklessly, and no evidence to show that the reckless driving was a foreseeable consequence of the theft. *Cf. Shaw v. H.M. Advocate,* 1953 J.C. 51; *S. v. Madlala,* 1969 (2) S.A. 637 (A.D.).

[75a] (1897) 5 S.L.T. 137.

[76] High Court at Glasgow, April 1932, unrep'd.

[77] Transcript of proceedings, 300–301.

the jury had believed that he had only agreed to keep watch on condition that no violence was used they would have been bound to acquit him: for violence would not then have been part of the plot he was in, nor even a foreseeable result of it since no weapons were carried. His mere presence outside could not, of course, make him party to any concert entered into inside by the other two.

5.46 *Error as to victim.* If A sets out to murder B and shoots C instead because he mistook him for B, A is guilty of murder, since his error is held to be irrelevant.[78] Similarly, if A and B set out to murder C, or A hires B to murder C, and B shoots at D whom he mistakes for C, A is in each case guilty of murder, for D's death is the result of the plot to kill C, and A is liable for B's error just as much as B is.[79] But if A gave B poison with which to kill C, or made arrangements for C and D to be at a particular place in order that B might kill C, and B intentionally killed D instead for his own private reasons, A would not be responsible in law for D's death, since the death would not arise out of the plot but out of B's independent intention.[80]

The question always is whether what in fact happened was a reasonably probable outcome of the original plot, and certain behaviour by B short of his acting on a private ploy may take him out of the limits of such reasonable probability. In the South African case of *R. v. Longone*,[81] A gave B poison to kill C. B put the poison in C's hut. He later learned that M was going to be in C's hut but took no steps to remove the poison or warn M. M took the poison and died. A majority of the Appeal Court held that M's death was not a reasonably probable result of A's plan, and A's conviction for the murder of M was quashed.[82]

5.47 *Concerted carelessness.* The same principles apply when death results from a concert to do something lawful in itself, but to do it carelessly. In *Geo. Barbier and Ors*[83] three men went shooting on a range: they did not put up the customary warning flags, or give any other warning that they were going to shoot: they shot in the direction of a public beach, and a girl was killed, having been hit by only one bullet. Lord Neaves told the jury that "if two or more persons went together to shoot, and shot in a reckless manner in the direction of a public place . . . and a death resulted, all would be guilty of culpable homicide, although it could not be proved who fired the fatal shot."[84] This, as stated, is too wide; there must be an agreement, not merely to shoot, but to shoot recklessly. All the members of a shooting party would not be guilty of homicide if one of them stupidly pointed a gun at a ghillie and killed him. Even if two of them independently were stupid enough to fire in the direction of some passers-by these two would not both be guilty of homicide. If it were known whose gun fired the fatal shot he would be guilty; if it were not known, both would have to be acquitted.[85]

---

[78] *infra*, para. 9.11.

[79] See *Hiu Chi-Ming v. R.* [1991] 3 All E.R. 897, PC. But see F.B. Sayre, "Criminal Responsibility for Acts of Another" (1930) 43 H.L.R. 689, 697.

[80] Hume, i, 280; Burnett, p.266.

[81] [1938] A.D. 532.

[82] See also *R. v. Calhaem* [1985] Q.B. 808.

[83] (1867) 5 Irv. 483.

[84] At 487–488.

[85] *cf. Docherty v. H.M. Advocate,* 1945 J.C. 89.

It does not matter in this connection whether or not the reckless discharge of firearms is a crime in itself even where no injury is caused. What is important is that where death is caused by the reckless actings of an individual that individual is guilty of homicide; accordingly, where death is caused by the reckless actings of a concert, all the members of the concert are guilty.[86]

Homicide in a brawl

The cases discussed above are all fairly simple, both in their facts and in the law applicable to them. A more complicated situation concerns a street brawl in which someone is killed. Such cases are usually distinguished by the presence of a number of people associated for the purpose of creating a disturbance or of committing some minor crime, by a deal of confusion as to how the victim was killed, and by the fact that one or more of the people so associated delivered the fatal blow or blows. **5.48**

The ideal approach to such a situation, especially where there is no pre-concert to do any violence, is no doubt that advocated in the *Digest*: to investigate the blows given by each of the persons assembled at the scene of the brawl.[87] Where such an investigation does yield results these results will normally be taken into consideration and an individualistic approach will be adopted, so that only those who actually took part in the attack on the deceased will be convicted of homicide. But this is a counsel of perfection: it is usually impossible to discover which of the accused struck the victim, and in such circumstances the approach adopted by the law is not entirely clear or consistent and seems to have varied somewhat over the past two hundred years. Sometimes the tendency has been to adopt a collectivist approach, to treat the death as the consequence of the brawl, and therefore to regard all the brawlers as guilty. At present, however, the law seems to favour an individualistic view based on the *mens rea* of each person involved[88] — at least relative to the question whether such a person can be convicted of murder or culpable homicide where there is no evidence that he personally struck the fatal blow. Concert is still essential, of course.[89] Without it, each person can only be responsible for his own acts.

---

[86] See *Sutherland v. H.M. Advocate (No. 1)*, 1994 S.C.C.R. 80.

[87] D. 48. 8. 17.

[88] See *Brown v. H.M. Advocate,* 1993 S.C.C.R. 382, which was decided after *Melvin v. H.M. Advocate,* 1984 S.C.C.R. 113, had held that in homicide art and part cases, it was possible to discriminate as between murder and culpable homicide according to the degree of recklessness with which each accused had associated himself. *Melvin* was not, however, referred to in *Brown. Cf. Kabalu v. H.M. Advocate*, 1999 S.C.C.R. 348.

[89] In *S. v. Safatsa*, 1988 (1) S.A. 868 (A), it was decided that if there could be shown a common purpose to kill, and if persons consciously sharing that purpose (adding this element from *S. v. Mgedezi*, 1989 (1) S.A. 687 (A.D.)) were proved actively to have associated themselves with the conduct of the mob before some members of that mob inflicted the fatal injuries, then those persons were as guilty of murder as those who had inflicted such injuries. The conduct of those who actually delivered the fatal blows was imputed to such persons. The more difficult situation, where a person joins in the activities of a mob after the fatal violence has been inflicted (or where there is no evidence to show when the fatal violence was inflicted, which will in effect amount to the same situation), was considered in *S. v. Motaung*, 1990 (4) S.A. 485 (A.D.). The opportunity was taken to reject the influential but minority view of Schreiner J.A. in *R. v. Mgxwiti*, 1954 (1) S.A. 370 (A.D.), at 382H to 383A, that the matter should be decided by applying the principle of ratification, *i.e.* "that whoever joins in a murderous assault upon a person must be taken to have ratified the infliction of any injuries which have already been inflicted, whether or not

5.49 *Hume's treatment of the problem.* Hume deals with two situations in this connection. The first is where "the felonious purpose is taken up suddenly, on a fortuitous quarrel among persons who were lawfully assembled for some other object", and someone is killed with a lethal weapon. In such cases Hume holds that anyone who co-operated in the killing, by using a weapon, or at least having one ready in his hand, is guilty of homicide, but that "a person shall not be liable to any punishment, unless he have in some measure been active in the assault."[90] Hume seems to require a spontaneous concert to kill or do serious violence, and he treats the display of weapons as evidence of the accused's adherence to that concert. He excludes from guilt those who do not use or brandish weapons, considering that they may have been involved only "out of curiosity or indiscretion, or at the worst with no more criminal purpose than that of raising a brawl in the street."[91] Mere presence as part of a group of brawlers, mere intention to brawl, is not enough to make one guilty of homicide if one or more of the brawlers uses weapons and kills someone.

5.50 The second situation with which Hume deals is that where there are no lethal weapons, and so no line can be drawn between those who had weapons and those who had not. He gives the following example:

> "[T]wo parties of men, all of them in liquor, meet and quarrel on the streets of a town, in the dusk of the evening. Words pass at first; and it soon comes to blows (owing to faults on both sides) with such instruments as the parties have with them, or can lay hold of at the time; and in this bustle a man is killed, it cannot, with certainty, be said how, or by whom, but probably through a succession of injuries, done by several persons. In these circumstances, it would plainly be unjust to punish every one capitally, who is proved to have struck or at all to have meddled with the sufferer . . . the fair result is, to inflict an arbitrary pain on those who struck the man, and entirely to acquit the others."[92]

Hume seems deliberately to have made the facts confused, and he includes among the reasons for his solution that it was probably partly

---

in the result these turn out to be fatal either individually or taken together." This was, and is, an attractive theory, since as far as the injuries inflicted on the deceased are concerned, it need only be shown that the deceased was not dead when the accused, appreciating the mob's common purpose, actively associated himself with their actions. It is, of course, very difficult in such situations to show (a) when the fatal blow or blows were delivered and (b) whether or not any blows delivered by A shortened the life of the victim. There is also much to be said for the view that if A actively joins a murderous assault, there is no good reason for making his responsibility depend on a fact of which he was very probably ignorant — *viz.* whether the fatal blow had already been delivered: but this argument will clearly not do, since it leads to the conclusion that it equally would not matter if the victim was already dead before A joined the attack (*cf. Collins v. H.M. Advocate,* 1991 S.C.C.R. 898). The court in *Motaung* decided in any event that it was contrary to principle to make persons liable for what had been done before they joined the mob: this smacked of retrospective criminal liability. Since it could not be shown in *Motaung* when the fatal injuries had been inflicted, the convictions of the appellants for murder could not be sustained, and verdicts of attempted murder were substituted. Scots law adopted the same general approach in *McLaughlan v. H.M. Advocate,* 1991 S.C.C.R. 733 (although the case involved assault to the danger of life rather than homicide). *Cf. Kabalu v. H.M. Advocate,* 1999 S.C.C.R. 348.

[90] Hume, i, 270–271.

[91] *ibid.*, 271.

[92] Hume, i, 272.

the fault of the deceased anyway. Such a consideration may be irrelevant in strict logic, but in fact, of course, it will influence a jury and so affect their views on reasonable foreseeability. Hume's main grounds seem to be that the quarrel arose suddenly and that no lethal weapons were used. He apparently rejects the simple view that the fact that the members of the group were assisting each other in the attack is enough to make them art and part with each other.

Hume's approach is supported by at least two cases. The first is *Geo. Hutchieson and Ors*[93] in which a group of people were engaged in molesting and insulting passers-by in the street. The deceased intervened to protect one of their victims, and the group attacked him with stones and killed him. All the accused were convicted of rioting but none of homicide. The second case is *Thos. Marshall and Ors*[94] in which a group of Dundee apprentices got into a fight with some country masons. There were blows on both sides, and a mason was killed. In the absence of previous concert and of evidence that any of the accused had struck a fatal blow they were convicted of riot and assault, but not of homicide.[95] On the other hand, in *Swanston and Ors*[96] four men who had gone out on a poaching expedition were convicted of assaulting a gamekeeper to the danger of his life by striking him repeatedly with a gun. Lord Justice-Clerk Boyle told the jury that it was enough to convict them all that they had been poaching together, had all been there when the assault started, and that when one had been caught the others came to his help. He went on to say, "In a case of this kind, of several persons all similarly armed, where it is not proved by whose hand the most severe injury was inflicted, . . . three cannot be acquitted, because another and different injury was done by the fourth."[97] **5.51**

The modern treatment of the problem. It is difficult to pin down the modern law. The most recent case decision[98] relevant to brawls (although hardly on its facts involving a classic brawl situation) seems to favour an approach ultimately dependent on individual *mens rea*. It makes use of the idea of foresight. It does not lay any particular stress on the presence or absence of weapons; but at the same time, the decision was reached without considering Hume, and without consideration of the earlier twentieth century cases which had specifically addressed the issue of homicide in the course of a brawl. **5.52**

Prior to 1993, the best statement of the modern law was thought to be contained in Lord Moncrieff's opinion in *Docherty v. H.M. Advocate* in 1945.[99] Lord Moncrieff criticised an illustration given by the trial judge,

---

[93] (1784) Hume, i, 272.

[94] (1824) Alison, i, 64.

[95] *Cf.* also *Macpherson and Ors* (1808) Burnett, 281; Alison, i, 63–64.

[96] (1836) 1 Swin. 54.

[97] At 60.

[98] *Brown v. H.M. Advocate,* 1993 S.C.C.R. 382. *Cf. Mathieson v. H.M. Advocate,* 1996 S.C.C.R. 388.

[99] 1945 J.C. 89, 95–96. The passage in question is *obiter* since the facts of the case — three men went into a room, one was killed by a hatchet, one disappeared, and the third was tried for murder — are rather different from those of the brawl. The accused's conviction was quashed because there was no evidence that he had struck the fatal blow, and the jury were not explicitly directed that unless they found proof of concert they must acquit; *cf. H.M. Advocate v. Welsh and McLachlan* (1897) 5 S.L.T. 137; see *supra*, para. 5.44. Contrast *Morton v. H.M. Advocate,* 1986 S.L.T. 622.

Lord Jamieson, to the effect that, "If without premeditation two or three men set on to someone in the street with the intention, just perhaps entered into at the time, of causing him injury, and one stabs him fatally, then all are equally guilty although there was not really an intention, until the man came along, to attack him at all." This, said Lord Moncrieff, was "too widely and too unguardedly framed." He referred to Hume's treatment of the subject and to Anderson's statement that, "If a sudden brawl arise, *rixa per plures*, sticks and fists being used, and one draws a knife and stabs another, the friends of the man who used the knife are not guilty of murder if the injured man dies."[1] This, of course, is because in such circumstances the use of the knife is treated as unforeseeable.

Lord Moncrieff stated the law as follows:

> "It is true that if people acting in concert have reason to expect that a lethal weapon will be used — and their expectation may be demonstrated by various circumstances, as, for example, if they themselves are carrying arms or if they know that arms and lethal weapons are being carried by their associates — they may then under the law with regard to concert each one of them become guilty of murder if the weapon is used with fatal results by one of them. In view of their assumed expectation that it might be used, and of their having joined together in an act of violence apt to be completed by its use, they will be assumed in law to have authorised the use . . .
>
> . . . secondary responsibility for a criminal act arises only in cases of reasonable expectation."[2]

Lord Moncrieff confines himself to the use of lethal weapons, but his statement that "secondary responsibility . . . arises only in cases of reasonable expectation" would be capable of wider application, and indeed, with certain qualifications, is probably still the kernel of the modern law. It is notable that Lord Moncrieff requires a joining together in an act of violence, although not active participation in the violence. It is also notable that he talks of an "assumed expectation", *i.e.* of what is deemed to be the expectation of the accused. This assumption depends on reasonable foreseeability, on whether the jury treat the death as a foreseeable consequence of the group action, and this in turn may depend on the jury's view of the responsibility of the accused for the crime.

Although it cannot confidently be stated that Lord Moncrieff's exposition exactly represents the modern law, what he said (together with elements drawn from Hume) seemed to be supported by three unreported cases from the 1940s and 1950s.

5.53 *Three unreported cases.* The working of the law, as set out by Lord Moncrieff in *Docherty*,[3] can be seen in three unreported cases which resemble the typical brawl more or less in their respective facts, and which occurred when the punishment for murder was death, so that the question of concert was a vital one.

THE CROSBIE CASE. The first is that of *Crosbie and Ors.*[4] The facts of *Crosbie* are typical of the twentieth century street killing which was a

---

[1] Anderson, p.48.

[2] 1945 J.C. at 95–96.

[3] See para 5–52, *supra*.

[4] High Court at Glasgow, Dec. 1945, unrep'd. The case is reported on another point *sub nom. Lennie v. H.M. Advocate*, 1946 J.C. 79.

feature of Scottish, and particularly of Glasgow, crime of the period. The facts are confused, and most of the witnesses were unreliable, but the following is a sufficient summary of what happened. The accused were members of a group of five or more people who roamed the streets for about an hour before the murder creating disturbances, brandishing bayonets and other weapons, and threatening at least two persons. They ultimately debouched from a tramcar into a crowded street where they probably chased, or were chased by, a rival group. In any event, they chased after the deceased (who did not belong either to the Crosbie group or to their rivals), shouting cries of "Kill him" or "Get him", and waving bayonets. A few minutes later a group of people was seen standing round the deceased's body, and one of the accused came forward either from the edge of the group or from the other side of the road, brandishing a bloody bayonet and shouting "Here's your victim". Of the four accused, all of whom were charged with a breach of the peace, two assaults prior to the murder, and murder, those who had been seen brandishing weapons were convicted of all the charges, and one who had not been seen with a weapon was acquitted of the murder charge; the one who was seen waving the bayonet after the murder was hanged.

On these facts it is fairly simple to infer a concert to do serious harm to the deceased, albeit a concert formed only a short while before his death, and the result was consistent with Hume's version of the law. The presiding judge, Lord Mackay, approached the problem from the foreseeability point of view, and laid hardly any stress on the question of which accused was carrying weapons, or on what was actually done by each accused at the time of the killing. He directed the jury on concert as follows:

> "[I]f the Crown has proved that if there is a group of associated people with some common purpose, whether it be suddenly taken up or at more length considered, and in this case I shall say short of pre-concert — for instance pre-concert to kill anybody; that is not averred — but short of pre-concert, if they are found associated for a continuous time brandishing lethal weapons which should not be brandished in public streets, threatening the lieges or three particular people in the lieges with these weapons, terrifying the populace, and if they are doing that at four different places and times consecutively within an hour and a quarter, and on the last occasion one of their weapons is used to lethal purpose and others so grouped as to help in that lethal purpose . . . they cannot escape the consequences. If they have killed a man it does not matter that the Crown cannot put their finger on the right person, but there must be a group associated for that purpose."[5]

This is not altogether clear. The last sentence begs the question of the purpose of the group, and "so grouped as to help" is unsatisfactory — the question is "Did they help?" It is also clear from the general progress of the case, and the lack of any clear distinction between those who did and those who did not have or use weapons, that the *ratio* was not so much the formation of a spontaneous concert to attack the deceased as that, "If you go around the streets brandishing weapons someone will get hurt", and accordingly all the accused could have been

[5] Transcript of judge's charge, 43–44.

held responsible for the death. The alternative approach, that the jury could convict only persons seen using or waving bayonets at the time of the murder, does not seem to have been considered, perhaps because the evidence about who had weapons and what happened at the end was very confused, and such an approach might have led to the acquittal of all, or all but one, of the accused. The Crown took up the position that the jury should be asked to say whether the crime was murder or culpable homicide, but Lord Mackay directed them that there was no room for culpable homicide, and did not suggest that they might convict some of the accused of culpable homicide and some of murder.[6]

5.54 THE HARRIS CASE. The second case is *Harris and Ors.*[7] Three men — two brothers, Paul Christopher Harris and Claude Milford Harris, and a third man, Walter Drennan — were charged with assaulting Drennan's brother-in-law M. and a man Boyle, and with murdering a man Dunleavy by striking him with a broken bottle. The facts, so far as relevant to this discussion, were as follows. The three accused were together in a public house when Drennan announced his intention of going to see M who had the day before assaulted his wife, Drennan's sister. It seems clear that Drennan intended to assault M, and that the Harrises agreed to go along "and see fair play". At least some of the accused carried bottles, weapons recognised as lethal.[8] The three went together to where M stayed; Drennan went up to M's house, followed by Christopher, while Claude remained at the closemouth. At that stage something was said about "getting them one by one". In the house Drennan made to attack M who retreated while Boyle and the deceased, who were in the house, intervened. Drennan did not manage to strike M, but Christopher did. A running fight then seems to have developed between Boyle and Drennan, and between Christopher and the deceased, and it seems that when this fight reached the close, Claude joined in. In any event, Drennan and Boyle moved out into the street, and the Harrises and the deceased went through the close into the backcourt where they were seen to kick him. At some stage, probably in the close, the deceased received fatal wounds administered by one of the Harrises with a broken bottle, but there was no evidence about how this happened, or which brother used the bottle. In the course of the trial the Crown dropped the charge against Claude of assaulting M, and the judge directed the jury to acquit Christopher of the assault on Boyle, and to acquit Drennan of the murder. In the result, Drennan and Christopher were convicted of assaulting M and both the Harrises were convicted of murder (Drennan and Claude were acquitted of assaulting Boyle, for reasons that do not affect this discussion).

---

[6] It should also perhaps be noted that the case was heard at a time when street fighting by gangs of youths was rife in Glasgow, and that the authorities regarded this case, and the execution of one of the accused, as responsible for the subsequent decline in crimes of violence: see R.C. App.6, para. 78. The execution was the first in Scotland for seventeen years, and the trial the first example, at least in the twentieth century, of a conviction of more than two persons for the murder of one person. There were only three prior cases in the century in which two people had been convicted of murdering another in concert, and they were connected with robbery or housebreaking; in one of them, *H.M. Advocate v. Fraser and Rollins*, 1920 J.C. 60, both were hanged. I am indebted to Mr D.J. Stevenson, sometime Clerk of Justiciary, for this information; *cf.* R.C. App. 2, Table 5.

[7] High Court at Glasgow, Sept. 1950, unrep'd.

[8] So much so that L.J.-C. Thomson directed the jury that there was no room for a verdict of culpable homicide where a broken bottle caused death.

Lord Justice-Clerk Thomson adopted an individualistic approach to the matter, and did not stress the aspect of foreseeability. He did say, "Then, of course, you have the evidence that the Harrises were going with Drennan to beat [M] up, a thing which they had no right to do. People that take the law into their own hands must, I think — you are to judge — have in contemplation that there may be resistance to the act and that third parties may intervene",[9] and that the jury must ask themselves if the use of a broken bottle was "within the purview of the common purpose",[10] but he did not say that all the accused could be convicted of all the charges as they were in a concert to assault M and knew bottles were being carried. Instead, he directed the jury that to convict even the Harrises of murder they must find that the brothers had formed an agreement specifically to kill or grievously injure the deceased, saying that "If one of them killed the deceased while they were acting together with the common purpose of killing him or of doing him grievous bodily harm regardless of the consequences, then each is responsible for the acts of the other, but you must be satisfied . . . that they were acting in concert in that common criminal purpose",[11] and not, presumably, in any other, such as a purpose to assault Drennan's brother-in-law. Drennan was freed of responsibility for the death because he was not present at the time, and therefore was not in any concert to kill the deceased.

In the same way, although Lord Thomson said of the assault on M, "If you are satisfied that Drennan and Christopher had formed a common criminal purpose to combine and punish [M], then in virtue of that common criminal purpose Drennan is responsible for what Christopher did and Christopher is responsible for what Drennan did",[12] he obviously accepted the Crown view that Claude, who had also been in the concert, could not be charged with assaulting M, because he had remained downstairs, although his later actings made it clear that he had not in any way dissociated himself from the others.[13]

THE HAMILTON CIRCUS CASE. The third case is *Gallacher and Ors*,[14] **5.55**
and it is of interest because of the absence of any lethal weapon, and also, apparently, of any prior concert at all. The background of the case was a feud between the members of a travelling circus and some local inhabitants of Hamilton, and it is thought that the deceased was mistaken for a member of the circus staff. It seems that one of the local men started a fight with the deceased on the circus ground while the circus was being dismantled, and that a number of other men joined in.

---

[9] Transcript of proceedings, 383–384.

[10] At 375.

[11] At 373.

[12] At 361–362.

[13] In the appeal court on the hearing of an appeal by the brothers L.J.-G. Cooper said of the dropping of the charge against Claude of assaulting M and the direction to acquit Christopher on the charge of assaulting Boyle, "whether in these respects the two appellants were treated with undue leniency I need not consider. The jury had no opportunity of considering the matter . . . and they cannot therefore be convicted of inconsistency in reasoning", *i.e.* in acquitting in these instances and finding concert proved in relation to the murder charge: Opinion of L.J.-C. Cooper, 4, Criminal Appeal Court, Oct. 1950, unrep'd.

[14] High Court at Glasgow, Oct. 1950, unrep'd. The case is reported on another point in 1951 J.C. 38.

Ultimately, they all stood around the victim who was kicked to death. Three of the crowd were charged with murder and convicted.[15]

There was some evidence that each of these three had kicked the deceased but the presiding judge, Lord Keith, did not regard this as necessary for conviction, "if . . . any of the accused was part of a crowd or group engaged in the common purpose of assaulting this man", since "each is responsible for the consequences of that assault, although only one of them may have delivered the fatal kick. If the accused were in a kicking crowd animated by a common purpose, joining in the attack, assisting and encouraging, each and all are responsible for the consequences."[16]

Gallacher[16a] applies the rule of foreseeability to cases of "spontaneous concert" where there are no lethal weapons, and this seems to go beyond *Hutchieson*[17] and *Marshall.*[18] The *ratio* of *Gallacher*[18a] is that if A joins a group of people who are assaulting someone, and joins in with the purpose of aiding in that assault then, if the assault proves fatal, he is guilty of homicide whatever his own part in the assault was.[19] Whether his guilt is of murder or only of culpable homicide depends on how likely it was that the assault would prove fatal. The two verdicts were left to the jury in *Gallacher*[19a]; in *Crosbie*[20] and in *Harris*[21] the court took the view that the weapons used were so dangerous that those using them must be regarded as reckless, and so as guilty of murder.

5.56 *Modern authority.* The modern position must take into account the decision of the Appeal Court in *Brown v. H.M. Advocate.*[22] This was not apparently a case involving a typical brawl, although the actual incident in which the fatality occurred was described by one of the counsel at the appeal as "a confused melee".[23] The separated wife of the deceased and her male partner had gone to see the deceased on the basis of "sorting out her difficulties" with him. It was clear that this was understood to involve some sort of confrontation with him. It was not clear that there was any pre-existing plan to assault him, although the female accused had previously threatened him with violence. The male accused picked up a hammer, or iron bar, on the way to the confrontation — although it was not certain whether this was known to his co-accused. In the event, the confrontation was or became a violent one. Witnesses spoke of two persons kicking and punching the deceased. It was admitted by the male accused that he struck the deceased over the head with the hammer or iron bar he had taken with him: but that did not constitute the fatal blow. The deceased was killed by one stab wound straight to his heart, most probably effected by a knife. Neither accused admitted to having had any such weapon, still less to having used it (or even to having seen it used) on the victim. Despite the lack of numbers involved, the factual

---

[15] See R.C. App.4, para. 6. There was a fourth accused who was acquitted.
[16] Transcript of judge's charge, 37.
[16a] High Court at Glasgow, Oct. 1950, unrep'd.
[17] (1784) Hume, i, 272, see para. 5.51, *supra*.
[18] (1824) Alison, i, 64, see para. 5.51, *supra*.
[18a] High Court at Glasgow, Oct. 1950, unrep'd.
[19] *Cf. Ramnath Mohan v. The Queen* [1967] 2 A.C. 187 (P.C.).
[19a] High Court at Glasgow, Oct. 1950, unrep'd.
[20] See para. 5.53, *supra*.
[21] See para. 5.54, *supra*.
[22] 1993 S.C.C.R. 382.
[23] *ibid.*, opinion of L.J.-G. Hope at 390D.

situation was not too distantly removed from the situations involved in the cases discussed in the paragraphs immediately above, and might, therefore, have been governed by the principles thought to emanate from them. That was probably the approach taken by the trial judge who told the jury:

> "If . . . you are satisfied that there was here some concerted . . . attack by the two accused the next question you must ask for each of them in turn is what so far as this accused is concerned was the foreseeable scope of the joint attack and, in particular, were murderous weapons to be used so as to make death or serious injury within her or, as the case may be, his contemplation."[24]

He accepted that the concerted attack might well have been spontaneous rather than pre-planned, as befits a true brawl situation, but emphasised that what mattered, if there had been such an attack, was whether each accused had realised that murderous weapons would or might be used. If so, "the foreseeable scope of that joint attack was indeed a murderous one, whether or not it was he [or she] who actually wielded the knife which killed Douglas Brown".[25] Because of the way in which the fatal blow had been delivered — with precision to the victim's heart — the trial judge ruled out culpable homicide on the basis that the necessary wicked recklessness had been demonstrated. If the jury took the view that the hammer or iron bar "was a weapon which might foreseeably cause serious or fatal injury",[26] that would be sufficient to make the foreseeable scope of the joint attack a murderous one, and it would not matter that the fatal injury had been inflicted with a different type of lethal weapon.

Both accused were convicted of murder. Had the Hume[27] and *Crosbie*[28] approaches been adopted, it might have been possible to convict the male accused of murder since he admittedly had a weapon which the jury would have been entitled to classify as "murderous" or "lethal". The female accused might then have been convicted of assault (since the trial judge had ruled out culpable homicide for either of them). The trial judge's approach is, however, more closely allied to that of Lord Moncrieff in *Docherty*[29] or Lord Keith in *Gallacher*.[30]

In the event, the Appeal Court quashed the convictions on the ground of misdirection.[31] A verdict of culpable homicide was substituted in the case of each appellant. It seems that what the jury should have been told was that they must be "satisfied that they both [*i.e.* both accused] had in contemplation, as part of their joint purpose, an act of the necessary degree of wicked recklessness such as that the deceased would be stabbed by plunging a knife into his heart."[32] Although a stab wound directly to the heart showed wicked recklessness as far as the person delivering that blow was concerned, it did not do so for the other. Not only would the other person have to be aware that a knife was likely to

---

[24] *ibid.*, 385F.
[25] *ibid.*, 387E.
[26] *ibid.*, 387D.
[27] See paras 5.49 to 5.51, *supra*.
[28] See para. 5.53, *supra*.
[29] See para. 5.52, *supra*.
[30] See para 5.55, *supra*.
[31] Neither Hume nor any of the cases discussed above was considered or even referred to.
[32] *Brown v. H.M. Advocate,* 1993 S.C.C.R. 382, at 390F.

be used in the attack but also that it was likely to be used to inflict a wound of the sort actually inflicted before murder could be considered for that person. As the object of this investigation is the ascertainment that each person in an attacking group was aware that conduct of the correct degree of wicked recklessness was likely, the *ratio* of the case is independent of the use of weapons. It is doubtful, therefore, whether the accused in *Gallacher*[33] would today be convicted of murder. If an accused person might not "appreciate the full significance of the production and use of [a] knife",[34] still less might he do so in relation to an assault involving kicking. As long as there was a concerted assault, however, culpable homicide would remain as an option.[35]

5.57 *Conclusion.* It is difficult to reach a firm conclusion on this matter since *Brown*[36] does not consider the earlier cases of *Crosbie*,[37] *Harris*,[38] or *Gallacher*[39] (which in any event are not consistent *inter se*) nor the *dictum* of Lord Moncrieff in *Docherty*.[40] It was probably clear prior to *Brown*[40a] that it makes no difference whether the brawl is conducted with lethal weapons or not, so long as no one produces any weapons unexpectedly. It was also probably clear prior to *Brown* that it is not necessary for the Crown to show that any particular accused struck any blows in order to obtain a conviction against him. *Crosbie*[40b] and *Gallacher*[40c] might have been authorities for the view that anyone who joins in an operation of which death is a foreseeable result is guilty of homicide; but there was evidence in *Crosbie* and *Gallacher* that each convicted man struck a blow or brandished a weapon at some stage; and *Harris*[41] suggested that membership in a criminal enterprise which results in death is not enough, even where death is foreseeable.

It may be that the doctrine of responsibility for foreseeable consequences was used by the law[41a] only as a last resort, and only where no detailed information was available about the fatal assault. But little information about the actual assault or any prior plan was available in *Brown*, yet the court made a point of taking an individualistic approach based ultimately on each accused's contemplation of what the other was likely to do: if he was likely to kill someone by acting in a wickedly reckless manner, the other who contemplated such conduct yet continued with his part in the concerted operation would be guilty of murder if someone was in fact killed as contemplated.

---

[33] See para. 5.55, *supra*.

[34] *Mathieson v. H.M. Advocate,* 1996 S.C.C.R. 388, Lord Sutherland's direction to the jury at 393F. It is noteworthy that Lord Sutherland also told them, at 394A, that they must look at the state of mind of each accused to decide whether *he* had the necessary degree of wicked recklessness. This would go further than even the current English law — see *R. v. Powell; R. v. English* [1997] 3 W.L.R. 959. The situation might preferably be that each person in the group should have contemplated that an act of wicked recklessness was likely to be performed by another member of the group in the course of executing the common plan — yet continued with his part in the operation. See also *Kabalu v. H.M. Advocate*, 1999 S.C.C.R. 348.

[35] See *R. v. Nathan* [1981] 2 N.Z.L.R. 473. *Cf. Cadona v. H.M. Advocate,* 1996 S.C.C.R. 300.

[36] See para. 5.56, *supra*.

[37] See para. 5.53, *supra*.

[38] See para. 5.54, *supra*.

[39] See para. 5.55, *supra*.

[40] See para. 5.52, *supra*.

[40a] See para. 5.56, *supra*.

[40b] See para. 5.56, *supra*.

[40c] See para. 5.56, *supra*.

[41] See para. 5.56, *supra*.

[41a] As suggested in the second edition of this work at para. 5.55.

It is submitted that *Brown* in effect confirms that 'reasonable expectation' remains the key to the modern law. Where, for example, a lethal weapon has been used murderously by one of those involved in a concerted attack on the victim, the others who participated will equally be guilty of murder if they each anticipated not only that such a weapon would be carried and used, but also that it would be used either with intent to kill or in a wickedly reckless way. More generally and at a minimum, a secondary party's liability for murder depends on its being shown that he must reasonably have anticipated that one of his co-assailants might[42] act with the *mens rea* necessary for murder in Scotland. A person who is shown reasonably to have had such anticipation may not himself, of course, have intended or wished that any victim should be killed; he may even oppose such actions as he reasonably anticipates may happen. He may not himself, therefore, have the *mens rea* for murder.[43] But public policy considerations, which have almost certainly permeated judicial thinking in most of the cases discussed in the paragraphs above, clearly apply to justify his conviction for murder. As Lord Hutton said in *R. v. Powell; R. v. English*,[44] "the rules of the common law are not based solely on logic but relate to practical concerns and, in relation to crimes committed in the course of joint enterprises, to the need to give effective protection to the public against criminals operating in gangs." He who continues to play an active part in an assault, when he knows (or should know) that a co-assailant may use murderous violence, lends active support to an enterprise which he realises (or should realise) may end in murder. There are sound policy reasons, therefore, for discouraging him from doing so.[45]

Where, therefore, a person is engaged with another or others in a common purpose which is not itself a purpose to kill anyone and someone is killed in the course of carrying out that purpose, that person is guilty of murder, even though there is no evidence which part (if any) he played in the causing of the death, providing: (a) the killing was achieved by conduct of such wicked recklessness as to satisfy the *mens rea* of murder, (b) he foresaw[46] that such wickedly reckless conduct was possible (or perhaps probable[47]), and (c) he nevertheless continued to play his part in that common purpose. If these conditions are met, then the accused associates himself with conduct sufficiently reckless to satisfy the definition of murder. Due allowance must be made for appropriate **5.58**

---

[42] It probably goes too far to suggest that he must have anticipated that such a co-assailant *would* have so acted.

[43] This is a far more cogent argument in England, where the *mens rea* for murder is confined to intention: see *R. v. Powell; R. v. English* [1997] 3 W.L.R. 959.

[44] [1997] 3 W.L.R. 959, at 976E.

[45] The matter may not be so clear if the killing was carried out in a way fundamentally different from that anticipated. In *R. v. Powell; R. v. English* [1997] 3 W.L.R. 959, for example, English and Weddle had joined together to assault their victim with wooden posts. It was foreseeable that a blow from such a post might prove fatal. In the event, however, death was caused by a blow from a knife — which was considered sufficiently different from what English had foreseen (possible fatality from attack with wooden posts) to take the matter beyond even secondary liability for manslaughter. In Scotland, such "fundamental difference" might not avoid conviction for culpable homicide — as in *Brown v. H.M. Advocate*, 1993 S.C.C.R. 382, itself. *Cf. Kabalu v. H.M. Advocate*, 1999 S.C.C.R. 348.

[46] It is not clear whether objective foresight would suffice.

[47] Although degrees of probability have been rejected elsewhere: see *McAuliffe v. The Queen* (1995) 69 A.L.J.R. 621; *R. v. Powell; R. v. English* [1997] 3 W.L.R. 959.

defences such as provocation[48] or self-defence (which is not ruled out by willingly joining in an assault[49]); and, of course, if there is in fact evidence to enable distinctions to be drawn amongst those so engaged on the basis of individual actings at the time of the fatal assault, discriminatory verdicts may be returned.[50] If provision (a) above is not met, but the death is due to assault or simple recklessness in the carrying out of the common purpose, the person in question can probably be convicted of culpable homicide art and part, irrespective of his foresight provided, of course, he continued to play his part in that common purpose,[51] and the common purpose (or method of its execution) posed objective risk to human life.[52]

Accession After the Fact

5.59 Since guilt art and part is guilt of the whole crime and is the same as the guilt of the principal perpetrator of the crime, no one can be guilty art and part merely because of anything he did after the crime had been completed.[53] The act of hiding a murderer, or a body, does not in any sense "cause" the murder, and so cannot make the hider guilty of the murder.

The only way actings after the crime can affect art and part guilt is by providing evidence of a pre-existing agreement to help in the crime, evidence of prior concert. The pickpocket's accomplice who carries off the spoils is guilty of theft, not just because he takes away what he knows to have been stolen, but because his actings are evidence that he was in league with the pickpocket from the outset. If A knows that B is going to kill someone and offers to help him by disposing of the body, A may be guilty art and part of murder because of this prior agreement; but if A knows nothing of the murder until after it is over, and then agrees to hide the body out of friendship for B, he is not art and part in murder.[54] He may be guilty of a separate crime if what he does is in itself a crime, but that has nothing to do with being art and part in B's crime. The murderer's wife who commits perjury in order to save him from the gallows is guilty of perjury; she is not guilty of murder.[55]

---

48 See *Gray v. H.M. Advocate*, 1994 S.C.C.R. 225.

49 See *Boyle v. H.M. Advocate*, 1992 S.C.C.R. 824.

50 *Melvin v. H.M. Advocate*, 1984 S.C.C.R. 113. At 118, Lord Avonside thought that there should be striking differences in relevant conduct if discriminatory verdicts were to be justified. *Cf.*, *Kabalu v. H.M. Advocate*, 1999 S.C.C.R. 348.

51 Culpable homicide was the substituted verdict in *Brown v. H.M. Advocate*, 1993 S.C.C.R. 382, itself.

52 See *Sutherland v. H.M. Advocate (No.1)*, 1994 S.C.C.R. 80. *Cf. Kabalu v. H.M. Advocate*, 1999 S.C.C.R. 348, where the appellant's conviction for murder was quashed: he seems to have known that the deceased was to be pursued and assaulted, but not that murderous violence was to be used. In any event, he arrived at the scene of the killing after the fatal blows had been struck; and there was insufficient evidence that the appellant must have seen the extreme violence to which the deceased was subjected, and which eventually caused the death, before he delivered his own one or two kicks to the victim. The appellant's conviction was reduced to one of assault. No case is mentioned in the opinion of the Court.

53 *cf. Martin v. Hamilton*, 1989 S.C.C.R. 292.

54 *cf. Collins v. H.M. Advocate*, 1991 S.C.C.R. 898.

55 *cf.* Hume, i, 281–283.

CHAPTER 6

INCHOATE CRIMES

I — ATTEMPTED CRIMES[1]

The General Theory of Responsibility for Attempts

The essential difference between attempted crimes and completed crimes is, of course, that in the former the *actus reus* of the crime attempted is not in fact brought into being, although other crimes may be fully committed in the course of the attempt. The circumstances of an attempted murder, for example, may disclose the crimes of breach of the peace and assault, or they may disclose no completed crime at all; what is important is that they do not disclose the crime of murder. Punishment for attempted murder is independent of punishment for any other crimes which may have been committed in the course of the attempt and which may be punished in addition to it. 6.01

The justification for punishing attempts

In punishing persons for attempting to commit crimes the law is punishing them for something they did not do, for an unfulfilled intention. The justification for this can be stated in two ways. Firstly, it can be said that the man who intends to kill and does not succeed is just as wicked as the man who does succeed, and should be punished as severely as if he had succeeded — in the words of the *Digest*, anyone who did not kill a man but wounded him for the purpose of killing him, should be convicted of homicide.[2] But although it seems wrong that a wicked man should escape punishment because he has been "lucky" 6.02

[1] The literature on attempt is so extensive as to be excessive. It includes Gl. Williams, Chap. 14; J.C. Smith and B. Hogan, *Criminal Law* (9th ed., 1999, Sir J. Smith (ed.)), pp.306–326; R.A. Duff, *Criminal Attempts* (Oxford, 1996); E.M. Burchell and P.M.A. Hunt, *South African Criminal Law and Procedure* (3rd ed., 1997), Vol. 1, *General Principles of Criminal Law* (by J.M. Burchell), pp.342–357; F.B. Sayre, "Criminal Attempt" (1928) 41 H.L.R. 821; Thurman W. Arnold, "Criminal Attempts — The Rise and Fall of an Abstraction" (1930) 40 Y.L.J. 53; J.W.C. Turner, "Attempts to Commit Crimes", in *Modern Approach*, 273; H. Wechsler *et al.*, "The Treatment of Inchoate Crimes in the Model Penal Code, etc." (1961) 61 Col.L.R. 571; J.A.C. Thomas, "Sutor Ultra Crepidam", 1962 J.R. 127; P.R. Glazebrook, "Should We Have a Law of Attempted Crime?" (1969) 85 L.Q.R. 28; D.R. Stuart, "The *Actus Reus* in Attempts" [1970] Crim.L.R. 505; L.C.W.P., No. 50; L.C. Report No. 102, "Attempt, and Impossibility in Relation to Attempt, Conspiracy and Incitement", H.C. 646 (1980); I. Dennis, "The Criminal Attempts Act 1981" [1982] Crim. L.R. 5; R.J. Buxton, "Circumstances, Consequences and Attempted Rape" [1984] Crim. L.R. 25; R.A. Duff, "The Circumstances of an Attempt" (1991) 50 C.L.J. 100; K.J.M. Smith, "Proximity in Attempt: Lord Lane's Midway Course" [1991] Crim. L.R. 576.

[2] D. 48.8.1 (3).

enough not to succeed in his wicked intentions, it is nevertheless felt that he should not be punished as severely as if he had succeeded. This may be because it is felt that Providence has intervened to save him from the greater sin of having completed his crime, and that he is entitled to the "benefit" of this intervention[3]; or it may be, from a more strictly legal standpoint, because the law's main concern is with external harm, and in fact an attempt causes less harm than a completed crime.

Secondly, it is only common sense to lock the stable door once the horse has shown signs of intending to get out, and foolish to wait until it has gone: prevention is better than cure. If a man shows that he intends to kill someone, it is clearly foolish to leave him to get on with it. The law may not be able to intervene until he has actually tried to kill, but once he has tried there can be no objection to seeing that he does not remain at liberty to try again. Indeed, there is much more point in punishing someone for an attempted crime, than for a completed one. For once there is an attempt, "the offender appears to the legal system, on the strength of the act done, already so dangerous that the law dare not wait for further proofs of his dangerous character; the incompleted act furnishes a sufficient proof."[4] Success encourages, failure discourages, and punishment discourages still further, weakening the offender's aggressive tendencies, and so "the punishment of an attempted crime promises a much more effective and endurable result than the punishment of a completed crime."[5]

The "actus reus" of an attempted crime

6.03 Before the law inflicts punishment for an attempted crime it requires the commission of some overt act in pursuance of the attempt. This overt act is not required merely as evidence that A really was trying to commit the crime in question, as evidence of his intention; it is required in order to constitute the attempt, and there is no attempt until the requisite overt act has been committed. To be guilty of an attempted crime A must have intended to commit the crime,[6] and must have done certain things in pursuance of that intention. The existence of the intention, or even the expression of the intention to someone who might help in the commission of the intended crime, is insufficient.[7]

The law is forced by its very nature, as it were, to concentrate on what is in fact done and not just on what was intended, because what is in fact done is the standard on which it usually relies in ascribing responsibility. "Crimes", says Beccaria, "are only to be measured by the injury done to society. They err, therefore, who imagine that a crime is greater or less, according to the intention of the person by whom it is committed. . . . Upon that system, it would be necessary to form not only a particular code for every individual, but a new penal law for every crime."[8] The punishment of attempted crimes necessarily involves some departure

---

[3] *cf.* Hume, i, 179, "the benignity of our practice considers, that the man is not lost to society, and allows the offender an opportunity to repent, and make atonement for his crime."

[4] W. Ullmann, "The Reasons for Punishing Attempted Crimes" (1939) 51 J.R. 353, 363.

[5] *ibid.*, 364.

[6] At least this is so in most cases, but see *infra*, paras 7.78 *et seq.*

[7] Macdonald, p.254; *H.M. Advocate v. Dick* (1901) 3 Adam 344.

[8] Beccaria, p.25; see also N.Walker, *Sentencing in a Rational Society* (London, 1st ed., 1969), pp.16–17.

from this strict view of the irrelevance of intention, but the departure is far from complete. As a result there has grown up something like a definition of attempted crimes in terms of external situations as well as in terms of the accused's intention. An "attempted crime" has become almost an entity in itself with something like an *actus reus* of its own, and a person is not guilty of an attempted crime until he has brought about the appropriate "actus reus".[9]

The question in every case in therefore, "Does what the accused did amount to an attempted crime?" and in practice this question becomes "Has the accused reached the stage of attempt, has he gone far enough in the prosecution of his intention to have committed an attempted crime?" The answer given in any case depends on the theory adopted by the answerer regarding the criterion of criminal attempt. There are a number of different theories, some of which must now be considered in detail.

Theories of criminal attempts

The following are the most important theories of criminal attempts: **6.04**

(a) *The wrongful act theory*. This is the theory that A is guilty of an attempt to commit the crime *x* when in pursuance of his intention to commit *x*, he commits a completed crime *y*.

(b) *The unequivocal act theory*. On this theory A is guilty of an attempt to commit *x* when in pursuance of his intention to commit *x* he has done an act which is such that it can be unequivocally inferred from a consideration of that act that it was done with the intention of committing *x*.

(c) *The appropriate stage theories*. These are theories which hold that once A has advanced a certain stage towards the commission of *x* he has committed an attempted crime. In these theories it is assumed that before one comes to consider whether A has reached the appropriate stage it is known *aliunde* that his actions were performed with the intention of committing *x*. The appropriate stage may lie anywhere between the formation of the intention to commit *x* and the actual commission of *x*. In particular it can be placed either:

(i) at the beginning, at the point where A starts to put into effect his intention to commit *x* — the first stage theory; or

(ii) at an intermediate stage, usually described as that at which A passes from preparation to perpetration — the perpetration theory; or

(iii) at the end, when A has no more to do in order to bring about *x*, but to wait for matters to take their natural course — the final stage theory.

(a) *The wrongful act theory*

As a theory of attempts this can be easily dismissed; it clearly will not do. Whether or not, for example, the buying of poison constitutes attempted murder cannot depend on whether or not the buying of poison is itself a crime. On this theory, a man who breaks into his neighbour's house with the intention of raping his daughter will be guilty **6.05**

[9] The analogy is not, however, exact. See *infra*, para. 6.30.

of attempted rape as soon as he has forced his way into the house, although a man who goes into his own living-room in order to rape his guest will not be guilty of attempted rape until he starts to assault her.

There is no Scots authority in favour of this theory.[10] It is true that Hume opens his treatment of attempts by saying, "But the vicious will is not sufficient, unless it is coupled to a wrongful act", but he is only pointing to the necessity for an overt act before there can be an attempt. The examples he gives, such as that of a man shooting at someone and missing, are compatible with the theory he in fact develops at length, which is the final stage theory.[11]

6.06 *Preventive crimes.* Although the wrongful act theory is useless as a theory of attempt, it is important in the more general consideration of the ways in which the law can deal with unfulfilled intentions. It is the only theory which insists that a completed crime must have been committed before there can be any conviction at all, and it points the way to the creation of a substitute for attempted crimes. If A must have committed one crime before he can be guilty of attempting to commit another, why not just charge him with the crime he has committed, and so avoid the difficulties inherent in any law of attempt? And even if one does not accept the principle that there can be no attempt unless there has been a completed crime, why not deal with the attempt problem by making certain common steps on the way to certain crimes, crimes in themselves? Why not create preventive crimes? This course was recommended by Hume who said of "acts of matured and extensive preparation . . . attended with danger to the interests of trade", that "it is for the Legislature to interpose and provide a remedy, accommodated to the exigency of the case; and thus the evil is obviated, without infringing on the humane principle of the common law."[12] If, for example, the law wants to prevent people injuring others with lethal weapons it can do so, not by trying to show that anyone who carries a lethal weapon with the intention of using it is *ipso facto* guilty of attempted assault, but by making it a crime to carry a lethal weapon without lawful excuse.[13] Preventive crimes can also be created in spheres in which attempts would raise difficult problems, for example, to prevent the careless infliction of harm, as is done by making careless or drunken driving a crime in itself whether or not any harm is done.

Although this type of crime is normally created by statute, as Hume indicated it should always be created, and although it is unlikely in the extreme that the common law would today create a new preventive

---

[10] *cf. McKenzie v. H.M. Advocate*, 1988 S.C.C.R. 153, at 156 where L.J.-C. Ross appears to suggest that a completed fraud against a solicitor in relation to the raising of a civil action was "sufficient to make a relevant case of attempted fraud" against the defender in the action.

[11] Hume, i, 26–27.

[12] Hume, i, 29.

[13] Criminal Law (Consolidation) (Scotland) Act 1995, ss.47 and 49 (re-enacting Prevention of Crime Act 1953 and Carrying of Knives Etc. (Scotland) Act 1993). *Cf.* Knives Act 1997.

crime,[14] there are two nineteenth century cases of such common law creation.[15]

In *John Horne*[16] the High Court held that it was criminal for a forger of notes to sell them, as forged, to an accomplice. It is not altogether clear whether the court considered this to be a specific crime or whether they considered it to be a form of attempted uttering, but they did recognise that to make it attempted uttering would be to go beyond the general rules governing attempt, and some of the judges held the conduct in question criminal because, *inter alia,* "In itself, such a *dealing* was a criminal act, and one of a dangerous as well as a base nature."[17] The view that *Horne*[17a] created a preventive crime is supported by Alison[18] and by Macdonald,[19] both of whom regard the selling of forged notes to an accomplice as an independent crime. **6.07**

A clearer example of the common law creation of a preventive crime is *Chas Macqueen and Alex. Baillie*[20] where a charge of housebreaking with intent to steal was held relevant. Housebreaking with intent to steal filled part of the gap created by the fact that at that time attempted theft was not indictable, but it is in itself a substantive crime, and now that an attempt to commit any crime is criminal[21] it is relevant to charge attempted housebreaking with intent to steal.[22] **6.08**

"With intent." Mention of the crime of housebreaking with intent to steal leads to a consideration of the practice of charging accused persons with behaving in a particular way with intent to commit a crime. Where an accused is charged with doing *x* with intent to commit *y* there are four possible situations. **6.09**

(i) *x* is not in itself a crime, but the whole facts libelled disclose an attempt to commit *y*. In such cases the charge is just a charge of attempting to commit *y*. In *Coventry v. Douglas*[23] it was held that a

---

[14] See *H.M. Advocate v. Forbes*, 1994 J.C. 71, L.J.-G. Hope at 74G: "If new preventive crimes are needed, this is best left to the legislature." *Cf. H.M. Advocate v. Dick* (1901) 3 Adam 344; *H.M. Advocate v. Semple*, 1937 J.C. 41; *Quinn v. Cunningham*, 1956 J.C. 22 (though now overruled by *H.M. Advocate v. Harris*, 1993 J.C. 150).

[15] It seems also that one of the ways in which the common law developed in its earlier stages was by the creation of preventive crimes; see Lord Walker, "The Growth of the Criminal Law", 1958 J.R. 230. *Cf.* Thurman W. Arnold, *op.cit.*, n. 1, at p.75, where he says that considered apart from any particular crime, the law of criminal attempt "simply means that courts are permitted to fill in the gaps which a set of definitions inevitably leave when applied to human conduct. The power to interpret statutes performs a similar function, but the rules of statutory interpretation of criminal statutes are never considered as definitions of crimes. The power to punish for criminal attempts gives the court power to extend a criminal statute without distorting its language. It is necessary to our criminal system. To treat this power as the definition of a substantive crime is either to destroy it or hopelessly to confuse it." *Cf.* N.D. Walker, op.cit., loc. cit.

[16] (1814) Hume, i, 150–153.

[17] *ibid.* 152.

[17a] (1814) Hume, i, 150–153.

[18] Alison, i, 406.

[19] Macdonald, p.69.

[20] (1810) Hume, i, 102.

[21] Criminal Procedure (Scotland) Act 1995, s.294, replacing Criminal Procedure (Scotland) Act 1975, ss.63 (1) and 312 (o), which in turn replaced Criminal Procedure (Scotland) Act 1887, s.61.

[22] Macdonald, p.51. It is now also a crime to force open lockfast places with intent to steal, although this was never the subject of an express decision: see Macdonald, p.51.

[23] 1944 J.C. 13.

charge of putting one's hand into a receptacle "with intent to steal therefrom" was just a charge of attempted theft.

6.10 (ii) *x* is not itself a crime and the facts libelled do not disclose an attempt to commit *y*. In such a situation there is a crime only if "*x* with intent to commit *y*" is itself a specific crime, as in "housebreaking with intent to steal".[24] If "*x* with intent to commit *y*" is not a specific crime, the charge is irrelevant, since it discloses neither a completed nor an attempted crime. In *H.M. Advocate v. Semple*[25] S was alleged to have supplied abortifacients to a non-pregnant woman with intent to cause an abortion. It was accepted under the law which then pertained that this was not attempted abortion since the woman was not pregnant,[26] and accordingly the question before the court was whether supplying or administering (S was charged as being art and part in the attempt, he having supplied, and successfully instigated the woman to use, the drugs) abortifacients to a non-pregnant woman with intent to cause an abortion was itself a crime. The court declined to "create" this crime, holding that it was for the legislature to do so if they thought it necessary, and this approach shows that here, as in *Macqueen and Baillie,*[27] one has left the realm of attempts, and entered the realm of substantive crimes. Similarly in *H.M. Advocate v. Forbes*,[28] the accused was charged as follows: that he broke into a flat "occupied by *inter alia* [J.M.], aged 14 years, while in possession of a tube of cream, and did remove [his] clothing with the exception of a pair of boxer shorts, prowl around said flat, remove articles from a chest of drawers in a bedroom, cut holes in a sweatshirt and fashion it in the manner of a hood, all with intent to assault and rape said [J.M.]". It was accepted by the court that entering without damaging another's house was not criminal; it was also accepted that it was not criminal for a person to intend to commit a crime, and that housebreaking with intent to commit theft had been recognised as an exceptional nineteenth century creation. Two unreported cases which *ex facie* had presented as housebreaking with intent to commit fire-raising were regarded as most probably examples of attempts to commit fire-raising.[29] The court rejected the Crown's contention that it was an offence to break into another's house with intent to commit *a crime* there, and the matter was resolved by amending the charge to one of breach of the peace.[30] Given what the accused was alleged to have done in the premises (no evidence having been led since the sheriff upheld a preliminary plea to the relevancy of the charge), it was impossible to conclude on any plausible theory that the stage of attempted rape had been reached.

6.11 (iii) *x* is itself criminal and the facts libelled constitute an attempt to commit *y*. In such situations there has been an attempt to commit *y*, and such an attempt should be libelled in preference to libelling "*x* with

---

[24] *cf. Charles Costello* (1882) 4 Couper 602, a charge of the innominate offence of sending explosives with intent to cause injury.

[25] 1937 J.C. 41.

[26] *infra*, para. 6.53.

[27] (1810) Hume i, 102; see para. 6.08, *supra*.

[28] 1994 J.C. 71.

[29] The cases are *H.M. Advocate v. Margaret Morrison and Ors*, High Court at Glasgow, 1913, unrep'd and *H.M. Advocate v. Frances Gordon*, High Court at Glasgow, 1914, *unrep'd*.

[30] For criticism of the decision, see J. Ross, "Housebreaking with Intent", 1994 S.L.T. (News) 315.

intent to commit *y*". Hume commented that in his day "our lawyers have refrained . . . from libelling directly as for an *attempt* to murder, rob, ravish, or the like; and have thought it better to shape the charge as for the assault made, or other harm done, and to state the ultimate and flagitious purpose, as an accompaniment only or aggravation of the injury."[31] This practice is inadvisable, since it confuses this situation with the next type, where there is in fact no attempt at *y* but only the commission of *x* with intent to commit *y*.

(iv) *x* is itself criminal, but the whole facts do not disclose an attempt to commit *y*. The commonest examples of this type of charge are assault with intent to ravish and assault with intent to rob. Such charges are usually regarded as aggravations of assault, and this, it is submitted, is the best way of dealing with them.[32] **6.12**

Macdonald regarded this form of charge as having become obsolete in 1887, when it was made criminal to attempt to commit any crime, and said: "Formerly it was also the practice to treat assaults as being aggravated by intent to commit more serious crime, but the present practice is to charge assault and attempt to commit the more serious crime."[33] But attempted rape and attempted robbery were criminal prior to 1887, and nonetheless charges of assault with intent to commit these crimes were common.[34] And Macdonald is wrong in implying that it is no longer the practice to charge assault with intent to rob or to ravish.[35]

In practice, this form of charge is a halfway house to attempt, employed when A's intention is clear, but he has not yet reached the stage at which his conduct would constitute an attempted crime.[36]

---

[31] Hume, i, 26.

[32] Prior to 1887 a distinction was drawn between charges of *e.g.* "assault with intent to rob" and charges of "assault, especially with intent to rob", the former being regarded as a specific crime like "housebreaking with intent to steal," and the latter as an aggravated form of assault. The importance of the distinction was that it was competent in the latter case to convict of simple assault, while in the former if the intent was not proved A had to be acquitted altogether: see *Alex. Wright and Wm Moffat* (1827) Syme 136; *Purves and McIntosh* (1846) Ark. 178, L.J.-C. Hope at 180; *Jas. Kennedy* (1871) 2 Couper 138. Since the 1887 Act this distinction has disappeared. The normal form of charge is that "you did assault . . . and this you did with intent to rob," and a conviction of simple assault is competent on such a charge: Criminal Procedure (Scotland) Act 1887, s.60; now 1995 Act, Sched. 3, para. 9(3).

[33] Macdonald, p.117.

[34] Hume, i, 26; Burnett, p.107. It must be admitted that the distinction between *e.g.* attempted rape and assault with intent to ravish was not kept clear — in at least two reported cases of assault with intent to ravish the indictment averred that A attempted to rape the complainer: *Hugh McNamara* (1848) Ark. 521; *Jas.Kennedy* (1871) 2 Couper 138. *Cf. John Rae and Robt Montgomery* (1856) 2 Irv. 355.

[35] The 1887 Act itself preserved the competency of a conviction of assault with intent to kill or do serious injury on a charge of murder or serious assault: s.61; 1995 Act, Sched. 3, para. 10(3). Assault with intent to murder is still an accepted common law charge — see *e.g. Mary McCormack or Desson*, High Court at Edinburgh, 1939, unrep'd, a charge of throwing a child from a train which could presumably also have been charged as attempted murder. See also *James Morton Love*, High Court at Stirling, April 1959, unrep'd, a charge of attempting to strike with a knife with intent to murder.

[36] See Burnett, p.107, where he says that where it is doubtful if the facts amount to rape there should be alternative charges of rape, attempted rape, and assault with intent to ravish — these alternatives are now implied in any charge of rape: Macdonald, p.119; 1995 Act, Sched. 3, para. 10. A charge of assault with intent to rape may also be a useful way of avoiding the question whether someone who is impotent can be convicted of attempted rape: *cf. Waters v. State*, 23 A.L.R. (3d) 1339 (1967). Impossible attempts are discussed *infra*, paras 6.49 to 6.54.

(b) *The unequivocal act theory*

6.13 This theory holds that before a person can be convicted of an attempted crime he must have committed an overt act of such a nature that the only reasonable inference which can be drawn from a consideration of the act is that it was committed with the intention of going on to commit the crime attempted. The act must be "unequivocally referable" to the intention to commit the crime. This theory relies on the overt act as evidence of the criminal intent and the intent is held proved only if no other reasonable inference can be drawn from the act but the inference that it was done with that intention.

There is no Scottish authority in support of this theory, but as it was the theory held by Salmond[37] and also in a slightly modified from by Mr J.W.C. Turner, the editor of Kenny and of *Russell on Crime*,[38] and forms part of the background of Anglo-American thought on the subject, and as that background itself has considerable influence on the way Scots lawyers think, it requires to be considered.

The critical difficulty of this theory is that no act is unequivocally referable to anything when regarded in isolation. Salmond explains the theory by saying that the act must be "of such a nature that it is itself evidence of the criminal intent with which it is done. A criminal attempt bears criminal intent upon its face. *Res ipsa loquitur.*"[39]

But Salmond himself commences his exposition by saying that, "To mix arsenic in food is in itself a perfectly lawful act, for it may be that the mixture is designed for the poisoning of rats. But if the purpose is to kill a human being, the act becomes by reason of this purpose the crime of attempted murder",[40] although on Salmond's own test it is not attempted murder, since it is equivocal: it may be referable to an attempt to poison rats or to an attempt to poison a human being.

The theory is also peculiar in that it is, as Salmond himself accepts, ultimately a theory of evidence; it is not interested in the overt act as such, but only in the act as proof of criminal intention. If that is so, why does the theory accept only overt acts as proof of such intention? Salmond says that it is because of the danger of punishing a man for acts in appearance and in themselves perfectly innocent.[41] But, as Glanville Williams points out in a footnote to the 10th edition of Salmond,[42] this danger may be completely removed by a confession of criminal intention, and the accused still not be guilty of attempt on Salmond's view because of the equivocality of his acts. What in fact happens is, of course, that where the accused has confessed his intention, the court finds it easier than otherwise to treat his acts as unequivocally referable to that intention.

6.14 This sort of situation arose in the New Zealand case of *R. v. Barker*,[43] in which Salmond gave judicial expression to his theory. Barker had written a note to a young boy asking him to meet him for five minutes in

[37] See *Salmond on Jurisprudence*, (10th ed., London, 1947), pp.387–389. The passage dealing with attempts has been omitted from later editions.

[38] See J.W.C. Turner, *op.cit.* n.1 at 279; C.S. Kenny, *Kenny's Outlines of Criminal Law* (19th ed., J.W.C. Turner (ed.)), para. 63; *Russell on Crime* (11th ed., 1958), p.195. Mr Turner requires only that the overt act be prima facie evidence of intention.

[39] *op.cit.* pp.388–389.

[40] *ibid.* p.387.

[41] *ibid.* p.389.

[42] *ibid.*

[43] [1924] N.Z.L.R. 865.

a paddock and saying, "We can have some fun." The boy showed the note to his father, and when Barker wrote to the boy again suggesting a meeting arrangements were made for the police to be present. Barker met the boy and the two walked together for a short time until the police intervened and charged Barker with attempted sodomy and attempted indecent assault. Barker later confessed to an intention to commit sodomy. He was convicted of attempted sodomy, and his conviction was upheld by the appeal court, which held, for a number of reasons, that his behaviour constituted an attempt to commit that crime. Stringer J. adopted the unequivocal act theory and said that there must be facts which "indicate, of themselves, the intention to commit the offence",[44] but he seems to have adopted this test because "Until this stage is reached, the matter rests in mere intention, and there is a *locus poenitentiae*"[45]; that is to say, he confused the unequivocality theory with a final stage theory.[46]

Salmond J. himself came out unequivocally for the unequivocal act theory, but it is difficult to understand how he succeeded in applying it to the facts of *Barker*[46a] in such a way as to produce the conclusion that Barker was guilty of attempted sodomy. Barker's conduct in inviting the boy for a walk and going for a walk with him is in itself, it is submitted, as referable to an intention to take the boy for a walk, or to the zoo, or to kill the boy, or to many other possible intentions, as it is to an intention to commit sodomy. In fact, as Stringer J. suggested, the "guilty complexion . . . is probably due to the light cast upon [Baker's actings] by the subsequent confession of the accused, which, admittedly, could not legitimately be used for that purpose."[47]

The unequivocal act theory was expressly adopted at common law in England in *Davey v. Lee*[48] where the cutting of a fence at one side of a compound containing offices, houses, and some stores including a metal store was held to amount to attempted theft of metal. The court adopted Archbold's statement[49] that an attempt is complete where there is "an act which is a step towards the commission of the specific crime, which is immediately and not merely remotely connected with the commission of it, and the doing of which cannot reasonably be regarded as having any other purpose than the commission of the specific crime." In *Jones v.* **6.15**

[44] At 871.

[45] *ibid.*

[46] See *infra*, paras 6.28, 6.38.

[46a] [1924] N.Z.L.R. 865.

[47] At 871. The theory has now been abandoned in New Zealand and the law there now is that, "An act done or omitted with intent to commit an offence may constitute an attempt if it is immediately or proximately connected with the intended offence, whether or not there was any act unequivocally showing the intent to commit that offence": Crimes Act 1961 s.72 (3). It is interesting to note that in the English case of *R. v. Miskell* (1954) 37 Cr.App.R. 214, in which the facts were similar to those in *Barker* — a soldier met a boy and engaged in indecent conversation with him, they met again, the soldier said, "We'll take a walk", and was arrested — the accused was convicted of attempting to procure the boy for an indecent purpose, but Hilbery J. pointed out that the facts did not amount to an attempt to commit indecent behaviour. Gl. Williams also points out that to offer a girl money to go into a park has been held in New Zealand to be an attempt to have carnal knowledge of her: *R. v. Yelds* [1928] N.Z.L.R. 18, while to offer a girl money to enter a hut has been held not to be attempted indecent assault: *Moore* [1936] N.Z.L.R. 471; (1955) 18 M.L.R. 620. These examples make it clear that the theory is untenable.

[48] [1968] 1 Q.B. 366.

[49] 36th ed., para. 4104.

Brooks[50] the court held that where the accused were seen trying the doors of motor cars their guilt of attempting to take and drive away a car could and should be determined not merely by their admittedly equivocal attempt to open the door, which could have been a step towards stealing the contents of the car or merely towards "the purely innocent purpose of going to sleep in it", but also by their subsequent admission to the police of their intention to take the car. Lord Parker C.J. said:

> "[A]n expressed intention alone does not amount to an attempt; there must be an *actus reus* which is sufficiently proximate to the expressed intention, But that does not mean to say that the courts should disregard entirely as part of the surrounding circumstances and the evidence in the case the expressed intention of the respondents, both at the time and after the *actus reus*. It seems to me that that intention is relevant when the act concerned is equivocal in order to see towards what the act is directed. Once that is decided, then it still remains for the prosecution to show that the act itself is sufficiently proximate to amount to an attempt to commit the crime which it was the intention of the respondents to commit."[51]

(c) *Stage theories*

6.16 Theories which require that the accused shall have reached a certain stage in the commission of his intended crime before he can be convicted of attempt suffer from a difficulty not altogether unlike the main difficulty of the unequivocal act theory. These theories do not view the act in isolation, but they have to fix on a stage in the series leading up to the completed crime which they can characterise as the beginning of the commission of the crime, or the stage of perpetration, or the final stage. There is no agreed standard of measurement which will show, for example, whether the poisoner begins to commit murder when he buys the poison, when he puts it in the soup, or when he invites the victim to dinner. The standard is a variable one, and the decision in any case may well depend on whether the court feels that the accused deserves to be punished, rather than on the logical application of a principle. "No facts or events force us by their very nature to relate them in a particular way to some other fact or event. Between any two facts there may be a number of relations among which we may choose, and our choice will depend on our purpose."[52] In cases of attempt the purpose behind the choice is either to convict or to acquit the accused, and the decision to treat his acts as sufficiently closely related to the intended crime to constitute an attempt to commit it may often be itself the result of a decision to convict him, and conversely, the decision that his acts do not amount to attempt may often just follow on the decision that he ought not to be punished.

---

[50] (1968) 52 Cr.App.R. 614.

[51] At 617. In *R. v. Shivpuri* [1987] 1 A.C. 1, the House of Lords finally decided that the distinction between innocent and guilty acts considered objectively was "incapable of sensible application in relation to the law of criminal attempts" (*per* Lord Bridge of Harwich at 21H; see also 22C). English law is now governed by the Criminal Attempts Act 1981, s.1 of which provides: "If, with intent to commit an [indictable offence], a person does an act which is more than merely preparatory to the commission of the offence, he is guilty of [attempt]." Similar provision is made by s.3 for attempts under special statutory provisions.

[52] O.C. Jensen, *The Nature of Legal Argument* (Oxford, 1957), p.134.

Are there different stages for different crimes? Professor Jensen, following Mr. Justice Holmes, takes the view that the real criterion of attempt is simply public policy, the important factors being, as Holmes puts it, "the nearness of the danger, the greatness of the harm, and the degree of apprehension felt."[53] If this is so, it will be reasonable to relate the appropriate stage to the seriousness of the intended crime, or to the amount of danger involved in the acts already committed. In that case no principles drawn from a consideration of cases of attempts to commit crime *x* would be applicable to cases of attempts to commit crime *y*. The law might be, for example, that where the intended crime is trivial there is no attempt until the final stage has been reached, but where the intended crime is serious there is attempt as soon as the accused has started to put his intention into operation.[54] **6.17**

This type of approach is envisaged by Hume, who says of his own rules, "in some instances, there seems to be room for an exception to the ordinary rule, on account of the deep atrocity of the intended mischief, or the extensive, mature, and elaborate preparation and contrivance. The case has been put of one who has stored his neighbour's cellar with gunpowder, for the destruction of him and all his family; and that of a plot, in a state of great advancement, to burn and plunder a whole quarter of a certain town."[55] A similar approach lies behind the decision of the court in *John Horne*[56] that it is criminal to sell forged notes to an accomplice. The court justified their decision by reference, *inter alia*, to the "*daring* energy of disposition in the artist", describing the preparations in question as "important steps of a deep and an advanced conspiracy against the safety of trade."[57] As such, the court regarded them as punishable, even although they had not reached what is normally regarded as the stage of attempt.[58]

This approach has not survived into modern times. This is partly because the "deep and advanced conspiracy" can be dealt with by using the law of conspiracy without recourse to the law of attempt,[59] but mainly because it is more difficult to maintain such an approach in a system in which an attempt to commit any crime is statutorily declared to be criminal,[60] than it was in the time of Hume. In Hume's day attempts were criminal only in the case of serious crimes, and the fact that attempts to commit less serious crimes were not criminal at all could be viewed as the logical conclusion of this approach. There is no suggestion in any modern case that there is more than one standard for criminal attempts.[61]

---

[53] Holmes, *The Common Law* (Howe (ed.), London, 1968) p.56; *cf.* Jensen, *op.cit.*, pp.130, 163; *Swift and Co. v. U.S.*, 196 U.S. 375, 396 (1905); *Hyde v. U.S.*, 225 U.S. 347, 388 (1911).

[54] For an exposition of the view that general schematic treatment is impossible in relation to any of the problems involved in attempt, see J.A.C. Thomas, *op.cit.*, n.1; P.R. Glazebrook, *op.cit.*, n.1. The general theory approach is supported by Law Commission Report No. 102 ("Attempt, and Impossibility in Relation to Attempt, Conspiracy and Incitement", H. of C. 646, Session 1979–80) para. 2.6, referring to L.C.W.P. No. 50, 44–46.

[55] Hume, i, 29.

[56] (1814) Hume, i, 150; *supra*, para. 6.07.

[57] *ibid.*, 152.

[58] See also *Chas Costello* (1882) 4 Couper 602.

[59] See *infra*, paras 6.57 *et seq.*

[60] 1995 Act, s.294.

[61] Although "attempting to pervert the course of justice" falls into a special class of its own, being more akin to a completed crime than to an attempt: see Vol. II, Chap. 47.

(c) (i) *The first stage theory*

6.18 On this theory A has committed an attempted crime as soon as he has performed an overt act with the intention of committing a specific crime, providing that the act was regarded by him as a step towards the commission of that crime. On this theory if A buys poison as part of a deliberate scheme to poison B he is guilty of the attempted murder of B; but if he buys poison with a vague idea that it might come in handy one day should he ever make up his mind to poison B, he is not guilty of attempted murder, and will not be guilty until he has formed a specific plan to poison B and committed some further act in pursuance of that plan.

The theory adopts a subjective criterion — an overt act may constitute an attempt, provided it is part of a scheme to commit a particular crime; in order to decide whether a particular act or series of acts constitutes attempt it is necessary to know if the accused considered them as part of the carrying out of his intention to commit a crime. The fact that the conduct appears to be unequivocally referable to such a scheme will be evidence of the accused's intention, but no more. It has been said that on the unequivocal act theory, "If A intending to kill Z goes into the street with a loaded gun, but fails to find Z . . . A has not attempted to murder Z . . . [but] if a person goes out at night with apparatus specially fitted for committing mischief by fire, not only must he be presumed to intend to commit that crime, but he has already made a move towards his purpose sufficient to constitute an attempt."[62] The distinction is unfair, and the first stage theory avoids the necessity of making it. On the first stage theory, A will be guilty of attempted murder if in fact he was carrying the gun in order to go and kill Z with it; he will not be guilty of attempted fire-raising if he can bring evidence to rebut the presumption of fact that he intended to raise fire.

The first stage theory seems to fit the ordinary meaning of "attempt", since all it requires is that the accused shall have been seriously bent on the commission of a crime, and shall have in fact started to put his criminal intention into effect. On this theory a jury need ask themselves only, "Was the accused engaged in carrying out his intention to commit the crime when he was arrested?" This is a simple and easily understandable test and concentrates attention on the accused's state of mind which is what is being punished when attempts are punished. The theory also has the advantage that it enables wicked intentions to be punished, and so frustrated, more often than do the other theories which may require considerable harm to be done before the law can intervene.

A number of codes use language which could be interpreted as embodying this theory, perhaps because of the similarity between the theory and the ordinary meaning of "attempt". The French Noveau Code Pénal talks of attempts manifested "par un commencement d'exécution",[63] the Australian Northern Territory's Criminal Code of a person who "begins to put his intention into execution by means adapted to its fulfilment",[64] the New Zealand Crimes Act of "one who . . . does or omits an act for the purpose of accomplishing his object",[65] and the

---

[62] A. Gledhill, " 'Attempt' in Indian Criminal Law", *Indian Year Book of International Affairs*, 1955, pp.304, 305.

[63] Art. 121–5.

[64] Schedule 1, s.4.

[65] Crimes Act 1961, s.72(1).

Canadian Criminal Code of "one who, having an intent to commit an offence, does or omits to do anything for the purpose of carrying out the intention."[66]

But in fact all of these systems reject the first stage theory, and all for the same reason. They all distinguish acts of preparation from attempts, and agree that acts of preparation are not punishable.[67] It is felt that to punish mere preparation for the commission of a crime is to go too far, since it comes near to punishing mere intentions, which it is not the purpose of the criminal law to do. The American Law Institute's proposed Model Penal Code, however, deliberately sets out to extend the scope of attempts by "drawing the line between attempt and non-criminal preparation further away from the final act; the crime becomes essentially one of criminal purpose implemented by an overt act strongly corroborative of such purpose", and regards lying in wait, possessing materials, or even reconnoitring or soliciting an innocent agent as capable of constituting attempt.[68]

Although this theory is an inviting one, and although it may underlie decisions which are ostensibly made in reliance on other theories,[69] there is no authority for it in Scotland,[70] and its approach is out of tune with the general attitude of Scots law towards attempt, which requires an almost complete act of execution before there can be an attempted crime.[71]

---

[66] Art. 24(1).

[67] See *e.g.* Jean Predal et André Verinard, *Les grands arrêts du droit criminel*, Tome 1, "Les sources du droit pénal l'infraction" (Dalloz, Paris 1995), Chap. 30, pp.345–354; New Zealand Crimes Act 1961, s.72(2), "[t]he question whether an act done or omitted with intent to commit an offence is or is not only preparation for the commission of that offence, and too remote to consitute an attempt to commit it, is a question of law"; Canadian Criminal Code, Art. 24(2) — which is virtually in identical terms to those of s.72(2) of the New Zealand Crimes Act: see also A.W. Mewett and M. Manning, *Criminal Law* (2nd ed., Toronto, 1985), pp.171–175.

[68] Model Penal Code, T.D. 10, 25; O.D., s.5.01 (2). *Cf. People v. Rizzo*, 246 N.Y. 334 (1927); L. Hall and S. Glueck, *Cases on Criminal Law and its Enforcement*, 2nd ed. (St. Paul, Minn., 1958), p.400, where the accused planned to rob B of a payroll, and drove to various places in the hope of finding him. They were arrested before they found him and their convictions for attempted robbery were quashed on appeal. But in *People v. Gormley*, 248 N.Y. 583 (1927), Hall and Glueck, *op.cit.*, p.403, G was convicted of attempted robbery where he had waited for an hour for his victim to collect money from a bank and had been arrested before the victim arrived. The conviction was sustained on the ground that "It would be a travesty upon justice to permit [the accused] to escape punishment." L.C.W.P. No. 50 proposed the adoption of the Model Code's example as part of a rule that attempt is committed where the conduct is, or is believed to be, a "substantial step" towards the commission of the attempt: p.53 *et.seq.* This would have departed significantly from the then English rule which depended on "proximity": see *D.P.P v. Stonehouse* [1978] A.C. 55. The Working Party's proposal did not find favour with consultees, however, and the Law Commission in 1980 rejected its Working Party's approach and made different proposals (Law Commission Report No. 102, H. of C. 646, para. 2.30 *et seq.*) which were embodied in the Criminal Attempts Act 1981. Under s.1 of that Act, which remains current English law, a person is guilty of an attempt if he "does an act which is more than merely preparatory to the commission of the offence". The English Draft Criminal Code retains this formula (see cl.49(1)). For difficulties in implementing it, see, *e.g.*, *R. v. Geddes* [1996] Crim.L.R. 894 with commentary at 895–6, and *R. v. Tosti* [1997] Crim.L.R. 746 with commentary at 747.

[69] *e.g. H.M. Advocate v. Camerons* (1911) 6 Adam 456.

[70] Except perhaps, the highly special cases of *H.M. Advocate v. Mitchell* (1915) 7 Adam 589, and *H.M. Advocate v. Innes* (1915) *ibid.* 596, see *infra*, paras 6.23, 6.24.

[71] It is not, for example, criminal merely to forge a writ, or to copy secret information with fraudulent intent: *cf. H.M. Advocate v. Mackenzies* (1913) 7 Adam 189, L.J.-C. Macdonald at 196.

(c) (ii) *The perpetration theory*

6.19 Despite its wide adoption[72] this theory is highly unsatisfactory. It is an objective theory since it requires more than the combination of intention with an overt act — it requires a particular sort of overt act. That being so, it should be able to point to a quality which distinguishes the type of act it requires — an act showing that the accused has passed from the stage of preparation to that of perpetration. But it is unable to do this, and as a result it is so vague that it allows the court to adopt an individual approach to each case, and to decide whether or not there has been an attempt by reference to whether or not it wishes to punish the accused. If this were frankly admitted it might not be altogether a bad thing — it would be flexible and would take account of ordinary moral reactions — but it would not be a stage theory of attempt. In the same way, the theory can be used to introduce the tenable Holmesian theory that the criterion of attempt is public mischief,[73] but it would be better to adopt the Holmesian theory explicitly. For when judges continually talk about preparation and perpetration, and not about morality or public mischief, they end by convincing themselves that the words mean something; and the result is that in order to justify their decisions on attempt they employ the perpetration theory. But the theory is quite incapable of standing on its own, and it tends to be combined or confused with an unequivocal act theory when the court wish to convict, and with a final stage theory when they wish to acquit.[74]

6.20 *The theory in Scotland.* Hume talks at one stage of "ambiguous cases with respect to which it is very difficult to say where preparation ends, and perpetration begins", but he equates the beginning of perpetration with the final stage. For he says that it is not attempt to lie in wait for someone or to lurk in the night near a shop with a ladder and picklock, because until the person is assaulted or the lock of the shop picked, there is no "inception" of the crime, and "fear, remorse, a moment's confusion, some accidental alarm, might have prevented an attempt from being made."[75]

Again, in *H.M. Advocate v. Baxter*,[76] Lord Justice-Clerk Macdonald said that, "A man who has done something by way of overt act with the purpose of committing a crime, but does not complete it, is punishable for attempt to commit the crime", but his examples are of placing poison in a teapot, or sending a parcel of explosives through the post so that they will blow up on being opened. And it is these acts that he describes as "acts done by a person who is in course of committing the full crime, and the person attempting had by overt act directly taken steps, not

---

[72] This theory appears now to be the law of England: Criminal Attempts Act 1981, ss.1 and 3. See J.C. Smith and B. Hogan, *Criminal Law* (9th ed., 1999, Sir J. Smith (ed.)), pp.311–315.

[73] Holmes, *op.cit.*, *loc.cit.*, *supra*, n.53.

[74] *cf. R. v. Barker* [1924] N.Z.L.R. 865; O.C. Jensen, *op.cit.*, Pt. III, *passim*. A striking example of this is offered by two South African cases, in one of which it was held that a man about to put on a contraceptive beside a coloured woman with her skirt up and her bloomers down was not guilty of attempting to have intercourse with her because there was still an opportunity for him to change his mind, and in the other that a man lying undressed, in a state of erection, in bed with a naked coloured woman, was guilty of attempted intercourse: *R. v. N. and B.*, 1952 (4) S.A. 210 (P.T.D.) and *R. v. S. and Anr*, *ibid.*, 591 (N.P.D.).

[75] Hume, i, 29.

[76] (1908) 5 Adam 609.

merely to prepare for the perpetration of a crime, but to put his machinations into practical action."[77] It is clear from the examples and from the whole tenor of the case that the theory adopted was the final stage one.[78] Lord Macdonald also spoke in *Baxter*[78a] of a housebreaker seen by a watchman looking into a house with all his tools ready to break in, and said that such a man was not guilty of attempted housebreaking if he went away when the watchman caught sight of him.[79]

The leading authority in Scotland for the perpetration theory is the case of *H.M. Advocate v. Camerons.*[80] The accused were husband and wife, and they were charged with attempting to defraud an insurance company. The attempt involved an elaborate scheme much of which had been carried out before they were arrested. They had obtained possession of a necklace for a limited time during which they effected an insurance on it. Then, after they had given the necklace back, they pretended that the wife had been robbed of it, and even went so far as to produce simulated injuries on her. They then reported the "theft" to the broker who had arranged the insurance. The insurance company requested a formal claim, and although it appears that this was in fact made the Crown failed to prove it, and the case went to the jury on the assumption that there had been no claim. In these circumstances the accused were convicted of attempted fraud. **6.21**

The presiding judge was Lord Justice-General Dunedin, and as he consulted several other judges before directing the jury, his charge is of considerable weight as an authority.

Lord Dunedin approached the law by way of Hume's requirement of an inchoate act of execution. He then referred to Hume's example of scuttling a ship with the intention of defrauding underwriters. But although Hume regarded this as attempted fraud[81] Lord Dunedin did not appear to do so, since he treated the simulated robbery in *Camerons*[81a] as itself insufficient to constitute an attempt, although he said that "very little more will do".[82] He quoted Hume's statement about ambiguous cases in which it was difficult to say where preparation ends and perpetration begins,[83] and summed up his own view of the law by saying that "the root of the whole matter" was "to discover where preparation ends and where perpetration begins. In other words, it is a question of degree, and when it is a question of degree it is a jury question."[84] The jury, naturally enough in the circumstances, convicted

---

[77] At 615.

[78] And indeed probably the possibility of repentance version; *cf. infra,* para. 6.32.

[78a] (1908) 5 Adam 609.

[79] At 614.

[80] (1911) 6 Adam 456.

[81] Hume, i, 27.

[81a] (1911) 6 Adam 456.

[82] At 484–485.

[83] Hume, i, 29.

[84] At 485. This last statement is rather surprising — the question whether the stage of attempt had been reached was decided on relevancy in the earlier cases of *Sam. Tumbleson* (1863) 4 Irv. 426, and *H.M. Advocate v. Baxter* (1908) 5 Adam 609, and in the later cases of *H.M. Advocate v. Mackenzies* (1913) 7 Adam 189, and *H.M. Advocate v. Semple*, 1937 J.C. 41. Lord Strathclyde did, however, treat it as a jury question in *H.M. Advocate v. Mitchell* (1915) 7 Adam 589, and *H.M. Advocate v. Innes* (1915) 7 Adam 596, but that seems to have been on the issue of the accused's intention, the court having held that what had been done could constitute an attempt. The "stage question" is generally regarded as one of

the accused — naturally, because there could be no doubt that the accused had concocted and to a great extent carried out a deliberate and complex plot to defraud the insurers.

It is not clear, however, whether Lord Dunedin would have convicted the accused had the matter rested with him. He said to the jury:

> "Supposing that after getting that letter . . . saying that they wanted a formal claim . . . they said 'No, we have changed our minds, and we give it up; we are not to claim at all' — do you think there would have been much chance of convicting them? Well, of course, they are not in that happy position, but through the omission of the Crown to prove any claim they are in the same position, as you must just take it, as if they had been arrested after [the letters to the broker reporting the theft and asking that inquiries be made, the last of which ended 'We will now be able to show our hand more or less and, if necessary, declare war.']."[85]

Lord Dunedin was thus at least flirting with the final stage theory; he certainly thought that actual repentance would have prevented conviction; and he was apparently by no means convinced that on the proved facts there had been "perpetration", — the passage could be read as an indication to the jury to acquit. On the other hand the suggestion that once the robbery had been carried out "very little more" would do, and the treatment of the question as one of degree, make it clear that his Lordship was not directing the jury in terms of either the final stage theory, or the first stage theory. What he himself meant by perpetration, or where he thought it began in the case, it is impossible to tell.

6.22 *The status of the case as authority.* The case is of considerable persuasive authority but it is not technically binding. It conflicts with the decision in *H.M. Advocate v. Baxter*[86] and with the dicta in *H.M. Advocate v. Mackenzies*,[87] which will be considered shortly.[88] Again, although the phrase about preparation and perpetration has been used frequently since *Camerons*[89] all the later reported cases in which the accused have been convicted of criminal attempts have been final stage cases on their facts,[90] except for two prosecutions under the Trading with the Enemy Act 1914, which are highly special and cannot be relied on as authorities on general principles.

6.23 The Trading with the Enemy Act 1914, in conjunction with certain proclamations, made it an offence directly or indirectly to supply to or obtain from an enemy any goods. The Trading with the Enemy

---

law: *cf.* Report of Royal Commission on Draft Code, 1879, C–2345-Draft Code, s.74; New Zealand Crimes Act 1961, s.72 (2); Canadian Criminal Code, s.24 (2); L.C.W.P. No. 50, para. 78; and the current English law, where the matter is clearly one of fact — Criminal Attempts Act 1981, s.4(3), J.C. Smith and B. Hogan, *Criminal Law* (9th ed., 1999, by Sir J. Smith (ed.)), p.313: this also seems to have been the law prior to the introduction of the Criminal Attempts Act 1981 — see *R. v. Matthews* [1981] Crim.L.R. 325.

[85] At 485–486.

[86] (1908) 5 Adam 609; see para. 6.20, *supra*.

[87] (1913) 7 Adam 189.

[88] *Infra*, paras 6.36, 6.37.

[89] (1911) 6 Adam 456; see para. 6.21, *supra*.

[90] *H.M. Advocate v. Semple*, 1937 J.C. 41; *Angus v. H.M. Advocate,* 1935 J.C. 1; *Dalton v. H.M. Advocate,* 1951 J.C. 76; *Docherty v. Brown*, 1996 J.C. 48; see *infra*, paras 6.41, 6.42.

Amendment Act 1914, which came into force on November 27, 1914, applied the original Act to anyone who, since August 4, 1914, "attempted, or directly or indirectly offered or proposed or agreed, to trade with the enemy". In *H.M. Advocate v. Mitchell*[91] the charge was of attempting to trade with the enemy by sending a letter in October 1914 to a merchant in Hamburg inquiring about the prospects of obtaining goods from him, contrary to both Acts. The main question before the court was whether, assuming the November Act did not apply retrospectively, it was competent to charge an attempt to trade. A Full Bench held that such a charge was competent in view of section 61 of the Criminal Procedure (Scotland) Act 1887[92] which made any attempt to commit an indictable offence itself indictable. But it was also argued that the letter did not disclose an attempt to trade, and on that point Lord Justice-General Strathclyde said, "Now, having considered that letter, I have come to the conclusion that it is susceptible of bearing that interpretation. The question whether that was or was not in fact its meaning is one entirely for the jury."[93] The accused was convicted but the trial proceedings are not reported.

In *H.M. Advocate v. Innes*[94] I wrote to a neutral in October 1914 asking him to write to an enemy trader inquiring if he would buy from I. The charge was laid as one of proposing to supply goods, contrary to both Acts. It was argued that the letter constituted only preparation to commit the offence, but Lord Strathclyde held that while its writing would have been only preparation, its posting was an overt act by which "the proposal, or the attempt" may have been made, although it might be open to the accused to show that that was not his intention and that the posting of the letter indicated only preparation.[95] His Lordship went on to say that the Crown were not restricted to showing that the letter indicated a proposal to supply goods contrary to the amending Act, and that, "It may be that the letter when justly construed may indicate an attempt to supply goods to the enemy, and I can conceive many cases in which a proposal to supply goods may be precisely equivalent to an attempt to supply goods to the enemy."[96] **6.24**

The value of these cases as authority is, it is submitted, doubtful. *Mitchell*[96a] is a Full Bench case, but the Full Bench was convened to consider the effect of section 61 of the 1887 Act and not whether or not the stage of attempt had been reached, and *Innes*[96b] is only a single judge decision, albeit the judge was Lord Strathclyde. The cases deal with wartime legislation — Lord Dundas emphasised in *Mitchell*[96c] that the court was not concerned with a common law charge of attempting to trade with the enemy,[97] and with legislation which expressly provided that a proposal to supply goods was criminal, circumstances which made **6.25**

[91] (1915) 7 Adam 589.
[92] Now 1995 Act, s.294.
[93] At 594.
[94] (1915) 7 Adam 596.
[95] At 601.
[96] *ibid.*
[96a] (1915) 7 Adam 589.
[96b] (1915) 7 Adam 596.
[96c] (1915) 7 Adam 589.
[97] At 596.

it easy for the court to adopt a very extended interpretation of attempt. The suggestion that a proposal to supply goods may be precisely equivalent to an attempt, and the emphasis laid on the jury's conclusions as to the accused's intention in sending the letter, point to a first stage theory, but there is no authority for adopting this theory in Scots law and ample authority that an invitation or proposal to commit a crime is not an attempt.[98] If what Lord Strathclyde said in *Mitchell*[98a] and *Innes*[98b] represents the law, it is difficult to see why Lord Dunedin found *Camerons*[99] a difficult case, since the accused in *Camerons* had advanced far beyond the stage reached in the wartime cases.

6.26 *The objections to the theory.* The objections to the theory may perhaps be summarised as follows:

(1) It is meaningless. To "perpetrate" is to "carry through, execute, perform".[1] That is to say, attempt and perpetration are mutually exclusive. At least, the crime is not perpetrated until the last act is committed. To begin to perpetrate either means the same as to begin to carry out — in which case the Camerons had committed an attempt when they staged their robbery, if not earlier — or it means to carry out the last act, or, of course, it means nothing at all. Hume[2] took the view that the beginning of perpetration was the stage at which the last act was performed. The same view is probably taken by the learned editors of the 5th edition of Macdonald when they say that there is an attempt "when it is beyond the power of the man to prevent its consequences; or, *as it is sometimes put*, when it has advanced from the stage of preparation to that of perpetration."[3]

(2) It is vague. The distinction between preparation and perpetration is said to be one of degree, and that in itself means that it is bound to be difficult to apply. But it is more difficult than many other questions of degree, because even the points between which the variations in degree operate are unfixed. In most questions of degree there is a wide area in which it is clear on which side of the line we are. We may not know where a horse's tail ends and its body begins, but outside of a small part of the horse we know without any doubt which is horse and which is tail; and we know clearly what "horse" and "tail" mean. When it comes to preparation and perpetration the terms are so vague as to be undefinable without reference to the borderline cases themselves, and almost every point in the series can be regarded as the borderline. Any point between the time at which the Camerons obtained possession of the necklace they insured until the time they were arrested can be plausibly described as the point at which preparation ended and perpetration began. A difference of degree which presents difficult borderline cases is one thing, but a difference of degree which leaves nothing but a borderline is quite another.

---

[98] See especially *H.M. Advocate v. Mackenzies* (1913) 7 Adam 189, L.J.-C. Macdonald at 197.

[98a] (1915) 7 Adam 589.

[98b] (1915) 7 Adam 596.

[99] (1911) 6 Adam 456; see para. 6.21, *supra*.

[1] N.E.D.

[2] Hume, i, 27.

[3] Macdonald, p.1, italics added.

(3) It leads to unsatisfactory results. The result of trying to use the test is to produce a distinction without a difference. In the English case of *R. v. Robinson*[4] a jeweller staged a fake robbery and reported it to the police, all with the intention of defrauding his insurers. It was held that the police were third parties, the statement to them therefore merely preparatory, and, accordingly, that there had been no attempted fraud, no step taken in the commission of the crime. In *Comer v. Bloomfield*[5] A hid his lorry after he had crashed it, reported it to the police as stolen, and then wrote to his insurers asking if he could claim for theft. As it happened he was not covered for theft. There was held to be no attempted fraud. This is very difficult to distinguish from *Camerons*.[6] There is a distinction between *Robinson* and *Camerons*, but does it mean anything? Could it not have been said of Robinson as it was of the Camerons that one does not normally report the theft of insured goods without a view to a claim?[7] This sort of distinction is so slight and artificial that it is objectionable.[8] It is highly unsatisfactory that liability to punishment by the law should rest on distinctions so thin that they seem to be the result of pilpulistic casuistry and not of principle at all. **6.27**

(c) (iii) *The final stage theory*

This theory is the one supported by most of the Scots authorities, and so requires considerably more attention than has been given to the other theories. **6.28**

It may take one of two forms:

(1) *The last act theory.* This is the theory that the stage of attempt is reached once A has done all it is necessary for him to do in order to bring the crime to completion. On this theory it is attempted fire-raising to set light to a fuse leading to a barrel of petrol in the cellar of a house; it is attempted murder to send a box of poisoned chocolates through the post to the intended victim; it is attempted fraud to send a letter containing fraudulent statements on the strength of which a request is made for money. In all these cases something remains to be done — the house must burn, the victim eat the chocolates, the recipient of the letter send the money — before the crime is completely executed, but there is nothing more for the accused to do except sit back and hope that all goes well.

(2) *The possible intervention theory.* On this theory the stage of attempt has not been reached as long as it is possible for the accused to repent and, following on such repentance, to intervene and prevent the completion of the crime. Thus, in each of the above examples there would be no attempt — the accused might put out the fuse before the house took fire, he might telephone the persons to whom the poison or letter had been sent and warn them of the situation.

Attempt and repentance. Since the ground of punishment in attempted crimes is the criminal intention of the accused any theory of attempts must deal with the question of repentance. Repentance may be important in two types of situation — when the accused, having passed the **6.29**

---

[4] [1915] 2 K.B. 342.
[5] (1971) 55 Cr.App.R. 305.
[6] (1911) 6 Adam 456; see para. 6.21, *supra*.
[7] *cf. Camerons, supra,* at 486.
[8] See Gl. Williams, pp.625–627.

stage of attempt, abandons his plan and desists from any further action; or when, having completed his plan, he intervenes to prevent the occurrence of the intended consequence.

6.30 ABANDONMENT. The position in English law seems to be that once the stage of attempt has been passed, abandonment is irrelevant, since an attempted crime has been "fully" committed.[9] This approach concentrates on the analogy between acts constituting criminal attempts and the *actus reus* of a completed crime and argues that repentance after the stage of attempt has been reached is as irrelevant as repentance after the completion of a crime. But this, it is submitted, is fallacious; the acts constituting an attempt are not the same as an *actus reus*, and the English approach carries the analogy too far. What is punished in attempts is basically the intention, and not the acts constituting the attempt, and it is therefore unreasonable to refuse to give the accused credit for having abandoned that intention, providing of course that the abandonment was voluntary. It seems unfair and contrary to religious and moral ideas not to accept the accused's repentance, coming as it does before he has committed the harm in question.[10] The acceptance of such repentance is also desirable on utilitarian grounds — "On veut encourager le repentir."[11] This is recognised in a number of continental Codes,[12] and it is submitted that Scots law should adopt the same attitude.[13]

The question is, however, unlikely to arise in Scots law if it adopts a last act theory since such a theory avoids the difficulty by postponing the stage of attempt until it is impossible for the accused effectively to abandon his object.[14]

---

[9] J.C. Smith and B. Hogan, *Criminal Law* (9th ed., 1999, Sir J. Smith (ed.)), p.320; A. Ashworth, *Principles of Criminal Law* (3rd ed., 1999) pp.482–484; Gl. Williams, para. 199; A. Gledhill, " 'Attempt' in Indian Criminal Law", *Indian Year Book of International Affairs*, 1955, pp.304, 310. But see *R. v. Lankford* [1959] Crim.L.R. 209. L.C.W.P., No. 50, was undecided — see pp.102–103; but L.C. No 102 (1980), *Criminal Law: Attempt and Impossibility in Relation to Attempt, Conspiracy and Incitement*, decided that no change in the existing English law was justified.

[10] If, of course, it is preceded by the incidental commission of a completed crime, it cannot affect the responsibility for that crime, but that is quite independent of the question of responsibility for attempting the "ultimate" crime. In *Docherty v. Brown*, 1996 J.C. 48, at 50, L.J.-G. Hope stated that if a person had reached the stage of attempt, it made no difference whether he was then interrupted "or desisted before the crime was committed" — but there is no suggestion that his Lordship was expressing a considered or concluded view on the general issue being discussed here.

[11] H. Donnedieu de Vabres, *Traité de Droit Criminal et de Législation Pénale Comparée* (3rd ed., Paris, 1947), p.135.

[12] *e.g.* StGB, Art. 24(1); Nouveau Code Pénal, Art 121–5. See also George Fletcher, *Rethinking Criminal Law* (Boston, 1978), at p.184 *et seq.*

[13] The Model Penal Code makes it a defence that the accused "abandoned his effort to commit the crime or otherwise prevented its commission, under circumstances manifesting a complete and voluntary renunciation of his criminal purpose", but not if the renunciation is motivated by the emergence of circumstances increasing the difficulty of success or the likelihood of apprehension: see Model Penal Code, O.D. s.5.01(4). The limitation, which perhaps places too much stress on the "moral value" in a Kantian sense, of renunciation, would probably not be adopted in Scotland: see *H.M. Advocate v. Baxter* (1908) 5 Adam 609, L.J.-C. Macdonald at p.614.

[14] Strictly speaking, the stage of attempt should probably be set by reference to what the accused thinks is the last act necessary to achieve his purpose. Thus if A believes that he can kill B by pointing a gun at him without firing it, he cannot abandon his plan after he has pointed the gun — but this raises the question of attempts at the impossible. Ebki and

INTERVENTION. Suppose now that the accused has carried out the last act — he has shot at his victim, or sent him a poisoned cake, or a blackmailing letter. He can no longer abandon his plan, because there is nothing left to abandon; all he can do if he repents is to intervene and prevent events taking their natural course. If he succeeds in doing this — if he obtains medical attention for the man he has shot, or warns the man he intended to poison, or countermands his request for money and gives up the incriminating letters he is using for blackmail — he will have manifested his repentance in the best way possible in the circumstances, by preventing the completion of his crime and, in the case of murder, saving the victim's life. In such a situation, as in the case of abandonment, it seems reasonable to give the accused credit for what he has done and to treat him as having by his acts earned remission for his original attempt. This type of repentance must of course be voluntary, and so must probably precede the discovery of the attempt. **6.31**

Recognition of this type of repentance is not free from difficulty. It means for example that the man who shoots and misses cannot avoid guilt of an attempted crime — since he cannot abandon his completed plan, nor save his victim's life which is not in danger — while the man who shoots and wounds may avoid such guilt by intervention. There is a great deal to be said for adopting a solution which gives the court a discretion to impose a lesser penalty rather than the one current in Germany which treats intervention as rendering the accused free of all punishment.[15] On the other hand it may be said that successful intervention should result in freedom from blame, and unsuccessful but sincere intervention result in mitigation of penalty as it no doubt would in practice in Scotland.[16] Be that as it may, it is submitted that the law should give some recognition to successful intervention, both because it shows that the accused did not persist in his evil intention, and because it is socially desirable to give intending criminals an interest to prevent the

---

Finkin raise the more realistic situation where A shoots at B, meaning to kill him, misses B but refrains from discharging another bullet at him although A knows or at least believes that he has the means of doing so. As they put it: "According to conventional doctrine, A is to be punished for attempted homicide . . . [H]e did everything that in his view was necessary to commit homicide and can therefore no more desist from its further commission. By refraining from further shots he merely omits further attempts." They point out however that the Bundesgerichtshof has decided that A in such a case should have the defence of withdrawal under StGB 24(1) provided his initial shot and refusal to unleash another can be considered as parts of one course of conduct; but it is essential that A should have considered himself able to try again (even by some other means) since he can then be seen to have desisted voluntarily before the point of no return had been reached. It is highly unlikely that a Scots court would adopt such a subtle approach, and indeed it is one which would be difficult to apply in practice because of the difficulty of proof. It is also an approach which is controversial in Germany (see W.F. Ebki and M.W. Finkin, *Introduction to German Law* (Kluner, 1996), pp.399–400). The Scots approach in such a situation would probably be objective. It should also be noted that the fact that the accused may have envisaged the need to give up his attempt in certain circumstances does not prevent him having the necessary intention to carry out the crime. *Cf. People v. Wylie* [1976] 2 N.Z.L.R. 167, Woodhouse J. at 169: "It would be quite artificial to hold that a necessary criminal intent had not been established merely because it was associated with a lively and common-sense recognition that some seemingly auspicious environment might present sudden perils that would need to be met by instant retreat."

[15] StGb, Art. 24 (1).

[16] *cf. John Smith* (1871) 2 Couper 1, a charge of uttering by posting a forged cheque to B with instructions to cash it, where Lord Ardmillan said, "If he had telegraphed, or otherwise communicated his desire to stop the uttering of this cheque, he might have saved himself . . . I should have had great difficulty in excluding the power of revocation if an honest attempt had been made to recall the cheque": at 12–13.

consequences of their actions.[17] Of course, if the accused has committed a completed crime, such as assault, his guilt for that will be unaffected by his intervention.

6.32 *Possible repentance.* So far the discussion has been of actual repentance. But it can be argued that the law should not punish a man so long as it is possible for him to repent effectively, either by abandonment or by intervention. One of the reasons for the refusal to punish preparations for crimes is that it is felt to be wrong to deprive a man of his chance to repent his criminal desires. The last act theory leaves him this chance right up to the time he completes his part in the crime, until he fires the shot, or puts his hand into the pocket from which he intends to steal. But if repentance is central to one's theory of attempt, it can be argued that the possibility of intervention should also be treated as sufficient to prevent the stage of attempt being reached. On this view there would be no attempt until something had made it impossible for the accused to intervene effectively, whether the act of another, the mere passage of time or anything else. Where the test is actual repentance one asks, "Had the accused effectively repented when he was arrested?", but where the test is possible repentance one asks, "Would he have had time or been able to repent effectively had he not been arrested when he was?"

6.33 *Which form of the final stage theory is preferable?* It is submitted that the last act theory modified by the acceptance of abandonment or actual intervention as a valid plea in defence or at least in mitigation is the preferable form of the final stage theory, and that for two reasons.

(1) The last act theory is easier to apply. The last act theory offers a fairly easy way of fixing the stage of attempt in any given case. One need ask only — did anything remain for the accused to do in order to complete the crime? But on the possible intervention form of the theory it is not so easy to fix the relevant stage, because it is difficult to say when intervention has been excluded. Is it, for example, enough to constitute attempted murder that the accused shot at the victim, or must one allow the possibility of his repenting thereafter and sending for a doctor or an ambulance, or otherwise saving the victim's life? To allow actual repentance of this sort to extinguish or diminish guilt seems morally sound, and this will in any event happen so rarely that the law may feel entitled to make an exception to the last act theory in favour of such situations when they do occur. But to allow the mere possibility of such intervention is surely to adopt such an extreme attitude that one might as well abolish attempted crimes altogether.

(2) The possibility of intervention theory leads to paradox. Suppose A sends a bottle of poisoned wine to B in London with the intention of killing him; he is arrested the following day, by which time B has taken the poison and is seriously ill. A is probably guilty of attempted murder. Suppose now that at the time of A's arrest B has not yet taken the poison because of an unexpected delay in the post, or because the dinner party at which A expected the wine to be drunk was postponed, and the police telephoned B and prevented him from drinking the wine. In the second case intervention was still possible at the time of A's arrest, but it

[17] *cf.* H. Donnedieu de Vabres, *Traité de Droit Criminal et de Législation Pénale Comparée* (3rd ed., Paris, 1947), p.139.

seems illogical to convict him in the first case and not in the second, since in neither did he actually repent, and since he did exactly the same thing in both cases.

An even more paradoxical situation may be conceived. Suppose A and B simultaneously shoot X and Y respectively, intending to kill them, and X and Y receive similar serious wounds. A and B are arrested immediately after firing the shots. A is a lawyer and knows nothing of medicine, and it is impossible for him to do anything about X's wounds; B is an extremely clever surgeon and one of the few men who can save Y's life — is it to be said that A is guilty of attempted murder but B is not, and will not be so guilty unless he remains at liberty until someone else has saved Y's life?

Objections to the final stage theory.[18] The main objection to the theory is that it allows too many prospective criminals to escape punishment, and allows even those it does punish to advance very far in their criminal purposes before it can intervene to punish them for attempting to commit a crime. It thus renders nugatory the main purposes of the law of attempt — to prevent harm by catching the criminal before he has had a chance to do appreciable damage, and to punish intending criminals who have shown their dangerousness even though they have not succeeded in their intentions. If, however, one takes the view that the scope of the criminal law should be restricted rather than extended, and further that any extensions should be by way of clearly defined (and perhaps preferably statutory) rules and not be made by the judicial application of vague common law principles,[19] one will view the objections to the theory as positive advantages. **6.34**

Another objection is that the theory probably makes it impossible to convict anyone of attempting to commit a number of common crimes. This result is contrary to the principle underlying the rule that an attempt to commit any crime is punishable,[20] and also contrary to current practice. Convictions for attempted rape, for example, are not uncommon, but attempted rape cannot be committed on the final stage theory — either there has been penetration, in which case the crime has been completed, or there has not, in which case the last act, penetration, remains to be done and the accused can still change his mind and decide not to commit the rape. Similar objections can be made to any charge of attempted assault, and probably to any charge of attempting to commit a crime which is inseparable from the criminal conduct necessary to commit it, *i.e.* to any crime which is not a result-crime.[21] **6.35**

The difficulties raised by the theory are also clear in the case of theft. It seems reasonable to hold, as the law does, that it is attempted theft to place one's hand in a receptacle with intent to steal something therefrom.[22] But the modern crime of theft requires that the object to be stolen be appropriated, which in the case postulated involves the

---

[18] For a trenchant summary of these, see P.R. Glazebrook, *op.cit.*, para. 6.01, n.1, at pp.39–40.

[19] *cf. supra*, para. 6.06, n. 15; N. Walker, *op.cit.*, n.8.

[20] 1995 Act, s.294.

[21] *cf. supra,* para. 3.05. It has been held in England that there is no such thing as an attempt to demand money with menaces: *R. v. Moran* [1952] 1 All E.R. 803n; and see J.Ll.J. Edwards, "Criminal Attempts" (1952) 15 M.L.R. 345. 346 *et seq.*

[22] *Coventry v. Douglas*, 1944 J.C. 13.

unauthorised physical removal of that object from its receptacle.[23] It follows, therefore, that merely to place one's hand in a receptacle is not the last act necessary to the commission of the theft; the object must be removed. And once it is removed there is a completed crime. It may be said that once the pickpocket has put his hand in the victim's pocket this is virtually the last act, since the possibility of his repentance and withdrawal at that stage is so slight that it can be discounted: but how far must A go to reach this stage? If the object is in a desk drawer is it enough for him to open the drawer, or must he put his hand inside the desk? And if there are a number of objects in the desk and he is interested in only one of them, must he go the length of finding, or touching, that one? Again, if the object is not in a receptacle, but lying on a table, is it enough for him to stretch his hand out towards the object, or must he reach or touch the table, or the object?

This problem does not appear to have been considered in Scotland. The cases on attempt deal with result-crimes like murder, abortion and fraud, and the decisions in these cases have not yet been applied to crimes like rape and theft. It has just been taken for granted that rape and theft can be attempted — they are serious matters, they deserve punishment, and the law says that an attempt to commit any crime is criminal.[24]

The Scots Authorities on the Final Stage Theory

6.36 (1) *The possibility of intervention.* In *H.M. Advocate v. Baxter*[25] B sent abortifacients to X with instructions to use them to procure the abortion of Y. They were not in fact so used. B was charged with attempted abortion and Lord Justice-Clerk Macdonald had little difficulty in holding that the indictment was irrelevant. This decision may accord with the last act theory — B's guilt was only art and part and if X had not administered the drugs the last act had not been performed — but Lord Macdonald's language suggests that he was thinking in terms of the possibility of intervention. His reason for rejecting the suggestion that B had been guilty of attempt was that:

> "There was plenty of room for going back on what was done. The sender of the drugs might immediately afterwards have sent a letter to the man to whom they were sent forbidding him to use them for the purpose for which he sent them, and saying that, if he did not get an undertaking at once that they would not be so used, he would himself inform the police of the matter. It is quite plain that, if he had done that, it could not be said that an attempt to commit the crime had been made. If that is so, it is equally plain that it cannot be said an attempt was made if nothing took place."[26]

6.37 In *H.M. Advocate v. Mackenzies*[27] a husband and wife were allegedly involved in a scheme of the husband's to copy his employer's trade secrets and sell them to a trade rival. The husband was charged with

---

[23] See Vol. II, Chap. 14.

[24] Criminal Procedure (Scotland) Act 1887, s.61: now 1995 Act, s.294.

[25] (1908) 5 Adam 609.

[26] At 615.

[27] (1913) 7 Adam 189.

copying the secrets with intent to dispose of them, and the wife with offering to dispose of them and attempting to appropriate them. The charge against the husband was rejected as irrelevant because it was held that what he had done was not criminal, and accordingly the charge against the wife was dropped. But the court considered what her position would have been had the secrets been criminally obtained and had she known of this when she made the offer. The court took the view that she would not in that event have been guilty of attempted fraud, since she would only have expressed a willingness to commit fraud and could still have drawn back and repented of her proposal.[28] This is consistent with the last act theory — the wife had still to hand over the secrets and receive the money — but the impression given by the opinions is that they were based on the possible intervention theory.

Neither of these cases, it is submitted, is direct authority for the intervention theory. The remarks in *Mackenzies*[28a] are *obiter*, and the facts of *Baxter*[28b] are too bound up with the question of art and part guilt by counsel for it to be a clear authority on the application of the theory.

Apart from these two cases the theory is supported only by one or two dicta. The learned editors of Macdonald say that the stage of attempt is reached "when it is beyond the power of the man to prevent its consequences",[29] but go on to equate this with the stage of perpetration. In *H.M. Advocate v. Tannahill and Neilson*[30] it was said that for attempt there must be "some overt act, the consequences of which cannot be recalled by the accused",[31] but in that case there had been no more than a suggestion to a prospective accomplice that he and the accused might carry out a fraud. This dictum was repeated in *Morton v. Henderson*,[32] but there again the facts disclosed only a suggestion that a fraud should be committed.

It is accordingly submitted that the possibility of intervention version of the final stage theory does not represent Scots law.

(2) *The last act theory.* This theory receives the support of Hume who says: **6.38**

> "[E]ven when no harm ensues on the attempt, still the law rightly takes cognisance of it, *si deventum sit ad actum maleficio proximum*; if there has been an inchoate act of *execution* of the meditated deed; if the man have done that act, or a part of that act, by which he *meant and expected* to perpetrate his crime, and which, if not providentially interrupted or defeated, would have done so; and more especially still (but this is *not* indispensable,) where he has done something which must have its own course, and puts repentance out of his power."[33]

It is submitted that this is clear authority for the application of the last act theory and the rejection of the possible intervention theory. It is true

---

[28] At 197. The facts in *Mackenzies* would have constituted an "act preparatory" under a statute which punished such acts; *cf. R. v. Bingham* [1973] Q.B. 870.

[28a] (1913) 7 Adam 189.

[28b] (1908) 5 Adam 609.

[29] Macdonald, p.1: the passage first appears in the 5th edition.

[30] 1943 J.C. 150.

[31] Lord Wark at 153.

[32] 1956 J.C. 55, L.J.-G. Clyde at 58.

[33] Hume, i, 27.

that Hume speaks of "that act, or a part of that act", and it is not too clear what he means by "a part of that act", but his talk of what the man expected the act to accomplish and of a providential interruption, and the way in which he deals with the possibility of repentance, all clearly point to the last act theory.[34] So do most of his examples, such as giving a man a poisoned cup, throwing combustibles on stacks in a barnyard, and ineffectual instigation or subornation. He treats the scuttling of a ship as attempted fraud on the underwriters, but it is submitted that he is wrong in that and was probably influenced by the grave nature of the act of scuttling — such an act may be regarded by those who adopt the distinction as being merely preparatory, and so not even the first, far less the last, act of execution.[35] It is not attempted fraud even on Hume's definition of attempt.

The theory is also supported by Alison, who says: "In attempts at murder, the crime is to be held as completed if the pannel has done all that in him lay to effect it, although, owing to accident or any other cause, the desired effect has been prevented from taking place."[36] The cases which focus the problem concern attempts to commit murder by poisoning, and on this matter Alison's views are as follows:

> "Whether the mere purchase of poison, or the mixing it up *with a view to mingling it* with the food that is intended to be taken, are to be taken as a complete commission of the crime, seems much more doubtful. In other departments of law the analogous cases are against such a construction. An incendiary letter written, but not sent or disclosed, a libel lying in the author's desk not published, a letter offering a bribe and enclosing the bank-notes, but still in the pocket of the writer, are no points of dittay . . . Judging from these principles, there seems good ground to distinguish between those cases where the person meditating poison has merely purchased and mixed up the materials with that view, and those where he has actually *put them out of his hands*, and Providence or fortune only have prevented the effect. The one case is analogous to an incendiary letter written, but still in the pocket; the other, to such a letter put into the post-office, but intercepted on its route by some supervening accident."[37]

6.39 The last act theory is supported, as against the possible intervention theory, by two cases of attempted poisoning. The first is *Janet Ramage*[38] where R placed poison in a teapot full of tea which she found by the fire in the victim's house, and from which the victim was expected to drink her breakfast tea. Now at that stage R could still have prevented the crime — she could have come back and removed the teapot, or warned the victim — but she had done all she needed to do to poison the victim, she had only to wait for the victim to come and take her usual breakfast. The charge was held to be relevant.

6.40 A similar situation arose in *Samuel Tumbleson*[39] where T put poison in his wife's oatmeal and gave the poisoned oatmeal to someone to give to her. The indictment does not say what happened after the intermediary

[34] *cf.* R.A.A. McCall Smith and D. Sheldon, *Scots Criminal Law* (2nd ed., Edinburgh, 1997) at p.103.

[35] See *H.M. Advocate v. Camerons* (1911) 6 Adam 456, 484; *cf. supra*, para. 6.21.

[36] Alison, i, 165.

[37] *ibid.*, i, 167.

[38] (1825) Hume, i, 28.

[39] (1863) 4 Irv. 426.

was given the poison and the case must therefore be treated as if the accused had been arrested as soon as the poison was handed over, *i.e.* when he could still have countermanded his instructions about giving the oatmeal to his wife. The charge was held relevant on the ground that the accused had put machinery in motion which "by its own nature, is calculated to terminate in murder", and which was "let out of the party's hands to work its natural results".[40]

There are some modern cases which should be mentioned, which are consistent with both the last act and the possibility of intervention theories. The first is *H.M. Advocate v. Semple*[41] in which a charge of attempted abortion was held relevant where the abortifacients had in fact been administered, but no abortion had resulted. Two others concern the crime of subornation of perjury, where a crime is committed as soon as the witness to be suborned agrees to give false evidence.[42] Where he does not agree or where he agrees and then when it comes to the trial gives true evidence, the crime is attempted subornation — although in the latter case it should probably be subornation if he initially did agree to give false evidence, since in that event he was suborned for a time at least. The situation here is essentially similar to that in which a pistol is fired with intent to kill: "The conspiracy has had its course so far as depended on the suborner."[43] **6.41**

In *Angus v. H.M. Advocate*[44] the suborned witness had in fact given true evidence and A. was convicted of attempted subornation. In *Dalton v. H.M. Advocate*[45] D had asked someone to refuse to make a statement to the police, and there was considerable argument as to whether this was a crime. But it was accepted that if what was intended could be regarded as a form of subornation the accused had gone far enough to enable the court to convict him of attempt.[46] The important point about subornation in relation to attempt is that subornation is a form of incitement, and that the crime of incitement or attempted incitement[47] is complete once a suggestion has been made to someone that he should commit a crime. **6.42**

Finally, in *McKenzie v. H.M. Advocate*,[48] it was held that to raise civil actions based on false averments constituted an attempt to defraud the person called as defender. Although the case is not without difficulty (since the deception referred to in the indictment was addressed to solicitors rather than to the defender in the actions which were raised), the court appears to have considered that the accused had either performed their last act in the fraudulent scheme[49] or had put in train events which could not "be expunged or blotted out".[50]

---

[40] Lord Neaves at 430.
[41] 1937 J.C. 41.
[42] *cf.* Hume, i, 382, where he treats this as a crime *sui generis*.
[43] Hume, i, 382.
[44] 1935 J.C. 1.
[45] 1951 J.C. 76.
[46] The crime was charged as an attempt to pervert the course of justice, *cf. supra*, para. 1.34.
[47] See *infra*, para. 6.71.
[48] 1988 S.C.C.R. 153.
[49] *ibid.*, L.J.-C. Ross at 156.
[50] *ibid.*, L.J.-C. Ross at 155.

Conclusion

6.43 It was submitted in the first edition of this book that Scots law adopted the last act theory of attempts and that *Camerons*[51] was unsupported by authority, and did not represent the law. While the authorities do support this view, *Camerons*[51a] appears to have lost none of the affection with which it has been regarded by the courts.[52] It has one inestimable advantage as a working authority, and that is its vagueness. It offers an impressive-sounding and apparently precise rationalization for doing justice in any particular case: if the jury think the accused should be punished for what he did they will characterise what he did as perpetration; if they do not, they will characterise it as preparation. What was a question of law related to ideas about how restricted the scope of criminal law should be, becomes a value-judgment related to the jury's assessment of blameworthiness.[53] That such an approach is in line with that adopted in other areas of Scots law,[54] increases the likelihood that *Camerons*[54a] will be endorsed by the Criminal Appeal Court if and when the occasion arises. The author is thus constrained to admit that if Holmes' "friend the bad man" wants to know what the Scots courts are likely to do in fact,[55] the answer which his legal adviser would give him is that they will probably apply the preparation-perpetration test, which means that he will have to take his chance on the tribunal's assessment of his wickedness and dangerousness. The appeal court have still to pronounce on the matter, and it remains open, of course, for them to reassert the authority of the pre-*Camerons*[55a] cases, but such a result is unlikely.

Art and Part in Attempted Crimes

6.44 Samuel Tumbleson[56] is authority for the view that to give poison to an intermediary to give to the victim is attempted murder. This is because the intermediary in *Tumbleson*[56a] knew nothing of the accused's intention, and so was an innocent agent. To give poison to an innocent agent

[51] (1911) 6 Adam 456.

[51a] *ibid.*

[52] See, *e.g.*, *Barrett v. Allan*, 1986 S.C.C.R. 479, where it was held that to stand in a queue at a stadium turnstyle could constitute an attempt to enter the stadium, the test being whether "it was clear that acts more than preparatory acts to enter had begun" (*per* L.J.-G. Emslie at 481). See also *Guthrie v. Friel*, 1992 S.C.C.R. 932, L.J.-C. Ross at 936E: "It has often been observed that before a charge of attempting to do something can be established, the individual must have passed from mere preparation to perpetration." In the full bench case of *Docherty v. Brown*, 1996 J.C. 48, L.J.-G. Hope (at 50) and L.J.-C. Ross (at 57 and 60) seem to accept that the stage of perpetration must be reached — all without mentioning *Camerons* but at the same time referring to or quoting with approval from the passages from Hume and/or Alison which support the "last act" theory (see Lord Hope at 50 and Lord Ross at 54–55); of the other judges, Lord Sutherland (at 61–62) refers only to the stage of perpetration having to be reached, whilst Lord Cameron (at 67 and 71) apparently favours the "last act" theory. Lord Johnston did not deal with what the appropriate test should be.

[53] *cf. R. v. Smith (Roger)* [1975] A.C.476, Lord Reid at 499G: "It must be left to common sense to determine in each case whether the accused has gone beyond mere preparation."

[54] See *e.g.* the definition of murder, Vol. II, Chap. 23, and the law of insanity and diminished responsibility, *infra*, paras 10.07, 11.03.

[54a] (1911) 6 Adam 456.

[55] See O.W. Holmes, "The Path of the Law" (1897) 10 H.L.R. 457, 460.

[55a] (1911) 6 Adam 456.

[56] (1863) 4 Irv. 426.

[56a] *ibid.*

is like posting it or placing it on a conveyor belt which will take it to the victim. In such a situation there is no need to consider the act and will of the agent, and the intending poisoner has only to sit back and let events take their normal course, just as where he posts the poison or leaves it in a cup from which he expects the victim to drink.

The position is, it is submitted, quite different where A gives the poison to an accomplice who knows that the substance is poisonous and who is party to A's intention. It is true that in such a situation A need do nothing more himself; he need only wait for his accomplice to deliver the poison in the same way as he need only wait for the post office to do so. But where the agent is an accomplice one leaves the realm of individual action and enters that of conspiracies, and must therefore leave the logic and language of individual action and use that of conspiracies, of art and part. This means that one no longer talks of the actions of individuals, but of the conspiracy; so "personifying" the plot.[57] If one does that, it is clear that at the stage where A gives his accomplice the poison something still remains to be done in pursuance of the plot by the conspiracy and so, notionally, by A, before there is attempt. In such a situation A is not guilty of attempt until his accomplice "places the food on Z's table or delivers it to Z's servants". If the accomplice recants before he does this, there will have been no attempt of which A could be guilty. In this situation, although there is nothing more for A to do, A knows that a deliberate human act is still necessary before the crime can be completed, and an act of this kind by a willing accomplice is quite different from the operation of a conveyor belt or the act of a postmen or of any other innocent agent. One might say also that just as A is responsible for the acts of his accomplice so he is entitled to the benefit of the accomplice's inaction. A may, of course, be guilty of incitement or conspiracy, but not of attempt.[58]

The above situations are fairly simple, but between them, between the **6.45**
case of *Tumbleson*[58a] or the example of the post office, and the fully-fledged conspiracy, there fall a number of very difficult situations. One such arose in the South African case of *R. v. Nlhovo*.[59] There the accused gave poison to one N. telling him that it was medicine and that he was to put it in J.'s food because "J arrests me when I go and pick mealies and peaches". N never intended to put the poison in J's food; he took it straight to J and the two of them went to the police. The Appeal Court held that there had been no attempt to poison, but only an attempted incitement. One of the judges, Maasdorp J.A., considered Scots law in his opinion and referred to the case of *Walter Buchanan*.[60] This case is described by Hume as one of attempted poisoning by "giving poison to a third party, who did not know it for such, and soliciting him, but without success, to administer it" to the victim. In fact the poison was given to a dog who died of it. Maasdorp J.A. also referred to Macdonald's statement that it was attempted poisoning to "give poison to B, to be administered to C, whether B is a consenting party to the crime or not",[61] and concluded that Nlhovo would have been convicted of

---

[57] *supra*, para. 5.38.
[58] *cf.* Gl. Williams, para. 198.
[58a] (1863) 4 Irv. 426.
[59] [1921] A.D. 485; see also *R. v. Dick*, 1969 (3) S.A. 267(R.).
[60] (1728) Hume, i, 181; Burnett, p.10; Alison, i, 166.
[61] Macdonald, 3rd ed., p.144; 5th ed., p.108.

attempted poisoning in Scotland, a result he attributed to the influence of the Roman law's special treatment of attempts to commit flagitious crimes.[62]

It is submitted that Nlhovo would not be guilty of attempt in Scots law and that the case can be distinguished from *Buchanan*[62a] by making the distinction which Macdonald rejects, between giving poison to an ignorant agent and giving it to someone who knows it is poison. It is not clear how much N knew in *Nlhovo*[62b] nor, and this is more important, how much the accused thought he knew, but his actions, and the court's view that there had been incitement, suggest that although nothing was said the accused was aware that N knew he was being asked to poison J. If that was the case, it is submitted that a similar result would follow in Scotland, since the question would then fall to be decided from the point of view of the law of art and part. In such a situation the accused would not think of himself as doing all that was required of him to bring about J's death, but merely as entering into a conspiracy with N to poison J. There is authority in Scotland that to invite someone to commit a crime does not constitute an attempt to commit that crime,[63] and in practice a case like *Nlhovo*[63a] would probably be decided on that simple ground. If N had agreed to poison J and then been caught by the police or run down by a motor-car before he had done so, there would have been no attempted poisoning — that being so it would be strange if there were to be attempted poisoning because N. did not agree to poison J. As Solomon J.A. pointed out, when the poison was given to N the crime "was actually further away from being committed than if the prisoner had procured the poison with the intention of himself putting it into [J's] food."[64]

The distinction between *Nlhovo*[64a] and *Buchanan*[64b] depends on the accused's views about the state of knowledge of the person to whom he hands over the poison. Alison describes *Buchanan*[64c] as "an attempt to commit poison, through the hand of an ignorant person", and thus as similar to offering poisoned food to the victim, or leaving it in the victim's cup.[65] The failure of the innocent agent to "deliver the goods" is comparable to a breakdown in a conveyor belt, his unexpected discovery that he is carrying poison the same as such a discovery by a postman, and these do not affect the guilt of the intending poisoner.[66]

---

[62] See *R. v. Nlhovo, supra*, at 499–500.

[62a] (1978) Hume, i, 181; Burnett, p.10; Alison, i, 166.

[62b] [1921] A.D. 485; see also *R. v. Dick,* 1969(3) S.A. 267(R).

[63] *H.M. Advocate v. Tannahill and Neilson*, 1943 J.C. 150; *Morton v. Henderson*, 1956 J.C. 55.

[63a] *supra,* at 485.

[64] *Nlhovo, supra*, at 490.

[64a] [1921] A.D. 485.

[64b] (1728) Hume, i, 181; Burnett, p.10; Alison, i, 166.

[64c] *ibid.*

[65] Alison, i, 166.

[66] The position becomes difficult where the innocent agent does not accept the poison at all, whether because he thinks it may be poison or for any other reason. There is then something like a telephone on which one cannot get through, or a pillar box that will not take one's parcel, or, perhaps, a gun that will not go off. The difficulty is one of defining the last act. Is the "last act" the request that the agent deliver the poison, or the placing of the poison in his hands? Is it, similarly, the firing of a bullet from a gun, or the pressing of a trigger? Strictly speaking, it is probably the latter of the two alternatives in each case. In practice, however, it is probably attempt to pull a trigger that does not go off, but because of the similarity to cases of incitement, not attempt today — whatever the position may

Mens Rea in Attempt

This is dealt with in the chapter on *mens rea*.[67] 6.46

Attempt in Statutory Offences

Section 294 of the 1995 Act,[68] which provides that any attempt to commit an offence shall itself be an offence, is general in its terms, and should therefore apply to statutory offences as well as at common law. The fact, therefore, that a statutory provision creating an offence makes no reference to attempt is irrelevant, even if other provisions of the same statute do make such reference. For example, section 4 of the Road Traffic Act 1988 makes it an offence to drive or attempt to drive while unfit, section 178 merely makes it an offence to take and drive away a vehicle without consent,[69] and section 12 of the English Theft Act 1968 (as originally enacted) recognises the offence of attempting to take away a vehicle.[70] It has been argued that the express reference to attempt in section 4[71] and the recognition of it in the 1968 Act show that Parliament did not intend an attempt to commit an offence against section 178[72] to be an offence, but this argument was rejected by the High Court, partly because section 178(3)[73] gives power to arrest without warrant, but principally because of the general rule of Scots law enshrined in the 1975 Act and now in the 1995 Act.[74] It must also be the case that the principles applicable to common law attempts apply equally to attempts to commit statutory offences — and there are some modern dicta to support this view.[75] 6.47

There is one difficulty in applying section 294 of the 1995 Act to statutes which do not expressly deal with attempts, which is not usually present in applying the law of art and part to statutes which do not expressly deal with aiding and abetting. It is accepted that the person who is art and part is in Scots law guilty as a principal and so it is reasonable to apply to him the penalty provided in the statute for a principal,[76] but a person guilty of attempt is usually thought of as guilty 6.48

---

have been in 1728 — to ask someone to deliver poison if in fact he refuses to do so. It seems, incidentally, that in the eighteenth century it was attempted poisoning to deliver the poison to an ignorant third party, but that it was *capital* attempted poisoning if in fact the poison had been administered to the victim: Burnett, p.10.

[67] *infra*, paras 7.78 *et seq.*

[68] Re-enacting, so far as relevant to the present issue, the former ss.63(1) and 312(o) of the Criminal Procedure (Scotland) Act 1975.

[69] See s.29 of Road Traffic Act 1991, which adds subs. (4A) to s.34 of Road Traffic Offenders Act 1988 and which now indirectly recognises the existence of an offence of attempt to commit an offence under s.178.

[70] See s.12(3). This subsection has now been repealed (Police and Criminal Evidence Act 1984, Sched. 7, Pt. I), but was in effect restored by s.24(1)(c), (2)(d) and (3)(b) of the same Act of 1984. Subsequently, s.24(3)(b) was amended by Criminal Justice Act 1988, Sched. 15, para. 98 so as to exclude specifically s.12(1) of the Theft Act — but *cf.* now s.34(4A) of Road Traffic Offenders Act 1988, as added by Road Traffic Act 1991, s.29.

[71] or rather s.5 of the Road Traffic Act 1972, as the law then was.

[72] or s.175 of the Road Traffic Act 1972, as the law then was.

[73] or s.175(3) of the Road Traffic Act 1972, as the law then was.

[74] *Wilson and Forbes v. Morton*, High Court on appeal, July 1975, unrep'd.

[75] See *Docherty v. Brown*, 1996 J.C. 48. Lord Sutherland at 61, Lord Cameron at 64, and Lord Johnston at 72.

[76] See s.293 of the 1995 Act, *supra*, para. 5.11.

of a lesser offence than a person guilty of the completed crime, and so liable only to a lesser penalty. But if this is so, then in the absence of any specific provision in the Act for punishing attempts there is no statutory penalty for attempt, and it is therefore, at least in theory, impossible for the court to impose any penalty on a person convicted of an attempt to commit a statutory offence unless the Act itself lays down a penalty for attempt.

In England prior to the Criminal Attempts Act 1981[77] it was a common law misdemeanour to attempt to commit a statutory offence, but on conviction of such a misdemeanour only the common law penalties were available, so that if the statute did not provide for disqualification in the case of attempt, no disqualification could be imposed.[78] It would be a rather strange use of language to describe section 294 of the 1995 Act as creating a common law misdemeanour. These arguments do not seem to have been raised in *Wilson and Forbes v. Morton*[79] where the accused were disqualified for attempting to take and drive away a vehicle. The sentences were attacked as harsh and oppressive, but it seems to have been conceded that if the attempt was criminal, the sentencing provisions applicable to the completed offence applied also to an attempt.

Attempts to Do the Impossible

6.49 One of the most controversial problems in the law of attempt is the question of responsibility for attempts to commit crimes which are impossible of achievement.[80] Two general principles are fairly clear. Since the essence of attempt is that the intended crime has not occurred, the reason for its non-occurrence is not usually of importance, and it should not matter whether an assailant's shot misses because he is a bad shot or because the victim is out of range. Equally, it is clear that where the accused knows of the impossibility of what he is "trying" to do there can be no attempt. It is not the impossibility but the accused's knowledge

---

[77] See s.6 of the 1981 Act, which abrogated the common law.

[78] *Bell v. Ingham* [1969] 1 Q.B. 563. Disqualification is now specially provided for England by Sched. 2 to the Road Traffic Offenders Act 1988, Pt. II, para. 2, which also more particularly caters for disqualification for an attempt to steal a motor vehicle. See also Road Traffic Offenders Act 1988 s.34(4A) added by the Road Traffic Act 1991, s.29.

[79] See para. 6.47, n.74, *supra*.

[80] The amount of literature on this topic is, as endorsed by L.J.-C. Ross in *Docherty v. Brown*, 1996 J.C. 48 at 54, wholly out of proportion to its practical importance. See, *e.g.* J.C. Smith, "Two problems in Criminal Attempts" (1957) 70 H.L.R. 422, and "Two Problems in Criminal Attempts Re-examined — II" [1962] Crim.L.R. 212; Gl. Williams, paras 205–207; Hall, 586–599; Gl. Williams, "Criminal Attempts — A Reply" [1962] Crim.L.R. 300; B. Gill, "Impossibility in Criminal Attempts", 1965 J.R. 137; G.H. Gordon, "Another Attempt at the Impossible" (1974) 19 J.L.S. 246; G. Fletcher, *Rethinking Criminal Law* (Boston, 1978), pp.146–184; H.L.A. Hart, "The House of Lords on Attempting the Impossible", in *Crime, Proof and Punishment*, (Tapper (ed.), London, 1981), 1; Brian Hogan, "The Criminal Attempts Act and Attempting the Impossible" [1984] Crim.L.R. 584; Gl. Williams, "The Lords and Impossible Attempts, or *Qui Custodiet Ipsos Custodes*" [1986] C.L.J. 33; R.A. Duff, "Attempts and the Problem of the Missing Circumstances" (1991) 92 N.I.L.Q. 87; J.C. Smith and B. Hogan, *Criminal Law* (9th ed., 1999, Sir J. Smith (ed.)), pp.320–326; A. Ashworth, *Principles of Criminal Law* (3rd ed., 1999) pp.469–471; Law Commission Report on Attempt, and Impossibility in Relation to Attempt, Conspiracy and Incitement (Law. Com. No. 102, 1980); *R. v. Smith (Roger)* [1975] A.C. 476; *R. v. Donnelly* [1970] N.Z.L.R. 980; and the articles cited *supra*, para 6.01, n.1.

of it which is important. A charge of administering drugs with intent to cause an abortion, for example, is meaningless unless there is postulated "a belief in the mind of the panel that what he was supplying was something which was calculated to cause an abortion to take place."[81]

UNREASONABLE MISTAKE. There is a subsidiary problem concerning **6.50** the situation where the accused's belief in the possibility of success is so unreasonable that his actions do not constitute a danger at all, and it has been argued that in such cases there should not be liability for attempt. An example would be an attempt to poison by using salt, or to wound by sticking pins into an effigy. But although the particular acts in such a situation may be harmless, they reveal the accused as a man with criminal intentions, and such a man may after the failure of his impossible attempt adopt more successful means. It is submitted, therefore, that the reasonableness of the accused's error should not affect his guilt — although if it is sufficiently unreasonable it may indicate that he is insane or in need of mental treatment.[82]

Theories relative to impossibility. Efforts have often been made to find a **6.51** theory which would explain apparently contradictory decisions arrived at by the courts and also provide for those instances of impossible attempts where conviction seems "intuitively" wrong. In fact some of the older decisions were simply quite impossible to reconcile; whilst the "objective innonce" of conduct, which made it possible to argue that it was intuitively wrong to convict,[83] cried out for analysis[84] rather than incorporation within some overall plan. An instance of the former problem certainly arose in Scots law, since by 1928 it had been decided that a conviction for an attempt to procure an abortion was not possible where the woman in question had not in fact been pregnant at the relevant time,[85] whereas by 1933 it had been accepted that it was perfectly proper to convict of attempted theft in a case where a pickpocket placed his hand inside a pocket which contained nothing.[86] Later cases[87] seemed to suggest that both earlier decisions could be supported,[88] although there was no sensible way in which that could be done. The other notion of "objective innocence" incorporating an intuitive feeling that conviction would be wrong, was founded on such hypotheticals as Bramwell B.'s famous question to counsel for the

[81] *H.M. Advocate v. Semple*, 1937 J.C. 41, L.J.-C. Aitchison at 44.

[82] See *R. v. Davies and Anr*, 1956 (3) S.A. 52 (A.D.), Schreiner J.A. at 63; Hall, 593. Gl. Wiliams, p.652 and F.B. Sayre, "Criminal Attempt" (1928) 41 H.L.R. 821, 850, both take the view that such attempts should not be punished.

[83] See, *e.g.*, J.C. Smith, "Two Problems in Criminal Attempts Re-examined — II" [1962] Crim.L.R. 212 at 212.

[84] See para. 6.52, *infra*.

[85] *H.M. Advocate v. Anderson*, 1928 J.C. 1.

[86] *Lamont v. Strathern*, 1933 J.C. 33.

[87] See *H.M. Advocate v. Semple*, 1937 J.C. 41, L.J.-C. Aitchison at 45 and Lord Moncrieff at 49 (although neither judge specifically mentioned *Lamont v. Strathern*, the case simply being cited to them by counsel for the Crown) and the conspiracy case of *Maxwell v. H.M. Advocate*, 1980 J.C. 40, Lord Cameron at 44–45.

[88] It has now been authoritatively ruled by a bench of five judges that *H.M. Advocate v. Anderson* was wrongly decided, and the support it received in *H.M. Advocate v. Semple* was wrong: see *Docherty v. Brown*, 1996 J.C. 48 — considered at para. 6.56, *infra*.

prisoners in the English case of *R. v. Collins and Ors*,[89] *viz*., "Suppose a man takes away an umbrella from a stand with intent to steal it, believing it not to be his own, but it turns out to be his own, could he convicted of attempting to steal it?" Superficially, the answer seems obvious, since an affirmative response apparently entails the pointless conviction of the actor for an attempt to steal his own property; alternatively, the actor's conduct, when viewed objectively, appears to amount to no more than a person's taking possession of his own goods. It also seems possible to argue that an affirmative answer will involve conviction for intent alone. But whilst it can be conceded that liability for attempt cannot be based solely on intent but must be predicated also on the actor's conduct, the better view is that that conduct should be considered in terms of the facts as the actor believed them to be.[90] To take any other view would be to narrow the ambit of attempt unacceptably — as has now been recognised in both Scots and English law.[91]

6.52 *Particular theories relative to purpose or motivation.* Academic writings have been much exercised by the "problem" of "objectively innocent conduct", the underlying assumption being that it might be wrong to convict of attempt in such cases. The types of situation with which such writings are concerned are exemplified by the following: the man who has intercourse in the belief that she is 15 with a consenting girl of 18; the person who buys goods at a very cheap price in the belief that they are stolen when in fact they have been come by legitimately; the person who imports what he believes to be prohibited goods when in fact they are not prohibited at all; the man who, in the belief that he is still married to his first wife, marries another woman when in fact his first wife is dead. In cases such as these, the actor believes that he is committing a crime known to the law — under age sexual intercourse, reset, contravention of the law forbidding the importation of prohibited goods, bigamy — but, of course, must fail to do so. In each such case, it may be argued that his conduct, when considered objectively, is innocent and therefore should not be such as to convict him for an attempt to commit the relevant crime. But what was it that enabled that conclusion to be drawn? What further objective requirement had to be met? (Admission of subjective considerations at this point would, it was thought, not only confuse the *actus reus* element of attempts (thus raising again the issue of conviction for intent alone) but also, of course, force re-examination of the "objective" innocence of the conduct.)

---

[89] (1864) 9 Cox C.C. 497 at 498. See also *R. v. Percy Dalton (London) Ltd.* (1949) 33 Cr.App.R. 102, Birkett J. at 110, *viz.* "Steps on the way to the commission of what would be a crime if the acts were completed, may amount to attempt to commit that crime, to which, unless interrupted, they would have led; but steps on the way to the doing of something, which is thereafter done, and which is no crime, cannot be regarded as attempts to commit a crime."

[90] See B. Gill, "Impossibility in Criminal Attempts", 1965 J.R. 137, at 138–139, and Gl. Williams, "The Lords and Impossible Attempts, or *Quis Custodiet Ipsos Custodes*" [1986] C.L.J. 33 at 50 and 59; E.M. Burchell and P.M.A. Hunt, *South African Criminal Law and Procedure* (3rd ed., 1997), Vol. 1, *General Principles of Criminal Law* (J.M. Burchell (ed.)), at p.352, where reference is made to *R. v. Davies*, 1956 (3) S.A. 52 (A) — attempt to carry out an abortion when the foetus was already dead, *S. v. W.*, 1976 (1) S.A. 1 (A) — attempt to rape a dead woman, and *S. v. Ndhlovu*, 1984 (2) S.A. 23 (A) — attempted murder of a person already dead. Although the conduct in such cases would strain "objective innocence" to its absolute limits, the cases in fact stress the beliefs of the accused as the determinant factor.

[91] See paras 6.55 and 6.56, *infra*.

Professor Sir John Smith at one time espoused a test which referred to achievement of purpose.[92] He pointed out that most men do not set out to break the law, and would not feel cheated or disappointed if they found that they had achieved their aims without breaking the law. So, for example, the man who intends to buy goods he believes to be stolen will not feel disappointed in his purpose if he learns the goods are not stolen — he will have succeeded in doing what he set out to do, obtain possession of the goods — and Professor Smith argued that it was unreasonable to talk of attempt where there had been success. But there are difficulties with such an approach. Suppose A buys goods in the belief that they were stolen from B, because he particularly wants B's property, but it turns out that they belonged to C from whom they were lawfully obtained: he has failed in his purpose and so would presumably be guilty of attempted reset, but he would not be guilty if the goods had been lawfully obtained from B, which is not a very satisfactory distinction. The approach also leaves open the position of the man who does have as his object and purpose the commission of a crime. A may be interested in buying only stolen goods because he disapproves of private property, or in going through only a bigamous marriage because he wants to avoid legal obligations to his partner. In such a situation he will have failed in his object if the goods are not stolen or if the marriage is lawful — but is he therefore guilty of attempted reset or bigamy? And further, how is such an objective to be determined other than subjectively? It is on the latter basis that Smith's theory was criticised by Professor Fletcher, who was at pains to suggest an approach in purely objective terms.[93]

Professor Fletcher's own theory concerns the test of "rational motivation". As he puts it: mistaken beliefs are relevant to what the actor is trying to do if they affect his incentive in acting. They affect his incentive if knowing of the mistake would give him a good motive for changing his course of conduct."[94] Thus, if A bought goods in the belief that they were stolen, he could not be convicted of attempted theft unless knowledge of the truth — that the goods were not stolen — would have provided him with a good motive for cancelling the deal and casting about for another purchase which would better answer his requirements. As ordinary people acting rationally would be happy to have obtained the original goods, then it is assumed by this theory that conviction for attempt would not be justifiable where the belief that the goods were stolen turns out to be unfounded. This may be a more objective approach than that advocated by Smith; but the difficulties encountered with Smith's theory seem to apply equally well to that of Fletcher. Indeed Fletcher concedes that an accused person may have an unusual incentive, such as to acquire only stolen goods or to have intercourse only with a girl under 16, and that such an incentive may not be discoverable objectively.[95] This then returns his theory to a subjective

[92] J.C. Smith, "Two Problems in Criminal Attempts Re-examined — II" [1962] Crim.L.R. 212. He subsequently disowned this approach: see R.A. Duff, "Attempt and the Problem of the Missing Circumstance" (1991) 42 N.I.L.Q. 87, at 93 and n.38.

[93] G.P. Fletcher, *Rethinking Criminal Law* (Boston, 1978), pp.162–163. Smith's approach was initially defended and refined by Prof. R.A. Duff in his article "Attempt and the Problem of the Missing Circumstance" (1991) 42 N.I.L.Q. 87, at 93 *et seq*. Duff ultimately rejects it, however, in favour of a test of his own — *ibid*., at 96.

[94] G.P. Fletcher, *op.cit*., at p.161.

[95] *op.cit*., p.164.

standpoint — thus reneging on one of its claimed principal strengths. Further, and in addition to problems created by basing a theory of liability on motive,[96] Fletcher's approach seems to falter on its other claimed strength — *i.e.* that it fits in well with judicial intuition relative to the cases where conviction for attempt is justifiable. His theory in fact requires conviction, contrary to his own view of intuition, where particularly unreasonable means are mistakenly employed by the actor,[97] as again he is forced to concede,[98] and acquittal where the judicial view (and, therefore, intuition?) now favours conviction.[99] The theory of "rational motivation", then, is hardly free from difficulty and must be treated sceptically as a practicable test.

6.53 *Missing elements; factual and legal impossibility.* If the actor's assumed purpose or motivation proved an unsatisfactory way of distinguishing types of impossible attempts where the conduct was "objectively innocent," it might be thought (as indeed was once popular) that greater success would attend a shifting of focus to the nature of the missing factor which made the complete crime impossible. As Gill pointed out many years ago, however, protagonists of such an approach tended to confuse attempts with completed crimes.[1] The most popular argument ran that if any essential element of the *actus reus* of a crime was missing, then no matter what were the accused's beliefs, neither the crime itself *nor* an attempt in respect of it could be committed.[2] The missing element made both impossible. Thus, it might be said that the crime of procuring an abortion required that there be something to abort. If, therefore, the woman in question was not pregnant, the lack of that essential element made it impossible to convict the actor of even an attempt to commit the full crime, no matter what he did or believed. Of course the lack of

---

[96] Motive is generally treated as irrelevant by the criminal law and is difficult in any event to assess — see Gl. Williams, "The Lords and Impossible Attempts, or *Quis Custodiet Ipsos Custodes*?" [1986] C.L.J. 33, at 78–80.

[97] *cf.* para. 6.50, *supra*.

[98] G.P. Fletcher, *op.cit.*, at pp.165–166, where, in order to cater for the "intuitive" view that that (*e.g.*) attempt to kill by sorcery should not result in a conviction for attempt, he has to fall back on the "principle of aptness".

[99] *cf.*, *e.g.*, *Anderton v. Ryan* [1985] 1 A.C. 567 and *R. v. Shivpuri* [1987] A.C. 1. For further criticism of Fletcher, see R.A. Duff, "Attempt and the Problem of the Missing Circumstance" (1991) 42 N.I.L.Q. 87, at 96–98.

[1] B. Gill, "Impossibility in Criminal Attempts", 1965 J.R. 137, at 138–139: see also Gl. Williams, "The Lords and Impossible Attempts, or *Quis Custodiet Ipsos Custodes*?" [1986] C.L.J. 33, at 35–36, where he aptly contrasts the "actual facts" and "putative facts" theories — the latter, which emphasises the accused's beliefs as to what the facts were, being his preferred choice in attempts. See also, Gill, *op.cit.*, pp.141–142.

[2] See, *e.g.*, B. Hogan, "The Criminal Attempts Act and Attempting the Impossible" [1984] Crim.L.R. 584, at 585; *H.M. Advocate v. Anderson*, 1928 J.C. 1; *H.M. Advocate v. Semple*, 1937 J.C. 41 (in which *H.M. Advocate v. Anderson* was approved); *R. v. Smith* [1975] A.C. 476 (where the House of Lords quashed a conviction for attempted handling of stolen property since the property had ceased to be "stolen", on the basis either that the conduct was then not proximate to any known crime or that to decide otherwise would be to invent a new crime which Parliament had not authorised — see Lord Hailsham, L.C., at 490G-F, 492B-C; Lord Reid at 499H-500A, 500D-E; Lord Morris at 503G, 506C); *D.P.P. v. Nock* [1978] A.C. 979 (where the House of Lords quashed a conviction for attempt to produce cocaine from a substance which could not be made to yield it, but held out the possibility of conviction for attempt where charges were generally drawn — *e.g.* "attempt to produce cocaine" *simpliciter*: see Lord Diplock at 993B-C; Lord Russell at 993E; Lord Scarman at 995G) — all attempts to limit the width of the *ratio* in *R. v. Smith*, cited above.

such an element certainly closed the possibility of conviction for procuring an abortion; but it surely opened the very real possibility of conviction for attempt. It would be surprising indeed for a person, who had done his best to procure an abortion on a woman he had believed pregnant, to be guilty of nothing if his belief turned out to be unfounded. The better view would be that such a missing element ensured that conviction could never exceed that of an attempt at the crime in question. But to conclude that the very factor which opened the possibility of conviction for attempt should also preclude that possibility clearly runs contrary to common sense and confuses the requirements for an attempt with those of a completed crime. As decisions of the courts seemed both to accept and to deny such a conclusion,[3] it was possible that it was the precise nature of the missing element which required greater attention. In this way, a distinction was sought between missing elements which were factual and those which were legal. The former might then be regarded as involving criminal responsibility for attempt but not the latter.[4] Typical examples of the former were considered to be attempting to steal from an empty pocket, to kill by shooting an unloaded pistol, to cause an abortion by using a harmless substance. Typical examples of the latter were thought to be attempts to reset goods which were not stolen, to commit bigamy when one's first wife was dead, to defraud by representations which were true. But it was never clear why the distinction should have such an effect on liability for attempt, and the modern view is that there is nothing in this purported distinction or that it is pointless to make it.[5] The distinction is doubted since paradigmatic "legal" elements — for example, whether goods are stolen or not — seem no less factual than other "factual" elements. Whilst it is true, for instance, that the status of goods as stolen or not cannot be determined by observation, that status is one related to factual events, and, as Williams aptly put it, is a fact related to the history of those goods.[6] More importantly, however, it is probably pointless to endeavour to make such distinctions between legal and factual missing elements since it is the accused's beliefs which are crucial in impossible attempts — and not the actual facts, however these are described. Indeed, the modern view is that legal impossibility, in the sense of barring conviction for attempt, is confined to one situation — where the accused believes that he is committing a crime when no such crime is

---

[3] *cf., e.g., H.M. Advocate v. Anderson*, 1928 J.C. 1 and *Lamont v. Strathern*, 1933 J.C. 33 (empty pocket foreclosing theft but allowing conviction for attempt).

[4] There is also sometimes a distinction drawn between "absolute" and "relative" impossibility, the first being exemplified by shooting at a corpse and the second by shooting into an empty bed — see J. Hall, *General Principles of Criminal Law* (2nd ed., Indianapolis, 1960), p.589, but the distinction is not helpful. See *R. v. Davies and Anr.*, *supra*, Schreiner J.A. at 62.

[5] See, *e.g.*, B. Gill, *op.cit.*, at p.139; Law Commission, No. 102, "Criminal Law: Attempt, and Impossibility in Relation to Attempt, Conspiracy and Incitement", 1980, H. of C., 646, paras. 2.88. 2.89 and 2.98; Gl. Williams, "The Lords and Impossible Attempts, or *Quis Custodiet Ipsos Custodes*?" [1986] C.L.J. 33, at 55–56.

[6] Gl. Williams, *op.cit.*, at pp.72–73. It must be the case too that whether stolen goods have ceased to have that status relates to actual events, such as recovery by the owner or the police: see, *e.g.*, the scenario in *R. v. Smith* [1975] A.C. 476. See also A. Asworth, "Belief, Intent and Criminal Liability", in J. Eekelaar and J. Bell (eds.), *Oxford Essays in Jurisprudence* (3rd ser., Oxford, 1987) 1, at pp.24–26.

known either at common law or under statute.[7] And this is certainly sensible: for the law of criminal attempts cannot be used to expand the law by the invention of new crimes which existed only in the imagination of an individual.[8]

6.54 *Personal impossibility.* There is one other situation in which legal impossibility may be relevant, although its relevance would rest on technicalities and not on any principle. If A attempts to commit a crime which can be committed only by members of a special class, such as licensees, in the erroneous belief that he belongs to that class, it may not be possible to convict him of attempt, if only because the statutes creating the crime are directed only against members of the class. And this may apply also to a man who intends to commit bigamy but is unaware that his first wife has died or divorced him. Although there is recent judicial opinion in Scotland to the extent that such impossibility may still be arguable,[9] modern developments in the law which render a non-agent liable art and part for an offence which only an agent can commit[10] and which sanction the conviction for incest (art and part) of a person who was unrelated to the participants,[11] suggest that such an argument will be difficult to sustain.[12]

6.55 *The modern English law.* Prior to 1981, the law in England had adopted the general rule that there could be no conviction for attempt where the crime in question could not be completed owing to an essential element being missing from the *actus reus*.[13] It did not matter whether the missing element was describable as being "factual" or "legal": for example that goods were not stolen vis á vis handling was treated in the same way as the emptiness of a pocket relative to attempted theft.[14] It was made clear, however, that inefficient or insufficient means to accomplish one's criminal purpose would not bar a conviction for attempt.[15] It was also made clear that the general rule was not to be construed more widely than it need be, and there then arose a recognised difference in law between an indictment which charged attempted theft from a particular person's pocket and one which charged attempt to steal from persons generally by picking their pockets. In the

---

7 Gl. Williams, *op.cit.*, at pp.55 and 76; J.C. Smith and B. Hogan, *Criminal Law* (9th ed., 1999, Sir J. Smith (ed.)), p.320, *et seq.*; *R. v. Taaffe* [1984] A.C. 539; E.M. Burchell and P.M.A. Hunt, *South African Criminal Law and Procedure* (3rd ed., 1997), Vol. 1, *General Principles of Criminal Law* (J.M. Burchell (ed.)), at pp.353–355; *S. v. Palmos*, 1979 (2) S.A. 82 (A); Law Commission No. 102 (*supra*), *loc.cit.*: *cf.* B. Hogan, "The Criminal Attempts Act and Attempting the Impossible" [1984] Crim.L.R. 584, at 584.

8 It may be noted, however, that this same argument was illegitimately used relative to an extant statutory offence in England to justify the quashing of a conviction for attempt: *R. v. Smith* [1975] A.C. 476, see, *e.g.*, Lord Hailsham L.C. at 490F.

9 *Docherty v. Brown*, 1996 J.C. 48, Lord Cameron at 71.

10 *Templeton v. H.M. Advocate*, 1988 J.C. 32.

11 *Vaughan v. H.M. Advocate*, 1979 S.L.T. 49.

12 See paras 5.09 to 5.11, *supra*.

13 *R. v. Smith* [1975] A.C. 476, where a conviction for attempt to handle stolen goods (contrary to the Theft Act 1968, ss.2. 23(1)) was quashed by a unanimous House of Lords since, unknown to the accused, the goods in question had ceased to be stolen in terms of s.24(3) prior to the actual handling. See also *Mieras v. Rees* [1975] Crim.L.R. 224. If the completed crime was not impossible, then this rule did not, of course, apply: see *Cooper v. Miles* [1979] Crim.L.R. 42.

14 *R. v. Smith*, supra, Lord Morris at 506C.

15 *R. v. Smith*, supra, Lord Hailsham L.C. at 494B, Lord Reid at 500F-G. See also *R. v. Farrance* (1977) 67 Cr.App.R. 136, Watkins, J., at 142.

former, there could be no conviction unless the prosecution could prove that the particular pocket in question contained something which might have been taken, whereas in the latter there was no such obligation.[16]

The position which the law had adopted was widely regarded as unsatisfactory, a view which was endorsed by the Law Commission in 1980.[17] In recommending that the common law be abrogated and replaced by a new statutory code, the Commission affirmed that the basic principle governing liability for impossible attempts should be what the accused believed the facts to be[18] — thus favouring what Professor Williams referred to as the "putative fact" theory.[19] If, therefore, the accused intended to commit an offence, and did more than merely preparatory acts with a view to realising his intentions and believed that such acts would complete the *actus reus* of that offence, then the actual impossibility of his completing the *actus reus* was not to be a bar to his conviction for attempt.[20] In so concluding, the Commission accepted that certain "difficult" or "exceptional" cases would thus be brought within the law as they proposed it should be — such as buying goods in the belief that they are stolen when that is not in fact so, or "stealing" one's own umbrella or attempting to kill by sorcery.[21] But the commission was satisfied that it could not strike a formula which would extract such cases from attempts whilst at the same time ensure that their goal of reversing the existing law was fulfilled. Their solution, therefore, was to rely on prosecutorial discretion to eliminate cases where it was not sensible to undertake criminal proceedings for attempt.[22] The Commission was careful to insist, however, that a mistake of law — meaning a situation where a person mistakenly thought that what he was doing was the *actus reus* of a crime when no such crime existed in law — should be beyond the reach of attempt.[23]

The Law Commission's proposals were embodied in the 1981 Criminal Attempts Act which contains the current English law on the subject. That law specifically lays down that a person may be guilty of an attempt even though the facts were such that the commission of the offence was impossible, and further that where a person's intentions would constitute an intention to commit an offence only if the facts had been as he believed them, he is to be regarded as having had such an intention.[24] No distinction is made as between "legal" and "factual" facts, as is

---

[16] This was laid down in the conspiracy case of *D.P.P. v. Nock* [1978] A.C. 979: see Lord Diplock at 991–992; 992C and 993B-C.

[17] Law Commission No. 102, "Criminal Law: Attempt, and Impossibility in Relation to Attempt, Conspiracy and Incitement", H. of C., 646, 1980. In para. 2.93 of the Report, the Commission concluded that the existing English law was over-analytical, uncertain, capricious and out of line with the law in many other jurisdictions.

[18] *ibid*., para. 2.96.

[19] Gl. Williams, "The Lords and Impossible Attempts, or *Quis Custodiet Ipsos Custodes*?" [1987] C.L.J. 23, at 36.

[20] Law Commission, *supra cit.*, para. 2.96.

[21] *supra cit.*, para. 2.97.

[22] Law Commission, No. 102, *supra cit.*, para. 2.97.

[23] *ibid*., para. 2.98.

[24] Criminal Attempts Act 1981, ss.1(2) and (3), and 3 (4) and (5). The common law rules are abolished by s.6(1).

evidenced by the subsequent case law[25]; and there is no room for any construction which will allow exceptions for objectively innocent conduct,[26] or any theory concerning purposes or motivations.[27]

6.56 *Scots law.* The most recent of the four reported cases on impossible attempts is the five-judge decision of *Docherty v. Brown*.[28] Although five separate opinions were delivered, the account of the law laid down by Lord Justice-Clerk Ross had the express support of the Lord Justice-General,[29] and Lords Sutherland[30] and Johnston.[31] The issue at stake was whether the accused could be convicted of attempting to have a controlled drug in his possession with intent to supply it to another,[32] where, contrary to his belief, what he had taken possession of was not in fact a controlled drug at all. A large court was convened since the then current authorities were in conflict — *H.M. Advocate v. Anderson*[33] having decided that it could not be attempted abortion to administer abortifacients to a non-pregnant woman whom one had believed to be pregnant, and *Lamont v. Strathern*[34] that it was attempted theft to place one's hand in an empty pocket with intent to steal. In addition, the earlier three-judge case of *H.M. Advocate v. Semple*[35] had followed *Anderson*[35a] and considered it to be correct. There is no doubt at all that the judges in *Docherty v. Brown*[35b] benefited considerably from the modern English law, and that they were determined to lay down the law as a matter of principle[36] in a way which would avoid the difficulties and

---

[25] *R. v. Shivpuri* [1987] A.C. 1, reversing *Anderton v. Ryan* [1985] 1 A.C. 560. In *Anderton v. Ryan*, a majority of the House of Lords (Lord Edmund Davies, dissenting) had attempted to construe the Criminal Attempts Act 1981 such that it applied to situations such as a pickpocket placing his hand in an empty pocket — but not to "objectively innocent" ones. Lord Roskill had found it impossible to believe that Parliament had intended the absurd result of penalising "objective innocence" (see 580F-G), as had Lord Bridge (see pp.582H-583B. 584H) — although it will be recalled the Law Commission had specifically rejected making any such exceptions. In any event, as Lord Bridge conceded (at p.584C-D), the effect of the legislation, as so interpreted, would be to preserve as correct the actual decision in *R. v. Smith* [1975] A.C. 476. After considerable adverse academic comment, especially that of Professor Glanville William (see "The Lords and Impossible Attempts, or *Quis Custodiet Ipsos Custodes*?" [1987] C.L.J. 33), *Anderton v. Ryan* was quickly reversed.

[26] *R. v. Shivpuri* [1987] A.C. 1, Lord Bridge at 21G–22A.

[27] *ibid.*, Lord Bridge at 22D–23A. *Cf.*, Lord Hailsham at 12E-F, who, had the option of exercising the Practice Statement to reverse the House of Lords' previous account of the law not been available, would have favoured distinguishing *Anderton v. Ryan* on the basis that Mrs Ryan had intended merely to purchase a cheap video-recorder, and that it was not part of her purpose to buy one that had been stolen. It is submitted that, notwithstanding that Lord Hailsham was supported by Lord Mackay of Clashfern (see 23H–24A) on this point, no such distinction should be made for the reasons set out at para. 6.52 *supra*.

[28] 1996 J.C. 48.

[29] *ibid.*, at 51.

[30] *ibid.*, at 64.

[31] *ibid.*, at 75.

[32] Contrary to s.5(3) of Misuse of Drugs Act 1971. It is to be noted that s.19 of the 1971 Act makes specific provision for attempt.

[33] 1928 J.C. 1.

[34] 1933 J.C. 33.

[35] 1937 J.C. 41; see L.J.-C. Aitchison at 45: *cf.* Lord Fleming at 47 and Lord Moncrieff at 49.

[35a] 1928 J.C. 1.

[35b] 1996 J.C. 48.

[36] See 1996 J.C. 48, opinions of L.J.-C. Ross at 54, and Lord Johnston at 72, 74 and 75: this was a direct response to the submission of counsel for the appellant (against the sheriff's ruling that the charge was relevant) that there was no general rule in Scots law — each case depending on its own particular circumstances.

complexities engendered by the various theories discussed briefly in the preceding paragraphs.[37]

The first point to be noted is that the court accepted that there was a clear difference between a completed crime and an attempt to commit it.[38] This then led to rejection of the argument that it was not possible to convict of an attempt where an essential element missing from the *actus reus* of the crime in question made it impossible to commit the full offence. It followed that *H.M. Advocate v. Anderson*[38a] had been wrongly decided, and that it was equally wrong for the bench in *H.M. Advocate v. Semple*[38b] to have supported it.[39] Conversely, it was decided that the decision in *Lamont v. Strathern*[39a] was correct in law.[40] Of course, it might be thought that that case was distinguishable in that the conduct involved in it (placing one's hand in another person's pocket) was not objectively innocent. But, by quoting with approval passages from certain antipodean judgments, the court in *Docherty v. Brown*[41] clearly, and, it is respectfully submitted, correctly, indicated that the objective innocence of conduct was of no consequence in impossible attempts.[42] Lord Cameron also expressed the view that there was nothing to be gained in enquiring whether "impossibility" was due to a factual or legal matter[43] — a view shared inferentially by the Lord Justice-General and Lord Sutherland since they considered more generally that the reason for the failure to complete the offence in question was not of itself significant.[44]

The ground was effectively cleared, therefore, of unsatisfactory or unworkable theories, and the simple rule to be followed in cases of impossible attempts was shown to be no different from that applicable to attempts in general. As Lord Justice-Clerk Ross puts it: "for a relevant charge of an attempt to commit a crime, it must be averred that the accused had the necessary *mens rea*, and that he has done some positive act towards executing his purpose, that is to say that he has done something which amounts to perpetration rather than mere preparation. If what is libelled is an attempt to commit a crime which is impossible of achievement, impossibility is irrelevant except that there can be no attempt to commit the crime if the accused is aware that what he is trying to do is impossible. Except to that extent, impossibility has no

---

[37] See paras 6.51 to 6.54, *supra*.

[38] 1996 J.C. 48, see opinions of L.J.-C. Ross at 58, L.J.-G. Hope at 50, and Lord Sutherland at 61 and 63.

[38a] 1928 J.C. 1.

[38b] 1937 J.C. 41.

[39] 1996 J.C. 48, see opinions of L.J.-C. Ross at 57, 60 and 61; L.J.-G. Hope at 50; Lord Sutherland at 63 and 64; Lord Cameron at 70 and 71; and Lord Johnston at 74.

[39a] 1933 J.C. 33.

[40] 1996 J.C. 48, see opinions of L.J.-C. Ross at 57 and 61; and L.J.-G. Hope at 50.

[41] 1996 J.C. 48.

[42] *ibid.*, see opinion of L.J.-C. Ross at 59–60, quoting Murphy J. in *Britten v. Alpogut* [1987] V.R. 929 at 934, and especially at 938. This particular dictum (at 938), dealing with the irrelevance of "objective innocence", is also quoted by Lord Sutherland at 63.

[43] *ibid.*, at 71 — citing as his reasons those given in the 2nd edition of this book at 196.

[44] *ibid.*, L.J.-G. Hope at 50, Lord Sutherland at 61 and 62; see also Lord Cameron at 68, where his Lordship opines that *Lamont v. Strathern*, 1933 J.C. 33, would have been correctly decided even if "it were to have been proved that the thief's intent was fixed solely upon stealing from the other party some particular piece of property which he believed to be in the pocket, but which was not in fact so", thus avoiding any suggestion that the unconvincing compromise offered by the House of Lords in *D.P.P. v. Nock*, [1978] A.C. 979, should govern such cases (see para. 6.55, *supra*).

relevance."[45] One point which must be noted in *de facto* impossibility cases, therefore, is that the attempt charge must state (as it did in *Docherty v. Brown*[46]) that the accused believed facts and/or circumstances which if true would have rendered the crime in question possible of achievement.[47] It must also be borne in mind, of course, that the attempt must contemplate a genuine crime, and not what is wrongly believed by the accused to be an offence known to the law.[48] The similarity between Scots law after *Docherty v. Brown* and the English Criminal Attempts Act 1981 is striking and demonstrates the capacity of the common law to reach an acceptable and workable rule on a principled basis. It possibly goes too far, however, to suggest that the English legislation and the Scots common law are now entirely at one on this issue,[49] since the latter does not insist on "intention" being the solely acceptable form of *mens rea* in attempt.[50] But the court in *Docherty v. Brown* clearly agrees with the English Law Commission[51] that "difficult" cases where it would genuinely be pointless or even unjust to convict should be dealt with by the exercise of prosecutorial discretion and not by fruitless attempt to adjust the legal rule in order to accommodate them;[52] and it seems that Scots law agrees with the Criminal Attempts Act 1981 in accepting that the same rule applies both to common law and statutory offences.[53]

II — Conspiracy and Incitement

Conspiracy

6.57 Conspiracy "is constituted by the agreement of two or more persons to further or achieve a criminal purpose. A criminal purpose is one which if attempted or achieved by action on the part of an individual would itself constitute a crime by the law of Scotland."[54] The crime consists in the

[45] *ibid.*, at 60. See similar tests laid down by L.J.-G. Hope at 50; Lord Sutherland at 61, 62 and 63; Lord Cameron at 68; and Lord Johnston at 79.

[46] 1996 J.C. 48.

[47] *ibid.*, see L.J.-C. Ross at 58.

[48] The quotations from Murphy J. in *Britten v. Alpogut* [1987] V.R. 929 at 934 and/or at 938, approved by L.J.-C. Ross at 60, Lord Sutherland at 63, and Lord Cameron at 72, make this clear.

[49] See *Docherty v. Brown*, 1996 J.C. 48, Lord Sutherland at 63, *viz.*: "The state of the law in England now rests on s.1 of the Criminal Attempts Act 1981 . . . and I consider that the propositions set out in subsections (1) to (3) of section 1 correspond with the common law of Scotland."

[50] See *Cawthorne v. H.M. Advocate*, 1968 J.C. 32, and para. 7.78 *et seq.*, *infra*.

[51] Law Commission No. 102, "Criminal Law: Attempt, and Impossibility in Relation to Attempt, Conspiracy and Incitement", H. of C., 646, 1980, at para. 2.97.

[52] This is inferential from the opinions of L.J.-C. Ross and Lords Sutherland and Cameron in *Docherty v. Brown*, 1996 J.C. 48, and expressed in the opinions of L.J.-G. Hope at 51 and Lord Johnston at 74.

[53] *Docherty v. Brown*, *supra cit.*, Lord Sutherland at 61, Lord Cameron at 64, and Lord Johnston at 72.

[54] *Maxwell v. H.M. Advocate*, 1980 J.C. 40, *per* Lord Cameron at 43. In *Crofter Hand-Woven Harris Tweed Co. v. Veitch*, 1942 S.C. (H.L.) 1, at 5, Viscount Simon L.C., no doubt forgetting that he was sitting in a Scottish appeal spoke of conspiracy as being the agreement "to effect any unlawful purpose". Although Viscount Simon's wording was adopted by L.J.-C. Grant in *Wilson, Latta and Rooney* (High Court at Glasgow, Feb. 1968, unrep'd, Transcript of Proceedings, 1314), by L.J.-C. Wheatley in *Carberry* (High Court at Glasgow, Nov. 1974, unrep'd, Transcript of Judge's Charge, 12), and most recently *per* Lord Sutherland in *H.M. Advocate v. Al Megrahi*, 2000 S.C.C.R. 177 at 184A, Lord Keith in

agreement though in most cases overt acts done in pursuance of the offences are available to prove the crime.

Charges of conspiracy may perhaps be divided into three types, of which the third is the most important from the point of view of the development of the law of inchoate crimes.

(1) *Where specific crimes have been carried out in pursuance of the conspiracy.* Where the accused have conspired together to bring about a certain object by criminal means, and have in pursuance of that object committed certain crimes, they may be charged as art and part in those crimes without being charged with conspiracy.[55] The same is true where the conspiracy is simply to commit a specific crime, and the crime is committed. Where the crime has only been attempted, they may of course be charged with being art and part in the attempt. Charges of conspiracy in such cases used to be uncommon. The normal course was simply to charge art and part guilt. In *H.M. Advocate v. Martin*[56] there was a conspiracy among two free men and a prisoner to effect the prisoner's escape whereby the free men waited for the prisoner and took him away in their car when he came over a perimeter fence. Although it was averred that the accused had each "conceived the felonious intention" of carrying out the plan, there was no charge of conspiracy; the prisoner was charged with attempting to defeat the ends of justice by escaping, and the free men with attempting the same crime by "aiding and abetting" him. **6.58**

There have also been cases in which the accused were charged with conspiring to effect a certain object by means of a particular crime, and alternatively with committing the crime in pursuance of the conspiracy.[57] The Crown clearly cannot obtain a conviction against an accused for conspiring to commit a crime and also for being art and part in its commission, since that would be to convict him twice for the same conduct.[58]

In recent years it has become increasingly common to charge conspiracy even where specific offences have been committed by the conspirators.[59] The reasons for this change in practice are probably mixed. The desire of the Crown to give notice of its intention to lead evidence of meetings or correspondence, or other conspirings, may be one of them. **6.59**

---

his Charge to the jury in *Smith* (High Court at Glasgow, May 1975, unrep'd) explained that "agreement to effect an unlawful purpose . . . means an agreement to do an act which would be criminal if done by a single individual": Transcript of Proceedings, 2456–2457. See also *Sayers v. H.M. Advocate*, 1981 S.C.C.R. 312, Lord Ross's Charge to the jury at 315–316.

[55] *cf.*, alternative charge (2) of the indictment set out in *H.M. Advocate v. Al Megrahi*, 2000 S.C.C.R. 177, at 181D to 182E.

[56] 1956 J.C.1.

[57] *e.g. Margt Gallocher or Boyle and Ors* (1859) 3 Irv. 440: conspiracy to extort money by false accusations and perjury, and making false accusations and committing perjury; *Robt Sprot and Ors* (1844) 2 Broun 179: conspiracy to make certain people leave their houses by violence, and injuring someone; *John Rae and Thos. Little* (1845) 2 Broun 476: conspiracy to defeat the ends of justice by having someone else impersonate an accused at his trial, and fraud, the deception having been in fact carried out: *John Rattray & Ors*, (1848) Ark. 406: conspiracy to obtain and obtaining unlawful possession of a deed with intent to defraud, conspiracy to destroy and destroying a deed with intent to defraud, theft, and destroying a deed with intent to defraud.

[58] Although more modern indictments, perhaps because of the change in style, charge, *e.g.* conspiracy to pervert the course of justice *and* subornation of perjury in pursuance of the conspiracy: *Wilson, Latta and Rooney*, High Court at Glasgow, Feb. 1968, unrep'd.

[59] See, *e.g.*, charge (1) of the indictment set out in *H.M. Advocate v. Al Megrahi*, 2000 S.C.C.R. 177, at 178E to 181C.

Conspiracy may be libelled to provide for cases where the ultimate crime cannot be proved but the conspiracy can, but such a situation is unlikely to occur except where what happened might be said to fall short of being even an attempted crime. It may be that the conspiracy charge is thought of as an aggravation, so that a charge of conspiring to pervert the course of justice and in pursuance thereof committing an assault is more serious than a charge of assault. But there is no difference between such a "conspiracy and assault" charge and a charge of assault with intent to pervert the course of justice, although such an assault has itself been libelled as something done in pursuance of such a conspiracy.[60] Conspiracy may, of course, be libelled simply to bring to the notice of the public, and of judge and jury, the dastardly and dangerous disposition of the accused. Or it may be that conspiracy is charged because of the difficulty of disentangling the part played by each accused in a complicated scheme: the jury are left to sort it out after hearing the evidence. Conspiracy charges are arguably prejudicial, they are certainly confusing, and it may be doubted whether they achieve any purpose, at any rate outside such cases of quasi-treason as *McAlister* and *Smith*.[61]

In the nineteenth century it was the practice to charge *e.g.* conspiracy to defraud and alternatively fraud. It was also thought that it was incompetent to convict of *e.g.* murder on a charge of conspiracy to murder.[62] Modern practice has become increasingly confusing, presenting problems to judges in charging juries, to juries in understanding what verdicts are open to them, to clerks of court in knowing how to record verdicts and to accused persons in knowing of what they have been convicted.[63]

6.60 The modern law and practice started with the comparatively simple indictment in *Wilson. Latta and Rooney*.[64] The charge was in the following form:

> "[K]nowing that J.B. and W.W. . . . had been indicted . . . on a charge of murdering W.R. . . . , and that [their] . . . trial . . . was to be held at . . . you did, . . . with intent to secure [their] acquittal . . . conspire with each other to have false evidence given at said trial and thus to defeat the ends of justice and in pursuance of said conspiracy, did, (*a*) . . . knowing that [C] . . . was an essential witness at said trial suborn [her] to depone as a witness at said trial that . . . two unknown men wearing light raincoats had come to the door of [a] house and that it was one of said two unknown men who had murdered W.R., the truth being as you well knew that no such unknown men had come to the door of said house or had murdered

---

[60] *Milnes*, *infra.*, para. 6.62.

[61] *infra*, para. 6.64, nn. 84, 85. Clarity of narration and any necessary basis for connecting charges for evidential purposes could be as well or better achieved by an introductory narration that the accused, "Having formed a scheme to effect a certain purpose", committed certain crimes, by analogy with the common introductory phrase, "Having formed a fraudulent scheme."

[62] *Thos. Hunter and Ors* (1838) 2 Swin. 1; the famous case of the cotton spinners.

[63] An accused charged with conspiracy to pervert the course of justice in pursuance of which an assault was committed may well complain when convicted of assault that he was never charged with assault. *Cf. H.M. Advocate v. Al Megrahi*, 2000 S.C.C.R. 177 at 189F, where Lord Sutherland acknowledged that "the practice may be somewhat regrettable and may cause confusion, certainly to juries," but declared himself satisfied that the practice ("now a fairly regular practice") was not incompetent.

[64] High Court at Glasgow, Feb. 1968, unrep'd.

said W.R., (*b*) knowing that [M] . . . had been intimated as a witness for the defence at said trial, attempt to suborn [him] . . . to depone as a witness at said trial that he had visited his aunt . . . the truth being as you well knew that [he] had not visited his said aunt . . . and (*c*) . . . attempt to suborn [G] . . . to depone as a witness at said trial that . . . he had been in the company of said J.B. and W.W. . . . the truth being as you well knew that [he] . . . did not know, and had not been in the company of, said J.B. and W.W."

Put simply, the Crown were charging a conspiracy to pervert the course of justice and the commission of subornation and attempted subornation in pursuance thereof. The Crown conceded that it would have been incompetent to charge conspiracy and subornation cumulatively, and argued that there was only one offence charged, namely conspiracy. Equally, it would follow, it was incompetent for the jury to convict of both conspiracy and subornation. But the Crown argued that as section 60 of the Criminal Procedure (Scotland) Act 1887[65] provided that "any part of what is charged in an indictment constituting in itself an indictable crime shall be deemed separable to the effect of making it lawful to convict of such a crime", it was open to the jury to acquit of conspiracy and convict of subornation. This argument was upheld by Lord Justice-Clerk Grant, although he described the point as one of some difficulty, and said he was not clear why the indictment did not include an alternative charge libelling the matters narrated in heads (*a*)-(*c*) of the indictment as substantive crimes.[66]

This case may have settled the competency of convicting of the "heads" of a conspiracy where these constitute crimes, although the conspiracy is unproved.[67] What is still far from clear is the nature of the conviction where the conspiracy and narrated heads are proved. Far from adopting Lord Grant's suggestion of libelling alternative charges the Crown have gone on to produce more and more complicated indictments, which in the main have been unchallenged by defence counsel.[68]

In *Wilson, Latta and Rooney,*[68a] Lord Grant suggested to the jury that **6.61**
if, for example, head (*b*) of the indictment was not proved against an accused they should find him "guilty as libelled under deletion of head (*b*)".[69] This at least makes it clear that the conviction is for conspiracy. But if the facts narrated in the subheads are merely evidence of the conspiracy, the verdict is a kind of special verdict, convicting of the offence while rejecting some of the evidence, so perhaps they are better

---

[65] See now 1995 Act, Sched. 3, para. 9(2).

[66] See Transcript of Proceedings, 1299–1302.

[67] It seems, too, that even if the main conspiracy is unproved, an accused may be convicted art and part of some smaller "plot" to commit the offence narrated in the "head" of the indictment; his actual perpetration of it as a principal is unnecessary: see *e.g. Milnes*, High Court at Glasgow, Jan. 1971, unrep'd, Transcript of Judge's Charge, 15–16.

[68] *e.g. Smith, supra*, n.252; *Milnes, infra. Cf. H.M. Advocate v. Al Megrahi*, 2000 S.C.C.R. 177, where the competency of an indictment which libelled conspiracy to murder and murder cumulatively was challenged; Lord Sutherland, in rejecting the challenge, observed at 189F: "It is now recognised that the approach [to such an indictment] is to deal separately with the conspiracy and various substantive charges by returning verdicts separately on each of the charges." This suggests that cumulative guilty verdicts have now become acceptable: see para. 6.62, *infra*.

[68a] High Court at Glasgow, Feb. 1968, unrep'd.

[69] See Transcript of Proceedings, 1365.

regarded as aggravations of the conspiracy. Alternatively, it may be that by rejecting a head of such an indictment in relation to a particular accused the jury are saying that the actings there libelled were not part of the conspiracy as envisaged by that accused. This is consistent with the practice of charging juries in conspiracy cases in the same way as in art and part cases, and with the specific terms of the judge's charge in the *Milnes* case.[70] But it does make it unclear just how many conspiracies are involved in this sort of indictment. The scope of the conspiracy should be set out in the initial conspiracy charge and not in the narration of the evidence supporting it.

In fact, the jury in *Wilson Latta and Rooney*[70a] did not follow Lord Grant's suggestion. For example, the jury found one accused "Guilty as libelled on indictments (*a*) and (*c*), not proven on (*b*)" and this was recorded as "Guilty [as libelled] with the exception of head (*b*) which they find not proven."

6.62 Complicated as *Wilson Latta and Rooney*[70b] is, it shines with the clarity of crystal when set against the *Milnes*[71] case, the indictment in which is well worth reproducing. It contains the following charge:

> "J.A.M., N.M., R.M., D.B. and G.S.K. . . . the charges against you are that you, knowing that J.A.M., N.M., and G.S.K. had been charged with having . . . assaulted J.C. . . . [and] W.M. . . . and were to be tried for said crime and that [they] . . . would be witnesses for the prosecution at the trial, did . . . conspire to pervert the course of justice by inducing [them] to refrain from giving evidence at said trial incriminating you J.A.M., N.M. and G.S.K. and by intimidating and coercing them to refrain from giving said evidence, and by murdering said W.M. when said inducement, intimidation and coercion seemed to fail to prevent said evidence from being given and did in pursuance of said conspiracy (*a*) on various occasions in Glasgow personally and by agents, . . . corruptly offer to give [your] bail money . . . or £200 to [them] to refrain from giving said evidence and with intent to intimidate them threaten to shoot and murder them and blow up and put petrol bombs in their houses if they did not refrain from giving said evidence and further threaten that if they did give said evidence £100 would be paid to someone to murder them, (*b*) . . . drive a motor lorry . . . at [W.M.] . . . all with intent to intimidate them (*c*) . . . park motor lorries outside [a] house . . . or drive slowly past said house and stare at said house and beset said house in a manner calculated to intimidate said J.C. and W.M., (*d*) . . . drive a motor lorry . . . past . . . a friend of said J.C. and wave a hatchet or other similar instrument to the prosecutor unknown at him and . . . , get out of a motor lorry, . . . follow said [friend] and shout threats at him, knowing that he would report all said threats to said J.C. and with intent to intimidate [him], (*e*) . . . assault said W.M. and discharge a loaded shotgun at him to his severe injury and attempt to murder him, (*f*) . . . repeatedly discharge a loaded firearm in the vicinity of the house of . . . an uncle of said J.C. and W.M. knowing that [he] would report said

[70] *Milnes*, *supra*. Transcript of judge's charge, 13–14.
[70a] High Court at Glasgow, Feb. 1968, unrep'd.
[70b] High Court at Glasgow, Feb. 1968, unrep'd.
[71] *Milnes*, High Court at Glasgow, Jan. 1971, unrep'd.

> discharging of a loaded firearm to [them] and with intent to intimidate [them], and *(g)* . . . when said W.M. was taken and detained in Ward 6A of Stobhill Hospital as a result of said attempt to murder him ascertain his whereabouts in order to obtain access to him and acquire a stethoscope with intent to impersonate a doctor all with intent to make a further attempt to murder him; and all this you did with intent to pervert the course of justice and you did attempt to pervert the course of justice."

In the end of the day, as a result of some pleas of guilty and some abandonments by the Crown, one accused went to the jury on heads (*a*)-(*e*) and one on (*e*), all as part of the conspiracy charge. The jury were told that the crime charged was conspiracy to pervert the course of justice, and that the method allegedly used to carry it out was intimidation, coercion, and murder.[72] They were told to acquit one accused under heads (*f*) and (*g*) for lack of evidence. "On these two heads", said Lord Avonside, "you will find [him] not Guilty".[73] The "heads" were sometimes described by the judge as "heads", and sometimes as "charges".[74] The jury were told at one stage:

> "Just assuming — and again this is pure assumption — assuming that you found Ronald Milne guilty of conspiracy. You may then, depending on your view of the evidence before you, find him Guilty of the actings set our under heads (A) to (E), or some of them . . .I am merely using entirely random examples, but you might, for example find him Guilty under head (B) or head (D) and the rest Not Guilty or Not Proven; or, if this were your view, that the charges under heads (A) to (E) in the case of Ronald Milne, which I am merely taking as an example, are not proved, and in respect of that your verdict in relation to him would be Not Guilty or Not Proven. If you found charge (E) not proved against Brannan then your verdict in relation to that head is Not Guilty or Not Proven."[75]

They were told that if they found Ronald Milne guilty of conspiracy on all or some of heads (*a*) to (*e*), they would "find him guilty of conspiracy as libelled and guilty of the heads in which your verdict is that".[76] The actual verdicts were recorded as follows:

> "The jury unanimously find the panel Ronald Milne Guilty of conspiring to pervert the course of justice; on Head (A) by a majority Guilty; on Heads (B),(C) and (D) by a majority find said sub-heads not proven; unanimously Guilty of sub-head (E); and unanimously Not Guilty of sub-heads (F) and (G).
>
> And unanimously find the panel David Brannan Guilty of conspiring to pervert the course of justice, and unanimously Guilty of head (E)."

It is quite clear from the above mishmash that the Crown's concessions in *Wilson, Latta and Rooney*[77] have been lost sight of, and that cumulative verdicts are being returned in cases of this kind, whether they

[72] Transcript of judge's charge, 6.
[73] *ibid.* 7.
[74] See *ibid.* 8.
[75] *ibid.* 14.
[76] *ibid.* 37.
[77] *supra*, n.71.

are verdicts of several conspiracies or of conspiracy and a substantive offence. It is fortunate that given the Scottish sentencing structure, or lack thereof, it makes no practical difference in most cases. But what would have happened if head (*e*) of the *Milnes* case had been murder and not attempted murder?[78]

6.63 Perhaps two things should be stressed at this point:

(1) There can be a conviction for conspiracy even if none of the heads is proved.[79] As Lord Avonside said in *Milnes*,[80] "You can have a criminal conspiracy even if nothing is done to further it", and indeed that is the very essence of conspiracy.

(2) Where a head of a conspiracy charge does not amount to a crime, then whether or not it is proved no one can be convicted of it, although it might conceivably be treated as an aggravation of the conspiracy. So, if head (*g*) of *Milnes* had been proved, but the conspiracy had not, there could have been no conviction for (*g*).[81] Nor, if conspiracy had been proved, could there have been a conviction for conspiracy and (*g*). But presumably there might have been a conviction for conspiracy under head (*g*), or a conviction as libelled under deletion of heads (*a*) to (*f*), but these would have been convictions for conspiracy alone.

6.64 (2) *Where no specific crime is charged.* Charges of conspiracy sometimes do not set out any specific crime by means of which the conspiracy was to be effected, but merely state that it was to be carried out by criminal, or violent, means. In *Walsh and Ors*[82] there was a charge of conspiring to further the purposes of the IRA, "by the unlawful use of force and violence . . . and especially by means of explosive substances . . . to be used . . . for the purpose of endangering the lives and persons and destroying the property of the lieges."[83] In *MacAlister and Ors*[84] the conspiracy was alleged to be "to further by criminal means the purposes of an association of persons known as the Scottish Republican Army . . . with the intention of coercing Her Majesty's Government in Great Britain into the setting up of a separate government in Scotland, or with the intention of overthrowing Her Majesty's government in Scotland."

---

[78] *cf.*, *H.M. Advocate v. Al Megrahi*, 2000 S.C.C.R. 177, at 189F, where Lord Sutherland seems to accept the competence of cumulative guilty verdicts in such cases.

[79] Separate specification of heads is unnecessary to the conspiracy charge except to avoid the difficulty of leading evidence of crimes not narrated in the indictment: Renton and Brown's *Criminal Procedure* (6th ed.), para. 24.166; *Nelson v. H.M. Advocate*, 1994 S.L.T. 389.

[80] *supra*, n.71, Transcript of judge's charge, 7.

[81] Unless, horrible thought, it were held to constitute the crime of attempting to pervert the course of justice — see Vol. II, Chap. 47; *supra*, para. 1.32; see also *Smith*, High Court at Glasgow, Jan. 1976, unrep'd, where one of the heads of a conspiracy to further the purposes of the UVF by criminal means alleged that in pursuance of the conspiracy the accused travelled by boat from Scotland to Northern Ireland for the purpose of collecting the weapons libelled in an earlier head, an allegation introduced presumably to give notice of evidence, since to go in an empty boat to collect explosives is not an offence, or even an attempt. The accused who were involved only in this charge were in the event acquitted by direction of the judge who said of one of them, "The only charge against him was conspiracy and there was insufficient evidence to establish conspiracy against him."

[82] High Court at Glasgow, Aug, 1921, unrep'd. Reported on other points *sub nom., H.M. Advocate v. Walsh,* 1922 J.C. 82.

[83] A number of charges of this kind were brought against Sinn Feiners at about the same time as *Walsh*.

[84] High Court at Edinburgh, Nov. 1953, unrep'd, but see *MacAlister and Ors v. Associated Newspapers Ltd*, 1954 S.L.T. 14.

The charge then went on to allege that the accused "did in pursuance of said conspiracy obtain possession of and retain . . . explosive[s]" — which is not a crime except under a statute which was not libelled in the conspiracy charge — "for use . . . in destroying or damaging the property of Her Majesty's Government and endangering the lives and property of Her Majesty's Government and endangering the lives and property of the lieges." The conspiracy to coerce the Government probably amounted to treason, but treason was not charged, while the rest of the charge discloses no common law crime other than the conspiracy itself which consists in agreeing and perhaps preparing to commit the crimes of destroying property and endangering life.[85] *Walsh*[85a] and *MacAlister*[85b] are therefore modern authorities for the view that to conspire to further an object by criminal means is to commit the crime of conspiracy, and that any further criminal action is unnecessary.[86]

UNLAWFUL AND CRIMINAL MEANS. This type of conspiracy raises the **6.65**
question whether the crime is committed by an agreement to accomplish an object by means which are unlawful, but not criminal; that is to say, whether it is criminal to agree to do what if done by one person would not be a crime, although it might be a breach of the civil law such as a breach of contract. Macdonald's view is that only conspiracies to do what would be criminal if done by one person are criminal conspiracies[87] and this now appears to be the law.[88] By way of contrast, in both *Walsh*[88a] and *MacAlister*[88b] the presiding judges described a conspiracy as an agreement to do something "unlawful"[89] and in *Walsh*[89a] Lord Justice-Clerk Scott Dickson is reported as saying that a conspiracy was a "plan to do something that was contrary to law, and that might either be one of two things. It might either be a conspiracy to do something that was wrong in itself — a conspiracy to murder was wrong in itself — or it might be a conspiracy to carry out some object or purpose which was not criminal in

---

[85] Although the completed crime would not have been charged without any specification of the property destroyed or lives endangered. The relevancy and specification of the charge on *MacAlister* were not challenged, perhaps because of a fear that it might be converted into one of treason. In the "1975 version" so to speak, the charge was of conspiring to further by criminal means the purposes of an association of persons known as the Scottish Army of the Provisional Government or some other association to the prosecutor unknown with the intention of committing a number of listed offences, including theft of arms and explosives, bank robbery, the disruption of power supplies by the destruction of dams and power stations, the disruption of transport by the destruction of bridges and blowing up labour exchanges, as well as "obtaining firearms and explosives by various means" and causing violence and injury to lives and property. The indictment then alleged that "in pursuance of said conspiracy" the accused committed a number of offences of unlawful possession of explosives and firearms, a bank robbery, and three instances of threatening violence to potential witnesses: *Smith*, High Court at Glasgow, May 1975, unrep'd.

[85a] High Court at Glasgow, Aug. 1921, unrep'd.

[85b] High Court at Edinburgh, Nov. 1953, unrep'd.

[86] *Cf. Jas. Cumming and Ors* (1848) J. Shaw 17.

[87] Macdonald, p.185; *Smith., supra,* n.54.

[88] See the definition of conspiracy offered by Lord Cameron (reading the opinion of the court) in *Maxwell v. H.M. Advocate*, 1980 J.C. 40, at 43 (see para. 6.57, *supra*).

[88a] High Court at Glasgow, Aug. 1921, unrep'd.

[88b] High Court at Edinburgh, Nov. 1953, unrep'd.

[89] The *Scotsman*, Aug. 22, 1921; Transcript of judge's charge in *MacAlister, supra,* 20. In *Wilson Latta and Rooney, supra,* and in *Carberry, infra,* n.297, the reference to unlawful purpose in *Crofter hand-Woven Harris Tweed Co. v. Veitch, supra*, was quoted without comment.

[89a] High Court at Glasgow, Aug. 1921, unrep'd.

itself by illegal or criminal means".[90] "Illegal or criminal" may however have been merely tautologous, and the conspiracy in *Walsh*[90a] was charged as involving criminal means. In order to find a case of criminal conspiracy to do what would not be criminal if done by one man, one has to go back to the special case of workmen's combinations to raise wages by striking work. Burnett is of the view that these, and also combinations by employers to keep down the price of labour, were criminal even if unaccompanied by threats or violence.[91] The modern view is probably that of Anderson who quotes Burnett and then says, "It is clear, however, that such a combination would become criminal only when violence or threats were employed to effect its object."[92]

6.66 STATUTORY OFFENCES. There is no authority in Scotland on whether it is a common law crime to conspire to commit a statutory offence, and it remains to be seen whether the still developing law of conspiracy will be extended to such a situation.[93]

6.67 (3) *Conspiracy as a substitute for attempt.* Where two or more persons have unsuccessfully tried to carry out a crime, such as murder or fraud, they may be charged with conspiracy to commit the crime. And such a charge may be brought in cases where a charge of attempt would not lie either because, before 1887, an attempt to commit the crime in question was not indictable, or because matters had not reached the stage of attempt.[94] The position is that an agreement to commit a crime is a criminal conspiracy, even where no crime is committed in pursuance of the conspiracy, and conspiracy is thus, as Macdonald points out,[95] an extension of the law of attempt. Any overt acts libelled are libelled simply as evidence of conspiracy.

Hume treats conspiracy under the head of "falsehood" in his chapter on crimes against property,[96] saying that "process is properly brought under this generic name, for any sort of *conspiracy or machination,* directed against the fame, safety, or state of another, and meant to be accomplished by the aid of subdolous and deceitful contrivances, to the disguise or suppression of the truth", although his examples are of conspiracy to murder, or to make a false accusation. Alison has a heading "False Conspiracy", under which he deals with conspiracies to fix false charges on individuals.[97] But today conspiracy is not confined to any particular sort of crime; as soon as two persons have agreed together to commit a crime they are guilty of conspiracy.

6.68 This type of conspiracy has become more common in recent years. The case of *Lafferty*[98] offers a simple example of an indictment of this kind. The accused were charged that they did:

---

[90] The *Scotsman*, Aug. 22, 1921.

[90a] High Court at Glasgow, Aug. 1921, unrep'd.

[91] Burnett, pp.237–238; *cf.* Hume, i, 494–496.

[92] Anderson, p.73.

[93] In England a man may be indicted for conspiracy to commit a summary statutory offence: *R. v. Blamires Transport Services Ltd.* [1964] 1 Q.B. 278, a conspiracy to contravene the regulations relating to the keeping of drivers' log sheets. See also *R. v. Simmonds* [1967] 3 W.L.R. 367.

[94] It may also be combined with an alternative charge of attempt: *Euphemia Robertson and Ors.* (1842) 1 Broun 295 — conspiring and attempting to extort money by false threats to accuse of adultery, and attempted extortion.

[95] Macdonald, p.186.

[96] Hume, i, 170.

[97] Alison, i, 369–370.

[98] High Court at Glasgow, Nov. 1974, unrep'd.

> "[B]etween 1st April and 28th May 1974 both dates inclusive, on Main Street, Cambuslang, Lanarkshire, in the house occupied by you, David Cochrane, at 143 Main Street, Bridgeton, Glasgow, and elsewhere in Scotland, conspire with each other and with another person, to commit the crimes of assault and robbery at the premises occupied by the Clydesdale Bank Limited at 214 Main Street, Cambuslang, and in pursuance of such conspiracy did frequent and loiter near said premises, observe the movements of employees at and other persons using said premises, have in your possession wigs, and spectacles as implements of disguise, and an imitation firearm and air pistol, and all this you did with intent to commit the said crimes of assault and robbery."

A similar charge reached the Criminal Appeal Court in *Carberry*.[99] In **6.69** that case the accused were alleged to have stolen a car, kept pairs of gloves and nylon masks in it, and frequented and loitered in the area of a bank, observing its interior and the movements of its staff, all in pursuance of a conspiracy to commit assault and robbery in the bank. In charging the jury, Lord Justice-Clerk Wheatley said that the "nub of the question" was whether what the accused had done indicated by reasonable inference that they were acting "in furtherance of a conspiracy previously hatched by them".[1] It was conceded in the appeal that the jury were entitled to infer a conspiracy from the police evidence of three occasions within two days when a car rented by false pretences and carrying false registration plates, in which were gloves, a black pullover, tartan tammies and three pairs of nylon stockings, was driven by the accused to a place near the bank, and left in a convenient get away position, while the accused reconnoitred the bank. The defence was that all that was afoot was a reconnaissance to see whether it might be possible to commit a crime at the bank, and it was argued that the charge to the jury had impliedly directed them "that an agreement merely to investigate the possibility of committing a crime" constituted a conspiracy to commit it. The Appeal Court held that the charge did not carry that implication. They did not go on to say whether such a direction would be a misdirection, but seem to have accepted that it would. This, it is submitted, is correct.[2] A conspiracy is an agreement to commit a crime, not an agreement to consider the possibility of committing a crime. What must be stressed, however, is that the overt acts, if any, carried out in pursuance of the conspiracy are relevant in so far as they are evidence of such an agreement; whether or not they amount to an attempt to commit the crime is irrelevant. A reconnoitring expedition preliminary to the setting up of an agreement is presumably itself a sufficiently remote preparatory step not to constitute attempted conspiracy. In any event, attempted conspiracy may be limited to attempts to induce people to take part in an already formulated plan.[3]

---

[99] Criminal Appeal Court, Feb. 1975; see 1976 S.L.T. 38.

[1] Transcript of judge's charge, 17.

[2] *cf.* Lord Keith's direction to the jury in *Smith*, High Court at Glasgow, May 1975, unrep'd, Transcript of Proceedings, 2478–2479, that to find conspiracy the jury "would have to be satisfied . . . that matters went beyond the putting forward by one man of his idea to another man with a view to the matter being discussed and possibly agreed upon at another date. There must be actual agreement." *Cf. R. v. O'Brien (Patrick)* (1974) 59 Cr.App.R. 222.

[3] *infra*, paras. 6.71, 6.80.

6.70 IMPOSSIBILITY. In *Maxwell v. H.M. Advocate*,[4] the accused were convicted of conspiracy to bribe members of a licensing board to transfer a gaming licence. They appealed on the ground that the conspiracy was incapable of success since at the relevant time the transfer of gaming licences was a matter for the sheriff and not for the licensing board. The appeal failed. Lord Cameron said that a conspiracy was an agreement to achieve a criminal purpose, and that it was the criminality of the purpose and not the result which made the agreement criminal. A conspiracy whose purpose was to corrupt public officials was therefore criminal, whether or not it could have the desired result. This seems, with respect, an odd use of "purpose": the purpose was to get the licence transferred; bribery was the means of effecting that purpose. But, semantics aside, there was clearly a conspiracy to achieve the desired result by criminal means, and there is no question that the means proposed were criminal, and no question of error or impossibility in so far as the intention of giving bribes to public officials was concerned. The case is therefore distinguishable from, *e.g.*, a conspiracy to obtain a passport by arranging a bigamous marriage where the parties in question are in fact, unknown to the conspirators, free to marry. Lord Cameron distinguished the English case of *D.P.P. v. Nock*[5] where the House of Lords held that it was not a criminal conspiracy to conspire to produce cocaine from a powder from which such production was in fact impossible. But there is no reason why that should not be a criminal conspiracy in Scotland by analogy with the current Scots law on impossible attempts;[6] and indeed there is no reason why "impossibility" should be treated as any more relevant to criminal conspiracy than it is to criminal attempt.[7]

Incitement

6.71 Despite the circular wording of the 1995 Act that, "Attempt to commit any indictable crime or offence punishable on complaint shall itself be an indictable crime or offence punishable on complaint",[8] it is not possible to extend the boundaries of attempted crime by charging an accused with attempting to commit the indictable crime of attempting to commit a crime, such as murder. That would involve an infinite regress.[9] But although conspiracy is an inchoate crime in that it does not require the putting into effect of any criminal purpose, it is in itself a substantive crime. That being so, it is a crime to attempt to form a conspiracy. This crime is usually called incitement (or instigation), or attempted incitement (or instigation).[10] Whether it is called attempted conspiracy, incitement or attempted incitement, is unimportant. It seems to be the practice to charge attempted incitement where the person incited resists the instigation, although once the invitation has been made to him there

---

[4] 1980 J.C. 40.

[5] [1978] A.C. 979.

[6] See para. 6.56, *supra*. *Nock* has in any event been reversed by statute — see Criminal Law Act 1977, s.1(1), as substituted by Criminal Attempts Act 1981, s.5(1). See J.C. Smith and B. Hogan, *Criminal Law* (9th ed., 1999, Sir J. Smith (ed.)), pp.277–278. There is a residuary category of common law conspiracy in England to which that statutory provision does not apply — see Smith and Hogan, pp.272–273.

[7] See *Docherty v. Brown*, 1996 J.C. 48, discussed at para. 6.56, *supra*.

[8] s.294 — reading both subsections thereof together.

[9] *cf. Walter Duthie Ure* (1858) 3 Irv. 10, Lord Ivory at 14.

[10] In the U.S.A., the relevant equivalent to "incitement" seems to be "solicitation": see, *e.g.*, W.B. LaFave and A.W. Scott, *Criminal Law* (2nd ed., 1986), p.486 *et seq.*; M.P.C., O.D., para. 5.02.

has been a completed, even if unsuccessful, crime. This position is recognised in the particular instance of incitement known as subornation of perjury,[11] but the same reasoning applies to any form of incitement. Where the invitation is one to enter an existing conspiracy it may be charged as "attempt to induce A.B. to enter said conspiracy",[12] or as "attempt to instigate and attempt to conspire with A.B."[13] What is important is that as soon as one person approaches another with an invitation to join in the commission of a crime, that first person has committed an indictable offence, call it attempted conspiracy, attempted incitement, incitement, or what you will.[14]

Since at least part of the reason for having the crime of incitement, and part of the justification for intervening at a stage well short of attempt, is the protection of the person incited from corruption it is possibly the law that there is no crime of incitement where the person incited is not aware that he is committing a crime.[15] Nor is there an attempted conspiracy in such a case since there cannot be an innocent conspirator.[16] The fact, however, that the person incited needs little or no persuasion is probably irrelevant, although in such a case a charge of attempted conspiracy might be more appropriate.

There is no case law on incitement to commit the impossible, but the law is doubtless the same as for attempt[17] and conspiracy.[18] The position is different, however, in England since common law rules continue to apply to incitement.[19]

---

[11] *cf.* Hume, i, 382, on subornation.

[12] *MacAlister, supra.*

[13] *cf. Kay and Strain*, High Court at Glasgow, May 1952, unrep'd., *infra*, para. 6.77.

[14] In *Baxter v. H.M. Advocate*, 1998 S.L.T. 414, it was decided that it was unnecessary for the inciter to have given any definite final instructions to commit murder in order for him to have been convicted of inciting the commission of that crime: it would be sufficient, depending on the circumstances, for him to have encouraged or requested another person to commit the crime (see L.J.-G. Rodger at 416B-C). In so concluding, the court quoted with approval from Homes J.A. in *S. v. Nkosiyana*, 1961 (4) S.A. 655 (A.D.) at 658H–659A, *viz*.: "[I]n criminal law, an inciter is one who reaches and seeks to influence the mind of another to the commission of a crime. The machinations of criminal ingenuity being legion, the approach to the other's mind may take various forms, such as suggestion, proposal, request, exhortation, gesture, argument, persuasion, inducement, goading, or the arousal of cupidity. The list is not exhaustive." (The final sentence of the foregoing quotation was not reproduced by the court in *Baxter*, but there is no reason to suppose that "invitation" would be insufficient for the *actus reus* of incitement.) The *mens rea* of the crime is a serious intention on the part of the inciter that the incitee should commit the crime in question. The reworking of the test in *S. v. Nkosiyana* in E.M. Burchell and P.M.A. Hunt, *South African Criminal Law and Procedure* (3rd ed., 1997), Vol. 1, *General Principles of Criminal Law* (J.M. Burchell (ed.)), at 359, *viz*.: "An inciter is one who unlawfully makes a communication to another with the intention of influencing him to commit a crime" — may be a little too understated for the purposes of Scots law. In any event, *Dolus eventualis* (recklessness in Scottish terms) may be acceptable as the *mens rea* for incitement in South African law — see Burchell and Hunt, at pp.360–361.

[15] *R. v. Curr* [1968] 2 Q.B. 944 L.C.P.W. No. 50, paras 93 and 101; J.C. Smith and B. Hogan, *Criminal Law* (9th ed., 1999, Sir J. Smith), p.271: *cf. supra.* para. 5.05.

[16] *cf. Churchill v. Walton* [1967] 2 A.C. 224.

[17] See para. 6.56, *supra*.

[18] See para. 6.70, *supra*.

[19] Neither the Criminal Law Act 1977 (as amended) so far as relevant to conspiracy, nor the Criminal Attempts Act 1981 applies to incitement. Thus, *e.g.*, *D.P.P. v. Nock*, [1978] A.C. 979, was applied in *R. v. Fitzmaurice* [1983] 1 Q.B. 1083. See also M. Cohen, "Inciting the Impossible" [1979] Crim.L.R. 239.

Cases of conspiracy and incitement

6.72 The starting point for the use of conspiracy as an extension of the law of attempt seems to be the case of *Elliot and Nicolson*[20] in 1694. N wanted to poison his wife and induced E to provide poison for that purpose. This plot failed, and N and his mistress M then concocted a scheme to have N's wife accused of poisoning him, and got E to make out a receipt for poison in the name of N's wife. There were thus two conspiracies, one to murder (which may have reached the stage of attempt), and one to fix a false charge of attempted murder, and the court treated them as together involving a capital crime.

6.73 The case of *Nicol Muschet and Campbell*[21] is a clearer case of a charge of conspiracy where attempt could not be charged. M bribed C to obtain false evidence of M's wife's adultery. C did this by drugging Mrs M, placing a man in bed beside her, and calling in two honest people to witness this. As Hume points out, there could be no charge of attempted subornation since the witnesses would not have committed perjury had they given evidence of what they had seen. The crime was accordingly punished as "a false conspiracy and machination, or crime of its own sort".[22]

6.74 In 1720, in the case of *W. and A. Fraser*[23] there was an example of a charge of incitement where the persons incited had refused to take any part in the proposed crime. The charge was of "having invited or solicited others to set fire" to a barn.

6.75 Again, a century later, in 1818, in *Roderick Dingwall,*[24] the accused was charged with "attempting to prevail upon" a surgeon "to enter into a conspiracy to commit murder, by furnishing poison for that purpose". D had asked the surgeon for poison for his wife, and asked him also to visit the wife and advise her to take the poison. D was charged with attempted murder, with procuring poison with intent to murder, and with attempted conspiracy, but only the last was held relevant.

6.76 It seems, therefore, that by the early nineteenth century it was recognised that attempted conspiracy was a crime, but the matter appears to have lain dormant until the case of *H.M. Advocate v. Tannahill and Neilson* in 1943.[25] T was charged with forming a scheme whereby contractors would charge the Government for work they had in fact done for him, and with attempting to defraud the Government. He was also charged with instigating and attempting to induce the contractors to render false accounts and to defraud the Government. Lord

[20] Hume, i, 170–171.
[21] (1721) Hume, i, 170.
[22] *ibid.*
[23] Hume, i, 136.
[24] Hume, i, 27, 28–29.
[25] 1943 J.C. 150. In *H.M. Advocate v. Semple,* 1937 J.C. 41, a charge of instigating a non-pregnant woman to take drugs with intent to cause her to abort was rejected as irrelevant, and other similar charges involving pregnant women were charged as attempted abortion. Similarly, inciting an idiot to kill someone was taken as art and part murder in *Wm Ross and Robert Robertson* (1836) 1 Swin. 195. *Cf. Eliz. Thomson,* High Court at Stirling, Aug.1939, unrep'd.

Wark directed the jury that in the absence of an overt act of fraud they could not convict of attempted fraud, but that they could convict of the attempted inducement.

The position of attempted inducement and attempted conspiracy were discussed on a plea to the relevance of the first charge in the case of *Kay and Strain.*[26] The accused were police officers, and they were charged with approaching one F with a scheme to defraud an insurance company. The scheme was that the two accused would enter F's home (the fact that the house belonged to Mrs F was regarded as immaterial) and "steal" his wife's fur coat, after which F. would get his wife to make a claim on the insurance company, and the accused would share in the proceeds.[27] F pretended to comply with this scheme, but in fact he informed the police, and Kay and Strain were caught while removing the coat from F's house — they were charged with theft as well as with conspiracy and were convicted of theft. The first charge was of attempting to instigate F to defraud the insurance company, of attempting to conspire with him for that purpose, and of entering the house and "removing" the coat in pursuance of the conspiracy.[28] **6.77**

The charge of attempted inducement and attempted conspiracy (the two things were treated as being one and the same) was held relevant by Lord Keith who followed *Tannahill.*[28a] He went on to say:

> "It is unnecessary to consider what the basis of the doctrine is, whether it is something of a half-way house between preparation and perpetration, a recognition of acts that may mark the end of preparation and the prelude to perpetration, or whether it is that because conspiracy to commit a crime is itself a crime, an attempt, although unsuccessful of course, an attempt to engage in conspiracy or to instigate someone else to conspire in a crime is an attempt to commit a crime. Hume deals with the matter on p. 27 although I confess that . . . it is not by any means easy to distinguish passages referring to attempts to commit a crime from passages which may refer to unsuccessful instigation to a crime, there are [detailed references] to at least two cases which support the view that instigation to commit a crime in which the instigation is unsuccessful, may of itself be a crime."[29]

It is submitted that to treat attempted incitement as a half-way house between preparation and perpetration would be unsatisfactory. This is not only because the distinction between preparation and perpetration is

---

[26] High Court at Glasgow, May 1952, unrep'd. The accused were acquitted on that charge, and so the matter was not discussed on appeal.

[27] It was argued that as the coat was Mrs F's and she was not in the plot, the coat would in fact be stolen and that there was no question of fraud, but this argument was rejected.

[28] There was no charge that the two accused conspired with each other to instigate F to enter the conspiracy, or to steal the coat. The second charge was a simple charge of art and part theft, and the allegation in the first charge that they "stole the coat in pursuance of the conspiracy" merely narrative, and not a charge of theft.

[28a] 1943 J.C. 150.

[29] The two cases are *Fraser* and *Dingwall*, see paras 6.74 and 6.75, *supra*. The original entries from the Acts of Adjournal relative to *Dingwall* were produced to Lord Keith and satisfied him that the instigation there had been unsuccessful.

itself unsatisfactory,[30] but also because it does not explain why this half-way house should exist only where more than one person is involved, or is sought to be involved, in the crime. It is much simpler to treat the charge in *Kay and Strain*[30a] as disclosing an attempt to commit the crime of conspiracy, or an attempt to incite someone to commit the crime of fraud.

6.78 Furthermore, if attempted incitement is merely a half-way house to perpetration, it is a kind of attempt to commit the ultimate crime, and so does not have to be specifically libelled, since on any indictment charging a crime the jury can convict of an attempt to commit that crime. This approach would come perilously near to making attempted incitement an attempt to attempt to commit a crime. But there is authority that where a conviction is sought for incitement, the incitement must be charged specifically. In *Morton v. Henderson*[31] the accused were charged with attempting to defraud bookmakers by "requesting" a racing dog's owner to "impair the racing ability of his greyhound . . . by administering to it a concoction", and it was held that these acts did not disclose attempted fraud, since matters had not reached the stage of attempt. But it was observed by the High Court that if the complaint had been appropriately framed[32] the accused could have been convicted of attempted incitement.

Conspiracy, incitement and attempt

6.79 The effect on the law of attempt of the existence of the crimes of conspiracy and incitement is considerable. When a single criminal reaches the stage of attempt he becomes guilty of an inchoate, uncompleted crime. Up to that stage he is guilty of nothing at all; at that stage he has still not committed a crime, but only attempted to do so. But when two criminals agree to commit a crime, then, although matters are much more inchoate and uncompleted than when, for example, a would-be poisoner invites his victim to dinner, they have committed a completed crime, the crime of conspiracy. And this is so, whether the aim of the conspiracy is to blow up the Houses of Parliament, to coerce the Government, to defraud bookmakers, or to steal a stick of rock from a child. The crime of conspiracy probably arose from the danger to society involved in large-scale political conspiracies, and as a result the term "conspiracy" has a considerable emotive effect — a conspiracy to do something sounds much worse than an attempt to do it, may even sound much worse than simply doing it. But this emotive element, which led, for example, to making trade unions illegal, and to Hume's suggestion that the rules regarding attempted crimes should suffer exception in the case of deeply atrocious or extensive plots,[33] has been forgotten in the later, logical, approach to the concept of conspiracy. Once it is accepted that the mere agreement of a large group of people to attain their ends by violence is an example of the crime of conspiracy, it follows logically that any agreement by two or more people to commit any crime is an example of the crime of conspiracy. The mistake, if

---

[30] *supra*, paras 6.26, 6.27.
[30a] High Court at Glasgow, May 1952, unrep'd.
[31] 1956 J.C. 55.
[32] *cf.*, *e.g.*, the charge in *Baxter v. H.M. Advocate*, 1998 S.L.T. 414.
[33] Hume, i, 29.

mistake there be, is in thinking of conspiracy as a "logical" crime at all, rather than as the reaction to certain special kinds of threat to the whole structure of society, or to the administration of justice.

The recognition of the crime of attempted conspiracy, which again follows logically from the existence of conspiracy, takes matters even further, for it means that merely to invite someone to commit a crime is criminal. As soon as one criminal asks another to join him all the principles underlying the reluctance of the law to punish people for attempts and its insistence on the actual execution of a considerable part of the criminal plan before it will do so, go by the board.[34] Yet these principles cannot be said to be valid where one criminal is involved, and invalid as soon as he tries to bring in a second to join him. It is true that to commit attempted conspiracy there must be a final act — the act of asking someone to join the criminal plot — but once the invitation has been given there is a completed crime. **6.80**

Whatever the objections to its existence, attempted conspiracy is a crime, and for aught yet seen, is a crime in every case in which it occurs, whatever the object of the conspiracy, provided of course it is criminal. It may or may not be attempted robbery to lie in wait for the victim[35]; it is almost certainly not attempted robbery to reconnoitre the bank which has been selected for plunder. But if two intending robbers engage in reconnoitring, conspiracy to rob can and will be inferred.[36] This means that the law is much more strongly armed against intending criminals than an adoption of the last act theory in attempt would lead one to think: the strict rules of attempt apply only to the solitary criminal who does not seek anyone else's aid in his crime. This development seems to be comparatively new. Hume's difficulty in reconciling the law of attempt with the necessity to forestall extensive conspiracies,[36a] the High Court's difficulty in holding it to be criminal for a forger to sell forged notes as such to someone who bought them for the purpose of uttering,[37] the approach of the court in *H.M. Advocate v. Baxter*,[38] the absence of any suggestion of a charge of conspiracy in *H.M. Advocate v. Camerons*,[39] all suggest that the early cases were not regarded as containing any general principle regarding conspiracies and incitements. It may be that the time has come to relate the development of the law of conspiracy to the law of attempt, and to consider whether Scots law should encourage the development, since it minimises the number of cases where the strict law of attempt prevents the law from administering deserved punishment, or whether it should discourage it as being contrary to the general spirit of a law which requires at the very least extensive and advanced preparations as a pre-requisite for the punishment of prospective criminals.

---

[34] See, *e.g.*, the incitement to murder case of *Baxter v. H.M. Advocate*, 1998 S.L.T. 414, where conviction was justifiable even though the inciter had done little more than discuss with the person incited possible methods of killing the identified victim and his likely fee.

[35] *supra*, para. 6.18.

[36] See *supra*, para. 6.69.

[36a] Hume, i, 29.

[37] *John Horne* (1814) Hume, i, 150–153.

[38] (1908) 5 Adam 609.

[39] (1911) 6 Adam 456.

CHAPTER 7

THE CRIMINAL MIND

MENS REA

The basic principle of the common law in criminal matters is that *actus non facit reum nisi mens sit rea* — no act is punishable unless it is performed with a criminal mind, *i.e.* by a person whose state of mind is such that it makes his actings criminal. So, for example, the killing of someone by a lunatic is not punishable, because the lunatic's state of mind is such that he has no *mens rea*. This principle reflects the deontological outlook of the common law, and demonstrates the close connection between the common law and ordinary moral judgments. *Mens rea* can be defined amorally as "a legally reprehensible state of mind",[1] but the test of reprehensibility is essentially a moral one, so that the ascription of *mens rea* is a moral judgment. 7.01

Mens rea and dole

The nearest Scots term to "*mens rea*" is "dole", but "dole" as used by Hume has a somewhat different meaning from "*mens rea*" as used in modern English textbooks and in some modern Scots cases. For Hume "dole" was a general wicked disposition, rather than a state of mind specific to a particular crime. The term is still used in Scots law from time to time in its old sense.[2] In *Cawthorne v. H.M. Advocate*,[3] Lord Guthrie said: 7.02

> "*Mens rea*, or dole, in our criminal law is the wicked and felonious intention which impels the criminal to commit a crime. It is a state of mind which results in a criminal act, and I fail to see how there can be a distinction between the wickedness resulting in murder, and the wickedness resulting in an attempt to murder. Hume in his book on Crimes, vol. i, p. 21, describes dole as 'that corrupt and evil intention, which is essential (so the light of nature teaches, and so all authorities have said) to the guilt of any crime.' "

"*Mens rea*" is generally used in modern discussions to refer to the "mental" requirements of a particular crime, the intention, recklessness, knowledge, etc., required for that crime. Its only use as a general term describing a requirement common to all crimes is in connection with insanity, where we speak of an absence of *mens rea* although the specific requirements as to intent, etc., may be present because "*mens rea*" is

---

[1] Kenny, para. 11; see also *R. v. Kingston* (1994) 99 Cr.App.R. 286, HL, esp. the opinion of Lord Mustill at 293.
[2] *cf.* T.B. Smith, pp.131 *et seq.*
[3] 1968 J.C. 32 at 36–37.

absent by reason of mental illness. To use the Scots term "dole" to refer to the mental element in crime would be confusing, and for that reason, as well as because most of the literature on the subject is not Scots, the English term "*mens rea*" will be used.

Three possible meanings of mens rea

7.03 When a man is described as possessing a criminal mind this may mean one of three things: (1) that he is a man of wicked or criminal character in general; (2) that a particular act of his reveals him as a wicked man, or as a man of criminal propensity; (3) that he committed a particular act in a particular state of mind which is regarded by the law as sufficient to make that act a particular crime. So far as the law is concerned it is of course criminality and not wickedness which is important, but the first two meanings of the phrase are closely connected with ideas of moral wickedness, and tend to be expressed in the language of morality. In addition, there is a strong tendency even in modern Scots law to equate criminality with wickedness, and to determine the existence or degree of criminality in certain situations by reference to the wickedness of the accused's conduct.[4]

7.04 (1) *General character.* One may call a man a person of criminal mentality when one means that he is a criminal by nature. This is a judgment of what sort of man he is taken to be, by and large. One can look back on a man's life and say, "He was a decent chap; mind you he did one or two things that were not altogether admirable, but on the whole he was a good man. His bad deeds were really out of character." Conversely one can say, "He was a really wicked man, a right criminal, even although he was kind to dogs and once saved someone's life." Crippen was of a quiet and kindly disposition, but the murder of his wife was nonetheless a wicked act; Hitler may have performed many "little, nameless, unremembered acts of kindness and of love," but he was nonetheless of a wicked disposition.

This type of judgment has no bearing on a man's responsibility, moral or legal, for any particular act. Its only relevance to the law is that it may influence the judge in passing sentence. It is by way of this sort of assessment that a judge may feel justified in treating a particular criminal leniently because he is by and large a good man. A man who has otherwise led a blameless life may be less severely punished for a particular crime than would a hardened offender who had committed the same crime.

7.05 (2) *General mens rea.* Instead of looking to a man's whole life, one may judge his character from the point of view of one particular act, and ask only if that act was done out of wickedness or criminality of disposition. The act is then evidence of the criminality of the agent's nature. This approach treats the criminal mind as a general characteristic of the man involved which has been exhibited in the commission of a crime, just as kindness is a general characteristic exhibited in particular acts of charity.

This is what Hume means by dole, which he describes as "that corrupt and evil intention, which is essential (so the light of nature teaches, and

---

[4] See. *e.g.*, *Smart v. H.M. Advocate*, 1975 J.C. 30; *cf. Lord Advocate's Reference (No. 2 of 1992)* 1993 J.C. 43. See also Sheldon, "Dole, Directness and Foresight in Causation: Lord Advocate's Reference No. 1 of 1994", 1996 J.R. 25.

so all authorities have said) to the guilt of any crime."[5] The requirement of dole, Hume says, does not mean that there must be "evidence of an intention to do the very thing that has been done, and to do it out of enmity to the individual who has been injured," but only that there must be circumstances which "indicate a corrupt and malignant disposition, a heart contemptuous of order, and regardless of social duty."[6] Because this approach treats the criminal mind as a general characteristic, revealed by a particular act, but capable of being extended to cover other acts, it is referred to in this book as "general *mens rea*."[7]

This way of treating *mens rea* is open to serious objections. Criminal responsibility is concerned with actions and not with character, and it is not concerned with motive, which is the clue whereby a man's character can be related to his actions. There is a difference in character between the man who commits bigamy out of a sense of religious duty and the man who commits it out of a desire to deceive and seduce, but both are equally guilty of the crime.

The idea of general *mens rea* may nonetheless still have some importance in Scots law. There are some cases in which the presence or absence of what is sometimes called "evil intent"[8] may affect responsibility. In determining, for example, whether a particular case of "theft by finding" is indeed theft, or whether consent is a defence to a particular charge of assault, the court may rely on an assessment of the accused's moral state rather than on the application of the definition of the crime in question.[9] The presence or absence of general *mens rea*, of a wicked disposition, is also one criterion which distinguishes murder from culpable homicide in Scotland, but this may be seen as an example of the more common use of general *mens rea* as a factor whose absence constitutes a mitigating feature in the situation.

The notion of general *mens rea* also makes possible legal doctrines which depend on the transferring of a criminal mind directed to one crime from that crime to another, so that a person who accidentally does X while criminally doing Y may be deemed to have done X criminally,

---

[5] Hume, i, 21.

[6] Hume, i, 21–22.

[7] This is not quite the meaning attached to the term by F.B. Sayre, "The Present Signification of *Mens Rea* in the Criminal Law" in *Harvard Legal Essays* (Cambridge, Mass., 1934), 399, 411.

[8] *Smart v. H.M. Advocate, supra. Cf. Lord Advocate's Reference (No. 2 of 1992)*, 1993 J.C. 43, where, notwithstanding the meaning assigned there to the expression (*i.e.* that the acts of the accused were deliberate irrespective of his motive), the court continues to treat "evil intent" as the appropriate way of referring to the *mens rea* of assault. See also the use of that expression in the relatively modern assault cases of *Roberts v. Hamilton*, 1989 J.C. 91; *Guest v. Annan*, 1988 S.C.C.R. 275; *Peebles v. Macphail*, 1990 S.L.T. 245; *H.M. Advocate v. Harris*, 1993 S.C.C.R. 559, L.J.-C. Ross at 564F, Lord McCluskey (diss.) at 569A-B, *cf.* Lord Murray at 566D; *Quinn v. Lees*, 1994 S.C.C.R. 159. *Cf. Morton v. H.M. Advocate*, 1986 S.L.T. 622, where a jury's verdict of guilty of culpable homicide "without evil intent" was considered by the appeal court to be a proper verdict of culpable homicide (as opposed to murder) in the circumstances of the case..

[9] On motive, see *infra*, para. 7.20; on dishonesty in theft, see Vol. II, Chap. 14; on consent in assault, see Vol. II, Chap. 29. Similar approaches can be seen in England in the Theft Act 1968, s.21 (1)(*b*), and *R. v. Feely* [1973] 1 Q.B. 530 as explained in *R. v. Ghosh* [1982] Q.B. 1053.

but although there are traces of this in Scots law[10], it has never attained the importance, scope or rigidity of the common law felony-murder doctrine.[11]

7.06 (i) CONSTRUCTIVE CRIME AND TRANSFERRED MENS REA. If the requirement of *mens rea* is satisfied by the presence of a "corrupt and malignant disposition," then the requirement is the same for all crimes. This means that if a man breaks into a house and negligently kills the householder, his killing of the householder must be a crime. For the *actus reus* — the killing — is present; and so is the *mens rea*, because the house-breaking is a circumstance exhibiting the necessary corrupt and malignant disposition. Although this rule does not operate in Scotland to make the killing of the householder constructive murder, *i.e.* to transfer the intent to break in to the killing so as to make the latter intentional, it might still operate to make it constructive culpable homicide where without the element of housebreaking it might not be a crime at all, although this is unlikely nowadays.[12]

This idea of general *mens rea* is also one of the reasons that recklessness is sometimes treated as equivalent to intention. A reckless indifference as to whether one's acts will cause harm may exhibit a corrupt and malignant disposition, as where A attacks another with a weapon, regardless of the possibility that he may kill him. If, then, he does kill him there is a murder, since the killing has been done in circumstances indicating a criminal mind.[13]

7.07 (ii) MITIGATION. Where a crime has been committed in the absence of circumstances indicating corrupt and malignant disposition or wickedness, or, as it is often called, malice, then, even although it has been intentionally committed, and so is *reus* according to modern ideas of *mens rea*, the court will almost certainly take the absence of malice into account in passing sentence. Now in homicide the sentence can be reduced only if the crime itself is reduced by the jury from murder to culpable homicide, and accordingly there have grown up recognised grounds on which a jury may make this reduction. There are certain circumstances which are almost compulsory mitigating factors, matters of law rather than of that general discretion which a judge employs when

---

[10] See, *e.g.*, *Roberts v. Hamilton*, 1989 J.C. 91 (although the type of crime actually committed there, assault, was the same as the one intended); *cf. Blane v. H.M. Advocate*, 1991 S.C.C.R. 576 (intention to set fire to moveables not transferable to actual but unintended destruction of heritage): *Blane* was upheld on this point in the full bench case of *Byrne v. H.M. Advocate*, 2000 S.L.T. 233, the tone of which strongly suggests the absence of any general doctrine of transferred intent in Scots criminal law: on fire-raising, see Vol. II, Chap. 22.

[11] Now abolished in England: Homicide Act 1957, s.1, but still lingering on in, *e.g.* the United States (see W.R. LaFave and A.W. Scott, *Criminal Law* (2nd ed., St. Paul, Minn., 1986) pp.622 *et seq*; and in truncated form in Canada: Criminal Code, s.230.

[12] *cf. Lourie v. H.M. Advocate*, 1988 S.C.C.R. 634, and see Vol. II, Chap. 26. The notion that transferred intent could apply in fire-raising was rejected in *Blane v. H.M. Advocate*, 1991 S.C.C.R. 578, which in turn was upheld on this point in *Byrne v. H.M. Advocate*, 2000 S.L.T. 233.

[13] *cf. Brown v. H.M. Advocate,* 1993 S.C.C.R. 382, where an intent to cause serious injury with a weapon was considered not necessarily sufficient to show the required level of recklessness for murder — at least in a case involving concert. The correctness of that consideration was questioned in *Coleman v. H.M. Advocate*, 1999 S.C.C.R. 87, but the Appeal Court reserved its opinion on the matter. See para. 5.56, *supra* and Vol. II, Chap. 23.

he takes general character into account. These circumstances do not affect the accused's responsibility for his actings, but they do affect his liability to punishment. A man who killed in circumstances which exhibit such mitigating factors was not liable to capital punishment, but only to what used to be called an "arbitrary penalty," to imprisonment or fine in the modern law. Since the Murder (Abolition of Death Penalty) Act 1965 these mitigating factors mean that a man need not be sentenced to life imprisonment for murder, but may be sentenced only to a specified term of imprisonment or other specified penalty for culpable homicide.[14]

The circumstances which are regarded as mitigatory in this way are so regarded because they show that the crime was committed, not out of malice, but from some other cause such as the accused's mental state or his reaction to provocation. This idea of the requirement of general *mens rea* for a murder conviction also influences the Crown authorities in deciding whether to charge an accused with murder or with culpable homicide. It is probably because of the absence of malice that it is thought that the survivors of suicide pacts and those who commit euthanasia would be charged only with culpable homicide in Scotland.[15]

(3) *The particular act.* The modern usage of *mens rea* is quite indepen- **7.08**
dent of moral wickedness, or even of any idea of general criminal depravity. *Mens rea* is "not the desire to do wrong but the intent to do that which causes social injury".[16] Each crime has its own *mens rea*, the mental state appropriate to its commission, so that "it is quite futile to seek to discover the meaning of *mens rea* by any common principle of universal application running alike through all the cases".[17] In Stephen's famous sentence, "The truth is that the maxim about 'mens rea' means no more than that the definition of all or nearly all crimes contains not only an outward and visible element, but a mental element, varying according to the different nature of different crimes."[18] As Glanville Williams puts it, *mens rea* is merely "the mental element necessary for the particular crime".[19]

In most circumstances this is the sense in which "*mens rea*" is used in Scotland but, as has been already suggested, the idea of a "general *mens rea*" still has some importance: the presence of general *mens rea* is necessary for murder; its absence may be necessary before certain defences, such as consent, are available. Its absence may make what would otherwise be theft or embezzlement non-criminal; its presence may well be sufficient to make otherwise innocent behaviour into the crimes of breach of the peace or attempt to pervert the course of justice.

THE PARTICULAR ELEMENT.[20] It is often assumed that all the elements **7.09**
of any particular crime require the same *mens rea* in the sense of all requiring knowledge or intention, etc., but although this is generally the

---

[14] This refers, of course, to voluntary culpable homicide, intentional homicide under mitigating circumstances, and not to involuntary or negligent homicide. The difference between murder and involuntary culpable homicide is a difference in responsibility, that between murder and voluntary culpable homicide merely a difference in liability to punishment.

[15] *cf.* R.C. Evid. of Lord Cooper, Q. 5428.

[16] F.B. Sayre, *op.cit.* at p.402.

[17] *ibid.* p.404.

[18] Sir J.F. Stephen, *History of the Criminal Law* (London, 1883), Vol. II, 95.

[19] Gl. Williams, p.31.

[20] *supra*, para. 3.06.

case at common law it is not universally or necessarily so. It is not clear, for example, that a belief, based on an error of fact, that one's first marriage no longer subsists is always a defence to bigamy,[21] or that it is a defence to a charge of fraud that one did not know whether the representations were false or not,[22] or that, should the question ever arise at common law, culpable ignorance as to age would be a defence to a charge of constructive rape of a girl under twelve — it is certainly not a defence to the statutory offence of unlawful carnal knowledge of a girl under thirteen.[23] *Mens rea* must therefore be considered separately not merely with reference to each crime but with reference to each element of each crime.[24]

7.10 IMMATERIAL ELEMENTS. *Mens rea* is required only for those elements which are peculiar to the particular *actus reus*; it is not required for general factors such as those relating to jurisdiction which are common to all crimes. It is not necessary, for example, to inquire whether A knew he was in Scotland when he committed the crime, or was reckless or negligent as to where he was, and it is similarly unneccessary to ask if he had *mens rea* regarding the age of criminal responsibility. It is no answer to a charge of incest with one's niece that one thought one was in England where such connection is not criminal, or to any charge that one wrongly believed one was under whatever is the minimum age of criminal responsibility. Such matters are treated in the American Law Institute's Model Penal Code as "immaterial", a "material element" being an "element that does not relate exclusively to the statute of limitations, jurisdiction, venue or to any other matter similarly unconnected with (i) the harm or evil, incident to conduct, sought to be prevented by the law defining the offense, or (ii) the existence of a justification or excuse for such conduct."[25]

The fact that the accused's conduct was contrary to law may also be regarded as an immaterial element, although it is usually dealt with under the heading of error.[26] The law does not require any *mens rea* to break the law, but only a *mens rea* to behave in a certain way: if that way is criminal then the agent is guilty whether or not he knows that, for example, bigamy is criminally punishable, or that the law considers his particular way of raising money as a criminal form of fraud or extortion.[27] Whether or not incidental errors as to the legal relationship between people or between people and things, for example, an error as to the legal ownership of the article in a theft charge, or the relationship of parties in an incest or rape charge, are relevant depends on the particular *mens rea* required for the element in question.

7.11 *The degrees of mens rea.* *Mens rea* may consist in intention or knowledge, in recklessness, or in negligence. These form a descending order, and a requirement of negligence is satisfied by the presence of

---

[21] *cf.* Hume, i, 461–462.

[22] See Vol. II, Chap. 18.

[23] See Vol. II, Chaps 33 and 36.

[24] *cf.* cl. 20(1) of the Draft English Code, which reads: "Every offence requires a fault element of recklessness with respect to each of its elements other than fault elements, unless otherwise provided." (Law Commission No. 177, "A Criminal Code for England and Wales", H. of C. No. 299 (1989), vol. 1.) *Cf.* also Model Penal Code, T.D. 4, 123–124; O.D. s.2.02(1); Gl. Williams, 52.

[25] Model Penal Code, O.D. s.1.13 (10).

[26] See *infra*., paras 9.16 to 9.24.

[27] Contrary to English law in relation to extortion: Theft Act 1968, s.21(1)(*b*).

recklessness or of intention or knowledge, and one of recklessness by the presence of intention or knowledge, but not vice versa.[28]

Crimes are often referred to as crimes of intent, crimes of recklessness, or crimes of negligence. In such phrases the degree of *mens rea* referred to is that required for the central element[29] of the crime.

7.12 *The basic common law principle.* Although it is true that *mens rea* in the sense of one state of mind required for all forms of criminal responsibility does not exist, and that instead there are only a number of *mentes reae* varying from crime to crime and from material element to material element,[30] the maxim *actus not facit reum nisi mens sit rea* is still of paramount importance. It serves as a reminder of the moral nature of the criminal law and also offers an ideal against which particular rules of that law can be measured. There is a presumption that criminal guilt involves moral blame, and it is for those who wish to impose punishment in the absence of such blame to show good reason for displacing the presumption.[31] It is still true that, in the words of Mr Justice Jackson in *Morissette v. U.S.*,[32]

> "The contention that an injury can amount to a crime only when inflicted by intention is no provincial or transient notion. It is as universal and persistent in mature systems of law as belief in freedom of the human will and a consequent ability and duty of the normal individual to choose between good and evil. A relation between some mental element and punishment for a harmful act is almost as instinctive as the child's familiar exculpatory 'But I didn't mean to' ".

There is a presumption that all common law crimes require *mens rea.*[33] Again, all common law crimes are crimes of intent unless they are specifically recognised as crimes of recklessness, except for culpable homicide, which can sometimes be committed negligently and even in certain circumstances in the absence of any *mens rea* at all directed to a fatal result.[34]

Nor is the requirement of intention restricted as a rule to the central element: it usually extends to all the material circumstances of the offence. It is not usually enough to show that A intended to do the act prohibited, he must have done so with knowledge of the other material elements of the *actus reus*.[35] If he is voluntarily in possession of property which is in fact stolen, but knows nothing of its provenance, he is not guilty of reset. The act in relation to which A's intention is to be measured is the *actus reus* as defined by the law. "A man may know that he is doing a thing under one description, and not under another",[36] and

---

[28] *cf.* Model Penal Code. O.D. s.2.02(5).

[29] *supra,* para. 3.06.

[30] See F.B. Sayre, "Mens Rea" (1932) 45 H.L.R. 974; Sir J.F. Stephen, *op.cit., loc. cit.;* Hall, p.70–77.

[31] See *infra,* paras 8.06 to 8.13 on the position in statutory offences.

[32] 342 U.S. (1952) 246 at 250–251.

[33] See, *e.g. Blane v. H.M. Advocate,* 1991 S.C.C.R. 576, L.J.-G. Hope at 581D; *Patterson v. Lees,* 1999 S.C.C.R. 231, Lord Sutherland at 235G-236A.

[34] See Vol. II, Chap. 26.

[35] But this is not always so in some peculiar crimes like sedition or breach of the peace, where it may be enough to show that a certain result was objectively likely, or in crimes like assault to severe injury or to the danger of life,
where the result is regarded as only an aggravation and requires no *mens rea*.

[36] G.E.M. Anscombe, *Intention* (Oxford, 1963), para. 6.

therefore unless A is aware that the goods are stolen he has not intentionally received stolen property. The common law is not, however, quite as interested in cognition as in volition, and may in some cases accept recklessness as a sufficient cognitive *mens rea* in crimes of intent. For example, recklessness as to whether goods are ownerless may be sufficient for theft, or as to the subsistence of a prior marriage for bigamy.

INTENTION[37]

Acting intentionally

7.13 A given action under a given description may be characterised as done intentionally, or as done with a certain intent or purpose. The more complex the description of the action the more convenient it is to

---

[37] I am particularly indebted to the late Professor A.H. Campbell for his helpful criticisms and suggestions on the subject of intention. There is a vast literature on intention and recklessness: see *e.g.* Gl. Williams, Chap. 2; Gl. Williams, *The Mental Element in Crime* (Jerusalem, 1965); J.C. Smith and B. Hogan, *Criminal Law* (9th ed., Sir J.C. Smith (ed.), 1999) Chap. 4, pp.52 *et seq*; P. Brett, *An Inquiry into Criminal Guilt* (London, 1963); R.A. Duff, *Intention, Agency and Criminal Liability: Philosophy of Action and the Criminal Law* (Oxford, 1990); Stephen Shute, John Gardener & Jeremy Horder (eds), *Action and Value in Criminal Law* (Oxford, 1993), esp. the chapters by Jennifer Hornsby, "On what's Intentionally Done", at pp.55 *et seq.,* and R.A. Duff, "Acting, Trying and Criminal Liability", at pp.75 *et seq.*; Andrew Ashworth, *Principles of Criminal Law* (3rd ed., Oxford, 1999), pp.159 *et seq.*; E.M. Burchell and P.M.A. Hunt, *South African Criminal Law and Procedure* (3rd ed. by J.M. Burchell, Cape Town, 1997), Vol. 1, Chap. 24; Law Commission Working Paper No. 31 (discussed in G.H. Gordon. "The Mental Element in Crime" (1971) 16 J.L.S. 282); Law Commission's Report on the Mental Element in Crime (Law Com. No. 89, 1978), and articles thereon in [1978] Crim.L.R. 588; Scottish Law Commission's Report on the Mental Element in Crime (Scot. Law Com. No. 80, 1983); Law Commission No. 177, "A Criminal Code for England and Wales", H. Of C. No. 299, 1989, esp. Vol. 1, cl.18 of the Draft Bill, and Vol. 2, paras 8.15 to 8–21; Rupert Cross, "The Mental Element in Crime" (1967) 83 L.Q.R. 215; R.M. Perkins, "A Rationale of Mens Rea" (1939) 52 H.L.R. 905; F.B. Sayre, "Mens Rea" (1932) 45 H.L.R. 974; D.R. Stuart, "Mens Rea, Negligence and Attempts" [1968] Crim.L.R. 647; J.C. Smith, "Intention in Criminal Law" (1974) 27 Curr.Leg.Prob. 93; D.J. Callaghan, "Responsibility for Recklessness" (1978) 31 Curr.Leg.Prob. 55; R.A. Duff, "Intention, Mens Rea and the Law Commission's Report" [1980] Crim.L.R. 147; also the same author's "Intention, Recklessness and Probable Consequences", *ibid.*404, and "Recklessness," *ibid.* 282; J.E. Stannard, "Subjectivism, Objectivism, and the Draft Criminal Code" (1985) 101 L.Q.R. 540; R.A. Duff, "The Obscure Intentions of the House of Lords" [1986] Crim.L.R. 771; Gl. Williams, "Oblique Intention", 1987 C.L.J. 417, and R.A. Duff's critique, "Intentions Legal and Philosophical", 1989 Ox.J.L.S. 76; R. Buxton, "Some Simple Thoughts on Intention" [1988] Crim.L.R. 484; I. Dennis, "Intention and Complicity: A Reply" [1988] Crim.L.R. 649 (being a response to G.R. Sullivan's "Intention, Purpose and Complicity" [1988] Crim.L.R. 641); Lord Goff of Chieveley, "The Mental Element in the Crime of Murder" (1988) 104 L.Q.R. 30, and Gl. Williams' rejoinder, "The *Mens Rea* of Murder: Leave it Alone" (1989) 105 L.Q.R. 387; W. Wilson, "A plea for rationality in the law of murder" (1990) 10 L.S. 307, G. Williams' response, "Rationality in murder — a reply" (1991) 11 L.S. 204, and Wilson's reply, "Rejoinder — a plea for excuses" (1991) L.S. 207; S.Field & M. Lynn, "The capacity for recklessness" (1992) 12 L.S. 74; Nicola Lacey, "A Clear Concept of Intention: Elusive or Elusory?" (1993) 56 M.L.R. 62, and a reply by J. Horder in, "Intention in the Criminal Law — A Rejoinder" (1995) 58 M.L.R. 678; J. Horder, "Varieties of intention, criminal attempts and endangerment" (1994) 14 L.S. 335; J.E. Stannard, "From Andrews to Seymour and Back Again" (1996) 47 N.I.L.Q. 1; A.P. Simester & W. Chan, "Intention Thus Far" [1997] Crim.L.R. 704. For some highly relevant philosophical questions see J.L. Austin, "A Plea for Excuses," reprinted in *Philosophical Papers* (2nd ed., Oxford, 1970), Chap. 8, and in A.R. White (ed.),*The Philosopy of Action*, (Oxford, 1968), Chap. 1; and the same author's unfinished "Three Ways of Spilling Ink," reprinted in *Philosophical Papers, supra,* Chap. 12. Some of the arguments in this chapter are developed in G.H. Gordon, "Subjective and Objective Mens Rea" (1975) 17 C.L.Q. 355.

analyse it into one or more single actions performed intentionally for a particular purpose. It is usually sufficient to describe A's assault on B as "A intentionally hit B" or even, because of the meaning of "hit", simply as "A hit B". But it is usually more helpful to describe A's murder of B as "A hit B with the intention of killing him". There are also certain offences which are described explicitly in terms of doing *x* with intent to achieve *y*, where it has to be shown that A did *x* intentionally with the purpose of bringing *y* about.[38] It should be noted, too, that A can sometimes do an act *xy* intentionally while not doing it with intent to bring about *y*. If A hits a policeman, whom he knows to be a policeman, he may do so with intent to hit a policeman, or he may do it because the victim, who happens to be a policeman, has run off with his wife.

To describe A's act as intentional is not, or not necessarily, to describe A's act as preceded by an act of intending.[39] An experienced driver who slows down, changes gear, turns his wheel, in order to turn a corner, does not hold a conference with himself, or come to a decision, or form an intention, to go through each of these motions before he performs them, but he performs them intentionally nonetheless. Indeed, if he is on his usual way home he probably does not even think about turning the corner, but that does not prevent his turn being properly describable as intentional.

A does *x* intentionally where he is aware of the circumstances which make up *x* (or at least would not claim ignorance if they were brought to his notice immediately), and where his conduct is voluntary and what happened was not an accident. Where A hits a policeman in the knowledge that his victim is a policeman, then he has done *x* intentionally, where *x* is "hitting a policeman"; if he does the same thing without knowing the victim is a policeman, he has done *x* intentionally where *x* is "hitting a man" or even "hitting a man who is a policeman", but not where it is "hitting a policeman". Lack of knowledge therefore prevents the characterisation as intentional of A's behaviour under a description which includes any element as to which he is ignorant.[40]

Acting with intent

To act with intent requires some much more positive mental state, although here again the mental state is more complex than the "ghost in the machine" idea of a mental event consisting of forming an intention at a particular time.[40a] **7.14**

It is this meaning of "intentional" which is referred to in Lord Hailsham's speech in *R. v. Hyam*[41] where he says:

> "I know of no better judicial interpretation of 'intention' or 'intent' than that given in a civil case by Asquith L.J. (*Cunliffe v. Goodman* [1950] 2 K.B. 237) when he said at p. 253:

---

[38] *cf. R. v. Belfon* [1976] 1 W.L.R. 741.

[39] *cf.* R. Buxton, "Some Simple Thoughts on Intention" [1988] Crim.L.R. 484, at 490 where it is argued that the root of true intention is premeditation, *i.e.* "rational reflection by the agent on the likely consequences of his action, followed by a desire on his part to act so as to bring about those consequences": the view expressed is that intention is a valid concept only in relation to future consequences of action, since "intentionally" doing present actions means no more than that those actions are done voluntarily. *Cf. supra,* para. 3.09.

[40] *cf.* G.E.M. Anscombe, *op.cit.*

[40a] See para. 7.13, n.39.

[41] [1975] A.C. 55, 74B-C.

> 'An "intention" to my mind connotes a state of affairs which the party "intending" — I will call him X — does more than merely contemplate: it connotes a state of affairs which, on the contrary, he decides, so far as in him lies, to bring about, and which, in point of possibility, he has a reasonable prospect of being able to bring about, by his own act of volition.' "

It may be, however, that Asquith L.J.'s phrase "in point of possibility" should be replaced by "which he thinks".[42] Mother Hubbard deserves the credit of intending to feed her dog,[43] and the witch-doctor the discredit of intending to kill the man whose effigy he burns.

7.15 *Intention as a substitute for knowledge.* Where A's intention comprehends a particular element in a situation and his intention is realised, it does not matter whether he knew of the existence of that element, or only believed, or even hoped, that it existed.[44] If A intends to kill B and does so by putting arsenic in his tea, it does not matter whether A knew or only thought or hoped that arsenic was poisonous. Again, if A suffers from a "Lolita syndrome" and has intercourse with B who is fifteen because his intention is "to have intercourse with a fifteen-year-old", then A has acted intentionally both as regards the intercourse and as regards the age, even if he did not know but only assumed or hoped that B was of the desired age. If, then, it were a crime of intent to have intercourse with a fifteen-year-old and intention were required both as to the intercourse and the age, A could be convicted of that crime. If the crime were so defined as to require an intention to have intercourse with a girl of fifteen in the knowledge that she was fifteen, A could not be convicted since he lacked knowledge. In practice, however, crimes do not as a rule specifically require knowledge of a particular circumstance, but are satisfied with either intention or knowledge. It is, for example, a crime to have intercourse with one's sister, intending to do so, or doing so in the knowledge that she is one's sister. One possible exception, at any rate in theory, may be reset which requires knowledge that the property received is stolen, but in practice such knowledge would be imputed to anyone who retained the property in the hope or belief that it was stolen, although without any actual "knowledge" to support the hope or belief.[45]

---

[42] In adopting Asquith L.J.'s definition, Lord Ross told the jury in *Sayers v. H.M. Advocate*, 1981 S.C.C.R. 312 at 318, that intention connoted "a state of affairs which an individual decides so far as he can to bring about and which he has reason to think can be brought about by his own act".

[43] *cf. Lamont v. Strathearn*, 1933 J.C. 33, Lord Sands at 36.

[44] In the "code team's" report to the (English) Law Commission ("Criminal Law: Codification of the Criminal Law. A Report to the Law Commission" (1985), L.C. No. 143), the draft Bill annexed to it offered (at cl.22(a)) "a person acts in respect of an element of an offence — ... 'intentionally' when he wants it to exist or occur, is aware that it exists or is almost certain that it exists, or will exist or occur"; but the 1989 Draft Code, at s.18(b), provides that a person acts intentionally with respect to a circumstance when he hopes or knows that it exists, or will exist, *cf.* Model Penal Code, O.D. s.2.02(2)(a): "A person acts purposely with respect to a material element of an offense when . . . (ii) if the element involves the attendant circumstances, he is aware of the existence of such circumstances or he believes or hopes that they exist."

[45] It is assumed here that "true belief" is not identical with knowledge, that it is meaningful for a man to describe at any rate his own state of mind by saying, "I thought this was so, but I did not know it to be so", and that there is some generally acceptable way of distinguishing the two states. It is meaningful, for example, to say, "I believe that the Battle of Waterloo was fought on June 18, 1815, but I'm not sure," and then, after having consulted a reliable work of reference, "I know the date of the Battle of Waterloo"; or "I believe that that hat belongs to A but I would have to see if his initials are inside to be sure."

Intention, desire and foresight of certainty

Lord Hailsham followed his citation of Asquith L.J.'s definition[46] by saying: **7.16**

> "If this be a good definition of 'intention' for the purposes of the criminal law of murder, and so long as it is held to include the means as well as the end, and the inseparable consequences of the end as well as the means, I think it is clear that 'intention' is clearly to be distinguished alike from 'desire' and from foresight of the probable consequences."

Intention and desire. Glanville Williams speaks of intention as "that **7.17** species of desire on the part of a person that is coupled with his own actual or proposed conduct to achieve satisfaction".[47] The requirement of actual or proposed conduct is necessary in order to distinguish intention from mere wishful thinking. Intentions may be divided into present and future intentions. A schoolboy's intention to take up the medical profession may be distinguished from his desire to become an engine-driver because the former is linked in his mind with a proposed course of action. The law, however, is concerned with present intentions, intentions linked to conduct which is either actual or is proposed for the immediate future. In this sense, A may desire to go to London, but unless he makes more or less detailed and definite plans to go there, such as reserving a room in an hotel, or buying a railway ticket, or at least "sets himself" to do these things, he would not be said to be intending to go there.[48]

Intention, however, is not just a species of desire. As Lord Hailsham pointed out,[49] to desire an end is to intend the means adopted for the attainment of that end, even if the means are not themselves regarded as desirable. Again, a man is said to intend whichever of two possible courses of action he adopts, even although it would be true to say that the way he acted was not the way he "really" wanted, not the way in which he would have preferred to act.

The relation between intention and desire was discussed by the Judicial Committee of the Privy Council in the Australian case of *Lang v. Lang*.[50] It was there held that a husband who pursued a course of conduct which he knew would lead to his wife's leaving him intended her to leave him although he did not want her to go. Lord Porter said, "A man may well have incompatible desires. He may have an intention which conflicts with a desire: *i.e.* he may will one thing, and wish another, as when he renounces some cherished article of diet in the interest of

---

46 *supra*, para. 7.14.

47 Gl. Williams, p.36.

48 The law is usually concerned with fulfilled intentions, and with the question of whether a particular result was caused or a particular act committed intentionally. Even where the law deals with unfulfilled intentions, as in attempts and crimes like "loitering (or in its modern form 'being found' on premises) with intent to steal," it is confined to intentions which are coupled with some conduct directed to bring them about, and usually to situations where the projected fulfilment is imminent. It is unlikely, for example, that a man who goes into a garden one day in order to reconnoitre for a crime he means to commit the following day would be guilty of being there with intent to steal, although he might conceivably be guilty of attempted theft in theory if not in practice.

49 *supra*, para. 7.16.

50 [1955] A.C. 402.

health. But 'intention' necessarily connotes an element of volition: desire does not."[51]

7.18 *Foresight of certainty.* There is little difficulty in saying that A's intention to bring about *x* involves an intention to bring about everything necessary to bring about *x* — he who wills the end wills the means. If A constructs a plan to acquire something by telling a lie then, however much he regrets the necessity, he intends to lie. But there has been some controversy over the situation where what is involved is not so much a step on the way to the realisation of A's intention, as an inevitable concomitant of it. Glanville Williams gives the following example in support of his view that intention extends to consequences foreseen as certain:

> "[S]uppose that D, when he caused P's death, did not desire the death, but that he was determined to give P a push (*e.g.* because he wanted to stop P picking up a watch which they had both at that moment seen lying on the path), and knew that the push must cause P to fall over the cliff and so must cause P's death. This is foresight of certainty of consequence, without desire of it."[52]

In this particular example one is tempted to suggest that the problem will dissolve if the jury view the situation, as they almost certainly will, simply as one in which D intentionally pushed P over the cliff, and then apply the law of homicide.

The problem is often discussed with reference to the example of the man who blows up an aircraft in flight in order to obtain insurance moneys. "But if any passengers are killed he is guilty of murder, as their death will be a moral certainty if he carries out his intention. There is no difference between blowing up the aircraft and intending the death of some or all of the passengers."[53] Glanville Williams would convict in this case on the basis that foresight of certainty is a form of intention.[54] Howard has argued that certainty here is no more than a high degree of probability, and that foresight of certainty is only recklessness.[55] In jurisdictions, such as England, where recklessness will not suffice for murder, the question is rather more than academic. But the English courts have not fully endorsed Williams' view; provided that there is

---

[51] At 428. See *Gollins v. Gollins* [1964] A.C. 644, 666, where Lord Reid said that what was in issue in *Lang* was not "intention" but "wilfulness."

[52] *The Mental Element in Crime*, p.11. See also his article, "Oblique Intention", 1987 C.L.J. 417, and A. Ashworth, *Principles of Criminal Law* (3rd ed., 1999), pp.176–183. *Cf.* R.A. Duff, "Intentions Legal and Philosophical", 1989 Ox.J.L.S. 76.

[53] *R. v. Hyam, supra,* Lord Hailsham of St Marylebone L.C. at 74D.

[54] Gl. Williams, para. 18; *The Mental Element in Crime*, p.20 *et.seq.*: A. Ashworth, *op.cit., loc. cit*. See also Lord Diplock in *R. v. Lemon* [1979] A.C. 617, at 638E-F, who said (in a dissenting opinion) that in the late 19th century it was not "settled law that, where intention to produce a particular result was a necessary element of an offence, no distinction was to be drawn in law between the state of mind of one who did an act because he desired it to produce that particular result and the state of mind of one who, when he did the act, was aware that it was likely to produce that result but was prepared to take the risk that it might do so, in order to achieve some other purpose which provided his motive for doing what he did. [But] it is by now well settled law that both states of mind constitute 'intention' in the sense in which that expression is used in the definition of a crime whether at common law or in a statute." *Cf.* n. 56, *infra*.

[55] C. Howard, *Australian Criminal Law* (2nd ed., 1970) 45, 352.

foresight of death as a "virtual certainty", an English jury is permitted to "find" the necessary intention for a murder conviction.[56]

This suggests that the rule is evidential rather than substantive[57]; and the insistence upon such a high degree of certainty is designed to avoid any blurring of the line between intention and recklessness. In Scotland the man would be convicted of murder on the basis that his action "betrayed a disposition depraved enough to be regardless of the danger".[58] This approach makes it plain that what is really involved is not an inquiry into degrees of probability or certainty, but a moral judgment. As such, it makes it easy to distinguish the case of the bomb in the aeroplane from cases like that of the surgeon performing a highly dangerous operation "not as a means to killing his patient, but as the best, and possibly the only, means of ensuring his survival".[59]

The other context in which this problem arises is in relation to "with intent" crimes. There is a strong argument in principle for the view that when a crime is defined as requiring a particular intent, it requires that intent in the strict sense of purpose, or, as the Model Penal Code puts it, "conscious purpose", although not necessarily in the sense of desired or most desired purpose.[60] Nothing less than purpose can be required for crimes like housebreaking with intent to steal, or assault with intent to rape.[61] **7.19**

The difficulties about foresight of certainty seem to arise in situations which are not really cases of foresight at all, but cases where the offence is in effect, and sometimes almost in terms, one of doing *x* with intent to do *x*, and in which, therefore, A can be convicted by showing that he did *x* intentionally, *i.e.* that he was aware that what he was doing satisfied the description *x*.

As Professor S. Z. Feller has pointed out, "with intent" crimes have to be divided into those where the consequence flows naturally from the conduct, and those where the consequence lies outside the conduct itself and to achieve it a factor additional to the conduct is required. There is thus a difference between a crime like failing to report for military service with intent to avoid registration for such service, and a crime like assault with intent to ravish. The fact that assault with intent to injure falls into the second class is explained by the fact that the definition of assault covers conduct which does not cause any injury. Offences of the first class are really semantic freaks, caused presumably by a belief in the legislator that *mens rea* can be imported into them only by using the language of specific intent.[62]

---

56 *R. v. Woollin* [1998] 3 W.L.R. 382, HL. It is clear from this case that lesser degrees of certainty are more compatible with recklessness than intention, and that in certain prior cases — such as *R. v. Hyam, supra* — the courts had strayed too far in the direction of recklessness. See also *R. v. Moloney* [1985] A.C. 905; *R. v. Hancock* [1986] A.C. 455; *R. v. Nedrick* [1986] 1 W.L.R. 1025; and *R. v. Walker* (1990) 90 Cr.App.R. 226 — although all of these must now be read subject to the ruling by the House of Lords in *Woollin, supra*. In view of that ruling, the opinion of Lord Diplock, quoted at n. 54 *supra*, must be taken as an incorrect statement of current English law — at least in so far as murder is concerned. *Cf.* the English Draft Code, and its definition of murder (cl.54) which in turn depends on the definition of intention in cl.18(b)(ii).

57 See I. Dennis, "Intention and Complicity: A Reply" [1988] Crim.L.R. 649, at 649–650; A.P. Simester and W.Chan, "Intention Thus Far" [1997] Crim.L.R. 704, at pp.710–713.

58 See *infra*, para. 7.60.

59 *R. v. Hyam, supra*, Lord Hailsham of St. Marylebone L.C. at 74E.

60 But see *e.g. R. v. Vallance* (1961) 108 C.L.R. 56.

61 *R. v. Belfon* [1976] 1 W.L.R. 741.

62 See S.Z. Feller, "The 'Knowledge Rule'" (1970) 5 Israel L.R. 352, esp. 365–366; "Absenteeism 'With Intent to Avoid Military Service'" (1975) 29 *Ha-Praklit* 534 (Hebrew).

The best known example of this first type of case is *R. v. Steane*.[63] The accused had broadcast for the Germans during the war in order to save his family from the Gestapo. He was charged with doing an act likely to assist the enemy with intent to assist the enemy. His conviction was quashed on the ground that the crime was one requiring a specific intent which had to be proved by the prosecution, and that they had failed to prove that Steane's intention was to assist the enemy. There seems little doubt that *Steane* was wrongly decided.[64] Glanville Williams argues that, subject to the defence of duress, Steane should have been convicted either on the basis that he acted voluntarily knowing that what he was doing was assisting the enemy, or that he caused a result foreseen as certain.[65] The simple approach to *Steane* is to say that what the Germans asked him to do was to assist them, and that that was what he deliberately did; his motive is irrelevant, his proper defence coercion.[66] If his act is described as "assisting the enemy by broadcasting" it cannot be disputed that he acted intentionally.[67] As Glanville Williams put it:

> "[L]et me assume, . . . that the formula is restricted to acts done with intent (in the sense of desire or purpose) to assist the enemy. Steane's predominant intent was to save his family, and in order to do that he broadcast for the enemy. On any intelligible use of language, he intentionally (purposely) broadcast. He did not broadcast by mistake or accident or in a state of automatism. If it is thought too strong to say that he desired to broadcast, at least he knew he was broadcasting, which is enough to establish wilfulness or intent. No doubt he did so reluctantly, as the lesser of two evils; but many people go to work in the morning for precisely the same reason."[68]

Intention and Motive

7.20 Intention and motive often overlap. A motive can often be described in terms of intention, and for some jurists motive is just a special sort of intention. Salmond divided intention into what he called "immediate" and "ulterior" intent, the former relating to the act itself, and the latter to the object for which the act was done, for example to alarm, or for a joke, and he called the ulterior intent motive.[69] In this way, the objects of intention and the object of motive are seen as parts of a sequence of the means-end type; A intends the means which lead to the end chosen by his motive.

The application and the difficulties of this approach can be seen by considering the following situation. A buys a bottle of poison and a bottle of port; he puts the poison into the port, takes the poisoned port

---

[63] [1947] K.B. 997.

[64] For a contrary view, see W. Wilson, "A plea for rationality in the law of murder" (1990) 10 L.S. 307, 311–315; and *cf.* R.S. Tur, "Subjectivism and Objectivism: Towards Synthesis" in S. Shute, J. Gardner & J. Horder (eds), *Action and Value in Criminal Law* (Oxford, 1993), 213 at p.231.

[65] *The Mental Element in Crime*, pp.21 *et seq.*

[66] See *infra*, para 13.24 *et seq. Cf.* J.C. Smith, *Justification and Excuse in the Criminal Law* (London, 1989), pp.61–64.

[67] See R.A. Duff, "Intentions Legal and Philosophical", 1989 Ox.J.L.S. 76, at p.84.

[68] *The Mental Element in Crime*, p.22. See also A. Ashworth, *Principles of Criminal Law* (3rd ed., Oxford, 1999), p.181.

[69] *Salmond on Jurisprudence*, (11th ed., London, 1957), para. 137.

to his aunt's house, pours her a glass of it which she drinks, and she dies as a result. A inherits a fortune from her, and retires to a house in Majorca on which he has long set his heart. If in considering this sequence one stops at the purchase of the poison, one can say that A's intention was to purchase the poison, and his motive to kill his aunt, inherit her fortune and retire to Majorca. If A is tried simply for buying poison, assuming that to be in itself a crime, the relevant intention will be to buy poison, and the later "intentions" will be regarded as motive, and so as irrelevant. If it is a crime to buy poison, it is a crime to do so whether one does it to kill an aunt or to improve one's complexion. But if A is tried for killing his aunt his intention will be taken to be that of killing her, and only the desire to inherit her money and retire to Majorca will be regarded as motive. Motive so defined is any intention which succeeds in time of proposed realisation the intention to commit the crime charged. It is, so to speak, the post-ultimate intention, and is irrelevant.

A similar analysis can be made in the case of crimes requiring a particular purpose. In a charge of "buying poison with intent to kill" the last relevant intention would be the intention to kill, and all subsequent intentions would be classed as irrelevant motives. **7.21**

Motive as something other than intention. Salmond's analysis of motive makes the concept unnecessary and deprives it of any independent meaning except in so far as evidence of motive may help in assessing intention, and except in so far as it may affect punishment. On his view "motive" is just a word used for certain intentions in given situations: and the use varies from situation to situation, so that what is motive in situation S — a charge of buying poison — may not be motive in situation S1 — a charge of murder. Moreover the variation is subjective in the sense that it depends on the standpoint from which the sequence of events is viewed. **7.22**

But there is a meaning of motive which is not satisfactorily translatable into terms of intention. Motive in this sense is a compelling, or at any rate a propelling, psychological factor. A man who sacrifices his child from religious motives need not have any ulterior intention, need not wish to bring about any state of affairs following the sacrifice of the child. Psychological motives can sometimes be translated into intentions, but the translations are rarely satisfactory. "His motive was greed" does not mean quite the same as "His intention was to inherit money"; "His motive was jealousy" is only tortuously translatable into "His purpose was to achieve that peace of mind which he could obtain only by the death of his rival". To regard all motives as being so translatable is to ignore the possibility that an act may be done intentionally without any regard to consequences whatever. The atheist materialist who fulfils an unimportant promise made to a dead friend does so from a motive — the desire to keep his promise, or affection and respect for his friend — but he does not do so with any ulterior purpose. Motive in this sense is something different from intention. It is not something connected with a particular action making it intentional in the sense of providing a goal to which it can be seen to be directed. It is a psychological state which explains a man's actions, and his intentions, by reference to their source and not to their purpose. It is something more fundamental than ulterior intention, and indeed one may ask of a man's ulterior intention, "Why did he want that?" and answer in terms of his psychological make-up.

One can ask "Why did he want a house in Majorca?" and answer in terms of his sybaritic character.

A system which does not accept that bad means may be justified by being directed to good ends can ignore motive in the sense of ulterior intention. But if motive is thought of as the psychological origin of action and of ulterior intention alike, it cannot be altogether ignored except by a wholly utilitarian ethic. Motive in this sense is very important in connection with general *mens rea*, since if the motive is not that of evil doing, malice, defiance, or some similar "criminal" or "depraved" state of mind, general *mens rea* will be absent and there will be room for a strong plea in mitigation based on the accused's motive. It seems, too, that in Scotland motive may be important in determining whether or not "evil intent" is present, and this may in some cases go to responsibility as well as to mitigation.

Proof of intention

7.23 *Acting intentionally.* Certain descriptions of actions are so simple that to say "A did *x*" is to say "A did *x* intentionally"; the description of the action carries its own imputation of intentional behaviour, as when we say "A hit B". In order to prove that A hit B intentionally we need do no more than describe A's objective behaviour; there is no need to postulate or prove a prior mental event in which A "intended" to hit B. As Hart and Hampshire put it:

> "In any ordinary narrative describing ordinary actions done in normal circumstances, it would be pointless to say that a person did these things intentionally; for normally there is a fulfilled presumption that if a person does something, he does it intentionally. This is a feature of the whole conceptual scheme involved in our description of persons in terms of actions. If I am telling you simply what someone did, *e.g.* took off his hat or sat down, it would normally be redundant, and hence misleading, though not false, to say that he sat down intentionally. The primary point of saying that someone acted intentionally is to rebut a prima facie suggestion that he was in some way ignorant of, or mistaken about, some element involved in this action."[70]

In *R. v. George*[71] Ritchie J. distinguished assault from robbery by pointing out that:

> "In considering the question of *mens rea*, a distinction is to be drawn between 'intention' as applied to acts done to achieve an immediate end on the one hand and acts done with the specific and ulterior motive and intention of furthering or achieving an illegal object on the other hand. Illegal acts of the former kind are done 'intentionally' in the sense that they are not done by accident or through honest mistake, but acts of the latter kind are the product of preconception and are deliberate steps taken towards an illegal

---

[70] H.L.A. Hart and S. Hampshire, "Decision, Intention and Certainty" (1958) 67 *Mind* 6–7; *cf. R. v. Mowatt* [1968] 1 Q.B. 421, Diplock L.J. at 426–427.

[71] [1960] S.C.R. 871, 890. See also *Lord Advocate's Reference (No. 2 of 1992)*, 1992 S.C.C.R. 960, where it was held that the *mens rea* for assault was sufficiently established by the deliberateness of the conduct, but that the same could not necessarily be said for the aggravation of intent to rob or attempted robbery: L.J.-C. Ross at 965D-E and 966B-C; Lord Cowie at 968B-C; and Lord Sutherland at 970A-B, B-C.

goal. The former acts may be the purely physical products of momentary passion, whereas the latter involve the mental process of formulating a specific intent."[72]

Proof of accident will involve a redescription of what happened: the witness who said "A pushed B" has to be persuaded to say instead "A stumbled into B". The defence of mistake raises other problems, which are dealt with below in Chapter 9. The point stressed here is that to act intentionally is not necessarily to act after having formed a plan or made a decision to do so, and therefore proof that the act was intentional does not require proof of the formation of such a plan or the making of such a decision. It should be stressed, too, that what is important is the description of the conduct, and not its classification as a crime of "specific" or of "basic" intent.[73] Some forms of assault, *e.g.* by discharging at some distance from the victim a gun pointed at the ground, do not bear on their face, so to speak, an imputation of intention to injure.[74]

Acting with intent. Here, always in theory, and sometimes in practice, it is necessary to prove, not that any particular act of intending occurred, but that what was being done was being done of design. This is the kind of intention which is required in result crimes, and in crimes of doing *x* with intent to do or produce *y*. **7.24**

There is, however, a preliminary question as to whether intention in this sense is objective or subjective.

Objective intention. Intention is normally thought of as a state of mind. A intends to do *x* when he sets before his mind the idea of *x* as a first stage in the process of bringing it into effect. But, apart from confessions, the only way in which A's mind can be known is by observing how he acts. If his actions make sense when regarded as directed towards a particular result he will be said to have intended that result. Actions which do not appear to form part of a series leading up to a particular result do not appear to be intentional — although they may of course be voluntary. Accidents are not led up to. "Dressing carefully 'makes sense' as a preliminary to going to the City, but not as a preliminary to being knocked over by a bicycle".[75] On this view "A intends to bring about *x*" means only that if A's actions are observed they will be seen to form a coherent series leading up to *x*. All that can be seen of A's intentions is this series. In the same way "A won that game of chess intentionally" can be said to mean only that his moves were the moves which might have been expected to lead to victory.[76] One does not see a series of events which are A intending, or A thinking intelligently about, the game of chess. **7.25**

On this view the statement that a man is presumed to intend the natural consequences of his actions is hardly more than a tautology. It is

[72] Similarly, a description of behaviour as "taking and driving away a car" is a sufficient description and proof that the behaviour was intentional; but this is not enough if the charge is one of theft: see *R. v. Macpherson* [1973] R.T.R. 157. See also the different interpretations of "maliciously" in *R. v. Cunningham* [1957] 2 Q.B. 396 and *R. v. Cato* [1976] 1 W.L.R. 110.

[73] *cf. D.P.P. v. Majewski* [1977] A.C. 443, HL.

[74] *cf. R. v. Vallance* (1961) 108 C.L.R. 56, esp., Windeyer J. at 79–80.

[75] J.A. Passmore, "Intentions", *Proceedings of the Aristotelian Society* (1955), Supp.Vol. XXIX, 131, 132. The arguments in this paragraph are based on this article.

[76] *cf.* G. Ryle, *The Concept of Mind* (London, 1949), *passim.*

not an arbitrary rule about what people in fact intend, or even about what will be regarded as evidence of their intentions. It does not rest on the ground that the best evidence to be considered in seeking to discover a man's intentions is that of his external behaviour, or even that that is the only evidence; but on the ground that there is no meaningful description of intention except in terms of external action. Accordingly it would be self-contradictory to say "A's actions necessarily led up to *x* but A did not intend *x*".

7.26 *Subjective intention.* The extreme objective view has serious difficulties. It suggests that a man knows less about his own intentions than do the people who watch his actions. It means that no credence can ever be given to a confession which claims that the confessor's intentions were other than the intentions spelled out from observing his actions.[77] In fact, the courts do pay attention to confessions, and indeed go further and accept in principle that intention is subjective,[78] but in particular cases they are naturally reluctant to believe an accused person when he says he did not intend to do something but his actings point strongly to his behaviour having been intentional.

In practice, therefore, the right of the accused to give evidence does not help a great deal in proving intention, unless of course he confesses. For he is a suspect witness in fact, however much judges may instruct juries that he is a witness like any other, and at best his evidence is only something to be weighed against the other evidence in the case. "The wicked intent", says Macdonald,[79] "is an inference to be drawn from the circumstances of the deed as well as from any explanations by the man". As Windeyer J. said in *R. v. Vallance*[80]:

> "A man's own intention is for him a subjective state, just as are his sensations of pleasure or of pain. But the state of another man's mind, or of his digestion, is an objective fact. When it has to be proved, it is to be proved in the same way as other objective facts are proved. A jury must consider the whole of the evidence relevant to it as a fact in issue. If an accused gives evidence of what his intentions were, the jury must weigh his testimony along with whatever inference as to his intentions can be drawn from his conduct or from other relevant facts. References to a 'subjective test' could lead to an idea that the evidence of an accused man as to his intent is more credible than his evidence of other matters. It is not: he may or may not be believed by the jury. Whatever he says, they may be able to conclude from the whole evidence that beyond doubt he had a guilty mind and a guilty purpose. But always the questions are what did he in fact know, foresee, expect, intend."

---

[77] The objective view could also mean that a man may intend a result of a kind he does not know to be possible as where someone ignorant of electricity switches on a light or someone ignorant of the existence of railways pulls a lever in a signal box which operates a signal which leads to a collision between two trains. An objectivist might answer, however, that in extreme cases the agent's ignorance is itself an objective factor serving to negative the inference indicated by the other factors. The picture presented by the sight of a child or an animal pulling levers on a machine may be objectively different from that presented by the sight of a grown man doing the same.

[78] See *e.g. Boyle v. Ritchie*, 1999 S.C.C.R. 278, Lord Prosser at 281E & F; *Gollins v. Gollins* [1964] A.C. 644; *Wilson v. Inyang* [1951] 2 K.B. 799.

[79] p.1.

[80] (1961) 108 C.L.R. 56, 83.

Any other result would make it almost impossible for the Crown to establish intention beyond reasonable doubt where it was denied by the accused.

It should also be noted that in most of the situations with which the common law deals, intention of some nature is fairly easy to prove. One reason for treating intention to do grievous bodily harm as a sufficient *mens rea* for murder is that while intention to kill may often be difficult to prove, intention to do grievous bodily harm is usually apparent. Indeed, where the result is immediate and obvious there is little if any difference between saying A did *x* with intent to do *y* and a description of A's conduct as intentionally doing *y*. To quote Windeyer J. again:

> "In every case where intent is in question the question is what did the accused — the man before the court — intend. Of that, the acts he did may well provide the most cogent evidence. In some cases the evidence that the acts provide may be so strong as to compel an inference of what his intent was, no matter what he may say about it afterwards. If the immediate consequence of an act is obvious and inevitable, the intentional doing of the act imports an intention to produce the consequence. Thus to suppose that a sane man who wilfully cuts another man's throat does not intend to do him harm would be absurd. A sane man who intentionally belabours another with a knuckleduster while he is lying helpless on the ground and then stabs him with a knife, cutting his throat, cannot rationally be said not to have meant to do him grievous bodily harm at the least."[81]

Proof of knowledge

In order to be able to say that A did *x* intentionally, A must have known of *x*. Before turning briefly, since this is not a treatise on evidence, to consider how knowledge is proved, it is necessary to point out an ambiguity in "A knows *x*". It may mean, "A has at this moment the fact of *x* before his mind", or it may mean, "If A were asked whether *x*, he would know the answer". The latter sense of knowledge may be described as "dispositional" by analogy with the dispositional sense of a word like "fragile", which means "liable to break if struck".[82] English criminal law apparently uses knowledge in the former sense, a sense in which to say "A knows *x*" is to describe a mental event, is to say, so to speak, "A is at this moment knowing *x*".[83] Proof of knowledge in this latter sense is very difficult, if not impossible, and, it may be thought, of little importance. **7.27**

Knowledge may be of a particular fact: that gun is loaded; this watch is stolen; this woman is resisting my attempts to seduce her; the object I am pummelling is a man; or it may be of a generalisation: people are liable to die when you shoot them; women who struggle, cry out for help and fight back are usually not consenting to whatever is being done to

---

[81] *Parker v. R.* (1963) 111 C.L.R. 610, 648–649.

[82] See G. Ryle, *The Concept of Mind,* Chaps. 2 and 5. *Cf. Derry v. Peek* (1889) 14 App.Cas. 337, Lord Bramwell at 348.

[83] See *R. v. Ramsay* [1967] N.Z.L.R. 1005, 1012, 1015. *Cf.* L.C. No. 177, "A Criminal Code for England and Wales" (H. of C. No. 299, 1989), Vol. 1, Draft Criminal Code Bill, cl.18 "a person acts — (a) 'knowingly' with respect to a circumstance not only when he is aware that it exists or will exist, but also when he avoids taking steps that might confirm his belief that it exists or will exist;" see also Vol. 2, "Commentary", paras 8.10, 8.11.

them; and so on. The latter are of course connected to particular facts by means of a simple syllogism.

Knowledge, in the dispositional sense, of general laws of nature will normally be assumed, and will be excluded only by evidence of mental abnormality or some wholly exceptional circumstance. Knowledge of particular facts creates more problems. It seems to require more than just the kind of dispositional knowledge which suffices for knowledge of the general facts of life, but it does not necessarily require an act of knowing. If I pick up a gun which I know to be loaded and carry it along the road while discussing the speeches in *R. v. Morgan*[84] with my attractive companion, I do not cease to know that it is loaded when I am engaged in trying to understand or explain what Lord X said on page n, or even when I fall into contemplation of my companion's beauty. On the other hand, if I pick up the same gun some hours later when I have forgotten that it is loaded, can I be said then still to "know" that fact? It is no answer to a question like, "Did you know that throwing bombs into crowded hotels is liable to kill people?" to say, "Yes, but at the time I forgot". But that may be an answer to a question like "Did you know the gun was loaded?" Knowledge of the latter kind seems to require the fact to have been present to the agent's mind at some time sufficiently close to the time of the offence to be relevant. That, of course, does not help very much unless the borders of relevancy are defined, and such definition is very difficult. Perhaps the best one can say is that the "active knowledge" must have occurred at the time of some event which was part of the same series of events as the criminal conduct.[85]

The simpler the description of the action the easier it is for the Crown to prove, or it might be said for one to assume, A's awareness of it. It will take a plea of insanity or extreme intoxication to show that a man who was raining blows on another with a club was not aware of the presence of the victim or the weapon; and if it does come to insanity or intoxication they will be proved or disproved by more or less objective facts (a little less objective in the former case because of the nature of psychiatry but still things perceived by the senses): A's behaviour on other occasions, his apparent capacity to reason, his biochemical state, his reaction to drugs, etc. Intoxication will be determined by reference to evidence of drink or drugs taken and to the well-known signs of drunken or drugged instability. Where the Crown run into trouble is when they have to prove facts which are not self-evident, such as the fact that goods are stolen, and the so-called doctrine of recent possession is evidence of their difficulty and of the readiness of the law, having laid down a requirement of proof of actual knowledge, to set up a formula — the so-called doctrine of recent possession — which assists in meeting such a requirement.[86]

---

[84] [1976] A.C. 182.

[85] *cf. R. v. Sakhuja* [1973] A.C. 152. Where the criminal conduct consists of possession, it seems that the continuing nature of such conduct (see para. 3.50, *supra*) may suggest that "active knowledge" is required only at the outset of a period of possession, and this seems to be the law: see *Gill v. Lockhart*, 1988 S.L.T. 189, where cannabis resin was found by the police in the accused's golfbag some two years after he had placed it there. Although it had been accepted at the trial that the accused had forgotten he had put the drugs there, the Appeal Court ruled that knowledge continues as long as physical possession is maintained thereafter. This followed the reasoning in *R. v. Martindale* [1986] 1 W.L.R. 1042.

[86] See G.H. Gordon, "The Burden of Proof on the Accused," 1968 S.L.T. (News) 29, 40–43; B. Wootton, "The Changing Face of British Criminal Justice," in Morris and Perelman (ed.) *Law and Crime: Essays in Honour of Sir John Barry* (New York, 1972), 116.

It is, then, easy to prove the accused's knowledge of the self-evident. It might be thought equally easy to prove his knowledge of common-sense general principles such as that setting fire to a house is likely to damage it and injure its inhabitants. But this is so only in the "non-event" or dispositional sense of knowledge. If the accused is sane and sober he will agree on the properties of fire if he is asked; but it is much more difficult, if not indeed impossible in the absence of a confession, to prove that at a particular time he had before his mind the proposition, "Fire burns, damages and injures", together with the inference, "Therefore, if I set fire I shall probably cause damage and injury".

In order to hold that A acted intentionally, then, we point to the objective appearance of his behaviour and the self-evidence of the relevant circumstances, or to aspects of his behaviour from which we can infer his knowledge of other, less evident, circumstances, such as his care in applying the safety-catch of a loaded gun before he entered the car which was taking him to the bank and his releasing of it as he went into the bank, or the furtiveness with which he concealed his possession of the stolen bracelet. In order to hold that he acted with a particular intent, we shall point out that what he did was senseless unless he did have that intent. The latter is more difficult to prove than the former, because people do senseless things, but we are experienced in inferring intention from behaviour and the jury must just apply that experience. Provided there is some objective basis for their decision, some way of pointing to behaviour which indicates intention, their task is possible. And so long as the judge tells them simply to determine whether or not the accused acted intentionally or with a certain purpose, they will not be forced into determining the existence or non-existence at a specific time of a specific event in his mind.[87]

Intention, then, is subjective, but is proved objectively. Or at least this **7.28** is so in most cases. Since it is in the end subjective, the jury cannot be prevented from claiming intuitive knowledge of the accused's state of mind, or from believing his account of his state of mind against all the objective evidence. Or at least they should not be so prevented, if they are, as they are always said to be, the judges of fact. The law should not at one and the same time lay down a subjective criterion, and then require the jury to determine whether the criterion has been satisfied by reference solely to an objective standard, the standard of the reasonable man.[88] It has from time to time been said that a man is presumed to intend the natural consequences of his acts,[89] but in the first place this is

---

[87] English law has been much exercised in recent years with proof of intention to kill or do serious bodily injury for the purposes of murder. It is now clear that, where exceptionally it is necessary to give a jury a direction on the significance of intention, the defendant's foresight of the consequences of his actions can provide evidence from which the necessary intention may be found, provided the jury is sure that death or serious injury was a virtually certain result of those actions and the defendant appreciated that such was the case: see *R. v. Woollin* [1998] 3 W.L.R. 382, HL, esp. the opinion of Lord Steyn at 393B-C. This case modified the earlier test given in *R. v. Nedrick* [1986] 1 W.L.R. 1025 (by substituting 'find' for the word 'infer' relative to the necessary intent), but overruled the view expressed in *R. v. Walker* (1990) 90 Cr.App.R. 226, CA by Lloyd L.J. at 233 that "we are not persuaded that it is only where death is a virtual certainty that the jury can infer intention to kill". Prior attempts to lay down lesser degrees of certainty as sufficient to permit the inference of intention are no longer valid — see, *e.g.*, *R. v. Hyam* [1975] A.C. 55, HL, Lord Hailsham of Marylebone at 79B-C; *R. v. Moloney* [1985] A.C. 905, HL, Lord Bridge of Harwich at 929F-G.

[88] See *infra*, para. 7.54.

[89] *e.g.* Report of the Committee on Contempt of Court, Cmnd. 5794/1974, para. 68.

at most a presumption,[90] and in the second place it applies only if "natural" is read as meaning "blatantly highly probable": if this were not so, all crimes of intent would be reduced to crimes of negligence.[91]

There is, too, a value in insisting on the jury's privilege to prefer the accused's account to the evidence of his behaviour, although the criminal justice system might be in difficulties if juries were to exercise that privilege often. And that is its effect in maintaining the ordinary citizen's somewhat rash faith in the criminal trial as a way of getting at the facts, and, more importantly, his belief that if he were wrongly accused, he would be able to rely on a jury to realise that his protestations of innocence were true.

The vocabulary of Scots law

7.29 The terms used in Scots indictments before 1887 to indicate the *mens rea* of intentional crimes were "wickedly and feloniously", or "wilfully and maliciously", and in the case of fraud and similar crimes "falsely and fraudulently"; each of these terms is now implied "in every case in which according to the existing [*i.e.* pre-1887] law and practice its insertion would be necessary in order to make the indictment relevant".[92] There is, therefore, no longer any possibility of an objection being taken to the relevancy of a common law charge on the ground that it fails to libel any of these qualifications, or even that it fails to allege that an act was done "knowingly".[93] If the qualifications are not necessary to the guilt of the accused no objection can be taken to their absence; if they are necessary they are impliedly present.[94] As a result, there are no modern decisions on relevancy concerned with the pure question of the *mens rea* of any crime; the modern law must be derived from those charges to juries on the subject which are still extant, and from occasional appeals (or Lord Advocate's references) on the ground of misdirection.

7.30 *"Wickedly and feloniously".* This phrase, and also "wilfully and maliciously," were described by Lord McLaren in *Dingwall v. H.M. Advocate*[95] as "expletive expressions," and as having "in general . . . no particular meaning." This seems a little too harsh: Lord Young pointed out in the same case that "if the act was criminal or innocent, according as it was done, fraudulently or feloniously or not, then the allegation that it was done fraudulently or feloniously is no mere epithet",[96] and it is submitted that the same is true of the other qualifications.[97]

It is, however, almost impossible to give any precise legal meaning to "wickedly and feloniously". "Wickedly" is simply a term of moral disapprobation, and "felonious" which, despite its frequent use in

---

[90] *cf.* R.S. Tur, "Subjectivism and Objectivism: Towards Synthesis", in S. Shute, J. Gardner and J. Horder (eds.), *Action and Value in Criminal Law* (Oxford, 1993), p.213, at pp.228–231.

[91] See G.H. Gordon, *op.cit.,* 1968 S.L.T. (News) 29.

[92] Criminal Procedure (Scotland) Act 1887, s.8; 1995 Act, Sched.3, para. 3.

[93] *ibid.*

[94] See *H.M. Advocate v. Jas. Swan* (1888) 2 White 137.

[95] (1888) 2 White 27, 34. The actual decision in *Dingwall* was overruled in *Swan, supra.*

[96] *Dingwall, supra,* at 40–41.

[97] *cf. Roland Vance* (1849) J. Shaw 211, where a charge of culpable homicide bore that the killing had been done wickedly and feloniously. The court took the view that there had been culpable homicide but that the accused had not acted wickedly and feloniously, and accordingly directed the jury to acquit him.

Scotland from Hume onwards, is not a Scots term of art, means only "atrocious"[98] or "heinous". Lord Justice-Clerk Inglis observed in *Jas. Miller*[99] that "the settled meaning" of these words is "a quality of the act which is . . . charged; they express that which is essential to the constitution of the crime — a certain condition of mind on the part of the accused at the time of committing the act libelled."[1] But this does not tell us anything about that condition. The tautological nature of these words as they appear in indictments was recognised by Lord Inglis in the later case of *Elizabeth Edmiston*[2] when he said that:

> "Every crime is wicked and felonious, and the moment you arrive at the conclusion that the act charged against the prisoner is a crime, that of itself is sufficient proof of wicked and felonious intent. The words mean no more than that the act is criminal."[3]

"Wilfully and maliciously". This phrase has some more meaning. "Maliciously" is an ethical term which, strictly speaking, should have no legal meaning, unless in any special case its meaning of "spiteful" is important. It is just another word for "wickedly". But it does indicate the presence of "general *mens rea*".[4] It does not mean intentional. The offence of malicious mischief, for example, can be committed without any intention of doing injury; "it is enough if the damage is done by a person who shows a deliberate disregard of, or even indifference to, the property or possessory rights of others."[5] Reckless actions can be described as malicious if they exhibit wickedness of disposition. **7.31**

"Wilful" has a more precise meaning in Scots law, where it seems to be the word for "intentional", and means more than just "perverse" or "obstinate".[6] "Wilfully" in the Salmon Fisheries (Scotland) Act 1844 was interpreted as meaning "designedly and with a certain intent".[7] In a charge of wilfully making a false entry in a register contrary to the Registration of Births Act 1854, "wilfully" was said by Lord Justice-Clerk Moncreiff to mean "with the intention of doing the thing which is prohibited".[8] Lord Moncreiff went on to say, "As a general rule, where that which would not be in itself an offence is made a criminal act by the addition of the word *wilful*, the interpretation — the legal interpretation — of that term is, that it implies an intention to do the thing which was prohibited . . . You must be satisfied that he knew it was false, and intended to put in the register an entry which he knew was false." The meaning of "wilfully" in English criminal statutes is not free from difficulty,[9] and it has been used to include recklessness. In *Gollins v. Gollins*,[10] in discussing the meaning of "wilful" in an allegation of wilful constructive desertion, Lord Reid said of *Lang v. Lang*[11]:

---

[98] See N.E.D.

[99] (1862) 4 Irv. 238, 244.

[1] See also *Wilson v. Dykes* (1872) 2 Couper 183, L.J.-C. Moncreiff at 188–189.

[2] (1866) 5 Irv. 219, 222–223.

[3] See also *Peter Milne and John Barry* (1868) 1 Couper 28. "Wickedly and feloniously" are in effect only another way of saying "with what the law regards as sufficient *mens rea* to make the act criminal."

[4] *cf. supra*, para. 7.05.

[5] *Ward v. Robertson*, 1938 J.C. 32, L.J.-C. Aitchison at 36.

[6] See N.E.D.

[7] *Grant v. Wright* (1876) 3 Couper 282, Lord Young at 287.

[8] *Jas. Kinnison* (1870) 1 Couper 457, 461.

[9] *infra*, para. 8.18.

[10] [1964] A.C. 644, 666.

[11] [1955] A.C. 402.

"The man deliberately ill-treated his wife. He knew that this was likely to cause her to leave him but he desired or hoped that she would not leave. He did not act with the intention of driving her out, but he acted with the knowledge that that was what would probably happen. There are references to what a reasonable man would have known; but it is said that this man must have known, which I take to mean that it was proper to hold on the evidence that he did know. So in the result his desire to keep his wife or lack of intention to drive her out was irrelevant. The Act said nothing about intention: it used the word 'wilful.' So the decision was that if without just cause or excuse you persist in doing things which you know your wife will probably not tolerate, and which no ordinary woman would tolerate, and then she leaves, you have wilfully deserted her, whatever your desire or intention may have been."

There are some English cases which suggest that "wilfully" in a statutory offence is satisfied by an intention to do the thing prohibited even in ignorance of the circumstance which makes it forbidden, for example, by making an entry which is in fact false, although the accused did not know of its falsehood,[12] but, however that may be, Lord Moncreiff's interpretation of the term corresponds to its common law meaning. The old common law crime of wilful fire-raising, for example, is an intentional crime, distinguished from culpable and reckless fire-raising in that the former must be raised "wilfully, — with a purpose to destroy the thing to which it is applied" and not merely "*recklessly*, or from *misgovernance*."[13] For a person to commit wilful fire-raising, it has been said, he must "designedly and in cold blood, set fire . . . well knowing what he was about, and intending to do so."[14]

7.32 *"Wilful negligence"*. The requirements of design, intention, and knowledge, clearly set wilfulness apart from any form of negligence, however gross; wilfulness and negligence are categorically different. Yet in *Bastable v. North British Railway Co.*[15] this difference was ignored by four out of a court of five judges in the Court of Session who were considering the meaning of "wilful misconduct". Lord President Dunedin spoke of "that degree of negligence which comes under the description of wilful misconduct . . . the question is whether he is guilty of gross negligence which comes to be wilful misconduct."[16] But to regard gross negligence as equivalent to wilful misconduct is to use "negligence" in a most peculiar way. As Lord Johnston pointed out in his dissenting opinion, "In wilful misconduct . . . the will must be party to the misconduct. Negligence, even gross and culpable negligence, excludes the idea of will. Negligence done on purpose is a contradiction in terms."[17] To regard gross negligence as a sort of wilfulness is to use

---

[12] *Infra*, para. 8.18.

[13] Hume, i, 128. See *Byrne v. H.M. Advocate*, 2000 S.L.T. 233, a full bench decision which puts the matter beyond doubt.

[14] *Geo. Macbean* (1847) Ark. 262, L.J.-C. Hope at 263. It has been suggested in England that a man does not act wilfully and maliciously when he believes he is entitled to act as he does: *Younghusband v. Luftig* [1949] 2 K.B. 354. This is not so in Scotland so far as malicious mischief is concerned: *Clark v. Syme*, 1957 J.C. 1. It may be so in crimes of dishonesty, but in these cases the matter is better dealt with by way of the defences of claim of right or absence of fraudulent intent.

[15] 1912 S.C. 555.

[16] At 566.

[17] At 562.

"negligence" to mean "intention", and in that case "gross negligence" is no more a sort of negligence than a hot dog is a canine animal.[18]

"Deliberate carelessness". This is not to say that a person cannot be deliberately careless: but to produce a result by deliberate carelessness is not the same as to produce it intentionally. If A delberately enters a major road without stopping at the halt sign and collides with another car, his failure to halt is deliberate, and is a piece of deliberate carelessness since it involves a failure to take reasonable care quite apart from the offence involved in the act itself, but the collision with the other car is not intentional, but only reckless or negligent. **7.33**

"Wilful neglect". The matter is further confused by the associations of the phrase "wilful neglect". Neglect is not a form of negligence; to neglect to do something is simply to omit to do it, as is shown by sentences such as "He neglected to attend the meeting, because he preferred to go to the cinema instead". Neglect may be negligent or intentional: the man who neglects his children by deliberately keeping them short of food and clothing has neglected them wilfully; the man who keeps them short of food and clothing because he is too feckless to look after them properly has neglected them negligently, or so one would expect. But the offence of wilful neglect of a child in a manner likely to cause unnecessary suffering under the Children and Young Persons (Scotland) Act 1937, s. 12, is committed by neglect to seek medical attention or provide food and clothing, whether or not the accused was aware of the needs of the child or the risk involved in his neglect, provided that the failure itself was not inadvertent but intentional.[19] Wilfulness is required only to establish that there was in fact "neglect (or ill-treatment, abandonment, assault, etc.) which is wilful." But the neglect need not be "in a manner intended to cause," but only "in a manner likely to cause," suffering.[20] **7.34**

RECKLESSNESS

Carelessness

The criminal law is concerned with recklessness only when it involves objective carelessness. Recklessness, like negligence, becomes legally significant when joined to a careless act.[21] Sometimes the agent is **7.35**

---

[18] *cf.* J.W.C. Turner, "The Mental Element in Crimes at Common Law," in *Modern Approach*, 195, 208.

[19] *Clark v. H.M. Advocate*, 1968 J.C. 52, where the decision was reached following an interpretation of *R. v. Senior* [1899] 1 Q.B. 283 (see also *R. v. Lowe* [1973] Q.B. 702) declared wrong by the House of Lords in *R. v. Sheppard* [1981] A.C. 394. The current law in England is thus that 'wilful' in the context of wilful neglect means intentional or reckless (*cf.* the dissenting opinion of Lord Fraser in *Sheppard*). See also *R. v. Gittins* [1982] R.T.R. 363, where the ratio of *Sheppard* was applied to the Malicious Damage Act 1861, s.36. *Sheppard* was considered in the Scottish case of *H. v. Lees; D. v. Orr*, 1993 S.C.C.R. 900, but the case was concerned with the meaning of 'neglect' rather than 'wilful'. (*Cf.*, *Kennedy v. S.*, 1986 S.L.T. 679.).

[20] *Clark, supra*, L.J.-C. Grant at 56–7. The case is discussed in "Two Recent Scottish Decisions — I" (1970) 34 J.C.L. 192.

[21] See, *e.g.*, *Crowe v. H.M. Advocate*, 1989 S.C.C.R. 681, where, in a case involving the then statutory offence of causing death by reckless driving, the trial judge failed to direct the jury that they should establish objective carelessness prior to their consideration of recklessness.

referred to as careless; there is no accepted usage whereby "reckless" and "negligent" can be used only to describe people or mental states, and "careless" only used to describe actions. But it is sometimes convenient to distinguish between a careless act on the one hand, and a reckless or negligent agent on the other.[22] In a system which recognises subjective recklessness, the same careless act may be done either recklessly or negligently, depending on the mental state of the agent; but unless the act is careless the fact that it was done recklessly or negligently does not make it criminal.

7.36 *The standard of care.* The legal standard of care is usually set by reference to the "reasonable man"[23]; behaviour is careless when it falls short of the care which the reasonable man would exercise. There is some ground for saying that in modern times the criminal common law requires carelessness to be "gross" and that not every lapse from the standards of the reasonable man counts as carelessness,[24] but many of the reported cases deal with homicide where the rules regarding *mens rea* are very special and complicated. So far as other common law crimes are concerned, they probably do require something more than would suffice for the civil law, but that is because they are thought of as requiring recklessness, and recklessness in Scots law is often equated with gross negligence and therefore with gross carelessness.[25]

7.37 *Degrees of carelessness.* There are different degrees of carelessness, and different scales by which the degree of carelessness of any act can be measured. The simplest scale is constructed by reference to the number or importance of the precautions omitted. It is more careless for a motorist to turn his car to the right from a position on the extreme left of the road than merely to turn right from the proper position without giving a signal; and still more careless to turn without looking to see if the way is clear to do so; and it is more careless than any of these to turn right from the left of the road without giving a signal or seeing that the way is clear.

Carelessness can also be measured by reference to the magnitude ot the risk involved. Dropping a lighted match in an empty hut is not as careless as dropping it in a crowded cinema; playing with a gun is more careless in the presence of a child than in the presence of a dog. Another

---

[22] See A.R. White, "Carelessness, Indifference and Recklessness" (1961) 24 M.L.R. 592, (1962) 25 M.L.R. 437; P.J. Fitzgerald and Gl. Williams, "Carelessness, Indifference and Recklessness: Two Replies" (1962) 25 M.L.R. 49; D. Calligan, "Responsibility for Recklessness" (1978) 31 Curr. Leg. Problems 55; R.A. Duff, "Recklessness" [1980] Crim. L.R. 282.

[23] see *supra*, para. 4.18.

[24] *Paton v. H.M. Adv*ocate, 1936 J.C. 19. *Cf.* the trial judge's directions to the jury in *McDowall v. H.M. Advocate*, 1998 S.C.C.R. 343, at pp.344G-346D: this was a case of culpable homicide involving the driving of a motor vehicle in a culpable and reckless manner; the trial judge (at p.346D) simply referred to the accused's driving having to be sufficiently bad "as to meet the high test required for culpable homicide" — the *Paton* test was not mentioned at all.

[25] See, *e.g. H.M. Advocate v. Harris*, 1993 S.C.C.R. 559, Lord Prosser at 574E and 577E-F, where recklessness is equated with gross negligence for the purposes of culpable and reckless injury; and *Byrne v. H.M. Advocate*, 2000 S.L.T. 233, opinion of the court (of five judges) at 239 E, that "Mere negligence is not enough" for culpable and reckless fire-raising. See also *infra*, para. 7.54. The Model Penal Code requires a "gross deviation" from the standard of the law-abiding or reasonable person for recklessness and negligence respectively: O.D. s.2.02(2)(c) and (d).

important factor is the degree of the probability of the risk; it is more likely that a drunken motorist will cause damage than that a sober one will.

MINIMAL RISKS. Where the degree of risk involved is so slight, either in magnitude or in likelihood, that the reasonable man would disregard it, then disregard of it is not careless. This is so whether or not the particular agent foresaw or ought to have foreseen the risk. It has been held, for example, that the risk that a cricketer might injure someone by hitting a ball over the wall of a cricket ground on to the road was so slight that failure to guard against it was not negligent, even although balls had been knocked over the wall on earlier occasions.[26] **7.38**

EVERYDAY RISKS AND HAZARDOUS OCCUPATIONS. Most everyday pursuits involve some degree of risk. Statistically it may be said that driving a car involves a substantial risk of causing personal injury, and the same is true for example of work on oil rigs. But the law recognises that life must go on and that a certain degree of risk must be accepted as inevitable. Accordingly, it allows people to drive cars and work on oil rigs, and requires only that they take certain precautions to reduce the inherent risks. The law also recognises that people can be trained to take care, and permits people with the necessary skill to take substantial risks. Glanville Williams suggests that in cases of these two kinds the important factor is the "social utility" of the operation, and that what the law does is to balance this against the risks involved.[27] The "social utility" of any pursuit may, however, be very much a matter of dispute. Even those not sufficiently unprejudiced to doubt the social utility of cricket or rugby might be tempted to question whether, to take one of Professor Williams's examples, there is much social usefulness in the exhibition of skill involved in a music hall performer firing at a cigarette in his assistant's mouth. The music hall artiste is permitted to perform because the standard applied to him is not that of the average man but that of the average practitioner of his particular art. An untrained person who shot or threw a knife at someone else would be acting carelessly by the mere act of shooting or throwing at the victim, but the expert can do this without substantial risk because of his skill. If the expert does not exercise proper skill he is, of course, careless, and the standard required of him must be commensurate with the risk involved. **7.39**

It is for the legislature to decide whether any activity is sufficiently hazardous to merit complete prohibition, or to require specific regulation. The common law does not prohibit or regulate any otherwise lawful activity merely because it is dangerous, although it does make it a crime to behave in a way which endangers life.[28] The Road Traffic Acts are the best known example of statutory control of a dangerous everyday activity; in some cases, such as driving while unfit through drink or other

---

[26] *Bolton v. Stone* [1951] A.C. 850. *Cf. Carmarthenshire County Council v. Lewis* [1955] A.C. 549, Lord Reid at 565; *Muir v. Glasgow Corporation*, 1943 S.C.(H.L.) 3; *Blaikie v. British Transport Commission*, 1961 S.C. 44; *R. v. Caldwell* [1982] A.C. 341, HL, Lord Diplock, at p.354B-D.

[27] Gl. Williams, para. 26.

[28] See *H.M. Advocate v. Harris*, 1993 S.C.C.R. 559 (which also confirms that conduct which recklessly causes actual injury is equally criminal). For examples of behaviour which recklessly causes danger to life, see *Normand v. Robinson*, 1993 S.C.C.R. 1119; *Cameron v. Maguire*, 1999 S.C.C.R. 44; and, *MacPhail v. Clark*, 1982 S.C.C.R. 395,Sh.Ct.

disability, or while under age, or without passing a test of skill, the activity is regarded as so dangerous that it is prohibited, but so far as the healthy trained adult driver is concerned the law takes the view that if he observes the standard precautions the risks involved are of the kind which are necessarily attendant on modern life. If, however, road deaths and injuries were to increase greatly, there would be a valid argument for banning driving altogether. On the other hand, the fact that there is a near-certainty that certain socially useful activities, such as drilling for oil, will lead to a number of deaths does not mean that those who carry on these activities are guilty of culpable homicide, far less murder, as and when each death occurs. Their responsibility will be measured against the background of the relevant statutory regulations in relation to the particular circumstances of each death, and is likely to be limited to responsibility for any statutory offence that may have been committed by breach of a regulation.

7.40 CRIMINAL BEHAVIOUR. The Scots law of homicide provides for different standards of care according to whether the activity in the course of which death is caused is lawful or unlawful. This, however, is not the result of considering unlawful activities as involving a greater likelihood of death than lawful ones but of the application of the concept of general *mens rea.*[29]

7.41 JUSTIFIABLE RISKS. In addition to risks which are permitted because of their minimal nature, or which are accepted as part of life, there are risks which are permitted because they are regarded as justifiable on what is tantamount to the ground of necessity, because the risk is taken for the sake of a valuable benefit which there is a likelihood of producing. The classic example of such a risk is the case of a surgeon performing a dangerous operation. Macaulay restricts the class of justifiable risks to cases where the person who takes the risk does so for the sake of conferring a benefit and the victim consents to the risk.[30] There may, however, be cases where the consent of the victim is not necessary. A fireman may have to take risks in rescuing people, conscious or not, without asking their consent. The pilot of an aircraft which develops engine trouble may have to decide on a dangerous course of action without asking his passengers' consent, or that of the people over whose town he decides to fly or in whose streets he tries to land. The situation is like that in cases of necessity or compulsion even if, in the particular case, *e.g.* that of the surgeon, there is no actual compelling force. The risk is a "calculated" one, justified by reference to its social usefulness — because it is better to take it than to refrain from taking it. In such cases the agent must choose a course of action, and provided his choice is reasonable and he exercises due care and skill his behaviour will not be careless.

7.42 *Attendant circumstances.* So far carelessness has been discussed in relation to the results of an action, and this is its most common form. But a person can also be careless as to the existence of a particular fact which is an attendant circumstance of his behaviour. The "risk" in such a

---

[29] The application is itself tortuous in the extreme, and in many cases open to serious criticism: see Vol. II, Chap. 26.

[30] Macaulay, p.451.

case is not so much that a particular result will be produced, as that a particular state of affairs may exist. Carelessness in such cases involves a failure in a duty to know or a least to inquire into the existence of the fact in question. If the reasonable man would have made inquiry, then it is careless not to make inquiry, and it is equally careless to fail to take the steps a reasonable man would take in pursuing the inquiry. A superficial inquiry which fails to explore an obvious avenue of information involves carelessness as to the existence of the fact inquired into.

The duty to take care. Carelessness is legally relevant only where there is a duty to take care. So far as the criminal law is concerned carelessness as to consequences is relevant only when it leads to the creation of the *actus reus* of a "crime of carelessness" such as involuntary culpable homicide or reckless fire-raising. Carelessness as to attendant circumstances is relevant when it relates to an element of an *actus reus* the *mens rea* required in relation to which is either recklessness or negligence. **7.43**

THE RELATIVITY OF CARELESSNESS. Carelessness does not exist in the abstract but only in regard to a particular result or circumstance. A given act may be careless in regard to result *x* and not careless in regard to result *y*, and if *x* is not something in regard to which the law exacts a duty of care the carelessness is irrelevant. Normally the criminal law starts with a particular result and asks if it was caused carelessly. The result is usually something specific like the death of B, and in theory if A causes B's death while acting carelessly as regards the death of C but without any negligence towards B, he should not be convicted of negligently causing B's death. But some crimes are concerned with the creation of a general danger — it is a crime to endanger life carelessly even although no actual injury is caused — and in that situation the carelessness is judged in relation to the likelihood of causing any danger to life and not in relation to any particular person or any particular danger.[31] The ambit of carelessness is wider in some statutory crimes such as careless driving, but even there it is limited to behaviour which is careless with regard to the risk of accident and not, for example, of an uneconomically high consumption of petrol, or damage to one's own vehicle which is not such as to endanger others. **7.44**

Recklessness and negligence

A person who does something careless may do it either recklessly or negligently. (He may also, of course, do it with the deliberate intention of causing harm in which case his act can be dealt with as intentional.) In orthodox academic usage, recklessness and negligence are quite distinct: recklessness is advertent and involves foresight of the risk; negligence is inadvertent and involves an absence of such foresight.[32] Recklessness **7.45**

---

[31] Although in practice a prosecution would normally be brought only where some specific danger could be pointed out.

[32] See, *e.g.* A. Ashworth, *Principles of Criminal Law* (3rd ed., Oxford, 1999), pp.184–185, where the need for advertence in recklessness is based on "the principle of individual autonomy and the importance of respecting choice"; J.C. Smith & B. Hogan, *Criminal Law* (9th ed., by Prof. Sir John Smith, 1999), p.68; Joshua Dressler, *Understanding Criminal Law* (2nd ed., 1995), p.116; D.J. Callaghan, "Responsibility for Recklessness" (1978) 31 Curr. Legal Problems, 55: *cf.* J. Horder, "Two Histories and Four Hidden Principles of Mens Rea" (1997) 113 L.Q.R. 95; J.E. Stannard, "Subjectivism, Objectivism and the Draft Criminal Code" [1985] 101 L.Q.R. 540; R.S. Tur, "Subjectivism and Objectivism: Towards Synthesis" in S. Shute, J. Gardner & J. Horder (eds.), *Action and Value in Criminal Law* (Oxford, 1993), p.213.

which is defined so as to require actual foresight and acceptance of risk will be referred to as "subjective recklessness."

Scots criminal law does not appear to require subjective recklessness[33]; but such recklessness has been described as the "dominant" form in England,[34] and is the preferred approach of the Law Commission there.[35] Those States which have adopted the American Law Institute's Model Penal Code also subscribe to that interpretation of recklessness, since the Code narrates that a person acts recklessly with respect to a material element of an offense "when he consciously disregards a substantial and unjustified risk that the material element exists or will result from his conduct."[36] In so far as South African law's realisation of the concept of *mens rea* can be compared with that which pertains in the Anglo-American school of criminal law, it is noteworthy that *dolus eventualis* requires foresight of the possibility of a particular result ensuing from one's conduct.[37]

Recklessness is often said to involve indifference to the risk foreseen, and this indifference can be regarded as evidence of the accused's wickedness.[38] But indifference in the sense of "couldn't care less" is not essential to subjective recklessness. A man may be reckless even though he wishes fervently that the foreseen possibility will not become actual; so long as he knowingly takes the risk, he is reckless.[39] The driver in a hurry who goes through the traffic lights at red may hope and pray that the junction is clear, but he is acting recklessly in relation to the risk of colliding with a car crossing on the green.

7.46 THE GROSSNESS OF RECKLESSNESS. Prior to 1991, when there was a statutory offence of reckless driving,[40] a driver who deliberately ignored a halt sign or a red light knowing that there might well be traffic on the

---

[33] Subjective recklessness would obviously be sufficient if it could be shown to have existed, but it is very far from being necessary: see paras 7.58 to 7.62, *infra*.

[34] A. Ashworth, *Principles of Criminal Law* (3rd ed., Oxford, 1999), p.191. The subjective form of recklessness has been favoured by the English courts for at least the last 50 years (see, *e.g. R. v. Cunningham* [1957] 2 Q.B. 396) and it pervades the field of non-fatal offences against the person: see *R. v. Savage; R. v. Parmenter* [1992] 1 A.C. 699, HL. An objective form of recklessness is accepted in relation to s.1 of the Criminal Damage Act 1971 (see *R. v. Caldwell* [1982] A.C. 341, HL) while indifference is accepted as sufficient for recklessness in relation to the victim's consent in relevant sexual offences (see *R. v. Satnam* (1984) 78 Cr.App.R. 149,CA); it is also the case that recklessness in the type of manslaughter which involves breach of duty is taken to mean gross negligence (see *R. v. Adomako* [1995] 1 A.C. 171, HL — but these are all regarded as exceptions to the orthodox approach: *cf.* J.E. Stannard, "From Andrews to Seymour and Back Again" (1996) 47 N.I.L.Q. 1.

[35] See, *e.g.* L.C. No. 89 (1978), "Criminal Law: Report on the Mental Element in Crime", paras 60 and 65 (*cf.* "Report on the Mental Element in Crime" (1983) S.L.C. No. 80, para. 4.33); "A Criminal Code for England and Wales" (1989) L.C. No. 177, Vol. 1, Draft Code Bill, cl.18(c)(i) and (ii); Vol. 2, paras 8.18 to 8.20: see also "Offences Against the Person", Report 14 of the Criminal Law Revision Committee (1980), paras 11 and 12.

[36] O.D., s.2.02(2)(c).

[37] *Dolus eventualis* is a form of intention in South African law, under which the accused does not aim to create a particular result or have it as his object; instead he must foresee the possibility of its occurrence and accept the risk of its materialisation: it is that acceptance of the risk which is regarded as reckless in South African terms. See E.M. Burchell and P.M.A. Hunt, *South African Criminal Law and Procedure* (3rd ed., 1997), Vol. 1, *General Principles of Criminal Law* (by J.M. Burchell), at pp.225–239.

[38] *Cf.* Macdonald, p.89.

[39] *Cf.*, R.A. Duff, "Recklessness" [1980] Crim.L.R. 282.

[40] Reckless driving and causing death by reckless driving were carried over as offences from the Road Traffic Act 1972 (as amended by the Criminal Law Act 1977, s.50) to the

other road would have been reckless in the theoretical sense; but he would normally have been charged only with careless driving. This was because, rightly or wrongly, his behaviour was not regarded as exhibiting sufficiently gross carelessness to merit being treated as reckless. A man who goes through a halt sign at say 20 miles an hour is careless; one who goes through it at say 50 miles an hour might be treated as reckless. Briefly, one might describe the meaning of recklessness by saying that a driver who goes "too fast" is careless but one who goes "too damn fast" is reckless.[41] The element of "grossness" is more important in the Scots concept of recklessness than that of foresight. Foresight of a minor or frequently accepted risk does not turn negligence into recklessness, and the absence of foresight does not prevent gross caselessness being treated as recklessness.

RECKLESSNESS AND WICKEDNESS. Recklessness in Scots law may be at **7.47** basis a question of general *mens rea*, a sign of wickedness, and, if this is so, the grossness of the carelessness would be important as a pointer to the wickedness of the agent — a wickedness which might be revealed as much, if not more, by lack of foresight as by acceptance of risk. The modern case decisions do not, however, suggest that 'wickedness' is a necessary concomitant or indicator of recklessness — which is now viewed principally as a description of behaviour rather than an illustration of any wicked dispostion of the actor.[42]

"Conscious negligence." Some Continental legal systems have a third **7.48** category between recklessness and negligence, which is called "conscious negligence." A person is "consciously negligent" when he foresees the harm as possible, but does not believe it will occur. For example, the hunter who realises that he may kill a beater but thinks he is a good enough marksman to avoid this is consciously negligent if in fact he hits the beater.[43] So also is the seducer of a fifteen-year-old girl if, having considered the question of the girl's age, he comes wrongly to the conclusion that she is over sixteen.[44] This concept allows a distinction to be made between the man who realises that what he is doing is dangerous and does his best to avoid the danger by being as careful as he can while still doing what he wants to do, and the man who takes no steps at all to minimise the risk. A system which does not recognise "conscious negligence" will class the consciously negligent man as reckless since he foresees the risk, and will find it difficult to give him credit for any efforts he makes to avoid the danger.[45] The concept of

---

Road Traffic Act 1988; but both offences were replaced by offences of 'dangerousness' (as defined) under s.1 of the Road Traffic Act 1991 (which replaced the original text for ss.1 and 2 of the 1988 Act, and added a new definitional section, s.2A). The account of 'dangerousness' set out in s.2A of the 1988 Road Traffic Act reflects in part the objective way in which recklessness, relative to the former statutory offences, had been interpreted by the Scottish courts: see *Allan v. Patterson* 1980 J.C. 57, L.J.-G. Emslie at p.60.

[41] *cf.* Peter Brett, *An Inquiry into Criminal Guilt* (London, 1963), 95 *et seq.* where the author essays a philosophic defence of the concept of "gross recklessness."

[42] See paras 7.58, *et seq.*, *infra*.

[43] See E.M. Burchell & P.M.A. Hunt, *South African Criminal Law and Procedure* (3rd ed., 1997), vol. 1, *General Principles of Criminal Law* (by J.M. Burchell), pp.241–245; P. Logoz, "Pas de Peine sans Culpabilité" (1950) 2 J.Cr.Sc. 197, 202–203.

[44] H. Mannheim, "Mens rea in German and English Criminal Law" (1935) 17 J.Comp.Leg. and Int. Law 82, 91–93.

[45] It might, however, be able to take these efforts into account in some cases by holding that what was actually done was not careless because all possible precautions were taken.

conscious negligence is a very subtle one, and has proved very difficult to apply in practice[46]; it could hardly find a place in a system whose attitude to recklessness and negligence is as unsophisticated and unsystematic as is that of Scots law.

Subjective and objective recklessness

7.49 *The arguments in favour of subjective recklessness.* The adoption of subjective recklessness as a form of *mens rea* may be regarded as a compromise between a desire to limit criminal responsibility to purposeful behaviour, and a recognition that to do so would be impractical and result in unwanted acquittals. That this is so can be seen by the efforts made to call subjective recklessness intention, or to define intention so as to include states of subjective recklessness.[47] Where there is both foresight and acceptance of risk it may be said that A deliberately took the risk, or even that A intended to subject the victim to the risk,[48] and that in punishing subjective recklessness the law is punishing a form of intentional behaviour. Subjective recklessness may be said, at least where the probability of harm foreseen is required to be very high, to be little different from intention shorn of the element of desire. It has the advantage of limiting responsibility to situations where the accused acts out of deliberate choice in the knowledge that harm may well occur,[49] and where he is prepared or willing that it should occur.[50]

---

[46] H. Mannheim, *op.cit., loc. cit.*

[47] See, *e.g.*, L.C. No. 89 (1978), "Criminal Law: Report on the Mental Element in Crime", para. 44, where it was suggested that in all future legislation, intending a particular result should mean actually intending it or having no substantial doubt that one's conduct would have that result, which had (at the least) the disadvantage of defining intention in terms of itself. *Cf.* L.C. No. 177 (1989), "A Criminal Code for England and Wales", vol. 1, Draft Code Bill, cl. 18(b), where it is stated that a person acts "intentionally" with respect to "(ii) a result, when he acts either in order to bring it about or being aware that it will occur in the ordinary course of events." *Cf.* also L.C. No. 218 (1993), "Legislating the Criminal Code: Offences Against the Person and General Principles", Draft Bill, cl. 1 "A person acts — 'intentionally' with respect to a result when — (i) it is his purpose to cause it, or (ii) although it is not his purpose to cause it, he knows that it would occur in the ordinary course of events if he were to succeed in his purpose of causing some other result . . ." See also *R. v. Vallance* (1961) 108 C.L.R. 56. *Cf.* E.M. Burchell & P.M.A. Hunt, *South African Criminal Law and Procedure* (3rd ed., 1997), vol. 1, *General Principles of Criminal Law* (by J.M. Burchell), at p.223: "This form of intention [*dolus eventualis*] exists when the accused does not mean to bring about the unlawful circumstance or to cause the unlawful consequence which follows from his or her conduct, but foresees the possibility of the circumstance existing or the consequence ensuing and proceeds with his or her conduct."

[48] *R. v. Hyam* [1975] A.C. 55, Lord Hailsham of St. Marylebone L.C. at 77E. The English law on this matter is now to be found in *R. v. Woollin* [1998] 2 W.L.R. 382 (H.L.).

[49] See A. Ashworth, *Principles of Criminal Law* (3rd ed., Oxford 1999), pp.160 *et seq. Cf.* H.L.A.Hart, *Punishment and Responsibility* (Oxford, 1968) esp. Chaps. I and II.

[50] See L.C. No. 177 (1989), "A Criminal Code for England and Wales", vol. 1, Draft Code Bill, cl. 18(c), under which a person acts recklessly "with respect to (i) a circumstance when he is aware of a risk that it exists or will exist; (ii) a result when he is aware of a risk that it will occur; and it is, in all the circumstances known to him, unreasonable to take the risk . . ." *Cf.* Law Commission (L.C. No. 10), *Imputed Intent in Criminal Law: D.P.P. v. Smith* (H.M.S.O., 1967). *Cf.* also the Report of the Select Committee on Murder and Life Imprisonment, 1989, H.L. Paper 78, vol. III, para. 2024, where L.J.-G. Emslie gave evidence as follows: "The question for the jury is: 'Looking at the acts do you discover a mind as wicked and depraved as that of a deliberate killer?' It has got to be as near as no matter to the mind of a deliberate killer. I would certainly think in almost every case the classic definition of murder, which goes back to Hume, is given to a jury and judges may tend to add: 'What it comes to is this, if he did these terrible things you have heard about,

It must be said, however, that although reckless behaviour may resemble deliberate behaviour, it is not the same thing. One would not say that a person who deliberately took a risk caused the resultant harm purposefully.[51] It may be right to punish those who deliberately take risks but that is not, in terms of the subjective view itself, the same as punishing them for the resultant harm, far less punishing them in the same way as if it had been caused deliberately. Such an equivalence of punishment is easier to defend on an objective view of recklessness.

The difficulties of subjective recklessness. Subjective recklessness is a very difficult concept in practice. It rests on two basic assumptions: (a) that it is realistic to talk of proving that at a particular time a certain thought was going through the accused's mind; and (b) that there is a clear moral distinction between advertence and inadvertence. Both these assumptions are open to question. **7.50**

(a) There may well be cases of premeditated behaviour in which the agent consciously foresaw and deliberately accepted a risk. But they are few and atypical. And even they are not free from difficulty[52] — for one thing there is the question of the degree of risk involved.

In the ordinary murder case, however, where A assaults, inflicts grievous bodily harm on, and kills B, it is impossible to prove whether the necessary mental event of foreseeing took place, and very unlikely that it did take place.[53] Difficult as it is to prove intention, it is more difficult to prove actual foresight. The objective facts on which reliance is usually placed for proof of intention are the same as those on which reliance is placed for proof of recklessness. That is why it was said in *Cawthorne v. H.M. Advocate*[54] that recklessness was evidence of intention. If, then, *ex hypothesi*, intention is not proved, it is difficult to see how actual foresight can be proved. In practice the most that can be proved is not that A foresaw the result, but that "he must have foreseen, and in that sense did foresee."[55] And even this rests for its plausibility on an unspoken assumption that the agent thought about what he was doing — if he thought about it he must have foreseen. But how does one prove that he did think about it? It may well be that "a lack of confidence in the ability of a tribunal correctly to estimate evidence of states of mind and the like can never be sufficient ground for excluding from inquiry the most fundamental element in a rational and human criminal code,"[56]

---

are you satisfied on all the evidence that he did not care one way or t'other whether the victim lived or died? He did not even apply his mind to the question.' " (The High Court has subsequently distanced itself from the view that wicked recklessness conjures up a state of mind which is as wicked and depraved as that of a deliberate killer: see *Scott v. H.M. Advocate*, 1995 S.C.C.R. 760, L.J.-C. Ross at pp.764F-765C.)

[51] *cf.* Hall, pp.115–116.

[52] See *R. v. Hyam, supra.*

[53] See R. Cross, *op.cit., supra,* para. 7.13, n. 37.

[54] 1968 J.C. 32.

[55] *Pemble v. R.* (1971) 124 C.L.R. 107, Barwick C.J. at 120. See also *S. v. Grove-Mitchell.* 1975 (3) S.A. 417 (A.D.), Trollop J. at 422; *R. v. Parker* [1977] 1 W.L.R. 600. *Cf.* E.M. Burchell & P.M.A. Hunt, *South African Criminal Law and Procedure* (3rd ed., 1997), vol. 1, *General Principles of Criminal Law* (by J.M. Burchell), p.229: "The subjective test may be satisfied by inferential reasoning. That is to say, it can be reasoned that in particular circumstances the accused 'ought to have foreseen' the consequences and thus 'must have foreseen' and, therefore, by inference 'did foresee' them." This may be a step too far for many subjectivists; and indeed Burchell and Hunt go on to state (*ibid.*) that the South African courts "have warned against any tendency to draw the inference of subjective foresight too lightly."

[56] *Thomas v. R.* (1937) 59 C.L.R. 279, Dixon J. at 309.

but here we have a situation in which the precise mental event at issue is not only often unprovable, but in which its existence is, it is submitted, not fundamental.

At least one further difficulty is to determine what degree of risk has to be foreseen: it seems that in England it has to be something less than a virtual certainty, since 'virtual certainty' entitles a jury to 'find' intention for the purposes of murder[57] and perhaps no higher than 'any degree' of risk;[58] in South Africa, the courts do not seem to have decided conclusively whether foresight of a remote, as opposed to a real (or reasonable), possibility will suffice,[59]; while according to an Australian case possibility is not enough, there must be a probability.[60] If the degree required is high, it would have to be proved that the mental event on which responsibility is based included an appropriate calculation of the degree of risk, and this will be if anything more difficult to prove than the existence of advertence to some degree of risk.

7.51 (b) It may be doubted whether, accepting that someone who shot another, or beat him to death, or killed him by driving on in the knowledge that he was clinging to the bonnet, did not intend to kill the deceased, it matters that he did or did not actually foresee that what he was doing was likely to kill him. To be so callous as to give no thought to what one is doing in such a situation is arguably at least as bad as to foresee and accept the risk.[61] Yet the subjective solution requires that if the Crown cannot prove the occurrence of actual foresight the accused must be acquitted for lack of *mens rea*. The cynical might say that subjective recklessness is acceptabe only because juries will in fact make the necessary inference in the "right" cases, and because (at least in murder cases) even if they do not they will have to convict of manslaughter, and the judge will then do the right thing when it comes to sentence.[62]

The recklessness of the reasonable man

7.52 One way of approaching the problem of recklessness, and indeed of intention,[63] is to rely on the standard of the reasonable man. The phrase, "the accused must as a reasonable man have foreseen", is ambiguous,

---

[57] *R. v. Woollin* [1998] 3 W.L.R. 382, HL.

[58] See Andrew Ashworth, *Principles of Criminal Law* (3rd ed., Oxford 1999), p.184. The English Draft Code lays down that any degree of risk will be sufficient: L.C. No. 177, 1989, "A Criminal Code for England and Wales", Draft Code Bill, cl. 18(c).

[59] E.M. Burchell & P.M.A. Hunt, *South African Criminal Law and Procedure* (3rd ed., 1997), vol. 1, *General Principles of Criminal Law* (by J.M. Burchell), pp.231–232.

[60] *La Fontaine v. R.* (1977) 51 A.L.J.R. 145.

[61] See R.A. Duff, "Recklessness" [1980] Crim.L.R. 282, at pp.283–284, where it is argued that there is no dichotomy between a man's actions and his attitude to risk, and that "recklessness is a quality of a man's actions, not of some private world of attitudes and feelings: but he is reckless because his actions manifest a certain attitude" — namely, one of "practical indifference", *i.e.* "the indifference of one who is prepared to make himself the agent of a result, not because he wants it, but because he does not care about it". This does not, he argues, compel an objective rather than a subjective account of recklessness, since (at p.292), "the kind of practical attitude which is central to the notion of recklessness may be revealed in his failure to realise a risk as much as in his conscious risk taking."

[62] Problems arise only where the judge fails to give the jury the right direction: see *R. v. Wallett* [1968] 2 Q.B. 367, and indeed *D.P.P. v. Smith*, [1961] A.C. 290, itself in the Court of Appeal.

[63] *supra*, para. 7.26.

and its ambiguity can be exploited in order to apply an objective standard of recklessness while appearing to be applying a subjective one: this is done by confusing the use of the reasonable man as a test of the accused's credibility with his use as a standard of conduct.

The position of the reasonable man as a standard of carelessness has already been mentioned[64]; he is also important when one comes to ask if the accused in a given case acted recklessly. Recklessness, like intention, has normally to be discovered by reference to objective behaviour unless the accused's own evidence as to his state of mind is available and believed. And the courts are much more prepared to reject such evidence when recklessness is in issue than when it is a question of intention, even when they do not go so far as to treat recklessness as wholly objective. However much Scots law may equate recklessness and gross negligence, it seems still to regard itself as punishing a wicked state of mind when it punishes reckless conduct, but the measure of the wickedness is usually the degree of recklessness which in turn is the degree of objective carelessness.

Even in English law, where the approach to recklessness might accurately be described as 'not wholly subjective', the standard of the reasonable man has figured in the promotion of apparent injustice. Thus, the statutory offence of destroying or damaging another's property, being reckless as to whether it would be destroyed or damaged,[65] was considered by the House of Lords in *R. v. Caldwell*[66] to be committed not only where the defendant ignores a foreseen risk that his conduct will cause such damage or destruction, but also where he fails "to give any thought to whether or not there is any such risk in circumstances where, if any thought was given to the matter, it would be obvious that there was."[67] As Lord Diplock then proceeded to talk of the "ordinary prudent individual", and addressed himself to what might have alerted such individual's attention to the risk of the harmful consequences in question, it was readily assumed by later courts that the issue of recklessness was to be determined by use of the reasonable man as a standard.[68] It followed, therefore, that a fourteen year old girl of low intelligence, whose limited capacity for rational judgment was exacerbated by fatigue and cold, was to be convicted of recklessly causing criminal damage by fire since she had set a match (with the object of warming herself) to a quantity of flammable spirit poured by her onto

---

[64] *supra*, para. 7.36.

[65] Contrary to the Criminal Damage Act 1971, s.1.

[66] [1982] A.C. 341.

[67] *ibid.*, *per* Lord Diplock at 353H-354A.

[68] *cf.* Lord Diplock's remarks in *R. v. Shepherd* [1981] A.C. 394, at 404A-B: "The concept of the reasonable man as providing the standard by which the liability of real persons for their actual conduct is to be determined is a concept of civil law, particularly in relation to the tort of negligence; the obtrusion into criminal law of conformity with the notional conduct of the reasonable man as relevant to criminal liability, though not unknown (e.g., in relation to provocation sufficient to reduce murder to manslaughter), is exceptional, and should not lightly be extended: *Andews v. Director of Public Prosecutions* [1937] A.C. 576, 582–583. If failure to use the hypothetical powers of observation, ratiocination and foresight of consequences possessed by this admirable but purely notional exemplar is to constitute an ingredient of a criminal offence it must surely form part not of the actus reus but of the mens rea."

the floor of a garden shed.[69] It seems that the English courts were at first minded to extend the *Caldwell* test for recklessness, and thus the standard of the reasonable man, to some non-fatal offences against the person[70] until the Court of Appeal put an end to such expansion in *R. v. Spratt*.[71]

7.53 *The reasonable man as a test.* When the reasonable man is used as a test of subjective recklessness the position is that if the reasonable man would have foreseen the risk, it will be accepted as a fact that the accused foresaw it, unless there is strong evidence to the contrary. But if the accused can show that in fact he did not foresee the risk, then it is illogical to characterise him as reckless on the ground that a reasonable man would have foreseen it. As Hall says, "In the determination of these questions, the introduction of the 'reasonable man' is not a substitute for the defendant's awareness that his conduct increased the risk of harm any more than it is a substitute for the determination of intention, where that is material. It is a *method* used to determine those operative facts in the minds of normal persons."[72]

Since evidence of the accused's state of mind must normally consist of objective facts from which the jury will draw an inference as to his state of mind, the more careless the accused's behaviour the more likely it is that he will be regarded as reckless, since the more likely it will be that he foresaw the risk involved. A man who kills another by punching him on the jaw may be believed when he says that he did not foresee the risk of death; but a man who kills another by striking him on the skull with a hatchet will be hard put to it to persuade a jury that he did not realise that what he was doing might be fatal. In *Robertson and Donoghue*[73] Lord Justice-Clerk Cooper directed the jury that "In judging whether . . . reckless indifference is present you would take into account the nature of the violence used, the condition of the victim when it was used, and the circumstances under which the assault was committed."[74] All these are objective factors affecting the degree of the carelessness of what the accused did, viewed as something likely to cause death. The

---

[69] *Elliott v. C.* [1983] 1 W.L.R. 939. For discussion of the merits of the conviction in that case, see the contrasting views of J.E. Stannard, "Subjectivism, Objectivism and the Draft Criminal Code" [1985] 101 L.Q.R. 540, and S. Field and M. Lynn, "The capacity for recklessness" (1992) 12 L.S. 74. See also *R. v. Reid* [1992] 1 W.L.R. 793, HL, Lord Keith at p.796B and D-E, where it is opined that the Diplock formula in *Caldwell* may be modified if, *e.g.*, the defendant's capacity to appreciate risks had been adversely affected by some condition which was not compatible with fault on his part: *cf.* Lord Ackner's opinion, at 805C.

[70] See, *e.g. D.P.P. v. K* [1990] 1 W.L.R. 1007.

[71] [1990] 1 W.L.R. 1073. This decision effectively overruled *D.P.P. v. K., supra*, and probably continues to represent the law on the point, notwithstanding that *Spratt* was itself overruled on another more particular point by the House of Lords in *R. v. Savage; D.P.P. v. Parmenter* [1992] 1 A.C. 619.

[72] Hall, p.120. *Cf.* Gl. Williams, p.55. For an example of the use of the reasonable man as a test only see *S. v. Mini*, 1963 (3) S.A. 188 (A.D.) where the South African court altered a conviction of murder to one of culpable homicide where the reasonable man would have known that death might result from the accused's conduct — assault with a knife — but the court was not convinced that the accused "an ignorant Bantu", must have known it.

[73] High Court at Edinburgh, Aug. 1945, unrep'd. This case contains directions on a number of fundamental questions of criminal law; Lord Cooper's charge to the jury appears in C.H.W. Gane and C.N. Stoddart, *A Casebook on Scottish Criminal Law* (2nd ed., Edinburgh, 1988) at pp.182 and 496.

[74] Transcript of Judge's Charge, 21; Gane and Stoddart, *op.cit.*, at pp.496–497.

jury proceed by way of syllogism to infer from these objective factors that the accused was subjectively reckless, and the major premise is that a reasonable man would have foreseen the risk. So they argue: all reasonable men would foresee the risk of death as a result of what the accused did; the accused is (*ex hypothesi*) a reasonable man; therefore the accused foresaw the risk.

The reasonable man as a standard. There is, however, a temptation to decide *a priori* that if it ever becomes necessary to balance an accused's statement against the inference drawn from objective factors by the test of the reasonable man the result of the test will always be preferred. To take up this attitude is to use the reasonable man as a standard and not as a test, and is tantamount to saying that whether or not a particular accused is believed when he says his mental state was not what the mental state of the reasonable man would have been, he is nonetheless to be treated as if his mental state had been the same as that of the reasonable man. Whether or not the accused foresaw the risk he is regarded as (subjectively) reckless because the reasonable man would have foreseen it: the accused is therefore deemed to have foreseen it. **7.54**

This use of the reasonable man elides the necessity of any decision about the accused's state of mind; it makes the accused's statements about his state of mind not merely incredible, but irrelevant. As a result, either the law retains its subjective terminology but nullifies it by an irrebuttable presumption that the accused possessed the state of mind of the reasonable man; or it abandons subjective recklessness and defines the necessary state of mind as the state of mind which the reasonable man should have had, or alternatively proclaims that he who fails to acquire and act on the mental state and judgments of the reasonable man is guilty of *e.g.* murder because of that failure. Scots terminology vacillates among these possibilities, and between these and an outright acceptance of a substantive rule of law which ascribes guilt to the accused's wickedness without reference to any specific foresight, and applies the term "reckless" to that wickedness. Certainly in murder cases, Judges talk of a man using "reckless violence" and not of a man "using violence recklessly",[75] and emphasis is laid on the likelihood of violence causing death rather than on the accused's foresight of death.[76] Macdonald defines murder as being "constituted by any wilful act . . . whether intended to kill or displaying such wicked recklessness as to imply a disposition depraved enough to be regardless of consequences".[77] There is a difference between adopting openly a substantive standard of wickedness, and applying a reasonable man standard. For one thing the wickedness in question is that of the accused and not that of the reasonable man. What Barwick C.J. said in *Pemble v. The Queen*,[78] to the effect that the jury:

> "need also to be reminded that the accused's circumstances are relevant to the decision as to his state of mind, for example his age

---

[75] *H.M. Advocate v. Fraser and Rollins*, 1920 J.C. 60, Lord Sands at 63.

[76] See R.C. Evid. of Lord Keith, Q. 5130 where he talks of "violence that [*might*] be contemplated as likely to result in death".

[77] Macdonald, p.89. It does not seem to be yet settled whether this definition precludes the acceptability of any other form of *mens rea* for murder: see *Coleman v. H.M. Advocate*, 1999 S.C.C.R. 87.

[78] (1971) 124 C.L.R. 107, 120.

> and background, educational and social, his current emotional state and his state of sobriety. They should be expressly told that they need to be satisfied beyond any reasonable doubt that he must have foreseen, and in that sense did foresee, the consequences of the act he contemplated,"

can be applied to the jury's determination of whether the accused's failure to foresee displayed wicked recklessness. For another, the use of the reasonable man as a standard runs the risk of treating recklessness as just gross negligence, as indeed is virtually the case in modern Scots criminal law except in relation to murder. If the reasonable man is a standard, anyone who does something careless can be said to be acting recklessly, since in doing what is careless he is taking a risk the reasonable man would have foreseen and tried to avoid, and so must be treated as if he himself had foreseen the risk. That being so, the only distinction which can be made between recklessness and negligence is one of degree: where the act is very careless the agent is called reckless, where it is not so careless he is called negligent. Thus, phrases like "culpable, reckless and negligent" are not self-contradictory, but only examples of legal tautology, or at most of a *diminuendo*.

7.55 Another approach is to say that A is reckless when he either had or ought to have had foresight of the risk. The phrase "knew or ought to have known" is familiar in cases of civil reparation as referring to two equivalent states of mind, and the same equation has been made in the case of criminal recklessness.[79] In *Ward v. Robertson*[80] the appellant was charged with maliciously damaging crops in a field in which he had trespassed, and claimed in his defence that he did not think he was doing any harm. He was convicted in the lower court but on appeal to the High Court the conviction was quashed. Lord Pitman took the simple view that "A person who thinks he is doing no harm cannot rightly be convicted of doing something maliciously,"[81] but Lord Justice-Clerk Aitchison expressed himself in terms which are at once more sophisticated and more confused, in that they reveal the ever present danger of slipping almost imperceptibly from the use of the reasonable man as a test to his use as a standard. Lord Aitchison said:

> "If this had been a case of a person crossing over an ordinary growing crop, I should have taken the view that the magistrate was entitled to infer that the appellant must have had knowledge that what he was doing was something that was calculated to cause damage . . . The whole difficulty here is to say that the appellant had knowledge, or should have had knowledge, that by crossing this field he was doing, or was even likely to do, any damage".[82]

So his Lordship slips from a requirement of actual knowledge of a high degree of likelihood of harm to failure in a duty to know of what sounds like a lesser degree of likelihood, without any apparent concern at the

---

[79] The South African courts have rejected the equation — see *R. v. Bergstedt,* 1955 (4) S.A. 186 (A.D.), *R. v. K.*, 1956 (3) S.A. 353 (A.D.) — although foresight and recklessness are regarded as separable issues under *dolus eventualis* there: see E.M. Burchell & P.M.A. Hunt, *South African Criminal Law and Procedure* (3rd ed., 1997), Vol. 1, *General Principles of Criminal Law* (by J.M. Burchell), pp.228–239.

[80] 1938 J.C. 32.

[81] At 39.

[82] At 36.

equation of a state of knowledge with a state of ignorance. When the civil law equates "knew or ought to have known" it does so in a situation where negligence is all that has to be proved; but in a case like *Ward v. Robertson*[82a] the criminal law does so where it is accepted that negligence is insufficient, and where what is sought to be done is to make a man liable for a crime which usually requires an intention to cause damage.[83]

The "principle of disfacilitation"

The use of the reasonable man as a standard, with the consequent refusal to accept any account the accused gives of his mental state which conflicts with that standard, is not uncommon in the criminal law. It is seen most clearly in the law of provocation. The basis of the plea of provocation is that a man who kills because he has been goaded into losing self-control should not be punished as severely as someone who kills in cold blood. Accordingly, killing under provocation is not murder but only culpable homicide. In order to operate to reduce the charge from murder to culpable homicide, however, the "goading" must be such that it would have caused a reasonable man to lose self-control, and since the reasonable man is a universal and objective concept the law has been able to lay down the types of "goading" which are sufficient to support a plea of provocation. Any accused who loses self-control in circumstances other than those laid down by the law as sufficient to affect the reasonable man is not entitled to the benefit of the plea of provocation. The use of the reasonable man as a standard is clear in provocation because lawyers are prepared to admit that there may be cases in which it is true that the accused lost control because of the "provocation" offered, but where he must nonetheless be treated as if he had not lost control, because he has failed to measure up to the standard of control set by the reasonable man.[84] **7.56**

Where the question is whether the accused was reckless or negligent, the result of this approach is that an accused who fails to foresee what the reasonable man would have foreseen is treated as if he had foreseen it. The practical difficulties here are not so acute as in provocation nor are the results so unjust, because recklessness is normally alleged only where the carelessness is so gross that it is highly unlikely that the accused did not foresee the risk, but this in itself merely increases the danger of confusing an actual state of mind with an imputed one.

It is proposed to give the name "principle of disfacilitation" to the "rule" that where an accused's account of his mental state conflicts with

---

[82a] 1938 J.C. 32.

[83] And which Lord Aitchison conceded Hume thought of as always requiring such an intention: *Ward v. Robertson, supra,* at 36.

[84] *cf.* English law, which adjusted the rules (see the Homicide Act 1957, s.3) such that the reasonable man was to be treated as a person having the same sex and age as the defendant and who shared some, but not all, of the defendant's characteristics: see *R. v. Morhall* [1996] 1 A.C. 90, HL; *D.P.P. v. Camplin* [1978] A.C. 705, HL, which overruled the former rigid approach shown in *Bedder v. D.P.P.* [1954] 1 W.L.R. 1119. The House of Lords, however, has recently decided by a narrow majority that all of the defendant's characteristics are to be taken into account in determining whether his degree of self-control was that which would have been exercised by reasonable people, the true issue being one of whether his loss of control was a sufficient excuse to reduce the gravity of the offence from murder to manslaughter rather than one of whether particular characteristics of the defendant might meaningfully be assigned to a "reasonable man": see *R. v. Smith (Morgan)* [2000] 3 W.L.R. 654. Scots law has not followed such developments. The law of provocation is discussed in Vol. II, Chap. 25.

the standard of the reasonable man the accused's account is to be disregarded. The result of the application of this principle is that where the accused is telling the truth, and where the true facts should logically operate to acquit him or should at least operate in mitigation, they will not be allowed to do so. For example, where the truth is that the accused was goaded into loss of self-control and so ought to be regarded as having acted under provocation he will not succeed in a plea of provocation if the reasonable man would not have been provoked by what was done. The basis of the principle is the deterrent purpose of the law. The criminal law is designed to protect society from crime by punishing criminals, and it assumes that the deterrent effect of such punishment is significant. It must therefore discourage the acceptance of easy excuses, and restrict the scope of such exculpatory or mitigatory pleas as it does recognise. Again, it is important to warn juries against too ready acceptance of the accused's glib statements about his state of mind, especially where those statements conflict with what one would expect the state of mind of a reasonable man to have been.

So far the principle is unobjectionable, but where it operates to bar the jury from accepting the accused's story even when they are convinced of his credibility and have given proper weight to the objective probabilities it ceases to be so. It seems self-evident that it is objectionable to say that recklessness involves foresight but that a man who does not have such foresight will nevertheless be regarded as reckless because a legal fiction like the reasonable man would have foreseen the risk in question. This attitude is adopted partly because of the fear that if a jury is allowed to believe a particular accused who is telling the truth that may lead to other juries believing other accused persons who may not be telling the truth, and that if that happens accused persons may "get away with murder" by telling an appropriate story.

The term "disfacilitation" has been adopted because when judges direct juries to reject the accused's statements they often preface their direction with phrases like "It would be too easy for criminals if," or "It would be a very convenient place for criminals if ", an accused could commit a crime and then get away with it just by coming into court and saying that he was provoked, or mistaken, or intoxicated,[85] or did not mean it, or did not realise the danger of what he was doing.[86] Used in this way the principle of disfacilitation is an example of the principle of the thin end of the wedge, which has been described as the principle that "you should not act justly now for fear of raising expectations that you may act still more justly in the future — expectations which you are afraid you will not have the courage to satisfy."[87]

In applying the principle of disfacilitation the courts confuse adjective and substantive law. On the other hand it is unrealistic to divorce

---

[85] Fear of frequent jury acquittals if acute intoxication were to be generally recognised in law as negating an inference of *mens rea* has been discussed, and rejected as over-exaggerated by courts in both Australia (*The Queen v. O'Connor* (1980) 54 A.L.J.R. 349) and Canada (*Daviault v. The Queen* [1994] 3 S.C.R. 63). In both jurisdictions, the view has been taken that principle must be ranked above matters of policy. State and Federal legislatures in Australia and Canada have not necessarily agreed with the courts, however: for an admirable survey of the current position, see S. Gough, "Surviving without Majewski" [2000] Crim.L.R. 719.

[86] *cf. Dewar v. H.M. Advocate,* 1945 J.C. 5, L.J.-C. Cooper at 9; *Robertson and Donoghue*, High Court at Edinburgh, Aug. 1945, unrep'd, Transcript of judge's charge, 17–18; *Russell v. H.M. Advocate,* 1946 J.C. 37; R.C. Evid. of Lord Cooper, Q. 5418.

[87] F. Cornford, "Microcosmographia Academica," 15, quoted by A.L. Goodheart in "Shock Cases and Area of Risk" (1953) 16 M.L.R. 14.

substantive rules entirely from considerations of proof. There are a number of options open. If a fact is difficult to prove the law can decide that it is nonetheless so central that there should be no conviction except where it can be proved, or conversely that convictions are so necessary that proof of the fact should be dispensed with: it can then decide whether or not the accused should be allowed to disprove the fact in question. Alternatively, and this is probably the Scots approach to recklessness, it can decide that the fact is irrelevant anyway, and that what really matters is something different, such as behaviour which is grossly negligent in relation to particular consequences or dangers, or a grossly negligent failure to advert to the existence of a crucial fact or circumstance. What is objectionable is for the law to talk as if the fact were essential, and then to obviate the need to prove it by reference to the reasonable man.

Conclusion

If, then, it is objectionable to use the reasonable man as a standard to determine foresight, and unrealistic to adopt subjective recklessness, what is the answer? The answer may lie in a recognition that what is involved is indeed a question of substantive law. Reckless conduct is not, as it has sometimes been said to be, conduct from which intention can be inferred,[88] but neither is it conduct from which foresight and acceptance of risk can be inferred. It is conduct which can be described as reckless behaviour, by analogy with conduct which can be described as intentional. It may be that the best solution is to recast the criminal law so that *e.g.* there is an offence of inflicting serious injury which results in death, as indeed is virtually the case under the Road Traffic Act[89]; a partial solution might be to abolish the distinction between murder and culpable homicide.[90] **7.57**

Short of such radical measures, however, it was suggested in an earlier edition of this book[91] that Scots law could achieve some kind of solution by concentrating on the idea[92] that *mens rea* requires wickedness. The Crown would then have to prove, not that the reasonable man would have foreseen some risk, but that the accused's behaviour showed "a disposition depraved enough to be regardless of consequences",[93] or wicked enough to be deserving of conviction. Such wickedness could, of course, be evidenced by the existence of subjective recklessness where this could be established, but it might be proved without such subjective recklessness. There would need to be an inquiry into what circumstances were known to the accused, *e.g.* whether or not he knew the gun was loaded or that the cliff over which he pushed the deceased was a sheer 200 feet drop on to sharp rocks: such an inquiry would admittedly be a difficult one, but it would be inescapable. As Holmes said, "There must be actual present knowledge of the present facts which make an act dangerous",[94] and subject to what has been said above[95] about

---

88 *Cawthorne v. H.M. Advocate,* 1968 J.C. 32, Lord Guthrie at 37.

89 Road Traffic Act 1988, s.1 (see also s.2A), as substituted/added by the Road Traffic Act 1991, s.1.

90 See *R. v. Hyam* [1975] A.C. 55, Lord Kilbrandon at 98.

91 2nd. ed. (1978), para. 7.57.

92 See *supra*, para. 7.05.

93 *cf.* Macdonald, p.89.

94 Howe (ed.)*The Common Law* (London and Melbourne, 1968) p.45.

95 see paras 7.27 *et seq.*

knowledge, this is necessarily so in any crime which cannot be committed negligently. But the accused's knowledge of the laws of nature, such as that a shot from a loaded gun or a fall from such a cliff is likely to be fatal, would be assumed. To quote Holmes again: "If the known present state of things is such that the act done will very certainly cause death, and the probability is a matter of common knowledge, one who does the act, knowing the present state of things, is guilty of murder, and the law will not inquire whether he did actually foresee the consequences or not."[96]

Recklessness under such a system would not exist except in very bad cases,[97] which is probably one of the reasons[98] why there is little to indicate that Scots law has considered adopting such an approach; but, under the suggested approach, the law would be able to express the severe public disapproval of such cases without deeming the accused to have foreseen what he cannot be proved to have foreseen and probably did not foresee. And it would be seen to be determining the moral guilt of the agent himself, which is in line with the place traditionally[99] given to "evil intent" in Scots law.

Recklessness under Scots law

7.58 *Scope of recklessness.* There is no general rule in Scots law that recklessness is always a sufficient form of *mens rea* for any common law crime.[1] Assault, for example, cannot be committed other than intentionally,[2] and the same applies to wilful fire-raising.[3] One can be certain, therefore, that recklessness is definitely sufficient only where a crime has been recognised by the courts or the authoritative writers as one which answers to that form of *mens rea*. Offences such as culpable and reckless conduct causing injury or danger to others,[4] and culpable and reckless

---

[96] *op. cit., loc. cit.*

[97] Or unless there was subjective foresight, but even then the moral thrust of the law would require the risk to be very great, or the decision to take it one which in the circumstances exhibited gross depravity.

[98] Another may be the opportunity afforded for confusion with the special *mens rea* required for involuntary murder: see para. 7.60, *infra*.

[99] *cf., e.g. Lord Advocate's Reference (No.2 of 1992)*, 1992 S.C.C.R. 960; *H.M. Advocate v. Harris*, 1993 S.C.C.R. 559.

[1] *cf.* "A Criminal Code for England and Wales", (1989) L.C. No. 177, Vol. 1, Draft Code Bill, cl.20(1): "Every offence requires a fault element of recklessness with respect to each of its elements other than fault elements, unless otherwise provided." See also cl.19(2): "A requirement of recklessness is satisfied by knowledge or intention."

[2] *Lord Advocate's Reference (No. 2 of 1992)* 1992 S.C.C.R. 960, L.J.-C. Ross at 965D, Lord Sutherland at 969F. See also *H.M. Advocate v. Harris*, 1993 S.C.C.R. 559. English law takes the opposite view: *R. v. Venna* [1976] Q.B. 421.

[3] *Byrne v. H.M. Advovate*, 2000 S.L.T. 233 (Court of five judges). It may also be the case that 'indecent exposure' is satisfied only by intent — or at least that seems to have been assumed in the relatively modern cases of *McDonald v. Cardle*, 1985 S.C.C.R. 195, and *Niven v. Tudhope*, 1982 S.C.C.R. 365: alternatively, the need for 'awareness of the risk of exposure' or subjective recklessness may explain these decisions.

[4] Where reckless injury is charged, the injury may require to be significant: see *H.M. Advocate v. Harris*, 1993 S.C.C.R. 559, Lord Murray at 566B-C; *cf.* Lord Morison at 571F-G; and it may be that slight injury is insufficient to demonstrate the high level of culpability required: *cf. Quinn v. Cunningham*, 1956 S.L.T. 55. For examples of culpable and reckless conduct causing danger to others, see *MacPhail v. Clark*, 1982 S.C.C.R. 395; *Gizzi v. Tudhope*, 1982 S.C.C.R. 492; *Khaliq v. H.M. Advocate*, 1983 S.C.C.R. 483; *Ulhaq v. H.M. Advocate*, 1990 S.C.C.R. 593; *Normand v. Robinson*, 1993 S.C.C.R. 1119; *Cameron v. Maguire*, 1999 S.C.C.R. 44: and for examples involving injury, see *W. v. H.M. Advocate*, 1982 S.C.C.R. 152; *Kimmins v. Normand*, 1993 S.C.C.R. 476; *H.M. Advocate v. Harris*, 1993 S.C.C.R. 559.

fire-raising[5] speak for themselves; some offences, such as malicious mischief may be satisfied either by intention or by recklessness;[6] culpable homicide may certainly be committed recklessly[7] as well as in other ways[8]; but involuntary murder requires the rather special type of *mens rea* known as "wicked recklessness", which is referred to in classic form in the following passage from *Macdonald*: "Murder is constituted by any wilful act causing the destruction of life, whether intended to kill, *or displaying such wicked recklessness as to imply a disposition depraved enough to be regardless of consequences*".[9] What recklessness may mean in Scots criminal law, and what relationship it bears to the 'wicked recklessness' referred to in involuntary murder, will be considered in the following paragraphs.[10] It is fairly clear, however, that outside murder the law draws upon terminology from a common pool in order to give content to the concept of recklessness, irrespective of whether the crime in question is of common law or statutory origin[11]; and it is also clear that the complex, varied and subjective interpretations of that concept in English law[12] have so far been resisted by Scottish courts.[13]

Recklessness in culpable homicide. Culpable homicide can be committed where death is causally related to lawful or unlawful conduct, but 7.59

[5] See *Byrne v. H.M. Advocate*, 2000 S.L.T. 233 (Court of 5 judges).

[6] See *Ward v. Robertson*, 1938 S.L.T. 165. It has recently been decided that shameless indecency in the form of indecent exposure may be committed by deliberate conduct undertaken with reckless indifference as to whether others may observe that conduct: see *Usai v. Russell*, 2000 S.C.C.R. 57, opinion of the court at 64E. The decision followed upon a concession by the appellant that shameless indecency in general was satisfied by reckless indifference.

[7] See *H.M. Advocate v. Pearson*, 1967 S.C.C.R. (Supp.) 20, Lord Cameron (direction to jury) at 21; *McDowall v. H.M. Advocate*, 1998 S.C.C.R. 343.

[8] See Vol. II, Chaps 25 and 26.

[9] Macdonald, at p.89 (emphasis added). Whether there is any additional form of *mens rea* for murder remains unclear: see *Coleman v. H.M. Advocate*, 1999 S.C.C.R. 87, and Vol. II, Chap. 23.

[10] See paras 7.59 to 7.68, *infra*.

[11] See, *e.g.* the interpretation of 'recklessly' in the (then) statutory offence of reckless driving in *Allan v. Patterson*, 1980 J.C. 57, at 60, which was applied to the common law offence of recklessly discharging firearms to the danger of others in *Gizzi v. Tudhope*, 1982 S.C.C.R. 492, as also to culpable homicide in *Sutherland v. H.M. Advocate*, 1994 S.C.C.R. 80. It has also been applied to other statutory offences involving recklessness, including vandalism, contrary to s.78 of the Criminal Justice (Scotland) Act 1980 (now s.52 of the Criminal Law (Consolidation) (Scotland) Act 1995), see *Black v. Allan*, 1985 S.C.C.R. 11, and maliciously causing an explosion likely to endanger life or cause serious injury to property, contrary to s.2 of the Explosive Substances Act 1883), see *McIntosh v. H.M. Advocate*, 1993 S.C.C.R. 464. In recent years, the High Court has emphasised that an account of recklessness conceived for driving offences is not necessarily appropriate for common law offences of a very different nature — see *Cameron v. Maguire*, 1999 S.C.C.R. 44 (reckless discharge of firearms to the danger of others), and *Carr v. H.M. Advocate*, 1994 S.C.C.R. 521 (culpable and reckless fire-raising); but the terms used to denote, and probably the core conception of, recklessness have nevertheless remained fairly constant.

[12] See para. 7.45, n.34, *supra*.

[13] See *Allan v. Patterson*, 1980 J.C. 57, L.J.-G. Emslie at 60 (noting that this case predated the House of Lords decision in *R. v. Lawrence* [1982] A.C. 510); *McIntosh v. H.M. Advocate*, 1993 S.C.C.R. 464, where the English approach is clearly frowned upon, although it was not necessary at the end of the day to reach a concluded view on the matter. *Cf.* the virtual incorporation of the English definition of rape as a result of the Scottish cases of *Meek v. H.M. Advocate*, 1983 S.C.C.R. 476, and *Jamieson v. H.M. Advocate*, 1994 S.C.C.R. 181: see para. 7.62, *infra*.

is not the intended result of such conduct.[14] The present concern is with 'lawful act' culpable homicide, since where (for example)[15] a person assaults another in some minor way which nevertheless results in death, the *mens rea* for culpable homicide is the *mens rea* for assault, and the resultant death need not have been a reasonably foreseeable consequence of that assault.[16] With respect to lawful conduct (such as is involved in the operation of machinery or the carrying out of a medical procedure) which results in death, however, culpable homicide will be committed only if the accused's acts were 'recklessly' performed.[17] At one time mere negligent performance was sufficient: but in *Paton v. H.M. Advocate*,[18] Lord Justice-Clerk Aitchison stated: "Unfortunately, this law has to some extent been modified by decisions of the Court, and it is now necessary to show gross, or wicked, or criminal negligence, something amounting, or at any rate analagous, to a criminal indifference to consequences, before a jury can find culpable homicide proved."[19] This postulated a very high standard of culpability, particularly by virtue of its reference to 'criminal indifference to consequences' which suggests that an actual awareness of the risk of death may be required. As English authors have stated: "It is difficult to understand how a man can be indifferent to something the possibility of which he has not envisaged."[20] On the other hand, what is required in *Paton* need only be 'analagous' to such indifference, which suggests perhaps that something which is as 'wicked' or morally reprehensible as indifference will suffice. The *Paton* formula also, however, appears to substitute gross negligence for recklessness — which might suggest a purely objective approach to the matter:[21] while the general use of the qualifying epithet 'wicked' supports an approach in terms of general *mens rea*.[22] The test proffered in *Paton* is, therefore, somewhat vague and confusing; and it is notable that in the more recent but not dissimilar case of *McDowall v. H.M. Advocate*,[23] Lord Justice-General Rodger gives an account of recklessness in culpable homicide which ignores *Paton* and

---

[14] See Vol. II, Chap. 26.

[15] Assault is the most likely and most easily justifiable form of relevant 'unlawful act'; but other crimes such as theft and fire-raising may also fulfil the requirements for this type of culpable homicide: see *Mathieson v. H.M. Advocate*, 1981 S.C.C.R. 196; *Lourie v. H.M. Advocate*, 1988 S.C.C.R. 634; *Sutherland v. H.M. Advocate*, 1994 S.C.C.R. 80, none of which conclusively settles the matter.

[16] Macdonald, at p.96; *Mathieson v. H.M. Advocate*, 1981 S.C.C.R. 196, charge to the jury at 197. *Cf. Lourie v. H.M. Advocate*, 1988 S.C.C.R. 684.

[17] This seems to be the term of art commonly employed in 20th century indictments and cases: see, *e.g. Paton v. H.M. Advocate*, 1936 S.L.T. 298 (*cf.* the terms of the indictment, n.18, *infra*, with L.J.-C. Aitchison's reference to criminal negligence, at 299); *H.M. Advocate v. Pearson*, 1963 S.C.C.R. (Supp.) 20, Lord Cameron at 21; *Sutherland v. H.M. Advocate*, 1994 S.C.C.R. 80; *McDowall v. H.M. Advocate*, 1998 S.C.C.R. 343.

[18] 1936 S.L.T. 298, where the charge narrated culpable homicide by driving in a culpable and reckless manner and at excessive speed to the danger of the lieges. *Cf.* the charge in the more modern case of *McDowall v. H.M. Advocate*, 1998 S.C.C.R. 343.

[19] *ibid.*, at 299.

[20] J.C. Smith and B. Hogan, *Criminal Law* (9th ed. by Prof. Sir John Smith, 1999), at 460, where the English crime of 'reckless rape' is discussed in subjective terms: see *R. v. Satnam* (1983) 78 Cr.App.R. 149, Bristow J. at 154–155, where recklessness in relation to the victim's consent in rape was to be taken as indifference, in the sense of 'couldn't care less'; *cf.* the rather different view of *Satnam* taken by Andrew Ashworth, *Principles of Criminal Law* (3rd ed., 1999), at 355–356. See also para. 7.45, *supra*.

[21] Gross negligence is now the appropriate test for 'breach of duty' type manslaughter in England: *R. v. Adomako* [1995] 1 A.C. 171, HL.

[22] See para. 7.05, *supra*.

[23] 1998 S.C.C.R. 343.

is in part borrowed from tests favoured in non culpable homicide decisions. As his Lordship states: " what the jury had to consider was whether at the time of the crash, the appellant was showing a complete disregard of any potential dangers and of what the consequences of his driving might be so far as the public were concerned."[24] As his opinion makes plain, this test is satisfied by considering quite objectively what the accused did before, during and after the event which resulted in the fatality — although he also states that these objective matters are to be taken into account "when assessing his state of mind at the time of the accident." The objectivity of the whole exercise is also apparent in *Sutherland v. H.M. Advocate*,[25] where Lord Justice-General Hope approved the trial judge's direction that the act "had to be done in the face of obvious risks which were or *should have been* guarded against or in circumstances which showed a complete disregard for any potential dangers which might result."[26] It seems, therefore, that in relevant cases — *i.e.*, those involving lawful but carelessly executed conduct which results in death — *mens rea* is satisfied by an objective assessment of what the accused did in relation to the risks which would have been obvious to a reasonable man: if the accused's careless acts, thus assessed, indicate a complete or utter disregard for the safety of others, he may be convicted of culpable homicide. This assumes, of course, that a distinction can be made between this type of culpable homicide and murder: that a distinction can be made between 'complete disregard for the safety of others' and 'wicked recklessness'.

Wicked recklessness in murder. Where an intent to kill cannot be **7.60**
established, the *mens rea* of murder may still be satisfied if the acts of the accused show "such wicked recklessness as to imply a disposition depraved enough to be regardless of consequences."[27] This form of recklessness is confined to murder, and enables a jury to make a moral assessment of the accused's conduct in all the circumstances of the case. It allows a jury to determine whether the recklessess "is so gross that it indicates a state of mind which falls to be treated as [as] wicked and depraved as the state of mind of a deliberate killer."[28] If a 'lesser degree' of recklessness is revealed by its deliberations, then the jury may convict of culpable homicide on a murder indictment.[29] It may be, however, that

---

[24] *ibid.*, at 349C and D.

[25] 1994 S.C.C.R. 80. For this case to be relevant to the type of culpable homicide under consideration, it is assumed that it was correct to treat the fire-raising in the case as not unlawful since the property in question belonged to the accused; the trial judge took the view that the accused's intent to defraud insurers was insufficient to turn his acts into unlawful conduct for the purposes of culpable homicide, although it was accepted that there was a common law crime of setting fire to one's own property to defraud insurers (see Vol. II, Chap. 18).

[26] *ibid.*,at 92C-D, emphasis added. The trial judge's direction is adapted from the test for the former statutory offence of reckless driving set out in *Allan v. Patterson*, 1980 J.C. 57, L.J.-G. Emslie at 60 (see *infra*, para. 7.61).

[27] Macdonald, p.89.

[28] *Scott v. H.M. Advocate*, 1995 S.C.C.R. 760, — the quotation represents a statement made in the 2nd ed. of this work at para. 23–17, as now amended by L.J.-C. Ross's suggestions at 765B.

[29] See, *e.g. Dunn v. H.M. Advocate*, 1980 S.C.C.R. (Supp.) 242, L.J.-G. Emslie at 243; *Thomson v. H.M. Advocate*, 1985 S.C.C.R. 448, trial judge at 455; *Melvin v. H.M. Advocate*, 1984 S.C.C.R. 113, Lord Cameron at 117; *Malone v. H.M. Advocate*, 1988 S.C.C.R. 498, L.J.-G. Emslie at 508; *Brown v. H.M. Advocate*, 1993 S.C.C.R. 382, L.J.-G. Hope at 391F-G.

involuntary murder cannot be established in the absence of an intention to cause injury, and that an intention to cause serious injury is an important way of demonstrating 'wicked recklessness'[30]; but it has been said that there is still room for culpable homicide (at least in a case involving concert)[31] where the accused foresaw the use of lethal weapons in order to cause serious injury to the victim.[32] It may appear strange that such a vague concept as 'wicked recklessness' continues to be of material importance to the modern Scots law of murder[33]; but it enables a jury to reflect community values in the distinction between murder and culpable homicide — a distinction which in Scotland is primarily based on a moral judgment.[34] Certainly in cases where a person has attacked another but killed him unintentionally,[35] whether the verdict should be murder or culpable homicide will be settled by the jury asking itself if the accused's actions in the circumstances were sufficiently depraved as to imply that he is to be treated in the same way as a deliberate killer: this may appear to make the distinction between murder and culpable homicide in such a case at best unclear and perhaps depend on the degree of recklessness shown or inferred (assuming that it can make sense to talk of degrees of recklessness): but if it is correct that wicked recklessness primarily depends upon an intention to injure the victim seriously, then the actual choice is between 'wicked recklessness' (murder) and the substantive rule that a person who assaults another

---

[30] See Vol. II, Chap. 23. This may or may not, therefore, provide a method of distinguishing murder from culpable homicide where an assault is involved; but it certainly serves to distinguish murder from the type of culpable homicide discussed in para. 7.59, *supra*.

[31] See paras 5.39 to 5.41, *supra*.

[32] *Brown v. H.M. Advocate*, 1993 S.C.C.R. 382, L.J.-G. Hope at 391F-392A: doubts were expressed by the Crown as to the correctness of this in *Coleman v. H.M. Advocate*, 1999 S.C.C.R. 87; but Lord Coulsfield and L.J.-C. Cullen were of the view that that case did not provide an appropriate occasion to review what the Lord Justice-General had said in *Brown*.

[33] In the House of Lords' "Select Committee Report on Murder and Life Imprisonment" (H.L. Session 1988/89, Paper 78 — I, II, & III), Vol. I, para. 43, "wicked recklessness" was described as an "elusive concept" which was unsuited for incorporation in statutory form since "the very flexibility . . . which is seen as its virtue in Scotland precludes the use of precise and definite language which is normally and rightly expected in a statute defining a criminal offence." A 'statutory' definition was nonetheless proffered by B.A. Kerr, Q.C., (Vol. III, Q. 1423) as follows: "a state of mind at the material time so reckless as to indicate that he did not care whether his victim lived or died." English academic writers generally do not favour "strongly evaluative decisions about whether the label of murder is appropriate" for a killing being allowed to juries, and thus frown upon the notion of 'wicked recklessness' — see, *e.g.* Jeremy Horder, "Intention in the Criminal Law — A Rejoinder" [1995] 58 M.L.R. 678, at 688: see also W. Wilson, "A plea for rationality in the law of murder" (1990) 10 L.S. 307, at 315, where he writes, relative to 'wicked recklessness' that "[t]his test has rightly been denounced as failing to provide a clear dividing line between murder and manslaughter." *Cf.* Lord Goff of Chieveley, "The Mental Element in the Crime of Murder" (1988) 104 J.Q.R. 30.

[34] *cf. Broadley v. H.M. Advocate*, 1991 S.C.C.R. 416, L.J.-C. Ross at 423C-E, where the distinction is said to be objective and a question of facts and circumstances: but that does not preclude, of course, the evaluation of those facts and circumstances in moral terms. The advantage of jury-made moral evaluation, and thus the merit of that type of account of 'wicked recklessness', will be weakened if a judge is able to withdraw from a jury's consideration the alternative verdict of culpable homicide in a murder case — see, *e.g.*, *Broadley v. H.M. Advocate, supra*; *Parr v. H.M. Advocate*, 1991 S.C.C.R. 180: but it is now clear that withdrawal of such an alternative verdict should be considered by a trial judge only with great caution, and indeed only in cases where no reasonable jury could possibly fail to find wicked recklessness if the evidence in the case is accepted — see *Brown v. H.M. Advocate*, 1993 S.C.C.R. 382.

[35] This assumes the absence of any exculpatory or mitigatory defence.

and causes his death is always guilty of no less than culpable homicide.[36] In other words, 'wicked recklessness' is simply an esoteric form of *mens rea* peculiar to murder, and very different from 'recklessness' encountered elsewhere in the criminal law and in particular from that concept as it relates to the type of culpable homicide described above.[37]

Recklessness as to result in non-homicide crimes. In a number of non-homicide offences, recklessness as to a particular result is a key issue: but, with one modern exception,[38] there has been very little judicial analysis of the concept. In the offence of culpably and recklessly causing personal injury, for example, the courts have tended to regard recklessness as having the same significance as in culpable homicide.[39] Thus Lord Justice-General Clyde in *Quinn v. Cunningham*[40] emphasised that common law recklessness involved a high standard of culpability, which was exemplified in the culpable homicide case of *Paton v. H.M. Advocate*[41] and which amounted to "utter disregard of what the consequences of the act in question may be so far as the public are concerned".[42] This test, of 'utter' or 'complete' or 'total' or even 'culpable'[43] disregard of consequences, appears in *W. v. H.M. Advocate*,[44] *Harris v. H.M. Advocate*[45] and *Kimmins v. Normand*[46]; it also appears in relation to offences of culpable and reckless endangerment[47] and fire-raising.[48] As an alternative, and sometimes in addition, it is not uncommon for judges to refer to varying degrees of 'indifference' to the prohibited result[49]: but there is no evidence to suggest that the use of such a term involves the incorporation of an element of subjective awareness of risk into recklessness, and it may be that the practical difference between 'disregard' and 'indifference' is not significant. One 7.61

---

[36] *McDermott v. H.M. Advocate*, 1973 J.C. 8.

[37] See para. 7.59, *supra*.

[38] See Lord Prosser's opinion in *Harris v. H.M. Advocate*, 1993 S.C.C.R. 559, 574F-575A. His opinion is discussed later in this paragraph.

[39] The same seems to apply relative to the offence of culpable and reckless endangerment: see *MacPhail v. Clark*, 1982 S.C.C.R. 395, Sh.Ct.

[40] 1956 S.L.T. 55, at 56. This case was overruled on a different point (see n.42, *infra*) by *Harris v. H.M. Advocate*, 1993 S.C.C.R. 559, in which Lord Prosser (at 574E) confirmed that recklessness followed the meaning it bore in culpable homicide.

[41] 1936 S.L.T. 298.

[42] The view taken in *Quinn v. Cunningham* was that 'danger to the public' had to be averred and proved in reckless injury cases; but that is no longer necessary — see *Harris v. H.M. Advocate*, 1993 S.C.C.R. 559.

[43] 'Reckless' disregard is also occasionally found (*e.g.*, *Harris v. H.M. Advocate*, 1993 S.C.C.R. 559, Lord Prosser at 577E-F); but defining recklessness in terms of itself can hardly be regarded as particularly illuminating.

[44] 1982 S.C.C.R. 152, Lord Hunter at 155.

[45] 1993 S.C.C.R. 559, Lord Murray at 566B; Lord Morison at 572D.

[46] 1993 S.C.C.R. 476, where the relevant phrase is included in the complaint.

[47] See, *e.g. Cameron v. Maguire*, 1999 S.C.C.R. 44 (culpable and reckless discharge of firearms to the danger of others) which disapproved the test applied in the earlier but not dissimilar case of *Gizzi v. Tudhope*, 1982 S.C.C.R. 492. In *Gizzi*, the test formulated for the (now repealed) statutory offence of reckless driving was applied. *Cf. Ward v. Robertson*, 1938 S.L.T. 165 (malicious mischief) at 167 where L.J.-C. Aitchison stated that danger might be caused non-intentionally by acts which "showed a deliberate disregard of, or even indifference to, the property of others."

[48] See *Carr v. H.M. Advocate*, 1994 S.C.C.R. 521, L.J.-G. Hope at 526D.

[49] See, *e.g.*, *W. v. H.M. Advocate*, 1982 S.C.C.R. 152, Lord Hunter at 155. 'Criminal indifference' also appears as part of the formula in the culpable homicide case of *Paton v. H.M. Advocate*, 1936 S.L.T. 298, L.J.-C. Aitchison at 299, and a similar reference occurs in *Quinn v. Cunningham*, 1956 S.L.T. 55, L.J.-G. Clyde at 57.

apparent exception seems to concern those cases which involve the offence of culpable and reckless endangerment by supply of substances dangerous to health and life[50]: but that offence may be regarded as special in that the Crown chose to libel and prove that the accused in question were aware of the risks involved, *i.e.* that they knew the purpose of those who were supplied and knew that that purpose was dangerous to health and life. Subjective knowledge of the risks seems therefore to be a self-imposed requirement of that particular crime rather than something which the Crown would have to establish normally in respect of recklessness in Scots criminal law.

Statutory *mens rea* is considered elsewhere;[51] but it is appropriate here to deal with the case of *Allan v. Patterson*[52] since it suggests that recklessness should not have a different meaning as between statute and common law (unless the statutory context otherwise requires), determines that recklessness relative to a statutory offence (again unless the context otherwise requires) is to be treated objectively, and provides a model direction which has proved attractive in relation to common law crimes involving recklessness.[53] The case concerned the now repealed offence of reckless driving under the Road Traffic Act 1972.[54] Lord Justice-General Emslie, giving the opinion of the Appeal Court, stated as follows:

> "Inquiry into the state of knowledge of a particular driver . . . and into his intention at the time, is not required at all . . . All that is in issue . . . is the degree to which the driving in question fell below the standard to be expected of a careful and competent driver . . . and whether the degree is such as properly to attach . . . the label of 'recklessness' . . . Section 2, as its language plainly, we think, suggests, requires a judgment to be made quite objectively of a particular course of driving in proved circumstances . . . Before judges or juries can apply the adverb 'recklessly' to the driving in question they must find that it fell far below the standard of driving expected of the competent and careful driver and that it occurred either in the face of obvious and material dangers which were or should have been observed, appreciated and guarded against, or in circumstances which showed a complete disregard for any potential dangers which might result from the way in which the vehicle was being driven."[55]

---

[50] See *Khaliq v. H.M. Advocate*, 1983 S.C.C.R. 483; *Ulhaq v. H.M. Advocate*, 1990 S.C.C.R. 593.

[51] See Chap. 8, *infra*.

[52] 1980 J.C. 57.

[53] The *Allan v. Patterson* test for recklessness was followed in *Gizzi v. Tudhope*, 1982 S.C.C.R. 492 (*cf. Cameron v. Maguire*, 1999 S.C.C.R. 44) and *Sutherland v. H.M Advocate*, 1994 S.C.C.R. 80 (although this did not, of course, involve a non-homicide crime); it was also applied in other relevant statutory offences — *e.g.*, *Black v. Allan*, 1985 S.C.C.R. 11 (*cf. McIntosh v. H.M. Advocate*, 1993 S.C.C.R. 464).

[54] See s.2 (as substituted by the Criminal Law Act 1977, s.50). This did not amount to a 'result' crime as such (*cf.* the offence of causing death by reckless driving in s.1 — again as substituted under s.50 of the 1977 Act, and also now repealed), although the treatment of recklessness by the court in *Allan v. Patterson* suggests that the *mens rea* relates to dangers caused or exacerbated by the manner of driving. S. 2 (and s.1) were replaced by ss.1, 2 and 2A of the Road Traffic Act 1988 (as substituted/added by the Road Traffic Act 1991, s.1). There is little doubt that the 1977 substitutions were intended by Parliament to introduce an element of subjective *mens rea* to the original offences in accordance with orthodox English criminal law theory of the time; but the Scots courts refused to accept that any significant change had been made, and interpreted recklessness in a wholly objective way — as indeed did the House of Lords in *R. v. Lawrence* [1982] A.C. 510.

[55] 1980 J.C. 57, at 60.

This test contains a clear statement that a finding of a high degree of objective carelessness is a necessary,[56] but not sufficient, condition for recklessness to be established. What is required beyond that sort of carelessness is a risk association between it and material dangers (whether created by the manner of driving or circumstantially related to it) which makes driving in that manner totally unacceptable. The importance of this test is that it brings together the issues of gross carelessness, danger and risk, and the consequent unacceptability of the behaviour which combines them, as the basic ingredients of recklessness and does so in a wholly objective way: subjective recklessness[57] is plainly rejected by the case.[58] Nevertheless, this test has been weakened by the repeal of the offence to which it primarily related,[59] and by the degree to which it is not readily adaptable to the needs of differently constituted offences.[60] The most recent, and practically sole, judicial analysis of 'recklessness' appears in *Harris v. H.M. Advocate*, where Lord Prosser said:[61]

> "Recklessness and danger are not unrelated concepts. I see no need here to embark upon a definition of recklessness: in relation to reckless conduct causing injury or danger it has in my opinion the same meaning as it has in relation to culpable homicide, where death has been caused by reckless conduct, and is not a crime of intent, with the death being caused by an assault. Whether one uses the word recklessness, or such descriptions as gross negligence, that is a familiar concept which I think is readily conveyed to and understood by juries. But it involves an assessment of duties owed to others, which in turn depend upon the foreseeability of harmful consequences. Analysis probably becomes unreal; but I think that one can say that in deciding that some conduct has been reckless, one will always be at least very close to saying that it involved a failure to pay due regard to foreseeable consequences of that conduct, which were foreseeably likely to cause injury to others, and which could correspondingly reasonably be called dangerous in relation to them. If that is so, then (i) the category of reckless conduct which is not to the danger of others will be empty or nearly so; (ii) it will make little or no difference whether one considers the recklessness of the conduct before the danger that it causes, or the danger before the recklessness, since the two are in practical terms interdependent; and (iii) even where the libel is to the effect that reckless conduct has caused injury, or indeed death, so that there is no need to libel danger as the result of the conduct, a judgment as to whether the conduct constituted a danger to others will in fact have to be made in this sense, that the existence and foreseeability

---

[56] *cf. Crowe v. H.M. Advocate*, 1989 S.C.C.R. 681.

[57] See para. 7.45, *supra*.

[58] Whilst it is true that the court in *Allan v. Patterson* (at p.60) did state: "It will be understood that in reaching a decision upon the critical issue a judge or jury will be entitled to have regard to any explanation offered by the accused driver designed to show that his driving in the particular circumstances did not possess the quality of recklessness at the material time" — this has been confined to situations where the accused shows that he had no alternative but to drive as he did — *i.e.* that the recklessness can be justified or excused: see *McNab v. Guild*, 1989 S.C.C.R. 138.

[59] See n.54 *supra*.

[60] See *Cameron v. Maguire*, 1999 S.C.C.R. 44.

[61] 1993 S.C.C.R. 559, at 574E to 575A.

of possible harm to others will be inherent in deciding whether the conduct can properly be described as reckless. I am not persuaded that there is any real difficulty in all this. But in cases where actual injury has resulted from the allegedly reckless conduct, I think the possibility of danger is relevant not as a result, but as an inherent element in recklessness itself."

The juxtaposition of conduct, foreseeability and danger in the above passage is illuminating, and a succinct account might be constructed as follows: 'that an assessment of recklessness (or gross negligence) in relation to conduct, which has in fact unintentionally but foreseeably injured another or exposed others to the danger of injury, depends upon the extent to which the agent's conduct demonstrates a failure in his duty in the circumstances to avoid (or perhaps minimise)[62] such injury or danger of injury to others.'[63] Lord Prosser, it will be noted, did not consider that there were any real difficulties in approaching recklessness in such a way;[64] but there may be difficulties in recognising the existence and scope of duties in particular circumstances, and also in determining when and to what extent the actor had failed to obtemper them: on the other hand, such difficulties might be avoided if a broad and intuitive approach to these matters is simply entrusted to the jury's common sense (as is in any event the traditional Scottish way of directing juries). There is certainly no suggestion in Lord Prosser's account that the matter of recklessness, and especially the foreseeability of the danger on which it depends (or in respect of which it is interdependent), should be established other than objectively;[65] and his account has some advantage in clarity over conventional but vaguer expressions such as 'utter disregard for the consequences'; it also dispels any lingering myth that recklessness is compatible only with "such a state of reckless excitement as not to know or care what he was doing."[66] Lord Prosser's view does not, of course, clearly distinguish negligence from recklessness. But that is because Scots criminal law does not clearly distinguish between the two. When judges, therefore, refer to recklessness in terms of conduct which shows 'utter disregard of consequences' or 'gross negligence' or, perhaps, 'an unacceptable level of exposure of others to foreseeable danger of injury or property damage', they are in fact referring to the objective dangerousness of the conduct in the light of reasonably foreseeable risks, and not to a state of mind at all. Should it be necessary to do so, conduct of such dangerousness can be used to show general

---

[62] See para. 7.48, *supra*.

[63] Relative to crimes such as malicious mischief and culpable and reckless fire-raising, the account would require adjustment to refer to injury or danger to property belonging to others.

[64] *cf.* Ld. McCluskey (diss. on the main issue in the appeal as to whether or not the charges in the indictment were proper alternatives) at 569F: "Lord Prosser's discussion of the concepts of recklessness and danger, intent, gross negligence and the existence and foreseeability of possible harm to others — all of which the trial judge would have to consider explaining to the jury — serves to illustrate how unnecessarily sophisticated and remote from reality we are in danger of rendering the law where, in a matter of this kind, it should be simple and easy for juries to grasp."

[65] Thus, lack of thought, relative to (*e.g.*) obvious and material dangers which were effectively risked by the accused's conduct, can be as culpable as being aware of them and choosing to run the risk of their materialisation. See *Robson v. Spiers*, 1999 S.L.T. 1141, where Lord Prosser's views were employed to determine the recklessness of the accused's conduct.

[66] *George MacBean* (1847) Ark. 262, at 263, *per* L.J.-C. Hope, in the course of directing a jury in a case of culpable and reckless fire-raising.

mens rea: but the authorities do not suggest that a finding of wickedness on the part of the accused is required.

Recklessness in conduct-crimes. Recklessness does not arise in **7.62** "conduct-crimes".[67] Volitionally speaking, conduct is either deliberate or accidental. Particular conduct, however, may be criminal only if certain circumstances exist. If such circumstances appear as part of the *actus reus* of the offence, then *mens rea* should apply to them, in the sense that the accused's knowledge of their existence may have to be shown by the Crown. Such knowledge may be actual, as where it is admitted, or inferred from the facts known to, or assumed to be known by, the accused. Where the accused did not know of the existence of the circumstance, an issue of cognitive recklessness (and its sufficiency for conviction of the crime in question) may then arise.[68] Circumstances not subsumed by the *actus reus*, but relevant to the crime, will most probably amount to exculpatory issues for the accused to raise by way of defence. It is of some importance, therefore, how crimes are defined and whether those definitions specifically include particular circumstances[69]: if these are included, then the actor's belief that they did not exist may be sufficient to prevent proof of *mens rea* by the Crown. Thus in rape[70] and in indecent assault,[71] lack of consent on the victim's part is a definitional circumstance, and the current Scots law is that an absence of any belief that the victim was consenting is the essence of the crime. It follows, therefore, that an honest belief, even one founded on unreasonable grounds, is sufficient to prevent proof that the accused knew of that essential circumstance. The crucial issue, however, relates to the type of *mens rea* which satisfies the crime, and in particular the essential circumstance: for if the crime's definition allows for recklessness in relation to the circumstance, then a recklessly formed belief should establish the necessary *mens rea* element rather than defeat it. This in turn raises the question of whether recklessness requires subjective awareness of the risk that (*e.g.*) the victim may not be consenting, such that an attitude of 'couldn't care less' or 'indifference' will at the very least be required. English law is clear on the matter of rape, since the definition of the offence is statutory and provides that "A man commits rape if (a) he has sexual intercourse with a person (whether vaginal or anal) who at the time of the intercourse does not consent to it; and (b) at the time he knows that the person does not consent to the intercourse or is reckless as to whether the person consents to it."[72]

Scots law has accepted that recklessness, or indifference, as to the matter of consent in rape will not suffice for acquittal[73]; in doing so, however, it has followed and approved the opinion of the House of Lords in *D.P.P. v. Morgan*,[74] a case decided within a system of criminal

---

[67] *supra*, para. 3.05.

[68] See paras 7.63 *et seq.*, *infra*.

[69] On the subject of definitional minimalism and maximalism, see R.S. Tur, "Subjectivism and Objectivism: Towards Synthesis", in S.Shute, J.Gardner and J.Horder (eds.), *Action and Value in Criminal Law* (Oxford, 1993), p.213, at p.216 *et seq.*

[70] See *Meek v. H.M. Advocate*, 1983 S.C.C.R. 613; *Jamieson v. H.M. Advocate*, 1994 S.C.C.R. 181.

[71] See *Marr v. H.M. Advocate*, 1996 J.C. 199.

[72] Sexual Offences Act 1956, s.1(2), as substituted by the Criminal Justice and Public Order Act 1994, s.142. (Unlike English law, Scots law does not permit rape to include a male victim.).

[73] *Jamieson v. H.M. Advocate*, 1994 S.C.C.R. 181, L.J.-G. Hope at 186A-B.

[74] [1976] A.C. 182.

law which espouses a subjective approach to *mens rea* in general[75] and recklessness as to consent in particular.[76] There has been no actual discussion of what recklessness may mean in relation to consent in sexual offences, or of the way in which it may be proved, in any reported Scottish case. Consequently, the matter presents itself as part of the wider problem of cognitive recklessness.[77]

7.63 *Cognitive recklessness.* The problem here is whether an accused's failure to know a particular fact can itself be so blameworthy as to make him responsible for an offence which cannot be committed by simple negligence.[78]

In the absence of knowledge itself, responsibility may rest on four different substitutes: wilful blindness; advertent recklessness as to the existence of the circumstance in question; "wicked" recklessness in failing to be aware of the circumstances; unreasonably giving no thought to the matter.

7.64 WILFUL BLINDNESS. Wilful blindness probably exists where A deliberately shuts his eyes to the means of knowledge because he prefers to remain in ignorance. Wilful blindness should be restricted to the situation where the accused believes that a certain state of affairs exists, knows that he can confirm this belief by taking a simple step like asking a question, or walking round a corner to read a notice board, but does not do so because he wants to be able to plead ignorance. Such wilful blindness, or "connivance" as it is sometimes called,[79] is regarded as tantamount and equivalent to knowledge, and it is therefore important to restrict it to cases of the kind described. Where A genuinely does not know and has formed no firm view or beliefs, and does not bother to find out, he may be reckless but he is not wilfully blind. As Glanville Williams puts it:

> "A court can properly find wilful blindness only where it can almost be said that the defendant actually knew. He suspected the fact; he realised its probability; but he refrained from obtaining the final confirmation because he wanted in the event to be able to deny knowledge. This, and this alone, is wilful blindness. It requires in effect a finding that the defendant intended to cheat the administration of justice."[80]

As Lord Fleming said in *Knox v. Boyd*[81]: "Connivance or wilful blindness to sources of knowledge may be tantamount to actual knowledge." Lord Normand in the same case spoke in terms of "wilfully

---

[75] *cf. R. v. Caldwell* [1982] A.C. 341; *R. v. Lawrence* [1982] A.C. 510: these decisions are now regarded as anomalous and exceptional in English law; see A. Ashworth, *Principles of Criminal Law* (3rd ed., Oxford, 1999), at p.191.

[76] See especially *R. v. Satnam* (1983) 78 Cr.App.R. 149.

[77] See paras 7.63 *et seq., infra.*

[78] See G.H. Gordon (1975) 17 C.L.Q. 355, cited *supra*, para. 7.13, n. 37.

[79] See *e.g. Knox v. Boyd*, 1941 J.C. 82; *cf. James & Son Ltd. v. Smee* [1955] 1 Q.B. 78, Parker J. at 91.

[80] Gl. Williams, 159. See also *Evans v. Dell* [1937] 1 All E.R. 349, Lord Hewart C.J. at 353; *The Zamora (No. 2)* [1921] 1 A.C. 801, Lord Sumner at 812; *Ianella v. French* (1967–68) 41 A.L.J.R. 389, Windeyer J. at 400: "This case is not one of 'wilful blindness' . . . The appellant had not[,] realising that he might be in fault[,] recklessly refrained from proper inquiry."

[81] 1941 J.C. 82, 86.

shut[ting] his eyes . . . and deliberately refrain[ing] from putting a question".[82] Wilful blindness has been succinctly described by Professor J.C. Smith as "deliberately avoiding finding out what one believes may exist."[83] Such Scottish cases as there are, however, tend to extend wilful blindness to include lesser forms of culpable failure to inquire.[84] It usually arises in connection with regulatory offences, but there seems no reason for not applying it in, for example, cases of incest, rape[85] or even of reset.[86]

ADVERTENT RECKLESSNESS. Where A is not sure that a particular circumstance exists but appreciates that it may exist and decides to act nonetheless, he is advertently reckless. In such a situation he can be said to "accept the risk" that the circumstance exists, and it is easy to see why he should be punished if he causes criminal harm by reason of the existence of that circumstance, and punished as much as if he had known of its existence.[87] If A knows that B may be his sister and is prepared to have intercourse with her in that knowledge, and she is in fact his sister, it is reasonable to treat him in the same way as if he had known she was his sister, if only because this knowledge would not have made any difference to his behaviour. This is probably what is meant in English law by indifference or 'couldn't care less' in relation to reckless rape.[88] **7.65**

"WICKED" RECKLESSNESS. If gross negligence in cognition is to be treated as criminal recklessness it must be on the ground that there is a duty to ascertain that one's conduct is not criminal, and therefore to inquire into any circumstance which might make it so. A failure to make such inquiry would then constitute recklessness sufficient to show a wicked state of mind, if the failure was so gross as to display "utter" or "wicked" disregard, or "depravity". And this is unlikely to occur except in the face of such clear evidence that the conduct is criminal that the accused's claim of innocent ignorance or excusable error in unlikely to be believed anyway, as in the case of the rapist who insists that he was entitled to treat the woman's screams and struggles as evidence of perverse delight.[89] Short of something as extreme as that it is difficult to envisage cases of wicked recklessness through ignorance. It is no doubt **7.66**

---

82 *ibid.*

83 See note on *R. v. Thomas* [1976] Crim.L.R. 517.

84 See *infra*, paras 8.83 *et seq.*

85 See para. 7.62, *supra*.

86 *Friel v. Docherty*, 1990 S.C.C.R. 351.

87 See, *e.g. People v. Murray* [1977] I.R. 360, where it was held by the Irish Supreme Court that it would be capital murder (under then prevailing legislation) to murder a member of the Garda where the accused knew of the status of her victim or where she adverted to the possibility that he might be a policeman yet proceeded to shoot him dead in reckless disregard of that possibility. (In fact, neither of these could be established, and the accused's conviction for capital murder was quashed.).

88 See *R. v. Satnam* (1984) 78 Cr.App.R. 149, Bristow J. at 155: "If [the jury] come to the conclusion that he could not care less whether she wanted to or not, but pressed on regardless, then he would have been reckless". This case approved the earlier indecent assault case of *R. v. Kimber* [1983] 1 W.L.R. 1118, where Lawton L.J. (at 1123) referred to the defendant's 'attitude of indifference' or 'couldn't care less' as a state of mind (clearly a subjective state of mind) amounting to recklessness. Whether a recklessly formed belief in his victim's consent will require advertent recklessness before a conviction for rape or indecent assault can be returned has not yet been discussed in any reported Scottish case. (See para. 7.62, *supra*.).

89 *cf. R. v. Morgan* [1976] A.C. 182.

very careless to pick up the wrong key in a hotel and proceed to enter the wrong room, a room quite unlike one's own, and have intercourse with a woman asleep in the bed without noticing that it is the wrong woman and the wrong room, but it hardly exhibits wickedness or depravity. Again, if it does not occur to A that the cloakroom attendant is handing him the wrong coat he cannot be said to be showing a wicked disregard for the rights of others if he does not examine it carefully to see whether it is his own or not. But the whole concept of inadvertent recklessness as exhibiting a wicked state of mind is connected with result-crimes where there is a manifest and direct disregard of person or property; it cannot be easily carried over into cognitive recklessness where what is disregarded is often a particular legal relationship which does not affect the central element of the crime. Again, such recklessness is connected with the idea of physical harm, of destructiveness and violence, and it cannot easily be carried over into situations of dishonesty. It may be blameworthy to induce someone to buy goods by making false representations without inquiring whether they are true or not, but it is hardly a sign of depravity.

7.67 *Unreasonably giving no thought to the existence of a fact or circumstance.* The issue here has been described by the Law Commission as one of "heedlessness",[90] that being the title they would have given to the non-advertent type of recklessness referred to by Lord Diplock in *R. v. Caldwell*,[91] had they taken the view that that should be enacted as part of the proposed code. That case, of course, dealt with a failure to consider the results of actions; but where no thought is given as to the existence of a fact or circumstance which ought reasonably to have informed a decision to refrain from acting and on which the criminality of actions depends, such lack of thought may well be as blameable as adverting to the risk of the existence of the fact or circumstance and deciding to act in spite of that risk. Thus, for example, the person who has intercourse with a fifteen-year-old girl without pausing to consider what her age is may be as blameworthy as is the person who realises that the girl might be only fifteen but either comes to no conclusion about it or rashly and unreasonably concludes that she is in fact sixteen. Similarly, a man who proceeds to have sexual intercourse with a woman without giving any thought as to whether she might not be consenting (when in fact she does not consent) may be as blameable as the man who suspected that she might not consent but had intercourse with her in any event, having deliberately refrained from making the minor effort which would have been necessary to confirm his suspicions. It is probably arguable that 'lack of thought' can demonstrate a state of mind — such as indifference to the existence of the fact or circumstance (in the sense of the man who could not care less about whether it exists or not[92] or R.A. Duff's 'sufficient attitude of practical indifference'[93]) or even wickedness; but this suggests that the true criterion is indifference or wickedness, in respect of which lack of thought might be a principal adminicle of evidence. But lack of thought, about a fact or circumstance, may be sufficiently blameworthy in itself, provided the reasonable man would

---

[90] "A Criminal Code for England and Wales" (1989) L.C. No. 177, Vol. 2, para. 8.21.

[91] [1982] A.C. 341, at 353H-354A.

[92] As now seems to be the law in England relative to 'reckless rape': see *R. v. Satnam* (1989) 78 Cr.App.R. 149.

[93] See, *e.g.*, his article: "Recklessness" [1980] Crim.L.R. 282, at 284 *et seq.*

have given the matter serious consideration and thus, for example, would have had a reason for refraining from acting at all. This in turn suggests that the issue is one of negligence rather than recklessness, and that at the very least there will be consequent confusion between the two; but this is to presuppose that a firm distinction ought to be made between the two concepts, and (probably) that the distinction lies at the level of advertence. Scots law makes no such firm distinction relative to consequences of actions, holding that the difference between negligence and recklessness is one of degree;[94] and there is no reason to suppose that the matter is any different where failure to know a fact or circumstance, which is essential to the criminality of one's actions, is at stake.[95]

The position in Scots law. Cognitive recklessness has not been discussed in any reported case. The legal significance of the blameworthiness of failing to know a fact or circumstance which is of importance to a particular crime depends on the type of crime in question and its *mens rea* requirement. Involuntary murder requires "wicked recklessness",[96] and thus that form of *mens rea* must be established. "I didn't know the gun was loaded" might itself be evidence of "gross disregard" of the safety of others, and thus of recklessness: but it would be necessary to go further in order to convict of murder. In most cases, the man who does not know the gun was loaded is a different moral animal from the man who does; he will not, therefore, be seen as sufficiently wicked for murder, and will be convicted only of culpable homicide. In crimes other than murder, whether or not 'reckless ignorance' is sufficient for conviction will depend on whether the offence in question can be committed recklessly.[97] If the offence requires intention, cognitive recklessness cannot be a substitute for knowledge: if a pregnant woman takes pills knowing that they might be abortifacients and not caring whether they are or not, and they cause her to abort, she has caused her abortion recklessly and not intentionally, and if abortion requires that the drugs be taken with intent to procure a miscarriage, she is not guilty. In reset, where knowledge that the goods are stolen or otherwise dishonestly acquired is an essential part of the definition of the crime, wilful blindness seems to suffice in the absence of actual knowledge[98]: but no other substitute for knowledge should probably be acceptable.[99] Recklessness has been held to be relevant in rape. As Lord Justice-General Hope put it in *Jamieson v. H.M. Advocate*[1]: "It will not do if [the accused] acted without thinking; or was indifferent as to whether or not he had her consent . . . Difficult questions of fact may arise as to whether, if he can give no reasonable grounds for his belief, the accused genuinely believed at the time that the woman was consenting or was reckless or indifferent as as to the matter of consent. These questions are, however, for the jury to resolve". It may be, given the link which the court in *Jamieson* confirmed between its decision and the one pronounced by the majority of the House of Lords in *R. v. Morgan*,[2] that **7.68**

---

[94] See para. 7.61, *supra*.
[95] *cf.* the discussion at para. 7.62, *supra*.
[96] See para. 7.60, *supra*.
[97] *cf.* para. 7.62, *supra*.
[98] See *Friel v. Docherty*, 1990 S.C.C.R. 351.
[99] *cf.*, however, *Latta v. Herron*, 1967 S.C.C.R. (Supp.) 18; *Mackay Bros. v. Gibb*, 1969 S.L.T. 216: in both cases, wilful blindness and grossly negligent ignorance seem to have been confused, and the latter treated as if it were tantamount to knowledge.
[1] 1994 S.C.C.R. 181, at 186B and 187A.
[2] [1976] A.C. 182.

recklessness with respect to the victim's consent in rape should mean advertent recklessness in the sense subsequently upheld in *R. v. Satnam*[3] — *i.e.* 'indifference' or 'couldn't care less' — since the trial judge's direction to the jury in *Satnam*, in terms of Lord Diplock's opinion in *R. v. Caldwell*[4] on the objectivity of recklessness as to consent in rape, was disapproved of on appeal. But the grafting on to Scots law of the complex and difficult English conceptions of recklessness is a prospect not to be contemplated lightly. In most other situations, it is submitted that cognitive recklessness in Scots criminal law is satisfied by what can be described as gross 'heedlessness'.[5] Thus if an accused has given no thought to the existence of a critical fact or circumstance in a situation where a reasonable man would have done so, then that accused is reckless relative to his failure to appreciate its actual existence: and recklessness is distinguished from negligence simply by its degree. The question is not whether the accused was negligent in failing to appreciate the existence of the essential fact at issue, but whether his failure can be described as grossly negligent in all the facts and circumstances of the particular case.[6]

NEGLIGENCE

7.69 Negligence consists in an inadvertent failure to take reasonable care to avoid a result or discover the existence of an attendant circumstance. So far as the latter is concerned the negligence may consist in a careless failure to consider whether the circumstance exists or not, or in an erroneous belief carelessly arrived at as to its existence.

7.70 *Has negligence a subjective aspect?* The standard of negligence is objective, and is that of the reasonable man. But in considering liability for negligence the particular agent cannot be wholly ignored.

7.71 THE NEED FOR A VOLUNTARY ACT. Liability for negligence as for any other form of criminal behaviour must be based on voluntary conduct. In considering whether A is negligent in regard to a particular result it is necessary to ask whether that result was a foreseeable consequence of some voluntary behaviour on his part. If, therefore, A drives a car in an objectively careless fashion because he is in an epileptic fugue or is behaving automatically in reaction to being stung by a swarm of bees, he is not driving negligently because he is not, in any significant sense, driving at all.[7]

7.72 NEGLIGENCE AS A STATE OF MIND. It is sometimes said that negligence is not a state of mind, and is not a form of *mens rea* at all,[8] since it denotes an absence of consciousness of risk, a blank inadventence. But a negative state of mind can still be referred to as a state of mind, and it is

---

[3] (1989) 78 Cr.App.R. 149.
[4] [1982] A.C. 341, at 353H to 354G.
[5] See para. 7.67, *supra*.
[6] *cf.* C.M.V. Clarkson and H.M. Keating, *Criminal Law: Text and Materials* (4th ed., 1998), at pp.174–175.
[7] But the law is more complex than this simple model would suggest: see *supra*, paras 3.13 to 3.28.
[8] *cf.* Gl.Williams, 102.

convenient to list the possible forms of *mens rea* as intention, recklessness and negligence. It is in any event necessary to inquire into the defender's mental state to discover whether he acted negligently, if only in order to exclude intention.

DEGREES OF NEGLIGENCE. It is also sometimes argued that as inadvertence is something negative there cannot be degrees of negligence — all blanks are equally blank.[9] But although all blanks are equally blank, all blanks are not of the same size. 7.73

The degrees are strictly degrees of carelessness and not of negligence, but the degree of carelessness is indicative of the accused's criminality which ranges from minimal negligence to extreme recklessness. The man who omits one precaution may not be less inadvertent than the man who omits twenty, but he is inadvertent with regard to fewer things. Again, degrees of negligence may be measured by reference to the degree of harm regarding which there is inadvertence, so that inadvertence of the possibility of death is regarded as more criminal than inadvertence of the possibility of a lesser harm.[10]

Should negligence be punished? It is often argued that negligence is not blameworthy and should not be punished.[11] It is true that the moral blame involved in negligence is very different from that involved in intentional wrongdoing, but that is not to say that negligence is not blameworthy. Indeed, it might be said that in Scots law it is axiomatic that negligence does involve moral blame — the technical term for negligence is *culpa*, and a person is negligent only when he has failed in a duty to take care.[12] The basic justification for punishing negligence is the existence of a duty to take care that one's behaviour does not cause criminal harm.[13] Ordinary moral attitudes, too, regard negligence as blameworthy. There is a difference between "I'm sorry, it was an accident", and "I'm sorry, it was my fault". People are expected to observe certain standards of care. "Men do indeed resent what is occasioned through carelessness but then they expect observance as their due, so that carelessness is considered as faulty."[14] 7.74

"OUGHT IMPLIES CAN". One of the difficulties which exist in punishing negligence is the situation of the person who is incapable of prudence: since in the Kantian phrase, "ought implies can", such a person has no duty to be prudent. But negligence is objective, and such a person is penalised when he fails to live up to a standard he is incapable of attaining. This argument is logically sound, but has little practical application. The law sets a standard because it is impossible to determine how prudent a particular person is capable of being, and so in practice impossible to apply a rule that A must be as careful as he can. 7.75

---

[9] *cf.* J.W.C.Turner, "The Mental Element in Crimes at Common Law" in *Modern Approach,* 195, 211.

[10] *cf.* H.L.A. Hart, *Punishment and Responsibility* (Oxford, 1968), Chap.VI. See also Professor Hall's reply: J. Hall, "Negligent Behavior should be Excluded from Penal Liability" (1963) 63 Col.L.Rev. 632, 635 n.19.

[11] *cf.* Hall, pp.133–141; Gl. Williams, p.122; Kenny, para. 25.

[12] W.A. Elliott, "Reparation and the English Tort of Negligence" (1952) 64 J.R. 1; T.B. Smith, 663–665.

[13] See A. Ashworth, *Principles of Criminal Law* (3rd ed., Oxford, 1999), pp.198–200.

[14] B. Butler, *Fifteen Sermons,* (ed. W.R. Matthews, London, 1953), Sermon VIII, 126–127. See also P.J. Fitzgerald, "Crime, Sin and Negligence" (1963) 79 L.Q.R. 351.

The standard set is that of the average member of society, and is therefore a fair one in most cases. Where the accused is mentally abnormal he will be excused his failure to be ordinarily prudent: there is no ground for punishing an insane person for negligence any more than for other kinds of criminal behaviour. Again, where A is rendered incapable of prudence by some sudden onset of illness or external force, his behaviour will probably cease to be voluntary, and so should not be punishable.[15] It should also be remembered that most punishable instances of carelessness are statutory and concern carelessness in the carrying on of particular professions or occupations, and if a person is constitutionally incapable of carrying these on carefully he ought not to carry them on at all. If he does carry them on nonetheless and causes harm, he is properly punishable for his negligence in doing so: indeed he might well be treated as having been reckless.

There remains the constitutionally feckless man who in going about his ordinary business drops a match into a can of petrol or a brick on to someone's head because he is incapable of paying attention to what he is doing, or of appreciating the results of his actions. Such a person, if he exists outside the wards of mental hospitals and the pages of textbooks, may not be morally blameworthy. But he will not in practice be punished at common law, since the few common law crimes of negligence which there are — *e.g.*, culpable homicide and culpable injury — are not committed by simple negligence in the course of lawful behaviour.[16]

7.76 THE USEFULNESS OF PUNISHING NEGLIGENCE. It is also argued that it is pointless to punish negligence since someone who does not advert to what he is doing cannot be deterred by fear of punishment.[17] But it is a fact of experience that threat of punishment can make people more careful, and encourage them to be advertent. A motorist sets out on a journey knowing that if he has an accident he may well be involved not merely in physical and financial injury but in criminal proceedings as well, that if he does not keep a lookout for halt signs he may find himself in trouble even if he does not have an accident, and this surely makes him concentrate more and so reduces the incidence of inadvertence.[18]

The law uses punishment for negligence as a social instrument in order to enforce prudence by means of the deterrent effect of punishment. And it is quite consciously applied. In the early days of railways there were a number of prosecutions for culpable homicide arising out of railway accidents. In the first of these the Lord Advocate explained that because of the increasing number of railways it was important to make clear what the community had a right to expect from railway employees, and that, "It was right that it should be understood that accidents should be strictly looked into."[19] There are a number of examples of charges

---

[15] *cf.* the modern Scots law on this issue: see paras 3.13 to 3.28, *supra*.

[16] See para. 7.61, *supra*.

[17] *cf.* Hall, p.137. Hall argues that if punishment is to be used to deter negligence the punishment imposed would require to be higher than that imposed for intentional crimes, since the heavier the sanction, the greater the deterrence. This somewhat ingenuous argument ignores completely the consideration that legal punishment is retributive as well as utilitarian, and that careless behaviour is not regarded as deserving as severe punishment as intentional behaviour.

[18] Halt signs are an example of the policy of increasing carefulness by specifying certain precautions which must be taken on pain of punishment, whether or not harm results: see Gl. Williams, pp.123–124, but the law punishes failure to take these precautions whether such failure is intentional or not.

[19] *Jas. Boyd* (1842) 1 Broun 7, 16.

brought by the Crown because they felt it necessary to warn people of the possible consequences of particular forms of carelessness, such as the case of *Alex Dickson*[20] where the accused was charged with causing injury by erecting a faulty hustings. The Advocate-Depute asked for an acquittal after leading evidence, and said he had felt it his duty to bring the case before the public.[21]

THE PRESENT LAW. Despite the above it remains true that simple negligence is quite different from intention or recklessness, and it is difficult to feel entirely happy about punishing simple negligence at common law. This is partly because common law punishment implies that the accused is a criminal, and one does not think of the negligent wrongdoer as a criminal.[22] Again, although one may feel resentful or indignant at the result of carelessness, one may also feel sympathetic towards the unfortunate culprit who has caused a catastrophe inadvertently; one may feel indeed that, "There, but for the grace . . .". A tribunal conscious of its righteousness may condemn the murderer or thief with a clear conscience, but no one can have all that clear a conscience when it comes to negligence. So punishment for negligence at common law outside homicide cases is now confined entirely to gross negligence, which is classed as recklessness. In homicide the law's practice of judging conduct by results as well as by intentions led to negligent homicide being regarded as criminal, and in the nineteenth century the standard of negligence was the same as that in reparation law. But for a number of reasons, including the reluctance of juries and latterly judges to convict of culpable homicide caused negligently by persons going about their lawful business, culpable homicide is now restricted to cases of gross negligence, or to cases where the homicide is caused in the course of criminal conduct of some kind.[23] 7.77

These considerations do not apply in statutory offences. Conviction of a statutory offence involving negligence, such as careless driving, does not make one a "criminal"; it may be regarded simply as one of the hazards of modern life. Indeed, so many statutory offences can be committed without any *mens rea* at all that when punishment is made to depend on negligence the law appears to be making a gracious concession to the requirements of morality.

MENS REA IN ATTEMPTS

When it is said that A was guilty of an attempt to commit a particular crime what is usually meant is that he was trying to create the relevant *actus reus*. If this is the correct approach then only crimes of intent can be attempted. This would mean that, for example, if A inflicts gross injuries on B without intending to kill him, he is guilty of murder if B dies but not of attempted murder if B survives, a result which is 7.78

---

[20] (1847) Ark. 352.

[21] See also *Jas. Finney* (1848) Ark. 432, 439, a charge of causing injury by careless rock-blasting on which the accused was sentenced to two months' imprisonment, and *Geo. Armitage* (1885) 5 Couper 675, 677, a charge of culpable homicide by careless dispensing of medicine in which the accused was acquitted, more or less by direction of the judge.

[22] *cf. supra*, para. 1.13.

[23] See Vol. II, Chap. 26, and the remarks of Lord Young in *Wm. Drever and Wm. Tyre* (1885) 5 Couper 680, 687.

sometimes thought to be paradoxical, since the *mens rea* is the same in each case.

7.79 *English law.* The offence of attempt at common law in England was abolished by the Criminal Attempts Act 1981,[24] but the substituted statutory offence reflects the older law by referring to the appropriate *mens rea* as 'intent'.[25] No guidance is provided as to the meaning of that term; and the legislation could have been interpreted as requiring intent to be shown in respect of every element of the *actus reus* of the crime in question. The courts, however, have declined to accept such a limitation on attempts; but it has been affirmed that intent must be given its common law meaning.[26] This does not go so far as to allow, for example, conviction for attempted murder where the accused had intended to inflict serious bodily harm on his victim rather than kill him, even though either form of *mens rea* will suffice in England for murder itself.[27] It has been held both before and after 1981 that nothing short of an intention to kill will enable a person to be convicted of attempted murder.[28] But an intent to kill can be 'found'[29] where a jury considers that the defendant appreciated that death was a "virtual certainty" as a result of his conduct, and that concession applies to attempted murder just as it does to murder itself.[30]

The question remains open, however, as to which parts of the *actus reus* require to be intended in order that a conviction for attempt may be obtained. Two main theories have been espoused by the courts. The first requires a distinction to be drawn between the acts of the defendant (including, where appropriate, the results of his acts) and the circumstances essential to those acts being received as criminal. Under this theory, the requirements of the Criminal Attempts Act are satisfied if intent exists in relation to the acts of the defendant. With respect to essential circumstances, recklessness will be sufficient provided that it would be so for the completed crime.[31] In rape, for example, as currently defined in England,[32] a conviction for attempt requires intent as to the sexual intercourse; recklessness, however, will suffice relative to the victim's consent.[33] This theory, since anything less than intent in relation to acts or their consequences must result in acquittal of attempt, depends on acts and results being readily identifiable and not confusable with circumstances. This is far from being the case, however, especially with respect to statutory offences.[34] The alternative theory which has been

---

[24] s.6(1).

[25] s.1(1) begins: "If with intent to commit an offence to which this section applies".

[26] See *R. v. Pearman* (1984) 80 Cr.App.R. 259, CA, Stuart-Smith J., at p.263.

[27] *R. v. Cunningham* [1982] A.C. 566,HL.

[28] See *R. v. Whybrow* (1951) 35 Cr.App.R. 141, Lord Goddard C.J. at pp.147–148; *R. v. Walker* (1990) 90 Cr.App.R. 226, Lloyd L.J. at p.230.

[29] *R. v. Woollin* [1998] 3 W.L.R. 382, HL, Lord Steyn at p.393B-C, Ld. Hope at p.393F-G. The previous legal rule had referred to the drawing of an "inference" of intent to kill — see *R. v. Nedrick* [1986] 1 W.L.R. 1025, Lord Lane C.J. at 1028F.

[30] *R. v. Walker* (1990) 90 Cr.App.R. 226, Lloyd L.J. at p.231.

[31] See J.C. Smith and B. Hogan, *Criminal Law* (9th ed., by Sir J.C. Smith, 1999), p.308: Law Commission No. 177 (A Criminal Code for England and Wales), Vol. 1, cl.49(2); Vol. 2, paras 13.44, 13.45.

[32] See the Criminal Justice and Public Order Act 1994, s.142.

[33] *R. v. Khan* (1990) 91 Cr.App.R. 29.

[34] See R. Buxton, "The Working Paper on Inchoate Offences: (1) Incitement and Attempt" [1973] Crim.L.R. 656, at pp.662–663; J.E. Stannard, "Making Up for the missing element — a sideways look at attempts" (1987) 7 L.S. 194, at pp.198–199.

applied by the courts finds compliance with the Criminal Attempts Act if intent can be shown in relation to the 'missing element' which required the offence to be treated as one of attempt in the first place: other elements may be accompanied by whatever form of *mens rea* would suffice for the completed crime.[35] In truth, these (and other[36]) theories arise in order to avoid the undue restriction which would be involved were the *mens rea* for attempts to be strictly confined to 'intent'. The problem is how to allow for sufficient flexibility whilst adhering to an acceptable basis of principle, given the terms of the Criminal Attempts Act 1981.

As far as impossible attempts are concerned, the two theories discussed briefly above have difficulties in situations where recklessness suffices for at least part of the *actus reus* of the completed offence. This is exemplified in rape, where, for example, a man has sexual intercourse with a woman not caring whether she consents or not when in fact she does consent. The theory of acts and circumstances, which *Smith and Hogan* prefers,[37] compels conviction: provided there was intent to have sexual intercourse, recklessness as to consent suffices. But the apparent absurdity of convicting a defendant of attempted rape for an act of consensual sexual intercourse compels *Smith and Hogan* to rely on a particular interpretation of the Criminal Attempts Act 1981,[38] and Glanville Williams to rely on prosecutorial discretion,[39] to avoid the situation arising. Surely, however, the difficulty here is simply one of 'objective innocence', which is now an untenable basis for argument.[40] The 'missing element' theory appears to fare better in such cases since what is missing is the victim's lack of consent: for conviction there must be intention as to the victim's lack of consent whereas in such cases, of course, there is but recklessness.[41] The difficulty here, however, relates partly to what can be meant by 'intention' in relation to another person's consent,[42] and partly to the distinction which then seems to arise — for it would be necessary to be content with conviction when the defendant fails to achieve penetration and acquittal if he succeeds, a rather strange conclusion to say the least.[43]

---

[35] This theory was developed by J.E. Stannard in his article referred to in the immediately preceeding note, and adopted by the Court of Appeal in *Attorney General's Reference (No. 3 of 1992)* (1993) 98 Cr.App.R. 383, which involved analysis of attempted aggravated arson in terms of s.1(2) and (3) of the Criminal Damage Act 1971; see in particular Schiemann L.J. at p.390. The Court of Appeal's reasoning has been criticised in J.C. Smith and B. Hogan, *Criminal Law* (9th ed., by Sir J.C. Smith, 1999) at pp.308–309, principally since conviction for attempt would have been upheld where recklessness but not intent existed in relation to a consequence. Stannard's theory has itself been criticised: see R.A. Duff, "Recklessness in Attempts (Again)" (1995) 15 O.J.L.S. 309.

[36] See, *e.g.*, R.A.Duff, "Recklessness in Attempts (Again)" (1995) 15 O.J.L.S. 309, esp. at p.316 *et seq.*; G.R. Sullivan, "Intent, Subjective Recklessness and Culpability" (1992) 12 O.J.L.S. 381, esp. at pp.385–388; Jeremy Horder, "Varieties of intention, criminal attempts and endangerment" (1994) 14 L.S. 335. The courts have also evolved a theory of 'conditional intention' relative to attempted theft — see *R. v. Husseyn* (1977) 67 Cr.App.R. 131n; *Attorney General's Reference (Nos. 1 & 2 of 1979)* [1980] Q.B. 180 (C.A.): for criticism of this, see J.C. Smith and B. Hogan, *Criminal Law* (9th. ed., by Sir J.C. Smith, 1999), pp.309–311.

[37] J.C. Smith and B. Hogan, *Criminal Law* (9th. ed., by Sir John C. Smith, 1999), p.307–308. See also *R. v. Khan* (1990) 91 Cr.App.R. 29, Russell L.J. at pp.33–34.

[38] *ibid.*, p.334.

[39] Gl. Williams, "The Problems of Reckless Attempts" [1983] Crim.L.R. 365, at p.375.

[40] See paras 6.52, 6.53, *supra*.

[41] J.E. Stannard, "Making up for the missing element" (1987) 7 L.S. 194, at pp.199–200.

[42] See *ibid.*, at p.201, where Stannard rejects 'knowledge' or 'belief' in favour of 'purpose'.

[43] See *ibid.*, at p.199, examples (2A) and (2B).

7.80 *Scots law.* The basic English rule, now embodied in the Criminal Attempts Act 1981,[44] that attempt requires an intent to commit the crime in question, was accepted by Lord Sorn in *Geo. McAdam*.[45] In that case the charge was of assaulting a woman, striking and kicking her, fracturing her ribs, injuring her private parts, dragging her along the ground, throwing her into an ashpit and covering her with debris, "all to the danger of her life", and attempting to murder her. Lord Sorn directed the jury that responsibility for attempted murder depended on whether they thought it reasonable to infer that "the person who did the assault did it with the intent to kill",[46] and the jury convicted of assault to the danger of life.

In *John Currie*,[47] however, the opposite view was taken. The accused, who had stolen a car and were being chased by the police, were charged that they did,

> "[while] travelling in [the stolen car] . . . assault [constables] who, in the execution of their duty were travelling in a police car in pursuit of said stolen car . . . with a criminal disregard for the safety of said constables, repeatedly swerved said stolen motor-car into the path of said police car when both cars were travelling at speeds ranging from 70 to 100 miles per hour and did throw from said stolen car at said police car a number of business papers, a hammer . . . a tyre lever, two spanners and other articles . . . and push from said stolen motor-car into the path of said police car a car seat, all with intent to prevent said police car from pursuing said stolen car and to avoid your apprehension and with intent to cause said police car to crash and to cause injury to said constables, all to the danger of their lives,"

the whole being libelled as a charge of attempted murder. The accused's conviction for attempted murder was upheld by the appeal court, although it is not altogether clear whether this was because they accepted the trial judge's general proposition that the *mens rea* of murder and that of attempted murder were the same, or because they felt that any reasonable jury must have inferred an intent to kill. Lord Patrick said that "when one looks at that which the jury must have held proved to have happened, I cannot see that any other verdict was open to the jury in this particular case than that of attempt to murder . . . If they held that these things were done intentionally, then I cannot see that there was any room for any verdict save that of guilty of attempt to murder."[48]

7.81 The matter, however, must now be regarded as settled by *Cawthorne v. H.M. Advocate*.[49] The charge was that the accused assaulted a number of people "and did wilfully discharge several bullets from a loaded rifle at them to the danger of their lives and did thus attempt to murder them." The evidence, as summarised in the report of the case, was that "the

---

[44] See s.1(1).

[45] High Court at Glasgow, Jul. 1959, unrep'd. Reported on another point, 1960 J.C. 1.

[46] Transcript of Proceedings, 109.

[47] High Court at Glasgow, Dec. 1962, High Court of Appeal, Jan. 1963, unrep'd.

[48] Opn. of Lord Patrick, 3. By "intentionally" Lord Patrick must have meant that the stolen car was swerved and the things thrown at the police car deliberately, not "with intent to kill."

[49] 1968 J.C. 32.

panel had been living in a lodge on Knockie Estate with the lady known as Mrs. Cawthorne. On the evening in question there was a quarrel between them. He went outside and fired two shots from a .303 rifle, apparently with the purpose of frightening Barbara Brown. Mrs Cawthorne, Barbara Brown and the two Frasers, who had been called to help them, went into the study, closed the shutters and barricaded the door. The panel, knowing these four were in the study, fired at least two shots into the room, one through the shutters and one through the door, Both shots travelled across the room low enough to strike a person."

The accused appealed unsuccessfully against the trial judge's direction that attempted murder did not require intent to kill but was satisfied by recklessness. Although the opinions betray some confusion between recklessness as evidence of intention and recklessness as an independent *mens rea*, and between intention and "criminal intention" in the sense of *mens rea*,[50] there is no doubt that the case established that the *mens rea* for an attempted crime is the same as that for the completed crime.[51] As Lord Justice-General Clyde said:

> "In my opinion attempted murder is just the same as murder in the eyes of our law, but for the one vital distinction, that the killing has not been brought off and the victim of the attack has escaped with his life. But there must be in each case the same *mens rea*, and that *mens rea* in each case can be proved by evidence of a deliberate intention to kill or by such recklessness as to show that the accused was regardless of the consequences of his act, whatever they may have been. I can find no justification in principle or in authority for the view so persuasively put forward by Mr. Cowie that the *mens rea* in the case where life is actually taken can be established by evidence of a reckless disregard of the consequences of the act on the part of the accused, but that *mens rea* cannot be proved in that way where the charge is attempted murder. In the latter case chance or good fortune has resulted in a life being spared, but the wilful intent behind the act is just the same as if a life had in fact been forfeited."[52]

Although the approach in *Cawthorne* is not without support,[53] it may be argued that it introduces an unnecessary paradox into the criminal law to the effect that A can be guilty of attempting to do something he did not intend to do, *i.e.* of trying to do something he was not trying to do. Nor

---

[50] See G.H. Gordon, "*Cawthorne* and the Mens Rea of Murder," 1969 S.L.T. (News) 41.

[51] In *Docherty v. Brown*, 1996 J.C. 48, the judges (other than L.J.-C. Ross, who confines himself to the general term "mens rea" itself) refer to 'intention' as the appropriate *mens rea* for attempt. (See L.J.-G. Hope at p.50; Lord Sutherland at pp.61, 62 and 63; Lord Cameron at p.67; Lord Johnston at p.74.) The case, however, is concerned with impossible attempts and the clarification of the law thereanént; *Cawthorne* was not mentioned at all, and there is no reason to suppose that the court considered itself to be casting doubt upon the correctness of what was said there. If unknown to the accused in *Cawthorne* there had been no one in the room into which he directed his shots, or if everyone there had died or committed suicide for reasons unconnected with his conduct, it is difficult to see why 'intention to kill' should have been required just because the facts, contrary to his belief, made the completed crime impossible.

[52] At 36.

[53] It is followed in South Africa: *R. v. Huebsch* 1953 (2) S.A. 568 (AD); E.M. Burchell & P.M.A. Hunt, *South African Criminal Law and Procedure*, Vol. 1, *General Principles of Criminal Law* (3rd ed., by J.M. Burchell, 1997), p.350; J. Burchell and J. Milton, *Principles of Criminal Law* (2nd. ed., 1997), at p.438; D.R. Stuart, *op.cit., supra,* para. 7.13, n. 37.

is there any need for this paradox — the ends of justice would have been sufficiently served by a conviction of assault to the danger of life, which would have avoided any inference as to *mens rea* except the simple one that the articles were deliberately thrown at the police car and the gun deliberately fired into the room, in *Currie* and *Cawthorne* respectively: the court's powers of punishment for such assaults are as wide as in the case of attempted murder, and the sentences actually imposed — ten years' imprisonment was the highest — would not have been out of place for a serious assault to the danger of life.[54]

7.82 *Possible limitations of the rule*. It may be possible to read *Currie*[54a] and *Cawthorne*[54b] as restricted to cases where there is an intent to cause some harm of the kind protected by the attempted crime or at least to commit a comparable crime, such as assault where the charge is attempted murder, but it may well be that the courts will extend it to other common law crimes of recklessness. Certainly, the opinions in *Cawthorne* do not suggest that any distinction between acts and circumstances is intended to be drawn relative to *mens rea* in attempts; and the current complexities of English law, notwithstanding the Criminal Attempts Act 1981,[55] may convince the Scots courts that the *Cawthorne* rule is on balance worthy of preservation rather than alteration.

So far as statutory offences are concerned, there seems to be some doubt in England whether intention is needed for an attempt, where the completed offence is one of strict responsibility.[56] Logically, *Cawthorne*[56a] could be read as meaning that no *mens rea* is needed for an attempt to commit an offence of strict responsibility, but in view of the court's dislike of such offences intention may well be required, at any rate in the case of "public welfare offences" by analogy with the position in conspiracy,[57] accession[58] and the commission of "acts preparatory".[59] In other crimes, however, such as sexual offences under Part 1 of the Criminal Law (Consolidation) (Scotland) Act 1995, there can be little doubt that no *mens rea* is required as to the age of the girl or other attendant circumstances, except where it is required for the completed offence.[60]

---

[54] One effect of *Currie* indeed has been to make almost all cases of assault to the danger of life, and many cases of assault to severe injury, into possible cases af attempted murder — it is difficult to accept that had this always been the law examples of aggravated assaults of these kinds would be so common and convictions for attempted murders by recklessness virtually unknown prior to 1962. See also *Strachan v. H.M. Advocate*, 1994 S.C.C.R. 341.

[54a] High Court at Glasgow, Dec. 1962, High Court of Appeal, Jan. 1963, unrep'd.

[54b] 1968 J.C. 32.

[55] See para. 7.79, *supra*.

[56] See para. 8.38, *infra*. See also Criminal Attempts Act 1981, ss.1(1), 3(3). It is believed that at common law in South Africa intention is required, since "liability for attempt stems from the common law which knows no exception to the rule *actus non facit nisi mens sit rea*": E.M. Burchell and P.M.A. Hunt, *South African Criminal Law and Procedure*, Vol. 1, *General Principles of Criminal Law* (3rd. ed., by J.M. Burchell, 1997), at p.350.

[56a] 1968 J.C. 32.

[57] *Churchill v. Walton* [1967] 2 A.C. 224; see also Criminal Law Act 1977, s.1(2).

[58] J.C. Smith and B. Hogan, *Criminal Law* (8th. ed., by Sir J.C. Smith, 1996), pp.141–142; *John Henshall (Quarries) Ltd. v. Harvey* [1965] 2 Q.B. 233.

[59] *Gardner v. Akeroyd* [1952] 2 Q.B. 743.

[60] See Vol. II, Chap. 36.

Attempted culpable homicide. It has been suggested that there is no such crime as attempted culpable homicide, and there is no record of any such charge.[61] The feeling that "attempted culpable homicide" is an oxymoron is due to the connotation of absence of intention in the phrase "culpable homicide", and the existence of this feeling indeed supports the view that *Cawthorne*[61a] is wrong. But standing *Cawthorne*[61b] there is no reason why, if the accused's *mens rea* is not gross enough for murder but is sufficient for culpable homicide, he should not be convicted of attempted culpable homicide.[62] **7.83**

---

[61] T.B. Smith, pp.163, 188.

[61a] 1968 J.C. 32.

[61b] *ibid.*

[62] But an attempted euthanasia which if successful would probably be charged as culpable homicide, would be charged as attempted murder, since there is no need to reduce the crime in the case of attempts in order to allow general mitigating factors to operate. See *H.M. Advocate v. Agnes Litster*, Edinburgh Sheriff Court, Jul. 1964, unrep'd. In fairly recent cases of attempted murder where the nature of the defence could have reduced a charge of murder to one of culpable homicide, the courts have declined to advance attempted culpable homicide as a possible verdict — see *Brady v. H.M. Advocate*, 1986 S.L.T. 686; *Salmond v. H.M. Advocate.*, 1991 S.C.C.R. 43 (provocation): *H.M. Advocate v. Blake*, 1986 S.L.T. 661 (diminished responsibility), the appropriate verdict being one of assault.

CHAPTER 8

MENS REA IN STATUTORY OFFENCES AND CORPORATE RESPONSIBILITY

I — MENS REA IN STATUTORY OFFENCES[1]

8.01 The basic common law principle that *actus non facit reum nisi mens sit rea*[2] does not extend to all statutory offences, and the rules regarding *mens rea* in statutory offences form a branch of the law somewhat separate from the general common law of *mens rea*.

In dealing with statutory offences it is particularly necessary to bear in mind that each offence consists of different elements so that *mens rea* must be considered with regard to each element separately.[3] Failure to do so may lead to the common mistake of asking whether a particular statutory offence, viewed as a unitary whole, either does or does not require *mens rea* for its commission, instead of asking whether a particular element of the offence must be committed intentionally, or whether knowledge of a particular element is necessary. There is also a tendency to concede that a particular offence does require *mens rea*, and then to nullify the concession by saying that the requirement of *mens rea* is satisfied by "an intention to do the act prohibited",[4] by which is meant an intention regarding what is taken to be the central element of the offence.[5] This works in the following way: suppose it is an offence for A to sell silk stockings but lawful for him to sell stockings of any other kind and that he does in fact sell B a particular pair of stockings which unknown to A are silk — if, then, A intended to sell these particular stockings to B and did not, for example, mistakenly put in B's parcel a pair of stockings he had set aside with the intention of dealing with them otherwise than by sale, A can be said to have *mens rea*, to act intentionally, although he lacked *mens rea* regarding the one circumstance which rendered his act illegal. To adopt this attitude is to pay lip service to the rule that even in statutory offences there is a presumption in favour of *mens rea*, while imposing in practice what is virtually strict responsibility.

---

[1] For a general discussion of the problem of *mens rea* in statutory offences, see J.Ll.J. Edwards, *Mens Rea in Statutory Offences* (London, 1955); Colin Howard, *Strict Responsibility* (London, 1963); Hyman Gross, *A Theory of Criminal Justice* (Oxford, 1979), pp.342–374.

[2] *supra*, para. 7.01.

[3] See, *e.g.*, *Shanks and McEwan (Teesside) Ltd v. The Environmental Agency* [1997] 2 All E.R. 332, which deals with an offence under s.33 of the Environmental Protection Act 1990; and, *Salmon v. H.M. Advovate; Moore v. H.M. Advocate*, 1998 S.C.C.R. 740, which deals *inter alia* with the *mens rea* requirements of certain offences under the Misuse of Drugs Act 1971.

[4] See *e.g. Law Society v. United Service Bureau Ltd* [1934] 1 K.B. 343; *Kat v. Diment* [1951] 1 K.B. 34.

[5] *supra*, para. 3.06.

8.02 In order to determine the position in any particular offence it is necessary to look to the terms of the statute concerned. As a result, it is impossible to lay down any generally valid rules of interpretation. The courts themselves make use of one or more of a number of criteria in deciding whether any offence requires *mens rea*, the most important of which are the wording of the statutory provision creating the offence, the gravity of the offence, the nature of the penalty, and the object of the statute.[6] It is therefore usually possible to hold that a particular offence does or does not require *mens rea*, as the court wishes, by selecting the appropriate criterion, in much the same way as courts are able to rationalise their *ad hoc* judgments on causality by choosing among a number of available criteria.[7] The situation is made even more unsatisfactory in relation to statutory *mens rea* because the courts tend also from time to time to regard it is self-evident that a particular provision necessarily implies either *mens rea* or its absence, as the case may be, and what is self-evident to one judge may not be so to another.[8] The result is, as Glanville Williams points out,[9] that the decisions are idiosyncratic and irreconcilable, and the courts often arrive at a decision by reference to their interpretation of the requirements of public policy. Fairly recent English cases including those at the highest level do, however, indicate that the presumption in favour of *mens rea* is now regarded as very strong.[10]

8.03 *Strict and vicarious responsibility.* The exclusion of *mens rea* may take two forms — it may involve either strict responsibility[11] where A is convicted of an act done by him without *mens rea*, or vicarious responsibility where A is convicted of an act done by B because A is held to be responsible for B on the principle *qui facit per alium facit per se*: vicarious responsibility usually goes hand in hand with strict responsibility, but it is possible to have vicarious responsibility for an offence

---

[6] See *Mousell Bros. Ltd v. L. and N.W.Ry.* [1971] 2 K.B. 836, Atkin J. at 845; *Sherras v. De Rutzen* [1895] 1 Q.B. 918, Wright J. at 921. *Cf. Gordon v. Shaw* (1908) 5 Adam 469, Lord McLaren at 477–478. Modern English authorities tend to relate the 'nature of the penalty' to the degree of the risk which the statutory provision seeks to prevent: see *Gammon (Hong Kong) Ltd v. Attorney General of Hong Kong* [1985] A.C. 1, a Privy Council decision which has been frequently referred to with approval in subsequent cases — *e.g. Wings Ltd v. Ellis* [1985] A.C. 272; *R. v. Wells Street Magistrates* [1986] 1 W.L.R. 1046; *Seaboard Ltd v. Transport Secretary* [1993] 1 W.L.R. 1025, Stoughton L.J. at 1030D; *R. v. Blake* [1997] 1 W.L.R. 1167; *R. v. Paine* (1998) 1 Cr.App.R. 36; *Harrow London Borough Council v. Shah* (1999) 2 Cr.App.R. 457.

[7] *supra*, para. 4.01.

[8] *cf. e.g. Gordon v. Shaw* (1908) 5 Adam 469, Lord McLaren at 478, Lord Kinnear at 481; *Paul v. Hargreaves* [1908] 2 K.B. 289 and *Fraser v. Heatly*, 1952 J.C. 103; and the classic pair of irreconcilables: *Cundy v. Le Cocq* (1884) 13 Q.B.D. 207, and *Sherras v. De Rutzen* [1895] 1 Q.B. 918. The same judge may even reach conflicting views in regard to the same offence in different cases — *cf. Evans v. Dell* [1937] 1 All E.R. 349, Goddard J. at 354; *Reynolds v. G.H.Austin and Sons Ltd* [1951] 2 K.B. 135; *Browning v. J.W.H. Watson (Rochester) Ltd* [1953] 1 W.L.R. 1172.

[9] Gl. Williams, p.260.

[10] *Sweet v. Parsley* [1970] A.C. 132; *R. v. Warner* [1969] 2 A.C. 256, Lord Reid diss., at 271–280; *cf. Tesco Ltd v. Nattrass* [1972] A.C. 153; but see also *Alphacell Ltd v. Woodward* [1972] A.C. 824; *Gammon (Hong Kong) Ltd v. Attorney General of Hong Kong* [1985] A.C. 1, PC, opinion of the Board at 14B-C — as approved by the House of Lords in *Wings Ltd v. Ellis* [1985] A.C. 272; *R. v. Wells Street Magistrates* [1986] 1 W.L.R. 1096, QBD; *R. v. Blake* [1997] 1 W.L.R. 1167, CA; *R. v. Paine* (1998) 1 Cr.App.R. 36, Court Martial Appeal Court.

[11] This is often called absolute responsibility, but Gl. Williams' use of the term "strict" is preferable since, as he points out, certain defences, such as infancy or duress, remain open even in cases of so-called absolute responsibility: Gl. Williams, p.215.

which requires *mens rea* on the part of the actual offender, in which case B's *mens rea* will be imputed to A. The general principles governing the applicability of strict and vicarious responsibility are the same; and the distinction between the two is further blurred by the existence of a number of offences which consist in A's selling articles by the hand of B, or causing or permitting B to do something, or even bringing about or permitting a state of affairs where the person at fault is B, where although A's responsibility is technically primary since it is he who is the seller in law or who causes or permits, or is the person with legal responsibility for what happened, in fact the prohibited act is done by B.

Most of the Scots cases on statutory *mens rea* are concerned with vicarious responsibility, but the question of strict responsibility is logically the prior one, and it is proposed to deal with it first.

Strict Responsibility

Strict responsibility and human rights

In Canada, a requirement for *mens rea* has virtually become a principle of fundamental justice. Prior to 1982, the law there was that offences were of three sorts: 'true crimes', where *mens rea* (including negligence) was essential and had to be established by the Crown; public welfare offences of 'strict liability', where it was unnecessary for the Crown to prove *mens rea* on the part of the accused but where it would be presumed nevertheless that the accused had the defence of showing on the balance of probabilities that he had had a reasonable belief in a mistaken set of facts, or that he had exercised due diligence to avoid any contravention; and absolute offences, where even the defence of absence of fault was foreclosed, but which required express creation by the legislature in question.[12] Statutory offences, other than those of express absolute liability, were thus either 'true crimes' or offences to which a defence of due diligence (or error) was presumptively applied. In 1982, the Canadian Charter of Rights and Freedoms was enacted,[13] and set out in particular that no one was to be deprived of his liberty "except in accordance with the principles of fundamental justice",[14] and that every person charged with an offence had "the right to be presumed innocent until proven guilty according to law."[15] Statutory or Criminal Code offences which violated such rights or freedoms might be declared of 'no force and effect' by the courts,[16] unless the violation in question could be justified under section 1 of the Charter, which reads: "The Canadian Charter of Rights and Freedoms guarantees the rights and freedoms set out in it subject only to such reasonable limits prescribed by law as can be demonstrably justified in a free and democratic society." **8.04**

The effect of the Charter has been to guarantee subjective *mens rea* as an essential element in offences where conviction carries considerable

---

[12] *R. v. City of Sault Ste Marie* [1978] 2 S.C.R. 1299.

[13] The Charter appears as Schedule B to the Constitution Act 1982, and became effective on April 17, 1982.

[14] Section 7. The text reads: "Everyone has the right to life, liberty and security of the person and the right not to be deprived thereof except in accordance with the principles of fundamental justice."

[15] Section 11(d).

[16] Constitution Act 1982 [Canada], s.52(1).

stigma or heavy penalties.[17] In all other offences, where imprisonment is a possible penalty following conviction, it has been held that at the very least a minimum level of fault must be establised; that minimum level is negligence, and can be satisfied where, again at the very least, a defence of due diligence is permitted to the accused.[18] Unless, therefore, a legislature creates an absolute liability offence which carries no prison sentence, the law in Canada recognises that a requirement of *mens rea* is a principle of fundamental justice. At the very least, a Canadian regulatory offence must make provision for a defence of due diligence; but such a defence, if the accused must carry the persuasive burden of showing lack of negligence, will probably infringe the presumption of innocence right guaranteed by section 11(d) of the Charter, and will thus have itself to be justifiable under section 1.[19]

The European Convention on Human Rights is not worded in the same way as the Canadian Charter, and in particular it makes no express reference to principles of fundamental justice. Accordingly, given the present state of Convention jurisprudence, it is simply not possible to be certain whether strict or absolute liability is contrary to Articles 5 or 6 of the Convention.[20] The following discussion assumes, therefore, that strict liability is not incompatible with Convention rights.

Statutory interpretation

8.05 *The words of the statute.* The most important factor in determining whether or not an offence requires *mens rea* is the wording of the relevant enactment: if Parliament enacts that *mens rea* is required, or that its absence is irrelevant, then the courts will act accordingly, and any question of injustice or absurdity will be disregarded.[21] There are,

---

[17] Murder would fulfil either criterion. In *R. v. Vaillancourt* [1987] 2 S.C.R. 636, where the accused and an accomplice set out to commit a robbery, the accused knew that his accomplice had a firearm but had insisted that the weapon be unloaded; indeed, prior to the carrying out of the offence, he insisted upon being given (and was given) possession of the bullets which his accomplice had. Unknown to the accused, the accomplice had retained some bullets, which he then used to shoot and kill someone during the course of the robbery. At the time, the Canadian Criminal Code adhered to the "felony-murder" rule, under which the accused was denied a defence to a murder charge based on personal lack of *mens rea* in relation to such a killing. The Supreme Court of Canada held however that that rule violated s.7 of the Charter.

[18] See *Re B.C. Motor Vehicle Act* [1985] 2 S.C.R. 486, where a statutory offence, which imposed absolute liability on those who drove on a highway without possessing a valid driving licence but which carried a penalty of imprisonment, was held to violate s.7 of the Charter. It was also held that s.1 could not be used to rescue such a provision except in the most exceptional circumstances, such as war or natural disaster.

[19] See the leading case of *R. v. Wholesale Travel Group Inc.* [1991] 3 S.C.R. 154, where the accused was charged with making false or misleading representations to the public (contrary to s.36(1)(a), as read with the defence under s.37.3(2), of the Competition Act 1970), in that he advertised that holidays were available from him at wholesale prices, an offence punishable by imprisonment. The Crown's contention was that the holidays in question were in fact being offered at a price which exceeded the prices paid for them by the accused in the course of his business. The Supreme Court treated as *pro non scripto* certain provisions which could have resulted in conviction even in the absence of negligence. They then considered a provision which declared that the accused would not be convicted if he established that he had taken reasonable precautions and exercised due diligence to prevent contravention. The Supreme Court decided by a majority that this constituted a reversal of the onus pertaining to the fundamental requirement of *mens rea*, that it was thus contrary to the "presumption of innocence" right under s.11(d) of the Charter, but that the violation involved was justifiable in context under s.1.

[20] See P. van Dijk and G.J.H. van Hoof, *Theory and Practice of the European Convention on Human Rights* (3rd ed., 1998), pp.341–353, 458–462.

[21] *Sweet v. Parsley, supra,* Lord Reid at 148.

however, many statutes whose terms are not explicit, and it is in relation to them that difficulties of interpretation arise.

THE PRESUMPTION IN FAVOUR OF MENS REA, AND WORDS OF ABSOLUTE PROHIBITION. The cases show that there are two opposing ways of approaching the interpretation of a statutory offence. The first is by way of a presumption that *mens rea* is always required, so that a statute will not be read as abrogating this fundamental requirement in the absence of clear words excluding *mens rea*: the second is by way of a literal interpretation of the statute, so that, if the statute uses what have been called "words of absolute prohibition," it will be improper for the courts to read into it words such as "knowingly" which would imply *mens rea*.[22] To take a simple provision: if a statute provides that "No person shall supply liquor to a policeman on duty", this can be interpreted as requiring *mens rea* since there is nothing in its phraseology to exclude the presumption in favour of *mens rea*,[23] or it can be interpreted as creating strict responsibility since it says simply that a certain thing shall not be done, and it would be improper to "rewrite" it as "No person shall knowingly".[24] The general adoption of either method of interpretation would lead to consistency, although the adoption of the literal approach might lead to consistent injustice, but in practice the courts have vacillated between the two approaches, sometimes even in construing the same statute.[25] **8.06**

As a matter of theory and general principle the proper approach is by way of the presumption in favour of *mens rea*. Such an approach is in accord both with moral requirements and with the accepted method of construing penal statutes[26] and its correctness has been clearly affirmed in the two leading Scots cases on the question.[27] It has also been stressed by the House of Lords in *Sweet v. Parsley*. Lord Reid said, "there has for centuries been a presumption that Parliament did not intend to make criminals of persons who were in no way blameworthy in what they did"[28]; Lord Morris of Borth-y-Gest said: "it would not be reasonable lightly to impute to Parliament an intention to create an offence in such a way that someone could be convicted of it who by all reasonable and sensible standards is without fault",[29] while Lord Diplock said that the mere fact that Parliament has made the conduct a criminal offence gives rise to some implication about the mental element of the conduct proscribed.[30] His Lordship added:

> "This implication stems from the principle that it is contrary to a rational and civilised criminal code, such as Parliament must be presumed to have intended, to penalise one who has performed his

---

[22] *Hobbs v. Winchester Corporation* [1910] 2 K.B. 471. *Cf. Reynolds v. G.H. Austin & Sons Ltd* [1951] 2 K.B. 135, Humphreys J. at 143.

[23] *Sherras v. De Rutzen* [1895] 1 Q.B. 918; *cf. R. v. Cugullere* [1961] 1 W.L.R. 858; *Lim Chin Aik v. The Queen* [1963] A.C. 160.

[24] *cf. Cundy v. Le Cocq* (1884) 13 Q.B.D. 207.

[25] *cf. Sherras v. De Rutzen* and *Cundy v. Le Cocq, supra; Anderson v. Rose,* 1919 J.C. 20 and *Beattie v. Waugh*, 1920 J.C. 64.

[26] *cf. L.N.E.R. Co. v. Berriman* [1946] A.C. 278, Lord Simonds at 313.

[27] *Mitchell v. Morrison*, 1938 J.C. 64; *Duguid v. Fraser*, 1942 J.C. 1: both cases of vicarious responsibility.

[28] [1970] A.C. 132 at 148G.

[29] At 153F.

[30] At 162G.

duty as a citizen to ascertain what acts are prohibited by law (ignorantia juris non excusat) and has taken all proper care to inform himself of any facts which would make his conduct lawful."[31]

But there are many reported cases in which the literal approach has been adopted,[32] and at least until recently one could say that on balance the presumption in favour of *mens rea* was more honoured in the breach than in the observance. It seems now to be accepted that, as Lord Goddard C.J. said in *Brend v. Wood*[33]: "It is of the utmost importance for the protection of the liberty of the subject that a Court should always bear in mind that, unless a statute, either clearly or by necessary implication, rules out *mens rea* as a constituent part of a crime, the Court should not find a man guilty of an offence against the criminal law unless he has a guilty mind." Nevertheless, those types of statutory offences which were held to involve strict responsibility at a time when the courts were perhaps more prone to adopt the literal approach than they have been in more recent times still involve strict responsibility, and new statutes creating similar offences are still construed as involving strict responsibility except where *mens rea* is specifically provided for. These statutes include all offences in relation to sale, such as offences under the Food and Drugs Acts, Acts regulating the sale of medicines and poisons, weights and measures legislation, anti-pollution legislation and other offences directed at public nuisances and offences under the Licensing Acts, as well as offences under the Road Traffic Acts, and so cover a very wide field. Statements supporting the presumption in favour of *mens rea* are often followed, therefore, by a reference to the class of

---

[31] At 163 C-D; *cf. R. v. King* [1962] S.C.R. 746, Ritchie J. at 762. For an account of the Canadian position, both before and after the adoption of the Canadian Charter of Rights and Freedoms, see para. 8.04, *supra*, and in particular — *Beaver v. The Queen* [1957] S.C.R. 531; *The Queen v. City of Sault Ste Marie* [1978] 2 S.C.R. 1299; *Re B.C. Motor Vehicle Act* [1985] 2 S.C.R. 486; *R. v. Vaillancourt* [1987] 2 S.C.R. 636; and *R. v. Wholesale Travel Gp.Inc.* [1991] 3 S.C.R. 154. For the law in South Africa, see *Amalgamated Beverage Industries Natal (Pty) Ltd v. Durban City Council*, 1994 (3) S.A. 170 (A), noting that a corrected version of Botha J.'s dissenting opinion appears at p.646; and E.M. Burchell and P.M.A. Hunt, *South African Criminal Law and Procedure* (3rd ed., 1997), Vol. 1, *General Principles of Criminal Law* (J.M. Burchell (ed.)), p.289 *et seq*., which notes *inter alia* the move away from strict liability in that country.

[32] *e.g. Gordon v. Shaw, supra: Howman v. Russell*, 1923 J.C. 32; *McLaren v. Smith*, 1923 J.C. 91; *Alphacell Ltd v. Woodward* [1972] A.C. 824; and see *Chalmers v. MacGlashan* (1886) 1 White 1, Lord Young at 7. See also dicta such as the following: "in construing a modern statute this presumption as to mens rea does not exist": *Hobbs v. Winchester Corpn* [1910] 2 K.B. 471, Kennedy L.J. at 483; and the similar observation by Stephen J. in *Cundy v. Le cocq, supra,* at 210; "It has been laid down over and over again that where a statute absolutely prohibits the doing of an act it is sufficient to show that the person accused did the forbidden act intentionally and that it is not necessary to go further and prove what is commonly known as mens rea or any intention other than to do the thing forbidden": *Law Society v. United Service Bureau Ltd* [1934] 1 K.B. 343, Avory J. at 349; "Where a statute forbids the doing of a certain act, the doing of it in itself supplies mens rea": *Kat v. Diment* [1951] 1 K.B. 34, Lord Goddard C.J. at 42; "[I]f a statute contains an absolute prohibition against the doing of some act, as a general rule mens rea is not a constituent of the offence": *Harding v. Price* [1948] 1 K.B. 695, Lord Goddard C.J. at 701; and Humphreys J.'s remark in the same case that knowledge is prima facie not a necessary ingredient of a statutory offence: at 702. See also the same judge's remark in *Reynolds v. G.H. Austin and Sons Ltd* [1951] 2 K.B. 135 at 143, that "[I]t is important that the rule should not be relaxed . . . that when there is an absolute prohibition against the doing of an act scienter forms no part of the offence." .

[33] (1946) 62 T.L.R. 462, 463.

statutes which do not require *mens rea*,[34] and, as was said in one Scottish case, there is no novelty about excluding *mens rea*.[35] Indeed, the two leading Scots authorities for the existence of the presumption[36] are themselves cases in which it was held not to apply, and there is no reported Scots case in which the court held that *mens rea* was necessary where the statute used words of absolute prohibition.[37]

The current approach is perhaps summed up in a passage in Lord Pearce's speech in *Sweet v. Parsley* where his Lordship said:

> "The notion that some guilty mind is a constituent part of crime and punishment goes back far beyond our common law. And at common law mens rea is a necessary element in a crime. Since the Industrial Revolution the increasing complexity of life called into being new duties and crimes which took no account of intent. Those who undertake various industrial and other activities, especially where these affect the life and health of the citizen, may find themselves liable to statutory punishment regardless of knowledge or intent, both in respect of their own acts or neglect and those of their servants. But one must remember that normally mens rea is still an ingredient of any offence. Before the court will dispense with the necessity for mens rea it has to be satisfied that Parliament so intended. The mere absence of the word 'knowingly' is not enough. But the nature of the crime, the punishment, the absence of social obloquy, the particular mischief and the field of activity in which it occurs, and the wording of the particular section and its context, may show that Parliament intended that the act should be prevented by punishment, regardless of intent or knowledge."[38]

EXPRESS EXCLUSION OF MENS REA. It is rarely if ever that a statute expressly excludes *mens rea*. Section 301 of the Customs and Excise Act 1952 dealt with false declarations and provided a higher penalty where the offence was committed knowingly or recklessly, and this was said to involve strict responsibility where the offence was committed other than knowingly or recklessly.[39] **8.07**

---

[34] See *Mitchell v. Morrison, supra,* L.J.-C. Normand at 71; *Duguid v. Fraser, supra,* L.J.-C. Cooper at 5. Two of the outstanding cases in favour of a requirement of *mens rea* are *Sherras v. De Rutzen, supra,* and *Lim Chim Aik v. The Queen* [1963] A.C. 160, and the latter adopted as one of the basic principles of the law a statement by Wright J. in the former that "There is a presumption that mens rea, an evil intention, or knowledge of the wrongfulness of the act, is an essential ingredient in every offence; but that presumption is liable to be displaced either by the words of the statute creating the offence or by the subject-matter with which it deals": [1895] 1 Q.B. 918, Wright J. at 921.

[35] *Hunter v. Clark,* 1956 J.C. 59, L.J.-G. Clyde at 63.

[36] *Mitchell v. Morrison; Duguid v. Fraser, supra.* But see *MacLeod v. Hamilton,* 1965 S.L.T. 305.

[37] *Haig v. Thompson*, 1931 J.C. 29 was a case of vicarious responsibility; *MacLeod v. Hamilton, supra,* is a very special case: see (1965) 29 J.C.L. 283.

[38] [1970] A.C. at 156E-G; see also *Sherras v. De Rutzen* [1895] 1 Q.B. 918, Wright J. at 921–922.

[39] *Attorney-General's Reference* (*No.* 3 of 1975) [1976] 1 W.L.R. 737: the view was taken that the section created two offences, one, which was indictable, requiring *mens rea* and the other being a summary offence of strict responsibility. The offence was reformulated in 1979 in a way which supports that view: see Customs and Excise Management Act 1979, s.167(1)-(3).

8.08 IMPLIED EXCLUSION OF MENS REA. It is common for modern statutes to provide that certain circumstances shall constitute a defence to an offence created by the statute. Such a provision has two general effects: the offences to which it applies will be treated as offences of strict responsibility subject only to the special defence, so that unless the defence is made out responsibility is strict[40]; and the offences to which it does not apply will often be treated as offences involving strict responsibility in all circumstances.[41]

Similarly, where certain provisions of a statute use terms like "knowingly" or "with intent to defraud" and others do not, the other provisions may be treated as involving strict responsibility.[42] Section 174 (1)(a) of the Road Traffic Act 1988 makes it an offence "knowingly" to make a false statement in order to obtain a driving licence, and section 174 (5)(a) an offence to make a false statement *simpliciter* in order to obtain a certificate of insurance; the latter offence has been held not to require knowledge of the falsity of the statement.[43]

8.09 *The gravity of the offence.* The modern law of strict responsibility stems mainly from cases dealing with offences under the Licensing Acts which were regarded as being not so much crimes as breaches of the licensee's certificate which carried a penalty, and so as at most only quasi-criminal; accordingly it was thought that the maxim *actus non facit reum* did not apply with such force to them as to ordinary crimes. Many statutes which have been interpreted as not requiring *mens rea* do concern comparatively trivial offences which are usually punished in the first instance with a fine. Many of them also concern public welfare offences[44] which bear little resemblance to the traditional old-fashioned crimes in respect of which the maxim was originally formulated. It is true that the more trivial and the more "public welfare" in character an offence is the more likely it is not to require *mens rea*, but offences of strict responsibility are by no means confined to such offences. Certain sexual offences under the Criminal Law (Consolidation) (Scotland) Act 1995, for example, strongly resemble the common law offences of rape and lewd practices and carry long sentences of imprisonment, but they are offences of strict

---

[40] See *e.g.* Food Safety Act 1990, s.21; Weights and Measures Act 1985, ss.33, 34; Trade Descriptions Act 1968, s.24; *McNab v. Alexanders of Greenock Ltd*, 1971 S.L.T. 121; *Clode v. Barnes* [1974] 1 W.L.R. 544; Hallmarking Act 1973, s.1; *Chilvers v. Rayner* [1984] 1 W.L.R. 328; Wildlife and Countryside Act 1981, s.1(2); *Kirkland v. Robinson* [1987] Crim.L.R. 643. *Cf. Salmon v. H.M. Advocate; Moore v. H.M. Advocate,* 1998 S.C.C.R. 740.

[41] See *e.g. Hunter v. Clark*, 1956 J.C. 59.

[42] *Bank of New South Wales v. Piper* [1897] A.C. 383; *Chajutin v. Whitehead* [1938] 1 K.B. 506; *Alphacell Ltd v. Woodward* [1972] A.C. 824, Lord Pearson at 842 G-H. But see *Sweet v. Parsley* [1970] A.C. 132, Lord Reid at 149 D-E. (*Cf. Gammon (Hong Kong) Ltd v. Attorney General of Hong Kong* [1985] A.C. 1, opinion of the Board at p.17G, where it is stated that the existence of other offences in the same statute with *mens rea* words attached proves nothing, since in complex legislation a range of offences and different ways of expressing them is bound to be encountered.) C. Howard justifiably offers the following comment on this mode of construction: "This myopic mode of statutory construction purports to be a method of discovering the intention of the legislature, which is thereby credited with an ineradicable passion for creating intellectual puzzles entitled to about the same measure of respect as a parlour game": Howard, *op.cit.*, p.63.

[43] *R. v. Cummerson* [1968] 2 Q.B. 534, interpreting the similarly worded provisions under s.275 (1)(a) and (2)(a) of the then current Road Traffic Act 1960.

[44] See *supra*, para. 1.11.

responsibility.[45] Even public welfare offences such as those under the Food Safety Act 1990, the Trade Descriptions Act 1968, or the Licensing Acts may have serious consequences to an accused in the loss of goodwill or even the loss of his right to carry on his business. At the time when it was decided in England that responsibility for driving while disqualified was strict the offence carried a mandatory penalty of imprisonment except in special circumstances.[46] And in *R. v. St. Margaret's Trust Ltd*[47] the Court of Criminal Appeal was not deterred from holding that legislation imposing restrictions on hire-purchase transactions created an offence of strict responsibility by the fact that the offences were punishable by imprisonment. Generally speaking, therefore, as Lord Moncrieff pointed out in *Mitchell v. Morrison,*[48] the distinction between crimes and "acts which in the public interest are prohibited under a penalty" is too subtle to be of use.[49]

The object of the statute. THE PROTECTION OF THE PUBLIC. It is **8.10**
sometimes said in support of the application of strict responsibility that the statute is designed to protect the public.[50] But this is an unsatisfactory criterion for at least two reasons. In the first place the things against which the public are protected are so various that they cannot all be classed together: they include protection from physical injury from defective motor-vehicles, bad driving by overworked drivers, carelessly dispensed poisons, adulterated food, and badly managed or equipped mines and factories; pecuniary injury from short weight or other forms of fraud; attacks on feminine virtue; and that peculiar area of morality which is concerned with the evils of drink. In the second place, all crimes are created in order to protect the public. Moreover, whatever the subject-matter of the statute, the courts may require *mens rea* where the penalty is severe and stigmatic, or where to dispense with *mens rea* would leave large sections of the public liable to conviction in situations where they were blameless.[51]

REGULATORY OFFENCES. There are probably four classes of statutory **8.11**
offences which are accepted as involving strict responsibility unless *mens rea* is specifically provided for, the first three at least of which may be reasonably described as "the regulation for the public welfare of a particular activity."[52] These are statutes regulating trade in the interests

---

[45] See, *e.g.*, ss.6, 7, 8, 10; *cf.* incest and related offences under ss.1–3 (see Vol. II, Chap. 35). Ignorance of her condition would probably be a defence for a person charged with concealment of pregnancy: see Vol. II, Chap. 27. *Cf. Harding v. Price* [1948] 1 K.B. 695.

[46] Road Traffic Act 1930, s.7 (4); *Taylor v. Kenyon* [1952] 2 All E.R. 726. This is regarded in Canada as a clear indication of a requirement of *mens rea*: *R. v. King* [1962] S.C.R. 746, Ritchie J. at 761; *Re B.C. Motor Vehicle Act* [1985] 2 S.C.R. 486; *R. v. Wholesale Travel Gp.Inc.* [1991] 3 S.C.R. 154. See also *Sweet v. Parsley* [1970] A.C. 132.

[47] [1958] 1 W.L.R. 522. See also *R. v. Pierre* [1963] Crim.L.R. 513; *Yeandel v. Fisher* [1966] 1 Q.B. 440.

[48] 1938 J.C. 64, 72.

[49] See, however, the minority opinion of Cory J. (L'Heureux Dubé concurring), where the distinction is vigorously defended, in the Canadian case of *R. v. Wholesale Travel Gp.Inc.* [1991] 3 S.C.R. 154.

[50] *e.g. Mitchell v. Morrison*, 1938 J.C. 64, L.J.-G. Normand at 71; *Fraser v. Heatley,* 1952 J.C. 103, L.J.-C. Thomson at 107; *Alphacell Ltd v. Woodward* [1972] A.C. 824, Lord Salmon at 848D.

[51] *Sweet v. Parsley, supra,* esp. *per* Lord Reid and Lord Pearce.

[52] *Lim Chin Aik v. The Queen* [1963] A.C. 160, 174.

of public health and welfare, conditions of safety and employment, potential nuisances such as environmental pollution, and traffic.

The courts are more likely to apply strict responsibility where the offence is directed at a particular class of people carrying on a particular occupation:

> "If a person sets up as say a butcher, a publican, or a manufacturer and exposes unsound meat for sale, or sells drink to a drunk man, or certain parts of his factory are unsafe, it is no defence that he could not by the exercise of reasonable care have known or discovered that the meat was unsound, or that the man was drunk or that his premises were unsafe. He must take the risk and when it is found that the statutory prohibition or requirement has been infringed he must pay the penalty. This may well seem unjust but it is a comparatively minor injustice, and there is good reason for it as affording some protection to his customers or servants or to the public at large. Although this man might be able to show that he did his best, a more skilful or diligent man in his position might have done better, and when we are dealing with minor penalties which do not involve the disgrace of criminality it may be in the public interest to have a hard and fast rule."[53]

8.12 ENFORCEMENT. Even in cases of these kinds, however, strict responsibility may be excluded if its application would mean that a class of persons could be convicted of contraventions which they could not avoid by care. One reason for the imposition of strict responsibility on traders is that it will encourage them to be on the alert to avoid contravening the statutes regulating their activities, so that conversely where no amount of care can avoid an innocent contravention there should not be strict responsibility. The accused in *Lim Chin Aik v. The Queen*[54] had entered Singapore illegally in contravention of an order declaring him to be an illegal immigrant. He was, however, unaware of the existence of the order, and there was no way in which he could, by exercising care, have made himself aware of it, since it had not been published. His conviction was quashed by the Judicial Committee of the Privy Council who held that the contravention was of a kind which could not be avoided by due care, and which therefore required *mens rea*.[55]

8.13 The accused in *Sweet v. Parsley*[56] was the sub-tenant of a farmhouse who was charged with a contravention of the Dangerous Drugs Act 1965 by being concerned in the management of premises used for cannabis smoking. Lord Pearce pointed out that if *mens rea* was not required for the offence:

> "The innocent hotel-keeper, the lady who keeps lodgings or takes paying guests, the manager of a cinema, the warden of a hostel, the matron of a hospital, the house-master and matron of a boarding school, all these, it is conceded, are, on the prosecution's argument, liable to conviction the moment that irresponsible occupants smoke

---

[53] *R. v. Warner* [1969] 2 A.C. 256, Lord Reid at 271–272.

[54] [1963] A.C. 160.

[55] For a further discussion of the relationship between negligence and strict responsibility see *infra*, paras 8.33 *et seq.*

[56] [1970] A.C. 132.

cannabis cigarettes. And for what purpose is this harsh imposition laid on their backs? No vigilance by night or day can make them safe. The most that vigilance can attain is advance knowledge of their own guilt. If a smell of cannabis comes from a sitting-room, they know that they have committed the offence. Should they then go at once to the police and confess their guilt in the hope that they will not be prosecuted? They may think it easier to conceal the matter in the hope that it may never be found out. For if, though morally innocent, they *are* prosecuted they may lose their livelihood, since thereafter, even though not punished, they are objects of suspicion. I see no real, useful object achieved by such hardship to the innocent. And so wide a possibility of injustice to the innocent could not he justified by any benefit achieved in the determent and punishment of the guilty. If, therefore, the words creating the offence are as wide in their application as the prosecution contend, Parliament cannot have intended an offence to which absence of knowledge or mens rea is no defence."[57]

Trade regulation. Originally it appears to have been thought that strict responsibility was restricted to offences dealing with trades which were regulated by licence, such as the licensing trade itself. One of the grounds of the decision in *Mitchell v. Morrison*[58] was that the business of road haulage was regulated by licence, and that the failure to keep proper records was a breach of a condition of the licence, and so involved strict responsibility.[59] In *Duguid v. Fraser*[60] one of the reasons given for treating the offence of overcharging contrary to a price control Act as one of strict responsibilty was that the courts had power to disqualify a person from trading on a third conviction for such an offence, which was regarded as making the offence analogous to a breach of a licence.[61] An offence relating to the carrying on of a business, trade or profession, however, may involve strict responsibility whether or not the business, etc., is regulated by licence, and whether or not the accused is himself the licensee or person carrying on the trade. It is probably an offence of strict responsibility for an unregistered veterinary surgeon or dentist to practise or to hold himself out as registered.[62] **8.14**

Where a "trade" statute penalises either "all persons" or all persons in a particular capacity, such as drivers of vehicles, the employees of a trader may themselves be strictly responsible for any breach of an absolute prohibition. The holder of a goods vehicle licence and his drivers were formerly both strictly responsible for any failure to keep proper records of their journeys,[63] although the licence-holder now has

---

[57] At 157A-C.

[58] 1938 J.C. 64.

[59] See especially L.J.-G. Normand at 68–71.

[60] 1942 J.C. 1.

[61] L.J.-C. Cooper at 5–6.

[62] Veterinary Surgeons Act 1966, s.19; Dentists Act 1984, ss.38, 39. An unregistered doctor commits an offence only if he wilfully and falsely holds himself out to be registered, an offence requiring *mens rea*: Medical Act 1983, s.49; *Younghusband v. Luftig* [1949] 2 K.B. 354, the difference being due probably to the fact that it is not an offence for an unqualified person to practise medicine.

[63] Goods Vehicles (Keeping of Records) Regulations 1935, reg. 6 (S.R. & O.1935/314), Rev. XX, 492; *Mitchell v. Morrison, supra.*

the benefit of a defence.[64] In *Fraser v. Heatley*[65] it was held that an employee who was in charge of a coal lorry which carried short weight was guilty of an offence of strict responsibility under section 273 (2) of the Edinburgh Corporation Order Confirmation Act 1933, which, like section 29 of the Weights and Measures Act 1889,[66] provided that "the person in charge of the vehicle" should be liable to a penalty. Lord Justice-Clerk Thomson took the view that the protection of the public required that responsibility should be strict and that there was no warrant in the Act for discriminating in favour of an employee. Again, both a chemist and his unqualified assistant are strictly responsible for the sale of non-medicinal poisons by the latter.[67]

8.15 *Pollution, etc.* In *Alphacell Ltd v. Woodward*[68] the accused were manufacturers who had installed machinery to avoid polluting the river on whose banks their factory stood. The machinery failed, and they were convicted of causing polluting matter to enter the river. This was held to be an offence of strict responsibility, being described as "not criminal in any real sense, but [an act] which in the public interest [is] prohibited under a penalty"[69]; and as an offence "in the nature of a public nuisance".[70] That the law laid down in *Alphacell Ltd* is also the law applicable in Scotland was accepted without discussion both by counsel and the court in *Lockhart v. N.C.B.*[71]

8.16 *Road traffic offences.* Most offences under the Road Traffic Acts and the regulations made thereunder are offences of strict responsibility even when they are not concerned with regulating any business. It is true that all road traffic is licensed and that it is illegal to drive a motor vehicle without a licence, but strict responsibility extends to offences for which disqualification from driving is not competent, as well as to persons who do not hold licences, and the reason given for treating road traffic offences strictly is the safety of the public. One of the few Scots cases which deals exclusively with strict responsibility is *Howman v. Russell,*[72] a charge of driving without lights,[73] where the lights of the accused's car had been blown out by the wind unknown to him and through no fault of his. Lord Justice-General Clyde's opinion sets out clearly the literal approach which results in strict responsibility. He said:

> "When the substance of the statutory regulation is to forbid the use of a vehicle unless it complies in construction or equipment with

---

[64] Transport Act 1968, s.98(4): the employer has to prove that he gave proper instructions and from time to time took reasonable steps to secure that those instructions were being carried out.

[65] 1952 J.C. 103.

[66] These provisions were repealed by the Weights and Measures Act 1963, which in turn was repealed by the Weights and Measures Act 1985.

[67] *cf. Tomlinson v. Bremridge* (1894) 1 Adam 393; Poisons Act 1972, ss.3 and 8.

[68] [1972] A.C. 824.

[69] Viscount Dilhorne at 839G, quoting *Sherras v. De Rutzen* [1895] 1 Q.B. 918, Wright J. at 922. Sim. Lord Salmon at 848 D-E.

[70] Lord Pearson at 842H, again quoting *Sherras v. De Rutzen, supra.*

[71] 1981 S.L.T. 161; see *infra* para. 8.30.

[72] 1923 J.C. 32.

[73] The charge was under the regulations made under the Locomotives on Highways Act 1896, but the decision applies to the modern provisions under the Road Vehicles Lighting Regulations 1989 (S.I. 1989 No.1796), contravention of which being an offence under the Road Traffic Act 1988, s.42(1).

certain statutory requirements, it is not, in my opinion, possible to say that an offence has not been committed because the defect in the prescribed construction or equipment of the vehicle happened to be unknown to the driver at the time. The question is not whether the accused was wilful (which in this case he certainly was not), or negligent (of which in this case I see no sign), or had any intention of contravening the statute or the regulation (it is common ground, I think, that the accused in this case was innocent of any such intention). The question is whether he was driving a motor-car which — for whatever reason — did not have a lighted lamp at its rear. If he was, he contravened the regulation and statute — however technical his offence, and however inappropriate for either prosecution or penalty the case may be."[74]

Howman v. Russell[74a] applies to all offences against the Road Vehicles (Construction and Use) Regulations 1986,[75] except where the particular regulation provides a special defence, and also to other road traffic offences such as driving while uninsured.[76] It is not so clear that it applies to all offences connected directly with the manner of driving the vehicle.[77] It applies to failure to comply with a traffic sign,[78] but it may be queried whether it applies to the offence of neglecting or refusing to comply with a police officer's signal.[79] There is authority that it is not an offence to fail to give precedence to a pedestrian on a pedestrian crossing unless there is some degree of negligence,[80] but later cases have suggested that responsibility is strict[81] and the position is confused.[82]

It may be, however, that on its own facts *Howman v. Russell*[82a] is open to reconsideration in the light of the suggested defence of acts of God referred to in *Alphacell Ltd v Woodward.*[83]

Health and Safety at Work legislation. The principal legislation (Health and Safety at Work etc. Act 1974), which is gradually replacing earlier statutes (principally for present purposes the Mines and Quarries Act 1954, the Factories Act 1961 and the Offices, Shops and Railway Premises Act 1963) by regulations and codes of practice,[84] appears to **8.17**

---

[74] At 35. *Cf.* W.S. Gilbert on the offence of "encompassing the death of the heir-apparent" in *The Mikado* — "Unfortunately, the fool of an Act says 'compassing the death of the heir-apparent'. There's not a word about a mistake, or not knowing, or having no notion, or not being there. There should be, of course, but there isn't. That's the slovenly way in which these Acts are always drawn.": *The Mikado*, Act II. This passage is also quoted by Lord Hailsham, L.C., in *Wings Ltd v. Ellis* [1985] A.C. 272, at 288D-F, in relation to s.14 (1)(a)(ii) of the Trade Descriptions Act 1968.

[74a] 1923 J.C. 32.

[75] S.I. 1986 No. 1078. See, *e.g., MacNeill v. Wilson*, 1981 J.C. 87 (use of vehicle with insecure load, under the prior but similar S.I. 1978 No. 1017).

[76] The suggestion in *Thomas v. Galloway*, 1935 J.C. 27, *per* Lord Anderson at 32–33, that responsibility depends on an assumed or implied knowledge has no foundation.

[77] See Vol. II, Chap. 30.

[78] *Brooks v. Jefferies* [1936] 3 All E.R. 232.

[79] See Road Traffic Act 1988, s.35.

[80] *Leicester v. Pearson* [1952] 2 Q.B. 668.

[81] See *Hughes v. Hall* [1960] 1 W.L.R. 733; *Burns v. Bidder* [1967] 2 Q.B. 227. See also "Zebra" Pedestrian Crossings Regulations 1971 (S.I. 1971 No. 1524), reg.8; the "Pelican" Pedestrian Crossings Regulations and General Directions 1987 (S.I. 1987 No. 16), regs. 16, 17; and, the Road Traffic Regulation Act 1984, s.25(2).

[82] See Vol. II, Chap. 30.

[82a] 1923 J.C. 32.

[83] [1972] A.C. 824.

[84] See Halsbury's Laws of England, (4th ed., reissue, 1993), Vol. 20, para. 402.

accept strict liability[85] for failure to discharge certain duties. But the duties in question[86] are qualified by reference to what "is reasonably practicable" or are discharged by using "the best practicable means" of preventing whatever is at stake.[87] No general defences are laid down by the principal Act, although this is not the case under the earlier statutes referred to above.[88]

Words implying mens rea

8.18 *"Wilfully".* There has been some difference of opinion among English judges as to the meaning of "wilfully" in a statute[89] and they have on occasion said that "wilfully" involves no *mens rea* other than what is involved in doing the forbidden act intentionally, even without knowledge of the circumstances making it forbidden,[90] but the accepted modern view is that "wilfully" involves full common law *mens rea* and is excluded by a claim of right.[91] It has been said of "wilful" that it "connotes intention and knowledge"; but the problem is to determine in the particular circumstances what is to be intended and what known.[92] It has been held that a person who boards a ship which is flying a quarantine flag is not guilty of wilfully neglecting or refusing to obey the quarantine regulations if he has not seen the flag.[93] In *Wilson v. Inyang*[94] the court went so far as to hold that if an accused believed he was entitled to describe himself as a naturopath physician he could not be convicted of wilfully and falsely using the title of physician, even if his belief was unreasonable. *Wilson*[94a] represents an application of the principle set out in *Younghusband v. Luftig,*[95] which dealt with the same offence, that a person does not act "wilfully and falsely", "if he honestly believes that he was within his rights" in doing as he did.[96] More recent cases support the view that "wilfully" is satisfied by subjective recklessness, does not require malice or a desire or purpose to bring about the prohibited result, and is excluded by the presence of a lawful excuse for one's conduct.[97]

8.19 There is little Scots authority on the matter, but what there is appears to support the approach of the English court in *Younghusband v. Luftig.* In *Jas. Kinnison,*[98] a charge against a registrar for knowingly and wilfully

---

[85] See 1974 Act, s.33(1)(a): *cf.* s.8: "No person shall intentionally or recklessly interfere with or misuse anything provided in the interests of health, safety or welfare".

[86] see, *e.g.*, ss 2–4, 6 and 7.

[87] See, *e.g.*, s.5. Under s.40 of the 1974 Act, the onus of proving compliance with the standard imposed by the duty in question lies on the accused.

[88] See Mines and Quarries Act 1954, s.157; Factories Act 1961, s.155; and Offices, Shops and Railway Premises Act 1963, s.67 which provides a general defence of due diligence.

[89] See Gl. Williams, para. 53.

[90] *e.g. Law Society v. United Services Bureau Ltd* [1934] 1 K.B. 343, Avory J. at 349; *Cotterill v. Penn* [1936] 1 K.B. 53.

[91] See Gl. Williams, pp.319 and 322, but *Wells v. Hardy* [1964] 2 Q.B.477 is a decision to the contrary.

[92] *Iannella v. Fench* (1967–68) 41 A.L.J.R. 389, Barwick C.J. at 393.

[93] *Bullock v. Turnbull* [1952] 2 Lloyd's Rep. 303.

[94] [1951] 2 K.B. 799.

[94a] *ibid.*

[95] [1949] 2 K.B. 354.

[96] Lord Goddard C.J. at 369. But *Arrowsmith v. Jenkins* [1963] 2 Q.B. 561 and *Wells v. Hardy* [1964] 2 Q.B. 447, may represent a return to the older outlook.

[97] See *R. v. Cunningham* [1957] 2 Q.B. 396; *Arrowsmith v. Jenkins* [1963] 2 Q.B. 561; *Rice v. Connolly* [1966] 2 Q.B. 414; *R. v. Mowatt* [1968] 1 Q.B. 421; *Clixby v. Pountney* [1968] Ch. 719; *R. v. Solanke* [1970] 1 W.L.R. 1; cf. *Willmott v. Atack* [1977] Q.B. 498.

[98] (1870) 1 Couper 457.

making a false entry contrary to sections 60 and 62 of the Registration of Births, Deaths and Marriages (Scotland) Act 1854, Lord Moncreiff said that "wilfully" meant "with the intention of doing the thing which is prohibited",[99] but went on to refer to the common law offence of wilful fire-raising as analogous, which indicates that he regarded "wilfully" as retaining its common law meaning. In *Grant v. Wright*[1] the High Court upheld an acquittal of a fisherman on a charge of unlawfully and wilfully taking salmon, apparently on the grounds that the salmon was caught accidentally while the accused was fishing legally for other fish, and that he believed he was entitled to keep the salmon. But the judgment of the court, delivered by Lord Young, is obscure, and one cannot confidently point to the case as anticipating *Younghusband v. Luftig.*[1a] Lord Young did, however, say that whether or not there was wilfulness was a question of fact, and that "wilfully" meant "designedly, and with a certain intent",[2] which again suggests full common law *mens rea*.

"Maliciously". The requirement of "maliciousness" is satisfied by reck- **8.20**
lessness. It has nothing to do with malice in the sense of spite. Its meaning is the same as in the common law crime of malicious mischief.[3] The English courts have construed "maliciously" in cases under the Offences Against the Person Act 1861 and the Malicious Damage Act 1861 as requiring either intention or recklessness, and as not being satisfied by mere negligence.[4]

"Falsely". It seems reasonable to say, as did the court in *Derbyshire v.* **8.21**
Houliston,[5] that to "give a false warranty" involves *mens rea*. Later cases, however, make it clear that this is not so. It was held, for example, that the offence of causing or permitting a false invoice to be given under the Fertilisers and Feeding Stuffs Act 1893 could be committed by someone who was unaware of the falsity of the invoice, and had even taken steps by having the goods analysed to ensure that the invoice was correct.[6] This "neutral" interpretation of "falsely" may be supported by the fact that certain statutes talk expressly of "knowingly" making a false statement.[7]

"Fraudulently". The words "fraudulently" or "with intent to defraud" **8.22**
have their common law meaning. Pecuniary loss is not a necessary element: if B asks A for an article of a particular description and A

---

[99] At 461.

[1] (1876) 3 Couper 282.

[1a] [1949] 2 K.B. 354.

[2] At 287.

[3] *Ward v. Robertson*, 1938 J.C. 32.

[4] *R. v. Cunningham* [1957] 2 Q.B. 396; *R. v. Welch* (1975) 1 Q.B.D. 23; *R. v. Savage; R. v. Parmenter* [1992] 1 A.C. 699; Gl. Williams, para. 30.

[5] [1897] 1 Q.B. 772.

[6] *Laird v. Dobell* [1906] 1 K.B. 131. See also *Patel v. Comptroller of Customs* [1966] A.C. 356; *R. v. Cummerson* [1968] 2 Q.B. 534. *Cf. Korten v. W. Sussex C.C.* (1903) 72 L.J.K.B. 514. The charge in *Mitchell v. Morrison*, 1938 J.C. 64 was in effect a charge of making a false entry and the case was treated as involving strict responsibility although the point at issue was concerned with vicarious responsibility.

[7] *e.g.* Social Security Administration Act 1992, ss.111A, 112 and 112(1A), as added and/or amended by the Social Security Administration (Fraud) Act 1997, ss.13 and 14, and Sched. 1, para 4; Road Traffic Act 1988, s.174 (1) as contrasted with (5); *R. v. Cummerson, supra,* para. 8.08. See also Civic Government (Scotland) Act 1982, s.7(4); *Buchman v. Normand*, 1994 S.C.C.R. 929.

falsely applies that description to another article in order to persuade B to take it, A is guilty of applying a false description with intent to defraud, whether or not the article offered is of equivalent value to the article requested.[8]

"Fraud" is a concept which is almost meaningless in the absence of *mens rea*, and, generally speaking, a man does not act fraudulently if he believes that he is telling the truth, or if he has no intention of deceiving anyone.[9]

In *Galbraith's Stores, Ltd v. McIntyre*[10] the accused were charged with a weights and measures fraud, their servant having sold a made-up packet of butter weighing less than the weight asked by the purchaser. It was held that there had been a false representation as to weight, but that the accused had acted without intent to defraud as they had taken reasonable means to secure that customers were aware that these packets were not sold by weight, and the servant had acted in breach of his instructions in not telling the purchaser this.[11]

In *Haddow v. Neilson Brothers*[12] the accused sold his products in a bottle which bore the brand name of another firm, to which he attached a label with his own name. It was found, however, that he had no intention of deceiving the public, although he had been warned that he should not use these bottles, and the court was therefore prepared to accept that he had acted without intent to defraud.

The Scots courts took an independent line in construing one English statute — the Vagrancy Act 1824 — which was at one time applied to Scotland.[13] Section 4 of that Act provided a penalty for "Every person pretending or professing to tell fortunes, or using any subtle craft . . . by palmistry or otherwise, to deceive and impose on any of Her Majesty's subjects." It had been held in England that on a charge of pretending to tell fortunes no intent to deceive need be shown,[14] but in *Farmer v. Mill*[15] the High Court followed the earlier case of *Smith v. Neilson,*[16] and held that such an intent was necessary. The question depended on the grammatical interpretation of the section, but the Scots decisions avoided creating an offence of pretending without intent to deceive.

A statute may, of course, expressly provide that an intent to defraud shall be deemed to exist in certain circumstances. Section 22 of the Post Office Act 1953, for example, provides that any officer who reissues a money order previously paid shall be deemed to have issued it with fraudulent intent.

When a statute penalises fraudulent behaviour it may be argued that this should be limited to deceit designed to frustrate the aims of the Act. Thus it was successfully maintained in one English case that fraudulent use of a vehicle excise licence required evidence of intent to avoid paying the duty in question.[17] That decision was, however, reversed by the

---

[8] *Starey v. Chilworth Gunpowder Co.* (1889) 2 Q.B.D. 90.

[9] *cf. Brend v. Wood* (1946) 62 T.L.R. 462.

[10] (1912) 6 Adam 641.

[11] One may feel that the court would not have been so lenient in more modern times.

[12] (1899) 3 Adam 104.

[13] See Prevention of Crime (Scotland) Act 1871, s.15. Section 4 of the Vagrancy Act was repealed *quoad* Scotland by the Civic Government (Scotland) Act 1982, Sched. 4.

[14] *Stonehouse v. Masson* [1921] 2 K.B. 818.

[15] 1948 J.C. 4.

[16] (1896) 2 Adam 145.

[17] *R. v. Manners-Astley* [1967] 1 W.L.R. 1505, interpreting s.17(1) of Vehicles Excise Act 1962 (equivalent to the current s.44 of Vehicles Excise and Registration Act 1994).

House of Lords in *R. v. Terry*,[18] where it was declared, following earlier authority,[19] that intent to cause a person performing public duties (such as a police officer) to do what he would not have done or refrain from doing what he otherwise would have done but for the deceit was sufficient.

"Knowingly". The most important word in the context of statutory *mens rea* is "knowingly", since the question at issue in most cases on this branch of the law is whether the accused's ignorance of the circumstances which rendered his act criminal constitutes a defence. "Knowingly" implies such knowledge. A cannot, for example, be convicted of knowingly possessing explosives unless he knew that what he had was explosive in character,[20] of knowingly making a false statement unless he knew that what he said was untrue,[21] or of knowingly harbouring uncustomed goods unless he knew they were liable to duty.[22] Nor can even a licensee be convicted of knowingly permitting drunkenness on his premises, unless he possessed the necessary knowledge: it is not enough that his employee to whom he had delegated the running of the public-house had the necessary knowledge.[23] In coming to the conclusion that "knowingly" must mean what it says, the court disapproved of dicta in the earlier case of *Greig v. MacLeod*,[24] but did not exercise its power to overrule the case itself, holding that the result in it "appears to be sound in the light of the facts found proved". Since these facts were that liquor was supplied to a child by a servant in and with the accused's "presence and actual personal knowledge", and that "No notice was displayed in the . . . shop warning assistants to be careful to observe [the Act] . . . and sufficient instruction . . . had not been given" to the servant not to supply liquor to children, it seems that the court in *Noble v. Heatly*[24a] thought that failure to institute a system to ensure observance of the statute was sufficient *mens rea* to constitute "knowingly permitting". While there is authority for the view that such a failure may in certain circumstances constitute permission[25] because it amounts to wilful blindness, and though there may be no difference between "permit" and "knowingly permit"[26] it may be doubted whether the facts in *Greig v. MacLeod* come up to wilful blindness. Perhaps, however, it must be assumed that they were so viewed by the court in *Noble v Heatly.*[27] **8.23**

OFFENCES DEPENDING ON PRIOR KNOWLEDGE. In *Harding v. Price*[28] A was charged with failing to report a road accident, contrary to section 22 of the Road Traffic Act 1930.[29] A was unaware that he had been **8.24**

---

[18] [1984] A.C. 374, interpreting s.26(1) of the Vehicles Excise Act 1971.

[19] *Welham v. D.P.P.* [1961] A.C. 103.

[20] *R. v. Hallam* [1957] 1 Q.B. 569; *Black v. H.M. Advocate,* 1974 S.L.T. 247.

[21] *cf. Napier v. H.M. Advocate,* 1944 J.C. 61, 73.

[22] *McQueen v. McCann*, 1945 J.C. 151; *R. v. Hussain* [1969] 2 Q.B. 567.

[23] *Noble v. Heatly*, 1967 J.C. 5. As it happens, the Act in question contained a provision that in a charge of the kind brought in *Noble v. Heatly* it was for the licensee to prove that "he and the person employed by him took all reasonable steps to prevent drunkenness": Licensing (Scotland) Act 1959, s.187, but that section was not founded on in *Noble v. Heatly.*

[24] (1907) 5 Adam 445.

[24a] 1967 J.C. 5.

[25] *infra*, paras 8.81 *et seq.*

[26] See *infra*, para. 8.83.

[27] *cf. Knox v. Boyd*, 1941 J.C. 82, 86; *Thornley v. Hunter*, 1965 J.C. 22.

[28] [1948] 1 K.B. 695.

[29] Now Road Traffic Act 1988, s.170 (as amended by the Road Traffic Act 1991, Sched. 4, para. 72).

involved in an accident as the sound of the impact had been drowned by the noise of his own engine. It was held that despite the fact that "knowingly" did not appear in the section, while it had appeared in the section of the Motor Car Act 1903 which section 22 replaced, ignorance was a good defence.[30] Lord Chief Justice Goddard said that although an absolute prohibition usually excluded *mens rea*, "there is all the difference between prohibiting an act and imposing a duty to do something on the happening of a certain event. Unless a man knows that the event has happened, how can he carry out the duty?"[31] It may be doubted whether the difference is as vast as Lord Goddard thought, or indeed whether it is more than verbal in many cases, but the decision itself is welcome as enabling the courts to avoid the manifest injustice of penalising someone for not reporting something of which he was unaware. Even if the reason for A's ignorance is that he was driving carelessly and failing to keep a proper lookout he will not for that reason alone be guilty of the offence of failing to report the accident, although he will be guilty of careless driving in relation to the accident: so long as his unawareness is not the result of wilful blindness he should have a good defence.[32]

Harding v. Price[32a] itself followed an earlier case in which it was held that a person could not be convicted of failing to report that one of his animals was diseased unless he knew of the disease[33] and if, as is submitted, these cases are correct, the case of *McLaren v. Smith*[34] will require to be reconsidered. It was a prosecution for a contravention of an order made under the Diseases of Animals Act 1894, which provided that "If any animal on a vessel has a limb broken . . . the master . . . shall forthwith cause [it] to be slaughtered." The order also provided that the person in charge of the animal should report its injury forthwith to the master. The stevedore who was in charge of the animal was convicted of failing to report to the master and the master was convicted of failing to have the animal slaughtered. The conviction of the master was upheld on the grounds (a) that an imperative unconditional personal obligation had been laid on him, (b) that he had washed his hands of responsibility and made no effort to see that the order was enforced, and (c) that he was liable for the failure of his officers, including the stevedore, to carry out the order. Lord Anderson dissented, holding that the master could be convicted only if he had instructed the person in charge not to report injuries to animals. The decision of the court can be supported on the ground that the facts were treated as disclosing wilful

---

[30] Once there is evidence to establish that the defendant caused the accident, a presumption is raised that he knew the accident had occurred, and the evidential burden to show lack of knowledge passes to him: see, *e.g.*, *Selby v. Chief Constable of Avon and Somerset* [1988] R.T.R. 216.

[31] [1948] 1 K.B. at 701.

[32] *Harding v. Price, supra*, Lord Goddard C.J. at 702. In *Sutherland v. Aitchison*, 1975 J.C. 1, the driver heard a bump as he squeezed past another car on a single track road. He thought the bump was caused by his exhaust hitting a stone and therefore drove on. In an appeal against conviction for failing to stop, since he had in fact hit the other vehicle, it was held that "the fact that some noise was heard was sufficient to indicate to a reasonable man . . . that he should stop to see if in point of fact he had been involved in an accident" (*per* L.J.Cl. Wheatley at 6). No case was referred to in the opinion of the court; but it seems that where something happens that should alert the accused to the possibility that the circumstances may be such as to require him to do something, he is not entitled to act on a belief that those circumstances do not exist, but is bound to make inquiry.

[33] *Nichols v. Hall* (1873) L.R. 8 C.P. 322.

[34] 1923 J.C. 91.

blindness, but it is submitted that it cannot be supported on the ground that the master's ignorance of the condition of the animal was irrelevant. Lord Anderson's view that the statutory duty of the master does not emerge until he has knowledge of the animal's condition is supported by *Harding v. Price*[34a] and is, it is submitted, correct.[35]

"Unlawfully". The words "unlawfully", or "without lawful authority", or "without lawful excuse", have no direct bearing on *mens rea*. They refer rather to the *actus reus*. Sexual intercourse with a mental defective, for example, is unlawful where the parties are not married.[36] Similarly, a person takes a postal packet unlawfully if he has no legal right or authority to take it, or to take it in the circumstances in which he does take it.[37] Whether or not a belief that the circumstances are such as to make the act lawful, such as a belief that one was married or had been duly authorised to act as one did, is a defence depends on whether the offence is otherwise regarded as involving strict responsibility.[38] **8.25**

Offences involving possession. Where A has with him or otherwise has in his possession an article which is of a character which renders his possession of it criminal, such as a salmon taken out of season, a prohibited drug, or an offensive weapon, the question of *mens rea* and in particular the question of knowledge may arise in two ways. A may not know that he has possession of the article at all, or he may not know that it is of such a character as to render his possession illegal. In offences of strict responsibility lack of knowledge of the latter kind is irrelevant. It has been said that belief that unclean salmon was lawfully caught is not a defence to a charge of unlawful possession[39]; A can be convicted of possessing fictitious stamps although he does not know they are fictitious,[40] or of possessing an altered passport although he believes it was properly issued to him in the ordinary way.[41] Again, A may be convicted of possessing diseased meat although he was unaware of its nature,[42] and one of the earliest cases on strict responsibility concerned a conviction for possessing adulterated tobacco without knowledge of the adulteration.[43] **8.26**

Whether any particular offence of possessing is an offence of strict responsibility will fall to be decided on the same principles as apply to other kinds of offences. Some statutes explicitly speak of "knowingly" possessing,[44] and in practice a statute which merely speaks of "possessing", or *a fortiori* of things being found in a person's possession, may well be treated as imposing strict responsibility.

34a [1948] 1 K.B. 695.

35 As the duty to report is laid specifically on the person in charge of the animal the master's conviction cannot be justified by imposing on him a vicarious responsibility for the stevedore's failure.

36 Mental Health (Scotland) Act 1984, s.106. *cf. Henry Watson* (1885) 5 Couper 696.

37 Post Office Act 1953, s.53.

38 *cf. Winkle v. Wiltshire* [1951] 1 K.B. 684.

39 *Chalmers v. MacGlashan* (1886) 1 White 1, Lord Young at 7.

40 *Winkle v. Wiltshire* [1951] 1 K.B. 684.

41 *Chajutin v. Whitehead* [1938] 1 K.B. 506.

42 *Blaker v. Tillstone* [1894] 1 Q.B. 345; *cf. Dickson v. Linton* (1882) 2 White 51; *Hobbs v. Winchester Corpn* [1910] 2 K.B. 471.

43 *R. v. Woodrow* (1846) 15 M. & W. 404.

44 *e.g.* Post Office Act 1953, s.28; Explosive Substances Act 1883, s.4; see *R. v. Hallam* [1957] 1 Q.B. 569.

Normally, knowledge of the former kind — that is, knowledge that one has the article in one's possession — will be necessary in order to establish the *actus reus* of possession,[45] and A could not be convicted of having offensive weapons with him in a van unless he knew they were there,[46] or of being in possession of prohibited drugs unless he knew he was in possession of the articles concerned, whether or not the Crown must show also that he knew of their prohibited character. It seems, too, that to say that A knows he is in possession of a particular article does involve attributing to him some knowledge of the nature of the article, but just what knowledge is a very difficult question. In *Lockyer v. Gibb*[47] it was held that a person who knew that she had a bottle with tablets in it but did not know that these tablets were drugs was guilty of the strict responsibility offence of possessing a prohibited drug.[48] In *R. v. Warner*[49] Lord Pearce said:

> "I think that the term 'possession' is satisfied by a knowledge only of the existence of the thing itself and not its qualities, and that ignorance or mistake as to its qualities is not an excuse. This would comply with the general understanding of the word 'possess'. Though I reasonably believe the tablets which I possess to be aspirin, yet if they turn out to be heroin I am in possession of heroin tablets. This would be so I think even if I believed them to be sweets. It would be otherwise if I believed them to be something of a wholly different nature. At this point a question of degree arises as to when a difference in qualities amounts to a difference in kind. That is a matter for a jury who would probably decide it sensibly in favour of the genuinely innocent but against the guilty."[50]

Moreover, possession of a box containing an article would not entail possession of its contents if A thought the box was empty, or contained other things.[51] The effect of *R. v. Warner*[51a] seems to be that there is a very strong inference of fact that a person in possession of a parcel is also in possession of its contents, on the assumption that if he does not open the parcel at the first opportunity to find what is in it, he is to be taken to have accepted possession of the contents. During the time before that opportunity, or if he has no right to open the parcel, he may displace the prima facie inference of possession of the contents by

---

[45] *supra*, para. 3.39. In addition to such knowledge, a sufficient degree of control over the article seems also to be required for possession to be established. See, *e.g.*, *McKenzie v. Skeen*, 1983 S.L.T. 121 (a case of 1977 reported by request in 1983); *Salmon v. H.M. Advocate; Moore v. H.M. Advocate*, 1998 S.C.C.R. 740 — both cases concerned with possession of prohibited drugs contrary to the Misuse of Drugs Act 1971. See also *Bellerby v. Carle* [1983] 2 A.C. 101, which emphasised the need for proof of control relative to the offence of possessing for use for trade false or unjust weighing or measuring equipment.

[46] *R. v. Cugullere* [1961] 1 W.L.R. 858.

[47] [1967] 2 Q.B. 243.

[48] See *supra*, para. 3.39. Nowadays, such an accused might be able to make use of the defence, under s.28(3)(b)(i) of the Misuse of Drugs Act 1971, which was not available at the time when *Lockyer v. Gibb* was decided. The defence is only required, however, once the Crown has proved possession: see *Salmon v. H.M. Advocate; Moore v. H.M. Advocate*, 1998 S.C.C.R. 740.

[49] [1969] 2 A.C. 256.

[50] At 305 F-G.

[51] Thus, if a box in fact contained prohibited drugs but was thought by the accused to contain pornographic or pirated video tapes, he should be acquitted as not possessing the contents: see *Salmon v. H.M. Advocate; Moore v. H.M. Advocate*, 1998 S.C.C.R. 740.

[51a] [1969] 2 A.C. 256.

showing that he would not have accepted possession had he known what kind of thing the contents were.[52]

But it is not clear whether in cases like that of having an offensive weapon, where the possession is illegal only in a public place, it would be a defence for A to say that he put the weapon voluntarily into his pocket in a private place the day before his arrest, but forgot all about it when he went out in public and did not realise he had it with him when he was arrested.[53] Where possession at any time and place is an offence such a defence might well not be accepted even in relation to a charge of possessing at the time of arrest.[54] But in either case it would be necessary for the Crown to show that A at some time came voluntarily and knowingly into possession of the articles in question. It was accepted in *Lockyer v. Gibb* that "a person cannot be said to be in possession of some article which he or she does not realise is, for example, in her handbag, in her room, or in some other place over which she has control",[55] and this was approved by all their Lordships in *R. v. Warner*[55a] and indeed conceded by the Crown. As Lord Morris of Borth-y-Gest put it in his dissenting speech[56]:

> "In *Lockyer v. Gibb* Lord Parker, at p. 248, gave the illustration of something being slipped into a person's basket. While the person was unaware of what had happened there would be no possession. But in such circumstances, on becoming aware of the presence of the newly discovered article, there would be opportunity to see what the article was: whether the opportunity was availed of or not, if the article was deliberately retained there would be possession of it."

But there are some cases in which, on the basis of the concept of a general duty of inquiry, such as was laid down in *R. v. Warner* in relation to knowledge of the contents of a package, negligence might be a sufficient *mens rea*, because the object of the statute creating the offence is to prevent danger or injury to others as a result of the presence of the prohibited article. An example of this is provided by section 66 of the Mines and Quarries Act 1954 which prohibits the possession of matches in certain underground mines. The point is undecided, but if A has matches in a mine in his pockets or haversack it would not be unreasonable to convict him in the absence of knowledge, on the ground that he ought to have taken steps to see that he was free of contraband before going into the mine, whether or not he had originally come into possession of the matches voluntarily. It would still be a defence to a charge of this kind that someone else had placed the matches in A's pocket or haversack without his knowledge or connivance, but only if the

---

[52] Lord Pearce at 307 G.

[53] *cf. Crowe v. Waugh*, 1999 S.C.C.R. 613, where it seems to have been accepted that an offence of having an article with a blade or sharp point with one in a public place is committed irrespective of knowledge or intent: the statutory defence of 'good reason' for having it with one was a question of fact and circumstance, although forgetting it was in one's jacket was unlikely to succeed.

[54] See *Gill v. Lockhart*, 1987 S.C.C.R. 599, where placing prohibited drugs in a golf bag some two years prior to their discovery by the police and forgetting in the interim that they were there, was not sufficient to avoid conviction for illegal possession.

[55] [1967] 2 Q.B. 243, Lord Parker C.J. at 248 E.

[55a] [1969] 2 A.C. 256.

[56] [1969] 2 A.C. 256, at 289 D.

circumstance were such that A could not with reasonable care have discovered this before going into the mine.[57]

8.27 *Offences involving an objective standard.* Offences of strict responsibility should be distinguished from offences which merely penalise a person who behaves in a way which offends against an objective standard of behaviour. This is the position in all offences involving carelessness, such as careless driving where an excusable ignorance of a mechanical defect in the car is a defence,[58] or offences against the Protection of Animals (Scotland) Act 1912, section 1, where it must be shown that the accused knew or ought to have known that what he was doing would cause unnecessary suffering.[59]

Defences

8.28 Generally speaking the prosecution must show even in offences of strict responsibility that the accused was a person legally capable of committing a crime, and that the offence arose as a result of his voluntary act or omission.

Personal factors. A person under the age of criminal responsibility cannot commit any offence, including an offence of strict responsibility.[60] The same is probably true of a person who is legally insane,[61] although the two defences are not altogether analogous. Nonage is a plea in bar and depends on a clear statutory provision[62]; insanity as a plea in bar, like any other plea in bar, is in the same position as nonage, but insanity as a defence may depend on showing that the accused was incapable of *mens rea*, in which case it should strictly speaking be irrelevant in an offence of strict responsibility. But it is almost inconceivable that insanity would not be accepted as a defence in an offence of strict responsibility. Self-induced intoxication would not be a defence, unless perhaps it was so gross as to exclude the volition necessary to constitute criminal conduct.[63]

8.29 *Voluntary act.* The form of involuntariness usually referred to as non-insane automatism has been recognised in Scotland since the case of *Ross v. H.M. Advocate*.[64] It was there considered as a complete defence and one that demonstrated a lack of *mens rea* rather than *actus reus*[65];

---

[57] In *R. v. Cugullere, supra,* the possibility of a "planting" of the offending article in this way was used as a reason for requiring knowledge, but such a requirement is not necessary in order to avoid punishing a man for involuntary possession of this kind. In the case of weapons or drugs there is no general duty on a man to take care, either at all times or even before entering a public place, to ensure that he is not in possession of prohibited articles, but in the case of a miner going into a mine such a duty seems reasonable.

[58] *R. v. Spurge* [1961] 2 Q.B. 205. This would also have been the case relative to the now repealed offence of reckless driving: *cf.* dangerous driving (which replaced reckless driving) under the Road Traffic Act 1988, ss.1 and 2, as substituted by Road Traffic Act 1991, s.1; see *R. v. Strong* [1995] Crim.L.R. 428, and Vol. II, Chap. 30.

[59] *Easton v. Anderson*, 1949 J.C. 1; see Vol. II, Chap. 32.

[60] *cf.* Gl. Williams, p.215.

[61] *Sweet v. Parsley* [1970] A.C. 132, Lord Diplock at 162G.

[62] 1995 Act, s.41.

[63] Gl. Williams, p.574. As a result of *Brennan v. H.M. Advocate*, 1977 J.C. 38, *infra*, paras 12.12 *et seq.*, it is difficult to say what the position of voluntary intoxication is in offences of strict liability.

[64] 1991 J.C. 210. See paras 3.18 *et seq., supra*.

[65] See para. 3.19, *supra*.

but the case was not concerned with statutory offences, still less ones of strict liability, and the attitude of Scots law to the issue of involuntariness in relation to strict responsibility offences may be regarded as open. It is submitted, therefore, that, subject perhaps to one exception,[66] no statutory offence can be committed unless there is an *actus reus* which consists of or is the result of voluntary conduct on the part of the accused. A may be convicted of using a car with faulty brakes although he knows nothing of the state of the brakes, but not if he was unaware that he was driving the car because, for example, he was in a state of automatism.[67] Similarly, A may be convicted of having intercourse with a girl of fifteen whom he had every reason to believe to be seventeen, but not if he was unaware that he was having sexual intercourse because he was asleep or hypnotised.[68]

Similarly, whether or not duress in the ordinary sense of threats or pressure constitutes a defence in any offence of strict responsibility, it would be a defence to show that the accused acted under such compulsion as to render his behaviour involuntary.[69]

The one exception to the requirement of a voluntary act is the case of *R. v. Larsonneur.*[70] The accused in that case was an alien who was refused permission to remain in the United Kingdom and went to Ireland. She was deported from there and brought by Irish police to England where she was handed over to the English police. She was charged with the offence of "being found" in the United Kingdom after having been refused leave to land, contrary to the Aliens Order 1920, the offence having been committed when she was returned by the police. Lord Hewart C.J. said simply that the Act penalised persons found in the United Kingdom and she had been found there. This decision is so ludicrous, one might almost say ingenuous, that it is to be hoped it will not be followed in Scotland. Indeed, it will probably not now be followed in England either, as it is inconsistent with the decision of the Judicial Committee of the Privy Council in *Lim Chin Aik v. The Queen*.[71]

Impossibility. It is not clear to what extent impossibility is a defence in crimes of strict responsibility. In a number of cases dealing with the duty to remove leaders from salmon nets during the weekly close season opinions were expressed that it would be a defence to show that because of gales or other weather conditions it was impossible to carry out the duty.[72] But it has been held not to be a defence to a charge of driving a car without lights that the lights were blown out by a gale.[73] The position **8.30**

---

[66] *infra.*

[67] *Hill v. Baxter* [1958] 1 Q.B. 277; *Sweet v. Parsley, supra*, Lord Diplock at 163A. In view of *H.M. Advovate v. Cunningham*, 1963 J.C. 80, as it survives following *Ross v. H.M. Advocate*, 1991 J.C. 210, this may have to be treated as a plea of insanity if the automatic state is due to a non-external factor and an acquittal is desired: see paras 3.20 to 3.25, *supra*, but if that is so it would be acceptable in offences of strict responsibility whatever the general attitude is to defences of insanity in such cases.

[68] *cf. Simon Fraser* (1878) 4 Couper 70; *Sweet v. Parsley, supra, loc. cit.* Again, if a butcher displayed tainted meat while he was in a somnambulistic state he would not be guilty of an offence of strict responsibility: see R.M. Jackson, "Absolute Prohibition in Statutory Offences" in *Modern Approach*, 262 at 270.

[69] Gl. Williams, 215; *Sweet v. Parsley, supra, loc. cit.*; see *infra*, para. 13.29.

[70] (1933) 29 Cox C.C. 673. *Cf.* the account of the case given by Rakesh C. Doegar, "Strict Liability in Criminal Law and *Larsonneur* Reassessed" [1998] Crim.L.R. 791.

[71] [1963] A.C. 160.

[72] *Don v. Johnston* (1897) 2 Adam 416; *Macrorie v. Forman and Ors.* (1905) 4 Adam 682; *Middleton v. Tough* (1908) 5 Adam 485, L.J.-G. Dunedin at 490.

[73] *Howman v. Russell*, 1923 J.C. 32; see *supra*, para. 8.16.

may be that where a statute requires the doing of a particular thing impossibility is a defence, but where a statute provides that a certain thing shall be used or a certain activity carried on only under certain conditions, an offence is committed unless the conditions are complied with, and impossibility of compliance is no defence: the person who carries on the activity does so, as it were, at his own risk.

In the New Zealand case of *Kilbride v. Lake*[74] it was held that the accused was not guilty of failing to display a certificate of fitness on his car where the evidence was that when he parked the car the certificate was there, and it had gone by the time the police arrived. Woodhouse J. held that no *actus reus* had been proved. Such a decision is hard to reconcile with such cases as *Howman v. Russell.*[75] Since then, however, the attitude of the English courts has changed, and where a statutory offence imposes strict responsibility on a particular person for a certain state of affairs, it may be a defence to show that the state of affairs was the result of the operation of natural forces, "acts of God", or perhaps the act of persons over whom the accused had no control. The possibility of these defences was referred to in *Alphacell Ltd v. Woodward,*[76] where the offence was "causing" polluting matter to enter a stream. But the use of the term "causing" did not create any speciality[77]; it has always to be shown that the accused caused the *actus reus*. The defence of act of God may be equated with impossibility. The suggested defence of third party intervention raises broader issues, since it would limit strict responsibility in offences of this kind where a "personal" duty is laid upon a particular person to cases where the offence was actually the fault of the accused or one of his employees (or some other person acting on his behalf). Defences of this kind are often inserted in statutes creating strict liability offences of *e.g.* sale,[78] but the dicta in *Alphacell*[78a] suggest that some such defence is always open, although its scope remains unknown. *Alphacell*[78b] was followed in *Lockhart v. N.C.B.*[79] where the accused were convicted of causing polluting material to enter a river from a mine which they had ceased to occupy, so that they were no longer able to carry out the pumping operations necessary to prevent pollution. This was viewed almost as a "self-inflicted" impossibility, and it does not, therefore, apply to acts of God or third parties. It seems to presuppose, however, that the inaction of third parties is an irrelevant consideration.[80]

8.31 *Necessity and coercion.* These pleas are applicable to offences of strict liability. In *Tudhope v. Grubb*[81] the defence of necessity was upheld where the accused who had an excess of alcohol in his blood tried to drive his car in order to escape from an assault; and in *Moss v. Howdle,*[82] the Appeal

74 [1962] N.Z.L.R. 590.

75 *Supra.* For a critique of the arguments in *Kilbride v. Lake*, see M. Budd and A. Lynch, "Voluntariness, Causation and Strict Liability" [1978] Crim.L.R. 74.

76 [1972] A.C. 824, Lord Wilberforce at 834F; Lord Pearson at 845D where his Lordship referred to intervening acts of trespassers and acts of God; Lord Cross of Chelsea at 846 F-H; Lord Salmon at 847 F.

77 See *infra*, para. 8.73.

78 *infra*, para. 8.68.

78a [1972] A.C. 824.

78b *ibid.*

79 1981 S.L.T. 161.

80 See para. 8.73, *infra*.

81 1983 S.C.C.R. 350, Sh.Ct.: for the defence of necessity, see Chap. 13, *infra*.

82 1997 S.C.C.R. 215.

Court accepted that a defence of necessity was available in all offences, including the strict liability offence of driving a motor vehicle on a road at more than the permitted speed. In the recent case of *Dawson v. Dickson*,[83] however, the Appeal Court held that necessity did not depend solely on the objective circumstances but also upon the accused's applying his mind to the dilemma before him and making a conscious decision to break the law in view of those objective circumstances. Curiously, this leads to the conclusion that although the offence may be proved against him objectively, an accused person who is charged with a strict liability offence and who pleads necessity by way of defence must show evidence of favourable "*mens rea*", as it were, in relation to that defence.

Statutory. A number of statutes specifically provide defences to what are otherwise offences of strict responsibility. The result of these defences is usually to limit responsibility to cases where the accused has acted negligently. Some statutes make it a defence for the accused to show that he neither knew nor had reasonable cause to believe or, in some cases, to suspect that the circumstances were such as to render his actings criminal.[84] Other statutes provide that it shall be a defence for the accused to show that he acted diligently or took all reasonable steps to comply with the statute.[85] In many cases the accused must show diligence on his own part and also that the contravention occurred through the fault of someone else,[86] and in the case of offences under section 6(4)(a) of the Food Safety Act 1990 it is a defence to show (*inter alia*) "that he did not know and had no reason to suspect" or "could not reasonably have been expected to know" the truth.[87] Section 26 of the Weights and Measures Act 1963 made it a defence to certain charges under that Act for the accused to show that the offence "was due to a mistake, or to accident or some other cause beyond his control" and that he took all reasonable precautions and used all due diligence to avoid the offence; but the defence was not repeated in the legislation which replaced that Act.[88] **8.32**

The purpose of strict responsibility

It is undeniable that strict responsibility involves injustice and moral absurdity. Why then has it been imposed by the courts? For the courts are more to blame than Parliament for the existence of offences of strict responsibility, because of their resort to the literal interpretation of provisions creating offences and their refusal to read these provisions as subject to an overriding presumption that *mens rea* is required in all offences. The reason, it is suggested, is the desire to punish negligence, and the peculiar position of negligence as *mens rea*. The law of Scotland is perhaps not altogether unfamiliar with the notion of negligence as a **8.33**

---

83 1999 S.C.C.R. 698.

84 *e.g.* Medicines Act 1968, s.67; Army Act 1955, s.195; Mental Health (Scotland) Act 1984, s.106; *cf.* Gaming Act 1968 s.23; Weights and Measures Act 1985, s.34; Misuse of Drugs Act 1971, s.28; *infra*, para. 8.36.

85 *e.g.* Mines and Quarries Act 1954, s.65, which requires that the contravention — loss of or damage to safety lamps — be reported.

86 *e.g.* Food Safety Act 1990, s.21(3); Trade Descriptions Act 1968, s.24; Agriculture Act 1970, s.82.

87 See Vol. II, Chap. 19.

88 See the Weights and Measures Act 1985, and contrast ss.34 and 35 thereof with s.26 of the repealed Weights and Measures Act 1963.

sufficient *mens rea* for common law offences, even if this is to some extent due to a failure to distinguish negligence from recklessness — one can plausibly read the nineteenth century cases as imposing responsibility for negligence in a number of crimes, including culpable homicide, fire raising, and culpably endangering life — but even so, *mens rea* normally connotes intention or recklessness. In England criminal responsibility for negligence at common law extends at most to manslaughter and one or two fairly recondite offences.[89] As has been argued[90] it is reasonable to describe negligence as a form of *mens rea*, but the prevalent English view is that negligence is not *mens rea*, and that the common law crimes of negligence which do exist are anomalous.[91]

When, therefore, the courts were faced with a statute which, for example, prohibited the sale of adulterated food, and it seemed clear that the statute would be useless unless negligence were sufficient for conviction, they found themselves in a difficulty. There are, as has been said,[92] two ways of construing such a provision: by reading it as subject to the requirement of *mens rea*, or by reading it literally. If negligence is not a form of *mens rea* the first reading will exclude negligence, so the only way to include negligence is to adopt the second reading, which involves strict responsibility. To read words like "No person shall sell" as an elliptical form of "no person shall knowingly sell" is a proper exercise of the power of interpretation by applying the presumption in favour of *mens rea*, but to read them as "no person shall negligently sell" is to rewrite the Act and insert words Parliament did not intend to be there. There are some indications in two early Scots cases involving vicarious responsibility that negligence would be a sufficient *mens rea* in a statutory offence,[93] but the problem was not fully dealt with, and in general the Scots courts have simply followed the English cases on *mens rea* in statutory offences.

If these suggestions are correct, they explain why judges have from time to time said both that it was necessary to interpret a statute strictly, and that the prosecution should not have been brought, or that the penalty should be only nominal in a particular case, because of the complete moral innocence of the accused.[94]

8.34 The views of the Judicial Committee of the Privy Council in *Lim Chin Aik v. The Queen*[95] are of great interest in this connection. In that case their Lordships held that there was nothing that the accused could have done which would have avoided the contravention, and that therefore the offence was one requiring *mens rea*. Their view was that the ordinary presumption in favour of *mens rea* was displaced where the imposition of strict responsibility would assist the enforcement of the statute because there was something an accused could do, by supervision or inspection, or improvement of his methods, or by exhortation of his employees, which could promote the observance of the regulations. On the other

---

[89] Gl. Williams, para. 41; J.C. Smith and B. Hogan, *Criminal Law* (9th ed., 1999, Sir J. Smith (ed.)), Chap. 5 (pp.90–96).

[90] *Supra*, para. 7.72.

[91] Gl. Williams, paras 14, 36; J.C. Smith and B. Hogan, *op.cit.*, *loc. cit.*

[92] *supra*, para. 8.06.

[93] *Wright and Wade v. Rowan* (1890) 2 White 426; *Neilson v. Parkhill* (1892) 3 White 379.

[94] *Parker v. Alder* [1899] 1 Q.B. 20. *Hobbs v. Winchester Corpn* [1910] 2 K.B. 471; *Howman v. Russell*, 1923 J.C. 32; *R. v. St Margaret's Trust Ltd* [1958] 1 W.L.R. 522.

[95] [1963] A.C. 160. For the facts see *supra*, para. 8.12.

hand, "Where it can be shown that the imposition of strict liability would result in the prosecution and conviction of a class of persons whose conduct could not in any way affect the observance of the law, their Lordships consider that, even where the statute is dealing with a grave social evil, strict liability is not likely to be intended."[96] Their Lordships deprecated the practice of imposing strict responsibility allied with a nominal penalty, and indicated that this method of dealing with the problem of the innocent offender should be resorted to only in exceptional cases.[97]

The Judicial Committee here indicate that where the *class of persons* concerned — in *Lim Chin Aik*[97a] persons declared illegal immigrants — can do nothing to avoid innocent contraventions the offence should require *mens rea*, and where the class of persons concerned, such as traders in food, can take precautions the offence should be one of strict responsibility. The individual innocent member of a class of the second kind they regard as exceptional. But most strict responsibility offences are of the second kind and most cases of injustice can at present be dealt with only in the way the Committee deprecate and feel should be applied only in exceptional cases. Most strict liability offences are cases where, "The accused, if he does not will the violation, usually is in a position to prevent it with no more care than society might reasonably expect and no more exertion than it might reasonably exact from one who assumed his responsibilities."[98]

The argument from the possibility of avoidance by care to the imposition of strict responsibility is in any event a *non sequitur*, for all that is needed to enforce care is to make negligence criminal. It may be that for practical reasons the onus of showing that the offence was not due to the accused's fault should lie on him, but it is not necessary to impose strict responsibility in order to penalise negligence, and if only negligence is penalised the innocent individual will receive the acquittal which is his due, instead of a sort of grace and favour dispensation by way of a nominal penalty.[99] If the criminal law is to have a moral foundation it must deal separately with individual cases and not impose punishment on an individual because he belongs to a class which can assist law enforcement by taking precautions or because his offence is one which can usually be avoided by care, if he himself, in the particular case, offended without any culpability.

Another suggestion which has been made, especially by Lord Diplock **8.35**
in *Sweet v. Parsley*,[1] is that it should always be a defence to an offence of strict responsibility for the accused to show that he acted under a reasonable mistake of fact. This appears to be the law in Australia, although the passage which is most often cited was in fact an *obiter*

---

[96] [1963] A.C. at 175.

[97] See also *R. v. Warner* [1969] 2 A.C. 256, Lord Reid at 278c.

[97a] [1963] A.C. 160.

[98] *Morissette v. U.S.*, 342 U.S. 246 (1952), Jackson J. at 256.

[99] The only sphere in which the courts have adopted this approach has been in connection with offences of permitting. They have been able to do this by way of interpreting the concept of permission as including failure to prevent, without becoming involved in any general creation of responsibility for negligence: see *infra*, para. 8.77.

[1] [1970] A.C. 132. This is still regarded as the leading authority on strict liability in England — see A. Ashworth, *Principles of Criminal Law* (3rd ed., 1999), p.173.

dictum. It is a statement by Dixon J. in *Proudman v. Dayman*[2] that, "As a general rule an honest and reasonable belief in a state of facts which, if they existed, would make the defendant's act innocent affords an excuse for doing what would otherwise be an offence." The adoption of this "half-way house", as it has been called, has been viewed with some sympathy by members of the House of Lords,[3] but it seems that the courts will not take it upon themselves to alter the general principle that the burden of proof of *mens rea* lies on the Crown.[4] It may, however, be possible to adopt the New Zealand approach which places only an evidential burden on the accused to produce some evidence of an honest belief based on reasonable grounds that her act was innocent.[5] A similar approach was favoured by the minority of the Supreme Court (Chief Justice Lamer and Justices McLachlin and La Forest) in the Canadian case of *R. v. Wholesale Travel Gp Inc.*[6] The majority, however, maintained the correctness (and indeed constitutionality) of the decision in *R. v. City of Sault Ste Marie*,[7] where the Supreme Court divided offences into three categories — those requiring *mens rea*; strict liability offences, in which *mens rea* need not be established by the Crown but the defence of reasonable care or reasonable mistake is available to the defendant; and absolute liability offences in which the defendant cannot exculpate himself by showing he was free of fault: and the Court held that public welfare offences were to be regarded as offences of strict liability unless the legislature clearly made them offences of absolute liability.[8]

The attractiveness of these solutions, and especially of the *Proudman v. Dayman* version, is that they meet the objection that to require *mens rea* would place an impossible burden on the Crown.[9] One of the problems about many strict responsibility offences is that, unlike most common law offences, the commission of the act does not in itself raise any inference of *mens rea*[10]; there is therefore need for some presumption to make it possible for *mens rea* to be established at all. Faced with a choice between abandoning the golden rule of *Woolmington v. D.P.P.*[11] that the onus of proof is on the Crown, or creating offences which do not require *mens rea*, the courts have chosen the latter. Perhaps only Parliament can create the halfway house, as indeed it has done in specific statutes.

---

[2] (1941) 67 C.L.R. 536, 540; *cf. Bank of New South Wales v. Piper* [1897] A.C. 383, 389–390: "the absence of mens rea really consists in an honest and reasonable belief entertained by the accused of the existence of facts which, if true, would make the act charged against him innocent."

[3] *R. v. Warner* [1969] 2 A.C. 256, Lord Reid at 280 B-E; *Sweet v. Parsley, supra,* Lord Reid at 150 B-E, Lord Pearce at 157 D-H; *Tesco Ltd v. Nattrass* [1972] A.C. 153, Lord Reid at 169 D-E.

[4] See especially *R. v. Warner, supra*, Lord Pearce at 303 A-C; *Sweet v. Parsley, supra*, Lord Pearce at 158A; *contra* Lord Diplock at 164 D-G.

[5] *R. v. Strawbridge* [1970] N.Z.L.R. 909; Lord Diplock thought that this was also the Australian position: see *Sweet v. Parsley, supra*, at 164 H.

[6] [1991] 3 S.C.R. 154.

[7] [1978] 2 S.C.R. 1299. See also *R. v. Vaillancourt* [1987] 2 S.C.R. 636, and para. 8.04, *supra*.

[8] Offences of absolute liability are unconstitutional in Canada if they carry the possibility of a prison sentence: see *Re B.C. Motor Vehicle Act* [1985] 2 S.C.R. 486, and para. 8.04, *supra*.

[9] *Sweet v. Parsley* [1970] A.C. 132, Lord Reid at 150 B; Lord Pearce at 156–157; *Alphacell Ltd v. Woodward* [1972] A.C. 824, Visc. Dilhorne at 839 E; Lord Salmon at 848 G.

[10] *cf. supra,* para. 7.23.

[11] [1935] A.C. 462, now adopted in Scotland: *Lambie v. H.M. Advocate*, 1973 J.C. 53.

There is a growing tendency for Parliament to recognise that responsibility for statutory offences should extend only to negligence and should not be strict, and this explains the special defences which are now often found in statutes creating offences of strict responsibility,[12] and which place on the accused the burden of establishing the absence of negligence. Unfortunately, Parliament has acted in a patchy and piecemeal fashion: the precise defences open vary from statute to statute, sometimes even from section to section.[13] Sometimes, indeed, the same incident can be charged under different statutory provisions which carry different defences.[14] If, as appears to be increasingly accepted, it is sufficient for the protection of the public in most cases to restrict responsibility to cases where there has been some degree of negligence, it would be much more satisfactory for Parliament to provide that it should be a defence to any statutory offence that the accused acted with all due diligence and neither knew nor had reasonable cause to suspect he was committing an offence. The relevant section of the Offices, Shops and Railway Premises Act 1963[15] which provides that, "It shall be a defence for a person charged with a contravention of a provision of this Act . . . to prove that he used all due diligence to secure compliance with that provision" might well be applied to all statutory offences.[16] If, for any sufficient reason, Parliament wished to impose strict responsibility for any offence it should be able to do so only by an express provision.[17] **8.36**

It should be noted too that the offences in *R. v. Warner*[18] and *Sweet v. Parsley*[19] are now clearly not strict liability offences. This is as a result of the provisions of the Misuse of Drugs Act 1971 which, generally speaking, makes it a defence to a possession offence to prove lack of knowledge, suspicion or reasonable ground for suspicion,[20] and limits the responsibility of persons concerned with premises to activities knowingly permitted by them.[21]

The English Law Commission at one time suggested the adoption of a rule that unless an offence was specifically stated to be one of strict liability in relation to any element, it was to be taken to require negligence for that element, unless of course it specifically required intention or recklessness.[22] Negligence could be treated as established in the absence of contrary evidence,[23] but the intention of the Law **8.37**

---

[12] *supra*, para. 8.32.

[13] A number of anomalies of this kind have been removed by the Weights and Measures Act 1985, ss.33 and 34.

[14] See *e.g.* with respect to offences of misdescribed or falsely described goods, Trade Descriptions Act 1968, ss.1–4, and 24; Weights and Measures Act 1985, ss.33 and 34; Food Safety Act 1990, ss.15 and 21.

[15] s.67.

[16] *cf.* C. Howard's suggestion that punishment should follow only on an unreasonable failure to comply with the statute: *op.cit.*, p.58.

[17] For an example of Parliament leaving the problem to the courts see the Under Secretary's comment in the debate on s.12 of the Criminal Justice Act 1967: "The absence of the word 'knowingly' does not mean automatically that *mens rea* is excluded. It depends very much on the total context. My immediate view is that *mens rea* would be required but that is something which would have to be left to the interpretation of the courts": *Hansard*, H.C., Vol. 751, col.767, July 26, 1967.

[18] [1969] 2 A.C. 256.

[19] [1970] A.C. 132.

[20] Misuse of Drugs Act 1971, s.28. See *Salmon v. H.M. Advocate; Moore v. H.M. Advocate*, 1998 S.C.C.R. 740.

[21] *ibid.*, s.8.

[22] L.C.W.P. No. 31, Proposition 3.

[23] *ibid.,* Proposition 4.

Commission was that this should place only an evidential burden on the defendant.[24] What was not clear was how it was envisaged that that burden would be discharged, and it may be that if it was enough for the accused to say he took what care he could, or even that he took certain specific precautions, the burden of proving negligence would remain "intolerable", while if he had to lead evidence to support his assertions one might as well have placed the persuasive burden on him. Whether the precautions he took were such as to show that he was taking care was presumably an objective question, but it would seem that it would be for the Crown to prove beyond reasonable doubt that they were insufficient to exclude negligence.[25]

One danger of substituting this approach for the standard statutory defence in which the accused has to prove that he exercised care is that Parliament, given the choice between requiring the Crown to prove negligence and imposing strict liability, may elect for strict liability.[26] In any event, the more recent Draft Code produced by the Law Commission adandons the approach discussed above in favour of a general presumption that an offence requires the fault element of recklessness for each of its elements "unless otherwise provided"; this seems by and large to favour the present vague rule whereby there is simply a presumption in favour of *mens rea* which Parliament may displace either expressly or by implication.[27]

Attempts and art and part guilt[28]

8.38 It has been said in England that a person cannot be convicted of attempting to commit an offence of strict responsibility unless he possessed full *mens rea* and acted intentionally.[29] This is in line with the English view that any common law attempt requires intention even although the completed crime can be committed recklessly.[30] It would seem to follow from this that *mens rea* is required for an attempt to commit an offence of strict responsibility, and it has been held that conspiracy to commit such an offence requires *mens rea*.[31] (There may, however, be strict responsibility for attempt where what is in issue is knowledge of a criminative circumstance, such as the age of a girl in a sexual offence.[32]) The Scots courts have rejected this view in common law crimes,[33] but it is to be hoped that they will follow the English courts in statutory offences, if only out of a reluctance to extend the ambit of strict responsibility.

---

[24] pp. 19–20.

[25] True, they have to do this where the offence consists of negligence, as in careless driving, but there the jury are merely asked to apply a description to proved behaviour, where the behaviour bears negligence on its face, so to speak.

[26] See G.H. Gordon, "The Mental Element in Crime" (1971) 16 J.L.S. 282.

[27] See Law Commission No. 177 (1989), *A Criminal Code for England and Wales*, Vol. 1, cl. 20(1), (2); and Vol. 2 (Commentary), paras 8.25 and 8.28.

[28] See *supra*, Chaps 6 and 5 respectively.

[29] Gl. Williams, para. 84. *Cf. Gardner v. Akeroyd* [1952] 2 Q.B. 743, itself a case of vicarious responsibility.

[30] *R. v. Whybrow* (1951) 35 Cr.App.R. 141.

[31] *Churchill v. Walton* [1967] 2 A.C. 224.

[32] *cf. R. v. Collier* [1960] Crim.L.R. 204; J.C. Smith and B. Hogan, *Criminal Law* (9th ed., 1999, Sir J. Smith (ed.)), pp.307–309.

[33] *supra*, paras 7.78 *et seq.*

It is also the law in England that a person cannot be convicted of **8.39** aiding and abetting an offence of strict responsibility unless he acted with *mens rea* — either intention or knowledge,[34] or advertent recklessness.[35] In the Scottish sheriff court case of *Valentine v. Mackie*,[36] A was convicted of aiding and abetting the driver (of the car in which he was a passenger) to drive with an excess of alcohol in his blood, on the basis that, given that A and the driver had been drinking together and that the car was being driven erratically, a reasonable man in A's position would have realised that the driver was likely to be over the limit. This followed the earlier English decision in *Carter v. Richardson*.[37] The English view of the required *mens rea* is now, however, more subjective,[38] and it is clear that aiding and abetting requires proof that the defendant was aware "that his act would or might bring about the commission of the principal offence".[39] It is possible to be art and part guilty of a crime of carelessness in Scotland,[40] and where A and B are engaged in a joint enterprise which is so carelessly conducted as to involve the commission of an offence of strict responsibility, both might be convicted. But art and part guilt is inconceivable without some *mens rea* on the part of the aider and abettor, and so far as "deliberate" offences like driving while disqualified or uninsured or with faulty brakes are concerned, the aider and abettor must have knowledge of the illegality. An apparent exception to this rule is to be found in *Salmon v. H.M. Advocate; Moore v. H.M. Advocate*,[41] where it was held that a person accused of being art and part in the somewhat unusual offence of being "concerned" in the supply of prohibited drugs to another need be shown to have known only that something was being supplied from A to B and that he was concerned in its supply: it did not have to be shown that he knew that the object of the supply was a prohibited drug.[42] This exception can probably be explained by the fact that the offence in question[43] is one which arguably imposes direct liability upon those who, in relation to less widely drawn offences, would be prosecutable only by way of art and part: in short, it is questionable whether art and part liability is applicable to this particular offence,[44] and thus decisions relative to art

---

[34] *Johnson v. Youden* [1950] 1 K.B. 544; *Ackroyds, etc., Ltd v. D.P.P.* [1950] 1 All E.R. 933; *Ferguson v. Weaving* [1951] 1 Q.B. 814; *John Henshall (Quarries) Ltd v. Harvey* [1965] 2 Q.B. 233. See also J.C. Smith and B. Hogan, *Criminal Law* (9th ed., 1999, Sir John Smith (ed.)), at pp.137–138.

[35] See, *e.g.*, *D.P.P. v. Andrews* [1990] R.T.R. 269; *Blakeley v. D.P.P.* [1991] R.T.R. 405.

[36] 1980 S.L.T. (Sh.Ct.) 122.

[37] [1974] R.T.R. 314, where the defendant was the supervisor of a learner driver whom the supervisor knew to have been drinking, and the court held on appeal against conviction that the jury had been entitled to infer that the supervisor knew also that the driver had been drinking to such an extent that it was probable that the level of alcohol in his body exceeded the permitted limit.

[38] See *Blakelely v. D.P.P.* [1991] R.T.R. 269.

[39] *ibid.*, McCullough J. at 415 H.

[40] *supra*, para. 5.47.

[41] 1998 S.C.C.R. 740.

[42] *ibid.*, L.J.-G. Rodger at 762E-763B. This case rejects assumptions or dicta favouring the ordinary rule in *McCadden v. H.M. Advocate*, 1986 S.C.C.R. 16; *Tudhope v. McKee*, 1987 S.C.C.R. 663, Lord McDonald at 666–667; *Rodden v. H.M. Advocate*, 1994 S.C.C.R. 841, L.J.-C. Ross at 844F.

[43] Section 4(3)(b) of the Misuse of Drugs Act 1971.

[44] See *Clements v. H.M. Advocate*, 1991 S.C.C.R. 266, L.J.-G. Hope at 273A and 274A-B; *H.M. Advocate v. Hamill*, 1998 S.C.C.R. 164, Lord Marnoch at 166A.

and part charges in respect of it should not be regarded as necessarily displacing the normal rule that the accused should have knowledge of the illegality.

Vicarious Responsibility

8.40 The position of vicarious responsibility for crime is in many ways similar to that of strict responsibility: both involve convicting someone in the complete absence of any *mens rea* on his part. Both, therefore, involve obvious injustice, and in some ways vicarious responsibility is less defensible than strict responsibility.[45] The latter at least requires some conduct on the part of the accused,[46] while the former does not. Vicarious responsibility represents a departure from the fundamental moral principle that "the soul that sinneth it shall die".[47] A person may, of course, be convicted at common law for someone else's conduct, but that happens only when he is art and part in it and therefore blameworthy as an accomplice. Vicarious responsibility under statute deals with cases where this element of conspiracy or accession is absent.

The general considerations regarding the application of strict responsibility apply equally to vicarious responsibility, and vicarious responsibility extends to the same groups of offences as does strict responsibility, although there are also some offences of vicarious responsibility which are not offences of strict responsibility so far as the actual offender is concerned.[48]

8.41 It has been said that vicarious responsibility has no place in criminal law but is restricted to situations like breaches of a public-house licensee's certificate which are only quasi-criminal.[49] Vicarious responsibility was developed mainly in licensing cases,[50] but it applied also in certain other nineteenth-century statutes such as the Salmon Fisheries (Scotland) Act 1868,[51] the Sale of Food and Drugs Act 1875[52] and the Army Act 1881.[53] Licensing offences themselves became offences in the normal meaning of the term, and not merely breaches of a certificate, after the passing of the Licensing (Scotland) Act 1903,[54] but they did not cease to involve vicarious responsibility. In *Mackenna v. Sim and Ors.*[55]

---

[45] For an attack on the concept of vicarious responsibility see A.D. Gibb, "Vicarious Liability for Crime", 1955 S.L.T. (News) 21. And see also K.W.B.M., "Vicarious Crime", 1938 S.L.T. (News) 25.

[46] Except perhaps in rare cases like *R. v. Larsonneur, supra*, para. 8.29.

[47] Ezekiel, Chap. 18, following Deut., Chap. 24, v. 16.

[48] *Mousell Bros Ltd v. London and N.W.Ry.* [1917] 2 K.B. 836; *Allen v. Whitehead* [1930] 1 K.B. 211; *G. Newton Ltd v. Smith* [1962] 2 Q.B. 278.

[49] *e.g., Linton v. Stirling* (1893) 1 Adam 61, Lord McLaren at 70; *Wilson v. Fleming* (1913) 7 Adam 263, L.J.-G. Strathclyde at 270; *Gair v. Brewster* (1916) 7 Adam 752, L.J.-G. Strathclyde at 756; *Kidd v. Murray*, 1954 S.L.T. (Notes) 24.

[50] Although there were earlier revenue cases involving penalties for offences, *e.g., Advocate-General v. Grant* (1953) 15 D. 980; *The Queen v. Gilroys* (1866) 4 M. 656. See also *Lord Advocate v. D. and J. Nicol*, 1915 S.C. 735.

[51] *Don v. Johnston* (1897) 2 Adam 416.

[52] *Fitzpatrick v. Kelly* (1873) L.R. 8 Q.B. 337 (decided under the similarly worded previous legislation, the Prevention of Adulteration of Food and Drugs Act 1872 — replaced by the 1875 Act).

[53] *O'Brien v. Macgregor* (1903) 4 Adam 202.

[54] *cf. Ferguson v. Campbell*, 1946 J.C. 28, L.J.-C. Cooper at 32.

[55] (1916) 7 Adam 732. See also *Gair v. Brewster* (1916) 7 Adam 752; *Soutar v. Hutton* (1916) *ibid.* 758.

vicarious responsibility was imposed for a breach of a defence regulation relating to licensing hours which carried a penalty of imprisonment without the option of a fine, and which could therefore not be described as in any way only quasi-criminal.[56] Since then vicarious responsibility has been applied in Scotland to offences by sailors for which an absent master has been convicted,[57] and offences by salesmen for which an absent shopkeeper has been convicted,[58] as well as to numerous offences by the holders of various kinds of licence under the Road Traffic Act, which are clearly dealt with by the Act as offences rather than breaches of a licence,[59] and which do not necessarily or even normally involve forfeiture of the licence[60]: it has been extended even further in England to include an offence requiring an intent to defraud.[61]

As in the case of strict responsibilty, whether or not an offence **8.42** involves vicarious responsibility can be decided only by reference to the statute creating the offence. There is a presumption against vicarious responsibility,[62] but there are a number of types of offence in which it is normally found. Vicarious responsibility may be created expressly by a statute, or may be implied from a consideration of the words and the object of a statute. It may also be imposed by means of the interpretation of words like "sells" to include both the person who is in law the contracting party and the employee or agent who actually conducts the transaction, and by means of creating offences of "causing" or "permitting" something to be done contrary to law, which, although formally offences of primary responsibility, in practice involve vicarious responsibility.

Statutory interpretation

Express words. Vicarious responsibility is frequently imposed expressly. **8.43** Section 67 (2) of the Licensing (Scotland) Act 1976 provides that where an employee or agent of a licence-holder commits certain specified offences,[63] proceedings may be taken against the licence-holder in respect of the offence. The Mines and Quarries Act 1954 provides that if certain sections of the Act are contravened the manager of the mine and certain other specified persons shall be guilty of an offence,[64] and section 155 of the Factories Act 1961 makes similar provision for the guilt of the occupier of a factory in which a contravention of that Act takes place.[65]

---

[56] The decision was explained by reference to "the nation's efficiency in a time of unexampled stress", but it is difficult to believe that the war effort was so seriously impaired by drinking after hours as to justify in itself a departure from the ordinary principles of the law.

[57] *Smith v. Ross*, 1937 J.C. 65.

[58] *Duguid v. Fraser,* 1942 J.C. 1 — although reference was made to the possibility of loss of the right to trade on a third conviction, the *ratio* of the case is much wider, and does not depend on the trade being in any way licensed, *infra,* para. 8.48.

[59] *Pace* L.J.-G. Normand in *Mitchell v. Morrison, infra.*

[60] *Bean v. Sinclair*, 1930 J.C. 31; *Macmillan v. Western S.M.T. Co. Ltd*, 1933 J.C. 51; *Clydebank Co-operative Society Ltd v. Binnie*, 1937 J.C. 17; *Mitchell v. Morrison*, 1938 J.C. 64.

[61] *Mousell Bros. Ltd, supra.* But see *Vane v. Yiannopoullos* [1965] A.C. 486.

[62] *Mitchell v. Morrison*, 1938 J.C. 64; *Duguid v. Fraser*, 1942 J.C. 1.

[63] Set out in Sched. 5 to the Act. See also Representation of the People Act 1983, s.159.

[64] s.152 (1). See also Management and Administration of Safety and Health at Mines Regulations, S.I. 1993 No. 1897.

[65] See also Offices Shops and Railway Premises Act 1963, s.63; Betting Gaming and Lotteries Act 1963, s.10 (1).

Some Acts have contained provisions that in the event of certain contraventions occurring a person in a certain situation should be "deemed" guilty of an offence.[66]

8.44 *By implication.* In deciding whether a statutory offence involves vicarious responsibility in the absence of express words creating such responsibility the courts, while taking into account the presumption against vicarious responsibility, must have regard "to the object of the statute, the words used, the nature of the duty laid down, the person upon whom it is imposed, the person by whom it would in ordinary circumstances be performed, and the person upon whom the penalty is imposed."[67] Where a duty is laid on a person in a particular capacity, such as the owner of goods sent by rail,[68] the holder of a road service licence[69] or the occupier of fishings,[70] it is likely that there will be vicarious responsibility, particularly if the duty is one which would normally actually be performed by an employee on behalf of the person on whom the duty is laid by statute,[71] or where no penalty is provided for the person who actually commits the offence but only for the person on whom the duty is imposed.[72]

On the other hand, the fact that a contravention is likely to occur through the activities of other people, especially people who are not employees of the accused, and over whom he has little or no control, can be an argument for interpreting the offence so as to require *mens rea*. As Lord Morris of Borth-y-Gest said of the argument that the offence of being concerned in the management of premises used for the smoking of cannabis did not require *mens rea*:

> "The implications are astonishing. Parliament would not only be indirectly imposing a duty upon persons concerned in the management of any premises requiring them to exercise complete supervision over all persons who enter the premises to ensure that no one of them should smoke cannabis, but Parliament would be enacting that the persons concerned in the management would become guilty of an offence if, unknown to them, someone, by surreptitiously smoking cannabis eluded the most elaborately devised measures of supervision. There would not be guilt by reason of anything done nor even by reasons of any carelessness, but by reason of the unknown act of some unknown person whom it had not been found possible to control. When the range of possible punishments is remembered the unlikelihood that Parliament intended to legislate in such way becomes additionally apparent."[73]

---

[66] *e.g.* Children and Young Persons (Scotland) Act 1937, s.17(3), which was repealed by Licensing (Scotland) Act 1959 but re-enacted as s.143(3); the present Act, Licensing (Scotland) Act 1976, which repealed in turn the 1959 Act, contains no equivalent provision. See also Sea Fisheries Act 1883, s.20 (which was repealed by the Sea Fisheries Act 1968, s.22 and Sched.2); see *Smith v. Ross*, 1937 J.C. 65.

[67] *Mousell Bros Ltd v. L. and N.W.Ry.* [1917] 2 K.B. 836, Atkin J. at 845.

[68] *Mousell Bros Ltd, supra.*

[69] *Bean v. Sinclair*, 1930 J.C. 31; *G. Newton Ltd v. Smith* [1962] 2 Q.B. 278.

[70] *Don v. Johnston* (1897) 2 Adam 416.

[71] *Mousell Bros Ltd; G. Newton Ltd, supra.*

[72] *G. Newton Ltd, supra. Cf. Benassi v. McLennan* (1906) 5 Adam 220; *Graham v. Strathern*, 1927 J.C. 29; *Spires v. Smith* [1956] 1 W.L.R. 601.

[73] *Sweet v. Parsley* [1970] A.C. 132, 155 F-H.

Where the offence is one which arises in the course of the carrying on of a trade or business vicarious responsibility is frequently imposed. Where the trade or business is conducted under licence this is almost always so. The position in such cases is set out by Lord Justice-General Clyde in *Bean v. Sinclair*[74] as follows: **8.45**

> "If a trader is, in virtue of statutory restrictions, allowed to carry on his trade only under certain conditions, the trader is, in my opinion, answerable for any breach of those conditions committed in the course of his trade. A breach is none the less committed in the course of *his* trade because the actual delinquent is a servant or other person acting within the authority committed to him by the trader. It is in this way that the maxim *qui facit per alium facit per se*, although it does not strictly apply in criminal cases, has been said to apply in the 'class of delicts in which, as in cases under the Licensing Acts, the offence is the acting in contravention of the trade conditions to which by Act of Parliament the master of the business is bound to conform . . .'[75] If a trader is allowed to carry on his trade only on certain conditions, and the conditions are breached in some particular, it follows that the trade is being carried on illegally in that particular; in other words, the trader is trading in a manner not permitted by law, and is therefore necessarily liable to the penalty for contravention, whether he commits the breach personally or not."[76]

Lord Clyde's remarks were expressed in the context of a case involving breach of a licence to operate a transport undertaking, but there is no reason to restrict the principle involved to licensed trades. Vicarious responsibility has been extended in England to make the owner of goods sent by rail responsible for statements made by the employee who actually dispatched them,[77] and in Scotland to the occupiers of salmon fishings for the failures of their employees to observe the byelaws relating to the weekly close time.[78] It may be, however, that the courts will be more reluctant to impose vicarious responsibility in relation to unlicenced trades than in the case of trades regulated by licence. In *Haig v. Thompson*[79] the owner of a house in respect of which a closing order had been made was charged with letting it or permitting it to be occupied contrary to the provisions of the now repealed Housing (Scotland) Act 1925, section 9. The transaction had been carried out with the knowledge of the owner's husband, but there was no evidence that he had acted with her approval, although he had clearly acted in the course of her business. The court applied the presumption against vicarious responsibility and refused to hold that the accused was responsible for her husband's actings. However morally praiseworthy the result, the case is difficult to reconcile with other authority, particularly as the person who was in law party to the lease was the accused, although it is true that the husband himself could also have been charged.[80] In cases involving "sale" and similar words vicarious responsibility is normal, and *Haig v. Thompson*[80a] could well have been regarded as a case of this kind.

---

74 1930 J.C. 31, 36–37.
75 *Hogg v. Davidson* (1901) 3 Adam 335, Lord McLaren at 338.
76 See also *Hall v. Begg*, 1928 J.C. 29, L.J.-G. Clyde at 32.
77 *Mousell Bros Ltd, supra.*
78 *Don v. Johnston* (1897) 2 Adam 416.
79 1931 J.C. 29.
80 L.J.-C. Alness at 32.
80a 1931 J.C. 29.

8.46 It has been held in England that where a bankrupt sends his agent to obtain goods and the latter fails to disclose the bankruptcy, the bankrupt is vicariously guilty of obtaining credit without disclosing his bankruptcy, although he had told the agent to make the disclosure and believed he had done so.[81] This appears to be an extremely harsh decision, although the offence is one of strict responsibility and the duty of disclosure is clearly laid on the bankrupt, and it may be that the Scots courts would not follow it.

Offences involving sale, etc.

8.47 Statutory provisions frequently penalise the sale or delivery of, the using, keeping or possessing, or other forms of dealing in, things in certain circumstances. If these words are given what Glanville Williams calls an "extensive interpretation" the result is to impose vicarious responsibility on the person who is legally the party to the transaction or activity which is in fact carried on by his employee or agent.[82]

8.48 SALE. The commonest example of this form of vicarious responsibility is the case of sale. It is well recognised that the person who is regarded as the seller in the civil law of contract is also criminally responsible for a sale carried out on his behalf, even although the statute provides only that "No person shall sell", and does not go on to specify "by himself or by his employee or agent".[83] Examples of this form of vicarious responsibility can be found in cases under the Food and Drugs Acts,[84] weights and measures legislation,[85] the Pharmacy Acts,[86] and wartime price regulations,[87] as well as under licensing laws.[88] Where, however, a statute provides that a person shall not "sell or allow any other person to sell", the practice is to charge the principal with allowing his employee to sell.[89] It has also been held that a purchase by an agent is a purchase by his principal.[90]

Words like "supply" or "dispatch" or other similar terms usually receive the same extensive interpretation as "sell" itself, but the cases on supply and dispatch have been under the Licensing Acts where provision is specially made for transactions by the licensee himself or by his employee or agent.[91]

---

[81] *R. v. Duke of Leinster* [1924] 1 K.B. 311; *cf. R. v. Salter* [1968] 2 Q.B. 793.

[82] Gl. Williams, para. 96. In such cases both the principal and his employee may be regarded as having contravened the statute: Gl Williams, pp.276, 347, but see *Spires v. Smith* [1956] 1 W.L.R. 601, and *G. Newton Ltd v. Smith* [1962] 2 Q.B. 278.

[83] The suggestion by the court in *Tomlinson v. Bremridge* (1894) 1 Adam 393 that liability is confined to the servant seller is *obiter*, depends on the interpretation of the Pharmacy Act 1868 as excluding vicarious responsibility in respect of one section because it expressly invokes it in respect of other sections, is of no general validity, and in any event conflicts with the later case of *Bremridge v. Turnbull* (1895) 2 Adam 29.

[84] *e.g. Lindsay v. Dempster* (1912) 6 Adam 707; *Wilson v. Fleming* (1913) 7 Adam 263; *Macleod v. Woodmuir Miners Welfare Society Social Club*, 1961 J.C. 5; *Skinner v. MacLean*, 1979 S.L.T. (Notes) 35.

[85] *e.g. Galbraith's Stores Ltd v. McIntyre* (1912) 6 Adam 641; *Brander v. Buttercup Dairy Co.*, 1921 J.C. 19; *Robertson v. Gray*, 1945 J.C. 113.

[86] *Bremridge v. Turnbull* (1895) 2 Adam 29.

[87] *City and Suburban Dairies v. Mackenna*, 1918 J.C. 105; *Duguid v. Fraser*, 1942 J.C. 1.

[88] *e.g. Philip v. Lamb* (1893) 1 Adam 4; *Hogg v. Davidson* (1901) 3 Adam 335; *Gair v. Brewster* (1916) 7 Adam 752; *Soutar v. Hutton* (1916) *ibid.* 758; *Hall v. Begg*, 1928 J.C. 29.

[89] *e.g. Greig v. Macleod* (1907) 5 Adam 445.

[90] *Macaulay v. MacKirdy* (1893) 3 White 464 where a sale to someone acting on behalf of an inspector was held to be a sale to the inspector. See also *Cheyne v. French*, 1948 J.C. 151.

[91] *Gair v. Brewster* (1916) 7 Adam 752; *Mackenna v. Sim* (1916) 7 Adam 732; *Herriot v. Auld*, 1918 J.C. 16; *Nicol v. Smith*, 1955 J.C. 7. *Cf. McAleer v. Laird*, 1934 J.C. 79.

"USE". It is not clear to what extent vicarious responsibility underlies **8.49** the interpretation given to offences predicated on 'use'. In England, there is a well established rule that this word has a restricted meaning where a statutory offence offers "causes or permits the use of" as an alternative to "uses" a specified item under qualifying circumstances.[92] Thus, for example, where a person drives a motor vehicle which has 'construction and use' defects[93] or in respect of which there is no or insufficient insurance,[94] he is a user of the vehicle; but so too is his employer provided that there is a true relationship of master and servant between the two and the driver is engaged in the course of his employer's business at the relevant time.[95] The former proviso is perhaps the more important of the two: it would not be sufficient to make a person other than the actual driver 'a user' if the driver was simply at the time contributing to that other person's business operation without being his employee. Under the rule, therefore, a person driving a vehicle for the benefit of himself and his fellow partner is the sole user of that vehicle, even where his fellow partner is a passenger in the vehicle at the time: partners do not employ one another, and thus the rule is not satisfied under which the non-driving partner can be a user.[96] *A fortiori* a businessman, who invites and authorises a friend to drive a truck owned by the business on a business ploy, is not a user since the actual driver is not his employee.[97]

On the other hand, if a statutory offence of 'using' does not offer a 'causing or permitting the use of' alternative, the rule identifying who may be users of the item in question is less restricted. In *F.E. Charman v. Clow*,[98] for example, a firm contracted with a self-employed individual to uplift and deliver a quantity of ash, utilising the individual's own truck. The firm did not supervise the collection, loading or delivery; nor did they satisfy themselves that the truck to be used had been inspected and passed as fit for the purpose in question. In fact, the driver delivered short weight to the firm's customer and it was discovered that the truck had not been inspected or passed as fit for the purposes of trade. As it was a statutory offence to use any article for trade unless that article had been inspected and stamped as fit for such purpose,[99] the question arose

---

[92] See *Crawford v. Haughton* [1972] R.T.R. 125, Lord Widgery C.J., at 129D; *Garrett v. Hooper* [1973] R.T.R. 1, Lord Widgery C.J., at 3E; *Passmoor v. Gibbons* [1979] R.T.R. 53, Drake J., at 55H; *Hallett Silbermann Ltd v. Cheshire C.C.* [1993] R.T.R. 32, Beldam L.J., at 37K; *West Yorkshire Trading Standards Service v. Lex Vehicle Leasing Ltd* [1996] R.T.R. 70, Dyson J. at 76D-E; *Jones v. D.P.P.* [1999] R.T.R. 1, Sullivan L.J., at 8C–9A, all decisions of the Divisional Court of the Queen's Bench. This trend of authority has been confirmed by the Court of Appeal in the civil cases of *Hatton v. Hall* [1997] R.T.R. 212, Henry L.J., at 216F-G, and *O'Mahoney v. Joliffe* [1999] R.T.R. 245, Simon Brown L.J. at 250E to 251A, both concerned with the now superseded Motor Insurers' Bureau (Compensation of Victims of Uninsured Drivers) Agreement 1972, cl. 6(1)(c)(ii).

[93] See ss.40A to 42 of the Road Traffic Act 1988, as added/substituted by the Road Traffic Act 1991, s.8.

[94] See s.143 of the Road Traffic Act 1988.

[95] See *Bennett v. Richardson* [1980] R.T.R. 358, Lord Widgery C.J., at 361E-G, in addition to the authorities listed in n.92, *supra*. For the position as to *mens rea* in such an offence, see para. 8.74, *infra*.

[96] *Bennett v. Richardson*, *supra*. Where a partnership is the employer of the driver, it has been held that a partner who takes no active part in the management or prosecution of the firm's business is nevertheless a person who uses the vehicle driven by the employee.

[97] He may, however, be guilty of causing or permitting such use by the driver.

[98] [1974] 1 W.L.R. 1384.

[99] Weights and Measures Act 1963, s.11(2), Sched. 5, para. 4. See now Weights and Measures Act 1985, s.11(2).

whether the firm, in addition to the driver, had been using the vehicle in contravention of the statutory provision. Lord Widgery, the Chief Justice, held that as the offence in question did not carry a 'causing or permitting' alternative, a wider significance could be given to 'use', and that the firm in this case were indeed using the vehicle and thus rightly convicted of the offence.

It is not clear why the English courts have favoured the rule set out above. Perhaps the conjunction of 'using' and 'causing or permitting the use' gives rise to the view that Parliament intended 'use' to refer more specifically to the actual user of the item in question since more "constructive" users can be dealt with for having 'caused or permitted' the actual use in contravention of the statutory provision. But this would favour an interpretation where, in relation to construction and use driving offences, for example, 'the user' would more properly be confined to the actual driver; this is not, however, what the rule states. Indeed, the rule is not regarded as a logical one in England,[1] but rather as a pragmatic one since a 'line had to be drawn somewhere'.[2]

Apart from its illogicality, the rule suffers from the drawback that it is not always clear whether a master and servant relationship exists in particular situations. Thus in *Howard v. G.T. Jones and Co. Ltd*,[3] a truck with an insecure load was driven on a road by a person hired to the company which owned the vehicle. He was the servant of an employment agency which had hired him out to that company for one month. The decision, upheld on appeal, was that the company could not be convicted of using the truck contrary to regulations since the driver was not the company's employee. But it would have been possible to regard him as the company's employee, albeit for a limited period, as was pointed out by Lord Justice Beldam in *Hallett Silbermann Ltd v. Cheshire C.C.*,[4] where he doubted whether the orthodox English rule was proper or fair. As his Lordship put the matter:

> "[To] determine the nature of an offence of using a vehicle in breach of regulations, it is not only necessary to consider the words and import of the regulation which makes the user unlawful but also permissible to have regard to the fact that they are more likely to be aimed at visiting primary responsibility on the person who is in a position to exert influence and control in preventing the threat to public safety which it is the purpose of the legislation to deter."[5]

This passage suggests an alternative approach in terms which would equate 'use' of a vehicle in the course of a business with ability to control and influence the way in which that vehicle conforms to safety regulations: but in so far as some offences of 'using' do not involve matters of public safety (using a vehicle on a road without insurance cover, for example[6]), the test is too limited. In any event, the actual case was complicated in that the vehicle in question consisted of a tractor unit owned by the driver and a trailer owned by a haulage company; the combined unit exceeded the permitted train weight; the driver, otherwise

---

[1] See *Garrett v. Hooper* [1973] R.T.R. 1, Lord Widgery C.J., at 3G-H; *Bennett v. Richardson* [1980] R.T.R. 358, Lord Widgery C.J., at 361E-G.

[2] *Crawford v. Haughton* [1972] R.T.R. 125, Lord Widgery C.J., at 129D-F.

[3] [1975] R.T.R. 150.

[4] [1993] R.T.R. 32, at 38F-G.

[5] *ibid.*, at 42B-C.

[6] See s.143 of the Road Traffic Act 1988.

self-employed, was under contract to the company to haul their trailers with his tractor unit for a three year period; the company determined the route, the load, the distribution of that load, and the trailer to be used; and the company regarded itself as the user for the purposes of an indemnity required by the roads authority in relation to such vehicles. Lord Justice Beldam also expressed the view that under some regulations "the words 'person who uses a motor vehicle' are intended to cover a person whose vehicle is being used for his purposes and on his behalf, under his instructions and control",[7] which would certainly have justified the court's view that conviction of the company in the case had been correct. But it might equally have been maintained that the company was the de facto employer of the driver and that the orthodox rule had been applied. This in any event was the view taken of the decision and of Lord Justice Beldam's opinion in *West Yorkshire Trading Standards Service v. Lex Vehicle Leasing Ltd*,[8] where it was denied that the earlier case had introduced any different or more flexible rule.

The English rule may, therefore, be considered as somewhat **8.50** unsatisfactory; it has nevertheless been followed in the sheriff court in Scotland in a case[9] which pre-dates but is similar in its facts to that of *Hallett Silbermann Ltd v. Cheshire C.C.*[10] The view was taken in the sheriff court that the opinion of the Appeal Court in *Swan v. MacNab*,[11] was to be read as supporting the English rule: but this may be doubted. In *Swan v. MacNab*,[11a] a vehicle belonging to a company was being driven on the company's business by one of its employees. The vehicle had defective brakes, and the company was charged as having used the vehicle in contravention of section 40(5) of the Road Traffic Act 1972.[12] The company's conviction for having so used the vehicle was upheld on appeal. Whilst it is true that the driver was the employee of the company and that he was driving on the company's business at the time,[13] the

---

[7] *Hallett Silbermann Ltd v. Cheshire C.C.* [1993] R.T.R. 32, at 43H-L.

[8] [1996] R.T.R. 70, Dyson J., at 79D, and F-G. This case affirmed the correctness of the orthodox rule in the situation where a self-employed individual was contracted to drive a car transporter for the company which owned it. Notwithstanding that when driving for the company he wore the company's uniform and drove the company's vehicle as and when the company directed, the company was acquitted of using the vehicle contrary to construction and use regulations since the driver was not the company's employee. It has to be stated, however, that the driver paid his own tax and national insurance, determined for himself the route to be followed, and decided for himself how to load and unload the vehicle.

[9] *Valentine v. MacBrayne Haulage Ltd*, 1986 S.C.C.R. 692, Sh.Ct. The Crown marked, but subsequently abandoned, an appeal against the sheriff's decision that the company involved had no case to answer since the driver of the combined vehicle was not its employee.

[10] [1993] R.T.R. 32.

[11] 1977 J.C. 57.

[11a] *ibid.*

[12] "Subject to the provisions of this section and sections 41 and 42 of this Act a person . . . (b) who uses on a road a motor vehicle . . . which does not comply with . . . regulations or causes or permits a vehicle to be so used, shall be guilty of an offence." See now the Road Traffic Act ss.40A to 42, as amended/substituted by the Road Traffic Act 1991, s.8.

[13] It is also true that the court quoted from the opinion of Parker J. in *James and Son v. Smee* [1955] 1 Q.B. 78, and in particular approved the following passage: "[I]t seems clear that while the driver of a vehicle on the road uses that vehicle within the meaning of [the statutory provision], so also, if he be a servant, does his master . . . provided always that the servant is driving on his master's business. It cannot be said that only the servant uses and that the master merely causes or permits such use. In common parlance a master is using his vehicle if it is being used by his servant on his business, and there is still room for the application of the words 'causes or permits' since he may request or permit a friend to use the vehicle."

court rested its decision on an apparently wider basis than that which would merely follow the English orthodox rule. Thus, the court said:

> "In our opinion, therefore, the offence created by use of a vehicle in contravention of the regulation founded on is one of absolute liability, and is one which can be committed not only by the actual driver but by the owner of the vehicle on whose business or in whose employment the vehicle is being driven at the time."[14]

This would seem to place less emphasis upon the relationship of master and servant than characterises the English decisions — a conclusion which is reinforced by the court's denial that vicarious liability was involved in the company's criminal liability.[15] At the same time, there appears to have been imposed an additional restriction relative to the relevant particular statutory provision in that the user, other than the driver, must own the vehicle in question. This is given added credence by *Dickson v. Valentine*,[16] where the appellant bought a car from an individual whose son advised that it needed repair. He therefore drove it away with the consent of the appellant. The car was later found parked on a road. No one was driving it at the time; but since the appellant had effected no insurance cover for the vehicle, she was convicted of using it without insurance. At the subsequent appeal, it was argued that the principle which allowed a person other than the driver of a vehicle to be nonetheless a user of that vehicle should be confined to cases of master and servant. The Appeal Court, however, demurred as follows:

> "In our opinion . . . the concept of two people having simultaneous use of a car is not to be confined to situations of master and servant. That principle could equally apply to such cases as principal or agent, parent or child or indeed two friends between whom there was an arrangement that one should use the car on behalf of, or in the interests of, the other."[17]

The court also made plain that it preferred a wide significance to be given to 'use' such that the term meant "have the use of".[18]

8.51 It is difficult, given the absence of recent reported appeals in this area, to be certain of the exact Scottish rule; but such authority as there is strongly suggests that Scots law favours a flexible interpretation of 'use', whether or not 'cause or permit' appears as an alternative in the legislative provision.[19] Given that the English rule is sometimes difficult to apply and is capable of leading to distinctions which are difficult to justify, there seems little reason to follow it. Further, there are situations recognised in English law where a passenger in or on a vehicle can be considered as using that vehicle, where the master-servant relationship is inapplicable as between that passenger and the driver. In *Cobb v. Williams*[20], for example, the owner of a car was considered as using it

---

[14] 1977 J.C. at 63.

[15] *ibid.*, at 61. The liability is instead said to be "primary even if simultaneous".

[16] 1988 S.C.C.R. 325.

[17] *ibid.*, at 328.

[18] *ibid.* This was based on Lord Parker C.J.'s opinion in the earlier case of *Elliott v. Grey* [1960] 1 Q.B. 367.

[19] *Pace* the sheriff court decision of *Valentine v. MacBrayne Haulage Ltd*, 1986 S.C.C.R. 692.

[20] [1973] R.T.R. 113.

when he was being driven home in it from the golf course by a friend: he was taken to be directly using it for his own purposes, and it may be that his ownership of the vehicle was material in that it provided him with management and control. Although it has often been stated that the basis of such liability is the existence of a joint venture between driver and passenger (especially, but not limited to, a joint venture of a criminal nature),[21] this clearly will not do without qualification. Since offences of 'using' are usually of strict liability, a simple 'joint venture' criterion might well involve passengers in buses and taxis acquiring criminal liability if the vehicles in which they were travelling happened to be uninsured or to have, for example, defective brakes.[22] If, as most would agree, it cannot have been intended to cast 'user' liability so widely, then more than a joint interest between driver and passenger that the vehicle should progress from one place to another will be required: and it is submitted that the modern English authorities are correct to conclude that a passenger in a vehicle is not a user of that vehicle for the purposes of criminal liability under a statutory provision unless he is able to exercise a sufficient degree of control or management over the vehicle itself.[23] An owner is clearly able to exercise such control or management, unless unusually the situation is such as to prevent him doing so: but there is no reason why ownership should be the exclusive criterion, and indeed it has not been the exclusive criterion in the English cases.[24] If a firm operates a vehicle on its business, and employs or hires or requests a person to drive that vehicle, that firm as well as the driver should be regarded as a user of it since it can be assumed that the firm controls and manages all aspects of its business, including the operation of its vehicles and their state of conformity with legal requirements. The circumstances would have to be special for such an assumption to be rebutted; but it should on principle always be sufficient to absolve such a firm from relevant criminal liability as a user if, for example, an employee drives one of the firm's vehicles without the authority of the firm on a private ploy of his own.[25]

"KEEP". It was accepted even by the dissenting judges in *Mitchell v. Morrison*[26] that an obligation to "keep records" involved vicarious responsibility for the failure of an employee to keep the records **8.52**

---

[21] *Leathley v. Tatton* [1980] R.T.R. 21, DC (joint enterprise to steal a car); *cf., B. (A Minor) v. Knight* [1981] R.T.R. 136, where learning in the course of a journey in which one was being driven home that the vehicle in question was stolen was insufficient to support the contention that the passenger was a user of the vehicle. *Cf.* also the civil cases of *Stinton v. Stinton* [1995] R.T.R. 167; *Hatton v. Hall* [1997] R.T.R. 212; *O'Mahoney v. Joliffe* [1999] R.T.R. 245.

[22] See opinion of Henry L.J. in *Hatton v. Hall* [1997] R.T.R. 212, DC, at 217G-218A.

[23] *Hatton v. Hall* [1997] R.T.R. 212, Henry L.J. at 218–219; *O'Mahoney v. Joliffe* [1999] R.T.R. 245, Simon Brown L.J. at 250E-251A. Although these are both civil cases, it was stressed by Simon Brown L.J. that there was no difference in approach between the criminal law interpretation of 'use' and the meaning to be given to the same word in the civil matter under discussion in these two appeals.

[24] See the cases referred to in n.23, *supra*, where joint ventures between driver and passenger were of such a nature as to give rise to the inference that the passenger had an element of control and management over the vehicle in question. Whether the actual control and management was sufficient to make the passenger a 'user' was considered to be a question of fact in *O'Mahoney v. Joliffe*.

[25] See *Phelon and Moore Ltd v. Keel* [1914] 3 K.B. 165, and the cases discussed *infra*, para. 8.60. See also Gl. Williams, para. 96. Contra *Strutt v. Clift* [1911] 1 K.B. 1.

[26] 1938 J.C. 64.

properly.[27] Where it is an offence to keep open a business except under certain conditions, it is the owner of the business and not the person who actually opens the shop who is liable for keeping open in breach of the conditions.[28] Similar conditions apply to "carrying on" a business.[29]

8.53 *Possession.* A may be guilty of possessing an article which, unknown to him, is in the possession of his employee acting in the course of A's business.[30]

8.54 *Other words.* A similar extensive interpretation may be given to other words describing activities similar to those listed above. It has been held in England that it is the transport operator and not his drivers or conductors who are responsible for offences in connection with the "carrying" of passengers,[31] and that the licensee of a theatre "presents" a play where the presentation is unlawful because of alterations made without his knowledge.[32] Some words, however, so clearly denote personal activity that they are not capable of this type of interpretation. It is extremely unlikely, for example, that it will be held that A can vicariously "drive" a car in fact driven by his employee.[33]

Vicarious mens rea

8.55 Most examples of vicarious responsibility are concerned with offences of strict responsibility; they involve imputing B's mental state to A only in so far as B's mental state is relevant to show that his conduct was sufficiently voluntary to constitute an *actus reus*. But vicarious responsibility has been extended, at least in England, to include offences requiring *mens rea*. These cases raise difficult problems of construction and interpretation, apart altogether from the moral and semantic difficulties involved in convicting A of "knowingly" or "fraudulently" doing something when he did not have the requisite knowledge or fraudulent intent. Cases involving vicarious responsibility of this kind must be distinguished from cases of permission,[34] and also from cases where a corporation is charged as a primary offender which raise the separate question of the circumstances in which the mental state of an employee is to be imputed to the company.[35]

8.56 Most of the cases of this kind arise under the English Licensing Acts and are based on a doctrine of "delegation" which has no application to Scotland.[36] There are, however, two English cases which do not fall into this group, one of which, indeed, has long been regarded as the leading

---

[27] See esp. Lord Moncrieff at 73.

[28] *Benassi v. McLennan* (1906) 5 Adam 220. *Linstead v. Simpson*, 1927 J.C. 101 depends on the view that the making of an isolated sale does not constitute the carrying on of a business.

[29] *cf. Linstead v. Simpson, supra.*

[30] *O'Brien v. Macgregor* (1903) 4 Adam 202. *Cf. Dickson v. Linton* (1888) 2 White 51; *Neilson v. Parkhill* (1892) 3 White 379.

[31] *Spires v. Smith* [1956] 1 W.L.R. 601. *Cf. Graham v. Strathern*, 1927 J.C. 29.

[32] *Grade v. D.P.P.* [1942] 2 All E.R. 118. See also *Lovelace v. D.P.P.* [1954] 1 W.L.R. 1468.

[33] Gl. Williams, p.281.

[34] *e.g. Greig v. Macleod* (1907) 5 Adam 445.

[35] See Gl. Williams, pp.274, 856; *infra*, paras 8.89 to 8.99.

[36] *Noble v. Heatly*, 1967 J.C. 5, *supra*, para. 8.23.

case on vicarious responsibility, *Mousell Bros Ltd v. L. and N.W. Ry.*[37] This was a prosecution under sections 98 and 99 of the Railway Clauses Act 1845, which impose a duty on "Every person being the owner or having the care of" goods sent by rail, to render an exact account of the goods, and provide a penalty "if any such owner or other such person" gives a false account with intent to avoid payment of the due tolls. The accused company were convicted, as owners, of an offence under this section in respect of false information given by their manager with intent to avoid payment, on the ground that the wording of the section showed that a penalty was imposed on the owner of the goods for an act of his employee where the employee acted with the requisite intent.[38] Glanville Williams suggests that this case represents an early stage in the development of corporate criminal responsibility, and that a similar case would be decided today on the principle that the intention of a superior servant is imputable to the company.[39] However this may be, the case was decided on general principles of vicarious responsibility, and the only part played by the fact that the accused was a company was that the court rejected an argument that a company could not be guilty of an offence involving intent to defraud, by holding that the intent involved was that of the employee. Viscount Reading C.J. said in terms that a company was the same as any other principal.[40] Moreover, the manager was not regarded as a "superior servant", and the problem was posed by Viscount Reading as being whether the directors of the company could be liable for their servant manager.[41] *Mousell*[41a] has not been followed in a similar situation in Scotland, but it is generally regarded both in Scotland and England as a leading case on vicarious responsibility, and the criteria set out by Atkin J. for deciding whether vicarious responsibility applies and in terms of which *Mousell* was itself decided are accepted in Scotland.[42]

The most recent case on the question is *G. Newton Ltd v. Smith.*[43] It **8.57** was a prosecution under section 134 of the Road Traffic Act 1960, which made it an offence for the holder of a public service vehicle licence "wilfully or negligently" to fail to comply with the conditions of the licence. A driver employed by the accused knowingly departed from the route he was permitted to take under the licence, and the accused were convicted of wilful failure to comply with the licence.[44] This was on the ground that the duty was laid on them, that any contravention would normally be committed by an employee, and that no penalty was

---

[37] [1917] 2 K.B. 836.

[38] Atkin J. at 845.

[39] Gl. Williams, p.274. See *infra*, para. 8.92.

[40] At 845.

[41] At 842.

[41a] [1917] 2 K.B. 836.

[42] See *e.g. Mitchell v. Morrison*, 1938 J.C. 64, esp. Lord Mackay at 81, a dissenting judgment. In *Vane v. Yiannopoullos*, [1965] A.C. 468, Lord Evershed "discarded" *Mousell* from consideration since it did not involve the word "knowingly," and on the view that "in the judgments (as I read them) the emphasis as regards liability was not in any real sense or substance founded on the words 'with intent' in section 99": [1965] A.C. at 502.

[43] [1962] 2 Q.B. 278. This case was not referred to in the House of Lords in *Vane v. Yiannopoullos, supra*, presumably because it did not concern the interpretation of "knowingly".

[44] It was agreed that a conviction of negligent failure would be bad.

provided for the employee. Both *Mousell*[44a] and the licensee cases were referred to by the court, but the decision proceeded on the authority of *Mousell*[44b] rather than on the fact that what was involved was a breach of a condition of a licence.[45] In this case too the actual offender was clearly not a superior servant of the company. As this case deals with a section of the Road Traffic Acts it is likely to be followed in Scotland despite the apparent absurdity of convicting A of doing wilfully something of which he was unaware.

8.58 *The Scots cases.* Vicarious *mens rea* has not been authoritatively discussed in Scotland and the only cases in which it has arisen at all have been licensing cases involving permission. In *Greig v. Macleod*[46] a licensee was charged with knowingly allowing his assistant to sell drink to a child,[47] the facts being that the drink had been sold when the licensee was in another part of the premises and without his knowledge. The licensee was convicted, but the case was decided on the meaning of "permission" and on the ground that a failure to give instructions not to sell to children constituted permission.[48]

The cases of *Patrick v. Kirkhope*[49] and *Campbell v. Cameron*[50] both concern comparable situations, but neither deals with the question of vicarious *mens rea. Patrick v. Kirkhope*[50a] concerned a charge of keeping open after licensing hours and knowingly permitting disorderly conduct, but it was decided on the ground that the barman who was the actual offender had been acting outwith the scope of his employment. *Campbell v. Cameron*[50b] was a charge against a licensee of knowingly permitting his manager to be drunk on the premises, and it was held that this particular offence required personal knowledge. The observation that in the case of a drunken customer the persons to whom a licensee delegates authority are in exactly the same position as himself is *obiter*, and was in any event concerned with a specific statutory provision that in order to escape liability in such cases the licensee must "prove that he and the persons employed by him took all reasonable steps" to avoid the contravention.[51]

There are also two cases dealing with road service licences, but in one of them — *Macmillan v. Western S.M.T. Co. Ltd*[52] — the offence was treated as one of strict responsibility, and the decision depended on and confused the concepts of causing and permitting, and the other — *Clydebank Co-operative Society Ltd v. Binnie*[53] — was also a permission

---

[44a] [1917] 2 K.B. 836.

[44b] *ibid.*

[45] The fact that the defenders might lose their licence was used as an argument *against* conviction, but rejected, the court observing that the Traffic Commissioners were not bound to withdraw the licence, and giving the impression that they did not consider it an appropriate case for withdrawal: see Lord Parker C.J. at 285–286.

[46] (1907) 5 Adam 445. But see now *Noble v. Healy, supra*, para. 8.23.

[47] See now Licensing (Scotland) Act 1976, s.68. There is now vicarious responsibility subject to a defence of due diligence or absence of reason to suspect the customer's age: *ibid.*, ss.67 (2), 71, Sched. 5.

[48] And see now *Noble v. Heatly*, 1967 J.C. 5, *supra.*

[49] (1894) 1 Adam 360.

[50] (1915) 7 Adam 697.

[50a] (1894) 1 Adam 360.

[51b] (1951) 7 Adam 697.

[51] Licensing (Scotland) Act 1903, s.98. *Cf. Soutar v. Auchinachie* (1908) 5 Adam 647.

[52] 1933 J.C. 51.

[53] 1937 J.C. 17.

case, and may have been decided on the separate principle that the knowledge of its superior servants is imputable to a company, and/or on the ground that the accused were wilfully blind.[54] It appears, therefore, that there is no Scots authority for the imposition of vicarious *mens rea* in the absence of specific statutory provision.[55]

Express statutory provision. Parliament can, of course, provide specifically for vicarious *mens rea*. Section 8(2)(b) of the Poisons Act 1972 provides that any material fact known to the accused's employee shall be deemed to have been known to the accused; and in the offence of knowingly permitting drunkenness on his premises it used to be for the licence-holder "to prove that he and the persons employed by him took all reasonable steps to prevent drunkenness in the premises."[56] **8.59**

Possession. It appears to be accepted that A may be convicted of possessing an article if it is in the possession of his employee, and therefore in so far as possession implies knowledge, the knowledge of the employee is imputed to A in such cases.[57] But it has also been held that possession requires a certain degree of control over the article, and it may be that neither employee nor employer has sufficient control. In *Bellerby v. Carle*,[58] the House of Lords confirmed that joint licensees were not in possession of beer dispensing equipment which was in fact operated by employees of the same company for which those licensees worked, since, despite the licensees being the only persons under the licensing Acts lawfully authorised to deliver intoxicating substances to customers, the equipment in question was supplied and maintained by a third party. The licensees thus did not have a sufficient degree of control to have in their possession for use for trade "measuring equipment which was false or unjust"[59] in that short measure was in fact being supplied to customers. Since the case contains some rather special circumstances, it is not certain how it affects the general view of vicarious possession. **8.60**

It is also not clear whether A could be convicted of "knowingly" possessing an article where the only person who had the necessary knowledge was his employee.[60]

The scope of vicarious responsibility

Before A can be held vicariously responsible for B's actings it must be shown that B stands in such a relationship to A that it is proper to make A responsible for him. The appropriate relationship is sometimes **8.61**

[54] *cf.* Gl. Williams, p.163. See *infra*, para. 8.83.

[55] See *Noble v. Heatly, supra.*

[56] Licensing (Scotland) Act 1959, s.187. See now Licensing (Scotland) Act 1976, ss.78 and 67(2).

[57] *cf. Dickson v. Linton* (1888) 2 White 51; *O'Brien v. Macgregor* (1903) 4 Adam 202.

[58] [1983] 2 A.C. 101.

[59] Weights and Measures Act 1963, s.16(1). (See now the Weights and Measures Act 1985, s.17.) There were in fact two offences under the subsection — using such measuring equipment and having it in one's possession for use; subsection (2) allowed a defence, but only to those who used the equipment in the course of their employment by another person and who did not know, could not have been expected to know, and had no reason to suspect that the equipment was false or unjust. The defence was thus inapplicable to possession for use, and it appears to have been concluded that that offence must be of strict liability — a conclusion which may well have had a considerable bearing on the House of Lord's decision. .

[60] See *O'Brien v. Macgregor, supra,* L.J.-C. Macdonald at 207.

described in terms of "delegation" and sometimes in terms of "scope of employment". It usually makes little difference which term is used since a person who is acting within the scope of his employment is acting as a delegate. But there may be cases of delegation outwith the relationship of employer and employee, and the concept of delegation is more fundamental than that of scope of employment. As a rule the term "delegation" is used mainly in connection with cases involving vicarious *mens rea*, and "scope of employment" in cases involving sale.

8.62 *Scope of employment.* In order to show that *e.g.* a sale actually carried out by B is truly a sale by A, it is necessary to show that B acted on behalf of A. Normally this means showing that B carried out the sale while employed by A and acting in the course of his employment. But there are cases in which A is not responsible although B acted in the course of his employment as that concept is understood in civil law. An employer is civilly liable for delicts committed by his employee in the course of his employment even if these delicts are carried out as part of a private criminal scheme — if a solicitor's clerk embezzles for his own gain moneys received by him in his capacity as clerk the solicitor is civilly liable to the client for his loss.[61] It appears, however, that the employer is not criminally responsible for any offences committed by an employee acting in pursuance of a private ploy. In *Patrick v. Kirkhope*[62] it was held that a licensee was not responsible for acts done by his barman when the latter entertained friends after hours: in *Herriot v Auld*[63] the accused's employee secreted liquor in the premises and took it out after hours to give to his friends, and the licensee was held not to be responsible.[64] Again, in *City and Suburban Dairies v. Mackenna,*[65] where a person who was employed to make sales sold goods in excess of the permitted price, accounted to his employer for the permitted price and pocketed the difference himself, the employer was acquitted. The decision in *Courage v. Smith*[66] that in a charge against a licensee in respect of a sale by a waiter on licensed premises it is not necessary to exclude the possibility of a private deal may depend on the wide wording of the section under consideration, but even so appears to conflict with the earlier cases which were not before the court.

Even where the sale is made on behalf of the employer and for his benefit the latter is not responsible if the employee is acting outwith the scope of his employment. In *Greenhill v. Stirling*[67] a waitress served two of her own friends with drink on a Sunday and accounted for the price to the licensee, but the latter was acquitted on the ground that the waitress had acted for her own convenience and outwith the scope of her employment, and on the ground that she had acted contrary to the licensee's instructions.[68] In *Lindsay v. Dempster*[69] a vanman employed

---

[61] *Lloyd v. Grace, Smith and Co.* [1912] A.C. 716.

[62] (1894) 1 Adam 360.

[63] 1918 J.C. 16.

[64] Although Lord Johnston delivered a strong dissenting judgment in which he expressed the opinion that the licensee was responsible for the deceit and disobedience of his servant.

[65] 1918 J.C. 105.

[66] 1960 J.C. 13.

[67] (1885) 5 Couper 602.

[68] *cf.* also *Galloway v. Weber* (1889) 2 White 171. And see *Duff v. Tennant*, 1952 J.C. 15.

[69] (1912) 6 Adam 707.

only to deliver goods already ordered by the customer from his employer himself sold adulterated milk to an inspector. The employer was acquitted on a charge of selling the milk by the hands of the vanman on the ground that the latter had acted outwith the scope of his employment in making a sale, although there was no suggestion that he did not intend to account for the money. Again in *Auld v. Devlin*[70] a licensee was acquitted of an offence in respect of a sale made by a message boy engaged by the licensee's shopman and not authorised to make sales, although the price was paid into the licensee's business.[71]

BREACH OF INSTRUCTIONS. Where B is employed by A and acts on A's behalf within the scope of that employment, it will be very difficult for A to escape responsibility for any offence of vicarious responsibility committed by B. The fact that the sale was made to a friend of the barman in breach of instructions and in circumstances where the sale would not have been made but for the friendship is not enough to take it out of the scope of the barman's employment.[72] There are indications throughout the cases that it may be a defence for an employer to show that his employee acted in breach of express instructions, but they are *obiter*[73]; some were made in cases where the employee was also held to be acting outwith the scope of his employment,[74] and others arose in cases in which it was held that it had not been proved that the instructions given were sufficiently specific.[75] The general principle is that it is no defence to show that the employee acted in disobedience of his instructions, the question being always not whether the employee acted as he was instructed or as he ought to have done, but whether he acted within the scope of his employment.[76] In order to succeed in a defence of this nature the employer must prove that he gave "express and particular" instructions; it is not enough to show merely that the employee was prohibited from making illegal sales, or sales outwith licensing hours, or that it was a term of his contract that he should observe the conditions of his employer's licence.[77] The cases do not indicate what kind of instructions would be sufficiently express and particular, but it is submitted that they must be such that the employee's disobedience puts his actings outwith the scope of his employment[78]: in other words, that the defence of express instructions is only another form of the defence that the employee acted outwith the scope of his employment.[79] **8.63**

---

[70] 1918 J.C. 41.

[71] *cf.* the English cases of *Phelon and Moore Ltd v. Keel* [1914] 3 K.B. 165; *Whittaker v. Forshaw* [1919] 2 K.B. 419; *Wilson v. Murphy* [1937] 1 All E.R. 315; *Barker v. Levinson* [1951] 1 K.B. 342; *Jack Motors Ltd v. Fazackerley* [1962] Crim. L.R. 486. But contrary opinions were expressed in *Moore v. I. Bresler Ltd* [1944] 2 All E.R. 515.

[72] *Simpson v. Gifford*, 1954 S.L.T. 39.

[73] *cf. Middleton v. Tough* (1908) 5 Adam 485, 494.

[74] *Greenhill v. Stirling; Lindsay v. Dempster, supra.*

[75] *Ferguson v. Campbell*, 1946 J.C. 28; *Duff v. Tennant*, 1952 J.C. 15; *Byrne v. Tudhope*, 1983 S.C.C.R. 737: *cf., Ahmed v. MacDonald*, 1994 S.C.C.R. 320.

[76] *Galloway v. Weber* (1889) 2 White 171; *Linton v. Stirling* (1893) 1 Adam 61; *Patrick v. Kirkhope* (1894) 1 Adam 360; *Simpson v. Gifford, supra.* The defence of disobedience to instructions has also been rejected in England — *e.g. Commissioners of Police v. Cartman* [1896] 1 Q.B. 655; *Collman v. Mills* [1897] 1 Q.B. 396.

[77] *Duff v. Tennant; Ferguson v. Campbell, supra.*

[78] *cf. Galloway v. Weber, supra,* L.J.-C. Macdonald at 174–175.

[79] The presence or absence of instructions may, however, be relevant in cases involving permission, *infra*, para. 8.81.

8.64 Section 8 of the Poisons Act 1972 specifically provides that it is not a defence to a charge under certain sections of that Act to show that an employee acted without his employer's authority, and that any material fact known to the employee shall be deemed to have been known to the employer, but it is submitted that it is still a defence to show that the sale was not made on the employer's behalf and so was not a sale by the accused employer at all.

8.65 *Responsibility for a fellow employee.* Vicarious responsibility usually arises because the offence involved is committed in the course of the accused's business, and therefore in the normal case it can never be said that one employee is vicariously responsible for the actings of another, even if one is a "superior servant".[80] The manager of a branch store is not responsible for an illegal sale made by an assistant in the store, for the sale is a sale not by or on behalf of the manager, but by the assistant on behalf of the owner of the chain of stores.[81] In *Shields v. Little*[82] the accused was the manager of a public-house who was charged with selling drinks without a licence. It was held that he was in fact covered by the previous manager's licence, but the court indicated that if there had been no licence the guilty party would have been the public-house owners and not the manager.

It was in *Shields v. Little*[82a] that Lord Cooper said that there was no authority that vicarious responsibility attached to a superior servant for a contravention by another servant of the same employer,[83] but where a special capacity is involved a servant who possesses that capacity may be responsible for the acts of another servant, not because of the relationship of "superior" and "inferior" servant, but because of the principle of delegation. The accused in *Ferguson v. Campbell*[84] was the secretary of a limited company which owned a public-house of which he was licence-holder; he was convicted of supplying liquor by the hands of the manager of the public-house, and the question of responsibility for a fellow-employee was not raised.[85] This has been accepted in England. In *Linnett v. Commissioner of Metropolitan Police*[86] the secretary and manager of a company were joint licensees of a public-house owned by the company, the manager being the person in actual control of the house, and the secretary was convicted of permitting disorderly conduct in the public-house on the ground that he had delegated his duties to the manager, although they were fellow-employees of the company. Also in *Bellerby v. Carle*,[87] Lord Brandon of Oakbrook, in delivering an opinion concurred in by the other judges of the House of Lords, said this: "where a licensee of licensed premises, who is alone permitted under the

[80] *Shields v. Little*, 1954 J.C. 25. *Cf. McIntyre v. Gallagher*, 1962 J.C. 20.

[81] In *Lord Advocate v. D. and J. Nicol*, 1915 S.C. 735, a civil action to recover a revenue penalty, the defenders were the owners of a ship the liquor licence for which was held by their steward. Waiters on the ship sold drink on Sundays in breach of the licence, but in the absence of the steward. It was held that the offence was not that the steward had sold the liquor in breach of his licence, but that the owners had sold it without being the holders of a licence.

[82] 1954 J.C. 25.

[82a] *ibid.*

[83] At 30.

[84] 1946 J.C. 28.

[85] See also *Bennett v. Hanks* [1954] Crim. L.R. 545.

[86] [1946] K.B. 290.

[87] [1983] 2 A.C. 101.

Licensing Acts to handle and hand over intoxicating liquor to a customer . . . , chooses to perform those acts through the agency of another person, such as a barmaid employed by the same company or other organisation as he is employed by, he is under the same criminal liability for such other person's acts as he would be if he had performed them himself."[88] It is submitted that these cases and views are correct and that where A is a licence-holder and is charged with an offence which can be committed only by a licence-holder he is responsible for the persons to whom he has delegated his duties as licence-holder, whatever his relationship with them. In such cases he is being charged not as the employer of the actual offender, but as the licence-holder. He is the only person who can be charged as a principal offender, since neither his employer nor the actual offender is a licence-holder, and it cannot be the law that a licence-holder is relieved from his obligations as such merely because he is himself the employee of the person on whose behalf the business is carried on.[89]

Responsibility for the fault of a stranger. Although A cannot be vicariously responsible for someone who is a stranger to him, and is neither his employee nor a person to whom he has delegated his powers or duties, there may be cases of strict responsibility in which the accused's failure to carry out his duty is due to the fault of a stranger, and in which it may be loosely and inaccurately said that A is being held responsible for the fault of the stranger. In *Parker v. Alder,*[90] where A was under a duty to deliver pure milk, milk sent by him in a pure condition to the railway station was adulterated by a stranger before it reached A's customer, and A was convicted of delivering impure milk. Lord Russell C.J. said that A was responsible for a dishonest stranger as much as for a dishonest employee.[91] **8.66**

On the other hand, it has been held in England that A is not responsible for strangers even in a charge involving strict responsibility, the charge of using a vehicle as an express carriage without a licence. In *Reynolds v. G.H. Austin and Sons Ltd*[92] the use was unlawful because the persons to whom the accused had hired the vehicle had advertised the trip for which they had hired it, thus making the vehicle an express carriage for that trip. The accused owners of the vehicle who were unaware of the advertisement were charged with using the vehicle as an express carriage. The court held that where a statute prohibited using, **8.67**

---

[88] *ibid.*, at 108A-B. His Lordship there approved what was stated in the earlier cases of *Goodfellow v. Johnson*, [1966] 1 Q.B. 83, and *Sopp v. Long* [1970] 1 Q.B. 518. It should be noted, however, that *Bellerby v. Carle* was not itself concerned with offences under the Licensing Acts but with the offence of possessing for use for trade any weighing or measuring equipment which is false or unjust, contrary to s.16(1) of the Weights and Measures Act 1963; and it was specifically held that just because a licensee is the only person who can lawfully use liquid measures for the sale of liquor does not in itself mean that he is in possession of them for the purposes of that offence (which is now contained in s.17 of the Weights and Measures Act 1985), for possession requires a certain degree of control over the measuring equipment (see opinion of Lord Brandon at 108D). The House of Lords seem to have been influenced by the fact that the section creates offences of using and possessing unjust measures, but provides a defence of lack of knowledge only in relation to use, making possession an offence of strict responsibility.

[89] See *Macdonald v. Smith*, 1979 J.C. 55. This may not apply in cases requiring *mens rea*.

[90] [1899] 1 Q.B. 20.

[91] At 25. See also *Quality Dairies (York) Ltd v. Pedley* [1952] 1 K.B. 275.

[92] [1951] 2 K.B. 135.

and also causing or permitting use, the same *mens rea* must be required for all three offences, and that as permission required *mens rea* so also must use. It followed therefore that where, as here, the circumstance which rendered the vehicle an express carriage was unknown to the accused, they could not be convicted of its unlawful use as such a carriage. The whole basis of *Reynolds*[92a] was undermined by *James and Son Ltd v. Smee*[93] which held that while permitting always requires *mens rea*, use does not: the court in *James*,[93a] however, did not overrule *Reynolds*[93b] but held that its essential feature was that the contravention arose from the actings of persons over whom the accused had no control. Glanville Williams suggests that the combined result of the two cases is that use involves *mens rea* when the statute also prohibits causing and permitting, provided that the contravention is not committed by one of the accused's servants.[94] The "use" must, of course, be a use by A before any question of responsibility arises — if A's employee uses the vehicle for his own purposes A is clearly not responsible, because A is not using the vehicle.[95] The situation involved in the express carriage cases is one where the use of the vehicle is a use by or on behalf of A, but the use is rendered unlawful because of the actings of a third party. *Reynolds*[95a] suggests that the fact that a contravention is likely to be due to someone over whom the accused has no control is good ground for excluding strict responsibility in construing any statutory provision. If, nevertheless, the courts do hold that there is strict responsibility, then responsibility would remain strict whether the contravention is due to the fault of A, or of his employees, or of strangers, or, as is sometimes the case in offences of strict responsibility, is not due to anyone's fault at all. *Alphacell Ltd v. Woodward*,[96] on the other hand, suggests that if strict responsibility is imposed because in the normal case any contravention will be due to persons under the accused's control, it will be a defence to show in any particular case that this was not so.

Statutory defences

8.68 The justification of vicarious responsibility has been said to be that it encourages employers to "keep themselves and their organisations up to the mark".[97] The rationale of creating offences involving vicarious responsibility in the field of consumer protection and public health and safety, said Lord Diplock in *Tesco Ltd v. Nattrass*[98] is that:

> "It is the deterrent effect of penal provisions which protects the consumer from the loss he would sustain if the offence were committed. If it is committed he does not receive the amount of any fine. As a taxpayer he will bear part of the expense of maintaining a convicted offender in prison.
>
> The loss to the consumer is the same whether the acts or omissions which result in his being given inaccurate or inadequate

---

[92a] *ibid.*
[93] [1955] 1 Q.B. 78.
[93a] *ibid.*
[93b] [1955] 1 Q.B. 78.
[94] Gl. Williams, p.283.
[95] *supra*, para. 8.51.
[95a] [1951] 2 K.B. 135.
[96] [1972] A.C. 824.
[97] *Reynolds v. G.H. Austin and Sons Ltd* [1951] 2 K.B. 135, Devlin J. at 149. See also *Lim Chin Aik v. The Queen* [1963] A.C. 160, 174, *supra* para. 8.34.
[98] [1972] A.C. 153, 194 B-D.

information are intended to mislead him, or are due to carelessness or inadvertence. So is the corresponding gain to the other party to the business transaction with the consumer in the course of which those acts or omissions occur. Where, in the way that business is now conducted, they are likely to be acts or omissions of employees of that party and subject to his orders, the most effective method of deterrence is to place upon the employer the responsibility of doing everything which lies within his power to prevent his employees from doing anything which will result in the commission of an offence."

Lord Diplock went on:

> "This, I apprehend, is the rational and moral justification for creating in the field of consumer protection, as also in the field of public health and safety, offences of 'strict liability' for which an employer or principal, in the course of whose business the offences were committed, is criminally liable, notwithstanding that they are due to acts or omissions of his servants or agents which were done without his knowledge or consent or even were contrary to his orders. But this rational and moral justification does not extend to penalising an employer or principal who has done everything that he can reasonably be expected to do by supervision or inspection, by improvement of his business methods or by exhorting those whom he may be expected to control or influence to prevent the commission of the offences (see *Lim Chin Aik v. The Queen* [1963] A.C. 160, 174; *Sweet v. Parsley* [1970] A.C. 132, 163)."[99]

In order to meet these points there are a number of kinds of defence which Parliament frequently provides in offences of vicarious responsibility and, as in the case of strict responsibility, the precise form of the defence varies from statute to statute, and even from section to section of the same statute. One frequently used defence is that found in the Trades Descriptions Act 1968[1] and is as follows:

> "In any proceedings for an offence under this Act it shall . . . be a defence for the person charged to prove:
> (a) that the commission of the offence was due to a mistake or to reliance on information supplied to him or to the act or default of another person, an accident or some other cause beyond his control; and
> (b) that he took all reasonable precautions and exercised all due diligence to avoid the commission of such an offence by himself or any person under his control."

A number of statutes require the accused to prove both his own diligence and that the contravention was due to the fault of a third party,[2] but due diligence is itself sufficient in some statutes,[3] and absence

---

[99] [1972] A.C. 153, 194 E-F.
[1] s.24.
[2] *e.g.* Food Safety Act 1990, s.21; Road Traffic Act 1988, Sched. 1, para. 4(2).
[3] *e.g.* Mines and Quarries Act 1954, s.156; Weights and Measures Act 1985, s.34.

of knowledge or consent in others,[4] while still others require both diligence and a lack of knowledge or connivance.[5]

8.69 It was at one time thought in England that a statutory defence of due diligence had to be made out not only in relation to the accused employer, but also to any employee to whom he had delegated the supervision of the regulated activity. It is now clear that this is not the case.[6] The only question at issue is whether in the whole circumstances, which may include the delegation of certain duties to an employee, the employer has exercised due diligence. As Lord Diplock put it in *Tesco Ltd v. Nattrass*[7]:

> "To exercise due diligence to prevent something being done is to take all reasonable steps to prevent it. It may be a reasonable step for an employer to instruct a superior servant to supervise the activities of inferior servants whose physical acts may in the absence of supervision result in that being done which it is sought to prevent. This is not to delegate the employer's duty to exercise all due diligence; it is to perform it. To treat the duty of an employer to exercise due diligence as unperformed unless due diligence was also exercised by all his servants to whom he had reasonably given all proper instructions and upon whom he could reasonably rely to carry them out, would be to render the defence of due diligence nugatory and so thwart the clear intention of Parliament in providing it."

8.70 There is some plausibility in the view that where the statute is expressed impersonally the defence must be shown to apply to both the actual offender and the person vicariously responsible, as for example where it provides that a penalty is exigible unless the accused shows that the contravention was committed "without intent to defraud" and not merely that *he* acted without such intent. The statutes alleged to have been contravened in *Galbraith's Stores Ltd v. McIntyre*[8] and *Brander v. Buttercup Dairy Co.*[9] had provisions of this kind, but their application to the servant was not considered by the court in either case.

Where, however, the defence includes a requirement of some specific action, it may be that failure by the employee to carry out this requirement will prevent the employer succeeding in the defence. In *Hemphill v. Smith*[10] the employer was charged with using a steam wagon so that it emitted smoke. The section of the Glasgow Police Act 1892 which created the offence also made it a defence to prove that the

---

[4] *e.g.* the now repealed Licensing (Scotland) Act 1959, s.139. The presence or absence of knowledge is a question of fact: *Nicol v. Smith*, 1955 J.C. 7. This is the only case dealing with the meaning of "consent", and held that where the accused licensee employed a competent manager and supplied him with the proper instructions she could not be said to have impliedly consented to an unlawful act of his merely because she trusted him and left the carrying on of the business to him.

[5] *e.g.* Licensing (Scotland) Act 1976, s.67(2); *Gorman v. Cochrane*, High Court on Appeal Nov. 1977, unrep'd.

[6] *Tesco Ltd v. Nattrass* [1972] A.C. 153 overruling *R.C. Hammett Ltd v. L.C.C.* (1933) 49 T.L.R. 209, and *Series v. Poole* [1969] 1 Q.B. 676.

[7] *supra* at 203 D-E.

[8] (1912) 6 Adam 641.

[9] 1921 J.C. 19.

[10] 1923 J.C. 23.

accused had used the best means to prevent smoke and had carefully attended to and managed the wagon so as to prevent smoke being emitted. The court found that the best means had been used by the accused's employers but that it had not been proved that their firemen had attended to the wagon's furnace properly, and they were convicted.

Attempts and art and part guilt

It seems that A cannot be vicariously guilty of an attempted crime.[11] **8.71**
In a sense all vicarious responsibility is a form of art and part guilt without *mens rea*, but normally only a particular person, such as a licensee, can be vicariously responsible in any case, and no one else can be art and part in his vicarious guilt unless he has *mens rea*. A person without *mens rea* cannot be vicariously guilty of a statutory offence of aiding and abetting where the principal offender is his employee.[12] Indeed, "art and part vicarious guilt" is almost inconceivable except in the case of joint licensees where both are more properly regarded as guilty as principals.[13] The difficult question of the possibility of art and part guilt in offences like licensing offences where there is *mens rea* has already been discussed.[14]

Causing and Permitting

Many modern statutes make it an offence to cause or permit **8.72**
something to be done or to occur in breach of the statutory requirements, such as the driving of a vehicle which is not properly insured, or the occurrence of disorderly conduct in a public-house. Where A is convicted of causing or permitting something to happen he is, in a sense, convicted of an offence for which he is primarily responsible, but in effect he is being convicted of something for which he is only vicariously responsible, for neither "cause" nor "permit" requires that A should be art and part in the offence in the common law meaning of "art and part".[15]

Causing

The term "cause" may be used in a statutory offence in a number of **8.73**
different ways.

---

[11] *Gardner v. Akeroyd* [1952] 2 Q.B. 743; *cf. supra*, para. 8.38.

[12] *John Henshall (Quarries) Ltd v. Harvey* [1965] 2 Q.B. 233.

[13] *cf. Linnett v. Commissioner of Metropolitan Police* [1946] K.B. 290.

[14] *supra*, paras 5.10 and 5.11.

[15] *cf. Vehicle Inspectorate v. Nuttall* [1999] R.T.R. 264, Lord Hobhouse at 277D, who, when discussing s.96(11A) of the Transport Act 1968, said: "The criminal liability of the employer under this section is dependant on his employee having contravened the relevant requirement as alleged. If the employee did not infringe the Regulations, then there can be no question of the employer being liable under this section of causing or permitting the alleged infringement. But the offence of causing or permitting is a separate offence only capable of being committed by the employer in distinction from the driver. It is not a vicarious or secondary liability. It is not an 'accessory' liability as that term is properly understood. It depends upon the conduct of the employer and his state of mind." It has been held, however, that an actual user, *e.g.* a driver, may be guilty of causing the use: *Baker v. Chapman* [1964] Crim. L.R. 316, but it is submitted that this is wrong in principle; it is also inconsistent with the decision that a driver cannot permit his own use of the vehicle: *James and Son Ltd v. Smee* [1955] 1 Q.B. 78.

Where A is charged with causing something to occur, the use of the word "cause" has no particular significance. There is no difference between making it an offence to pollute a river and making it an offence to cause polluting matter to enter a river, except from the point of view of literary style. The word "cause" here connotes only the causal nexus which must always be shown between the accused's activities and the *actus reus*. Whether or not *mens rea* is required in an offence of this kind is determined by the general considerations which apply to any other statutory offence. In particular, if Parliament makes it an offence to "cause or knowingly permit" something to happen, the omission of "knowingly" before "cause" will assist the courts to hold that the offence of causing is strict.[16]

Similarly, where the accused is responsible for a certain activity, at any rate if it is a licensed activity, there may be strict responsibility for causing certain things to occur. There is no difference between charging a licensee with selling something and charging him with "causing it to be delivered", or between charging him with failing to keep records or with failing to cause records to be kept.[17] In such cases the obligation is personal to the licensee and is strict.[18]

Where an offence of causing something to occur is strict, it is no defence that the forbidden result occurred because of a failure by someone else to take precautions, or that the accused was no longer in a position to prevent the result. In *Lockhart v. N.C.B.*,[19] the Coal Board were convicted of causing polluting matter to enter a river from disused workings which had some time before passed out of their control into that of someone else who had not kept up the precautions taken by the Board when they had been in occupation. It was held that as the Board had set up a system under which pollution was bound to occur in the absence of preventive measures they had caused the pollution. The only defences which might be open were acts of a third party or act of God; the mere fact that the accused could no longer legally enter the mine to take the necessary precautions was irrelevant. The High Court in this case accepted *Alphacell Ltd v. Woodward*[20] as representing Scots law.

Where the offence of causing something to occur involves conduct on the part of some person other than the accused, the Privy Council have held that the accused does not cause the occurence unless he has some express or implied control over that other person's actions; that the accused contributed to that other person's decision to act would be insufficient without some actual authority over him. Thus, where the accused were convicted of attempting to cause video-recorders to be taken out of Hong Kong, in that they had shipped the recorders to a point within Hong Kong territorial waters where a rendezvous with a China-bound fishing boat was expected but never materialised, it was decided that the Hong Kong Appeal Court was correct to quash the convictions since the accused had not been shown to have had any influence or control over the crew of that fishing boat. The crew's conduct would have had to have been the result of "actual authority, express or implied, of the party said to have caused it or [be the]

---

16 *Alphacell Ltd v. Woodward* [1972] A.C. 824.

17 *Sopp v. Long* [1970] 1 Q.B. 518; *Mitchell v. Morrison*, 1938 J.C. 64, as explained in *Ross Hillman Ltd v. Bond* [1974] Q.B. 435.

18 *supra, Smith of Maddiston Ltd v. MacNab*, 1975 S.L.T. 86.

19 1981 S.L.T. 161.

20 [1972] A.C. 824.

consequence of his exerting some capacity which he possesses in fact or law to control or influence [their] acts".[21]

Use, cause and permit. Where a statute makes it an offence "to use, or to cause or permit the use" of something, normally a vehicle, different considerations apply. The current rule is that while "use" does not require *mens rea*,[22] both causing and permitting do. This means that whether *mens rea* has to be shown in a prosecution of an employer for the state of a vehicle driven by his employee depends on whether he is charged with using or, as was at least at one time the normal practice in Scotland, with causing the use of, the vehicle.[23] **8.74**

"CAUSE". The concept of cause as understood in the interpretation of statutory offences of "causing and permitting" someone else's contravention involves an order or mandate from the causer, who must be "a person possessing some degree of control or authority to order or direct the use by another",[24] and causing probably occurs only when the use is made on behalf of the causer. The usual "cause" situation is that where A employs B to do something such as drive a vehicle, and so "causes" him to do so. The owner of a business involving the use of a vehicle would probably be regarded as causing every use made by his employees of the vehicle in the course of and within the scope of their employment whether or not he was aware of the particular journey. "Cause" involves something more than permission: A does not cause B to use a vehicle merely by allowing him to do so: it may be that every causing is also a permission — the matter does not seem to have been decided — but it is clear that not every permission is a causing.[25] Despite some uncertainty of judicial opinion it is submitted that the lessor of a vehicle does not cause it to be used by the lessee.[26] **8.75**

The "causing" is referred to the use of the vehicle or other form of conduct, and not to the circumstance rendering the use or conduct illegal. In ordinary language one might say that if a mechanic failed to repair, or deliberately created, a defect in a vehicle and the owner then innocently drove the vehicle while it was defective the mechanic was the cause of the owner's driving a defective vehicle. But the mechanic would not be guilty of causing the vehicle to be used while it was defective, as he had no control over its use by its owner.[27]

---

[21] *Attorney-General of Hong Kong v. Tse Hung-Lit* [1986] A.C. 876, at 883, approving the Australian case of *O'Sullivan v. Truth and Sportsman Ltd* (1956–1957) 96 C.L.R. 220 (where the publisher of a newspaper which contained prohibited material was acquitted of causing it to be offered for sale to the public simply by delivering it to a newsagent, since he had no actual authority to control or influence what the newsagent then did with it). See also para. 8.75, *infra*.

[22] *supra*, paras 8.49 *et seq*.

[23] See *Swan v. MacNab*, 1977 J.C. 57, in which the employers were convicted of using an unsafe lorry driven by their employee.

[24] *Hunter v. Clark*, 1956 J.C. 59, Lord Russell at 66. See also *Houston v. Buchanan*, 1940 S.C. (H.L.) 17, Lord Wright at 39; *Shulton (Great Britain) Ltd v. Slough B.C.* [1967] 2 Q.B. 471; *O'Sullivan v. Truth and Sportsman Ltd* (1956–57) 96 C.L.R. 220 where it was held that the printers of a newspaper did not "cause" it to be sold by a newsagent.

[25] In *Whitehead v. Unwins (Yorks) Ltd* [1962] Crim L.R. 323 where a farmer gratuitously lent his van to a company for the purpose of collecting cattle food and the van was driven by an employee of the company, the farmer was charged with permitting, the company with causing and the driver with using.

[26] *Mackay Bros v. Gibb*, 1969 J.C. 26; see (1970) 34 J.C.L. 280; *Farrell v. Moggach*, 1976 S.L.T. (Sh.Ct.) 8.

[27] *Shave v. Rosner* [1954] 2 Q.B. 113.

8.76 KNOWLEDGE. Where A is charged with causing a contravention to occur he must be shown to have ordered or authorised the activity in course of which the contravention occurs, and also to have knowledge that the use would be in contravention of the Act, *e.g.* to have knowledge of the unlawful condition of the vehicle.[28] The meaning of "knowledge" is probably the same as in cases of permission.[29] It remains to be seen whether to cause a vehicle to be used uninsured (or, perhaps, also to cause someone to drive without a licence[30]) will be treated as a strict responsibility offence: the likelihood is that it will be so treated for as long as permitting such an occurrence remains a strict responsibility offence.

Permitting

8.77 A person permits something when he allows it to happen although he is in a position to prevent or forbid it: one cannot permit something unless one could have meaningfully refused permission.[31] So, for example, the only person who can permit a vehicle to be used is someone who is either the owner or is for some other reason the person responsible for the "care, management and control" of it.[32] A garage owner does not "permit" his customer to drive away his car from the garage in a defective condition where the defect is due to the fault of the garage, since the garage owner cannot effectively forbid a man to use his own car.[33] But permission can continue in the absence of effective control by the permitter who may go abroad, or become ill, or even die, without the permission being thereby terminated.[34]

Permission may be express or implied. It is express where, for example, A lends B his car for a specific journey. But if A simply lends his car to B for a period without imposing any restrictions or conditions,[35] A permits every use made by B of the car, although whether this permission involves criminal responsibility for an unlawful use may depend on A's *mens rea* as to the illegality.[36]

Permission may also consist in merely standing by and allowing something to happen which one is in a position to prevent. If a barman stands by while unlawful drinking takes place on the premises, he is permitting it[37]; if a shopkeeper places in his shop a gaming machine which is capable of being operated illegally and stands by while it is so

---

[28] *Smith of Maddiston Ltd v. Macnab*, 1975 J.C. 48, overruling *Hunter v. Clark*, 1956 J.C. 59.

[29] *cf.*, *Vehicle Inspectorate v. Nuttall* [1999] R.T.R. 264, HL.

[30] See para. 8.80, *infra*.

[31] *Goodbarne v. Buck* [1940] 1 K.B. 771. It is sometimes said that the meaning of "permitted" varies with the statutory context: see, *e.g.*, *Vehicle Inspectorate v. Nuttall* [1999] R.T.R. 264, HL, Lord Nicholls of Birkenhead at 267G-268A, Lord Steyn at 272G-273A, and Lord Hobhouse of Woodborough at 277F. The meanings are said to range from 'allowed or authorised' to 'failed to take reasonable steps to prevent'. It is not clear why the significance of the word should depend on the statutory context, or why a particular meaning should be preferred in any particular statutory setting: but selection of a particular meaning may affect both the extent to which *mens rea* is required and the nature of the mental element which is sufficient.

[32] *Lloyd v. Singleton* [1953] 1 Q.B. 357.

[33] *Shave v. Rosner* [1954] 2 Q.B. 113.

[34] *Kelly v. Cornhill Insurance Co. Ltd*, 1964 S.C.(H.L.) 46.

[35] *cf.*, *Newbury v. Davis* [1974] R.T.R. 367, which was distinguished (if not impliedly disapproved) in *D.P.P. v. Fisher* [1992] R.T.R. 93.

[36] *infra*.

[37] *Finnegan v. Hart* (1916) 7 Adam 705.

operated, he has permitted illegal gaming.[38] A fortiori, where there is a clear duty to act to prevent contravention of regulations by employees — for example, the duty on a transport undertaking to examine its drivers' tachograph records to ensure that drivers' hours regulations are complied with — failing to obtemper that duty will amount to permitting such contraventions as have occurred.[39]

Knowledge. Before A can be convicted of permitting a statutory contravention it must be shown either that he knew, or at least that he ought to have known,[40] of the circumstances constituting the contravention. There are a number of cases which appear to conflict with this, but they all preceded *James and Son Ltd v. Smee*[41] and *Hunter v. Clark*[42] which for the first time clarified the meanings of "use", "cause" and "permit". **8.78**

MOTOR INSURANCE.[43] The offence of permitting a vehicle to be used without insurance may, however, be an exception, but it is submitted that it need not, and should not, be so regarded. In *Houston v. Buchanan*[44] the owner of a car insured only for business purposes gave his brother a general permission to use it, knowing of the limitation in the insurance policy, and knowing that his brother had used a former car of his for both business and private purposes: he was held to have permitted the use of the car by his brother for private purposes. Although Lord Wright[45] expressed the view that the requirements of the relevant statutory provision[46] were strict, this was, strictly speaking, *obiter*. Permission in such a situation arises in two ways: there is the permission of the use, which is a question of fact depending on the interpretation of "permit," and the permission of the contravention which, it is submitted, depends on the accused's state of knowledge as to the circumstance rendering the use illegal. The second question was not in dispute in *Houston*[46a] as knowledge of the illegality was conceded; what was in issue was whether the defender could be said to have permitted his brother to use the car "privately" by giving him an unconditional permission to use the car without making any mention of the insurance limitation. *Houston*[46b] is authority for the view that when A lends B something unconditionally he is to be held to have given him permission to use it in any way B wishes, but it does not follow that he is criminally responsible in respect of any unlawful use B makes of the article if A is unaware of the feature which makes the use illegal. Where a vehicle is lent or is given for use for one purpose and is used for another the lender or giver **8.79**

---

[38] *Vettraino v. Grosset*, 1948 J.C. 49, a case under the now repealed Gaming Machines (Scotland) Act 1917, but which was decided on general principles.

[39] See *Vehicle Inspectorate v. Nuttall* [1999] R.T.R. 264, HL. It may also be necessary to show that the actual contraventions were caused by the failure in duty: see opinion of Lord Hobhouse of Woodborough at 278E-279A.

[40] See *MacPhail v. Allan and Dey Ltd*, 1980 S.L.T. (Sh.Ct.) 136, where the accused company's transport manager had no system for checking whether drivers had valid licences. See also *Carmichael v. Hannaway*, 1987 S.C.C.R. 236.

[41] [1955] 1 Q.B. 78.

[42] 1956 J.C. 59.

[43] See A. Samuels, "Insurance under the Road Traffic Act" [1963] Crim. L.R. 327.

[44] 1940 S.C. (H.L.) 17.

[45] At 39.

[46] Then s.35 of the Road Traffic Act 1930 and now s.143 of the Road Traffic Act 1988.

[46a] 1940 S.C. (H.L.) 17.

[46b] *ibid.*

is not regarded as having permitted the unauthorised use.[47] Similarly, where A lends B a car on condition that B insures it he does not permit B's subsequent use of the car in breach of the condition.[48]

Houston[48a] is a decision by the House of Lords in a civil case, although it depended on the issue of criminal responsibility, and is not technically binding on the High Court. The leading authority in criminal law for the view that knowledge is unnecessary in insurance cases is *Lyons v. May*[49] in which the owner of a car asked his garage to have it driven back to his premises after they had repaired it, in the belief that, as was the normal case, the garage would be covered by insurance: the garage was not covered and the car owner was convicted of permitting their employee to use the car while uninsured. *Lyons*[49a] is still accepted as authoritative in England despite the later case of *James and Son Ltd v. Smee*,[50] but it is not technically binding on the Scots criminal courts. In view of *James and Son Ltd v. Smee*[50a] the principle of which was accepted by the Crown in *Hunter v. Clark*,[51] and reinforced in *Smith of Maddiston Ltd v. Macnab*[51a] it is submitted that *Lyons*[52] should not be followed, and that permission implies knowledge in insurance, as well as in other, cases. This would lead to the strange situation that if, for example, A buys a car which he reasonably but wrongly believes to be insured he is guilty of a contravention if he drives it himself but not if he allows his wife to drive it, but that is, as it were, the fault of the strict responsibility rule regarding use and not of the requirement of some form of *mens rea* for permission.

There may well be good grounds in public policy for treating negligence as sufficient *mens rea* in insurance cases whatever the position regarding other forms of permission, and for setting a very high standard of care.[53] But there seems no need to convict A where, for example, he believes B to be a person holding a driving licence and therefore covered by his policy, because B has shown him a fraudulently obtained licence, or in the *Lyons v. May*[53a] situation where he arranges with a reputable garage to return his car to him: he can hardly be expected to demand production of the garage's insurance policy, and even if he did and the garage was insured he would still, if responsibility is strict, be guilty if the

---

[47] *Sheldon Deliveries Ltd v. Willis* [1972] R.T.R. 217.

[48] *Newbury v. Davis* [1974] R.T.R. 367. In *D.P.P. v. Fisher* [1992] R.T.R. 93, at 97K-L, Watkins L.J. said that the *ratio* of *Newbury v. Davis* was to be "regarded with extreme caution" and was applicable "only in exceptional circumstances". Thus, that *ratio* was declared inapplicable where F lent his car to L on condition that L (whom F knew to be disqualified from driving) obtained someone with a valid driving licence and who was insured to drive the vehicle. It seems that at the very least, F would have had to communicate the condition to the person F selected to drive. As this had not been done, and F did not know who the driver would be, F was not entitled to an acquittal on a charge of permitting his car to be driven by a person who had no insurance. The decision is harsh; but the court emphasised the importance of not undermining the strictness of the offence under s.143 of the Road Traffic Act 1988. It is submitted that *D.P.P v. Fisher* should not be followed in Scotland.

[48a] 1940 S.C. (H.L.) 17.

[49] [1948] 2 All E.R. 1062.

[49a] *ibid.*

[50] [1955] 1 Q.B. 78. *Lyons* was followed in *Baugh v. Crago* [1975] R.T.R. 453.

[50a] *ibid.*

[51] 1956 J.C. 59.

[51a] 1975 J.C. 48.

[52] [1948] 2 All E.R. 1062.

[53] *cf. McArthur v. Henderson*, 1953 J.C. 37.

[53a] [1948] 2 All E.R. 1062.

garage owner sent a disqualified driver to return the car, even though neither he not the garage owner knew of the disqualification. It is difficult to see why there should be responsibility for permitting in such a case when other types of permission require some *mens rea*.

DRIVING LICENCES. It was held in *Ferrymasters Ltd v. Adams*[54] that the offence of causing or permitting someone to drive without a licence was in the same position as that of causing or permitting someone to drive uninsured. In *MacPhail v. Allan and Dey Ltd*,[55] however, the sheriff refused to follow that decision, holding it to be inconsistent with *Smith of Maddiston Ltd v. MacNab*.[56] **8.80**

THE MEANING OF KNOWLEDGE. So far as offences other than offences regarding vehicle insurance (or possibly driving licences) are concerned, *mens rea* is necessary, but it is not clear what is meant by this. In particular it is not clear what degree of constructive knowledge is sufficient for causing or permitting.[57] In *Roper v. Taylor's Central Garages (Exeter) Ltd*[58] Devlin J. said that constructive knowledge — the failure to make use of reasonable inquiries — generally had no place in criminal law,[59] but there are a number of dicta to the contrary.[60] *James and Son Ltd v. Smee*[61] is not itself decisive on this point. **8.81**

Glanville Williams takes the view that there must be knowledge or at least "technical recklessness",[62] and he is supported by *Hutchings v.*

---

[54] [1980] R.T.R. 139.

[55] 1980 S.L.T. (Sh.Ct.) 136.

[56] 1975 J.C. 48.

[57] The cases all concern permission since causing did not require *mens rea* until *Ross Hillman Ltd v. Bond* [1974] Q.B. 435 and *Smith of Maddiston Ltd v. Macnab, supra.*

[58] [1951] 2 T.L.R. 284.

[59] At 289. See also *Robinson v. D.P.P.* [1991] R.T.R. 315, where a conviction of an employer for permitting an employee to drive a vehicle with defective brakes was quashed on appeal, since the conviction had been based on the employer's failure to establish a proper system of inspection, maintenance and repair for his vehicles — *i.e.*, the conviction had been based on negligence: in the absence of proof of his actual knowledge or his recklessness *quoad* the brake defects, the conviction could not be sustained.

[60] *Underwood v. Henderson* (1898) 2 Adam 596; *Korten v. W. Sussex C.C.* (1903) 72 L.J.K.B. 514, Channell J. at 523; *Campbell v. Cameron* (1915) 7 Adam 697, L.J.-G. Strathclyde at 702; *Goldsmith v. Deakin* (1933) 50 T.L.R. 73; *Clydebank Co-operative Society Ltd v. Binnie*, 1937 J.C. 17, Lord Fleming at 26; *Evans v. Dell* [1937] 1 All E.R. 349, Lord Hewart C.J. at 353; *Churchill v. Norris* (1938) 158 L.T. 254, Humphreys J. at 257; *MacDonald v. Wilmae Concrete Ltd*, 1954 S.L.T. (Sh.Ct.) 33; *Mallon v. Allon* [1964] 1 Q.B. 385, Lord Parker C.J. at 394. In *Dundas and Anr. v. Phyn* (1914) 7 Adam 414 the statute specifically provided that negligence might be deemed permission, but L.J.-G. Strathclyde's statement (a) that he did not know how a man could permit that of which he was ignorant, and (b) that actual knowledge was unnecessary provided permission could be inferred from facts and circumstances, is typical of judicial attitudes. See also the confusing House of Lords case of *Vehicle Inspectorate v. Nuttall*, [1999] R.T.R. 264, where the opinions of Lord Nicholls of Birkenhead at 268D-F and Lord Hobhouse of Woodborough at 279C–280A seem to favour a deliberate failure to take reasonable steps to prevent a contravention of drivers' hours regulations as sufficient for conviction of an offence of permitting under s.96(11A) of the Transport Act 1968, whereas Lord Steyn at 273C states that nothing less than wilfulness or recklessness will suffice as the appropriate mental element: as Lord Slynn concurred in the opinion of Lord Steyn, and Lord Jauncey in the opinions of both Lords Steyn and Nicholls, the *ratio* of the case is somewhat uncertain; see the commentary on the case by J.C.S. in [1999] Crim. L.R., 675–676. It is also to be noted that Lord Steyn (at 273C–274B) quoted with apparent approval from Devlin J. in *Roper v. Taylor's Central Garages (Exeter) Ltd* [1951] 2 T.L.R. 284 at 289, whereas Lord Hobhouse (at 279D) dismissed Devlin J's. analysis of knowledge there as unhelpful.

[61] [1955] 1 Q.B. 78.

[62] Gl. Williams, p.166.

Giles,[63] *Wilson v. Bird,*[64] *Fransman v. Sexton,*[65] *Gray's Haulage Co. Ltd v. Arnold,*[66] and *Robinson v. D.P.P.*[67]

It appears, on the whole, that the operation of a system of working which makes it easy for employees to contravene a statutory prohibition and provides no effective method for the employer to enforce compliance with the statute will be regarded as sufficient for permission,[68] and that in imposing responsibility the courts may use the language of wilful blindness,[69] or of negligence, or a combination of both.[70] In *James and Son Ltd v. Smee*[70a] it was said that the requirement of knowledge was satisfied by shutting one's eyes and allowing one's servant to do something where a contravention is likely, not caring whether it takes place or not.[71]

8.82 The more recent English cases tend to stress that wilful blindness, or at least recklessness in the sense of not making inquiries when one suspects a contravention, is necessary for permission.[72] In *Gray's Haulage Co. Ltd v. Arnold,*[73] a charge of permitting an employee to drive excessive hours, Lord Parker, C.J. said:

> "In my judgment, there is a tendency today to impute knowledge in circumstances which really do not justify knowledge being imputed. It is of the very essence of the offence of permitting someone to do something that there should be knowledge. The case that is always referred to in this connection is *James & Son Ltd v. Smee; Green v. Burnett* where, in giving judgment, I pointed out that knowledge is really of two kinds, actual knowledge, and knowledge which arises either from shutting one's eyes to the obvious, or, what is very much the same thing but put in another way, failing to do something or doing something not caring whether contravention takes place or not. Here, there is no question of actual knowledge at all, nor is it a case where there is a shutting of eyes to the obvious as, for instance, refraining from looking at the records which had to be kept of hours of work showing that the driver was not complying with the statute."

Similarly, in *Fransman v. Sexton,*[74] a charge of permitting the use of a car with defective brakes, Lord Parker stressed that:

> "If they are meaning merely this, that knowledge was being imputed to the appellant because in fact he had failed to discover the defect

---

[63] [1955] Crim. L.R. 784.

[64] [1963] Crim. L.R. 57.

[65] [1965] Crim. L.R. 556.

[66] [1966] 1 W.L.R. 534.

[67] [1991] R.T.R. 315.

[68] See esp. *Clydebank Co-operative Society Ltd v. Binnie,* 1937 J.C. 17. The court in *Noble v. Heatly*, 1967 J.C. 5, appear to have regarded failure to give instructions as enough for "knowingly allowing" in *Greig v. Macleod* (1907) 5 Adam 445.

[69] *Lawson v. Macgregor*, 1924 J.C. 112.

[70] *Clydebank Co-operative Society Ltd v. Binnie, supra.*

[70a] [1955] 1 Q.B. 78.

[71] [1955] 1 Q.B., Parker J. at 91. See also *Ross v. Moss* [1965] 2 Q.B. 396, and *Vehicle Inspectorate v. Nuttall* [1999] R.T.R. 264, Lord Steyn at 274F.

[72] Lord Diplock's remark — *Sweet v. Parsley* [1970] A.C. 162 D-E — that permission requires knowledge or at least "reasonable grounds for suspicion" must be regarded as inaccurate: see *R. v. Souter* [1971] 1 W.L.R. 1187.

[73] [1966] 1 All E.R. 896, at 898A.

[74] [1965] Crim. L.R. 556.

> and might have taken steps which would have revealed a defect, then in my judgment the test is completely wrong. Knowledge is not imputed by mere negligence but by something more than negligence, something which one can describe as reckless, sending out a car not caring what happens."

These statements were approved in *Hill and Sons (Botley and Denmead) Ltd v. Hampshire Chief Constable*,[75] in which the Divisional Court quashed a conviction for permitting the use of a vehicle with defective brakes where the only evidence of *mens rea* was a failure to institute a follow-up system to check that the maintenance system laid down by the defendant company had been carried out. Of this Lord Widgery C.J. said: "I think that the absence of such a further check might amount to negligence, but certainly I would not think that, as a matter of law, the absence of that further check could be described as recklessness sufficient to justify the inference that the managing director was wilfully closing his eyes to the obvious."[76]

The most recent decision of relevance by the House of Lords provided the opportunity for a definitive and clear statement of the law.[77] Unfortunately, the judicial opinions taken as a whole do not provide such a statement. Lord Steyn was of the view that in an offence of permitting under section 96(11A) of the Transport Act 1968,[78] "[n]othing less than wilfulness or recklessness will be sufficient" and that "[i]n practice recklessness will be the relevant *mens rea*".[79] He was then at pains to indicate where the line should be drawn between recklessness and negligence, since he had clearly implied that negligence would not suffice. After quoting from Devlin J. in *Roper v. Taylor's Central Garages (Exeter) Ltd*,[80] he made it plain that the line was to be drawn where a defendant deliberately refrained from making inquiries since he suspected that the results of such inquiries would show information of which he preferred to remain in ignorance.[81] As Lord Steyn concluded: "if the defendant's state of mind is one of not caring whether a contravention of the provision of the Regulation took place that would generally be sufficient to establish recklessness and that . . . is the necessary mental element . . . If recklessness in at least this sense is not established no offence is committed."[82] It seems fairly clear that if all that was proved was that the defendant failed to make such inquiries as a reasonable and prudent employer might make — *i.e.* that the defendant had been negligent — that would be insufficient. Lord Steyn's opinion stands, however, in sharp contrast to that of Lord Hobhouse, who said: "The relevant question in this type of case will normally be not what he did or did not know but what the performance of his duty required him to know. Absent any special factor such as accident or innocent mistake

---

75 [1972] R.T.R. 29.

76 *ibid.*, at 35F-G.

77 *Vehicle Inspectorate v. Nuttall* [1999] R.T.R. 264.

78 Section 96(11A) reads: "Where, in the case of a driver of a motor vehicle, there is in Great Britain a contravention of any requirement of the applicable Community rules as to periods of driving, or distance driven, or periods on or off duty, then the offender and any other person (being the offender's employer or a person to whose orders the offender was subject) who caused or permitted the contravention shall be liable".

79 [1999] R.T.R. at 273C.

80 [1951] 2 T.L.R. 284, at 288–289.

81 See *Evans v. Dell* (1937) 53 T.L.R. 310, Lord Hewart C.J. at 313, as quoted by Devlin J. and reproduced by Lord Steyn at 273F.

82 [1999] R.T.R. at 274B.

of fact . . . he will not be able to escape criminal responsibility for his acts and omissions, nor will he be able to rebut the case made against him."[83] His final conclusion puts his views beyond doubt, *viz.*: "The failure to take the requisite precautions both constitutes the *actus reus* and, in practical terms, satisfies the requirement of providing prima facie proof of *mens rea*."[84] It follows that Lord Steyn would not, whereas Lord Hobhouse would, be content with negligence as the mental element of permitting in this case. Lord Nicholls agreed with Lord Hobhouse, Lord Slynn agreed with Lord Steyn, and Lord Jauncey agreed with both Lord Hobhouse and Lord Steyn: it is thus very difficult to understand the *ratio* of the case, notwithstanding that their Lordships were united as to the disposal of the appeal itself; and the value of the case as an authority must, therefore, be limited.

8.83 The Scottish cases talk in terms of wilful blindness, but they do suggest that something less than what Lord Steyn, and closer to what Lord Hobhouse, considered necessary in *Vehicle Inspectorate v. Nuttall*[85] may be enough for permission. Consequently they suggest also that there is still a difference between "permit" and "knowingly permit",[86] a difference that may or may not now be recognised in English law.[87]

In *Clydebank Co-operative Society Ltd v. Binnie*[88] the charge was of permitting the use of a motor-vehicle as an express carriage without a licence. The circumstance which made the vehicle an express carriage was an arrangement made by the person who hired the vehicle from the accused company. This arrangement was not known to the company or to their driver. They were convicted of permitting the use, because they should have known from the circumstances of repeated journeys that each passenger was paying his own fare and that the hire was not being paid by the lessee. Lord Justice-General Normand said that, "they had a duty to consider and inquire" whether their vehicle was being legally used, and concluded: "They were, in short, in the position of persons who either know or ought to have known that this journey which Miss Woods had organised was a journey towards the cost of which other persons would contribute, and, if so, they must be held as a matter of law to have permitted a breach of the statute."[89] Lord Fleming said: "I think it is also true that if a person has good reasons for supposing that a prohibited thing is happening and, being able to prevent it, does nothing, he may be held to permit it."[90]

8.84 *Clydebank Co-operative Society Ltd v. Binnie*[90a] may be accommodated within the confines of reckless wilful blindness, although it does suggest that it might be enough to show that the accused "ought to have known". The narrowness of the line between wilful blindness and negligence can be seen in *Mackay Brothers v. Gibb*[91] in which car-hirers

---

[83] *ibid.*, at 279D.
[84] *ibid.*, at 280A.
[85] [1999] R.T.R. 264; see para. 8.82, *supra*.
[86] See *Mackay Bros v. Gibb*, 1969 J.C. 26, Lord Wheatley at 33.
[87] See *Alphacell Ltd v. Woodward* [1972] A.C. 824, Viscount Dilhorne at 840D; *R. v. Thomas and Thomson* (1976) 63 Cr.App.R. 65; *cf.*, J.C. Smith and B. Hogan, *Criminal Law* (9th ed., 1999, Sir J. Smith (ed.)), pp.102–103.
[88] 1937 J.C. 17.
[89] At 25.
[90] At 26.
[90a] 1937 J.C. 17.
[91] 1969 J.C. 26.

were charged with permitting a car to be used with a faulty tyre. The evidence was that the person responsible did not check the depth of tread on the tyres before hiring-out the car. He said that they had appeared to be in good order, but was disbelieved. Stress was also laid on his ignorance of what the permitted depth was. This ignorance, and the ignorance of the actual depth of tread on the car, might be regarded by Glanville Williams as recklessness,[92] but it is a far cry from the state of mind in which a person refrains from making inquiries for fear of confirming a belief that he is acting illegally. Lord Justice-Clerk Grant said that the appearance of the tyres was not decisive, and went on to say that what mattered was:

> "that the garage controller took no steps to ascertain the minimum depth of tread laid down by law or to measure the tread of what was obviously a very well-worn tyre. To my mind this is a case of the garage controller wilfully turning a blind eye to the high likelihood of the event which in fact occurred, namely, the user of the car on the date charged with a tyre having a tread with a depth below the minimum. He may have had no actual knowledge, but notional or constructive knowledge is enough, and there was, in my opinion, such knowledge here."[93]

Lord Wheatley said:

> "When, as here, such an employee is so lacking in care that he fails to examine the tyres of a car which he is hiring to a customer, is completely ignorant of the requirements of the law regarding the permissible standard of wear in the tyres, and allows a car to leave the garage with a tyre which is defective, he was guilty of what has been called wilful blindness, which is, I suppose, a form of notional knowledge. In acting thus, he permitted the offence, and in the circumstances his knowledge must be transmitted to his employers, the appellants."[94]

In *Smith of Maddiston Ltd v. Macnab*,[95] Lord Justice-General Emslie **8.85**
said:

> "Knowledge in this connection includes the state of mind of a man who shuts his eyes to the obvious and allows another to do something in circumstances where a contravention is likely, not caring whether a contravention takes place or not. It may be inferred where the permittor has given no thought to his statutory obligations at all (*Houston v. Buchanan*, 1940 S.C. (H.L.) 17, *per* Lord Wright, at p. 40)."

The first sentence of the above quotation reflects the criterion of wilful blindness, but the second reads rather like the common law attitude to recklessness.[96] The inference of knowledge from lack of thought might also be justified on the rather tortuous argument that A is presumed to know the law and therefore his failure to inquire is a failure by someone who knows that inquiry may reveal illegality, and that that is to be taken

---

92 See Gl. Williams, paras 54 and 55, critically discussed in J.C. Smith, "The Guilty Mind in the Criminal Law" (1960) 76 L.Q.R. 78.

93 At 30–31.

94 At 33.

95 1975 J.C. 48, at 53.

96 See *supra*, paras 7.58 to 7.68.

to be a failure motivated by a fear of discovering the illegality,[96a] an argument which is not in fact mentioned by the court at all. *Houston v. Buchanan*[97] is, of course, of little value as an authority, since it long preceded the modern law of permitting and dealt in any event with the special case of motor insurance, apart altogether from the fact that knowledge of illegality was not in issue in *Houston v. Buchanan*.[98]

Perhaps the most that can be said is that the Scottish cases are not as clear as some of the English cases quoted above.[99] In particular, there is no Scottish case which says so plainly as does *R. v. Souter*[1] that it is not enough that reasonable grounds for suspicion existed: the question is whether in fact the accused suspected. A requirement of actual suspicion would mean reading *Mackay Bros v. Gibb*[2] as a case in which the tyre was so clearly bald that the garage controller must have suspected its illegality,[3] although there were no findings in fact to that effect. The second sentence quoted from *Smith of Maddiston Ltd*[4] remains somewhat wide, but may be treated as *obiter*, that case being concerned primarily with whether *mens rea* was required at all in offences of causing, rather than with what constituted *mens rea* in offences of causing or permitting.

8.86 VICARIOUS PERMISSION. The question to be considered under this head is whether in a charge against A of permitting, B's *mens rea* can be imputed to A where B is A's servant or delegate. In England it may be so imputable in cases under the Licensing Acts even where the statute uses the words "knowingly permits",[5] but generally not in other cases.[6] The English licensing cases have no application in Scotland,[7] but there are some confusing road traffic cases, particularly in connection with express carriages.

96a See n.92, *supra*.

97 1940 S.C. (H.L.) 17.

98 *supra*, para. 8.79.

99 Paragraph 8.82. More recent Scottish cases continue to be equivocal, although in *Carmichael v. Hannaway*, 1987 S.C.C.R. 236, L.J.-C. Ross did say that the employer in question had sent his driver to pick up a load when he must have known that a contravention was likely and when he did not care whether a contravention took place or not. See also *Brown v. W. Burns Tractors Ltd*, 1987 S.C.C.R. 146, where a female clerical assistant was held to be a person to whom an important part of the administration of the accused's company had been delegated, she being responsible to the directors for supervising the company's drivers in relation to their work and rest hours and tachograph records, and the company were convicted of causing a large number of contraventions of the relevant Regulations by their drivers. The court also accepted that the contraventions had been so many and so flagrant that the accused must be regarded as having been wilfully blind to their assistant's behaviour. *Cf. MacPhail v. Allan and Dey Ltd*,1980 S.L.T. (Sh.Ct.) 136, where Sheriff R.J.D. Scott said: "[Constructive, notional or imputed knowledge] can be inferred where someone allows another to do something when a contravention is likely or where he gives no thought to the statutory obligation at all or where he has good reason to suppose that a prohibited thing is happening and does nothing to prevent it." The case was probably concerned with negligence in fact, although the statement as to what would suffice for knowledge is particularly wide.

1 [1971] 1 W.L.R. 1187.

2 1969 J.C. 26.

3 *supra*, para. 7.53.

4 *supra*.

5 *Allen v. Whitehead* [1930] 1 K.B. 211; *Linnett v. Commissioner of Metropolitan Police* [1946] K.B. 290; Gl. Williams, para. 95. *Cf. Vane v. Yiannopoullos* [1965] A.C. 486.

6 Gl. Williams, p.166.

7 *Noble v. Heatly*, 1967 J.C. 5.

In *Evans v. Dell*[8] the owners of a vehicle were acquitted because they and their driver were unaware of the circumstance which brought its use within the scope of the law relating to express carriages, namely, that the journey had been advertised to the public by the persons who had hired the vehicle.[9] But in *Browning v. J.W.H. Watson (Rochester) Ltd*[10] where what made the use of the vehicle illegal was the presence in a private party of two uninvited Ministry of Transport inspectors, the owners were convicted although they and their driver were unaware of their presence. It was held (a) that the driver did not know of their presence only because he failed to inquire, (b) that the owners had failed to take any precautions against unauthorised persons entering the vehicle, and (c) that the offence was in any event one of strict responsibility; but it was later said that the *ratio decidendi* was the owner's failure to take precautions.[11]

In *Forsyth v. Phillips*,[12] a charge of permitting employees to drive in excess of the permitted hours, the court held that the knowledge of the drivers could be imputed to the employers, although there was also wilful blindness on the part of the employers to the behaviour of their drivers and the case could have been decided on that point.

The Scots cases suggest that for the purpose of fixing an accused with **8.87**
guilt of permission, there may be imputed to him the knowledge of his employees, unless the statute talks of "knowingly" permitting.

In *Maxwell v. Malcolm*[13] a publican was convicted of suffering women of bad fame to assemble in his public-house. It was not proved that the accused even knew the women were there, nor that the barmaid who served them knew their characters. The magistrates convicted "from the suspicious manner" in which the barmaid gave evidence of her ignorance of the women's characters. The High Court upheld the conviction. Lord Deas, with whom Lord Adam concurred, said there could be no question that the licensee was responsible for his servant, the question was whether the servant knew or reasonably ought to have known.[14] The Lord Justice-Clerk seems to have treated the case as one of strict responsibility.[15]

The knowledge founded on in *Clydebank Co-operative Society Ltd v. Binnie*[16] was knowledge "through their manager",[17] but no point was taken on this, nor on the specialty of the accused being a company.

The most important case is again *Mackay Bros v. Gibb*,[18] although it is difficult to assess because it preceded *Tesco Ltd v. Nattrass*[19] and *Readers' Digest Association Ltd v. Pirie*,[20] but it does suggest that

[8] [1937] 1 All E.R. 349.
[9] This decision is supported by *Reynolds v. G.H. Austin and Sons Ltd* [1951] 2 K.B. 135, itself a decision on use.
[10] [1953] 1 W.L.R. 1172.
[11] *James and Son Ltd v. Smee* [1955] 1 Q.B. 78, 92–93.
[12] [1964] Crim.L.R. 229.
[13] (1879) 4 Couper 289.
[14] At 293.
[15] See also *Galloway v. Weber* (1889) 2 White 171; *Macmillan v. Western S.M.T. Co.*, 1933 J.C. 51.
[16] 1937 J.C. 17.
[17] L.J.-G. Normand at 24.
[18] 1969 J.C. 26.
[19] [1972] A.C. 153.
[20] 1973 J.C. 42; see *infra*, para. 8.104.

vicarious *mens rea* can suffice for permission. The actual permitter was the accused's garage controller: his precise position in the hierarchy is not stated, but reference was made in the case to another person as "a responsible representative" of the appellant firm who was the person cautioned and charged. Lord Justice-Clerk Grant treated the case as one of direct responsibility, the appellants being a firm who could act only by the hands of their partners and employees.[21] Lord Wheatley, on the other hand, did treat the case as one of vicarious responsibility, and said: "If a person is employed by a firm as garage controller and part of his responsibility is to hire out cars to customers, his employers are responsible for his actings and in my opinion his knowledge or notional knowledge must be attributed to them."[22]

8.88 *Supervening illegality.* Suppose A lends B his car in the knowledge that B is covered by the insurance policy on the car, and that the car's brakes are in good condition. If subsequently B is disqualified and so ceases to be covered by the insurance policy, or the car's brakes become defective, and B continues to drive the car, is A guilty of permitting B's contraventions of the Road Traffic Act? It is submitted that he is not. Common sense and justice require this answer and there is nothing in cases like *Houston v. Buchanan*[23] to require any different result.[24]

II — Corporate Responsibility

8.89 As far as human persons are concerned, strict liability permits conviction even though the accused had no *mens rea* relative to the issue or issues in respect of which the offence in question is strict,[25] and vicarious liability permits conviction where someone other than the accused perpetrated the act which, or omitted to do what, the offence in question requires.[26] It follows that actual capacity for *mens rea* at the appropriate time or actual capacity to act, or omit, at that time is not an essential requirement where strict or vicarious liability is applicable. Thus where the law recognises non-human personality, as it does, for example, in relation to duly constituted companies and (in Scotland) partnerships,[27] it would seem that the prosecution of *personae fictae*[28] for strict or vicarious liability offences poses no greater problems than are encountered where human beings are prosecuted for such offences. But vicarious liability and strict liability are exceptional in criminal law which

---

[21] 1969 J.C. at 31; see also Lord Milligan at 35.

[22] *ibid.*, at 33.

[23] 1940 S.C. (H.L.) 17, *supra*, para. 8.79.

[24] It may unfortunately be the law that if B continues to drive after A has terminated his permission but before he knows of this termination and there is no other illegality involved, B is guilty of driving without insurance: see *Kelly v. Cornhill Insurance Co. Ltd*, 1964 S.C. (H.L.) 46, Lord Reid at 58, but this has no bearing on the situation considered in the text.

[25] See paras 8.01 to 8.02; 8.04 to 8.39, *supra*.

[26] See paras 8.40 to 8.71, *supra*. If the offence requires *mens rea*, then the mental state of the actual perpetrator will also require to be attributed to the accused: see paras 8.03 and 8.55 *et seq.* (esp. 8.58), *supra*.

[27] Such entities will generally be referred to in the following paragraphs as "corporations" and subsumed by the epithet "corporate"; see also para. 8.91, *infra*.

[28] This term is used to denote corporations in *Meridian Global Funds Management Asia Ltd v. Securities Commission* [1995] 3 W.L.R. 413, by Lord Hoffmann at 418C.

is generally designed with individual responsibility in mind. If there is a case for a wider criminal liability on corporations,[29] the question then arises as to the way in which *personae fictae* are to be convicted of offences, whether under statute or common law, where the assumption is that the accused will personally have acted in a certain way in a certain state of mind. Corporations are legal abstractions which are never able to act or have *mens rea* in any human sense: if, therefore, they, as opposed, or in addition, to the individuals employed by them, are to be primarily liable, there are probably but two main methods of finding a solution to the question posed — either the acts and *mentes reae* of actual human beings have to be attributed to them, or the way in which they can be made liable must be tailored to the sorts of organisation which they are. The former would involve a derivative liability, which, at its most extreme might simply echo vicarious liability;[30] the latter, however, would create a more direct liability — but at the expense of the paradigm of modern criminal responsibility with its emphasis upon individual human accountability.

The case for corporate responsibility. What is at issue here is corporate **8.90** responsibility as a primary offender. The difficulty about making a corporation primarily responsible is said to be that as it has no mind it is incapable of forming a criminal intent of its own. Corporate responsibility for offences of strict responsibility may be distinguished just because of the absence of any need for *mens rea*,[31] although even an offence of strict responsibility requires some voluntary conduct, and if a corporation is capable of committing such offences it may be argued that it should also be capable of committing offences involving *mens rea*. Again, a corporation can be responsible in civil law for a delict which requires "actual fault or privity",[32] and even for one which requires malice.[33] A corporation can be guilty of an offence of permitting a statutory contravention by reason of wilful blindness,[34] and that being so it is difficult to see any ground for holding that a corporation cannot be guilty of a statutory offence requiring actual knowledge or intention, and if a corporation can commit a statutory offence requiring *mens rea* it should be capable of committing a common law offence.[35] A corporation can also be guilty of contempt of court,[36] but this may be regarded as special.

There are social arguments for and against making corporations criminally responsible: on the one hand it means punishing, in the case of a company for example, the shareholders by inflicting a fine on the company for the acts of, for example, its directors or managers; on the other hand it seems only fair that if the company carries on its business criminally for the purpose of making profits, the company's funds as well

---

[29] See para. 8.90, *infra*.

[30] *cf.* J. Ross, "Corporate Criminal Liability: One Form or Many Forms?", 1999 J.R. 49, at 49–50.

[31] *cf. Macmillan v. Western S.M.T Co.*, 1933 J.C. 51.

[32] *Lennard's Carrying Co. Ltd v. Asiatic Petroleum Co. Ltd* [1915] A.C. 705. But *cf. Melias Ltd v. Preston* [1957] 2 Q.B. 380.

[33] *Gordon v. British and Foreign Metaline Co.* (1886) 14 R. 75.

[34] *Clydebank Co-operative Society Ltd v. Binnie*, 1937 J.C. 17.

[35] Whether it may be convicted of *any* common law offence is a separate issue. See p.372, n.39, and paras 8.95 and 8.107, *infra*.

[36] *Stirling v. Associated Newspapers Ltd*, 1960 J.C. 5.

as the person and property of its servants should be penalised.[37] It is also relevant to consider that a corporation is regarded in other branches of the law as a person and that it does have an identity and, in many cases, a "public image" which is of value to it: it may therefore be salutary to convict the company and not to allow it to hide its reputation behind the skirts of the individual directors.[38]

From the strictly legal point of view, however, there appear to be no good grounds for excluding criminal responsibility. An individual car-owner who permits the unlawful use of his car is liable to be fined: why should the position be different where the owner is a corporation? A corporation which runs nightclubs and arranges to bring young girls to this country to enable them to remain here by arranging marriages which proceed on false declarations to a registrar would, it is submitted, be guilty of contravening section 44 of the Criminal Law (Consolidation) (Scotland) Act 1995, and if the marriages were bigamous would, it is submitted, be guilty art and part of bigamy.[39] It is true that a company cannot be imprisoned and perhaps therefore cannot be convicted of a crime for which the only punishment is imprisonment, but such crimes are very rare.

8.91 *What is a corporation?* It is submitted that any body for the prosecution of which a competent procedure exists can be convicted of a crime. In Scotland, such procedures exist in the case of any "body corporate" so far as solemn procedure is concerned,[40] and in the case of any "partnership, association, body corporate, or body of trustees"[41] so far as summary procedure is concerned. "Body corporate", however, seems for this purpose to include a firm in any event.[42]

8.92 *Who are the corporation?* A corporation can only act by its servants, and so far as vicarious responsibility is concerned it is responsible for the actings on its behalf of any of its servants in the course of their employment. So far as primary responsibility is concerned, however, responsibility is usually confined to particular persons within the corporation who are identified as being that corporation in terms of what was done (or omitted) and the *mens rea* with which it was done (or omitted); but this depends upon the approach to corporate liability favoured by

---

[37] See, *inter alia,* L.H. Leigh, *The Criminal Liability of Corporations in English Law* (London, 1969); J. Andrews, "Reform in the Law of Corporate Liability" [1973] Crim.L.R. 91.

[38] See A. Ashworth, *Principles of Criminal Law* (3rd ed., 1999), pp.120–121; *cf.* J.C. Smith and B. Hogan, *Criminal Law* (9th. ed., 1999, Sir J. Smith (ed.)), p.186. See also N. Lacey, C. Wells and D. Meure, *Reconstructing Criminal Law* (1st ed., 1990, London), pp.243–252; and *ibid.* (2nd ed., 1998, London, N. Lacey and C. Wells (eds)), at pp.512–523.

[39] See para. 5.02, *supra*. *Cf.* J.C. Smith and B. Hogan, *Criminal Law* (9th ed., 1999, Sir J. Smith (ed.)), p.184: "There are . . . offences which it is quite inconceivable that an official of a corporation should commit within the scope of his employment; for example, bigamy, rape, incest and, possibly, perjury." See also E.M. Burchell and P.M.A. Hunt, *South African Criminal Law and Procedure*, Vol. 1, *General Principles of Criminal Law* (3rd. ed., 1997, J.M. Burchell (ed.)), at p.300: "Surely it would be verging on the absurd to think of a corporation being held guilty of rape or bigamy?" Whether or not such things are inconceivable or absurd must depend, however, on the theory of corporate liability adopted: *cf.* para. 8.107, *infra.*

[40] 1995 Act, s.70.

[41] 1995 Act, s.143.

[42] *Mackay Bros v. Gibb*, 1969 J.C. 26; *Douglas v. Phoenix Motors*, 1970 S.L.T. (Sh.Ct.) 57.

the criminal law.[43] Where a statute makes it a defence to prove that a contravention was due to the fault of another person, and also provides that where an offence committed by a corporation has been committed with the connivance of "any director, manager, secretary, or other similar officer" of the corporation the conniver is also guilty, then any servant of the corporation not falling within that definition is an "other person." And the term "manager" means someone managing the corporation's affairs as its directing mind and not *e.g.* the manager of one store in a large chain of supermarkets.[44]

Derivative Approaches to Corporate Liability

Directing mind and will. "A limited company, as such, cannot carry on business. It can only do so by employing human beings to act on its behalf. The actions of its employees, acting in the course of their employment, are what constitute the carrying on of business by the company."[45] This statement underlines the basic principle of corporate liability in modern English law — that, assuming that a corporation can be criminally liable for the particular offence in question,[46] the acts and mental states of its employees are attributed to the corporation as a legal person and thus become its acts and mental states. The elements of criminal liability are thus derived from the corporation's human employees, but not necessarily from any of them irrespective of position. If a corporation were to be criminally liable for the acts of each and every one of its employees, the result might be very onerous: in *R. v. British Steel*,[47] for example, the defendant company operated 40 plants and employed some 50,000 persons. To meet this problem, it was until quite recently common to treat a corporation anthropomorphically, such that employees could be divided into those who represented its hands and thus performed the practical work associated with its business, and those who exercised its powers and thus represented its directing mind and will.[48] Only the latter's acts and mental states were to be attributed to the company.[49] The advantage of **8.93**

---

[43] See R. Mays, "The Criminal Liability of Corporations and Scots Law: Learning the Lessons of Anglo-American Jurisprudence" (2000) 4 E.L.R. 46, and paras 8.93 *et seq.*, *infra*.

[44] *Tesco Ltd v. Nattrass,supra,* Lord Morris of Borth-y-Gest at 178F; Visc. Dilhorne at 188B; Lord Pearson at 191A; see para. 8.97, *infra*: see also *R. v. Andrews-Weatherfoil Ltd* [1972] 1 W.L.R. 118, Eveleigh J. at 124C-D. For an example of responsibility attaching to a municipal corporation for the actings of one of its officials, see *Morris v. Wellington City* [1969] N.Z.L.R. 1038.

[45] *In Re Supply of Ready Mixed Concrete (No. 2)* [1995] 1 A.C. 456, HL, *per* Lord Nolan at p.474G: see also Lord Templeman at p.465C-D. For a general discussion of this approach, see J. Ross, "Corporate Criminal Liability: One Form or Many Forms?", 1999 J.R. 49.

[46] See para. 8.90, and n.39 there, *supra*; and para. 8.107, *infra*.

[47] [1995] 1 W.L.R. 1356, CA.

[48] See *Lennard's Carrying Co. Ltd v. Asiatic Petroleum Co. Ltd* [1915] A.C. 705, HL, Visc. Haldane L.C. at 713; *H.L. Bolton (Engineering) Co. Ltd v. T.J. Graham and Sons Ltd* [1957] 1 Q.B. 159, CA, Denning L.J. at 172; *Tesco Ltd v. Nattrass* [1972] A.C. 153, HL, Lord Diplock at 199–200; *Seaboard Ltd v. Transport Secretary* [1994] 1 W.L.R. 541, HL, Lord Keith of Kinkell at 545G-H.

[49] This rule applies also where a corporation is a victim of crime — although the group of persons then thought of as representing the mind and will of the corporation may be different: see *R. v. Rozeik* [1996] 1 W.L.R. 159, CA, where a finance company was the alleged victim of an offence of obtaining property by deception; if the company's branch manager knew of the deception — and it seemed that he did — the question lay whether

this rule is its (apparent) simplicity: identification of senior management officers[50] of any corporation should enable that corporation's criminal liability to be determined, since if any of those officers was criminally responsible for what had been done in the course of his employment, then so was the corporation. The rule also preserved the accepted paradigm of criminal responsibility by concentrating on the acts and *mentes reae* of individuals; thus special treatment for corporations was avoided. In practice, however, it is often uncertain whether a particular employee has sufficient status within a corporation to count as the mind of that corporation: in one case, for example, the person, whose omission and mental state would have been sufficient, if attributed, to make the corporation criminally liable, was one of 2,900 section engineers employed by that corporation.[51] It is probably clear that members of the board of directors represent the directing mind of the relevant corporation; but to cut off the search for eligible persons at board level in a corporation of any significant size would probably go far towards securing immunity for that corporation from criminal conviction, since a director is unlikely to know of, let alone to have authorised, some particular defalcation of employees more junior than himself. This approach also suffers from the disadvantage that it requires at least one individual of the correct status to be found personally at fault, *i.e.* one such person who can be regarded as the perpetrator — again often a difficult matter in large modern corporations with many employees and many different management levels. Nevertheless, the American Model Penal Code follows a somewhat similar rule relative to offences other than "violations"[52] or specific statutory offences where a general vicarious liability is applicable in respect of any employee who acted on behalf of the corporation and within the scope of his office or employment[53]: apart from these exceptions,[54] a corporation is liable when the commission of an offense was "authorized, requested, commanded, performed or recklessly tolerated by the board of directors or by a high management agent acting

---

his knowledge might be attributed to the company itself: the appeal against conviction succeeded, but on the basis that the trial judge had told the jury that if *any* employee of the company had been deceived, then the company would also have been deceived — a ruling which did not accord at all with the directing mind theory.

[50] It seems clear that the English courts equate the directing mind of a corporation with its senior management, including (and sometimes being confined to) those having places on the board of directors — see, *e.g.*, *R. v. British Steel* [1995] 1 W.L.R. 1356, CA, opinion of the court (Steyn L.J.) at 1363B. See also *Seaboard Ltd v. Transport Secretary* [1994] 1 W.L.R. 541, HL, Lord Keith of Kinkell at 546E-F: the appeal succeeded in this case precisely because the Justices had convicted on the basis of fault by a person who was not a member of the company's senior management.

[51] *R. v. British Steel* [1995] 1 W.L.R. 1356, CA. In fact, the court decided that the offence in question was one of "absolute" liability subject to an objective defence of reasonable practicability, and that the corporate appellant was therefore criminally liable for the acts or failures of all its employees, regardless of position in the corporate hierarchy.

[52] Defined at para. 1.04(5) of the MPC (1985).

[53] M.P.C. (1985), para. 2.07(1)(a) and (4). It seems that corporate vicarious liability is applied to all Federal offenses in the U.S.A., such that a corporation is liable for the criminal conduct of any of its employees or agents provided that the offense was committed within the scope of the person's employment and the corporation benefited from its commission: see J. Gobert, "Corporate Criminality: New Crimes for the Times" [1994] Crim.L.R. 722, at 722; C. Wells, "Corporations: Culture, Risk and Criminal Liability" [1993] Crim.L.R. 551, at 563.

[54] And see also M.P.C. (1985) para. 2.07(1)(b).

in behalf of the corporation within the scope of his office or employment."[55]

Aggregation. One significant weakness of the "directing mind and will" approach[56] concerns its dependence on a positive outcome to the search for an individual who has criminal responsibility for the offence in question. (Provided he is of sufficient status to be regarded as the mind or part of the mind of the corporation which employs him, his act or omission and his mental state can be attributed to that corporation.) It has often been pointed out, however, that that search is unlikely to be successful outwith small, owner-managed companies because of the diversity of organisational structure found in large modern corporations, and that, in any event, blame is unlikely to be the preserve of, or necessarily deserved by, a single individual.[57] To overcome these problems, it has been suggested that a corporation should be criminally liable for the combined acts or failings, and the composite *mens rea*, of its employees. As Clarkson and Keating put it: "Under this doctrine one aggregates all the acts and mental elements of the various relevant persons within the company to ascertain whether, aggregated together, they would amount to a crime if they had all been committed by one person."[58] This begs the question of what is meant by "relevant persons", and, in so far as such persons are to be equated with senior management, this account might reproduce some of the significant restrictions on corporate liability imposed by the 'directing mind and will' model. There is also the problem that the aggregation doctrine departs from the paradigm case of criminal responsibility in terms of which the conduct and *mens rea* of an individual are to be considered and not the cumulation of parts of those elements from a number of persons; and it was indeed on this basis that the doctrine was rejected by the Divisional Court in *R. v. H.M. Coroner for East Kent, ex parte Spooner.*[59] In form, the doctrine follows the derivative approach of the 'directing mind and will' model considered above[60]: but in fact it seems to pass from an **8.94**

---

[55] *ibid.*, at para. 2.07(1)(c); a "high management agent" is defined as an officer of the corporation or unincorporated association or a partner in a partnership, or other agent of the corporation or association having duties of such responsibility that his conduct may be assumed to represent the policy of the corporation or association (see para. 2.07(4)).

[56] See para. 8.93, *supra*.

[57] See, *e.g.*, C.M.V. Clarkson, "Kicking Corporate Bodies and Damning their Souls" [1996] 59 M.L.R. 557, at 557–558, where it is pointed out that one of the few successful prosecutions in England of companies for manslaughter involved a small, owner-managed company — *Kite and O.L.L. Ltd, The Independent*, Dec. 9, 1994, unrep'd. *Cf. D.P.P. v. P. & O. European Ferries (Dover) Ltd* (1991) 93 Cr. App.R. 73. See also C. Wells, "The Corporate Manslaughter Proposals: Pragmatism, Paradox and Peninsularity" [1996] Crim.L.R. 545, at 547; J.Gobert, "Corporate Criminality: Four Models of Fault" (1994) L.S. 393, at 394.

[58] C.M.V. Clarkson and H.M. Keating, *Criminal Law: Text and Materials* (4th ed., 1998), at p.240. See also S. Field and N. Jörg, "Corporate Liability and Manslaughter: Should We be Going Dutch?" [1991] Crim.L.R. 156, at 161 and 167, where it is stated that the aggregation doctrine applies in Dutch law.

[59] (1989) 88 Cr.App.R. 10. This case concerned the judicial review of decisions reached by the coroner during the inquest into the loss of life following the sinking of the ferry "Herald of Free Enterprise" at Zeebrugge in 1987. The disaster was probably caused by the cumulative negligence and failures of many persons employed by the corporation which owned the ferry: see *D.P.P. v. P. & O. European Ferries (Dover) Ltd* (1991) 93 Cr.App.R. 73, where there was an unsuccessful attempt to prosecute the ferry owners for manslaughter.

[60] See para. 8.93, *supra*.

attributional to a direct liability model of responsibility where the corporation is made to answer for its own shortcomings as evidenced by the collective acts and failures of its personnel.

8–95 *Interpretative attribution.* The 'directing mind and will' approach attributes to a corporation the criminal responsibility of a human being who represents the controlling mind of that corporation and who acted in the course of his employment or office.[61] If the actual culprit is not of sufficient status within the organisational structure, the corporation will escape liability, although the culprit himself remains answerable to the law. This certainly represented the orthodox approach of English law to corporate criminal responsibility for most of the twentieth century: but the decision of the Privy Council in the civil case of *Meridian Global Funds Management Asia Ltd v. Securities Commission*[62] strongly suggests that the orthodox English view is too narrow and is based on an erroneous interpretation of the prior authorities. The opinion of the Court, read by Lord Hoffmann, is appropriately introduced in the following passage:

> "Any statement about what a company has or has not done, or can or cannot do, is necessarily a reference to the rules of attribution (primary and general) as they apply to that company. Judges sometimes say that a company 'as such' cannot do anything; it must act by servants or agents. This may seem an unexceptionable, even banal remark. And of course the meaning is usually perfectly clear. But a reference to a company 'as such' might suggest that there is something out there called the company of which one can meaningfully say that it can or cannot do something. There is in fact no such thing as the company as such, no ding an sich, only the applicable rules. To say that a company cannot do something means only that there is no one whose doing of that act would, under the applicable rule of attribution, count as an act of the company."[63]

The Court's 'primary rules' of attribution are those to be found in the company's constitution, such as that a decision taken by the Board of Directors will amount to an act of the company in question; the 'general rules', on the other hand, are those rules of law which apply also to human beings, such as rules of agency and vicarious liability (if such liability is applicable, as it is generally in tort or delict).[64] The Court's opinion continues by stating that many rules of law are so worded as to exclude agency or vicarious liability, as, for example, where a legal rule "requires an act or state of mind on the part of the person 'himself' as opposed to his servants or agents . . . [as] is generally true of the criminal law which ordinarily imposes liability only for the *actus reus* and *mens rea* of the defendant himself."[65] Where, therefore, the general rules of attribution are excluded expressly or by necessary implication by the terms of a legal rule, and assuming that (for example) the board of directors has not sanctioned a contravention of that rule, the question then arises as to whether that rule is applicable to corporations at all.

---

[61] See para. 8.93, *supra*.

[62] [1995] 3 W.L.R. 413. Although the case is a civil one, it is made plain by Lord Hoffmann, in delivering the opinion of the Privy Council, that the decision is intended to apply to criminal cases: see in particular what Lord Hoffmann states at 418C.

[63] *ibid.*, at 418H-419A.

[64] *ibid.*, at 418C-D.

[65] *ibid.*, at 418C.

The court accepts that certain rules may not be so applicable, and mentions in particular the sort of offence which carries only a punishment of community service. (Reference might also have been made, of course, to murder, for which the only available penalty is imprisonment for life.) It seems that whether or not such a rule is applicable to a corporation (in the absence of any express statement, such as in a statute, that it is so applicable) will depend on a court's interpretation of the content and policy of the rule: and once it has been determined that it does so apply, the crucial issue then arises as to "whose act (or knowledge, or state of mind) [is] for this purpose intended to count as the act etc. of the company? [And one] finds the answer to this question by applying the usual canons of interpretation, taking into account the language of the rule (if it is a statute) and its content and policy."[66] In this way, a court may fashion a special rule of attribution which is tailored to the particular substantive rule of law in question.

Thus far, the above exposition is capable of leading merely to an **8.96** endorsement of the 'directing mind and will' approach to corporate liability; but it is clear that that was not the Privy Council's intention, for they proceed to demolish any such view. In particular, the case of *Lennard's Carrying Co. Ltd v. Asiatic Petroleum Co. Ltd*[67] is examined and reinterpreted. That case was concerned with section 502 of the Merchant Shipping Act 1894 under which a ship owner's liability for loss of cargo might be avoided if he could show the loss occurred without his actual fault or privity.

Where a company was the owner of the ship in question it was necessary to consider whose (if anyone's) fault or privity (or the lack of it) was to be considered as that of the company. The opinion of Viscount Haldane in the case has traditionally been regarded as one of the foundations of the 'directing mind and will' model of corporate liability. As reinterpreted by the Privy Council, however, Viscount Haldane is shown to have rejected the applicability of vicarious liability in view of the language of the relevant section of the 1894 statute, and also to have rejected the suggestion that that section did not apply to a company as owner of a ship. "Instead, guided by the language and purpose of the section, he looked for the person whose functions in the company, in relation to the cause of the casualty [fire in the ship due to the unseaworthy nature of the ship's boilers], were the same as those to be expected of the individual ship owner to whom the language principally applied. Who in the company was responsible for maintaining the condition of the ship, receiving the reports of the master and ship's agents, authorising repairs etc? That person was Mr. Lennard, whom Viscount Haldane L.C., at pp. 713-714, described as the 'directing mind and will' of the company. It was therefore his fault or privity which section 502 attributed to the company."[68] In short, it was fortuitous that a person answering to that description was the person pointed out by the specific rule of attribution applicable to section 502: and it had not been Viscount Haldane's intention to express "a general metaphysic of companies".[69] The important consideration was thus the identifying of

---

[66] *ibid.*, at 419E-F.

[67] [1915] A.C. 705.

[68] *Meridian Global Funds Management Asia Ltd v. Securities Commission* [1995] 3 W.L.R. 413, at 421C-D.

[69] *ibid.*, at 421E.

the person pointed out by the appropriate rule of attribution rather than the identifying of a person of particular status within an anthropomorphic concept of a corporation, and it had been wrong for Lord Justice Denning in *H.L. Bolton (Engineering) Co. Ltd v. T.J. Graham and Sons Ltd*[70] to perpetuate such a concept by distinguishing between the hands of a corporation and its brain and nerve centre for the purpose of attributing liability.

8.97 In a similar way, the case of *Tesco Ltd v. Nattrass*[71] is explained by the Court in *Meridian Global Funds Management Asia Ltd v. Securities Commission*[72] not as one of the leading authorities supporting the 'directing mind and will' approach but rather as an application of the 'particular rule of attribution' model, the particular rule being derived from the relevant substantive law's content and policy. The substantive law there was contained in section 11(2) of the Trade Descriptions Act 1968, which proscribed the offering of goods for sale at a price less than that for which they were actually being sold, and in section 24(1) thereof, which allowed a defence to a shop owner who proved that the contravention of section 11(2) was occasioned by another person whilst he (the shop owner) took all reasonable precautions and exercised all due diligence to avoid such a contravention on the part of himself or any person under his control. In the case, the contravention was caused by the negligent conduct of the manager of a store owned by a company whose senior management had exercised due diligence to prevent any such contravention. The question, therefore, was posed whether the exercise of due diligence applied to a store manager employed by the company as well as to the senior management of that company. In other words, the question lay as to whether one employee's lack of due diligence could be attributed to the company, thus destroying the basis of its defence under section 24(1). The decision that it was not to be so attributed is consistent with the 'directing mind and will' model; but the Privy Council's view in *Meridian*[72a] is that the House of Lords in *Tesco*[72b] considered the content and policy of the legislation and arrived at a rule of attribution which was consistent rather with the scheme of consumer protection which the Trade Descriptions Act espoused — namely, the encouragement of a sufficient supervisory scheme by senior management to avoid contraventions of section 11(2): had the view been taken that any lack of diligence by any employee negatived the statutory defence, that defence would have been rendered pointless, and the intention of Parliament — to set up a morally justifiable (as opposed presumably to an absolute) scheme of consumer protection — would have been defeated.[73]

---

[70] [1957] 1 Q.B. 159, at 172.

[71] [1972] A.C. 153.

[72] [1995] 3 W.L.R. 413.

[72a] *ibid.*

[72b] [1972] A.C. 153.

[73] *ibid.*, at 419G-420E. The Privy Council also explains (at 420E-H) the decision in *In re Supply of Ready Mixed Concrete (No. 2)*, [1995] 1 A.C. 456, HL, where restrictive trade agreements entered into against the express instructions of senior management of the companies involved, and without their knowledge, were nevertheless to be attributed to those companies, as the result of the application of a rule of attribution arrived at after due consideration of the content and policy of section 35(1) of the Restrictive Trade Practices Act 1976; of that case, it was said that that policy would have been of little value

In *Meridian*[74] itself two men, below the level of the board of directors or of the managing director of the investment company by whom they were employed, used company funds to buy shares in a quoted company which they planned to acquire for their own purposes. They did not intend that the board or the managing director should discover what they had done; but the company thus became a substantial shareholder in a quoted company and, under the provisions of the New Zealand Securities Amendment Act 1988, was required officially to register that fact at once. The company failed to do so since it was unaware of the transactions which had made it such a shareholder. In terms of the approach favoured by the Privy Council, the content and policy of the legislation was considered and used to generate the rule of attribution under which the conduct and knowledge of the two employees was attributed to their employer company. The policy was plainly to compel immediate disclosure of such share holdings, for the information of the fast moving financial markets in which the company operated, and such legislative intention would be defeated if the knowledge of employees, who had the authority of the company to act as they had done, was not attributed to that company.[75] **8.98**

The Privy Council in *Meridian*[75a] were at some pains to emphasise that their decision was not intended to suggest that, where an employee of a corporation has the authority of that corporation to act as he did, knowledge of what he did is automatically to be attributed to that corporation: rather "It is a question of construction in each case as to whether the particular rule requires that the knowledge that an act has been done, or the state of mind with which it was done, should be attributed to the company."[76]

There is little doubt that the subtle approach favoured in *Meridian*[76a] represents an improvement on the narrow focus of the 'directing mind and will' method of deciding when a corporation will have criminal liability where a substantive rule is applicable to corporations but vicarious liability is inapplicable: but the actual decision in the case could be, and was by the New Zealand Court of Appeal, justified under the 'directing mind and will' approach, since at least one of the two employees had previously been managing director of the company and could still have been described as a senior manager at the relevant time. The *Meridian*[76b] approach also relies on interpretation of the relevant substantive legal rule in order to assess the policy which drives that rule; the particular attributive rule is then formed in accordance with that **8.99**

---

if it could be defeated by senior management's lack of knowledge of the conduct of their unit, area and sales managers. But the case was ultimately concerned with whether the companies in question were in breach of injunctions obtained against them by the Director General of Fair Trading, and thus in contempt of court: and it may be that in relation to contempt proceedings, companies are vicariously liable for the conduct of their employees — see *Z Bank v. D1 & Ors.* [1994] 1 Lloyds Rep. 656; *cf. Seaboard Ltd v. Transport Secretary* [1994] 1 W.L.R. 541, HL. See also the Privy Council's approval in *Meridian* of the decision in *Moore v. I. Bressler Ltd* [1944] 2 All E.R. 515.

[74] [1995] 3 W.L.R. 413.

[75] *ibid.*, at 423B-D. The court said that it did not matter that the employees had acted for a corrupt purpose and did not want their employers to know of their actions.

[75a] *ibid.*

[76] *ibid.*, at 423E.

[76a] *ibid.*

[76b] *ibid.*

policy. Courts are, of course, well used to assessing legislative intention by consideration of statutory rules in accordance with allowable construction techniques; but unless corporate liability is to be confined to statutory crimes, it is not particularly easy to see how the content and policy of common law crimes can be assessed in order to generate an appropriate rule of attribution. At the end of the day, this approach perhaps allows too much discretion to courts at too many points to command universal acceptance; and it will be greeted with dismay by those who search for a general rule of universal application.[77]

Direct Corporate Liability

8.100 It has been said of derivative approaches to corporate responsibility that the courts have used them "in a regressive manner that has all but insulated large companies from criminal liability",[78] and consequently that other ways of thinking should be adopted. In recent years too, a series of incidents such as ferry capsizings and rail crashes involving significant loss of life have highlighted the relative inability of English prosecutors, using the orthodox approach to corporate liability,[79] to convict of manslaughter the corporations which operated the ferries or rail services in question.[80] There are perhaps two significant suggestions as to how these difficulties might be overcome — by creating special offences for corporations, which will cater directly for the differences there are between human and corporate accused, and by finding a special type of moral responsibility in the policies and institutional practices of corporations: both lead to direct corporate criminal liability without the need to identify particular employees as culprits, and both, in so far as the United Kingdom is concerned, lie in the realm of law reform.

8.101 *Corporate offences.* A pattern for special corporate offences may be found in existing statutes such as the Health and Safety at Work Act 1974. In sections 2 and 3, for instance, employers are required to conduct their business operations in ways which, so far as reasonably practicable will maximise the safety of their own employees as well as of other persons who are affected by such operations; and offences are created for employers who (or which) fail in these duties. In short, it is not necessary, as is so often the case in offences designed primarily for human accused, that a particular result be proved or shown to have been intended: instead, it is the failure in duty which matters for the purposes of conviction.[81]

The Law Commission has fairly recently proposed an offence of this nature to cover the difficulty of prosecuting corporations for manslaughter in England. The proposed offence of "corporate killing" is

---

[77] *cf.* the opinion of Lord Maxwell in *Dean v. John Menzies (Holdings) Ltd*,1981 J.C. 23, at 37 *et seq*.

[78] J. Gobert, "Corporate Criminality: four models of fault" (1994) 14 L.S. 393, at 393. This statement preceded the Privy Council's decision in *Meridian Global Funds Management Asia Ltd v. Securities Commission* [1995] 3 W.L.R. 413; see paras 8.95 to 8.99, *supra*.

[79] *i.e.*, the directing mind and will model: see para. 8.93, *supra*.

[80] See, *e.g.*, C.M.V. Clarkson, "Kicking Corporate Bodies and Damning Their Souls" (1996) 59 M.L.R. 554.

[81] See J. Gobert, "Corporate Criminality: New Crimes for the Times" [1994] Crim.L.R. 722, at 724–726.

committed if "management failure" causes, or is one of the causes of, the death of a human being; and such failure is reflected in conduct which falls far below the standard to be expected of the corporation in the circumstances. The offence is predicated on the definition of "management failure" which is stated to be present when the way in which the corporation manages and organises its operations fails to ensure the health and safety of its own employees or others affected by those operations. The suggested punishment is a fine or, perhaps, an appropriate remedial order.[82] Clearly, the offence concentrates on direct corporate liability rather than on liability derived from the defalcations of particular employees; but the proposal has been criticised in that it fails to identify what is meant by 'management' within a corporation,[83] and also runs the risk of trivialising corporately caused human death by diverting attention away from the loss of life itself.[84]

Corporate fault. Some commentators who are opposed to the creation **8.102**
of special offences for corporations, or who highlight problems associated with such offences, believe on principle that conventional criminal law is, or should be, applicable to corporations provided that the notion of *mens rea* is adapted to corporate realities[85]: and indeed it may be noticed that derivative accounts of corporate liability, at least where vicarious responsibility would not apply in relation to individual accused, involve the piling of fiction upon fiction. C.M.V. Clarkson argues that corporations themselves can be seen as "culpability-bearing agents who through their rules, policies and operational procedures can exhibit the required degree of *mens rea* and be blamed therefor."[86] It may be riposted that such rules, policies and procedures are nothing other than the productions of the servants and agents of the corporation in question, and the productions of particular individuals at that. But James Gobert has argued that a particular policy or practice may emerge from a corporation without that policy or practice being derived from any individual within that corporation.[87] As it has also been put: "[T]he policies, standing orders, regulations and institutional practices of corporations are evidence of corporate aims, intentions and knowledge that are not reducible to the aims, intentions and knowledge of individuals

---

[82] Law Commission No. 237, *Legislating the Criminal Code: Involuntary Manslaughter* (H. of C. No. 171, Session 1995–96), Pt. VIII, Chap. 4, esp. paras 4(1), (2). This new offence is to be a non-mandatory alternative to the proposed new offences of reckless killing and killing by gross negligence which the Commission propose as replacements for the current English common law offence of involuntary manslaughter.

[83] See Celia Wells, "The Corporate Manslaughter Proposals: Pragmatism, Paradox and Peninsularity" [1996] Crim.L.R. 545, at 552–3.

[84] See C.M.V. Clarkson, "Kicking Corporate Bodies and Damning their Souls" (1996) 59 M.L.R. 557, at 569–570; J. Ross, "Corporate Criminal Liability: One Form or Many Forms?" 1999 J.R. 49, at 61–62. *Cf.* James Gobert, "Corporate Criminality: New Crimes for the Times" [1994] Crim.L.R. 722, at 726.

[85] See, *e.g.*, R. Mays, "The Criminal Liability of Corporations and Scots Law: Learning the Lessons of Anglo-American Jurisprudence" (2000) 4 E.L.R. 46, esp. pp.56–58, and the Appendix at pp.72–73 where a suggested new approach to corporate criminal liability is worked out in some detail; C.M.V. Clarkson, "Kicking Corporate Bodies and Damning their Souls" (1996) 59 M.L.R. 557; J. Gobert, "Corporate Criminality: New Crimes for the Times" [1994] Crim.L.R. 722, at 726 *et seq.*

[86] *Op.cit.* at 571.

[87] J. Gobert, *op.cit.*, at 723. See also J. Gobert, "Corporate liability: four models of fault" (1994) 14 L.S. 393, at 408.

within that corporation. Such regulations and standing orders are authoritative, not because any individual devised them, but because they have emerged from a decision making process recognised as authoritative within the corporation"[88]; and, as it has been suggested, "[a] company should be criminally liable where a crime is authorised, permitted or tolerated as a matter of company policy or *de facto* practice", although the author thereof concedes that finding such a policy may pose considerable difficulties.[89] Australian Federal Law[90] seems to endorse the same general idea in that it lays down that in an offence of intention, knowledge or recklessness, fault is to be attributed to a corporation which expressly, tacitly or impliedly authorised or permitted the commission of such an offence, and includes the case where 'corporate culture' authorised or permitted it. The legislation then proceeds to indicate that 'corporate culture' can be found in the attitudes, policies, rules, course of conduct or practices within the corporate body — either as a whole or in that part of the corporation where the offence occurred. Such approaches avoid the problem of finding individuals within the corporation who are themselves blameworthy as individuals by focusing instead on the notion of corporate moral responsibility.[91] It is difficult to imagine, however, the adoption of such ideas by United Kingdom courts without the assistance of legislation.[92]

Scots Law

8.103 Scots law accepts that a "limited company can only act through its employees or servants",[93] and that partnerships can only "act by the hands of their partners and employees".[94] It follows that corporate bodies including partnerships can generally be convicted of crimes only where there is some rule which permits the acts (and, where required, *mens rea*) of the actual human culprit to be attributed to them.

---

[88] S. Field and N. Jörg, "Corporate Manslaughter: Should We be Going Dutch?" [1991] Crim.L.R. 156, at 159.

[89] J. Gobert, "Corporate Criminality: New Crimes for the Times" [1994] Crim.L.R. 722, at 728.

[90] Federal Criminal Code Act 1995, s.12.3, as narrated and commented upon by C. Wells in "The Corporate Manslaughter Proposals: Pragmatism, Paradox and Peninsularity" [1996] Crim.L.R. 545, at 552–553.

[91] See S. Field and N. Jörg, "Corporate Manslaughter: Should We be Going Dutch?" [1991] Crim.L.R. 156, at 159.

[92] A more radical approach to corporate liability is suggested by Fisse and Braithwaite, whose views are conveniently summarised in C.M.V. Clarkson and H.M. Keating, *Criminal Law: Text and Materials* (4th ed., 1998) at pp.240–241. Basically what they propose involves corporate fault found in the inability of a corporation satisfactorily to identify and discipline those employees in fact responsible for an offence, the corporation having been ordered by a court to do such things; the premise is that the corporation is better able than anyone else to identify the culprits. This type of approach is rejected by R. Mays in his article "The Criminal Liability of Corporations and Scots Law: Learning the Lessons of Anglo-American Jurisprudence" (2000) 4 E.L.R. 46, at pp.53 and 57.

[93] *Docherty v. Stakis Hotels Ltd; Stakis Hotels Ltd v. Docherty*, 1991 S.C.C.R. 6, L.J.-C. Ross at 14C. See also *Duguid v. Fraser*, 1942 S.L.T. 51, Lord Jamieson at 54. *Cf. Industrial Distributions (Central Scotland) Ltd v. Quinn*, 1984 S.L.T. (Notes) 240, where admissions by two directors of a company that their company was responsible for VAT offences were taken to be admissions by the company. For a critical account of the Scots law relative to corporate criminal liability, see R. Mays, "The Criminal Liability of Corporations and Scots Law: Learning the Lessons of Anglo-American Jurisprudence" (2000) 4 E.L.R. 46, at pp.49–54.

[94] *McKay Bros v. Gibb*, 1969 S.L.T. 216, L.J.-C. Grant at 219. See also *Douglas v. Phoenix Motors*, 1970 S.L.T. (Sh.Ct.) 57. A local authority may also be body corporate — *cf. Armour v. Skeen*, 1977 S.L.T. 71.

Statutory offences. Where a statutory offence is one attracting vicarious liability and liability is also strict, no additional rule of attribution is required: nor is it then necessary to identify the precise culprit, provided he was an employee of the corporation and was acting at the time within the scope of his employment.[95] It seems that strict liability offences also pose no particular problems for corporate liability[96]: but where some form of *mens rea* is required, as in offences of permitting something to occur where knowledge must be shown, a rule of attribution would seem to be necessary. The case law is such, however, that no clear rule has emerged, other than that the knowledge of *some* employees may be attributed to the employing corporation. In *Clydebank Co-operative Society Ltd v. Binnie*,[97] for example, where the driver of a hired vehicle knew that the hirer was allowing other passengers to be picked up on the journey to a sanatorium (but did not know that they were paying separate fares, which was the crucial fact relative to the offence), and the driver told the transport manager what he knew, that manager's wilful blindness relative to the existence of the crucial fact was imputed to the company which employed them both and owned the vehicle: the company was thus guilty of permitting the vehicle to be used as an express carriage without being in possession of an appropriate licence. It is not clear if the driver's knowledge would have sufficed for the company's conviction; but the impression gained from the case is that it might not have been sufficient. *Clydebank Co-operative Society Ltd v. Binnie*[97a] was quoted as authority by Lord Justice-Clerk Grant in the case of *Mackay Bros v. Gibb*,[98] where a partnership was charged with having permitted the use of a car which had a tyre with an insufficient depth of tread. Since the 'garage controller' employed by the firm had not checked the tyre before hiring out the car to which it was attached, and since he was inexcusably ignorant of the law's requirements as to tyre condition, he and thus the firm were held to have satisfied the essentials of the offence: the garage controller's wilful blindness, and thus constructive knowledge, were imputed to the firm.[99] These two cases do not make clear whether an employee must be of a particular rank or status within the corporation for his acts and *mens rea* to be attributed to that corporation; and it is certainly not clear that the person whose knowledge (or constructive knowledge) was so attributed could be described as the directing mind and will[1] of either of the corporate bodies in question. The case of *Readers Digest Assoc. Ltd v. Pirie*[2] does, however, contemplate the relevance of the directing mind and 8.104

---

[95] *cf.*, *Wilson v. Allied Breweries Ltd; Wilson v. Chieftain Inns Ltd*, 1986 S.C.C.R. 11.

[96] See *Macnab v. Alexanders of Greenock*, 1971 S.L.T. 121, esp. L.J.-C. Grant at 124–125.

[97] 1937 S.L.T. 114. See also *Macdonald v. Wilmae Concrete Co. Ltd*, 1954 S.L.T. (Sh.Ct.) 33.

[97a] *ibid.*

[98] 1969 S.L.T. 216.

[99] The *ratio* of the case is somewhat blurred by the opinions of Lord Wheatley and Lord Milligan: the former referred to there being "vicarious knowledge" (at p.220), whilst the latter (*ibid.*) believed the offence in question to be one of absolute liability. See also *Brown v. W. Burns Tractors Ltd*, 1986 S.C.C.R. 146, where the High Court, in a "causing and permitting" case, upheld the Crown's argument that the wilful blindness of a clerical assistant could, in the circumstances, be attributed to the employing company: as Lord Hunter, with whom L.J.-C. Ross and Lord Robertson agreed, stated at p.149, "Mrs. Locke was in the position not merely of an employee of the respondent company, but also of a person to whom had been delegated an important part of its administration and control".

[1] See para 8.93, *supra*.

[2] 1973 S.L.T. 170.

will theory to statutory offences where knowledge is required: unfortunately, the court there decided the appeal without having to reach a concluded opinion on the attribution of knowledge; but Lord Justice-Clerk Wheatley did refer to the House of Lords decision in *Tesco Ltd v. Nattrass*[3] in rejecting the suggestion that the knowledge of a junior employee could be attributed to the appellant company.[4]

8.105 *Common law crimes.* As far as common law crimes are concerned, no question of strict or vicarious liability arises: *mens rea* is always required. It follows that if a corporation is to be convicted of such a crime, the acts and *mens rea* of a servant or agent must be considered to be the acts and *mens rea* of the corporation by virtue of some rule of attribution. Scots law has accepted that a corporation can be guilty of attempted fraud. In *Purcell Meats (Scotland) Ltd v. McLeod*,[5] a limited company was charged with attempting to perform various acts "by the hands of persons unknown" and thus with attempting to commit fraud. The company unsuccessfully raised objections before the sheriff court to the competency and relevancy of the complaint, but appealed the sheriff's decision on these objections to the High Court. The principal ground of appeal was that it was incompetent to charge a corporate body with a common law crime, since a corporation was incapable of forming the necessary *mens rea* for such a crime. This submission was not in fact addressed by the court, since the Crown accepted at the appeal that the *mens rea* necessary for attempted fraud would have to be proved against the company, and that the success of the prosecution would depend on whether, at an eventual trial, they could show that the "persons unknown" referred to in the complaint were of such status within the company as to enable the trial judge to conclude that the acts (and presumably *mens rea*) of such persons were the acts of the company itself. The Crown also referred to the House of Lords case of *Tesco Ltd v. Nattrass*[6] and in particular to a passage from the speech of Lord Reid there,[7] where his Lordship refers to the 'directing mind and will' rule of attribution.[8] Lord Justice-Clerk Ross, in delivering the opinion of the court stated as follows:

> "Having regard to what Lord Reid said in that passage we are of opinion that in the present case it will only be once the facts have emerged that it will be possible to conclude whether the persons by whose hands the particular acts were performed were of such status and at such a level in the company's employment that it would be open to the sheriff to draw the conclusion that the acts fell to be regarded as acts of the company rather than acts of the individual. It may not be easy for the Crown to establish its case, but in our opinion from the point of view of the competency and specification of this charge, it is sufficient now that the charge libels that the acts in

---

[3] [1972] A.C. 153.

[4] *ibid.*, at p.176; Lord Kissen, at p.178, also refers briefly to *Tesco Ltd v. Nattrass*. It is of interest that the sheriff at first instance took the view that since all the relevant information lay somewhere within the company's organisation, the company did have the knowledge that the goods in question were unsolicited. This would have amounted to an application of the aggregation doctrine (see para. 8.94, *supra*); but Lord Kissen, at p.178, expressly repudiated the sheriff's view.

[5] 1986 S.C.C.R. 672.

[6] [1972] A.C. 153.

[7] *ibid.*, at p.170, quoted in *Purcell Meats* at pp.675–676.

[8] See para. 8.93, *supra*.

question were done by the hands of persons unknown. If the acts were done by persons who were not employed by the company or by employees who had no authority to do the acts, the Crown may fail."[9]

This case is authority, therefore, for the competency of a charge of attempted fraud brought against a corporation. It does not decide the larger issue as to whether *any* common law crime may be committed by a corporate body.[10] It does, however, endorse the 'directing mind and will' approach to corporate liability, although it provides no guidance as to the required status of the person whose acts and *mens rea* are to be taken as those of his employer corporation: he must, of course, be an employee (not necessarily identifiable by name by the prosecutor) of that corporation acting within the scope of his authority as such an employee. The only authority, apart from *Tesco Ltd v. Nattrass*,[10a] mentioned (albeit rather briefly) by the court is that of *Dean v. John Menzies (Holdings) Ltd.*[11]

Dean v. John Menzies (Holdings) Ltd.[11a] In this case, a limited company was charged with the common law offence of shameless indecency by selling or exposing for sale in its retail shops certain magazines alleged by the Crown to be of an indecent or obscene nature. The subject of the appeal in the case was a sheriff's decision that the charge was incompetent since a corporation could not commit a common law offence since all such offences required *mens rea*.[12] Lords Stott and Maxwell declined to decide the broad question of whether a corporation could commit such an offence, and instead confined their attentions to the more particular question of whether a limited company could be guilty of the specific crime in fact charged. They both answered that question in the negative, but for somewhat different reasons. Lord Stott took the view that there were some offences which could not be committed by corporations[13] and that the specific crime charged in this case was such an offence. In his view, the central feature of that crime was the quality of shamelessness which the accused must be shown to have possessed; and it was simply not possible for a non-human person to exhibit a sense of shame.[14] Lord Maxwell agreed that the offence charged involved a type of behavioural trait of which only human beings were capable, but thought that it might be possible to attribute that trait to a corporation in accordance with the general theory of corporate liability.[15] He accepted, in other words, that fictions were used in law to attribute to a corporation human characteristics which, by its very nature, it could not actually have; but he was unable to endorse the Crown's contention that there was a clear, single fiction which applied in this case and which would render competent the charge against the **8.106**

---

[9] 1986 S.C.C.R. at p.676.

[10] See para. 8.107, *infra*.

[10a] [1972] A.C. 153.

[11] 1981 J.C. 23.

[11a] *ibid.*

[12] The sheriff's view was that since a corporation had no mind, it could not be shown to have *mens rea* or dole.

[13] See para. 8.107, *infra*.

[14] See 1981 J.C. at pp.35–36.

[15] See para. 8.103, *supra*.

company.[16] Instead, with reference to Scottish and English authority, he was of opinion that the courts did not employ any single fiction (or rule of attribution). As he put the matter: "It seems to me that the approach of the courts has been this. Where the plain requirements of justice, the express provisions of statute, or the presumed intentions of Parliament require human characteristics to be attributed to corporations the courts provide the necessary fictions tailored to give effect to those requirements, provisions or intentions."[17] In particular, he did not consider that the Scottish cases[18] showed any clear or consistent fiction: and thus he found it difficult "to hold that the present complaint is competent because of a fiction, without knowing with reasonable precision what the fiction is."[19] His final conclusion is this: "In the light of the authorities cited to us I am not satisfied that the common law of Scotland recognises any clear single fiction which would, for purposes of criminal responsibility, in all matters attribute to a company the kind of human characteristics and conduct alleged in this complaint."[20]

Unlike the majority of the court, Lord Cameron in his dissenting opinion addressed himself to the issue of whether a corporation could be guilty of common law offences. In concluding that it could, he emphasised that it was the purpose of rules of attribution to enable corporations to be vested with capabilities otherwise not consistent with their personality. "It is trite law . . . that a company is legally capable of many deliberate actions within the limit of its powers as set out in its Articles of Association, these powers being exercised by those who are the 'directing mind' or 'will' of the company."[21] He also emphasised that in his view *mens rea* (or wicked intent) was as much an inference from the circumstances as an actual state of mind,[22] and that, therefore, from the point of view of dole, there was not necessarily the wide gap between an individual and a corporate accused as was sometimes suggested. Thus armed, he was able to conclude that the offence in question was such that a corporation might be convicted of committing it: shamelessness was an objective and not a subjective consideration, and could be proved if the sale or exposure for sale to the public was done either with the intention of depraving or corrupting the purchasers or deliberately, in

---

[16] The Crown appears to have favoured the 'directing mind and will' rule of attribution, although Lord Maxwell pointed out that the Advocate-Depute at times seemed to base his argument on the policy of the company to stock and expose for sale such magazines as were the subject of the complaint: see 1981 J.C. at pp.38–39 and 44–45. *Cf.* para 8.102, *supra*.

[17] 1981 J.C. at p.39. Of the stated issues, the one which is solely applicable to common law crimes is the first, *viz*. "the plain requirements of justice" — which was in fact used by the sheriff in *Purcell Meats (Scotland) Ltd v. Macleod*, 1986 S.C.C.R. 672, at p.674, to justify his decision that attempted fraud was a charge which could competently be brought against a corporation: see para. 8.105, *supra*. It is perhaps noteworthy that Lord Maxwell, in the quoted passage, appears to anticipate the opinion of the Privy Council in *Meridian Global Funds Management Asia Ltd v. Securities Commission* [1995] 3 W.L.R. 413: see paras 8.95 *et seq*., *supra*.

[18] See para. 8.104, *supra*.

[19] 1981 J.C., at p.42.

[20] *ibid*., at p.45.

[21] *ibid*., at p.29. The references here to *Lennard's Carrying Co. Ltd v. Asiatic Petroleum Co. Ltd* [1915] A.C. 705, the opinion of Visc. Haldane at p.713, and to *H.L. Bolton (Engineering) Co. Ltd v. T.J. Graham and Sons Ltd* [1957] 1 Q.B. 159, the opinion of L.J. Denning at 172, confirm that Lord Cameron favoured the 'directing mind and will' rule of attribution, and that he also favoured the view that only those at board of director, or equivalent, level would count *quoad* that rule.

[22] *ibid*., citing Macdonald (5th ed., 1948), at p.1.

the knowledge that the content of the magazines was likely to deprave or corrupt them.[23]

It may be conjectured that if the competency of such a charge as was brought in *Dean v. John Menzies (Holdings) Ltd*[24] was to be argued afresh today, Lord Cameron's views would be likely to prevail over those of Lords Stott and Maxwell: there seems no particularly good reason for granting immunity to a limited company which retails obscene material in circumstances where an individual retailer would be liable to conviction.

Limitations on corporate criminal liability. *Dean v. John Menzies (Holdings) Ltd*[25] provides authority for the proposition that there are some offences which a corporation is incapable of committing. There may be a variety of reasons for this conclusion, not all of them convincing. If, for example, the only punishment for an offence is a period of imprisonment without the alternative of a fine, as is the case in murder,[26] a corporate body cannot be punished if convicted, and this *may* be considered to provide practical immunity from prosecution.[27] The same applies where the sole punishment available for a crime is corporal or one of community service, *i.e.* wherever the penalty is one which only a human being may undergo. In *Dean v. John Menzies (Holdings) Ltd*[27a] itself, Lord Stott[28] accepted that, in addition to shameless indecency, reset or perjury were probably not offences which corporations could commit; but he gave no reason why those two offences should be excepted. Perjury may be a justifiable exception in that a corporation cannot be put on oath; but it is difficult to see why, in appropriate circumstances and by use of an appropriate rule of attribution, a corporation could not be convicted of reset[29]: it would scarcely be a novelty for possession and knowledge to be attributable to a corporate body. Lord Cameron too seems to accept in the same case that there are crimes, such as rape, which are obviously and necessarily physical acts of a natural person[30]: but once it is accepted that corporations can only act through natural persons,[31] it is not easy to see why such a crime could not be attributed to a corporation in appropriate circumstances.[32] **8.107**

With respect to statutory offences, it may be the intention of Parliament that corporations should be excluded from liability. In *Gray*

---

[23] *ibid.*, at pp.32–33. As the crime of shameless indecency has been developed, Lord Cameron's account of the *mens rea* has proved to be correct: see, *e.g.*, *Paterson v. Lees*, 1999 S.C.C.R. 231, Lord Sutherland at p.236A.

[24] 1981 J.C. 23.

[25] 1981 J.C. 23.

[26] See 1995 Act, s.205. See also *Dean v. John Menzies (Holdings) Ltd*, 1981 J.C. 23, Lord Cameron at pp.29 and 33; Lord Stott at p.35.

[27] See *N.B. Ry. Co. v. Dumbarton Harbour Board* (1900) 3 Adam 121, L.J.-C. Macdonald at p.125, Lord Trayner at p.128, Lord Moncreiff at p.129. *Cf.*, J.M. Ross, "Corporate Liability for Crime", 1990 S.L.T. (News) 265, at 266, where it is pointed out that there is a confusion here between penalty and liability; see also R. Mays, "The Criminal Liability of Corporations and Scots Law: Learning the Lessons of Anglo-American Jurisprudence" (2000) 4 E.L.R. 46, at pp.62–63 and 69–70.

[27a] 1981 J.C. 23.

[28] 1981 J.C. 23, at p.35.

[29] See D. Whyte, "Corporate Criminal Liability", 1987 S.L.T. (News) 348.

[30] 1981 J.C. 23, at p.33.

[31] See para. 8.103, *supra*.

[32] See J.M. Ross, "Corporate Liability for Crime", 1990 S.L.T. (News) 265, at p.268, where the question is posed: "Were, for example, a film company to decide to make a film of a rape and to decide at the highest level to procure a rape for that purpose would it be beyond commonsense to charge the company with rape?".

v. Brembridge,[33] for example, the offence was so worded that it was unlawful for any person to assume or use the title chemist and druggist "unless such person shall be a pharmaceutical chemist . . . and be registered under the Act"[34]; and it was held that the offence in its terms could not, therefore, be committed by a company which had utilised the words 'chemist' and 'druggist' in its trading name, since only a human being could be qualified to be a pharmaceutical chemist. The court in that case seems to have regarded the immunity of corporations as the inevitable consequence of thoughtless Parliamentary drafting: but the Scottish courts have sometimes, not perhaps always justifiably, imputed to the legislature the intention to exclude corporations from criminal liability. In *Docherty v. Stakis Hotels Ltd; Stakis Hotels Ltd v. Docherty*,[35] for example, it was decided that regulation 32(2) of the Food Hygiene Regulations 1959 was such that a corporation, as opposed to an actual human being, could not be "a person having the management and control of a food business", and thus that where a limited company owned premises where a food business was conducted, it could not competently be charged with the relevant offence *as such a person*. There seems no good reason why the hotel company should not have been considered to have management and control though the hands of their manager — as the complaint narrated; if there is any reason for rules of attribution to have evolved, it is surely to provide for such circumstances.

8.108 INDIVIDUAL RESPONSIBILITY. Where the managers of a corporation commit a crime on its behalf they are criminally responsible whether or not the company is also charged. The High Court has approved of a situation in which both a one-man company and its director were fined for contravening a statute which provided that in the case of a contravention both the company and its directors should be responsible.[36]

8.109 *Statutory provisions.* Many modern statutes provide that where the statute is contravened by a body corporate both that body and its officers (usually its directors, managers, secretaries and other officers)[37] shall be responsible.[38] The main purpose of such provisions appears to be to create individual responsibility for what the corporation does rather than to create corporate responsibility for the acts of individuals.[39] Many statutes provide that where an offence committed by a corporation is proved to have been committed with the consent or connivance of, or to have been attributable to any neglect on the part of, any director, manager, secretary or other similar officer, he as well as that corporation will be guilty of the offence[40]; other statutes provide that all officers are responsible unless they can prove lack of knowledge or consent.[41]

---

[33] (1887) 1 White 445.

[34] Pharmacy Act 1868, s.1.

[35] 1991 S.C.C.R. 6.

[36] *Sarna v. Adair*, 1954 J.C. 141.

[37] A local authority director of roads is a "manager, secretary or other similar officer" of the authority: *Armour v. Skeen*, 1977 J.C. 15.

[38] See *Huckerby v. Elliot* [1970] 1 All E.R. 189.

[39] See Gl. Williams, para. 284.

[40] *e.g.* Trade Descriptions Act 1968, s.20; Misuse of Drugs Act 1971, s.21; Health and Safety at Work Act 1974, s.37; Social Security Administration Act 1992, s.115; Pension Schemes Act 1993, s.169. Neglect is attributable where the accused has failed to take steps to prevent the commission of an offence by a corporation, if taking these steps falls or should be held to fall within the scope of the functions of his office: *Wotherspoon v. H.M. Advocate*, 1978 J.C. 74. L.J.-G. Emslie at 78.

[41] *e.g.* Official Secrets Act 1920, s.8(5).

CHAPTER 9

ERROR

Error is of importance in the criminal law in two ways: as evidence that certain acts were not committed or certain results not caused intentionally, and as a factor which induces an agent to do certain things intentionally. **9.01**

Error as evidence of lack of intention

The criminal courts are concerned with error in this sense only where A has done something which he claims he did not mean to do, and where he supports his claim by reference to an error under which he laboured. As has been pointed out, A does an act intentionally only under a description of the act which is limited to circumstances of which he is aware. A cannot intentionally strike a policeman if he is unaware that he is a policeman, or intentionally have intercourse with a 15-year-old if he does not know her age. It does not matter whether his lack of knowledge is due to a failure to consider the question at all, or to a belief that the victim is a traffic warden, or aged 18, respectively. Similarly, he cannot be convicted of reset if he never applied his mind to the provenance of the goods.[1] If A has shot and injured B because he thought B was a scarecrow it follows that he did not cause the injury intentionally; if A takes B's coat because he thought it was his own, he does not take it with intent to steal.[2] In such cases it is not really necessary to have a separate doctrine of error; it is enough to say that it is clear on the facts that A did not act intentionally.[3] **9.02**

Error and recklessness and negligence

Where A's error is itself arrived at recklessly, it will be evidence of lack of intention, but will equally be evidence of recklessness. An error may be reckless either because A was aware of the possibility of the existence of the true facts but took no steps to find them out and so remained ignorant, or because he took grossly inadequate steps and as a result arrived at a grossly mistaken belief. A is probably also reckless where he realises the need for inquiry, or for taking certain particular steps by way of inquiry, but does not take them and so remains ignorant or mistaken.[4] The person who takes someone else's umbrella knowing **9.03**

---

[1] See *supra*, paras 7.13–7.15. *Cf.* J.C. Smith, "The Guilty Mind in the Criminal Law" (1960) 76 L.Q.R. 78 at 87.

[2] Hume, i, 73.

[3] *cf.* Gl. Williams, pp. 172–173. Equally, of course, where A is required to act knowingly the fact that he acted under error will be evidence of lack of knowledge.

[4] Gl. Williams endeavours to distinguish ignorance and mistake, and to show that while ignorance involves recklessness mistake excludes it. His argument is difficult to follow and is not wholly convincing: see Gl. Williams, paras 54–55, and J.C. Smith, "The Guilty Mind in the Criminal Law" (1960) 76 L.Q.R. 78. In any event it cannot be applied to Scots law where recklessness is considered as gross negligence.

not that it is but that it might be someone else's, and being unmoved by that knowledge, is probably guilty of theft.[5] Whether the person who fires unthinkingly into a bush in which a man is hidden is guilty of murder will depend on whether the circumstances exhibit sufficient recklessness; whether the unthinking seducer of the 15-year-old is reckless can, if necessary, be determined in the same way. What is important is the recklessness displayed: it does not matter whether the error takes the form of unthinking ignorance or a recklessly formed belief that the bush is empty or the girl 18, although it may be easier to displace an inference of recklessness in the latter case.[6] If A injures B because he believed his pistol was loaded only with blanks or because he did not know B was in his line of fire, he cannot be said to have injured B intentionally, but if his errors were themselves the result of a reckless disregard of the danger to others inherent in his conduct, he has injured B recklessly.[7] If A marries B in the mistaken belief that his first wife is dead, he does not act knowingly or intentionally with regard to his marital status, but if his belief is arrived at recklessly he acts recklessly with regard to the possibility of his second marriage being bigamous. Where the *mens rea* of any offence, or of any element of any offence, is recklessness, then reckless error is no defence. A's guilt will be determined by whether his behaviour, including his error, displays gross negligence or, of course, actual foresight and acceptance of the risk of error. It seems, for example, that a recklessly formed belief in a woman's consent would not be an answer to a charge of raping her where she did not in fact consent.[8]

9.04 Similarly, if A's error is arrived at negligently his actings will be negligent, but not reckless (unless the negligence is gross) or intentional.[9]

Error inducing intent

9.05 A may act intentionally because of an error as to the circumstances of his conduct, usually in the form of a mistaken belief in the existence of justifying or mitigating circumstances. If A kills B in the mistaken belief that B is about to kill him, he acts in self-defence and is not guilty of homicide[10]; if A kills his wife in the mistaken belief that she has just confessed to adultery he is guilty only of culpable homicide.

Proof of error

9.06 Where the Crown are obliged to prove that A acted with a particular knowledge, such as knowledge that the goods are stolen in reset, or the articles explosives in a charge of knowingly possessing explosives,[11] there

---

[5] *supra*, para. 7.65. See also Vol. II, Chap. 14.

[6] Gl. Williams would treat ignorance as always being reckless: but it is not easy to reconcile the example of the inhabited bush with the general approach to recklessness in England, and his justification of the seduction-type case depends on a strained application of the *ignorantia juris* rule: see Gl. Willaims, paras 54 and 55; J.C. Smith, *op.cit.*, 83–91.

[7] *cf. H.M. Advocate v. A.B.* (1887) 1 White 532; *David Buchanan* (1817) Hume, i, 192.

[8] *Jamieson v. H.M. Advocate*, 1994 S.C.C.R. 181, L.J.-G. Hope at 186B and 187A.

[9] In *R. v. Mkize*, 1951 (3) S.A. 28 (A.D.) the accused gave her husband poison in the belief that it was an aphrodisiac, a belief induced by her lover. It was held that she had poisoned her husband negligently because it was negligent to take her lover's word as to the nature of the substance, and she was convicted of culpable homicide.

[10] *Owens v. H.M. Advocate*, 1946 J.C. 119.

[11] Explosive Substances Act 1883, s.4; *R. v. Hallam* [1957] 1 Q.B. 569; *Black v. H.M. Advocate*, 1974 S.L.T. 247.

is no evidential burden on A to put error in issue. Of course the articles may be so obviously stolen or explosives that in fact once they have been put in evidence the tactical burden shifts. But in many reset cases the Crown have to bring evidence of extraneous circumstances from which knowledge can be inferred. Any evidence of ignorance or mistake on the part of A will go to prevent the Crown proving *mens rea*.

In other cases, however, the error may relate to matter of defence and it will be for A to introduce evidence of a mistaken belief. Whether a given case is one of this kind will depend on whether what is involved is a positive element of the offence requiring proof by the Crown, or a defeasing factor such as self-defence. Problems arise in relation to factors which are not easily characterised in this way, such as knowledge that the woman in a rape case is unwilling. Must the Crown show that A knew the woman was not consenting, or must A lead evidence that he believed she was willing? The answer will depend on whether knowledge of lack of consent is regarded as part of the definition of rape, or belief in consent is seen as a defence to rape.[12]

The effect of error

The general rule in error is that A is to be judged as if the circumstances were as he believed them to be. In this matter the law adopts as a basis the principle that the relevant duty in any situation is the agent's subjective duty: his duty in the circumstances as he sees them, and not his objective duty: his duty in the circumstances as they are.[13] **9.07**

Irrelevant errors

There are certain types of error which are irrelevant either because they do not affect *mens rea*, or for reasons of policy.[14] Errors of the first kind are usually grouped as errors as to crime, errors as to victim, and errors as to mode. The problems raised by these errors are sometimes treated under the heading of "transferred intent;" but as Scots law has either abandoned the doctrine of transferred intent or retained a very limited form of it,[15] these problems are discussed here as a part of the law relating to error. **9.08**

Error as to crime. If A intended to create a particular *actus reus*, and in fact created another, then, provided that the intended *actus reus* is contained within the created one, he may be convicted of the *actus reus* **9.09**

---

[12] In English law, the definition of rape is statutory, and shows that knowledge of lack of consent (or recklessness in respect of it) is included as part of that definition: thus s.1(2) of the Sexual Offences Act 1976 (as substituted by the Criminal Justice and Public Order Act 1994) reads: "A man commits rape if — (a) he has sexual intercourse with a person . . . who at the time of the intercourse does not consent to it; and (b) at the time he knows that the person does not consent to the intercourse or is reckless as to whether that person consents to it." It would appear that Scots common law has adopted much the same definition (apart from the non-gender specific nature of the victim): see *Meek v. H.M. Advocate*, 1982 S.C.C.R. 613; *Jamieson v. H.M. Advocate*, 1994 S.C.C.R. 181; paras 9.26 *et seq., infra*.

[13] *cf.* H.A. Prichard, "Duty and Ignorance of Fact" (1932) 18 Proc.Brit.Acad. 67; *Attorney-General for Northern Ireland's Reference No. 1* [1977] A.C. 105, Lord Diplock at 136C.

[14] It may also be the case that a mistake relates to some issue which is irrelevant as a matter of law: see, *e.g.*, *C v. H.M. Advocate*, 1987 S.C.C.R. 104 — error as to consent of a girl aged 11 held irrelevant to a charge of indecent assault, since a girl under 12 conceded to be incapable of consenting to indecencies done to her.

[15] See para. 9.10, *infra*.

intended.[16] A can be convicted only of a crime he has in fact committed, and then only if his *mens rea* was appropriate to that crime, but he may be convicted despite the fact that the objective situation constituted a different crime from that intended. If A has sexual intercourse with B and intends to do so against her will and believes her passivity to be due to fear on her part, and if she is in fact unconscious due to self-induced intoxication, he probably will escape conviction for rape (and perhaps attempted rape) but he can certainly be convicted of indecent assault, for indecent assault is contained in rape and he had the necessary *mens rea* for indecent assault.[17] But if he "rapes" B, who is dead, in the mistaken belief that she is alive, he cannot be convicted of rape, because he has not in fact committed rape, nor of whatever crime is constituted by that crime necrophilia, because he did not intend to commit: all that he can be convicted of is attempted rape,[18] provided that such an attempt is not excluded by the rules of the relevant legal system with regard to impossible attempts.[19]

9.10 TRANSFERRED INTENT. The classic transferred intent situation is where A intends to commit one crime, such as fire-raising or rape, and in the course of that crime the *actus reus* of another crime, usually homicide, occurs. The doctrine of transferred intent holds that the guilty mind revealed by the intention to commit the first crime can be transferred so as to make the homicide intentional[20]; this doctrine has now been abolished in England.[21]

In Scotland, a limited form of transferred intent was expressly applied by the High Court in *Roberts v. Hamilton*,[22] although the case is perhaps

---

[16] See J.C. Smith, *op.cit.* at 91.

[17] This example assumes that the decisions of the High Court in *Meek v. H.M. Advocate*, 1982 S.C.C.R. 613, and *Jamieson v. H.M. Advocate*, 1994 S.C.C.R. 181 have not so altered the definition of rape in Scots law that the earlier authorities of *William Fraser* (1847) Ark. 280, and *Charles Sweenie* (1858) 3 Irv. 109 are no longer valid. See Vol. II, Chap. 33.

[18] *S. v. W.*, 1976 S.A.L.R. 1; [1976] C.L.Y. 558. If A forcibly commits buggery on a woman he believes to be a man he will be guilty of indecent assault and perhaps also of attempted sodomy; see *supra*, paras 6.49 *et seq*.

[19] It is an offence under s.44(1) of the Criminal Law (Consolidation) (Scotland) Act 1995 to make certain false statements on oath, while s.44(2) of the Act penalises certain false statements made otherwise than on oath. If A and B agree that B will make a false statement, and A thinks that the statement is not one which has to be made on oath, but in fact B is put on oath, then A is not art and part in B's crime — he cannot be convicted of contravening subs. (1) because he lacked *mens rea*, and he cannot be convicted of contravening subs. (2) because no such contravention occurred. The most he can be convicted of is an attempt to incite B to contravene subs. (2), assuming such an attempt is criminal: see Criminal Law (Consolidation) (Scotland) Act 1995, s.45, and Vol. II, Chap. 47. This particular difficulty would not arise at common law, for A could be convicted of fraud even although he wrongly believed that the fraudulent statement was going to be made on oath, perjury and fraud not being mutually exclusive.

[20] See *e.g. D.P.P. v. Beard* [1920] A.C. 479; and J. Hall, *General Principles of Criminal Law* (2nd ed., Indianapolis, 1960), 259–260 for the felony-murder misdemeanour-manslaughter rule.

[21] Homicide Act 1957, s.1. English law retains, however, the doctrine of "transferred malice", under which, *e.g.*, if A shoots at B intending to kill him but kills C instead either because he mistook C for B (*cf.* para. 9.11, *infra*) or because his aim was bad (*cf.* para. 9.12, *infra*), he is guilty of C's murder: the crime intended and the one actually committed must be the same for this doctrine to apply: see *Attorney-General's Reference (No. 3 of 1994)* [1998] A.C. 245, HL, Lord Mustill at 253G-H; 259A; 262B-E (although the doctrine was not used in that case owing to the complication that the 'victim' was a foetus at the time of the deliberate injury (to its mother) which eventually caused its grossly premature birth and subsequent death).

[22] 1989 S.L.T. 399.

better described as one involving *aberratio ictus*.[23] The point at issue arose since the accused aimed a blow with a pole at A who was fighting with her son. She intended to hit A, but her blow went astray and took effect on B, who was attempting to separate the combatants. She was convicted of assaulting the actual recipient of the blow, and her conviction was upheld on appeal, on the ground that Hume's notion of transferred intent[24] was not confined to murder (as had been argued) but was equally applicable to assault; but the Court also held that the conviction could be sustained on the alternative ground favoured in the previous, and similar, case of *Connor v. Jessop*,[25] namely, that what actually happened was in the circumstances so likely to happen that criminal liability could not be avoided.[26] If, therefore, transferred intent remains a general doctrine of modern Scots criminal law, it has received little recent support beyond the situation where A intends to assault B but by some mischance effects the *actus reus* of the very same crime on C.[27] *Roberts v. Hamilton*[27a] stands virtually alone in modern times; and the need for the doctrine's use in situations of assault as exemplified in that case has been diminished by the development of the concept of reckless injury.[28] It is also significant that a court of five judges has recently and decisively rejected the application of such a doctrine to cases of wilful fire-raising,[29] a crime which, as is also true of assault, can be committed only intentionally.[30] It would appear, therefore, that a return to the classic form of the doctrine as favoured by Hume[31] is at present unlikely.[32]

Error as to identity of victim. This is generally irrelevant because the identity of the victim is generally not an element requiring *mens rea*, but where the identity or any particular characteristic of the victim *is* an element requiring *mens rea* error is relevant. In practice, error as to victim is relevant only when it involves an error as to the crime, or the degree of crime, involved. If A shoots at B believing him to be C, he is guilty of assaulting B, since to assault B is just as criminal as to assault C. Similarly, if A breaks into and steals from a bank believing it to be a warehouse, or has intercourse with a 14-year-old black woman believing her to be a 14-year-old white girl, the mistake is irrelevant. But this irrelevancy depends on the fact that the victims are in each case legally **9.11**

---

[23] See para. 9.12, *infra*.

[24] See Hume, i, 22.

[25] 1988 S.C.C.R. 624. There, the accused threw a glass at a person with whom he had been fighting; the glass, however, missed its intended target and hit an innocent bystander.

[26] The Court in *Connor v. Jessop*, *supra cit.*, followed Macdonald at p.2: "The principle is, that where the result which has happened was likely to occur, the perpetrator is answerable, and accordingly the circumstance of each case must determine the applicability of the rule." All Macdonald's examples relate to murder; and the reference to what was "likely to happen" is suggestive of recklessness or negligence rather than intention.

[27] This indeed seems closer to the English doctrine of transferred malice (see n.21, *supra*) than to Hume's conception of transferred intent.

[27a] 1989 S.L.T. 399.

[28] See Vol. II, Chap. 29.

[29] *Byrne v. H.M. Advocate*, 2000 S.C.C.R. 77, at 92A, following the like opinion in *Blane v. H.M. Advocate*, 1991 S.C.C.R. 576, L.J.-G. Hope at 582C–583A.

[30] For the *mens rea* of assault see *Lord Advocate's Reference (No. 2 of 1992)*, 1993 J.C. 43; *H.M. Advocate v. Harris*, 1993 J.C. 150; Vol. II, Chap. 29.

[31] See Hume, i, 22–25.

[32] See in particular *Byrne v. H.M. Advocate*, 2000 S.C.C.R. 77, the views of Lord Coulsfield (who delivered the opinion of the Court) at 91C-D.

equivalent. In a system which distinguishes parricide from murder and requires knowledge of the relationship Oedipus would no more be guilty of parricide than of incest. In Scots law between 1957 and 1965, when it was capital murder to kill a policeman on duty,[33] A was not guilty of capital murder if he killed a policeman on duty in the belief that he was a private citizen: he was guilty of non-capital murder.[34]

9.12 ABERRATIO ICTUS.[34a] The above cases of error of identity are cases where the criminal makes a mistake in identifying his victim, where *e.g.* A shoots at B believing him to be C. This is what is called *error in objecto*. But there are other cases where the mistake is not the mistake of the criminal but, so to speak, the mistake of the bullet — *aberratio ictus* — where A aims at B but accidentally hits C instead.

Hume makes no distinction between *error in objecto* and *aberratio ictus*, as the following passage makes clear:

> "A criminal charge may be good, though there is no evidence of a purpose to injure the very person who has been the sufferer on the occasion. For instance, in a trial for fire-raising, it cannot affect the judgment of the Court, nor ought it of the Jury, that the house which has been consumed is not the house of an enemy, which the pannel meant to destroy, and to which he applied the fire, but that of another person, to him unknown, and to which, by the shifting of the wind, or some other accident, the flames have been carried. The same is true in a case even of homicide, that crime to which a special malice may seem more natural than to most others. If John make a thrust at James, meaning to kill, and George, throwing himself between, receive the thrust, and die, who doubts that John shall answer for it, as if his mortal purpose had taken place on James"?[35]

The views thus expressed were upheld by the High Court in *Roberts v. Hamilton*,[36] a case of assault where a glass thrown by the accused at B missed its intended target and struck C instead. On the other hand, Hume's views have recently been rejected by the Court in relation to the crime of intentional fire-raising.[37] As assault is also a crime of intention and cannot be committed recklessly,[38] it is submitted that the same view of transferred intent should be taken in both crimes, and that that view should be the one preferred by the full bench in *Byrne v. H.M. Advocate*,[39] not only to avoid confusion but also since Hume's views are open to the following criticisms[40]:

---

[33] Homicide Act 1957.

[34] This would have been so even if capital murder was regarded merely as an aggravated form of murder in the way that theft by housebreaking is an aggravated form of theft, although the additional penalty was mandatory in the case of murder. *Cf.* StGB, Art. 16 (2).

[34a] For a criticism of this section, see J.H. Pain, "Aberratio Ictus. A Comedy of Errors — and Deflection" (1978) 95 S.A.L.J. 480, 482–484.

[35] Hume, i, 22. The case of *Isabella Graham or Bryce* (1840) Bell's Notes, 1 and *John Lees* (1833) *ibid*. are inconclusive as the charge was only culpable homicide.

[36] 1989 S.L.T. 399.

[37] *Byrne v. H.M. Advocate*, 2000 S.C.C.R. 77 (court of five judges), which upholds on this point (whilst disagreeing with it on others) the decision in *Blane v. H.M. Advocate*, 1991 S.C.C.R. 576.

[38] See *Lord Advocate's Reference (No. 2 of 1992)*, 1993 J.C. 43; *H.M. Advocate v. Harris*, 1993 J.C. 150.

[39] 2000 S.C.C.R. 77.

[40] Although it must be conceded that these criticisms did not find favour with the Court in *Roberts v. Hamilton*, 1989 S.L.T. 399.

(1) Difficulty arises in cases where there is neither intent nor recklessness so far as the actual crime is concerned. Where A shoots at B and kills C whom he knows to be standing beside B he may well be guilty of murdering C because he recklessly disregarded the possibility that C might be killed. In *Matthew Hay*[41] the accused was convicted of murder because he put poison in a pot in which a whole family's breakfast was being cooked, with the intention of poisoning the daughter but with the actual result of poisoning her parents. This, as Hume recognises, was a case of recklessness, "as he could not but see the hazard to the whole family".[42] In such circumstances, there is no need to invoke the doctrine of transferred intent. The doctrine is required where there is no recklessness regarding the actual crime, where the fire laid to A's house is carried to B's by sheer accident, or where C suddenly throws himself between A and B in circumstances in which A could not have foreseen this, or at any rate where it was not so likely as to make A reckless.[43]

(2) The doctrine depends on the idea of general *mens rea*.[44] It is made so to depend by Hume, and the only reason it has not been seen to conflict with the Scots attitude to transfer between crimes is that all victims are legally equal in Scots law.

(3) The law as stated by Hume can lead to some peculiar situations. It means that if a man shoots at his wife and the bullet ricochets and kills his child who has suddenly come into the room, he is guilty of murdering the child. But if he were about to shoot his wife because he had found her in adultery, he would be guilty only of culpable homicide, since the killing of his wife would only have been culpable homicide. The doctrine means that a man may be convicted of murdering someone of whose existence he was unaware, or "to whom he bore all manner of regard."[45] For these reasons the doctrine is objectionable, and for these reasons it is difficult to imagine that a jury could be persuaded to follow it, as Hume appears to have suspected when he said that the change of victim "ought" not to affect the jury. The obvious solution is to convict A of the attempted murder of B, and of the culpable homicide of C, if he was sufficiently negligent *quoad* C.[46]

---

[41] (1780) Hume, i, 22.

[42] The same may be true of the case of *Peter Robertson* (1798) Hume, i, 23 who threw a pair of tongs at a servant which missed her but killed his child, and who was convicted of culpable homicide.

[43] *cf. H.M. Advocate v. Brown* (1907) 5 Adam 312, where the accused sent a poisoned cake addressed to his intended victim which was actually eaten by the latter's servant. The indictment simply libelled the intent to poison the person to whom the cake was addressed and the actual death by poison of the deceased, and it was not suggested, so far as the report shows, that it was necessary to ask if the accused should have foreseen the likelihood of anyone else eating the cake. The indictment certainly suggests that the charge was based on pure transfer of intent. The case, however, was fought on the ground of insanity, and although an example of, is not an authority on, transferred intent.

[44] *supra*, para. 7.05.

[45] *Carnegie of Finhaven* (1728) Hume, i, 22.

[46] H. Mannheim, "Mens Rea in German and English Law" (1935) 17 J.Comp.Leg. and Int.Law, 82, 246. In *R. v. Mabena*, 1968 (2) S.A. 28 (R.,A.D.) the court held that it is murder if A attacks B in circumstances showing he must have realised he was likely to kill him but by mistake kills C in circumstances showing he ought to have realised that he was likely to cause serious injury to him. This was attacked in E.M. Burchell and P.M.A. Hunt, *South African Criminal Law and Procedure* (1970 ed.), Vol. 1, at 143, because the *mens rea* of murder was absent *quoad* C. Guilt in Scotland should also depend on the *mens rea quoad* C, however this is defined. (*Cf.* E.M. Burchell and P.M.A. Hunt, *South African Criminal Law and Procedure*, Vol. 1, *General Principles of Criminal Law* (3rd ed., 1997, J.M. Burchell (ed.)), pp.258 *et seq*., which *inter alia* narrates that South African law has turned its back on the *aberratio ictus* rule, founded as it was on the now discredited notion of *versari in re illicita*.)

9.13 (4) The real difficulty, as Mannheim points out,[47] is to justify the distinction between *error in objecto* and *aberratio ictus*. Why should the person who aims at B believing him to be C be in a worse position than the person who aims at B and hits C because he is a bad shot? It may be that both should be treated alike, but it can at least be said that it is easier to treat the bad shot as only negligent than it is so to treat the man who makes an *error in objecto*. To say that in *error in objecto* A intended to shoot the person in front of him is too simple, since in neither type of case did he intend to shoot C, and in both cases his shooting of C was in some sort an accident. But it seems reasonable to say that in *error in objecto* A intended to kill C although his intention was induced by the mistaken belief that he was B, but in *aberratio ictus* A does not intend to kill C at all. The simplest way of describing *aberratio ictus* is to say just that A carelessly shot C, and it seems reasonable for the law to adopt this attitude.[48] Again, where the error is *in objecto* it is more difficult, if not impossible, to distinguish the intended act from what happened, since both the intended and the actual shot have, so to speak, the same trajectory.[49]

There can be no great objection to treating *error in objecto* as irrelevant error; and in practice it would be very difficult to arouse any sympathy for the accused in such a case. But it does seem objectionable to deal with *aberratio ictus* by way of transferred intent, if only because transferred intent is objectionable, and there is no great difficulty in treating it in the way suggested. After all, if A had aimed at a tree and accidentally or carelessly hit C instead, he would not be guilty of murdering C. In cases of *aberratio ictus* it is easy to consider the situation without taking into account the original intention to shoot B: the intention to shoot B can be treated as no more important than the intention to shoot at a tree. To treat it as more important is very like adopting the old English doctrine of constructive malice.

The simple answer is probably that *aberratio ictus* is not an example of error at all but of accident, and accidents are not punished by the criminal law.[50]

9.14 *Error as to mode.* The position here is the same as in cases of error as to victim, although examples are rarer. If A sets out to kill B by knocking him on the head and then cutting his throat while he is unconscious, it does not matter if in fact the first blow kills B. But if it is capital murder to kill by shooting and non-capital murder to kill by drowning,[51] and A intends to wound B by shooting him, and then to throw him into the river and drown him, it may be important to know if the shot killed B, for then A will have created the *actus reus* of capital murder while

---

[47] H. Mannheim, *op.cit., loc cit.*

[48] *cf.* E.M. Burchell and P.M.A. Hunt, *South African Criminal Law and Procedure*, Vol. 1, *General Principles of Criminal Law* (3rd ed., 1997, J.M. Burchell (ed.)), pp.261 *et seq*.

[49] It remains to be seen what the result will be if A intending to kill B shoots at C whom he wrongly believes to be B, but misses him and instead hits B who happened to be standing nearby: see Donnedieu de Vabres, *Traité de Droit Criminal et de Législation Pénale Comparée* (3rd ed., Paris, 1947), p.84.

[50] *cf.* J.L. Austin, "A Plea For Excuses" reprinted in *Philosophical Papers*, 2nd ed. (Oxford, 1970), pp.175, 185n.; *The Philosophy of Action*, A.R. White (ed.) (Oxford, 1968), pp.19, 27n.

[51] As it was during the currency of the Homicide Act 1957.

intending only to commit non-capital murder, and if *mens rea* is required as to the capital nature of the crime, he cannot be convicted of capital murder.[52] Again, suppose A sets out to rob a safe and takes with him a substance he believes to be a non-expolosive corrosive intending to use it to melt the safe lock, and in fact the substance is explosive and the safe blows up. In such circumstances, it is submitted that the error would be relevant if A were charged with theft by opening lockfast places by means of explosives, but not if he were merely charged with theft by opening lockfast places.

ERROR AS TO MODE AND CAUSALITY. Error as to mode may be relevant even where there is no question of a different crime being committed, not because of the law of error but because of the law of causality. If A intends to kill B by shooting but B is in fact killed by a road accident while being taken to hospital for treatment, it may be that A is guilty only of assault and attempted murder.[53] Even if A puts B's wounded body into his own car and drives him off with the intention of burying him somewhere, and B who is still alive is killed in a road accident caused by A's negligence, A may be guilty only of attempted murder and careless driving. That at any rate is the logical result, but in practice A might be convicted of murder in the last example on the ground that he caused B's death and intended to kill him, despite the lack of concurrence between *mens rea* and *actus reus*. In *Shoukatallie v. The Queen*[54] the Privy Council had to consider the situation where A shoots B and then throws him into a river with the help of C who had not been concerned in the original shooting, both A and C believing wrongly that at the time B was thrown into the water he was dead. Their Lordships concluded that in such a case A would be guilty of murder but C would be guilty only of manslaughter. This follows an earlier case in which Lord Reid had described the argument that someone in A's position was not guilty of murder as "much too refined a ground of judgment," and treated A's actings as all part of one transaction.[55] **9.15**

Error of law. There is a general rule that, as a matter of policy, error of law is irrelevant. That is to say, it is not a defence to a criminal charge that A did not know that what he was doing was against the criminal law, or that he thought it was legal. Provided that A voluntarily performed an act or produced a result that was criminal, it does not matter that he **9.16**

---

[52] Unless it is shown that his shooting of B was reckless with regard to the possibility of its being fatal.

[53] *cf.* H.L.A. Hart and A.M. Honoré, *Causation in the Law* (2nd ed., Oxford, 1985), pp.77–78, 390–391; T.B. Smith, p.711; *supra*, para. 4.43.

[54] [1962] A.C. 81.

[55] *Thabo Meli v. R.* [1954] 1 W.L.R. 228. It has been held that the *Thabo Meli* rule applies only to cases where the act which caused death was itself part of the original plan for disposing of the body: *R. v. Chiswibo*, 1961 (2) S.A. 714; and only cases where there was an intention to kill: *R. v. Ramsay* [1967] N.Z.L.R. 1005. But see *R. v. Church* [1966] 1 Q.B. 59; *S v. Masibela*, 1968 (2) S.A. 558 (A.D.); E.M. Burchell and P.M.A. Hunt, *South African Criminal Law and Procedure*, Vol. 1, *General Principles of Criminal Law* (3rd ed., 1977, J.M. Burchell (ed.)), 295–297.

thought it was not a crime.[56] *Clark v. Syme*[57] is an example of this. C was charged with maliciously killing a sheep and pleaded in defence that he thought he had a legal right to kill the sheep because it was trespassing on his land. In rejecting this defence Lord Justice-General Clyde said:

> "If . . . it was not clear whether the [accused] knew that by doing what he did he was doing or was likely to do damage, the Crown might fail; for the necessary wilfulness might not then be present. But in this case no such doubt could possibly arise. The [accused] in this case acted deliberately. He knew what he was doing . . . The mere fact that his criminal act was performed under a misconception of what legal remedies he might otherwise have had does not make it any the less criminal."[58]

9.17 ERROR OF LAW AND ERROR OF FACT. The distinction between error of law and error of fact is a difficult one.[59] Suppose A marries again during the lifetime of his first wife in the belief that bigamy is not a crime, B does so in the belief that he is free to marry again because his

---

[56] Hume, i, 26; J.C. Smith and B. Hogan, *Criminal Law* (9th ed., 1999, Sir J. Smith (ed.)), pp.82–84. A similar rule pertains in Canada: see Canadian Criminal Code, s.19 — to which there are exceptions, see, *e.g.*, *Regina v. Jorgensen* [1995] 4 S.C.R. 55. In South African law, a mistake (or, indeed, ignorance) of law may negative *mens rea*, provided the mistake is an honest one and relates to an essential element (of which "unlawfulness" is always one) of the offence: *De Blom* 1977 (3) S.A. 513 (A); there is no requirement for the mistake to be reasonable, which accords well with the South African subjective account of *mens rea*: see E.M. Burchell and P.M.A. Hunt, *South African Criminal Law and Procedure*, Vol. 1, *General Principles of Criminal Law* (3rd ed., 1977, J.M. Burchell (ed.)), pp.254–255: see also R.C. Whiting, "Changing the Face of Mens Rea" (1978) 95 S.A.L.J. 1: the court's view in *De Blom* was that "At this stage of our legal development it must be accepted that the cliché that 'every person is presumed to know the law' has no ground for its existence and that the view that 'ignorance of the law is no excuse' is not legally applicable in the light of present day concept of mens rea in our law." See also *Williams v. N.C.,* 325 U.S. 226 (1944); *Ajami v. Attorney-General* (1959) 3 Isr.S.C. 198; *Reynolds v. U.S.*, 98 U.S. 145 (1878).

In the curious case of *Secretary of State for Trade and Industry v. Hart* [1982] 1 W.L.R. 481, an English Divisional Court seems to have accepted that error of law could result in an acquittal. The defendant was charged with acting as a company auditor when he knew he was disqualified by reason of being a director of the company, contrary to section 13(5) of the Companies Act 1976, which provided that "No person shall act as auditor of a company at a time when he knows that he is disqualified". The Court held that it was necessary for conviction not merely that the accused knew he was a director, but that he knew that directors were disqualified from acting as auditors. Woolf, J. said, at 485F, "The words in their ordinary interpretation are wholly consistent with a view of the subsection which means that a person in the position of the defendant must be aware of the statutory restrictions which exist against his holding the appointment." And as Ormrod L.J. put it at 487–488, "If that means that he is entitled to rely on ignorance of the law as a defence, in contrast to the usual practice and the usual rule, the answer is that the section gives him that right. Whether it does so intentionally or not is another matter." It may, therefore, be the law that where a statute requires knowledge of some particular circumstance which involves a rule of law, ignorance of that rule of law is a defence where it leads to lack of the knowledge required by the statute.

In *Attorney-General's Reference (No. 1 of 1995)* [1996] 1 W.L.R. 970, the Court of Appeal distinguished *Hart* on the basis that the offence in question had been an unusual one in which the statutory wording had specifically required that the knowledge of the unlawfulness of what the defendant had been doing had to be shown.

[57] 1957 J.C. 1.

[58] At 5.

[59] In South Africa, the distinction does not have to be made, since both types of error can negative intention: see E.M. Burchell and P.M.A. Hunt, *South African Criminal Law and Procedure*, Vol. 1, *General Principles of Criminal Law* (3rd ed., 1977, J.M. Burchell (ed.)), 254 *et seq.*

first wife has divorced him, C does so in the belief that his first wife has obtained a decree of judicial separation against him which he thinks leaves him free to marry, D does so in the belief that his first wife is dead. It is clear that A is guilty of bigamy and D is not,[60] but the position of B and C is far from clear. It was at one time thought that in England B and C were both guilty of bigamy,[61] although it is now clear that B is not[62]: there is no authority on the point in Scotland.[63] B would certainly be acquitted, his mistake being one of what is sometimes called "private law", a mistake restricted to the legal relationship of the particular parties. In C's case the error might be regarded as one of "general law", an error as to the effect of a separation decree, and therefore irrelevant, so that he would be convicted. But it is submitted that the distinction between B and C should be rejected as technical and both be acquitted on the ground that they accepted the criminality of bigamy but believed themselves free to remarry. If the law is that B and C are both not guilty, error of law is irrelevant only where A is aware of the true circumstances surrounding his conduct including any "legal" circumstances, but wrongly believes that his behaviour in these circumstances is not criminal. Where through an error of law A mistakes the nature of these circumstances, that error would be relevant.[64] There may be cases in which it is difficult to distinguish errors of the type committed by A from errors of the type committed by C, but the general principle suggested is that the only irrelevant error is one of the type "Persons are not liable to punishment for polygamy", or "It is not a crime to cause personal injury to someone else."[65]

Erroneous inferences of law. Where A is not mistaken about the facts **9.18** but draws an erroneous legal inference from them his error is an error of law. This particular situation has not been clearly focused in any reported case, although it has arisen in three of the leading cases on error.[66] It is seen most clearly in connection with self-defence. Whether or not retaliation in self-defence is justifiable is a question of law, and if on the facts as the accused believes them to be self-defence is not justified it is irrelevant for the accused to say that he thought it was. It would also be an error of law for A to infer wrongly that he was entitled

---

[60] Assuming, if it is necessary to do so, that D's error is reasonable — see *infra*, paras 9.26 *et seq.*; see also Vol. II, Chap. 45.

[61] *R. v. Wheat and Stocks* [1921] 2 K.B. 119.

[62] *R. v. Gould* [1968] 2 Q.B. 65; *R. v. King* [1964] 1 Q.B. 285; Gl. Williams, para. 115; J.Ll.J. Edwards, "*Mens Rea* and Bigamy", 1949 *Current Legal Problems* 47. *Cf. Thomas v. R.* (1937) 59 C.L.R. 279: the accused was acquitted where he wrongly believed his first marriage to be invalid because he thought his first wife had obtained only a decree nisi and not a decree absolute, and wrongly believed that she was therefore not free to marry him. It was held in the Canadian case of *The Queen v. Prue* [1979] 2 S.C.R. 547 that as the offence of driving while disqualified was one requiring *mens rea*, it required knowledge of the disqualification, even where the disqualification was an automatic consequence of the accused's earlier convictions. Where, therefore, the accused knew that he had been convicted but had not been told that he was disqualified, he was not guilty of driving while disqualified, his error being treated as one of fact. The case is, however, complicated by reason of the disqualification being the result of provincial legislation while the offence of driving while disqualified is a federal one.

[63] *cf.* T.B. Smith, p.137.

[64] *cf.* Gl. Williams' distinction between error of civil and error of criminal law: Gl. Williams, para. 116.

[65] See the discussion of error of morals, *supra* para. 2.08.

[66] *Dewar v. H.M. Advocate*, 1945 J.C. 5; *Owens v. H.M. Advocate*, 1946 J.C. 119; *Crawford v. H.M. Advocate*, 1950 J.C. 67.

to appropriate certain property, but such an error would be relevant because errors of law are relevant where they exclude the special intent required in crimes of dishonesty.

9.19 ERROR OF LAW IN CRIMES OF "SPECIAL INTENT". Even if errors of "general law" are rejected as irrelevant in the bigamy example given, they would still be relevant in any crime in which they negatived a specific element of the crime. If A takes B's goods in the belief that they are rightfully his because he has made a mistake about the general law of succession or the legal effect of a hire-purchase contract, his taking is not *"fraudulosa"* and therefore, leaving aside any question of recklessness, is not theft. This is the basis of the defence of claim of right in crimes of dishonesty.[67]

Paterson v. Richie[68] is a difficult case. The accused was charged with fraudulently obtaining a widow's pension to which she was not entitled, since she was cohabiting with another person as man and wife and as such was disqualified from claiming a pension. The defence was that although she was living with someone else she did not hold herself out as his wife and so believed that she was not disqualified by the statute. The sheriff-substitute took the same view of the meaning of the statute as the accused and acquitted her. The Crown appealed and the court upheld the sheriff substitute on the ground that there had been no fraudulent intent. But they went on to say that the accused and the sheriff-substitute had misinterpreted the law and that in future any widow in the accused's position would be convicted, since the court had given public notice of the true meaning of the statute. This approach rather suggests that error of law is a defence in cases of dishonesty only where the law is in doubt.[69] But this is difficult to justify. The defence of claim of right is a recognised exception to the irrelevance of error of law, and there is no warrant for limiting the exception by reference to the obscurity of legislation or the knowledge of judges. Whether or not A acts fraudulently must depend on A's state of mind and not on that of Parliament or his judges. No doubt the more abstruse the law the easier it will be to persuade a tribunal of fact that there was error, but once they are so persuaded that should be an end of the matter.

9.20 *The reason for the irrelevance of error of law.* The rule that error of law is irrelevant is comparable to the principle of objective duty in moral philosophy: A's duty is to do what is right and not what he wrongly believes to be right. This principle itself has many difficulties[70]: why should a person for whom bigamy or child sacrifice is a religious duty be

---

[67] Hume, i, 73–75. An error may, however, be so general as to be irrelevant even in cases of dishonesty. It is clearly no defence to say that A believed theft was not a crime, but suppose A believes that a certain article has been abandoned by its owner and is unaware that all abandoned property in Scotland belongs to the Crown. If in that situation he appropriates the property believing he is entitled to do so, is he guilty of theft? See *Kane v. Friel*, 1997 S.C.C.R. 207, where such an issue was raised but the case decided on the basis that there was insufficient evidence to suggest that the accused must have known that the items they found were things which someone might have wished to retain. See also Vol. II, Chap. 14.

[68] 1934 J.C. 42.

[69] Or perhaps even where the error is shared by the trial judge: see Lord Anderson at 47.

[70] *cf. supra,* para. 2.07.

morally blameworthy for acting conscientiously? And the difficulties are increased when it is criminal responsibility and not moral blameworthiness which is in question. It may seem reasonable to say that a murderer should be punished whether or not he knows murder is criminal, but this is due partly to the fact that it is difficult to believe that anyone does not know murder is criminal. The position is not quite so clear when it comes to bigamy, and it is not at all obvious why an Englishman who brings his niece to Scotland and there has intercourse with her should be convicted of a crime if he did not know that such intercourse which is not criminal in England is criminal in Scotland. And most law-abiding citizens will agree that it is unfair to punish someone for breach of a parking regulation of which he was excusably ignorant.[71]

The rule about error of law is sometimes supported by reference to the principle of disfacilitation,[72] as by Hume when he says, "The law which cannot know the truth of his excuse, and which perceives the advantage that might be taken of such gross pretences, for the indulgence of malice, presumes his knowledge of that which he is not excusable for being ignorant of,"[73] but this is open to the same objections as any other reference to disfacilitation. The best basis for the rule is the idea of "inexcusable ignorance", of a duty to know the law, although a failure to find out whether one's behaviour is criminal or not should not, strictly speaking, involve responsibility for more than recklessness or in some cases negligence. Hume recognised this, since he refers to the rule as an example of the maxim "*culpa lata equiparatur dol*",[74] but this maxim does not apply in modern criminal law.

The only other basis on which the rule can be founded is simply that the administration of the criminal law would be extremely difficult if it could be enforced only on those who know it. In other words, public policy requires that the law should disregard any plea that the accused did not know that what he was doing was struck at by the criminal law.

Entrapment

It appears that Scots law may recognise a limited form of a defence of entrapment, or at least accept that certain evidence of the commission of a crime is inadmissible where it has been obtained by entrapment, *i.e.* by a police officer or other person in authority disguising himself and inciting the accused to commit a crime, *e.g.* by supplying him with controlled drugs, or with liquor in breach of the licensing laws. Such a defence will succeed only where it can be said that the accused would not have committed the offence but for the inducement, and was not already predisposed or willing to commit crimes of the kind involved. A distinction is also drawn between proper police activities designed to detect and stop a course of criminal activity already embarked on, and activity designed to pressurise, encourage or induce the commission of an offence of a kind the accused would not otherwise be involved in.[75] **9.21**

RELIANCE ON OFFICIAL ADVICE. There is a growing acceptance in Canada and the United States of the view that where A acts illegally on the advice of an official who has advised him that his proposed **9.22**

---

[71] *cf. MacLeod v. Hamilton*, 1965 S.L.T. 305.

[72] *supra*, para. 7.56.

[73] Hume, i, 26.

[74] *ibid.*

[75] See *Weir v. Jessop (No. 2)*, 1991 S.C.C.R. 636; *Tudhope v. Lee*, 1982 S.C.C.R. 409, Sh.Ct.; *Cook v. Skinner*, 1977 J.C. 9. For a general discussion of entrapment, see *Amato v. The Queen* [1982] 2 S.C.R. 418.

behaviour is legal, A has a defence of error of law, based on the idea of estoppel by a public official.[76]

In England such circumstances operate only in mitigation[77]; there is one old Scottish case which lends some support to the defence, although it was treated in *Arrowsmith*[78] as a case of mistake of fact, and involves a specific statutory defence. The case is *Roberts v. Local Authority for Inverness.*[79] The accused was convicted of moving cattle from one local authority area to another without a licence. His defence was that when he applied for a licence the responsible inspector told him that because of an amalgamation of local authorities no licence was needed for the journey in question. He admitted knowledge of the regulation prohibiting unlicensed movement. The ruling statute made it an offence to contravene the regulation "without lawful authority or excuse", and the High Court quashed the conviction. Lord Justice-Clerk Macdonald said:

> "It is quite plain that in this case the appellant acted in perfect *bona fides* upon Mr. Thompson the inspector's statement that no licence was necessary, and the inspector also evidently acted in perfect good faith as the administrator of the Contagious Diseases Animals Acts. In these circumstances, the only question that I should propose that we should answer is whether the appellant, having proved that he went to the inspector and was informed by him that no licence was necessary, was in the position of a person having lawful excuse for what he had done . . . I have no hesitation in saying that there is in the facts found proved sufficient to warrant us in finding that there was a lawful excuse for what the appellant did."[80]

9.23 UNPUBLISHED LAW. Most discussions about error of law assume that the law in knowable, and there is Privy Council and American Supreme Court authority that the rule regarding error of law does not apply when the law is not published and the accused had no means of discovering it.[81] The Privy Council have also said, however, that the publication of an order in terms of the Statutory Instruments Act 1946 is sufficient to impose a duty to know it, and to render irrelevant any plea of ignorance,[82] which is perhaps a little unrealistic in view of the difficulties which face the layman, and often enough the lawyer too, who seeks to discover which statutory instruments are operative at any time. Similarly, the assumption of the High Court of Justiciary that the recipients of widows' pensions are familiar with the law reports, or even with the usually garbled accounts of decisions which appear in the press, is somewhat unrealistic.[83]

---

[76] See the instructive opinion on this matter by Lamer C.J. in *R. v. Jorgensen* [1995] 4 S.C.R. 55 (although the majority of the Supreme Court of Canada declined to express a view on the matter). See also the Model Penal Code, O.D., art. 2.04 (3); *Raley v. Ohio*, 360 U.S. 423 (1959); *Cox v. Louisiana*, 379 U.S. 559 (1965); see Gl. Williams, para. 106; L.D. Houlgate, "Ignorantia Juris: A Plea for Justice" (1967) 78 *Ethics* 32; "Applying Estoppel in Criminal Cases" (1969) 78 Y.L.J. 1046.

[77] *R. v. Arrowsmith* [1975] Q.B. 678; *Surrey C.C. v. Battersby* [1965] 2 Q.B. 194; *Redbridge London B.C. v. Jacques* [1970] 1 W.L.R. 1604; *Cambridge County Council v. Rust* [1972] 2 Q.B. 426.

[78] *supra.*

[79] (1889) 2 White 385.

[80] At 391–392.

[81] *Lim Chin Aik v. The Queen* [1963] A.C. 160; *Lambert v. California*, 355 U.S. 225 (1957). *Cf. MacLeod v. Hamilton, supra.*

[82] *Lim Chin Aik*, *supra*, at 171.

[83] See *Paterson v. Richie*, 1934 J.C. 42, *supra*, para. 9.19.

CLASS AND PARTICULAR LAW. *Lim Chin Aik v. The Queen*[84] raises the question of the position of a law which concerns only one person or a limited class of persons. In that case the accused was charged with failing to obtemper an unpublished ordinance making it illegal for him to remain in Singapore. In *Lambert v. California*[85] the charge was that the accused, being a convicted criminal, had failed to register her address, and the Supreme Court held by a majority that the provision creating this offence was unconstitutional, since it did not provide for *mens rea*. The court were influenced by the passivity of the criminal conduct involved, and its lack of any connection with any activity, but *Lambert*[85a] is nonetheless an example of a relevant error of law: the accused knew that she belonged to the class of persons bound to register, *i.e.* knew she was a convicted criminal, what she did not know was that members of that class were bound to register, which seems clearly to be an error of law and not of fact. There is no Scots authority on the matter, but it is unlikely that in, for example, a charge under section 21 of the Firearms Act 1968 against a discharged prisoner for possessing a gun within five years of his discharge it would be a defence to show that the accused did not know of the statutory provision. The position in *Lim Chin Aik*[85b] is, however, different. Where an ordinance refers only to one person it may or may not be properly called law, but ignorance of the ordinance is at once ignorance of fact and of law, since the two merge: knowledge that the accused belongs to the class is the same as knowledge of the prohibition since the class is a class of one and the prohibition an individual one. In such a case, it is submitted, whether or not the ordinance is duly published, ignorance of its publication should be a defence, assuming of course that the offence requires *mens rea*, as it was held in *Lim Chin Aik*[85c] such offences always should.[86] **9.24**

Immaterial error. Error regarding immaterial elements, such as whether or not one is within the jurisdiction of a particular court or system is immaterial. **9.25**

Unreasonable error

In theory the relevance of unreasonable error may depend on the part the error plays in the case. If the Crown are required to prove a certain *mens rea*, then the existence of an error which negatives that *mens rea* should be relevant whether or not is unreasonable,[87] As Lord Hailsham of St Marylebone said in *Morgan*: **9.26**

> "Once one has accepted, what seems to me abundantly clear, that the prohibited act in rape is non-consensual sexual intercourse, and that the guilty state of mind is an intention to commit it, it seems to me to follow as a matter of inexorable logic that there is no room either for a 'defence' of honest belief or mistake, or of a defence of honest and reasonable belief or mistake. Either the prosecution proves that the accused had the requisite intent, or it does not. In

---

[84] [1963] A.C. 160.
[85] 355 U.S. 225 (1957).
[85a] *ibid.*
[85b] [1963] A.C. 160.
[85c] *ibid.*
[86] *supra*, para. 8.34.
[87] *R. v. Mkize*, 1951 (3) S.A. 28 (A.D.).

> the former case it succeeds, and in the latter it fails. Since honest belief clearly negatives intent, the reasonableness or otherwise of that belief can only be evidence for or against the view that the belief and therefore the intent was actually held."[88]

Although Lord Hailsham talks of "intention", his reasoning would still apply if the term "knowingly" were used instead.

The above "theory" has become the practical reality of modern English law. Where a defendant alleges that he had an honest, but mistaken, belief as to the victim's consent,[89] or age[90] where relevant, in relation to a sexual offence, then, assuming that the Crown must show an intention on the part of the defendant to commit the sexual act in question on a non-consenting or under-age victim, that belief, if accepted by the jury, should prevent the prosecution from proving its case. As Chief Justice Lamer said in a recent Canadian case, "the defence of honest but mistaken belief in consent is simply a denial of the *mens rea* of sexual assault."[91] The subjective belief of the defendant, if genuinely held, is all that is required. As Lord Nicholls of Birkenhead said, "over the last quarter of a century, there have been several important cases where a defence of honest but mistaken belief was raised. In deciding those cases the courts have placed new, or renewed, emphasis on the subjective nature of the mental element in criminal offences. The courts have rejected the reasonable belief approach and preferred the honest belief approach."[92] It may be thought that honest mistakes relative to matters of defence, such as the need for self-defence, would lie outside the *mens rea* of assault or murder, and thus be at least eligible for different treatment: but the courts in England have taken the view that "an essential element of all crimes of violence [is] that the violence or threat of violence be unlawful."[93] In this way, the *actus reus* of assault is regarded as the application of *unlawful* force to another, such that the *mens rea* for the crime is the intentional application of *unlawful* force. If, therefore, the defendant has an honest though mistaken, belief in the need for self-defence, he intends to apply *lawful* force and will have to be acquitted.[94] It must be concluded, therefore, that the unreasonableness of an error in English law is generally irrelevant, although the grounds for a belief may provide evidential support for the belief's genuineness.

9.27 UNREASONABLE ERROR IN SCOTS LAW. Prior to the decision of the Appeal Court in *Meek v. H.M. Advocate*,[95] it could probably have been stated with some confidence that Scots law accepted that for an error to

---

95 1982 S.C.C.R. 613, see para. 9.32, *infra*.

88 [1976] A.C. 182, 214E-G; see also *Wilson v. Inyang* [1951] 2 K.B. 799.

89 *R. v. Morgan*, *supra cit.* (rape); *R. v. Kimber* (1983) 77 Cr.App.R. 225 (indecent assault).

90 *B. (A Minor) v. D.P.P.* [2000] 2 W.L.R. 452, HL (inciting a child under the age of 14 to perform an act of gross indecency on the defendant, contrary to the Indecency With Children Act 1960, s.1(1)).

91 *R. v. Davis* [1999] 3 S.C.R. 759, para. 80 (a case of indecent assault).

92 *B. (A Minor) v. D.P.P.* [2000] 2 W.L.R. 452, at 456D-E.

93 *Beckford v. The Queen* [1987] 3 All E.R. 425, PC, at 431.

94 *R. v. Gladstone Williams* (1983) 78 Cr.App.R. 276, CA: the Privy Council has applied the same reasoning to murder — *Beckford v. The Queen*, *supra cit. Cf.* the view of the Australian High Court in *Zecevic v. D.P.P.* (1987) 61 A.L.J.R. 375, that a belief in the need for self-defence must have an objective component, *i.e.*, reasonable grounds; Lord Steyn in *B. (A Minor) v. D.P.P.* [2000] 2 W.L.R. 452, at 471, found such an approach to be attractive, but eventually rejected it since it would have run counter to the way in which English law had developed.

be relevant it had to be reasonable.[96] But it was (and is) by no means clear what was meant by "reasonable" in this connection. It could not mean that any error the reasonable man would not make was irrelevant, since that would make all crimes crimes of negligence in any question involving error. General principles of morality and the rules of logic require that negligent error should exclude recklessness and intention, and that reckless error should exclude intention.

CARELESS ERROR. There are certainly a number of culpable homicide cases which show that the Scots courts have recognised that a negligent error excludes intention and also excludes at any rate murderous recklessness. In *Williamina Sutherland*[97] S. killed a child by folding up a bed in which, unknown to her, the child was lying. She was charged only with culpable homicide, and her ignorance of the child's presence was regarded as irrelevant, but it was said that it would have been of "vital consequence" had the charge been murder.[98] Again, in *Edmund F. Wheatley*[99] W killed someone by carelessly dispensing French instead of English quantities of medicine, and in *H.M. Advocate v. Wood*[1] death was caused by a chemist who carelessly did not read the labels on his bottles and so dispensed strychnine instead of a medicine: both accused were charged with culpable homicide.[2] **9.28**

There is little authority on the effect of error on recklessness in general,[3] but a reckless error must exclude intention. Whether or not reckless error should excuse from responsibility depends on whether recklessness is a sufficient *mens rea* for the element in question. It might be, for example, that a reckless error as to the abortifacient nature of a substance administered to a pregnant woman would not affect guilt, while a reckless belief that the woman was not pregnant would be a good defence.

FANTASTIC ERROR. It is submitted that, where Scots law continues to require that errors be based on reasonable grounds,[4] "unreasonable error" is confined to a very limited class of errors which are so unreasonable that they can be described as "fantastic," that indeed in many cases they would provide evidence that the accused's state of mind was disturbed. Put another way, unreasonable errors are errors which no ordinary normal person could honestly make, the "ordinary normal person" being someone much less prudent, careful and conscientious than the "reasonable man"; and this in turn means that no jury will believe that such error existed unless they also believe the accused to be in some way abnormal. A's error is irrelevant when it is founded "on fantastic notions of his own devising,"[5] or "in the violent passions of the man, or his blind prejudices in his own favour."[6] Except for references to **9.29**

[96] See Macdonald, at p.11, where he spoke of mistake "based on reasonable grounds"; T.B. Smith, p.138.

[97] (1856) 2 Irv. 455.

[98] Lord Cowan at 457.

[99] (1853) 1 Irv. 225.

[1] (1903) 4 Adam 150.

[2] See also *H.M. Advocate v. A.B.* (1887) 1 White 532, where the accused was killed by discharging a gun he believed to be empty, and the similar case of *David Buchanan* (1817) Hume, i, 192.

[3] See *Dewar v. H.M. Advocate*, 1945 J.C. 5; *infra*, para. 9.31.

[4] See para. 9.32, *infra*.

[5] T.B. Smith, p.138.

[6] Hume, i, 74, dealing with the defence of claim of right.

the defence of claim of right in crimes of dishonesty there is hardly any treatment of unreasonable error in Scots law prior to the 1940s, and there is still no authoritative general account of the law on this question. But in so far as can be discovered the law appears to be as stated.

Error in relation to self-defence

9.30 In *Owens v. H.M. Advocate*[7] O was charged with murdering a man F, and pleaded in defence that he had acted in self-defence because he believed that F was threatening him with a knife. At the trial Lord Jamieson directed the jury that if O was "completely wrong" in thinking that F had a dangerous object in his hand they should reject the plea of self-defence. This direction was overruled by the Criminal Appeal Court and O's conviction quashed. Lord Justice-General Normand said:

> "In our opinion self-defence is made out when it is established to the satisfaction of the jury that the panel believed that he was in imminent danger and that he held that belief on reasonable grounds. Grounds for such belief may exist although they are founded on a genuine mistake of fact. In the present case, if the jury had come to the conclusion that the appellant genuinely believed that he was gravely threatened by a man armed with a knife but that [F] actually had no knife in his hand, it would, in our opinion, have been their duty to acquit."[8]

In the later case of *Crawford v. H.M. Advocate*[9] it was said that for a mistake to be relevant it "must have an objective background and must not be purely subjective or of the nature of a hallucination."[10] As Professor Smith suggests[11] "these observations should not be construed too sweepingly, but against the background of the particular case, where the defence really rested on a somewhat remote apprehension of danger" — the accused stabbed his father repeatedly while the latter was unarmed and had only used strong language and made some threatening gestures towards the accused. The main issue in the appeal was whether the trial judge had acted correctly in withdrawing the defence of self-defence from the jury. *Crawford*[11a] is concerned with unreasonable self-defence and not unreasonable error, with an erroneous inference of law and not with an error of fact. *Crawford*[11b] is in a way the opposite of *Owens.*[12]

In *Owens* it was accepted that on the facts as the accused believed them self-defence was justifiable, and the dispute was whether his account of the facts could be accepted; in *Crawford*[12a] the accused's view

---

[7] 1946 J.C. 119.
[8] At 125.
[9] 1950 J.C. 67.
[10] L.J.-G. Cooper at 71.
[11] T.B. Smith, p.138.
[11a] 1950 J.C. 67.
[11b] *ibid.*
[12] 1946 J.C. 119.
[12a] 1950 J.C. 67.

of the facts was accepted as correct, and the dispute was whether on these facts self-defence was justifiable. In any event it is clear from *Owens*[12b] that a mistake about objective facts does not preclude the defence of error — if it did, such a defence would have only a very restricted application. The dictum in *Crawford*[12c] was intended to exclude the purely subjective error and the hallucinatory error, and "objective background" must be interpreted accordingly. It is submitted that it means only that the surrounding circumstances in which the error is made must be such that the accused's error is one a normal man might genuinely make, as they were in *Owens*[12d] where the deceased had risen from his bed and followed the accused out of the room after the two men had quarrelled.

THE CASE OF DEWAR. In *Dewar v. H.M. Advocate*[13] D was the manager of a crematorium who was charged with the theft of lids from coffins entrusted to him for cremation along with the bodies they contained. Instead of burning the lids D removed them from the coffins and appropriated them. His defence was (a) that he had believed that the removal of lids was a common practice, a belief which he admitted at the trial was unfounded in fact, (b) that the coffins were "abandoned" to him to do as he pleased with, and (c) that he thought that in any event he was entitled to treat the lids as ownerless scrap and to appropriate them, more or less as a perquisite of his position, erroneously believing that this too was a common practice. In directing the jury at the trial Lord Justice-Clerk Cooper told them that they must consider not only the fact that D.'s explanation was false but also "whether he ever had any colourable ground for holding such a view, or whether the statements made by him . . . with regard to the practice of the crematorium movement, were made recklessly without any justification for belief in their accuracy."[13a] So far as D's belief that he was entitled to appropriate the lids was concerned Lord Cooper told the jury that they must consider "whether he may have entertained an honest and reasonable belief, based on colourable grounds",[13b] and then read them the passage from Hume in which the latter excludes beliefs "directly in the face of the law" and grounded only in the accused's blind prejudice or violent passion.[14] **9.31**

Parts of Lord Cooper's charge can be seen as supporting the view that error is irrelevant only when it is "fantastic", but the reference to recklessness creates difficulties. It appears that Lord Cooper accepted that a defence of belief in entitlement to appropriate could succeed even where it was based on a mistake of fact (and this view gains support from the later decision of the Criminal Appeal Court in *Owens v.*

[12b] 1946 J.C. 119.

[12c] 1950 J.C. 67.

[12d] 1946 J.C. 119.

[13] 1945 J.C. 5.

[13a] At 8.

[13b] *ibid.*

[14] Hume, i, 74, *supra.* D was convicted and his appeal dismissed. The Criminal Appeal Court, however, went much further than Lord Cooper and indicated that in their view Lord Cooper had erred in favour of the accused in allowing the defence of error to go to the jury at all.

H.M. Advocate[15]), but that he thought the mistake must not be reckless. It must be remembered, however, that what was in issue here was cognitive *mens rea* as to the element of ownership in theft, and if Lord Cooper was correct in excluding reckless error that may be because recklessness is a sufficient *mens rea* for this element, and not because reckless error is always irrelevant as being unreasonable.

The Appeal Court thought that Lord Cooper had been lenient to the accused, and indicated that the defence of error was probably wholly irrelevant. This seems, however, to have been based on the view that what was being urged was an error of law, supported at most by a belief that what was being done was common practice.

Dewar also holds that it is for A to prove his belief. But Scots law now recognises the difference between the evidential and persuasive burdens,[16] and this part of *Dewar* should be interpreted as applying only to the evidential burden which lies on someone who asserts any claim of right.

9.32 THE CASE OF MEEK. In *Meek v. H.M. Advocate*,[17] a number of men were convicted of the rape of a young woman. Their appeals were based on the refusal of the trial judge to direct the jury that if they found that the accused had honestly but mistakenly and even unreasonably believed in the woman's consent at the time of the intercourse, then the accused should be acquitted. The Appeal Court took the view that the evidence had presented the jury with two irreconcilable accounts of the events — one, on the part of the complainer, alleging non-consensual intercourse in the face of objection and distress, and the other, on the part of the accused, telling of willing compliance in a sexual orgy: there was thus no reason for any defence of error to be considered, especially since the defence had not been conducted on such a basis. The Court went on, however, to say this:

> "We have no difficulty in accepting that an essential element in the crime of rape is the absence of an honest belief that the woman is consenting. The criminal intent is, after all, to force intercourse upon a woman against her will and the answer to the certified question given by the majority of their Lordships in *Morgan*[18] is one which readily accords with the law of Scotland. The absence of reasonable grounds for such an alleged belief will, however, have a considerable bearing upon whether any jury will accept that such an 'honest belief' was held."[19]

The Court seems to have accepted, therefore, that the law laid down by a bare majority of the House of Lords in *R. v. Morgan*[20] is also the law in Scotland: an honest and even unreasonable error as to a woman's consent would be sufficient to acquit the accused on a charge of rape. The role of 'reasonable grounds' was but a minor evidentiary one,

---

[15] *supra. Dewar* was not referred to in *Owens* — an example of the tendency to compartmentalise the law by reference to fact situations to the detriment of any general view based on principle.

[16] *Brown v. Rolls Royce*, 1960 S.C. (H.L.) 22; G.H. Gordon, "The Burden of Proof on The Accused", 1968 S.L.T. (News) 29 and 37; *Lambie v. H.M. Advocate*, 1973 J.C. 53. *Cf.* also *R. v. Kundeus* [1976] 2 S.C.R. 272.

[17] 1982 S.C.C.R. 613.

[18] *R. v. Morgan* [1976] A.C. 182; see para. 9.26, *supra*.

[19] *Meek v. H.M. Advocate*, 1982 S.C.C.R. 613, at 618.

[20] [1976] A.C. 182; see para. 9.26, *supra*.

relating to credibility; that role was certainly not a substantive one, as had seemed to be the case relative to the self-defence and theft cases,[21] which were in fact not mentioned in the Court's opinion at all. In spite of the Court's opinion on error being an *obiter dictum*, and notwithstanding the criticism which followed the decision,[22] the case was in practice regarded as authority for the rule that an honest belief in consent, even though not based on reasonable grounds, is sufficient for an acquittal in a case of rape; and that authority was confirmed in *Jamieson v. H.M. Advocate*.[23] *Jamieson* is an important decision in the context of error since the Court does consider the self-defence cases,[24] and accepts that they provide "ample authority that a person who claims that he acted in self-defence because he believes that he was in imminent danger must have reasonable grounds for his belief."[25] On the question of consistency of these cases with the rule promulgated in *Meek*,[26] the Court stated, that (although they had not been addressed to any extent on this issue): "we are not to be taken . . . as casting any doubt on the soundness of the dicta in those cases. Nor are we to be taken as suggesting that in any other case, where a substantive defence is based on a belief which is mistaken, there need not be reasonable grounds for that belief. The reason why, in rape cases, the man's belief need not be shown to be based on reasonable grounds for his belief to be relevant as a ground of acquittal is because of the particular nature of the *mens rea* which is required to commit the crime."[27]

This seems to intimate an intention to confine the "honest belief" approach to the crime of rape rather than allow it to extend to other crimes such as murder, assault or even theft (although the Court did not mention theft or the case of *Dewar v. H.M. Advocate*[28]). It must be doubted, however, whether the distinction sought to be made between rape and other crimes is sustainable: no such distinction has been made in England in relation to error,[29] and it has been convincingly asserted that there is none to be drawn.[30]

The general position following *Meek*[31] and *Jamieson*[32] is somewhat difficult to assess; but it now seems that the outcome will depend on the nature of the issue to which the mistaken belief relates. If that issue happens to be one of the essential elements of the offence which the Crown must establish to prove its case, there is perhaps little difficulty in accepting that an honest error, whether reasonably based or not, can hardly be consistent with success for the prosecution[33]; but if that issue is

---

[21] See paras 9.30 to 9.31, *supra*.

[22] *E.g.*, C.H.W. Gane, *Sexual Offences* (Edinburgh, 1992), pp.40–45.

[23] 1994 S.C.C.R. 181. The view of 'honest error' in the case has also been applied to a case of indecent assault: see *Marr v. H.M. Advocate*, 1996 S.C.C.R. 696.

[24] *Owens v. H.M. Advocate*, 1946 J.C. 119; *Crawford v. H.M. Advocate*, 1950 J.C. 67; and *Jones v. H.M. Advocate*, 1990 J.C. 160.

[25] 1994 S.C.C.R. 181, at 186F.

[26] 1982 S.C.C.R. 613.

[27] 1994 S.C.C.R. 181, at 186F-187A

[28] 1945 J.C. 5.

[29] See para. 9.26, *supra*.

[30] See P.W. Ferguson, "The Mens Rea of Rape", 1996 S.L.T. (News) 279, at 280.

[31] 1982 S.C.C.R. 613.

[32] 1994 S.C.C.R. 181.

[33] The difficult matter of a recklessly formed error remains, however, although its effect must surely depend on whether recklessness is a sufficient form of *mens rea* for the element to which the error relates. The court in *Jamieson* certainly seems to have assumed that recklessness (as opposed to indifference or complete lack of thought) in relation to the victim's consent is sufficient thus far for conviction of rape: see 1994 S.C.C.R. 181, at 186B–C and 187A.

one which is extraneous[34] to the elements of the offence, and on the assumption that the Crown has proved or is able to prove those elements to the required standard, the evidential burden will lie on the accused to show some objective background for his alleged error — *i.e.,* he will have to demonstrate more than an 'honesty of belief' in order to dent the prosecution's case. The problem with this approach, however, is that it does not explain why an honest belief is sufficient in the one situation but not in the other.[35] There is also the difficulty that the approach which the Scottish courts seem to favour depends upon the way in which particular crimes are defined; but the definitions of many common law crimes are often uncertain even today, such that it is sometimes difficult to be sure what is or is not an element of a particular crime: and given that the courts have the undoubted ability to develop common law crimes, the difficulty referred to is simply compounded.

9.33 *Error as a specific statutory defence.* Where a statute provides that a belief "on reasonable grounds," or even a "reasonable belief," in certain facts is a defence to an offence, "reasonable" means much more than "not fantastic"; it probably means a belief such as a reasonable man might have held and acted on, and it excludes negligent mistake.[36] In *H.M. Advocate v. Hoggan*,[37] which dealt with reasonable belief that a girl was over 16 as a defence to a charge of unlawful carnal knowledge, Lord Justice-Clerk Macdonald suggested that the accused would have to prove that he was told the girl's age was over 16 by her mother whom he knew well, or was shown the wrong birth certificate, or had some other strong foundation for his belief, and that it was not enough for him just to say that the girl looked over 16.[38] Some statutes restrict the defence even more and provide that the accused shall be convicted unless he had "no reasonable cause to suspect" the truth,[39] and in such a case the accused would have to show not merely that it was reasonable for him to hold the belief he did but that no reasonable man would have suspected the contrary, which places a very heavy onus on him.

---

[34] In *Jamieson,* 1994 S.C.C.R. 181, at 186G, the court refers to a matter of "substantive defence".

[35] *cf.* the views of Bridge J., giving the opinion of the Court of Appeal in *R. v. Morgan* [1976] A.C. 182, at 191–192, where he attempts to justify the requirement of reasonable gounds where an evidential burden lies on the defendant. On appeal, however, the majority of the House of Lords did not accept that such a distinction followed from a consideration of the differences between the persuasive and evidential burdens of proof.

[36] *cf.* C. Howard, *Strict Responsibility* (London, 1963), *passim.*

[37] (1893) 1 Adam 1.

[38] See also *H.M. Advocate v. Macdonald* (1900) 3 Adam 180. In practice, however, juries usually accept the accused's word for his belief in this type of case if he impresses them favourably and the girl seems to have been as much to blame as he.

[39] *e.g.*, Betting Gaming and Lotteries Act 1963, s.10(5).

CHAPTER 10

INSANITY

I — INSANITY AS A DEFENCE

10.01 The Scots law on insanity as a defence to a criminal charge must be regarded as still unsettled although it has been considerably clarified in two modern reported cases, one a High Court trial[1] and the other a decision of the Second Division of the Court of Session on the effect of insanity as a defence to an action of divorce for cruelty.[2] The only reported decision of the Criminal Appeal Court on the subject is concerned with states of mind caused by voluntary intoxication, and deals with insanity in general by citing with approval Hume's distinction between insanity, which requires "an absolute alienation of reason", and drunkenness.[3] This limited reference to an 18th century work is not very relevant to a general discussion of modern concepts of insanity; the reported cases conflict with each other, and are very few in the twentieth century; the evidence given to the Royal Commission on Capital Punishment is very vague. The general tendency of the law in the past has been to wash its hands of the whole matter and abide by the decision of medical experts, but at the same time it is felt that there is a legal criterion somewhere by which it can be determined whether or not a man is legally irresponsible as a result of mental illness, and that not all psychotic patients are necessarily irresponsible, although no one can say what the criterion is, or just what types of mental illness do render a man irresponsible. In this state of affairs it is proposed to deal with the subject by discussing generally the problems raised by insanity before turning to the Scots cases on the subject, and to conclude by giving some indication of what the present law is.

Insanity and Irresponsibility

The basis of the defence of insanity

10.02 Insanity is recognised in all advanced systems of jurisprudence as a factor which may prevent a person being held responsible for his actions.[4] Violent disputes have raged on the question of what degree or

---

[1] *H.M. Advocate v. Kidd*, 1960 J.C. 61.

[2] *Breen v. Breen*, 1961 S.C. 158. See also *Mackenzie v. Mackenzie*, 1960 S.C. 322. So far as divorce law was concerned these cases were superseded by the Divorce (Scotland) Act 1964, s.5 (2)(a). See now Divorce (Scotland) Act 1976, s.1.

[3] *Brennan v. H.M. Advocate*, 1977 J.C. 38. For Hume's treatment see *infra*, paras 10.22, 10–23.

[4] For a historical account, see N. Walker, *Crime and Insanity in England* (Edinburgh, 1968), Vol. 1.

type of insanity is necessary or sufficient to free an accused from criminal responsibility for what would otherwise be crimes. These disputes have been intensified and very much complicated by the great advances made in the study of the human mind and its motivations in the past century, but they were present long before that. In 1800, in defending James Hadfield who had shot at the King in order that he might be hanged and so obey a divine command to sacrifice himself without incurring the sin of suicide, Thomas Erskine said:

> "It is agreed by all jurists, and is established by the law of this and every other country, that it is the REASON OF MAN which makes him accountable for his actions; and that the deprivation of reason acquits him of crime. This principle is indisputable; yet so fearfully and wonderfully are we made . . . so difficult is it to trace with accuracy the effect of diseased intellect upon human action, that I may appeal to all who hear me, whether there are any causes more difficult, or which, indeed, so often confound the learning of the judges themselves, as when insanity, or the effects and consequences of insanity, become the subjects of legal consideration and judgment."[5]

10.03 *Legal and medical insanity.* It has been said that criminal responsibility is "purely an artifact of the law", and that it cannot, therefore, be directly affected by new psychological knowledge.[6] This view can lead to a sharp distinction between what are sometimes known as legal and medical insanity, though the distinction should be between legal responsibility and medical insanity,[7] or, as it is now called, mental illness.[8] The law is concerned to know not just whether the prisoner was mentally ill when he committed the crime, but also whether his mental state was such as to render him legally irresponsible. Just as a lunatic can make a good will in a sane interval, or a person suffering from delusions about his paternity contract a good marriage, so a lunatic may, at least in theory, be responsible for committing a crime in a lucid interval, or a person suffering from delusions be responsible for his actions when these are concerned with something unconnected with the delusion. The law is concerned with the accused's responsibility, not his mental health.

But although the law asks "Is he responsible?" and not "Is he mad?" and although that is a legal and not a medical question, psychiatric knowledge may be of great assistance in answering the legal question, since it can show whether the accused's mental state was such that he fulfilled the requirements laid down by the law as sufficient to render a person responsible or irresponsible. The law is, of course, entitled to say, "We only hold a man to be irresponsible when, as a result of mental disease, certain conditions, *a, b* and *c*, are satisfied", and then it would not matter if psychiatrists proved that certain people in whom these conditions were not present were insane because of the presence of

---

[5] *Jas. Hadfield* (1800) 27 St. Trials, 1281 at 1309–1310.

[6] *cf.* G. Ellenbogen, "The Principles of the Criminal Law Relating to Insanity" (1948) J. of Cr.Sc., Vol I, 178, 192.

[7] See *e.g. U.S. v. Brawner* 471 F. 2d 969 (1972); *Brennan, supra.* Contrast the proposals of the Report of the Butler Committee on Mentally Abnormal Offenders, Cmnd. 6244, 1975, paras 18–26 *et seq.*

[8] See Mental Health (Scotland) Act 1984, ss.1, 17–18. Mental illness now includes personality disorder for the purposes of these sections: Mental Health (Public Safety and Appeals) (Scotland) Act 1999 (asp 1) s.3.

other conditions, *d* and *e*. But if the law wishes to keep pace with medical knowledge, and to conform to certain general principles of responsibility, such as the necessity for free-will as a precondition of responsibility, it will not adopt this approach, and psychiatry may lead the law to recognise that conditions *d* and *e* also exclude responsibility because, for example, they negative free-will in whatever sense the law understands that term. It will not matter then that at one time the law said, "A man is irresponsible only if his mental disease produces conditions *a, b* and *c*", since these conditions will not be a closed class, but be capable of extension in the light of later knowledge. It is only if the original conditions are treated as ultimate and self-justifying that development is impossible; if they are regarded as conditions which exemplify the general principles of responsibility there is nothing to prevent additions being made to them. And if later knowledge shows that one or more of the original conditions are not such as to exclude responsibility there is nothing to prevent their being subtracted from either.

"LEGAL INSANITY". It has long been recognised that a person might **10.04** be medically insane without being legally irresponsible. Conversely, it is recognised that a person might be irresponsible without being insane: that is to say, that someone who was in such a mental state as not to be responsible for his actions may be entitled to a simple acquittal where he was not mentally ill but suffering instead from some temporary condition such as unconsciousness induced by poisonous fumes.[9] Since *H.M. Advocate v. Cunningham*,[10] however, the law appears to be that where anyone's irresponsible state is due to a mental disease or pathological condition, rather than some external factor like poisonous fumes, he is not entitled to an acquittal except on the ground of insanity. The law is familiar with the case of persons who are sane at the time of their trial being acquitted on the ground of insanity because they were insane at the time of their crime, but *Cunningham*[10a] may go further and hold that some persons who are, and always were, sane but who were not responsible for their actions at the time of the offence are to be treated as insane. So sane people, like the diabetic who commits an offence while in a coma, may be regarded as having been legally insane at the relevant time if, as a result of their condition, their responsibility was affected to the same degree as it requires to be affected to justify a verdict of not guilty by reason of insanity in the ordinary case of insanity.

SCOTTISH LEGISLATION. The criminal law of insanity grew up **10.05** alongside the "civil" concept of "certifiable insanity" which was a condition rendering the patient liable to compulsory detention in a mental hospital. The modern Scottish legislation retains the concept and the language of "insanity" for the purpose of acquittals[11] and findings of unfitness to plead on the ground of insanity,[12] but replaces it in the

---

[9] *H.M. Advocate v. Ritchie*, 1926 J.C. 45; *Ross v. H.M. Advocate*, 1991 J.C. 210, discussed in paras 3.18 to 3.22, *supra*.

[10] 1963 J.C. 80. This aspect of *Cunningham* was not overruled by *Ross v. H.M. Advocate*, 1991 J.C. 210. An accused in such an irresponsible state may, of course, prefer to be convicted and may therefore not plead irresponsibility.

[10a] *ibid.*

[11] See the 1995 Act, ss.54(6), 55(3) and (4), 57.

[12] See the 1995 Act, s.54(1).

"civil" law by that of "mental disorder".[13] A person is liable to compulsory admission to hospital if he suffers from mental illness[14] which, in terms of section 17(1) of the Mental Health (Scotland) Act 1984, is of such a nature or degree that it warrants detention, provided it is appropriate for him to receive medical treatment in a hospital and it is necessary for his health or safety or the protection of others that he should receive such treatment which cannot be provided unless he is detained. The change was no doubt brought about partly for euphemistic reasons and for the sake of the "image" of mental illness, but even if persons liable to detention for mental illness under section 17 are just persons who would formerly have been described as certifiably insane,[15] the modern legislation clearly distinguishes the requirements of section 17 from the requirements of insanity in the criminal law.[16] For sections 58 and 59A of the 1995 Act contemplate the situation of a person who has been convicted of an offence and who also fulfils the grounds for detention under section 17(1) of the 1984 Act — *i.e.* that he suffers from a "mental disorder" (which covers mental illness, including personality disorder, as well as mental handicap)[17]: such a situation empowers the court to order his admission to hospital. The legislation, therefore, adopts the view that a man may be "medically insane" and yet liable to conviction.[18]

Whether or not a man is "legally insane" remains a question to be decided on medical evidence as to his mental state, but the relevant state ought to be defined by the law and not by the doctors. In the normal case,[19] however, legal insanity is the result of mental disease and so is closely linked to medical notions of mental disorder. In practice, therefore, the position may still be not very different from what it was

---

[13] See the Mental Health (Scotland) Act 1984, s.1. Section 1(2), as amended by the Mental Health (Public Safety and Appeals) (Scotland) Act 1999 (asp 1), s.3(1)(a), which states that " 'mental disorder' means mental illness (including personality disorder) or mental handicap however caused or manifested." It is noteworthy, however, that the modern "interim" and "temporary" hospital orders rely on "mental disorder" rather than "insanity": see 1995 Act, ss.53(1) and 54(1); see also committal to a hospital under s.52.

[14] This term is more appropriate to the present discussion than the alternative "mental handicap".

[15] *i.e.*, prior to the Mental Health (Scotland) Act 1960, s.24, which was superseded by the Mental Health (Scotland) Act 1984. It appears, however, that s.24 of the 1960 legislation applied to people who would not have been "certifiable" previously.

[16] In this chapter the term "insanity" except where it refers to "legal insanity" is used to describe mental illness of a degree which would formerly have warranted certification. It is a convenient term and is, of course, the one used in discussions of the matter prior to the inception of the modern law in the Mental Health (Scotland) Act 1960 (now consolidated in and amended by the Mental Health (Scotland) Act 1984). But as Lord Hunter remarked in the civil case of *Ramsay v. Ramsay*, 1964 S.C. 289, 298 "any attempt to define insanity is likely to be defeated by the constant search which goes on from generation to generation to discover euphemisms for that condition."

[17] Section 59A was added to the 1995 Act by the Crime and Punishment (Scotland) Act 1997, s.6(1). "Mental illness" was extended to include personality disorder by the Mental Health (Public Safety and Appeals) (Scotland) Act 1999 (asp 1), s.3(1)(a).

[18] Section 58 of the 1995 Act does not apply to murder, or to any other offence with a fixed penalty, which means that in such cases a "hospital order" (see s.58(4)) cannot be made unless the accused is insane "legally" (see s.57): but a person liable to detention under s.17(1) of the 1984 Act might be acquitted of murder on the ground of diminished responsibility, and could then be dealt with under s.58 on conviction for culpable homicide. Section 59A permits the court to make a "hospital direction" in addition to a sentence of imprisonment, and the exercise of the power is restricted simply to persons who are convicted on indictment of an offence punishable by imprisonment.

[19] See *Brennan v. H.M. Advocate*, 1991 J.C. 38, para. 10.41, *infra*; but *cf.* paras 3.18 *et seq.* (esp. para. 3.22), *supra*.

when Lord Cooper told the Royal Commission that "However much you charge a jury as to the McNaghten Rules or any other test, the question they would put to themselves when they retired is — 'Is the man mad or is he not?' "[20]

THE REASON FOR TREATING THE INSANE AS IRRESPONSIBLE. The ultimate reason for acquitting the man who is irresponsible because of his insanity is the same as that for acquitting persons on the ground of necessity or coercion, or because they acted under error of fact. A person is treated as irresponsible, either because the law recognises that in the circumstances it would be unfair to regard him as morally to blame, or because there would be no point in punishing him. Bentham includes insanity among those cases where punishment is inefficacious, because it could produce no preventive effect.[21] In the same way the Criminal Law Commissioners included the insane among those to whom the principle that the object of the penal law is the prevention of injury through fear of suffering has no operation.[22] Dixon J. said in *R. v. Porter*[23]: "It is perfectly useless for the law to attempt, by threatening punishment, to deter people from committing crimes if their mental condition is such that they cannot be in the least influenced by the possibility or probability of subsequent punishment." The various theories and the cases on insanity have been viewed in the light of two questions, which may be just two sides of the one question — "Is it fair to blame the accused?" and "Is there any point in punishing the accused?" Professor Hart has, however, argued convincingly that the punishment of the insane may have some point, at least to the extent that it supports the general deterrence function of the law. The effect of general deterrence is weakened by the existence of defences or excuses, and is therefore weakened by the defence of insanity. The defence is retained because the requirements of deterrence here give way to the values of fairness and justice: it is unfair to punish the insane man, because he did not choose to break the law.[24] **10.06**

Knowledge or control

Formulations of the insanity defence refer either to the accused's lack of knowledge or to his lack of capacity to control his behaviour, or to both. Cognitive tests of insanity are directed to showing that A lacked *mens rea* in cases where this lack of *mens rea* is provable and explicable only on the basis of mental illness, or at least of some pathological condition which affected A's reason. In cases of this kind A is truly "not **10.07**

---

[20] R.C. Evid. of Lord Cooper, Q. 5479. Lord Cooper's own suggested test: "Is he not responsible for his actions by reason of a defect of reason?", *ibid.* Q. 5475, does focus attention on responsibility rather than madness, but it is tautologous and offers no help in determining when the question should be answered in the affirmative.

[21] Bentham, *Principles*, XIII, 9.

[22] 7th Report of Her Majesty's Commissioners on the Criminal Law, 1843, Parl. Papers, xix, 17.

[23] (1936) 55 C.L.R. 182, 186.

[24] *Punishment and Responsibility* (Oxford, 1968) Chap.I. *Cf.* N. Lacy, *State Punishment* (London and New York, 1988), p.74: "Insane offenders must thus be removed from the ambit of normal criminal regulation not because they lack normal capacities of understanding and control, but because they do not and cannot participate in the normal discourse which underpins the enterprise of criminal justice", an approach which also offers an explanation of the rule that the insane cannot be tried: see R.A. Duff, *Trials and Punishments* (C.U.P., 1986).

guilty on evidence of mental disorder"[25]; the peculiarity of the case is that the result of such an acquittal may not be discharge but compulsory detention in a mental hospital.[26] Control tests are directed to showing that although A had *mens rea*, in the sense that he knew what he was doing, he was unable to apply this knowledge to control his behaviour: he could not help acting as he did. If free choice is an essential prerequisite of responsibility, this type of insanity must produce an acquittal.[27]

There appear to be, however, cases which do not fall clearly within either of these tests, in which insanity is nonetheless regarded by some legal systems, including the Scots, as relevant. Such cases can perhaps be squeezed into the classic formulations, but the effort required to do this suggests that the real explanation of their relevance is something different. We acquit the depressive who after long brooding decides — *i.e.* chooses — to kill his family;[28] but if we say this is because although he knew what he was doing, he did not *really* know, he lacked a *sane* understanding, or he did not appreciate what he was doing, are we talking meaningfully or circularly? And if we say this is because he could not stop himself, how do we distinguish his "mad" choice from the sane choice of a man who kills his family rather than have them be devoured by wolves, captured by cannibals, or for that matter sent to the Gulag Archipelago? The depressive is acquitted because he arouses pity and not blame, because we are prepared to make a moral judgment which ascribes his conduct to illness, and therefore, or perhaps *ipso facto*, we do not regard him as a proper object of condemnation. Lord Cooper's question, "Is the man mad or not?", should perhaps be rephrased as, "Is the man to be blamed or not?"

> "The application of [tests of insanity], however they are phrased, to a borderline case can be nothing more than a moral judgment that it is just or unjust to blame the defendant for what he did. Legal tests of criminal insanity are not and cannot be the result of scientific analysis or objective judgment. There is no objective standard by which such judgments of an admittedly abnormal offender can be measured. They must be based on the instinctive sense of justice of ordinary men."[29]

---

[25] See Report of Butler Committee, *supra*, n. 7, paras 18.17 *et seq.* The English Draft Criminal Code (L.C. No. 177, "A Criminal Code for England and Wales" (1989) H. of C., No. 299, Vol. I) attempts to give effect to the Butler proposals, but with some amendments: see cls 34–39. See in particular cl.36: "A mental disorder verdict shall be returned if — (a) the defendant is acquitted of an offence only because, by reason of evidence of mental disorder [as defined in cl.34] or a combination of mental disorder and intoxication, it is found that he acted or may have acted in a state of automatism, or without the fault required for the offence, or believing that an exempting circumstance existed; and (b) it is proved on the balance of probabilities (whether by the prosecution or the defendant) that he was suffering from mental disorder at the time of the act."

[26] 1995 Act, s.57.

[27] Indeed in *U.S. v. Currens*, 290 F. 2d 751 (1961), the control test was treated as *the* test: has A lost the capacity to control his behaviour? *Cf.* the English Draft Criminal Code (L.C. No. 177, "A Criminal Code for England and Wales" (1989) H. of C., No. 299, Vol. I) at cl. 35, *viz.*: "(1) A mental disorder verdict shall be returned if the defendant is proved to have committed an offence but it is proved on the balance of probabilities (whether by the prosecution or by the defendant) that he was at the time suffering from severe mental illness or severe mental handicap [both as defined in cl. 34]. (2) Subsection (1) does not apply if the court or jury is satisfied beyond reasonable doubt that the offence was not attributable to the severe mental illness or severe mental handicap."

[28] *cf. H.M. Advocate v. Sharp*, 1927 J.C. 66.

[29] *Holloway v. U.S.*, 148 F. 2d 665, Arnold, J.A. at 666 (1945).

In *U.S. v. Eichberg*[30] Bazelon C.J. said:

> "The only acceptable explanation of our deference to the jury on the issue of responsibility lies in the special nature of the jury's role in resolving that issue. With respect to responsibility the jury has two functions. In the first place it measures the extent to which the defendant's mental and emotional processes and behaviour controls were impaired at the time of the unlawful act. The answer to that question is elusive but no more so than many other facts that a jury must find . . . The second function is to evaluate that impairment in light of community standards of blameworthiness, to determine whether the defendant's impairment makes it unjust to hold him responsible. The jury's unique qualification for making that determination justifies our unusual deference to the jury's resolution of the issue of responsibility."

Again, in *Brennan v. H.M. Advocate,*[31] the Court of Criminal Appeal said:

> "We ask ourselves first of all the fundamental question: What is insanity, according to the law of Scotland, for the purpose of a special defence of insanity at the time? The question has nothing to do with any popular view of the meaning of the word insanity, nor indeed is it a question to be resolved upon medical opinion for the time being. It is, on the contrary, a question which has been resolved by the law itself as matter of legal policy in order to set, in the public interest, acceptable limits upon the circumstances in which any person may be able to relieve himself of criminal responsibility."

Cognitive insanity and the M'Naghten Rules

It has long been recognised that madmen are subject to delusions: **10.08** they see things, or hear voices, they may believe that the devil is pursuing them[32] or that they have received divine commands to sacrifice themselves.[33] The simplest way to approach this problem was to treat insane delusions as analogous to errors of fact, with this difference, that the insane man, being *ex hypothesi* unreasonable, might successfully plead unreasonable error, and might plead error of law if he was incapable of knowing the law. If A kills a man in the belief that he is killing the devil he is entitled to be acquitted since it is, presumably, no crime to kill the devil.

The rules regarding the application of the law of error to the insane were schematised in the notorious M'Naghten Rules. These rules were set out by the English judges in answer to questions asked by the House of Lords following the acquittal of Daniel M'Naghten on the ground of insanity after he had killed the Prime Minister's secretary — whom he took for the Prime Minister — because he had an insane belief that the Government were persecuting him.[34] Despite their unusual origin they are regarded in England almost as if they were part of a statute; they

---

30 439 F. 2d 620, 624–625 (1971).
31 1977 J.C. 38.
32 *cf. Robt Thomson* (1739) Hume, i, 40.
33 *e.g. Jas. Hadfield* (1800) 27 St. Trials 1281.
34 (1843) 10 Cl. & F. 200.

have been followed in Canada, New Zealand, India, Pakistan, Ceylon and in parts of Australia and of the United States.[35] They have been said to be the law of Scotland[36] although today they are almost certainly not law in Scotland, or at any rate are not the whole Scots law on insanity. They set out clearly and definitely a particular legal attitude to what might be called insanity of the intellect, insanity affecting the patient's capacity for knowledge, and as such they merit consideration. They, or something like them, are almost bound to form part of any law which lays down detailed rules for judging the responsibility of the insane. In any event, it is impossible to consider the subject of insanity in the criminal law of an English-speaking country without discussing them, although there is nothing new that can be said about them. They may be accepted, criticised or rejected, but they cannot, perhaps unfortunately, be ignored.

10.09 *The Rules.* The essential parts of the Rules are as follows:

1. Persons who labour under partial delusions only, and are not in other respects insane, and who act under the influence of an insane delusion, of redressing or revenging some supposed grievance or injury, or producing some public benefit are nevertheless punishable if they know at the time of committing the crime that they were acting contrary to the law of the land.
2. Every man is presumed to be sane and to possess a sufficient degree of reason to be responsible for his crimes until the contrary be proved.
3. To establish a defence on the ground of insanity it must be clearly proved that at the time of committing the act, the accused was labouring under such a defect of reason, from disease of the mind, as not to know the nature and quality of the act he was doing, or, if he did know it, that he did not know he was doing what was wrong. If the accused was conscious that the act was one that he ought not to do, and if that act was at the same time contrary to the law of the land, he is punishable.
4. A person labouring under a partial delusion only and not in other respects insane must be considered in the same situation as to responsibility as if the facts with respect to which the delusion exists were real.[37]

The strength of the Rules lies not only in their similarity to the rules of the ordinary law of error, which makes them easily comprehensible to lawyers and easy to use in legal contexts, but also in their apparent coincidence with ordinary moral judgment. The core of the Rules is the requirement that the insane person did not "know the nature and quality of the act he was doing, or, if he did know it, that he did not know he was doing what was wrong". This seems to be in accord with moral thinking — if a man knows what he is doing and knows it is wrong, it seems proper to blame him for doing it.[38] "You knew what you were doing, and you knew that Mummy said you weren't to do it" is a familiar enough justification for punishment.

---

[35] See R.C.App.9, paras 3–5.

[36] *Jas. Gibson* (1844) 2 Broun 332.

[37] See 2 Broun. App.1.

[38] The controversy over whether wrong means morally wrong, or contrary to law, can be left to Anglo-American lawyers: see *R. v. Windle* [1952] 2 Q.B. 826.

Indeed the Rules might be thought to be quite indulgent to the criminal in some cases. They appear to adopt a subjective attitude to right and wrong, and allow the defence that the accused did not know he was doing wrong: if Himmler had suffered from a mental disease which led him to believe that it was right and proper to exterminate certain people he would be entitled to be regarded as morally irresponsible, for his actings were moral judgments based on the same principles as are enshrined in the Rules. What more, it might be asked, can be demanded in the way of consideration for the mentally ill? Surely someone who knowingly does wrong must be regarded as blameworthy, and in adopting the Rules the law is merely reflecting this.

The weakness of the Rules. The Rules rest, however, on assumptions now rejected by all psychologists.[39] **10.10**

They depend on the view that a man can be insane with regard to one matter and perfectly sane in regard to everything else. They assume that while a man's judgment may be so warped that he believes his neighbour is trying to make him impotent by black magic, he may yet be sane enough to be responsible for killing that neighbour.[40]

They mean that "a person whose cognitive capacity is intact but whose psychotic delusions have led him to homicide cannot gain protection from the Rules unless it can be shown in court that he did not know what he was doing, or that he did not know that killing was a crime. Thus many offenders who are undoubtedly insane do not fall within the M'Naghten criteria."[41] It has also been said that " 'our mental institutions, as any qualified psychiatrist will attest, are filled with people who to some extent can differentiate between right and wrong' or who can tell the difference between a human neck and a lemon but who are still out of touch with reality to a significant degree. Because of the apparent absolutism of the test, some psychiatrists are tempted to shape their testimony to fit the definition of insanity, although few of them believe that incapacity is ever complete."[42]

The Rules concentrate entirely on knowledge, and assume that the knowledge of an insane man is the same as that of a sane man, that the sufferer from delusions who knows that it is wrong to kill his imagined persecutor knows this in the same way as a sane man knows it is wrong to kill his real enemy. The Rules say that the test of responsibility is

---

[39] See, *e.g.*, R. Blueglass, P. Bowden and N. Walker (eds), *Principles and Practice of Forensic Psychiatry* (Churchill Livingstone, 1990), at p.219, where it is stated that a disease of the mind "on its own (*e.g.*, schizophrenia) without a defect of reason arising from it, would not support the insanity defence [under the *M'Naghten Rules*], reflecting an outmoded 19th century view that reason controls behaviour." See also J.R. Mason and R.A. McCall Smith, *Law and Medical Ethics* (5th ed., London, 1999) at p.530. The inadequacy of the Rules has even been recognised in the House of Lords: see *Williams v. Williams* [1964] A.C. 698, as well as the Court of Session: *Breen v. Breen*, 1961 S.C. 158. The distance between legal and psychiatric notions may raise an issue under Art. 5 of the European Convention on Human Rights: see P.J. Sutherland and C.A. Gearty, "Insanity and the European Court of Human Rights" [1992] Crim.L.R. 418.

[40] See R. Blueglass, P. Bowden and N. Walker, *op.cit.*, at p.222: "Under the rules a man of good cognitive state suffering from gross paranoid delusions, for example, is excluded from the defence. Such a man although completely lacking insight and disabled by illness would almost certainly know what he was doing and that it was legally wrong."

[41] S.Dell, "Wanted: An Insanity Defence that Can be Used" [1983] Crim.L.R. 431, at 431.

[42] J. Dressler, *Understanding Criminal Law* (2nd ed. 1995), at pp.320–321, in part quoting from *United States v. Freeman*, 357 F.2d 606, at 618 (1966).

knowledge of right and wrong, and that therefore an insane man who knows right and wrong is responsible, But it is not possible to treat this knowledge in isolation from the diseased part of the accused's mind, or to regard it as sane knowledge. It is tempting to say that "However mad he was, he was sane enough to know he was doing wrong", but to do so is to forget that his knowledge may have been tainted by his insanity.

The strict application of the Rules leads to some peculiar results. Hadfield, for example, was so clearly insane that after the defence evidence had been led the judge advised the Crown to accept a plea of insanity, but he knew he was doing wrong — that was why he did it, he wanted to be hanged. M'Naghten himself might not have been regarded as irresponsible in terms of the Rules, for had his delusion been real, had the Government really been persecuting him, that would have been no justification for murdering the Prime Minister. Cases like *Hadfield*[43] show how ridiculous the Rules can be in operation. As Maudsley remarked of a similar case in which the judge applied the Rules and said the accused's desire to be hanged showed that he knew the nature and consequences of his act, "He was in due course executed; the terrible example having been thought necessary in order to deter others from doing murder out of a morbid desire to indulge in the gratification of being hanged."[44]

Even if the utilitarian aspect of the matter is left aside, and the problem dealt with by reference to the idea of blameworthiness, the Rules will clearly not do. An example of this is the case of *Straffen*[45] who killed little girls to annoy the police, *i.e.* in the knowledge that it was wrong to do so. A medical witness said of him that: "He might be likened to a child who burns some very valuable documents because he likes to see them blaze, but who does not appreciate that they are valuable, although he knows it is wrong to do it."[45a] It seems clearly wrong to blame Straffen in the same way as one would blame a sane man who went about killing little girls.

10.11 *"Sane understanding".* The above objection to the Rules can be met without fundamentally altering them, and without recognising any form of insanity other than intellectual insanity. All that is needed is to recognise that an insane man cannot reason properly, and so can never know the nature and quality of his act, or its wrongness, in the way a sane man would. The result of this would probably be to make it the law that to be responsible a man must have "a sane understanding of the circumstances of his act".[46] This would be in line with the Faculty of Advocates' view of the modern Scots law as expressed in their Memorandum to the Royal Commission.[47] It would also accord with the views

---

[43] (1800) 27 St. Trials 1281.

[44] H. Maudsley, *Responsibility in Mental Disease* (London, 1874), p.159.

[45] Fairfield and Fullbrook (eds), *Trials of John Thomas Straffen*, (London and Edinburgh, 1954).

[45a] *ibid.,* p. 182.

[46] We might go on to say "and no one so mentally ill as to require hospitalisation can have such an understanding," and this indeed is the approach proposed by the Butler Committee — *op.cit.*, n.7, paras 18.26 to 18.36, and suggested in the first edition of this work. But unless it is specifically shown that A lacked understanding of the circumstances and nature of the particular offence, one does not have a standard of responsibility at all, but a form of the "biological" test, such as operates in *e.g.* Norway: J. Andenaes, *The General Part of The Criminal Law of Norway* (London, 1965) p.255; and in a sense in ss.58 and 59A of the 1995 Act.

[47] R.C. Evid., Memorandum of the Faculty of Advocates, para. 12.

expressed by Dixon J. in the Australian case of *Sodeman v. The King*[48] where he said, "In general it may be correctly said that, if the disease or mental derangement so governs the faculties that it is impossible for the party accused to reason with some moderate degree of calmness in relation to the moral quality of what he is doing, he is prevented from knowing that what he does is wrong."

The same result could perhaps be achieved by concentrating on the need for the accused to know the quality of his act. It could be said that an insane man cannot know the quality of his act, because he cannot have a sane appreciation of its nature. Straffen, for example, knew he was killing, but did not know the quality of his act, in the sense that he did not appreciate the seriousness of that he was doing.[49]

Volitional insanity and irresistible impulse

If the Rules are regarded as a complete statement of the law on insanity and not merely as a formulation of the rules regarding delusional or cognitive insanity, they are open to a much more fundamental objection than their failure to recognise that knowledge of right and wrong is insufficient unless accompanied by a sane understanding of the circumstances of the crime. They are open to the objection that they treat man as a purely cognitive being, and ignore the volitional and emotional aspects of human nature. Modern psychology recognises that a man may be sufficiently disturbed emotionally to be insane and yet have his intellectual faculties unimpaired as such. Henderson and Gillespie point out in their textbook that: **10.12**

> "There is no mental disorder, however partial, that does not have its reverberations throughout the rest of the affected mind. Consequently the purely intellectual criterion of responsibility falls to the ground, for the intellect as intellect may be unimpaired, but an emotional disturbance will alter, or impede, or nullify its effect on conduct. Conversely, intellectual defect means deficient emotional control."[50]

Since the criminal law is not concerned with thought but with conduct, any rules regarding responsibility which ignore volition cannot be satisfactory.

The obvious solution to the problem is to add to the Rules a statement that where an accused is incapable of controlling his actions as a result of mental illness he shall not be regarded as responsible. This seems to follow from the general rule that a person cannot be blamed for failing to do the impossible; and also from the utilitarian consideration that punishment or the threat of it will no more persuade a man to resist an irresistible impulse than it will persuade a one-legged man to win an Olympic race. Irresistible impulse is accepted as a defence in South Africa, in Germany and in the Model Penal Code.[51] The defence

---

[48] (1936) 55 C.L.R. 192, 215.

[49] *supra*: he was nonetheless convicted, but that may have been because he had done the same thing before and succeeded in a plea of insanity in bar of trial, and public feeling ran high. He was not hanged but reprieved and sent to prison.

[50] D.K. Henderson and R.D. Gillespie's *Textbook of Psychiatry* (9th ed., London, 1962), pp.551–552.

[51] See R.C. App.9, paras 3–12; St.GB Art. 20. It is also accepted by the Model Penal Code: O.D. s.4.01 (1); T.D. 4, 157. Incidentally, it is not accepted in France. Although Art. 122–2 of the Nouveau Code Pénal, which deals with insanity, also talks of "contrainte à laquelle elle n'a pu résister", this has been interpreted so as to apply only to external compulsion: Jean Pradel et André Verinard, *Les grands arrets du droit criminal: Tome 1, Les sources du droit pénal: L'infraction* (Paris, 1995), p.498.

is normally expressed by reference to a mental illness which renders the accused incapable of acting according to his knowledge of the wrongness of the act.[52] It is probably accepted in Scotland.[53] It has been rejected in England as "fantastic",[54] and although it has the support of the Royal Commission on Capital Punishment,[55] it has been rejected by the Judicial Committee of the Privy Council.[56]

The phrase "irresistible impulse" is an unfortunate one, since it conjures up the idea of a single impulse operating irresistibly on one occasion so that, even if there were a posse of policemen at A's elbow, he would still give way to the impulse. Such an occurrence is in the highest degree unlikely, and if the concept were to be limited to that sort of case it would be of little or no practical importance. What is really in issue is lack of capacity to control conduct, as in the case of the depressive, or the addict. An addict's craving for his drug does not cease to be "irresistible" just because he can postpone its gratification until the policeman has gone away.

10.13 *The objection to a volitional (control) test.* The main difficulty in accepting a control test is one of proof. Before it can be accepted it must be shown that A's capacity for self-control has been so seriously reduced as to make his condition comparable to that of someone acting under superior external force. It has to be shown not merely that he did not resist his desire to kill or rape or steal or forge, but that he could not have done so: and indeed that he and his like cannot be helped to resist their impulses by threat of punishment. Barbara Wooton has argued forcibly that it is impossible to distinguish those who cannot from those who will not,[57] but while this might be true in the context of the psychopathic gangster there are some cases where we are prepared to treat the offender as lacking free will. The most striking case is that recorded by Dr Guttmacher of the soldier who appealed to the chaplain because of his overpowering desire to kill an officer and who soon afterwards shot an officer in the presence of two military policemen.[58] It

---

[52] *e.g.* South African Criminal Procedure Act, s.78(1) — "A person who commits an act which constitutes an offence and who at the time of such commission suffers from a mental illness or mental defect which makes him incapable (a) of appreciating the wrongfulness of his act; or (b) of acting in accordance with an appreciation of the wrongfulness of his act, shall not be criminally responsible for such act". StGB Art. 20 — "Ohne Schuld handelt, wer . . . unfähig ist, das Unrecht der Tat einzusehen oder nach deiser Einsicht zu handeln." Model Penal Code, O.D. s.4.01: "A person is not responsible for criminal conduct if at the time of such conduct as a result of mental disease or defect he lacks substantial capacity either to appreciate the criminality [wrongfulness] of his conduct or to conform his conduct to the requirements of law." This may be wider in application than the limited idea that an impulse is irresistible only if it could not have been resisted on the particular occasion if the accused had had a policeman at his elbow, but the latter is an unrealistic limitation of volitional insanity. See also E.M. Burchell and P.M.A. Hunt, *South African Criminal Law and Procedure*, Vol. 1: *General Principles of Criminal Law* (3rd ed., 1997, Cape Town, J.M. Burchell (ed.)) pp.174–175.

[53] See *infra*, para. 10.37.

[54] *R. v. Kopsch* (1925) 19 Cr.App.R. 50, Lord Hewart C.J. at 51.

[55] R.C. Recommendation 18.

[56] *Attorney-General for South Australia v. Brown* [1960] A.C. 432. See also the English Draft Criminal Code (L.C. No. 177, "A Criminal Code for England and Wales" (1989) H. of C., No. 299, Vol. I) cl. 34 *et seq.*

[57] *Crime and the Criminal Law* (London, 1963), p.74.

[58] See Model Penal Code, T.D. 4, p.175.

seems, too, that we accept that the addict lacks control of his craving.[59] It may be, however, that the control test depends on the view that the criterion for freedom of choice is corrigibility.[60] Or, to put it another way, the control test may operate only in situations where blame seems inappropriate, and may just be another way of describing such cases. It will, at the very least, be easier for the addict to establish irresponsibility by reason of lack of control than it will be for the robber or shoplifter: for as a general rule drug-addiction is not affected by threat of punishment or promise of reward, while stealing is. This leaves it open to a particular accused to show that his stealing is of the nature of an addiction for the result of which it would be unfair to blame him, but such proof will not be easy. There is the further difficulty that irresistibility is relative and, if only for that reason, most "control" type cases are perhaps better treated in the context of diminished responsibility.[61]

The control test shares with the product test[62] the difficulty of defining disease. That difficulty may exist in relation to M'Naghten-type insanity at the stage of deciding whether to acquit *simpliciter* or to acquit by reason of mental disorder. But it arises in the control- and product-type tests at the stage of deciding whether to acquit or convict. And definitions of disease in this area tend to be circular, being based either on the distinction between morally reprehensible and morally neutral conditions, or on the distinction between conditions susceptible to medical treatment and those susceptible to social treatment, a distinction which is, of course, blurred by the practice of modern psychiatry to use social treatments like group-counselling and other case-work methods, which are distinguishable from moral exhortation and good works, if at all, only by their greater sophistication.[63]

The need to recognise the defence. Unless the law is prepared to say that **10.14**
there is no such thing as "irresistible" impulse it is difficult to see how it can refuse to accept it as a defence. The existence and strength of any insane impulse must be regarded as a question of medical fact, just as the existence and strength of mechanical compulsion is regarded as a question of physical fact. To adopt any other attitude is to insist that the concept of free will means that everyone is always free to do or refrain from any action in any circumstances, and that is a very extreme view. Lord Justice-Clerk Hope once told a jury that they might be sure that the accused was not tempted beyond what he was able to bear.[64] But even Lord Hope later recognised that an accused might be "unable, by the visitation of God, to do what his duty to God requires — to struggle and overcome his passions, which every man possessed of reason may".[65]

---

[59] And should therefore be acquitted of any offence which arises out of his subjection to it: *cf. Robinson v. Cal.*, 370 U.S. 660 (1962); *Powell v. Texas*, 392 U.S. 514 (1968). Whether his acquittal should be by reason of insanity depends on the law's definition of mental disorder.

[60] *cf.* Nowell-Smith, *Ethics* (Harmondsworth, 1954), Chap. 20.

[61] On this whole problem see A. Ross, *On Guilt, Responsibility and Punishment* (Berkley 1975), Chaps 4 and 5.

[62] *infra*, paras 10.15 *et seq.*

[63] *cf.* the Butler Committee's comments on the treatment of psychopaths: *op.cit.* n.7, para. 5.38.

[64] *Jas. Gibson* (1844) 2 Broun 332, 361.

[65] *Geo. Lillie Smith* (1855) 2 Irv. 1, 62. By way of contrast, for an account of the move away from volitional insanity in the United States (following the controversial verdict in the case of *U.S. v. Hinckley* 672 F.2d. 115, 1982) see R.D. Mackay, *Mental Condition Defences and the Criminal Law* (Oxford, 1995), pp.108–131: see also J. Dressler, *Understanding Criminal Law* (2nd ed., 1995), p.316 *et seq.* for a general critical account of the insanity defense in the U.S.A.

The causal approach

10.15 One influential modern view of the problem of insanity and crime is that the question cannot be decided by reference to rules or formulae. This view is reflected in the recommendation of the Royal Commission on Capital Punishment that the Rules should be abrogated, and the jury left to decide if "the accused was suffering from disease of the mind . . . to such a degree that he ought not to be held responsible."[66] This is too vague, but the modern approach can perhaps be described by saying that wherever the accused's crime was caused by his insanity he should be treated as irresponsible. If the accused's conduct is caused by insanity, punishment would be pointless because it would not affect the cause of the crime. Alternatively, it can be said that where the accused's crime is caused by illness it is caused by something for which he is not to blame, unless he lives in Erewhon. If the answer to "Why did he do it?" is "Because he was mentally ill", there can be no responsibility. And because serious mental illness affects a person's whole personality this will usually be the answer when an insane man commits a crime.

Unless this type of approach is adopted it is difficult to include among the irresponsible those who act not on sudden impulse but after long brooding on imagined wrongs or their own miserable condition, like the man who kills his family to save them from the result of his poverty,[67] the depressive who finally kills the girl he has seduced, or the woman who kills her child while suffering from puerperal insanity. This approach is implicit in present Scottish practice, but it is not expressly the law of Scotland.[68]

10.16 THE NEW HAMPSHIRE RULE. Of the many states whose laws were considered by the Royal Commission on Capital Punishment, only New Hampshire expressly adopted the view that insanity is to be decided on the facts without reference to any special tests, although the same attitude was adopted by Lord Justice-Clerk Moncreiff in a number of cases in the 1870s.[69] The law there is that:

> "Neither delusion nor knowledge of right and wrong, nor design or cunning in planning and executing the killing and escaping or avoiding detection, nor ability to recognise acquaintances, or to labour or transact business or manage affairs, is, as a matter of law, a test of mental disease: but . . . all symptoms and all tests of mental disease are purely matters of fact, to be determined by the jury . . . Whether the defendant had a mental disease, and whether the

---

[66] R.C. Recommendation 19. *Cf.* Lord Wheatley's charge to the jury in *H.J. Burnett*, High Court at Aberdeen, July 1963 unrep'd.: "[T]here is no exact definition of what constitutes insanity in the law of Scotland, and there are no rules regulating the matter": Transcript of Judge's Charge, 25.

[67] *cf. H.M. Advocate v. Sharp*, 1927 J.C. 66.

[68] The English Draft Criminal Code (L.C. No. 177, "A Criminal Code for England and Wales" (1989) H. of C., No. 299, Vol. I) seems to have abandoned causal criteria by requiring proof only that at the time of the offence the accused was suffering from severe mental illness or severe mental handicap: but the assumption is that a causal connection can be presumed because of the severity of the defendant's condition. Nevertheless, the presumption has been made a rebuttable one — see cls 35(1) and (2) of the Draft Bill, and paras 11.15 to 11.16 of the Commentary to the Code.

[69] *infra*, paras 10.32 to 10.35.

> killing of his wife was the product of such disease, are questions of fact for the jury."[70]

A similar view was at one time taken by the federal courts in the District of Columbia, where it has been held that an accused is not responsible if his crime was the product of mental disorder. This was said to be because "The legal and moral traditions of the western world require that . . . where [criminal] acts stem from and are the product of a mental disease or defect . . . moral blame shall not attach, and hence there will not be criminal responsibility."[71]

The advantages of the causal approach. The greatest advantage of the causal approach is that it enables the law to separate those whose crimes are committed from motives which are amenable to punishment from those who require not punishment but medical treatment in order to prevent a recurrence of their crime: an advantage which is increased by the consideration that treatment of the insane is more likely to be effective than punishment of the sane. **10.17**

The causal approach has the further advantage that it is flexible, and is sensible enough to leave the decision on the matter to those who know something about it: the medical experts. Only the doctors can know whether an accused is insane, and only the doctors can know whether he requires treatment or is amenable to punishment. Lawyers and doctors have always been suspicious of each other, especially in matters regarding insanity and irresponsibility. Lawyers tend to throw up their hands in horror at the idea of questions of legal responsibility being decided by doctors. But this is a misleadingly naïve attitude. The doctors do not decide responsibility; they only say whether the accused is mentally ill or not, and if he was ill, whether his illness affected his conduct. If it were the law that all insane criminals were irresponsible, this would be a legal principle, just as much as the Rules are legal principles. Lawyers may all consider themselves amateur psychologists, and in the old days when only raving lunatics were regarded as irresponsible it might have been easy for a lawyer to know if a particular accused was responsible or not, but today only an expert can pronounce on someone's mental health. The doctor who says the accused committed the crime because he was suffering from paranoia is no more answering a legal question than is the doctor who says the deceased died from poison, or the handwriting expert who says a particular signature is forged; all these experts do is to give the law the facts to which the relevant legal principle is to be applied. And this is so whether that principle is about responsibility and insanity, or about the criminal nature of poisoning or forgery. The New Hampshire Rule is no less a legal criterion than the Rules.

The difficulties of the causal approach. The product test has now been abandoned by the courts of the District of Columbia in favour of the Model Code's criterion of substantial capacity to appreciate the **10.18**

---

[70] *State v. Pike* (1869) 49 N.H. 399, Doe J.; R.C. App.9, para. 11. The modern law of New Hampshire is no different: see *State v. Abbott*, 127 N.H. 444; 503 A.2d 791 (1985). The State Criminal Code offers no separate definition of insanity, and indeed narrates that: "A person who is insane at the time he acts is not criminally responsible for his conduct. Any distinction between a statutory and common law defense of insanity is hereby abolished" (628:2.I).

[71] *Durham v. U.S.* 214 F. 2d 862 (1954), cited in H. Weihofen, *The Urge to Punish* (London, 1957). 7–8; but see now *U.S. v. Brawner*, 471 F. 2d 969 (1972) which rejected the *Durham* rule; *infra*, paras 10.18 *et seq.*

criminality of one's actions or to conform one's conduct to the requirements of law.[72] The abandonment of the test was due partly to its failure to prevent psychiatrists from usurping the jury's function by labelling behaviour as the product of disease, but also to weaknesses in the formulation of the "product" test itself.

10.19 THE CAUSAL LINK. The causal approach accepts that to succeed in a defence of insanity it is necessary to show that the criminal conduct was caused by mental illness: the mere co-existence of mental illness and criminal conduct is insufficient.[73] Even persons who suffer from severe mental illness behave in certain ways and at certain times just as they would have behaved had they not been suffering from the illness, and in these situations their conduct is not caused by their illness even in terms of *sine qua non* causation. But where the illness is severe, conduct of this kind is likely to be restricted to trivial matters, such as eating, or dressing, or performing other routine operations. The law, however, is concerned with extraordinary and important types of behaviour, and it may be possible to say that certain illnesses are so extensive as to affect any important decisions the patient may make, or his ability to control his behaviour in all important matters. In such a case it could be said that any unusual behaviour should be ascribed to the illness. What is "unusual" is a matter of fact in the circumstances of the case. If a thief developed a mental illness and continued to steal the stealing would not be ascribed to the illness, but if he began to indulge in serious violence after the onset of the illness it would be reasonable to ascribe that change in his behaviour to the illness. In any event, however difficult it may be in theory, the causal problem is not necessarily insurmountable in practice: the court will merely ask whether the mental illness was a cause of the criminal conduct, applying the same causal standards as are applied in other branches of the law. These standards may not be free from difficulty, but the difficulty is no greater with regard to mental illness than in any other situation.[74]

10.20 THE NATURE OF THE ILLNESS. Once the causal question is answered in the affirmative, however, a more fundamental difficulty arises: is the fact that this conduct was caused by a certain mental illness sufficient to support a defence of insanity? In the days of certifiable insanity it was assumed in practice that where the illness amounted to certifiable insanity the accused was entitled to succeed in his defence, and that where it was caused by something less it might support a plea of diminished responsibility or be quite irrelevant, but, except perhaps on rare occasions, it did not amount to a defence.[75] Now that certifiable insanity has disappeared the law has to make its own standards, and probably the only way the law can do this is by reference to the

---

[72] Model Penal Code, O.D., s.4.01 (1). The case which finally abandoned *Durham* is *U.S. v. Brawner*, 471 F. 2d 969 (1972). Bazelon C.J., the creator of *Durham*, would have preferred to replace it by asking whether there was such impairment of the accused's mental or emotional processes or behaviour controls that he could not justly be held responsible for his act: at 1032.

[73] The Model Penal Code rejects the New Hampshire Rule because it does not set out a causal criterion: Model Penal Code, T.D. 4, 159.

[74] The District Court in *Carter v. U.S.*, 252 F. 2d 608 (1957), did in fact adopt the test of "but for" causation.

[75] *cf. H.M. Advocate v. Sharp*, 1927 J.C. 66; *H.M. Advocate v. Savage*, 1923 J.C. 49; *H.M. Advocate v. Braithwaite*, 1945 J.C. 55.

consequences of the illness, by saying that where the illness has a certain effect on the patient he is to be regarded as legally insane: and the definition of that effect will be the definition of legal insanity. In *McDonald v U.S.*[76] the Federal District Court adopted a definition of this kind, which was reasserted in *Brawner*[77]: "Mental disease includes any abnormal condition of the mind which substantially affects mental or emotional processes and substantially impairs behaviour controls."

Conclusion. How then is legal insanity to be defined? To adopt a rigid test like the M'Naghten Rules or even to concentrate entirely on intellectual insanity is to cut oneself off from any advances which may be made in psychiatric medicine, while on the other hand to say as the Royal Commission did that the question should be whether the accused was suffering from disease of the mind to such a degree that he ought not to be treated as responsible[78] is to take refuge in an unhelpful tautology.[79] Probably the best that can be done is to adopt a modified form of the New Hampshire Rule and treat a person as legally insane whenever his actings are substantially caused by a mental disorder so severe as to affect his ability to appreciate his situation and behaviour or to translate his appreciation into action. The American Law Institute's Model Penal Code's formulation of the test appears to be appropriate in this regard. Section 4.01 (1) of the Official Draft provides that: "A person is not responsible for criminal conduct if at the time of such conduct as a result of mental disease . . . he lacks substantial capacity either to appreciate the criminality of his conduct or to conform his conduct to the requirements of the law." The Code suggests that "criminality" might be replaced by wrongfulness; it might be even better to replace it by a neutral term such as "nature," or simply to talk of capacity to appreciate his conduct. "Appreciation" is a wide enough term to cover all aspects of the conduct — its nature, its consequences, its moral value, and its legal effect. **10.21**

The key word in the proposed definition is "substantial". This recognises that something less than a total lack of capacity is sufficient, and at the same time that not every impairment of mental health is to be treated as insanity. But the Code does not define "substantial",[80] and in that respect fails to define legal insanity. Whether or not there is "substantial" incapacity is something which the court has to decide by weighing all the evidence against some undefined standard and deciding whether the accused's condition is such that he should properly be regarded as having acted under the influence of a serious mental illness. This, of course, is a return to the Royal Commission's tautology, although it does give a little more guidance than the latter formulation: indeed in the end it amounts to an acceptance of the situation described by Lord Cooper when he told the Royal Commission that whatever directions one gave a jury they would simply ask themselves, "Is the man mad or is he not?"[81]

---

[76] 312 F. 2d 847 (1962).

[77] 471 F. 2d 969 (1972).

[78] R.C. Recommendation 19.

[79] It may be that the tautology expresses the reality of jury behaviour, but it may be that the jury require rather firmer guidelines than the Royal Commission suggest if the proper balance is to be maintained between the demands of stability and predictability and those of flexibility. Even jury equity presupposes a background of strict law; see R.J. Simon, *The Jury and the Defence of Insanity* (Boston and Toronto, 1967).

[80] See T.D. 4, 159.

[81] R.C. Evid. of Lord Cooper, Q. 5479.

More enlightened attitudes to mental illness[82] and the abolition of capital punishment[83] have meant that the question behind the question asked in almost all British insanity cases has changed: it is no longer "should he hang?" but "What disposal would be most appropriate in the circumstances?" It is no longer the case that the stark choice is between prison or mental hospital.[84] Nor is it any longer necessary to have a finding of insanity and an acquittal before a hospital order (or hospital direction) can be made.[85] In these circumstances there is much to be said for going back to M'Naghten or something like M'Naghten, or even for abolishing the insanity defence altogether. The effect of the former would be to restrict insanity to cases where *mens rea* was absent. The effect of the latter would be to leave it open to the accused to show lack of *mens rea* by leading evidence of mental illness — and to be acquitted *simpliciter* as a result.[86] If he was mentally ill he could be dealt with as such by civil procedures. Mental disorder which did not lead to an absence of *mens rea* could be dealt with by a hospital order following on conviction. In homicide cases this result would require to be mediated by a reduction to culpable homicide on the ground of diminished responsibility, if a life sentence was felt to be inappropriate: but it is now possible to combine such a sentence with the type of hospital order known as a "hospital direction".[87]

The Scots Cases

From Hume to Lord Hope

10.22 Hume states that for the plea of insanity to succeed there must be "an absolute alienation of reason . . . such a disease as deprives the patient of the knowledge of the true aspect and position of things about him, — hinders him from distinguishing friend or foe, — and gives him up to the impulse of his own distempered fancy."[88] It is interesting that this definition, written before M'Naghten was heard of, is typical of what may still be the Scots approach to the problem. It starts off by setting a very high standard — absolute alienation preventing the patient from knowing not merely what he is doing, but what is going on around him, and then tacks on a remark which may or may not be capable of wider interpretation — that he should be activated by the impulse of his own distempered fancy. Hume later distinguishes "want of the ordinary command of temper" and "alienation of reason", pointing out that "To teach men to withstand the impulse of sudden rage, is one great object

---

[82] In Scotland, since the passing of the Mental Health (Scotland) Act 1960: see now the Mental Health (Scotland) Act 1984.

[83] Since the Murder (Abolition of Death Penalty) Act 1965.

[84] See 1995 Act, s.57.

[85] See 1995 Act, s.58 — which is not applicable where the sentence for the offence charged is one 'fixed by law' — and s.59A (as added by the Crime and Punishment (Scotland) Act 1997, s.6(1)).

[86] There would, of course, have to be provisions for an acquittal on the ground of unreasonable error where there was evidence of mental disease — but such evidence would clearly exclude wicked recklessness and so be unobjectionable in principle: see *supra*, para. 9.32.

[87] See 1995 Act, s.59A.

[88] Hume, i, 37. *Cf. Brennan v. H.M. Advocate*, 1977 J.C. 38.

of criminal justice; and a person cannot be considered as incapable of this discipline, who lives at large, as a member of society, and gains his bread by the exercise of an ordinary profession."[89] It is clear now that as a statement of fact this is too wide, but it might be inferred from what Hume says that where someone is in fact incapable of this discipline he is not a fit object of punishment. At any rate it seems to be going too far to say, as did Lord Dunedin, that nothing in Hume countenances a defence of irresistible impulse.[90]

So far as the specific subject of delusions is concerned, Hume seems to take a rather broader view than that taken in the Rules. Hume says, **10.23**

> "And though the pannel have that vestige of reason, which may enable him to answer in the general, that murder is a crime; yet if he cannot distinguish a friend from an enemy, or a benefit from an injury, but conceives everything about him to be the reverse of what it really is, and mistakes the illusions of his fancy in that respect for realities, . . . these remains of intellect are of no sort of service towards the government of his actions, or enabling him to form a judgment of what is right or wrong on any particular occasion. If he does not know the person of his friend, or is possessed with the vain conceit that his friend is there to destroy him, and has already done him the most cruel wrongs, and that all about him are engaged in a conspiracy to abuse him, as well might he be utterly ignorant of the quality of murder. Proceeding, as it does, on a false case, or a conjuration of his own fancy, his judgment of right and wrong is, as to the question of responsibility, truly the same as none at all. It is therefore only in this special sense, as relative to the particular thing done, and the condition of the man's belief and consciousness on that occasion, that an inquiry concerning his intelligence of moral good or evil seems to be material to the issue of his trial."[91]

It is not altogether clear what this means, but it could be argued that Hume is seeking for a criterion like that of a "sane understanding" of what the accused is doing, a view supported by his earlier remark that insanity must be such as to exclude a "competent understanding" of what the accused is doing.[92]

Most of the cases of insanity which Hume cites with approval concern persons "in a state of utter furiosity"[93] who are clearly irresponsible.[94] In *David Hunter*[95] the accused believed his victim had smothered his mother, and was said accordingly to have been "incapable of judging the propriety of his actions, or of reasoning with propriety upon them", which sounds more like a criterion of "sane understanding" than the stricter criterion of the Rules. Hume also seems to recognise the defence **10.24**

---

[89] *ibid.*, 41n.
[90] *Hansard*, HL, May 15, 1924, Vol. 57, col. 475.
[91] Hume, i, 37–38.
[92] *ibid.* 37.
[93] *ibid.* 39.
[94] *Sir Archibald Kinloch* (1795) Hume, i, 39; *Robert Spence* (1747) *ibid.*; *Jean Blair* (1781) *ibid.* 40; *cf. Robt Thomson* (1739) *ibid.*, who was subject to fits and who believed his victim was the devil, and who was in fact convicted and reprieved, although Hume apparently thought he should have been regarded as insane.
[95] (1801) Hume, i, 38.

of puerperal insanity,[96] in which case he is in advance of the Rules and of Lord Hope.[97]

The first case after those in Hume which is reported at any length is that of *William Douglas*,[98] who was found insane on a charge of wilful fire-raising. He had formerly been in a mental institution, and was said to be in such a condition that his disease could be rekindled by drink, and to have been unconscious of what had happened. The question of drink does not seem to have troubled the court, and the case contains no discussion of principle. In *Eugene Whelps*[99] the accused believed that he was a son of the Duke of York, and was the heir to the throne; he was also addicted to walking about barelegged and bearded. Lord Justice-Clerk Hope accepted the view that monomania of the kind the accused suffered from "may proceed to such an extent as to amount to general insanity", but added that the insanity must be shown to have led to the crime, and that unless the accused was so insane "as not to have been able to distinguish between right and wrong" he was responsible.[1]

The last case in this group is *Adam Sliman*.[2] The accused there knew the nature of murder in the abstract but could not apply his knowledge to the particular case since he believed that there was a conspiracy to injure him by supernatural means. Apparently, also, he did not realise that his victim was dead. He was found insane.

Up to the time the Rules were promulgated in England it cannot be said that they formed the law of Scotland, for although the Scots law seems to have proceeded on similar lines, it had no rigid formula and its operation, like that of the English law, seems to have been more liberal than would have been allowed by the Rules.

Lord Hope and the Rules

10.25 The introduction of the Rules as such into the law of Scotland was the work of Lord Hope, who was Lord Justice-Clerk from 1841 to 1858, and of whom it has been said that "from the impetuous and despotic character of his will, and his total incapacity for philosophical inquiry" he should have avoided such difficult subjects as insanity.[3] He certainly seems to have taken a much narrower view of insanity than any other Scots judge, and the driving force behind his attitude seems not to have been any psychological or legal principle, but a religious view that free-will was absolute, and that people must not be allowed to escape punishment for their sinfulness on the excuse that they were not responsible for their acts.

Lord Hope declared the Rules to be part of the law of Scotland in the case of *Jas. Gibson*.[4] Gibson set fire to a mill under the delusion *inter alia* that he was employed by a local aristocrat to punish monopolists, and that the Queen would herself set fire to the mill if he did not do so.[5] He

---

96 *ibid.* 41–42, and in case of *Agnes Crockat* (1756) *ibid.* 42, in which the accused was convicted, apparently, in Hume's view, because of the weak evidence regarding insanity, and reprieved.

97 *cf. Eliz. Yates* (1847) Ark. 238.

98 (1827) Syme 184.

99 (1842) 1 Broun 378.

1 At 381.

2 (1844) 2 Broun 138.

3 C. Scott, "Insanity in its Relation to the Criminal Law" (1889) 1 J.R. 237, 241.

4 (1844) 2 Broun 332.

5 See C. Scott, *op.cit.*, 251.

also believed that he was acting under divine command. Lord Hope told the jury that before they could find the prisoner insane they must be satisfied that there was an absolute alienation of reason. He then put the Rules into his own words as follows:

> "The man must believe, not that the crime is wrong in the abstract (for most madmen do admit murder to be wrong, and punishable in the abstract), but that *the particular act* committed under the influence of the motive which seems to have prompted it, was not an offence against the law . . . [The question for the jury is] if the delusion really went to that extreme length that he thought the particular act was not only praiseworthy in itself (for that is not by any means sufficient), but not a crime against the law, for which he could be punished."[6]

As an example of what would be sufficient Lord Hope gave the case of a man believing insanely that his victim was going to kill him — *i.e.* an error which if reasonable would result in the acquittal of a sane man.

Gibson[6a] is also authority for the view that there can be a partial insanity which is irrelevant to the question of responsibility:

> "The law does not recognise partial insanity in the ordinary sense of the term . . . if it appears . . . that the pannel, in reference to the particular act with which he was charged, and the motives which are thought (on the notion of insanity) to have prompted its commission, still well knew that he was punishable for his act, because it was an offence against the law, that is enough to negative insanity according to the rules of law."[7]

Gibson[7a] also contains an explicit rejection of the defence of irresistible impulse:

> "No such principle is recognised in law, as that a man allowing a fancy or morbid feeling to get possession of his mind and temper although it *disturbs* reason, while it does *not overthrow* it, will escape punishment, because, instead of resisting the temptations of such ill-regulated, morbid, distempered, and ungovernable feelings and passions, and prejudices (whether called delusions or not), he gives way to them, and indulges in their gratification and satisfaction . . . The man *chooses* to commit the act: he *gives way* to the suggestions and temptations which are strong, only because he has long indulged in such thoughts. Rely upon it, he was not tempted above what he was able to bear."[8]

The "religious" attitude is prominent in all Lord Hope's pronounce- **10.26**
ments on insanity. He was convinced that the existence of temptation, however overwhelming, was only the result of the patient's own wickedness. He gave strong expression to this view in *Eliz Yates*,[9] where a distracted and destitute girl drowned her ten-month-old illegitimate child after the father had refused to support it. The jury were told:

> "You are not . . . to allow yourselves to be led away by the false notions of what is insanity, which seem to be creeping, if not into

---

[6] 2 Broun at 356–357.
[6a] (1844) 2 Broun 332.
[7] At 359.
[7a] (1844) 2 Broun 332.
[8] At 360–361.
[9] (1847) Ark. 238.

> courts of justice, at least into moral discussions elsewhere. The gambler who destroys himself, because ruin is staring him in the face, is a responsible agent, and violates the laws of God. It is not insanity that is the cause of his crime — it is the distempered and disordered workings of a depraved nature within him . . . There are many cases arising from moral depravity and moral wickedness, which pass in the ordinary language of life as acts of insanity, which are nevertheless acts of a mind rebelling against the decrees of God".[10]

It is interesting that the suggestion, which is hardly more than implicit in these directions, that insanity which is the result of the accused's own evil ways is irrelevant, was never taken up by the law: there is no difference in legal responsibility between the man whose insanity is the result of syphilis, or even of drink, and the man whose insanity is the result of a wound received in the battlefield.[11]

10.27 Lord Hope expressed views similar to those in *Gibson*[11a] in *George Lillie Smith,*[12] and the Rules were followed in at least two later cases, although without the religious overtones. They were followed by Lord Justice-General McNeill in *Geo. Bryce*[13] where the accused, who was mentally subnormal, had killed a girl he believed to have been calling him a drunken blackguard. The test put in *Bryce*[13a] was whether he really believed "something had occurred which would be a ground for taking away the life of this unfortunate girl"[14] — *i.e.* the test of error.

The Rules were also followed in *Andrew Brown*[15] by Lord Justice-Clerk Inglis who spoke of knowledge of the act committed, or of its nature, more or less in the words of the Rules.[16]

The movement away from the Rules — 1852–69.

10.28 Although the Rules were being followed as late as 1866, there had been cases before then in which a broader view had been taken. This may be said to have begun as early as 1852 in *Isabella Blyth,*[17] where Lord Cockburn stopped the trial of the accused for matricide because he was satisfied of her insanity. It appears that she believed she was wasting away and going mad, and that she sometimes knew right and wrong and sometimes not. Nothing seems to have been said of her knowledge regarding the murder, and the case looks like one of murder following on a period of depressive brooding, so that it cannot be brought within the Rules.

---

[10] At 240–241.

[11] Provided in the case of voluntary intoxication the resulting insanity is not of a transitory nature: *Brennan, supra*; see *infra,* paras 12.05, 12.12 *et seq.*

[11a] (1844) 2 Broun 332.

[12] (1855) 2 Irv. 1 — the plea succeeded in this case.

[13] (1864) 4 Irv. 506.

[13a] (1864) 4 Irv. 506.

[14] At 526.

[15] (1866) 5 Irv. 215.

[16] At 217. *Cf.* also *John Caldwell* (1866) 5 Irv. 241.

[17] (1952) J. Shaw 567.

In *James Denny Scott*,[18] in the following year, Lord Cockburn gave as one of the classes of insanity the case "where the prisoner was under *an impulse, so irresistible to him, that he was not a free agent.* A man cannot be punished for doing an act which, from mental disease, he could not avoid doing."[19] **10.29**

Again, in *John McFadyen*,[20] Lord Cowan told the jury that the law was as laid down in *Gibson*[20a] but went on to say that they must ask the question, "Did the panel possess intellect enough to know the distinction between right and wrong . . . Or, if he knew that distinction, was he under disability, from want of sufficient rational power, to govern his actions, and to control his emotions and desires?"[21] **10.30**

Finally, in this group, comes *Alex Milne*,[22] in which Lord Justice-Clerk Inglis, after citing the Rules, said, "[I]f you are once satisfied that this man was under the influence of insane delusions at the time this act was committed, you have no occasion to inquire farther, whether he knew what was right from what was wrong . . . because . . . the law at once presumes . . . that he cannot appreciate what he is doing."[23] This reads like an acceptance of the modern medical view that acts of an insane man should be presumed to be caused by his insanity, although it is restricted in its terms to cases of delusional insanity. **10.31**

By the 1860s, therefore, there were at least two laws of insanity in Scotland, and whether or not an insane person was convicted was likely to depend more on which judge happened to try him, than on any accepted legal principle. The conflict could only be resolved by the reference of a case to the High Court, but naturally in a sphere where opinions were held as strongly as they were for example by Lord Hope, the judges preferred to apply their own ideas.

Lord Moncreiff and the causal approach

In a series of cases in the early 1870s Lord Moncreiff, who was Lord Justice-Clerk from 1869 to 1888, attempted to clarify the law of insanity, mainly by rejecting any rigid criterion and emphasising that the law must keep up with the advances of science. If it is the law today that the only question a jury need ask in deciding the responsibility of an accused who pleads insanity is, "Is he mad?"[24] the credit must go to Lord Moncreiff. **10.32**

The first case in which Lord Moncreiff discussed the question of insanity was that of *Eliza Sinclair or Clafton*,[25] who cut her two children's throats and then her own; the children died and she was charged with murder. Lord Moncreiff said:

> "When the doctors speak of a person doing a thing from uncontrollable impulse, they do not mean an impulse which his mental constitution is not strong enough to combat, or an impulse which

[18] (1853) 1 Irv. 132.
[19] At 142.
[20] (1860) 3 Irv. 650.
[20a] (1844) 2 Broun 332.
[21] At 665.
[22] (1863) 4 Irv. 301.
[23] At 343.
[24] *cf. supra*, para. 10.05, n.20.
[25] (1871) 2 Couper 73.

> the individual will not control; but one which through mental disease he has not the power of controlling, and therefore, in the doctors' view also, before a case can be brought under that category, mental disease must be proved to have been present . . .
>
> The question here is whether the unsoundness of the prisoner's mind prevented her from having the power to resist the impulse to kill her children when it occurred. It is certainly amply proved that there is such a form of insanity recurrent on pregnancy and lactation, and which is sometimes accompanied with homicidal and suicidal paroxysms. And if you can find . . . that the panel at the time of the commission of the crime, was labouring under such a paroxysm, I know of nothing in the shape of a legal proposition that can possibly prevent you from finding that she was of unsound mind."[26]

The whole tenor of this charge is in violent contrast to that of the charge in *Yates*;[27] on this matter Lord Hope and Lord Moncreiff belong to different worlds.

On the test of knowledge of right and wrong, Lord Moncreiff said, "I doubt this test will not advance us far; for the definition of what constitutes the knowledge of right and wrong, may be as hard as [the definition of her mental condition]. It must be in a sane knowledge."[28]

10.33 In *Archibald Miller*[29] Lord Moncreiff gave the following direction:

> "[I]t is entirely imperfect and inaccurate to say that if a man has a conception intellectually of moral or legal obligation, he is of sound mind. Better knowledge of the phenomena of lunacy has corrected some loose and inaccurate language which lawyers used to apply in such cases. A man may be entirely insane, and yet may know well enough that an act which he does is forbidden by law . . . It is not a question of knowledge, but of soundness of mind. If the man have not a sane mind to apply his knowledge, the mere intellectual apprehension of an injunction or prohibition may stimulate his unsound mind to do an act simply because it is forbidden . . . If a man has a sane appreciation of right and wrong he is certainly responsible; but he may form and understand the idea of right and wrong and yet be hopelessly insane. You may discard these attempts at definition altogether. They only mislead."[30]

10.34 Lord Moncreiff again expressed his dislike of tests of insanity in the case of *Jas. Macklin*,[31] where he said:

> "It may be asked, what are the indications from which unsoundness of mind may be inferred? I can lay down no general test which can be applied to solve such a question. At one time lawyers were apt to avoid all difficulty by enquiring whether a prisoner knew right from wrong; and as, in point of fact, except in acute mania or idiocy, there are very few lunatics who do not know right from wrong in the

---

[26] At 93.
[27] (1847) Ark. 238.
[28] At 91.
[29] (1874) 3 Couper 16.
[30] At 18.
[31] (1876) 3 Couper 257.

sense of being capable of appreciating and even acting on the distinction, much unreasoning inhumanity has been the result of this unscientific maxim. If it be said that a man is sane if he can form sound judgments on the subject of moral duty, that is only stating the problem in another form, and is not solving it; for a sane judgment on right and wrong can only be formed by a man of sound mind."[32]

Lastly, in the case of *Thos. Barr,*[33] Lord Moncreiff stressed that the problem was one of medical fact, and more or less expressly stated the causal criterion adopted in New Hampshire.[34] His Lordship said: **10.35**

"A man is said to be of unsound mind when his mind is diseased so that, in some at least of the ordinary relations of life, he is incapable, by reason of disease, of controlling his conduct and actions . . .

The question is, was this man's mind diseased — was he the victim of unsound thought, — thought which was the product of the working of an unsound mind . . .

If . . . the prisoner was acting under a conclusion that was not only unsound in the sense of not being well founded, but that it was a conclusion he had formed because his mind was insane, that, no doubt . . . would amount to evidence of insanity."[35]

The effect of these cases is to make the Rules quite irrelevant to the problem, and to replace them with the very general rule that the insane are not responsible for acts which are the product of their insanity. Lord Moncreiff's views accord with the views of modern psychologists and criminologists. Whether or not they accord with the view of the modern law of Scotland is a more difficult question. Judges have been loth to discard the misleading attempts at definition of which Lord Moncreiff spoke, and were, at any rate until very recently, still attached to the Rules. Indeed, Lord Moncreiff can be regarded as an eccentric in this branch of the law — a view which seems to have been adopted by Lord Keith when he said of the cases quoted, "one Judge . . . a long time ago . . . more or less gave the go-by to the M'Naghten Rules",[36] which rather suggests that Lord Keith thought it was so long ago that little heed need be paid to it.

From Lord Moncreiff to the Royal Commission

The cases in this period are few and by no means clear. It seems that when a brief direction of a more or less formal nature was required, the Rules were treated as the best way of expressing the law;[37] but where insanity was dealt with in any detail the common approach was by way of the Rules together with irresistible impulse. There is much to be said for the view that at any rate in the early part of the twentieth century the law was as stated by Lord Cockburn in *James Denny Scott* in 1853[38] — that **10.36**

---

[32] At 259–260.

[33] (1876) 3 Couper 261.

[34] *cf.* para. 10.16, *supra.*

[35] At 264–265.

[36] R.C. Evid. of Lord Keith, Q. 5190.

[37] *e.g. Alex Dingwall* (1867) 5 Irv. 466, 476; *Thos. Ferguson* (1881) 4 Couper 552, 557–8, in both of which the live issue was one of diminished responsibility.

[38] (1853) 1 Irv. 132.

insanity was relevant if it deprived the accused of the capacity to know he was doing wrong, or to know the nature and quality of his act, or if it deprived him of the power of controlling his actions.[39] Sometimes, however, as in *H.M. Advocate v. McClinton,*[40] the judge added to *James Denny Scott*[40a] a reference to *Miller*[40b] without apparently realising that *Miller*[41] represented a wholly different approach to the question, and could not just be tacked on to the Rules as could irresistible impulse.[41a]

There are a number of unreported cases which suggest that the influence of the Rules was still strong in this period. It seems that many judges started off with the Rules as the basic law of insanity, and then said something which sounded not unlike an admission of the defence of irresistible impulse, after which they might or might not add a reference to *Miller.*[41b] As a result, the only clear impression given is that the Rules were the law, though in some cases they might not be the whole law. Macdonald is typical of this approach. He begins by stating the Rules, and gives the case of the man who believes he is acting in self-defence or killing an evil spirit as an example of someone irresponsible through insanity, and then quotes from *Miller.*[42]

10.37 The Rules died hard, but there are a number of cases in this period in which they were dispensed with. Perhaps the most important of these is *H.M. Advocate v. Sharp.*[43] The point at issue was insanity in bar of trial, but the test was treated as being the same as that for the plea of insanity at the time of the crime. In *Sharp*[43a] the accused was intelligent and sane in most matters, but obsessed with the idea that the only way out of his poverty was to kill two of his children so as to relieve his wife of the burden of their support. He knew that this was criminal, but regarded it as a necessary sacrifice. Sharp was clearly suffering from depressive insanity[44] and it was accepted that he was certifiably insane. His plea of insanity was sustained by Lord Constable ostensibly on the ground that he had obviously "lost the sense of distinguishing between right and wrong in regard to the particular act which he was contemplating."[45] But, with respect, this is not convincing — his position seems to have been rather that of someone who felt he had to do something wrong as the only way out of an intolerable situation. Lord Constable went on,

---

[39] This was said to represent the developed law in an article in 1916: H.H. Brown, "Insanity in its Relation to Crime" (1916) 28 J.R. 119, 138.

[40] (1902) 4 Adam 1.

[40a] (1853) 1 Irv. 132.

[40b] (1874) 3 Couper 16.

[41] *ibid.*

[41a] There was a suggestion in *H.M. Advocate v. Robert Smith* (1893) 1 Adam 34, 42, that the accused succumbed to an impulse he was psychologically incapable of resisting, but the plea of insanity was abandoned and the case is not really an authority on irresistible impulse; it was decided on diminished responsibility.

[41b] (1874) 3 Couper 16.

[42] *supra.* Macdonald also gives the impression that not only *Gibson, supra* but also *Milne, supra,* support the Rules: Macdonald, 9. See also L.J.-C. Alness in *John Henry Savage*, High Court at Edinburgh, May 1923, rep'd on another point at 1923 J.C. 49, and in *William and Susan Newall*, High Court at Glasgow, September, 1927, unrep'd, and Lord Moncreiff in *John Maxwell Muir*, High Court at Dumfries, April 1993, rep'd on another point at 1933 J.C. 46.

[43] 1927 J.C. 66.

[43a] *ibid.*

[44] *cf.* A. McNiven, "Psychoses and Criminal Responsibility" in *Mental Abnormality and Crime,* 8, 15; W.C. Sullivan, *Crime and Insanity* (London, 1924), p.92.

[45] 1927 J.C. 66, Lord Constable at 68.

however, to reject the M'Naghten formulation of the law and to accept the views of Lord Moncreiff in *Archibald Miller*.[45a] He then held that Sharp could be treated as insane because, while he regarded his act as a justifiable and even meritorious one, he fully realised the penalty that would follow, and regarded it as a solemn sacrifice which he was called to make.[46] On its facts *Sharp*[46a] appears to be a good example of the causal approach, his irresponsibility being due to the fact that his behaviour was the product of depressive insanity.

In *H.M. Advocate v. Brown*[47] where the real question was again fitness to plead, Lord Justice-General Dunedin dealt with the question of insanity at the time of the crime by telling the jury that they could acquit the accused on the ground of insanity if they found that he was not "really responsible for his actions".[48] In *H.M. Advocate v. Cameron*[49] where there was again a question of unfitness to plead as well as one of insanity at the time of the crime, Lord Birnam directed the jury on the latter point by merely telling them that if on the evidence they came to the conclusion that the accused had been insane at the time of the crime they should find accordingly. These cases show that at least some judges accepted that there was no legal test of insanity in Scots law. This view gained further support from *H.M. Advocate v. Mitchell*,[50] although the defence there was that the crime had been committed during an epileptic fit which is fairly clearly a state of irresponsibility on any view. Lord Justice-Clerk Thomson said that in the circumstances there was no need for any detailed direction on insanity, and told the jury merely that since in a seizure, "when the patient is subject to the attack, his consciousness is so clouded that he does not know what he is doing and consequently cannot be regarded as responsible for his actions",[51] they need only ask themselves if in fact he was in a fit when he committed the crime. **10.38**

The Royal Commission

The witnesses who gave evidence to the Royal Commission on Capital Punishment had some difficulty in explaining to the Commission just what the Scots law on insanity was. **10.39**

The Faculty of Advocates suggested in their evidence that the law would hold a man responsible if he had "a sane understanding of the circumstances of his act",[52] but this is question-begging, unless it means that all insane persons are irresponsible, in which case it should have said so, and it ignores the question of volition.

The M'Naghten Rules loom large in the evidence of Lord Cooper and of Lord Keith. But it is not clear if this was because the Rules were regarded as a concise expression of the law of cognitive insanity, and adopted to that extent in Scotland, or whether it was just that they were

---

[45a] (1874) 3 Couper 16.
[46] 1927 J.C. at 69.
[46a] 1927 J.C. 66.
[47] (1907) 5 Adam 312.
[48] At 346.
[49] High Court at Perth, June 1946, unrep'd, see 1946 S.N. 74.
[50] 1951 J.C. 53.
[51] At 54.
[52] R.C. Evid. Memorandum of Faculty of Advocates, para. 12. The Faculty's definition is accepted by Prof. Smith: T.B. Smith, p.150.

a natural starting point for any discussion, especially in the comparative absence of modern Scots authority. Lord Cooper said at one point,"if you had the whole fourteen Scottish Judges here and asked them to produce the M'Naghten formula they would probably not be able to because it is not part of our law. We talk about it, but we do not use it as an authoritative formula",[53] but neither Lord Cooper nor Lord Keith could produce such a formula.

Lord Keith said that, "the M'Naghten Rules would be considered, but my impression is that the law is perhaps developing and is rather more flexible in that matter than it used to be, and that more regard would probably be paid to the actual evidence that was led by specialists on insanity, and that the jury would be directed in the circumstances of each particular case",[54] which seems, with respect, to sum up the situation as it was then, although it gives little weight to the views of Lord Justice-Clerk Moncreiff.

Lord Cooper's evidence was that, if he had to direct a jury,

> "I am not prepared to say that I would charge in the exact terms of the M'Naghten Rules . . . I would take as the broad rule only the third one, that insanity arises when a person is labouring under such a defect of reason from disease of the mind that he does not know the nature, and quality of the act he is doing, or if he does know it, he does not know he is doing wrong . . . I would embroider and elaborate that a bit and not leave it as if the last word of the decalogue had been uttered in the M'Naghten Rules, which are not part of the law of Scotland. You will appreciate my difficulty in answering more specifically, because the question so rarely arises and in fact has never arisen in my judicial experience.[55]
>
> . . . However much you charge a jury as to the M'Naghten Rules or any other test, the question they would put to themselves when they retired is — "Is the man mad or is he not?"[56]

The nearest Lord Cooper came to committing himself to any definite statement was to enlarge the Rules into a tautology when he said that in directing a jury,

> "I would certainly have to give . . . an explanation of the essence of what is in the M'Naghten Rules, probably with some embroidery, to the effect that the matter for their consideration was whether, on the expert testimony and the factual evidence the accused had shown the probability to be that he was not responsible for his actions by reason of a defect of reason."[57]

But this says only that the burden is on the accused to establish his irresponsibility, and that he must do so not quite by reference to the Rules, but yet in some way by reference to the Rules, which takes insufficient notice of Lord Justice-Clerk Moncreiff's rejection of the Rules altogether.[58]

---

[53] R.C. Evid. of Lord Cooper, Q. 5506.

[54] Q. 5189.

[55] Q. 5465.

[56] Q. 5479.

[57] Q. 5475.

[58] The Crown Office, incidentally, said that the Rules as laid down in *Gibson, supra*, represented the law, and here as elsewhere their Memorandum merely followed the inaccuracies of Macdonald: R.C. Evid. Memorandum of the Crown Agent, App.(d), para. 2. This statement is sufficiently belied by Crown Office practice to lose all value, and the Crown Agent was constrained in his oral evidence to admit that the rules had been modified in some judges' charges: Q. 1998.

Later cases. The most recent reported statement of the general law in a criminal case is that by Lord Strachan in *H.M. Advocate v. Kidd.*[59] Lord Strachan gave the following directions to the jury on the defence of insanity: **10.40**

> "The question really is this, whether at the time of the offence charged the accused was of unsound mind. I do not think you should resolve this matter by inquiring into all the technical terms and ideas that the medical witnesses have put before you. Treat it broadly, and treat the question as being whether the accused was of sound or unsound mind. That question is primarily one of fact to be decided by you, but I have to give you these directions. First, in order to excuse a person from responsibility for his acts on the ground of insanity, there must have been an alienation of the reason in relation to the act committed. There must have been some mental defect, to use a broad neutral word, a mental defect, by which his reason was overpowered, and he was thereby rendered incapable of exerting his reason to control his conduct and reactions. If his reason was alienated in relation to the act committed, he was not responsible for that act, even although otherwise he may have been apparently quite rational. What is required is some alienation of the reason in relation to the act committed . . .
>
> At one time, following English law, it was held in Scotland that if an accused did not know the nature and quality of the act committed, or if he did know it but did not know he was doing wrong, it was held that he was insane. That was the test, but that test has not been followed in Scotland in the most recent cases. Knowledge of the nature and quality of the act, and knowledge that he is doing wrong, may no doubt be an element, indeed are an element, in deciding whether a man is sane or insane, but they do not, in my view, afford a complete or perfect test of sanity. A man may know very well what he is doing, and may know that it is wrong, and he may none the less be insane. It may be that some lunatics do an act just because they know it is wrong. I direct you therefore that you should dispose of this question in accordance with the directions which I have given, which briefly are, that there must be alienation of reason in regard to the act committed, . . . the question is one for you to decide whether the accused was at the time of sound or unsound mind."

Lord Strachan's approach was followed by the Second Division (including himself) in the civil case of *Breen v. Breen*[60] where what was in issue was the relevance of a plea of insanity in an action of divorce for cruelty. The Second Division expressly stated that the M'Naghten Rules did not form part of Scots law.[61] The defender in *Breen*[61a] was certifiably insane but, as Lord Patrick said, "The case is not one of total alienation of reason, since the doctors are agreed that the defender knew the

[59] 1960 J.C. 61, 70–71.

[60] 1961 S.C. 158.

[61] See also Lord Cameron at 176, and *Mckenzie v. Mckenzie*, 1960 S.C. 322, *per* Lord Walker.

[61a] 1961 S.C. 158.

nature and quality of his acts and knew that they were wrong. Nevertheless, at the times when the acts in question were committed he was insane, and the acts were committed under the influence of his insanity."[62]

Lord Patrick did not, however, rest content with this statement of the causal theory, but went on to say that the defender was not responsible because his conduct "was influenced by his insanity, so that he was disabled from forming a rational decision in regard to it".[63] Lord Mackintosh said that insanity was not treated as a question of knowledge but of "soundness of mind".[64] Both Lord Mackintosh and Lord Strachan spoke of "alienation of reason" as well as "unsoundness of mind", and Lord Strachan repeated his rejection of the Rules, and also said that certifiability was not the test.[65]

The directions in *H.M. Advocate v. Kidd*[65a] have since been followed in a number of cases,[66] and the question lies whether they can be taken to represent the current position. They have been described as coming close to the M'Naghten Rules,[67] but although their language is in the main that of cognitive insanity, if they are viewed against the background of Scots law and in particular of Lord Moncreiff's views, they will be seen to be much wider than the Rules. They lay stress on the medical position — is the man insane or not — even if certifiability is not accepted as a criterion in itself, and they take into account capacity to control one's actings. They are consistent with the more general requirement of "sane understanding" of which the Faculty of Advocates spoke in their evidence to the Royal Commission,[68] and with Lord Moncreiff's view that mere "intellectual apprehension" is useless without a sane mind to apply one's knowledge.[69]

The opinion of the Appeal Court in *Cardle v. Mulrainey*,[70] however, casts doubts on whether the Scots law test for insanity is as liberal as the directions of Lord Strachan in *Kidd*[70a] would suggest. In effect, *Cardle v. Mulrainey*[70b] is concerned with the defence of non-insane automatism; but the court emphasised that that defence shared with insanity the requirement of a total alienation of reason, which was not only an essential requirement but to be distinguished from loss of control or inability to control one's actions. In the words of Lord Justice-General Hope, in delivering the opinion of the Court: "Inability to exert self-control, which the sheriff has described as an inability to complete the reasoning process, must be distinguished from the essential requirement that there should be total alienation of the accused's mental faculties of reasoning and of understanding what he is doing."[71] Even more telling perhaps is the reason given for there having been an absence of total

---

[62] 1961 S.C. at 182.

[63] At 185.

[64] At 193.

[65] At 196.

[65a] 1960 J.C. 61.

[66] *e.g.* in *H.M. Advocate v. Blake*, 1986 S.L.T. 661, *per* Lord Brand.

[67] J.Ll.J. Edwards, "Diminished Responsibility" in *Essays in Criminal Science*, G.O.W. Mueller (ed.) (N.Y. and London, 1961), 301, 306n.

[68] R.C. Evid., Memorandum of Faculty of Advocates, para. 12.

[69] *Arch. Miller* (1874) 3 Couper 16, 18.

[70] 1992 S.C.C.R. 658.

[70a] 1960 J.C. 61.

[70b] 1992 S.C.C.R. 658.

[71] 1992 S.C.C.R. 658, at 668E.

alienation of reason in the case itself: "Where, as in the present case, the accused knew what he was doing and was aware of the nature and quality of his acts and that what he was doing was wrong, he cannot be said to be suffering from the total alienation of reason in regard to the crime with which he is charged which the defence requires."[72] This suggests, but does not necessarily conclude, that insanity depends on the cognitive criteria found in the McNaghten Rules.[73] The court did not go so far as to overrule what Lord Strachan told the jury in *Kidd*[73a]: but the opinion of the court notes that "[a]n insistence in such absolute terms upon an utter or total alienation of reason may appear to be absent from some of the more recent discussions of the defence of insanity, and in particular from the passage in Lord Strachan's charge to the jury in *H.M. Advocate v. Kidd* at p. 70".[74] This is then followed by a quotation from *Brennan v. H.M. Advocate*[75] which supports the view that a total alienation of reason is required in insanity "as the result of mental illness, mental disease or defect or unsoundness of mind."[76]

It is difficult to assess the significance of the opinion in *Cardle v. Mulrainey*,[76a] especially as the court there apparently proceeds to equate total alienation of reason with "a total loss of control of the accused's actions".[77] Bearing in mind, therefore, that what was said about insanity in *Cardle v. Mulrainey* is strictly *obiter* (since the case is concerned with the defence of non-insane automatism); that the opinion of the court there concedes that the argument it had heard on the need for a total alienation of reason had been "relatively brief";[78] that the court did not say that Lord Strachan's directions in *Kidd* were not to be followed in relation to insanity; and that Scots law prefers common sense solutions to doctrine, it is tentatively submitted as follows: that the present law of Scotland is in broad agreement with the proposals of the American Law Institute's Model Penal Code[79] in requiring the absence of a proper "appreciation" of the situation, and of the ability to control one's actions in the light of such an appreciation.[80]

Brennan v. H.M. Advocate[81] adds little to the general law of insanity, except to stress that the accused's condition must be the result of disease, and to say that, "It is abundantly clear, too, whatever may be comprehended within the word 'disease' as Hume used it, that it does **10.41**

---

[72] *ibid.*, at 668D.

[73] See para. 10.09, *supra*.

[73a] 1960 J.C. 61.

[74] 1992 S.C.C.R. 658, at 668G to 669A.

[75] 1977 J.C. 38. On the effect of *Brennan* on the law of insanity, see para. 10.41, *infra*.

[76] *ibid.*, at 45, quoted in *Cardle v. Mulrainey*, *supra*, at 669C.

[76a] 1992 S.C.C.R. 658.

[77] 1992 S.C.C.R. at 669D. See also *H.M. Advocate v. Bennett*, 1996 S.C.C.R. 331, at 338A, where *Cardle v. Mulrainey*, *supra*, is said to be a case concerned with the need for loss of control to be total.

[78] 1992 S.C.C.R. at 668F.

[79] *supra*, para. 10.21.

[80] *cf.* the English Draft Criminal Code's definition of "severe mental illness" for the purposes of a "mental disorder verdict." The definition (see L.C. No. 177, "A Criminal Code for England and Wales" (1989) H. of C., No. 299, Vol. I), in cl. 34, is very wide but includes "(e) thinking so disordered as to prevent reasonable appraisal of the defendant's situation or reasonable communication with others." For an interesting discussion of the difference between appreciation and knowledge, see *The Queen v. Barnier* [1980] 1 S.C.R. 1124.

[81] 1977 J.C. 38.

not include deliberate and self-induced intoxication."[82] *Brennan*[82a] does not say what is comprehended in "disease", either by Hume or by the modern law, far less what effect the disease must produce, save that there must be "absolute alienation of reason in relation to the act charged".[82b] *Brennan*[83] rejects the "transitory effects on the mind of self-induced intoxication", but not, presumably, other forms of temporary mental unsoundness. Acute melancholia, brought about by an emotional disturbance, and lasting some 48 hours with lucid intervals, and at least exacerbated by drink, led to an acquittal on the ground of insanity in *James Mitchell*[83a] where the accused was charged with murdering his wife's lover.[84]

II — Insanity in Bar of Trial

10.42 The question of insanity in bar of trial is, strictly speaking, a procedural question,[85] but as it is not uncommon for cases of insanity in Scots criminal law to be dealt with by way of a plea in bar of trial, and as this is one reason why the Scots law of insanity and responsibility is comparatively unsettled, it is not inappropriate to discuss the plea in bar of trial in connection with the substantive law.

10.43 *The test of fitness to plead.* Persons who were certifiably insane have almost always been regarded as unfit to plead, and the court normally just accepted the evidence of recognised medical experts.[86] In the rare cases where a plea of insanity in bar of trial had not been accepted by the judge but had been left to the jury the directions given were very simple. In *H.M. Advocate v. Brown*[87] Lord Justice-General Dunedin told the jury they must decide whether the accused could "maintain in sober sanity his plea of innocence and instruct those who defend him as a truly sane man would do". In *H.M. Advocate v. Cameron*,[88] Lord Birnam told the jury merely that they must decide whether the accused was sane or not.[89] For a statement of the legal requirements which must be fulfilled before the plea can succeed one must turn to the cases dealing with sane persons who may be unfit to plead.

---

[82] At 43.

[82a] 1977 J.C. 38.

[82b] *ibid.*, at 43.

[83] *ibid.*

[83a] High Court at Glasgow, March 1960. unrep'd.

[84] *cf. Henry J Burnett, supra*, where the victim was the accused's mistress's husband, and where the alleged insanity lasted only for an hour, although there was some evidence of an earlier history of instability and of some neurological peculiarity. The jury convicted of murder, thus conferring on Burnett the distinction of being the last man to be hanged in Scotland.

[85] See Renton and Brown, Chap. 26.

[86] See R.C. Evid. of Lord Cooper, Q. 5491. *H.M. Advocate v. Cameron*, 1946 S.N. 73 is exceptional in that L.J.-C. Cooper declined to accept the medical evidence, but this may have been at least partly because the doctors had seen each other's reports. Under the modern law, the court is constrained to make its decision on the oral or written evidence of two medical practitioners (1995 Act, s.54(1)): for difficulties this may pose, see *McLachlan v. Brown*, 1997 J.C. 222.

[87] (1907) 5 Adam 312, 346.

[88] High Court at Perth, June 1946, unrep'd. Transcript of judge's charge, 24.

[89] The modern law does not contemplate that decisions on unfitness to plead will be undertaken other than by a judge: see 1995 Act, s.54; *Stewart v. H.M.Advocate (No. 1)*, 1997 J.C. 183, L.J.-C. Cullen at p.190G.

Non-insane unfitness. The principle behind the plea in bar is that everyone is entitled to a fair trial, and that the exercise of that right presupposes that the accused is capable of instructing counsel and of understanding the proceedings. A person may therefore be unfit to plead without suffering from insanity, or indeed from any mental disease at all.[90] There are two reported cases in Scots law in which the question of fitness to plead was raised in respect of deaf mutes, both of whom were found fit to plead and acquitted.[91] In the second of these cases Lord Wark directed the jury as follows: **10.44**

> "Now, what exactly is meant by saying that a man is unfit to plead? The ordinary and common case, of course, is the case of a man who suffers from insanity, that is to say, from mental alienation of some kind which prevents him giving the instructions which a sane man would give for his defence, or from following the evidence as a sane man would follow it, and instructing his counsel as the case goes along upon any point that arises. Now, no medical man says, and no medical man has ever said, that this accused is insane in that sense. His reason is not alienated, but he may be insane . . . although his reason is not alienated, if his condition be such that he is unable either from mental defect or physical defect, or a combination of these, to tell his counsel what his defence is and instruct him so that he can appear and defend him; or if, again, his condition of mind and body is such that he does not understand the proceedings which are going on when he is brought into Court upon his trial, and cannot intelligibly follow what it is all about."[92]

Although there remains doubt as to whether a purely physical defect will suffice,[93] the above direction has recently been affirmed by the Criminal Appeal Court as the proper test for unfitness to plead.[94] It seems to be the case, however, that a mental defect which results in loss of memory as to the act or omission charged will not *per se* suffice. Thus, in *Russell v. H.M. Advocate*[95] the court rejected a plea in bar of trial that the accused suffered from hysterical amnesia which prevented her from remembering anything about the circumstances of the offence — a series of frauds committed some years earlier. Lord Sorn rejected the plea on the ground that "In a plea in bar of trial there is involved the accused's

---

[90] In *Stewart v. H.M.Advocate (No. 1)*, 1997 J.C. 183, the Crown argued that insanity had to be given the same meaning — whether it was pled as a defence (1995 Act, s.54(5)) or in bar of trial (1995 Act, s.54(1)); but this was rejected by the trial judge (Lord Hamilton), and his decision on this point was not appealed. In any event, such an argument runs counter to the accepted law (*infra*).

[91] *Jean Campbell* (1817) Hume, i, 45; *H.M. Advocate v. Wilson*, 1942 J.C. 75. Although *Sharp v. H.M. Advocate*, 1927 J.C. 66, was a bar of trial case it proceeded on the definitions of insanity as a defence. The older cases on the plea-in-bar are reviewed in the Second Report of Committee on Criminal Procedure (Thomson Report), *supra*, Cmnd. 6218, 1975, para. 52.13.

[92] *H.M. Advocate v. Wilson*, 1942 J.C. 75, at p.79.

[93] In *Stewart v. H.M. Advocate (No. 1)*, 1997 J.C. 183, the trial judge (Lord Hamilton) at p.185G reserved his opinion on this matter.

[94] *Stewart v. H.M. Advocate (No. 1)*, *supra*; *McLachlan v. Brown*, 1997 J.C. 222. In both cases, the accused suffered from a mental handicap. There is earlier authority that mental defect does not constitute a bar to trial: *H.M. Advocate v. Breen,* 1921 J.C. 30; *Russell v. H.M. Advocate, infra,* L.J.-C. at 47 — but this is clearly wrong: an idiot cannot be treated as fit to be tried, and there is clear authority that deaf-mutism is relevant to fitness. See also *Barr v. Herron*, 1968 J.C. 20 as reported in (1968) 32 J.C.L. 113.

[95] 1946 J.C. 37.

capacity to understand the charge, and of that there is no doubt here. It also involves her capacity to appreciate the proceedings, and again there is no doubt as to her capacity to appreciate them, and to communicate with her counsel in the course of these proceedings."[96] These views were upheld by the Criminal Appeal Court[97] who refused to apply as a general rule Lord Justice-General Dunedin's statement in *H.M. Advocate v. Brown*[98] that an accused who cannot clearly remember what happened at the time of the offence is unfit to plead. As was pointed out, to accept Lord Dunedin's statement would mean that anyone who committed an offence while very drunk would be unfit to plead.

10.45 *The treatment of persons found unfit to plead.* Since 1995, a court which finds that an accused is insane so that his trial cannot proceed must order an "examination of facts",[99] the purpose of which being to establish in court beyond reasonable doubt that he "did the act or made the omission constituting the offence".[1] It must also be established on the balance of probabilities that there are no grounds which would lead to his acquittal.[2] The rules of evidence and procedure are equiparated to those which would pertain at a trial[3]; but this "examination of facts" is not a proceeding which would bring the plea of "tholed assize" into play.[4] A person found unfit to plead is liable to be tried should he regain sanity, although this is not likely to happen very often.[5] The present approach nevertheless represents a distinct improvement over the pre-1995 law, under which it was rather assumed, without the benefit of any examination of facts, that the accused had committed the offence charged. It is also the case that the modern law allows the court the same choice of disposal[6] in relation to those found unfit to plead as can be exercised relative to those acquitted on the ground of insanity.[7]

---

[96] At 39.

[97] And followed by the English court in *R. v. Podola* [1960] 1 Q.B. 325.

[98] (1907) 5 Adam 312, 344.

[99] 1995 Act, s.54(1)(b). *Cf.* the recommendations in Thomson Report, *supra*, Cmnd. 6218, 1975, para. 52.18.

[1] *ibid.*, s.55(1)(a). Presumably this excludes the issue of *mens rea* for the offence charged: *cf.*, *R. v. Antoine* [2000] 2 W.L.R. 703, HL, where, at p.714, Lord Hutton (in an opinion with which all the other Law Lords concurred) considered the terms of the Scottish legislation in arriving at his decision that in the equivalent English provisions the word "act" did not include "intent".

[2] *ibid.*, s.55(1)(b).

[3] *ibid.*, s.55(6).

[4] The 1995 Act itself proceeds on this assumption — see s.56(7).

[5] It happened in *H.M. Advocate v. Bickerstaff*, 1926 J.C. 65.

[6] Unless the crime charged is murder: 1995 Act, s.57(3).

[7] See 1995 Act, s.57: Renton & Brown, *Criminal Procedure According to the Law of Scotland* (6th ed., Edinburgh, 1996, Sir Gerald H. Gordon (ed.)), Chap. 26.

CHAPTER 11

DIMINISHED RESPONSIBILITY

THE GENERAL PRINCIPLE[1]

The doctrine of diminished responsibility has been said to be so simple that it "can be mastered by a single morning's comfortable reading",[2] but things are unfortunately not quite as simple as this suggests. Any discussion of diminished responsibility is likely to be bedevilled at the outset by the inaccuracy of the term itself which suggests wrongly that diminished responsibility affects responsibility in the sense of guilt, and not merely sentence. This fundamental error crept gradually into Scots law between 1867 and 1923[3] and seems now to have been taken over by English law.[4] That it is an error can be seen merely by reference to the fact that it is not and never has been necessary to give notice of a plea of diminished responsibility as a special defence as it would be if the plea went to conviction and not merely to mitigation.[5] **11.01**

Is the doctrine illogical? One result of treating diminished responsibility as a doctrine about responsibility has been a reaction against it as an illogical doctrine which should not have been allowed into the law, and which having been allowed in should not be extended or applied to any situation for which there is no exact precedent, with the result that it is said that the categories of diminished responsibility, so to speak, are not **11.02**

---

[1] For a brief account of diminished responsibility see Lord Keith, "Some Observations on Diminished Responsibility", 1959 J.R. 109. For a more critical and philosophical discussion with particular reference to psychopaths see Barbara Wooton (Lady Wooton of Abinger), "Diminished Responsibility: A Layman's View" (1960) 76 L.Q.R. 224, and J.Ll.J. Edwards, "Diminished Responsibility — A Withering Away of the Concept of Criminal Responsibility?" in *Essays in Criminal Science*, G.O.W. Mueller (ed.) (London, 1961), p.301. For a critical account of English law, see R.D. Mackay, *Mental Condition Defences in the Criminal Law* (Oxford, 1995), p.180 *et seq*. An account of the law in the United States may conveniently be found in Joshua Dressler, *Understanding Criminal Law* (2nd ed., 1995), pp.335 *et seq*.

[2] A. Koestler, *Reflections on Hanging* (London., 1956), p.83. *Cf.*, M.T. Morrow, "Ever Diminishing Circles", 2000 S.L.T. (News) 127.

[3] *cf. Alex. Dingwall* (1867) 5 Irv, 466; *John McLean* (1876) 3 Couper 334; *H.M. Advocate v. Aitken* (1902) 4 Adam 88; *H.M. Advocate v. Savage*, 1923 J.C. 49. *The Faculty Digest of Justiciary Cases for 1868–1925* does not use the term. It has a section headed "Abnormal State of Mind Falling Short of Insanity" which includes two cases of intoxication as well as the cases on what is now called diminished responsibility.

[4] Homicide Act 1957, s.2. *Cf.* the English Draft Criminal Code (L.C. No. 177, "A Criminal Code for England and Wales", 1989, H. of C., No. 299, Vol. 1), cl. 56(1), *viz.* "A person . . . is not guilty of murder if, at the time of his act, he is suffering from such mental abnormality as is substantial enough reason to reduce his offence to manslaughter."

[5] *cf. H.M. Advocate v. Cunningham*, 1963 J.C. 80; *John Small* (1880) 4 Couper 388.

capable of extension.[6] In *Kirkwood v. H.M. Advocate*[7] Lord Justice-General Normand attacked the doctrine as offending against the principle of non-contradiction: "The defence of impaired responsibility", he said, "is somewhat inconsistent with the basic doctrine of our criminal law that a man, if sane, is responsible for his acts, and, if not sane, is not responsible."[8] This argument rests on the view that a person must be characterised as responsible or not responsible, and that there can be no degrees of responsibility. This seems plausible, but if "punishable", or even "blameworthy", is substituted for "responsible" the plausibility disappears, and the doctrine can be seen for what it is, a special case of the rule that personal factors mitigate sentence.[9] There is nothing illogical or odd in accepting that there may be mental conditions which while not amounting to insanity[10] and so not involving irresponsibility do affect the patient sufficiently to make it only fair not to blame him so much as a normal man.[11] The existence of such conditions is recognised by psychiatric medicine, and all that the doctrine says is that degrees of mental illness produce degrees of culpability.[12] It may also be noted that the doctrine is by no means peculiar to Scotland: it is recognised in, for example, Germany,[13] apart altogether from its more recent acceptance in England.

There should be no more difficulty in saying that a man suffering from some mental weakness or illness is entitled to a mitigation of sentence than in saying that a man who acts under provocation is entitled to such a mitigation. In both cases the men are responsible and liable to conviction, but in both cases there are mitigating circumstances. The doctrine of diminished responsibility is based ultimately on general humanitarian grounds. It exists because, as has been said of provocation, the law shows a "tenderness to the frailty of human nature."[14] In its particular application to homicide it was, in the words of Lord Keith, "probably a reaction against imposing the capital sentence in all cases of murder, or in what might be treated as murder if the defence of diminished responsibility did not prevail."[15] It is based on human sympathy with the mentally abnormal.[16] What makes the doctrine seem anomalous is not the doctrine itself, but the anomalous nature of the law of murder which alone among Scots crimes retains a fixed penalty.[17]

11.03 *Diminished responsibility and murder.* The earliest cases of diminished responsibility

---

[6] *Carraher v. H.M. Advocate*, 1946 J.C. 108; *Kirkwood v. H.M. Advocate*, 1939 J.C. 36; *H.M. Advocate v. Higgins* (1913) 7 Adam 229.

[7] 1939 J.C. 36.

[8] At 40.

[9] See R.C. Evid. Memorandum of Faculty of Advocates, para. 13.

[10] See *supra*, para. 10.05.

[11] See M. Wasik, "Partial Excuses in Criminal Law" (1982) 45 M.L.R. 516.

[12] *cf.* Norwood East, *Society and the Criminal* (London, 1949), pp.37–39.

[13] See StGB Art. 21.

[14] *Cmwth v. Webster* (1850) 5 Cush. 296; Sayre, 785, 788.

[15] R.C. Evid. Q. 5206. Lord Keith later changed his mind and said there was no evidence to show that the doctrine was a reaction to capital punishment — *op.cit.* (1959) J.R. at 112, but whatever the origin of the doctrine there can be no doubt that its later development and its application to homicide are linked with capital punishment.

[16] *cf. H.M. Advocate v. Edmonstone* (1909) 2 S.L.T. 223, where Lord Guthrie told the jury that for diminished responsibility to operate the mental deterioration must be such as to entitle the accused to be dealt with unlike other men.

[17] *cf.* T.B. Smith, p.161.

were non-capital charges where the court imposed a reduced sentence in view of the accused's mental weakness. In capital cases mental weakness could be taken into account only by way of the royal prerogative of mercy, and it was common for juries to make recommendations to mercy on the ground of mental weakness. So far, no "doctrine" was necessary. Diminished responsibility as a doctrine started in 1867 with *Alex. Dingwall,*[18] where Lord Deas treated the accused's mental state as a mitigating factor entitling the jury to convict of culpable homicide instead of murder. It is quite clear, however, that even then there was nothing unique about diminished responsibility — it was just one of a number of factors which were put before the jury as justifying the lesser verdict. And when Lord Deas spoke about *Dingwall*[18a] in later cases, he referred to all the mitigating factors, and not only to the accused's mental state, as the reason for the reduction of the crime to culpable homicide.[19]

Because, however, the only way of giving effect to mental abnormality short of insanity in murder cases was by acquitting the accused of murder and convicting him of culpable homicide, diminished responsibility developed as a "doctrine" in the context of murder. Its position in that context is not unlike the position of provocation. Both are merely mitigating factors, but in both cases judges developed strict rules about when they could be invoked, about what was necessary to justify a reduction of murder to culpable homicide on the ground of diminished responsibility or of provocation. The anomalous position of the fixed penalty for murder meant that the effect of diminished responsibility on sentence had to be "justified", to be "rationalised" and to be given some conceptual basis in the law of murder which would explain how it could operate to produce an acquittal, and so apparently to affect responsibility. The way this was done was by reference to the *mens rea* of murder, not in the modern sense of intention or recklessness, but in the old sense of malice, wickedness or wilfulness, of "general *mens rea*",[20] in the same way as in the nineteenth century intoxication was regarded as a factor justifying the reduction of murder to culpable homicide.[21] In *John Tierney*[22] Lord Ardmillan said that "the man's control over his own mind might have been so weak as to deprive the act of that wilfulness which would make it murder."[23] Diminished responsibility, like provocation, operates where there is an intention to kill but the intention arises from a particular circumstance — weakness of mind or provocation — which deprives it of the heinousness which is necessary for murder. The culpable homicide for which persons of diminished responsibility are convicted is voluntary culpable homicide — where the homicide is involuntary there is no need to rely on diminished responsibility to avoid conviction for murder, although it could of course still be invoked in reference to penalty. And voluntary culpable homicide is not a different

---

[18] (1867) 5 Irv. 466.

[18a] *ibid.*

[19] See *Thos. Ferguson* (1881) 4 Couper 552; *Andrew Granger* (1878) 4 Couper 86.

[20] *supra*, para. 7.05.

[21] *cf. Margt Robertson or Brown* (1886) 1 White 93. *H.M. Advocate v. McDonald* (1890) 2 White 517; *H.M. Advocate v. Kane* (1892) 3 White 386. But see now *Brennan v. H.M. Advocate*, 1977 J.C. 38; *infra*, para. 12.12.

[22] (1875) 3 Couper 152.

[23] At 166.

crime from murder — it is just murder under mitigating circumstances, second degree murder.[24]

11.04 THE CATEGORY OF THE OFFENCE. Because voluntary culpable homicide has often wrongly been thought of as a different crime from murder diminished responsibility has been said to affect not merely sentence but also the category of the offence.[25] This raises the question whether diminished responsibility can alter the category of offence in crimes other than homicide. Macdonald thinks it might so operate in assault[26]; Lord Keith could find no reason why it should not so operate outside homicide, but rightly treated the question as largely academic.[27] Professor J.Ll.J. Edwards suggests that it might operate, for example, to reduce rape to indecent assault.[28] If, however, diminished responsibility is to have this effect it can probably be only in relation to offences which are inter-related in the same way as murder is to culpable homicide, that is to say in the case of wilful and reckless fire raising, or assault and reckless injury, and not where the difference between the offences is more a matter of *actus reus* as it is in the case of rape and indecent assault. In fact there is no example of the doctrine operating in this way outside homicide. In *J.F. Wilson*[29] the accused pleaded guilty to wilful fire raising and then invoked the doctrine, and it was not suggested that his plea should have been only to culpable and reckless fire raising. The reduction of category is only a device to avoid a fixed penalty, and is unnecessary where the crime charged does not have a fixed penalty or where, as in a number of crimes for many years prior to the Criminal Procedure (Scotland) Act 1887, it is capital in name but is not in fact capitally punished.[30]

---

[24] *cf. Thos. Ferguson* (1881) 4 Couper 552, Lord Deas at 558. Where the initial charge is one of attempted murder, there should be no problem in taking account of diminished responsibility at the stage of sentence, since attempted murder does not carry a fixed penalty. It is a sign of the hold which diminished responsibility has acquired as a doctrine, however, that the courts have advised juries not only that diminished responsibility applies to attempted murder but also that a successful plea of that nature will reduce attempted murder to assault: *H.M. Advocate v. Blake*, 1986 S.L.T. 661, Lord Brand at p.662K-L. (It seems that in terms of the doctrine attempted culpable homicide would have been an appropriate verdict in such cases — had the courts not taken the view that such a crime does not exist: *cf.* the provocation cases of *Brady v. H.M. Advocate*, 1986 J.C. 68, and *Salmond v. H.M. Advocate*, 1992 S.L.T. 156.).

[25] This phraseology was used by Lord Deas in *John McLean* (1876) 3 Couper 334, 337, which was not a murder case, presumably to justify his own actions in *Dingwall, supra*, and has been much used since.

[26] Macdonald, p.117. In *H.M. Advocate v. Blake*, 1986 S.L.T. 661, at p.662, Lord Brand treated attempted murder as an aggravation of assault, such that diminished responsibility, if established to the jury's satisfaction, simply removed that aggravation.

[27] *op.cit.* at 113.

[28] *op.cit.* at 305.

[29] (1877) 3 Couper 429.

[30] In *J.F. Wilson, supra* the accused pleaded guilty to wilful fire raising and was sentenced to 12 months imprisonment by Lord Young — he subsequently committed the crime again and was found insane; in *John Small* (1880) 4 Couper 388, Lord Adam allowed evidence to be led of mental weakness in a charge of post office theft despite the absence of any special defence of insanity; in *H.M. Advocate v. Fergusson* (1894) 1 Adam 517, evidence of mental weakness was led after a plea of guilty to fire raising, and L.J.-C. Macdonald gave this evidence "very considerable effect" in restricting the sentence to 12 months.
In *Archd Robertson* (1836) 1 Swin. 15 the jury convicted the accused of rape and added a recommendation to mercy, but rape was then capital and in any event the case precedes *Dingwall*, so no conclusions can be drawn from it.

IS THE DOCTRINE RESTRICTED TO MURDER? In *H.M. Advocate v. Cunningham,*[31] the High Court stated that diminished responsibility was restricted to murder cases. This statement was repeated, *obiter*, in *Brennan v. H.M. Advocate*.[32] Historically this is clearly inaccurate, but in any event the point is only verbal since their Lordships accepted that mental states short of insanity could operate in mitigation[33] — and if that is so it does not matter whether or not they are called diminished responsibility. In practice it is true, however, that diminished responsibility as a doctrine is confined to murder cases, and modern developments, particularly since the Mental Health (Scotland) Act 1960,[34] render the doctrine otiose except in cases of murder, because they provide a way of treating mentally ill patients without recourse to the doctrine. **11.05**

In *Henry John Burnett*[35] the jury were directed by Lord Wheatley that they could consider the plea of diminished responsibility only in relation to one of the charges against the accused: the charge of capital murder, because,"[i]n the normal case, in a non-murder case, a successful plea in diminished responsibility is only reflected in the sentence imposed by the Court, and that is a matter for the judge and not for the jury, but in a murder charge the penalty for murder is fixed by law, and the judge has no discretion."[36]

The treatment of persons of diminished responsibility. The nineteenth century way of dealing with persons of diminished responsibility was charmingly simple, not to say naïve. As Alison puts it, "[i]n such cases there is a mixture of guilt and misfortune; for the former he should be severely punished, for the latter the extreme penalty of the law should be remitted."[37] In other words, the penalty should be reduced in proportion to the degree of impairment of responsibility — the worse the accused's mental condition the less the sentence. This was the only way open in the nineteenth century, but it has the unfortunate result that it means that the more dangerous or lacking in self-control the accused is the less time he will spend in prison and the less protection will be afforded to the public. The nineteenth century solution is deontologically impeccable, but it takes no account of such utilitarian considerations as public safety. The whole question of the treatment of persons of diminished responsibility was dealt with by the Criminal Appeal Court in *Kirkwood v. H.M. Advocate*[38] where they upheld a sentence of life imprisonment on a person convicted of culpable homicide because of diminished responsibility, on the ground that the sentence was necessary for the protection of the public. Lord Justice-General Normand said that to maintain that "although an insane person might properly be detained indefinitely, a person who was not insane, but whose responsibility was impaired in a high degree, should be leniently treated without regard to the safety of his fellows . . . is . . . a *reductio ad absurdum* of the argument that the **11.06**

---

[31] 1963 J.C. 80.

[32] 1977 J.C. 38, at 47.

[33] See, *e.g.*, *Andrews v. H.M. Advocate*, 1994 S.C.C.R. 190 (indecent assault), and *Arthur v. H.M. Advocate*, 1994 S.C.C.R. 621 (assault).

[34] See para. 11.08, *infra*.

[35] High Court at Aberdeen, July 1963, unrep'd.

[36] Transcript of judge's charge, p.9.

[37] Alison, i, 652–653.

[38] 1939 J.C. 36.

punishment should be measured by the responsibility of the criminal to the exclusion of other considerations."[39] It was pointed out in *Kirkwood*[39a] that a life sentence was in fact an indeterminate sentence, and that the accused's ultimate release would depend on the state of his mental health. Although there have been cases since *Kirkwood*[39b] in which fixed sentences have been imposed, *Kirkwood*[40] is sufficient authority for and contains cogent arguments in favour of an indeterminate sentence in such cases.[40a] Since mentally ill prisoners should receive appropriate treatment in prison, *Kirkwood*[40b] in effect combined a mitigated penalty with what are called on the Continent security measures.[41] An indeterminate sentence is difficult to justify on retributive grounds except in the most serious cases, but if diminished responsibility is restricted to murder cases such a sentence can be justified either retributively or as a security measure.

11.07 Since *Kirkwood*[41a] there have, however, been two important changes in the law. One is the abolition of capital punishment for murder, the fixed punishment for which is now life imprisonment.[42] Where, in such a case, the accused is sufficiently dangerous to merit the treatment applied in *Kirkwood*[42a] the distinction between murder and culpable homicide is virtually abolished, and diminished responsibility no longer has any mitigating effect.

11.08 A more important change was the passing of the Mental Health (Scotland) Act 1960, section 55 (now section 58 of the 1995 Act), which provided that where a person is convicted of a crime the penalty for which is not fixed, *i.e.* a crime other than murder,[43] and his mental state

---

[39] *ibid*., at 41.
[39a] 1939 J.C. 36.
[39b] *ibid.*
[40] *ibid.*
[40a] See, *e.g.*, *Duff v. H.M. Advocate*, 1983 S.C.C.R. 461; *cf. L.T. v. H.M. Advocate*, 1990 S.C.C.R. 540.
[40b] 1939 J.C. 35.
[41] *Massregein der Sicherung und Besserung*: StGB Art. 61. In theory one can even provide for a punishment succeeded by security measures or vice versa; and in practice, something similar may be contemplated under s.59A of the 1995 Act. That section was added by the Crime and Punishment (Scotland) Act 1997, s.6(1) and permits the High Court or Sheriff Court to impose a 'hospital direction' on a person convicted on indictment of an offence punishable with imprisonment. Such a direction authorises the admission and detention of the convicted person in a hospital "in addition to any sentence of imprisonment which [the court] has the power or the duty to impose." Future release from hospital is subject to restrictions. The court must, however, be satisfied that the conditions for civil admission of that person under s.17(1) of the Mental Health (Scotland) Act 1984 are met. These conditions include that the person in question is suffering from mental disorder (*i.e.*, in terms of s.1(2) of the 1984 Act, as amended by the Mental Health (Public Safety and Appeals) (Scotland) Act 1999 (asp 1) s.3(1), mental illness (including personality disorder) or mental handicap); but the way in which diminished responsibility is now interpreted in Scotland means that most persons of diminished responsibility will meet that condition. As it is also a condition (see s.17(1)(b)) that admission to hospital should be necessary "for the health or safety of that person or for the protection of other persons", there seems here a true opportunity for combining punishment (suitably mitigated where possible) and public safety measures in relation to persons of diminished responsibility.
[41a] 1939 J.C. 36.
[42] Murder (Abolition of Death Penalty) Act 1965; see now the 1995 Act, s.205.
[42a] 1939 J.C. 36.
[43] Treason does not now have a fixed sentence (see the Crime and Disorder Act 1998, s.36). In any event, treason is governed by English law and presumably diminished responsibility does not apply to it.

is such as to make him a suitable person to be detained compulsorily in a mental hospital under the non-criminal provisions of the Act (now the Mental Health (Scotland) Act 1984), the court may commit him to hospital instead of dealing with him in any other way.[44] Now, because of the very restricted interpretation put on "diminished responsibility" at a time when it was distrusted by judges as a way of "getting off" a richly deserved hanging, and as conflicting with the principle of disfacilitation,[45] almost everyone to whom the doctrine applies will be a person to whom section 58 of the 1995 Act also applies. And the most appropriate way of dealing with such a person is by way of section 58 together with the imposition where appropriate of a restriction without limit of time on his future discharge from hospital in terms of section 59 of the Act, which means that he cannot be discharged without the consent of a Scottish Minister.

HAS DIMINISHED RESPONSIBILITY A FUTURE? There have been cases **11.09**
of diminished responsibility since the coming into effect of the Mental Health (Scotland) Act 1960 which have been dealt with by way of imprisonment, and it may be that there will continue to be occasional cases of diminished responsibility of a temporary nature, when the accused is not in a state justifying his detention in a mental hospital at the time of his trial,[46] but such cases are exceptional.[47] The principal effect of the doctrine of diminished responsibility is to enable the provisions of section 58 of the 1995 Act to operate in cases of homicide. A simple amendment deleting the restriction of the operation of section 58 to crimes where the penalty is not fixed by law would enable someone convicted of murder to be dealt with under the Act, and obviate the need for any special doctrine to reduce murder to culpable homicide before the court can take cognisance of a condition of mental illness short of insanity.

The most recent relevant legislative change, however, enables a person convicted on indictment of an offence punishable by imprisonment (including murder) to be imprisoned *and* detained compulsorily in a hospital.[48] The court achieves this by adding a 'hospital direction' to the custodial sentence. The qualifying conditions include that the person in question is suffering from a mental disorder sufficient to satisfy the provisions for non-criminal admission to hospital,[49] and this means that persons of diminished responsibility will almost always fall within this new disposal possibility. In murder cases, therefore, it is important that the special doctrine should continue to apply, since otherwise it seems possible for a person of diminished responsibility to be convicted of

---

[44] Under the 1995 Act, s.59A (added by the Crime and Punishment (Scotland) Act 1997, s.6), it is now competent for a court to combine a "hospital direction" with a prison sentence, where the accused has been convicted on indictment of an offence punishable with imprisonment. Murder is not excluded from the exercise of this power. See n.41, *supra*, and para. 11.09, *infra*.

[45] *supra*, para. 7.56.

[46] *e.g. H.M. Advocate v. Fiddes*, 1967 S.L.T. 2; *Strathearn v. H.M. Advocate*, 1996 S.C.C.R. 100.

[47] There might also be cases where a sentence would be necessary because no hospital was prepared to accept the accused, but a killer would almost always be accepted by the state mental hospital.

[48] 1995 Act, s.59A, added by the Crime and Punishment (Scotland) Act 1997, s.6(1). See n. 41, *supra*.

[49] See the Mental Health (Scotland) Act 1984, s.17(1), and n.41, *supra*.

murder, sentenced to life in prison, and made subject to a hospital direction — thereby defeating the mitigation of penalty to which his mental condition should lead.

The Development of the Doctrine

Its development up to 1900

11.10 Before *Dingwall.*[50] The idea of diminished responsibility occurred to Sir George Mackenzie who wrote: "It may be argued, that since the Law grants a total Impunity to such as are absolutely furious, that therefore it should by the Rule of Proportions, lessen and moderat the Punishments of such, as though they are not absolutly mad, yet are Hypocondrick and Melancholly to such a Degree, that it clouds their Reason."[51] But although the idea was present in 1678 (the date of the first edition of Mackenzie's work) its development can be traced only from a later date. It seems to have started in practice with an understanding that certain cases of mental weakness should be dealt with by way of a conviction accompanied by a recommendation to mercy.[52] The earliest example of this practice offered by Hume is the case of *Robt Bonthorn*,[53] a case of assault by a smuggler on a revenue officer, in which the jury found "that the intellects of the pannel are most remarkably weak, irregular and confused, and therefore recommend him to the mercy of the Court." This form of verdict was approved of by Hume, who also approved of the exercise of mercy in cases of weak intellect even where the jury had not specifically made any recommendation to mercy.[54] That this was a recognised way of dealing with the mentally weak also appears from Hume's comment on the acquittal on the ground of insanity in *Jas. Cummings*,[55] who killed a fellow-soldier apparently when under the influence of melancholia and drink. Hume, who disapproved of treating drunkenness like insanity, said, "It may be questioned, whether, under the whole circumstances of this case, it would not have been a more correct and a more salutary judgment, to convict him of the murder, and recommend him to the royal mercy."[56]

Bell's Notes to Hume state that "In offences inferring arbitrary pains, weakness of intellect is a relevant plea to use in mitigation",[57] and the cases cited in support of this statement[58] were said by Lord Justice-General Normand in *Kirkwood v. H.M. Advocate*[59] to be the origin of the

---

[50] (1867) 5 Irv. 466.

[51] Mackenzie, I, 1, 7, 2.

[52] *cf.* Lord Keith, "Some Observations on Diminished Responsibility", 1959 J.R. 109, 110.

[53] (1763) Hume, i, 38.

[54] *Alex Campbell* (1890) Hume, I, 38; *Susan Tinny* (1816) Hume, i, 41; *Robt. Thomson* (1739) Hume, i, 40; *Agnes Crockat* (1756) Hume, i, 42: both the latter earlier, it will be noted, than *Bonthorn*, which suggests that the verdict with recommendation followed on a practice of exercising mercy in cases of weak intellect.

[55] (1810) Hume, i, 40.

[56] Hume, i, 41. Hume offers similar comments on *Wm Gates* (1811) Hume, i, 41, and *Pierce Hoskins* (1812) *ibid.*, both of which involved drink, although Gates also suffered from melancholia.

[57] Bell's Notes 5.

[58] *Wm Braid* (1835), *Thos. Henderson* (1835), both Bell's Notes 5 and *Jas. Ainslie* (1842) 1 Broun 25.

[59] 1939 J.C. 36.

doctrine. This reference to these non-capital cases is useful as showing that Lord Normand recognised that the plea was at least originally regarded as a general mitigatory plea. The cases in Hume show that mental weakness was recognised as a mitigating factor in homicide cases as well, although its effect was confined to a recommendation to mercy.[60]

The law is made explicit, so far as capital offences are concerned, by Alison who states that, "If it appear from the evidence that the pannel, though partially deranged, was not so much so as to relieve him entirely from punishment, the proper course is to find him guilty; but, on account of the infirmity of mind, which he could not control, recommend him to the royal mercy."[61] Alison thus takes the view that there are cases where the law requires that there be mitigation, and so requires a recommendation. In two mid-nineteenth-century cases the jury were more or less directed to bring in a recommendation on the ground of the accused's weak intellect. In *Jas. Denny Scott,*[62] Lord Cockburn told the jury that "a conviction, though obstructed in its result by a recommendation, was the safest for the public, and the least opposed to the truth of the case."[63] In *John McFadyen,*[64] Lord Cowan said that "the safest verdict would probably be one of guilty, accompanied by such recommendation as the undoubted weakness of the pannel's intellect might appear to them to justify."[65] In both cases the recommendation was accepted. **11.11**

There are also three non-capital cases involving diminished responsibility in this period. In *Alex. Carr,*[66] a case of slandering and threatening judges, sentence was restricted because the accused's actings were not malicious but the result of constitutional weakness or perversity. In *Thos. Wild and Ors,*[67] a case of mobbing, there was a recommendation to leniency on the ground of weakness of intellect. And in *Dorothea Pearson or Rodgers,*[68] the accused was sentenced to only two months' imprisonment for child stealing after inquiry into her mental state following certification by the trial judge to the High Court which included Lord Deas. It appeared she was of morbid personality, but not insane. **11.12**

Dingwall[69] *and after.* It was but a short step from *Denny Scott*[69a] and *McFadyen*[69b] to asking the jury to bring in a verdict of culpable homicide instead of a verdict of murder with a recommendation to mercy. A culpable homicide verdict obviated any risk that the recommendation might be rejected, and also left the treatment of the accused in the hands **11.13**

---

60 In *Archd Robertson* (1836) 1 Swin. 15, a charge of rape, which was then a capital crime, the jury convicted and added a recommendation to mercy "in respect of the pannel's previous insanity and imbecility of mind": at 21. The Crown did not ask for the death sentence but this was mainly for reasons unconnected with the accused's mental state: see Vol. II, Chap. 33.

61 Alison, i, 652.

62 (1853) 1 Irv. 132.

63 At 143.

64 (1860) 3 Irv. 650.

65 At 666.

66 (1854) 1 Irv. 464.

67 (1854) 1 Irv. 552.

68 (1858) 3 Irv. 105.

69 (1867) 5 Irv. 466.

69a (1853) 1 Irv. 132.

69b (1860) 3 Irv. 650.

of the judge who could impose what he considered to be a suitable sentence, giving what weight he thought proper to the accused's mental state. This step was taken (although not expressly for these reasons) by Lord Deas in 1867 in the case of *Alex. Dingwall*,[70] which is generally recognised as the origin of the modern law on the subject. Although the doctrine was recognised by the High Court in the non-capital case of *John McLean* in 1876,[70a] it owes its existence in its modern form almost entirely to one judge, Lord Deas, who delivered the observations of the court in *McLean*,[70b] and who was the judge in six of the nine cases between 1867 and 1882 in which the application of the doctrine to homicide was evolved.[71]

The accused in *Dingwall*[72] was an alcoholic who stabbed his wife on Hogmanay after a quarrel which was caused because she had hidden his liquor and his money. He was kind to her when he was sober; he had suffered from occasional attacks of *delirium tremens*; he was sober at the time of the killing but claimed to remember nothing about it. In suggesting to the jury that they might bring in a verdict of culpable homicide Lord Deas mentioned the accused's mental condition as one among a number of mitigating factors. He set out the grounds which would justify a verdict of culpable homicide as being:

> "1st, The unpremeditated and sudden nature of the attack; 2d, The prisoner's habitual kindness to his wife, of which there could be no doubt, when drink did not interfere; 3d, There was only one stab or blow; this, while not perhaps like what an insane man would have done, was favourable for the prisoner in other respects; 4th, The prisoner appeared not only to have been peculiar in his mental constitution, but to have had his mind weakened by successive attacks of disease. It seemed highly probable that he had had a stroke of the sun in India, and that his subsequent fits were of an epileptic nature. There could be no doubt that he had had repeated attacks of *delirium tremens*, and if weakness of mind could be an element in any case in the question between murder and culpable homicide, it seemed difficult to exclude that element here . . . The state of mind of a prisoner . . . might . . . be an extenuating circumstance, although not such as to warrant an acquittal on the ground of insanity."[72a]

11.14 The next case, *John Tierney*[73] in 1875, is of interest only because the question of diminished responsibilty was raised by the Crown and not the defence; it was left to the jury by Lord Ardmillan, although he said he did not see much ground for it in the evidence.[74] No reference was made to *Dingwall*,[74a] and *Tierney*[74b] suggests that at least by 1875 the

---

[70] (1867) 5 Irv. 466.

[70a] (1876) 3 Couper 334.

[70b] *ibid.*

[71] His influence, like that of Lord Moncreiff in the case of insanity, shows how a single judge, if he happened to preside at appropriate trials, could influence the law and create a body of authority by repeating his views in a number of cases.

[72] (1867) 5 Irv. 466.

[72a] (1867) 5 Irv. at 479–480.

[73] (1875) 3 Couper 152.

[74] The jury convicted of murder with a recommendation to mercy, and Tierney was subsequently reprieved.

[74a] (1867) 5 Irv. 466.

[74b] (1875) 3 Couper 152.

climate of professional opinion was not unfavourable to reducing murder to culpable homicide on the ground of mental weakness. Lord Deas' views gained ready acceptance, it would appear, from his contemporaries, and were not seriously challenged until the twentieth century.

The next important case after *Dingwall*[75] is *John McLean*.[75a] The accused was an imbecile who had been weak minded from childhood, and had at one time been a certified lunatic. He was charged with theft by housebreaking, a crime which might have been still technically capital, but which had long ceased to be regarded as one for which a death sentence was appropriate, and he was convicted with a recommendation to leniency because of his "weak intellect". The case was reported to the High Court and the sentence of the High Court was imposed by Lord Deas in a speech in which he pointed out that it was quite proper for a judge to take mental weakness into consideration in passing sentence, whether or not there was a recommendation to leniency. He went on to say that, **11.15**

> "without being insane in the legal sense, so as not to be amenable to punishment, a prisoner may yet labour under that degree of weakness of intellect or mental infirmity which may make it both right and legal to take that state of mind into account, not only in awarding the punishment, but in some cases, even in considering within what category of offences the crime shall be held to fall."[76]

Lord Deas dealt with diminished responsibility in a number of murder cases after *McLean*.[76a] In *Andrew Granger*,[77] a case of *delirium tremens*, his Lordship said that "a weak or diseased state of mind, not amounting to insanity, might competently form an element to be considered in the question between murder and culpable homicide."[78] He then went on to describe *Dingwall*,[78a] pointing out that the accused there had been habitually kind to his wife and had acted in temporary irritation. The jury found Granger guilty of culpable homicide, "believing the act to have been committed when he was labouring under *delirium tremens*", and then added at Lord Deas' suggestion, "and therefore not amounting to murder".[79] Lord Deas repeated his reference to the other mitigating features in *Dingwall*[79a] when he referred to it in *Thos. Ferguson*.[80] He told the jury that *Ferguson* was a much more difficult case for the application of the principle than *Dingwall*,[80a] because the husband in *Dingwall* was habitually much kinder than Ferguson, and there was in *Dingwall* neither the deliberate preparation nor the ferocity in execution which were present in *Ferguson*. These remarks show that diminished responsibility was still regarded just as an element for consideration, as one of a **11.16**

---

[75] (1867) 5 Irv. 466.
[75a] (1876) 3 Couper 334.
[76] (1876) 3 Couper at 337.
[76a] (1876) 3 Couper 334.
[77] (1878) 4 Couper 86.
[78] At 103.
[78a] (1867) 5 Irv. 466.
[79] 4 Couper at 104.
[79a] (1867) 5 Irv. 466.
[80] (1881) 4 Couper 552.
[80a] (1867) 5 Irv. 466.

number of possible features which might reduce murder to culpable homicide. In discussing diminished responsibility in *Ferguson*[80b] Lord Deas said it,

> "was founded on a principle of natural justice, which recognised a distinction between what in other countries, equally enlightened as our own, was termed murder in the first and in the second degree, and which under our own humane system we could act upon better and more conveniently by the distinction between murder and culpable homicide. The undoubted fact that under an indictment for murder a verdict might be returned of culpable homicide, although not alternatively libelled, of itself sufficiently proved that we had in our law the principle . . . It was, however, a principle which required great care and discretion in its application."[81]

He then went on to distinguish the facts of *Dingwall*[81a] in the way described above.[82] The two subsequent cases of *Helen Thomson or Brown*[83] and *Francis Gove*[84] add little to the law, except that in these cases the only mitigating factor appears to have been the accused's mental weakness. In *Gove*[84a] Lord Deas said "There might be men of habits of mind who should not be punished with the capital sentence of death, as they would have been if in full possession of all their faculties . . . the prisoner's act was very like the act of somebody not free from some infirmity of mind."[85]

11.17 There are also some cases involving non-capital charges in this period but they add nothing to the development of the principle.[86] The next case of any importance is *H.M. Advocate v. Robt Smith.*[87] Smith was a farm-worker who was charged with murdering a fellow-worker and pleaded insanity. He was a sensitive man, much given to brooding. His fellow-servants had subjected him to a campaign of continual annoyance, and eventually he lost control when the deceased said "Boo" to him, and he shot him. Lord McLaren applied the law of diminished responsibility saying, with reference to *Dingwall*,[87a]

> "Now, if it were the law that a state of mental disturbance brought on by a man's own fault, by his own intemperance, going the length of producing a physiological disturbance of the brain, might to that extent excuse him, it seems to me that the same result must follow when the disturbance of the mental equipoise was not due to a man's own fault, but to his being subjected to a system of incessant persecution."[88]

Lord McLaren laid stress on physiological disturbance, and also relied on evidence that the accused had been "physiologically unable to

---

[80b] (1881) 4 Couper 552.
[81] At 558.
[81a] (1867) 5 Irv. 466.
[82] Ferguson was convicted of murder with a recommendation on the ground of weakness of mind, and subsequently reprieved.
[83] (1882) 4 Couper 596.
[84] (1882) *ibid.* 598.
[84a] *ibid.*
[85] At 599–600.
[86] See *supra*, n.30.
[87] (1893) 1 Adam 34.
[87a] (1867) 5 Irv. 466.
[88] 1 Adam at 50.

resist"[89] the provocation offered by the deceased. It is not clear just what "physiological " means here, but it may be a sign of a tendency to distrust merely "mental" conditions which cannot be shown to have any physiological foundation, in which case it foreshadows the modern attitude. The accused was convicted of culpable homicide and sentenced to penal servitude for life.[90]

The twentieth century cases

Aitken[91] to *Carraher.*[92] Cases decided in the first half of the twentieth century show an increasing distrust of the concept of diminished responsibility. The judicial approach to the plea, which was favourable in the nineteenth century, becomes affected by the fear that it will lead to many murderers escaping their just deserts, and by the view that the doctrine is illogical and anomalous, attitudes adopted by Lord Cooper and Lord Normand respectively, and as a result the doctrine has been restrictively interpreted in the twentieth century. The modern approach is due partly to the fact that modern psychiatry has discovered many abnormal conditions unknown in the nineteenth century which doctors consider as creating a state of diminished responsibility. Lawyers are afraid of these new-fangled notions with strange names,[93] and are also afraid that if they allow psychiatrists to determine the question of diminished responsibility they will find that all criminals will be characterised as being of diminished responsibility.[94] Such a result would destroy the doctrine entirely because there would then be no norm against which to measure diminution. **11.18**

It should also be remembered that diminished responsibility is in practice usually an alternative to a plea of insanity in murder cases, and the main reason for pleading insanity, at any rate until 1957, was to escape hanging. This result could be achieved more easily by a plea of diminished responsibility, and could in that way also be achieved without any risk of incarceration in a criminal lunatic asylum for an indefinite period, so that diminished responsibility was thought of as a way out of the difficulties of insanity, as a means of escape for the criminal who was not insane and who should really have been convicted of murder. Viewed in this way, it was naturally not regarded by judges with much favour.

Signs of this tendency appear earlier than the spread of modern psychiatric ideas. The restrictive outlook is present in the first reported twentieth-century case on the subject: *H.M. Advocate v. Aitken.*[94a] In that case a plea of insanity was lodged, but the defence asked only for a verdict of culpable homicide on the ground of the accused's mental state

---

[89] At 52.

[90] Lord McLaren also put diminished responsibility to the jury in *H.M. Advocate v. Abercrombie* (1896) 2 Adam 163, a case of infanticide where the accused was found insane.

[91] (1902) 4 Adam 88.

[92] 1946 J.C. 108.

[93] *cf.* R.C. Evid. of Lord Cooper, Q. 5468.

[94] The law is in part a reaction to the extreme claims made by some psychiatrists. In *H.M. Advocate v. Braithwaite*, High Court at Edinburgh, Nov. 1944, rep'd at 1945 J.C. 55, one witness said that all persons who committed crimes of violence were not fully responsible: Transcript of Evidence, 98; and in *H.M. Advocate v. Carraher*, High Court at Glasgow, Feb. 1946, rep'd at 1946 J.C. 108, a witness said that two per cent of the population were not fully responsible: *Trials of Patrick Carraher*, Blake (ed.) (Edinburgh, 1951) p.225.

[94a] (1902) 4 Adam 88.

as well as on the merits of the case. Lord Stormonth Darling directed the jury that:

> "The rule of law . . . to the effect that there might be a degree of insanity, not sufficient to destroy criminal responsibility, and yet sufficient to modify the quality of the crime, was one which had been undoubtedly received and acted on within comparatively recent times. But it was a rule which required to be applied with great caution. It could only be applied if a jury were satisfied that there was something amounting to brain disease."[95]

In *H.M. Advocate v. Graham,*[96] however, the doctrine was applied by Lord Justice-Clerk Macdonald, who expressed his admiration for Lord Deas and repeated to the jury the latter's account of the various mitigating features in *Dingwall.*[96a] In *H.M. Advocate v. Edmonstone,*[97] Lord Guthrie described diminished responsibility to the jury in terms of "enfeeblement of faculties", and of mental deterioration entitling the accused to be dealt with unlike other men.

The only other reported case in which a judge has explicitly refused to follow *Dingwall*[97a] is *H.M. Advocate v. Higgins*[98] in which Lord Johnston anticipated and surpassed Lord Normand's later criticism of diminished responsibility as illogical.[99] Such a refusal 50 years after *Dingwall*[99a] was possible only because of the absence of any Criminal Appeal Court, and Lord Johnston's rearguard action had no effect on the law.

11.19 H.M. ADVOCATE V. SAVAGE.[1] The most important case on diminished responsibility after *Dingwall,*[1a] and the one which seems to be responsible for the term itself, is *H.M. Advocate v. Savage.*[1b] This is not because of the facts of the case[2] but because the directions which Lord Justice-Clerk Alness gave on diminished responsibility have been adopted as the basis of the modern law, and come near to being the M'Naghten Rules of diminished responsibility. Lord Alness first told the jury:

> "[T]hat there may be such a state of mind of a person, short of actual insanity, as may reduce the quality of his act from murder to culpable homicide, is, so far as I can judge from the cases cited to

---

[95] (1902) 4 Adam at 94–95. The jury convicted with a strong recommendation to mercy.

[96] (1906) 5 Adam 212.

[96a] (1867) 5 Irv. 466.

[97] 1909, 2 S.L.T. 223, 224.

[97a] (1867) 5 Irv. 466.

[98] (1913) 7 Adam 229 — the facts were particularly revolting and unsympathetic and Higgins was hanged: see S. Smith, *Mostly Murder* (Edinburgh, 1959) Chap. 3.

[99] Lord Johnston said, "To say that that man is mentally capable of murder and this man only mentally capable of culpable homicide, that that man is capable of a capital offence but this one only of an offence not capital is a proposition which would, I think, unsettle the administration of criminal law . . . I can understand limited liability in the case of civil obligation, but I cannot understand limited responsibility for a criminal act. I can understand irresponsibility, but I cannot understand limited responsibility — responsibility which is yet an inferior grade of responsibility": at 232–233.

[99a] (1867) 5 Irv. 466.

[1] 1923 J.C. 49.

[1a] (1867) 5 Irv. 466.

[1b] 1923 J.C. 49.

[2] The accused was a confirmed drunkard and a methylated spirits addict, and his defence was really one of intoxication although he pleaded insanity; the evidence regarding his state of mind was conflicting, and he was in fact hanged: see Transcript of Evidence, High Court in Edinburgh, May, 1923.

me, an established doctrine in the law of Scotland. It is a comparatively recent doctrine, and, as has at least twice been said from the bench to a jury, it must be applied with care. Formerly there were only two classes of prisoner — those who were completely responsible and those who were completely irresponsible. Our law has now come to recognise in murder cases a third class . . . namely those who, while they may not merit the description of being insane, are nevertheless in such a condition as to reduce the quality of their act from murder to culpable homicide.[3]

Thus, before defining the meaning of the term "diminished responsibility" Lord Alness set out his attitude to it, an attitude which is typical of that adopted by his successors. They start off by regarding the doctrine as an upstart, something new and therefore to be regarded suspiciously: although a doctrine at least as old as 1867 was not all that new even in 1923 in a legal system which only began properly in 1797 with the first edition of Hume. Then they talk of the doctrine as doing something to the "quality of the act" as if it were an exculpatory plea and not a plea in mitigation of sentence, and go on from this to regard it as something special to homicide and so as something which must be capable of definition since it takes the accused's act out of one legal category into another. Moreover, one has the impression, an impression given more strongly by Lord Normand in later cases, that if earlier judges had not recognised the doctrine as often as they did the modern law would dispense with it altogether.

After his introductory remarks Lord Alness went on to define the doctrine in a passage which has become the *locus classicus* on the subject. He said:

"It is very difficult to put it in a phrase, but it has been put in this way: that there must be aberration or weakness of mind; that there must be some form of mental unsoundness; that there must be a state of mind which is bordering on, though not amounting to, insanity; that there must be a mind so affected that responsibility is diminished from full responsibility to partial responsibility — in other words, the prisoner in question must be only partially accountable for his actions. And I think one can see running through the cases that there is implied . . . that there must be some form of mental disease."[4]

The only authority quoted by Lord Alness for this definition is *H.M. Advocate v. Aitken*[4a] but the definition, which might be called the *Savage* formula, has itself become the authoritative origin of the modern law independently of its consistency or otherwise with the nineteenth century cases. It was accepted by a Full Bench of the High Court in *Carraher v. H.M. Advocate,*[4b] and before that had been adopted by Lord Cooper, who was not of the court in *Carraher,*[5] in *H.M. Advocate v. Braithwaite,*[5a] so that it has the authority both of Lord Normand and of Lord Cooper;

---

[3] 1923 J.C. at 50.
[4] At 51.
[4a] (1902) 4 Adam 88.
[4b] 1946 J.C. 108.
[5] *ibid.*
[5a] 1945 J.C. 55.

the recognised way of directing juries on diminished responsibility is to quote the *Savage* formula to them.[6]

11.20 In *Braithwaite*[6a] Lord Cooper, who was then Lord Justice-Clerk, also described the doctrine in his own words, which were later approved in *Carraher*.[6b] He said, "[O]ur law does recognise — although it is only latterly that it has done so — that, if he was suffering from some infirmity or aberration of mind or impairment of intellect to such an extent as not to be fully accountable for his actions, the result is to reduce the quality of his offence".[7] These words echo the *Savage*[7a] attitude, even to repeating 20 years later the allegation of *arrivisme*. Lord Cooper went on to emphasise the stress laid on "weakness of intellect, aberration of mind, mental unsoundness, partial insanity, great peculiarity of mind and the like."[8] He also spoke in terms of disfacilitation, saying that,

> "[I]t will *not* suffice in law . . . merely to show that an accused person has a very short temper, or is unusually excitable and lacking in self-control. The world would be a very convenient place for criminals and a very dangerous place for other people, if that were the law . . . [there must be] something amounting or approaching to partial insanity and based on mental weakness or aberration."[9]

It is at once the merit and the defect of the *Savage* formula that it is largely tautologous.[10] As Professor Weihofen says of Lord Cooper's summary in *Braithwaite,*[10a] it is "somewhat amorphous and even circular, for it seems to say only that he is not to be held fully accountable if he was not fully accountable."[11] The only significant parts of the formula are those referring to the type of mental state which is relevant, and they consist of phrases like "mental weakness", "mental aberration", and "unsoundness of mind", which are all very vague. Even "mental disease" is capable of wide and varying interpretation. "Disease" just means

---

[6] The *Savage* formula was approved by the Criminal Appeal Court in *Connelly v. H.M. Advocate*, 1990 S.C.C.R. 504, where the argument that it was out of touch with modern psychiatric medicine was rejected. Indeed, L.J.-G. Hope went on to express the view that the formula was sufficiently elastic or flexible to avoid rigidity and yet prevent the doctrine being abused (at p.509 D-E). Nevertheless, in *Williamson v. H.M. Advocate*, 1994 S.C.C.R. 358, the Appeal Court denied that Lord Hope could possibly have meant that the formula itself was to be interpreted in a flexible way — for that would simply result in the abuse which Lord Hope had wished to avoid. Both cases strongly emphasise that there must be adequate evidence of mental disorder for diminished responsibility to be established: see also the opinion of the Court in *Martindale v. H.M. Advocate*, 1992 S.C.C.R. 700. The strong implication from *Lindsay v. H.M. Advocate*, 1996 S.C.C.R. 870, is that the formula, and any associated rules (such as onus of proof), are now of such long standing that any change should be mooted and implemented by the Scottish Parliament, after due consideration by the Scottish Law Commission.

[6a] 1945 J.C. 55.

[6b] 1946 J.C. 108.

[7] 1945 J.C. at 56.

[7a] 1923 J.C. 49.

[8] 1945 J.C. 55 at 57.

[9] *ibid.* at 57–58.

[10] It is not, however, as tautologous as the question put to the jury in *H.M. Advocate v. Muir,* High Court at Dumfries, April 1933, see 1933 J.C. 46, 48: "was he, owing to his mental state, of such inferior responsibility that his act should have attributed to it the quality not of murder but of culpable homicide?".

[10a] 1945 J.C. 55.

[11] *The Urge to Punish* (London, 1957), p.192, n.22 to Chap. 4.

"illness" except when it is used to distinguish infectious diseases from other forms of illness, a use which is irrelevant here. Even "partial insanity" is a rather vague phrase, and if what is required is only "something . . . approaching to partial insanity",[12] the vagueness is intensified.

Although it is tautologous[13] and may thus be thought to have the effect of making the law of diminished responsibility as open a matter as that of insanity, the formula is usually regarded as restrictive, and does operate in a restrictive way. But if there is to be a formula at all, and there is no warrant in the earlier cases for a "formulistic" approach, the *Savage* one is itself comparatively innocuous, since its denotation is fairly wide and elastic. Unless the requirement of disease or borderline insanity were to be unduly stressed, it would probably allow the doctrine to keep pace with medical science. What would have to be guarded against would be any tendency to treat it as if it were a statute in the way in which the M'Naghten Rules have been treated in England. The most recent authorities strongly suggest, however, that the formula is not open to much in the way of flexibility, and that crucially there must be evidence of mental disorder — that being how the tautology in the formula should actually be resolved.[14]

Psychopathic personality and the case of Carraher.[15] The case of *Carraher v. H.M. Advocate,*[15a] a Full Bench case,[16] may, however, itself have had the effect of making the law of diminished responsibility, at any rate in theory, rigid and incapable of further development. It is the most important of all cases on diminished responsibility; it is a Full Bench case; and it purports to say the last word about diminished responsibility. **11.21**

The case appears to have decided:

(1) That "the plea of diminished responsibility, which . . . is anomalous in our law, should not be extended or given wider scope than has hitherto been accorded to it in the decisions"[17];

(2) That, in particular, persons suffering from the condition known as psychopathic personality are not to be regarded as of diminished responsibility.

The phrase "appears to have decided" is used advisedly for the following reasons which cast doubt on the authority of the case.

(a) The history and purpose of the doctrine of diminished responsibility show that it is incapable of being confined within a list of closed categories. As Professor T.B. Smith says, it is too protean for that.[18] It seems to be accepted that the law regarding insanity must keep pace

---

12 *Braithwaite, supra.*

13 This is fully accepted by the courts: see, *e.g.*, *Connelly v. H.M. Advocate*, 1990 S.C.C.R. 504, L.J.-G. Hope at 509B-C; *Williamson v. H.M. Advocate*, 1994 S.C.C.R. 358, L.J.-C. Ross at 362C-D.

14 See *Williamson v. H.M. Advocate*, 1994 S.C.C.R. 358, where the Court emphasised that in *Connelly v. H.M. Advocate*, 1990 S.C.C.R. 504, at 509 D-E, L.J.-G. Hope had not meant that the formula itself was to be interpreted with any degree of flexibility. See also *Martindale v. H.M. Advocate*, 1992 S.C.C.R. 700.

15 1946 J.C. 108.

15a *ibid.*

16 L.J.-G. Normand, Lords Carmont, Jamieson, Stevenson and Birnam.

17 L.J.-G. Normand at 1946 J.C. 118.

18 T.B. Smith, p.159.

with scientific developments[19]; and if the categories of diminished responsibility are closed, the strange result is reached that a system which has no rigid criterion for distinguishing the sane from the insane, the guilty from the innocent, has such a criterion for deciding whether an accused's mental condition is such as to merit some mitigation of punishment. And the criterion it has is the worst possible — nothing can ever amount to diminished responsibility in the future unless it amounted to diminished responsibility before 1946. Moreover, *Carraher*[19a] adopted this criterion at a time when the legislature was taking modern psychological knowledge more and more into account in dealing with criminals.[20]

For substantially these reasons Professor Smith takes the view that *Carraher*[20a] does not in fact close the categories of diminished responsibility, and that "the judges will be prepared to recognise the *consensus prudentium* in matters of science."[21] Similarly, Lord Keith says that the Scots courts have not gone the length of saying that the question whether a particular psychopath is suffering from diminished responsibility should not be left to a jury, but he recognises that "They have, however, come very near saying so" in *Carraher*.[22] It is to be hoped that Professor Smith is right, but it must be pointed out that psychopathic personality was not something new in 1946, but was as well recognised then as it was a few years later when the Royal Commission on Capital Punishment cast doubt on *Carraher*[22a] and accepted that at any rate some psychopaths could properly be regarded as persons with diminished responsibility.[23] The decision in *Carraher*[23a] was not, in any event, confined to the special case of the psychopath, which is admittedly a difficult one. The court set itself against any extension of the doctrine because it disapproved of the doctrine itself, and not merely of some advanced psychiatric views. Far from being interested in the *consensus prudentium* the court refused to appoint a psychiatric assessor for fear of substituting trial by doctors for trial by jury.

(b) It is not clear how much of the judgment in *Carraher*[23b] is *obiter*. The trial judge had left the question of diminished responsibility to the jury, and the appeal was mainly concerned with the relation between intoxication and diminished responsibility. The court suggested that it would not have disapproved had diminished responsibility been withdrawn from the jury, but these remarks are *obiter*.

But the case has been regarded as containing general authoritative pronouncements on diminished responsibility and on psychopaths.[24]

(c) The case was decided in an atmosphere of fear; fear that violence would reach alarming proportions in Glasgow unless the courts took a firm hand, and fear that psychiatrists were undermining the whole structure of the criminal law.

---

[19] *ibid*, p.160; *cf. H.M. Advocate v. Brown* (1907) 5 Adam 312, L.J.-G. Dunedin at 343.
[19a] 1946 J.C. 108.
[20] *cf.* Criminal Justice (Scotland) Acts 1949 and 1963; Mental Health (Scotland) Act 1960.
[20a] 1946 J.C. 108.
[21] T.B. Smith, p.160.
[22] *op.cit.*, 1959 J.R. at 115.
[22a] 1946 J.C. 108.
[23] R.C., para. 401.
[23a] 1946 J.C. 108.
[23b] *ibid.*
[24] *cf.* R.C. para. 382; T.B. Smith, p.158.

The case was decided only a short while after the first execution in Scotland for 17 years, and belonged to the same class of crime as that for which hanging had been reintroduced.[25] Carraher was a much worse and older criminal than the hanged man, and there were good grounds in public policy for treating Carraher (a lifelong criminal who had killed a man on an earlier occasion[26]) as fully responsible. To have allowed him to "escape hanging" would have looked like giving licence to habitual criminals to continue the sort of gang warfare the authorities had determined to stamp out.[27] It may therefore have been thought important to impress upon criminals that the defence of psychopathic personality was not open to them.

This attitude was also due to fear that psychiatrists were coming to the conclusion that all habitual criminals were psychopaths, and that to allow psychopathic personality to count as diminished responsibility would mean that the worse a man was, the less punishment he would receive.[28] Lord Normand said of the medical evidence in *Carraher*[28a] that it was "descriptive rather of a typical criminal than of a person of the quality of one whom the law has hitherto regarded as being possessed of diminished responsibility."[29] Lord Cooper told the Royal Commission on Capital Punishment that,

> "At the time of the *Carraher* judgment the lawyers had become alarmed at a flood of psychological or psychiatric evidence introducing, or attempting to introduce, as new special defences all kinds of psychological and mental abnormalities with names which were unknown to us and to the man in the street . . . It was in reaction to that, I think, that the *Carraher* decision was pronounced."[30] As Professor Smith puts it, the court was anxious about "the danger that unverified hypotheses of individual psychiatrists might lead to abuse of the defence of diminished responsibility."[31]

Recent cases involving severe personality disorders have not, however, sought to criticise *Carraher*[31a] in any way; and the Appeal Court has consistently rejected attempts to suggest that the legal requirements for diminished responsibility have been stated too rigidly in the past.[32] Indeed the Court has been at pains to emphasise the importance of mental illness to the doctrine, such that medical evidence of severe personality disorder[33] falls short of what is required unless there is also **11.22**

---

[25] The first case was that of John Lyon, one of the accused in *Crosbie and Ors.*, High Court at Glasgow, Dec. 1945, unrep'd, discussed *supra*, para. 5.53. It is in point to note that one reason for the lack of executions between 1929 and 1945 was the readiness with which the Crown and juries reduced charges of murder to culpable homicide.

[26] R.C., App.4, para. 14.

[27] *cf.* R.C. App.6, para. 78.

[28] *cf.* Lady Wooton, *op.cit.* (1960) 76 L.Q.R. 224.

[28a] 1946 J.C. 108.

[29] 1946 J.C. at 117.

[30] R.C. Evid. of Lord Cooper, Q. 5468. .

[31] T.B. Smith, p.160. English law accepts that a psychopath can be of diminished responsibility: *R. v. Byrne* [1960] 2 Q.B. 396. This would not be altered under the English draft criminal code (L.C. No. 177, "A Criminal Code for England and Wales", 1989, H. of C., No. 299, Vol. 1): see cl. 56.

[31a] 1946 J.C. 108.

[32] See, *e.g.*, *Connelly v. H.M. Advocate*, 1990 S.C.C.R. 504.

[33] This term tends to be used in modern times where psychopathic personality might have been referred to in the past.

clear evidence of mental disorder.[34] As was stated by Lord Justice-General Hope in *Connelly v. H.M. Advocate*:[35]

> "In my opinion the concept has been defined in terms which are sufficiently elastic or flexible to avoid the dangers of rigidity while at the same time preserving the doctrine from abuse. The question for the expert medical witness will be whether there is something in the mental condition of the accused which can properly be described as a mental disorder or a mental illness or disease. It is hard to see how the criteria for diminished responsibility could ever be met in the absence of evidence to this effect . . . The criminal conduct of the accused may be explained by immaturity on his part or by his vulnerability or lack of self-control when faced with stress, but these cannot in law diminish his responsibility for what he has done."

Any suggestion that Lord Hope's references to 'flexibility' and the 'danger of rigidity' might presage a softening of attitude to the doctrine's criteria was specifically denied by the Court in *Williamson*,[36] where it was once again concluded that, in the absence of mental or psychiatric illness or any mental disorder, "a serious personality disorder as evidenced by gross immaturity and seriously irresponsible conduct . . . is not an adequate basis for contending that the test in *H.M. Advocate v. Savage* has been met."[37]

11.23 *The Mental Health (Scotland) Act 1984.* This Act (as was also the case with its predecessor, the Mental Health (Scotland) Act 1960) does not directly affect the law of diminished responsibility, nor, unlike its English equivalent,[38] does it deal specifically with "psychopathic disorder". Its provisions do, however, directly affect the ability of a court in Scotland to make a hospital order[39] in relation to a person convicted of an offence.[40] That person must fall within the rules allowing the compulsory detention of those who are not criminals under section 17(1) of the 1984 Act. These rules include that the person in question must be "suffering from mental disorder of a nature or degree which makes it appropriate for him to receive medical treatment in a hospital and (i) in the case where the mental disorder from which he suffers is a persistent one manifested only by abnormally aggressive or seriously irresponsible conduct, such treatment is likely to alleviate or prevent a deterioration of

---

[34] See *Connelly v. H.M. Advocate*, *supra*; *Martindale v. H.M. Advocate*, 1992 S.C.C.R. 700; *Williamson v. H.M. Advocate*, 1994 S.C.C.R. 358. These cases stress that it must be through mental illness that the accused's responsibility comes to be diminished. In *Williamson*, at 359A, Lord Sutherland (correctly, it is submitted — see para. 11.25, *infra*) directed the jury that "organic brain damage or something of the kind" was an alternative to mental illness or disease.

[35] 1990 S.C.C.R. 504, at 509D-E.

[36] 1994 S.C.C.R. 358, at 361E–362E.

[37] *ibid*., at 362G–363A.

[38] Mental Health Act 1983, s.1(2).

[39] They also affect the ability of a court to impose a "hospital direction" on a person convicted of an offence on indictment and in respect of whom a prison sentence is to be imposed: see 1995 Act, s.59A (added by the Crime and Punishment (Scotland) Act 1997, s.6). This procedure is primarily intended, however, to avoid situations of the type which arose in *R. v. Secretary of State for Scotland*, 1999 S.C. (H.L.) 17; see also *A. v. The Scottish Ministers*, 2000 S.L.T. 873.

[40] See the 1995 Act s.58(1). In a summary case before a sheriff, the same rule applies under s.58(3) where the accused is found to have done the act or made the omission with which he is charged, but the sheriff refrains from convicting him.

his condition". As the court in question must be satisfied of that likelihood "on the written or oral evidence of two medical practitioners",[41] and given current psychiatric attitudes, it seems that psychopaths are unlikely to be dealt with by way of hospital orders[42]: but the law appears to consider that they are suffering from mental disorder. One may go further, however, and state that the law appears to consider that they are suffering from mental illness, since 'mental illness' is not only included within the definition of mental disorder but is also now itself inclusive of 'personality disorder'.[43] This is important since, if diminished responsibility at common law requires mental illness (as appears to be the case), and if the statutory law includes personality disorder within mental illness (as it plainly does), it may be more difficult in future for courts to maintain that psychopathic personality is not sufficient for diminished responsibility.

The question whether the law should recognise psychopathic personality involves difficult moral, philosophical, penological and even psychological questions which are beyond the scope of this work, but as the statutory law has now decided to recognise psychopathic disorder as a mental disorder, it is difficult to see why this recognition should stop short at the psychopath who commits murder.[44] In so far, however, as the

---

[41] See s.58(1)(a) of the 1995 Act.

[42] This conclusion is based on the view that psychopaths are not treatable in ways which are likely to alleviate or prevent a deterioration of their conditions; but what amounts to "treatment" is currently controversial: see *R. v. Secretary of State for Scotland*, 1999 S.C. (H.L.) 17. Even were psychiatric attitudes to change with the advent of appropriate treatments, a hospital order could not be made where a psychopath had been convicted of "an offence the sentence for which is fixed by law" (1995 Act, s.58(1)): it would be possible for a court to impose a 'hospital direction' under the Mental Health (Scotland) Act 1984 s.59A (added by the Crime and Punishment (Scotland) Act 1997, s.6(1)); but this must be combined with a prison sentence, which in a murder case could not allow for the mitigation of sentence which is inseparable from the common law notion of diminished responsibility.

[43] See s.1(2) of the Mental Health (Scotland) Act 1984, as amended by the Mental Health (Public Safety and Appeals) (Scotland) Act 1999 (asp 1), s.3(1).

[44] For a discussion of the problem of the psychopathic offender, see B. Wooton (Lady Wooton of Abinger), *Social Science and Social Pathology* (London, 1959), p.249 *et seq.*; "Diminished Responsibility: A Layman's View" (1960) 76 L.Q.R. 224; J.Ll.L. Edwards, "Diminished Responsibility," in *Essays in Criminal Science*, G.O.W. Mueller (ed.) (London, 1961), p.301; J.E. Hall Williams, "The Psychopath and the Defence of Diminished Responsibility" (1958) 21 M.L.R. 544; Gl. Williams, para. 170.

One fundamental difficulty in accepting psychopathic personality as an abnormal state is that it appears to be a personality defect, or at most a form of emotional instability, so that the psychopath's "excuse" seems to be his own character, and the acceptance of such an excuse conflicts with ordinary ideas of moral responsibility and free will — see *supra*, para. 2.16. A man's responsibility for his own character does not, however, extend to the result of a mental disease, and the question comes to be whether psychopathic personality is such a disease or is just a way of saying that a person has criminal tendencies. This is itself partly a matter of terminology but if psychiatrists can distinguish the psychopath from the merely wicked and can provide some form of treatment for him, however difficult it is to cure him, then it is for this purpose a disease, and is properly recognised by the Mental Health (Scotland) Act 1984.

At the time of the first edition of this book, in the 1960s, psychiatric opinion seemed to favour the treatment of psychopathic personality as a medically diagnosable and curable, or at least treatable, condition: see *e.g.* Sir D.K. Henderson's Memorandum of Evidence to the Royal Commission on Capital Punishment; *R. v. Byrne* [1960] 2 Q.B. 396. Psychiatrists are now much less optimistic about their ability to treat psychopaths, and the term itself may be so vague as to be at least an uncertain guide for lawyers. The current view appears to be that the proper place for most psychopaths is more likely to be a prison than a hospital, and it has been proposed that the relevant provisions of the mental health

common law continues to deny that a killer who is of psychopathic personality can be of diminished responsibility, such a killer is most likely to be dealt with by imprisonment for life.

Intoxication

11.24 It was held in *Brennan v. H.M. Advocate*[45] that, since the requirement of mental disease in insanity applies equally to diminished responsibility, a transient state of mind induced by voluntary intoxication can never constitute diminished responsibility.

A Note on Mental Handicap

11.25 It was held in *H.M. Advocate v. Breen*[46] that mental deficiency could not operate as a defence or in bar of trial under the now repealed Mental Deficiency and Lunacy (Scotland) Act 1913. *Breen*,[46a] however, does not affect the current law which speaks of "mental handicap" rather than "mental deficiency".[47] Since such handicap is a constitutional condition a person who is mentally handicapped at the time of the offence will be in the same state at the time of the trial, so that the question is normally raised in the context of a plea in bar of trial. In practice, persons suffering from severe mental handicap are treated as insane for the purposes of a plea in bar of trial.[48] It would indeed be almost impossible for the law to hold that a deaf mute who could not instruct a defence was to be deemed insane but that a mentally handicapped person in the same condition was to be put on trial. If the court had to deal with a special defence of insanity based on mental handicap it is submitted that it would deal with it in the same way as the ordinary special defence of insanity based on mental illness. If the mental deficiency is so severe as to deprive the accused of a sane understanding of his circumstances, or to bring him within the scope of whatever other definition of legal insanity is adopted, he will be acquitted on the ground of insanity. Again, if a person who is rendered irresponsible by arteriosclerosis or hypoglycaemia is to be acquitted on the ground of insanity, it is difficult to justify the conviction of someone rendered irresponsible by reason of mental handicap.

Despite the terminology of the *Savage* formula,[49] with its reference to conditions bordering on insanity, there is no doubt that mental handicap may, and usually does, constitute diminished responsibility.[50] The early

---

legislation should not apply to psychopathic offenders — Report of Butler Committee on Mentally Abnormal Offenders, Cmnd. 6244/1975, Chap. 5. See also s.4.01(2) of the Model Penal Code, which excludes from mental disease "an abnormality manifested only by repeated criminal or otherwise anti-social conduct".

[45] 1977 J.C. 38. *Cf. R. v. Fenton* (1975) 61 Cr.App.R. 261; *R. v. Egan* [1992] 4 All E.R. 470.

[46] 1921 J.C. 30: see L.J.-G. Clyde at 38; in *Breen* itself the plea offered was one in bar of trial.

[46a] *ibid.*

[47] Mental Health (Scotland) Act 1984, s.1(2).

[48] *cf.* R.C., para. 341, Recommendation 21; *Barr v. Herron*, 1968 J.C. 20; see 32 J.C.L. 113; Second Report of Committee on Criminal Procedure in Scotland, Cmnd. 6218, 1975, para. 52.13.

[49] *supra,* para. 11.19.

[50] *cf.* R.C., para. 343.

cases on diminished responsibility talk of "mental weakness",[51] and in *H.M. Advocate v. Breen*[51a] Lord Clyde referred to mental deficiency as presenting "a close analogy to the familiar appeal for a recommendation to leniency or mercy on the ground of the accused's proved weakness of mind."[52]

The Mental Health (Scotland) Act 1984 divides mental disorder into mental illness (including personality disorder) and mental handicap,[53] and so retains the distinction between the two. Of course, both the mentally ill and the mentally handicapped may be compulsorily admitted to hospital on the general ground that they are "suffering from mental disorder of a nature or degree which make it appropriate for [them] to receive medical treatment"; but in the case of those who are mentally handicapped, their handicap has to amount to severe mental impairment, or to be the sort of mental impairment where medical treatment "is likely to alleviate or prevent deterioration of [their] condition",[54] in addition to any other requirement.[55] Provided these conditions are met, a mentally handicapped person who has been convicted of a crime can be made the subject of a hospital order or hospital direction under sections 58 or 59A of the 1975 Act.

---

[51] *supra*, para. 11.10.

[51a] 1921 J.C. 30.

[52] 1921 J.C. at 38.

[53] s.1(2), as amended by the Mental Health (Public Safety and Appeals) (Scotland) Act 1999 (asp 1), s.3(1).

[54] 1984 Act, s.17(1)(a)(ii). Both "mental impairment" and "severe mental impairment" are defined in s.1(2) of that Act.

[55] On which, see 1984 Act, s.17(1)(b).

CHAPTER 12

INTOXICATION[1]

Introduction

12.01 The law regarding voluntary intoxication as a defence to a criminal charge is an unsatisfactory compromise among a number of attitudes and principles. On the one hand it is felt that drunkenness should never be taken into account in ascribing responsibility for crime, because it is a voluntary condition and is, moreover, a reprehensible one. Drinking is a vice, and it is a man's own fault if he commits a crime under the influence of drink. As Hume says, "[O]ne cannot well lay claim to favour, on the ground of that which itself shews a disregard of order and decency."[2] On the other hand, the man who gets drunk and commits a crime sometimes arouses sympathy rather than indignation. Take, for example, the young man who commits a crime, say indecent assault, as a result of drinking too much at his first alcoholic party. Talk of vice and wickedness seems out of place in such a situation, and it seems unduly harsh to treat him as if he were a deliberate criminal.

The law, too, is concerned at the number of crimes which are committed under the influence of alcohol. Alison said in 1832 that "such is the tendency to this brutalising vice, among the lower orders in this country, that if it were sustained as a defence, three-fourths of the whole crimes in the country would go unpunished; for the slightest experience must be sufficient to convince everyone, that almost every crime that is committed is directly or indirectly connected with whisky."[3] And in *Brennan v. H.M. Advocate*[4] the court commented that self-induced intoxication due to drink has been increasingly a factor in crimes of violence committed in Scotland.

Although the law grew up in the context of alcoholic intoxication, it applies to other forms of intoxication, such as those caused by drugs.[5]

12.02 *The causal question.* Whatever the nature and effect of the plea of intoxication it must be limited to cases of gross intoxication. The plea can apply only in those cases where the crime would not have been

---

[1] Some of the issues in this chapter are discussed further in G.H. Gordon, "Automatism, Insanity and Intoxication" (1976) 21 J.L.S. 310; see also J.W.R. Gray's articles, "A Purely Temporary Disturbance", 1974 J.R. 227, and "The Expulsion of *Beard* from Scotland: Murder North of the Border" [1979] Crim.L.R. 369.

[2] Hume, i, 45–46.

[3] Alison, i, 661. A similar view has fairly recently been expressed in the American Supreme Court, see *Montana v. Egelhoff*, 116 S.Ct. 2013 (1996), Scalia J. at 2020. *Cf.* Law Commission, Consultation Paper No. 127, *Intoxication and Criminal Liability* (1993) para. 1.10, and C.M.V. Clarkson and H.M. Keating, *Criminal Law: Text and Materials* (London, 4th ed., 1998), at pp.405–407, for some English statistical studies.

[4] 1977 J.C. 38.

[5] *R. v. Lipman* [1970] 1 Q.B. 152; *Brennan, supra; Donaldson v. Normand*, 1997 S.C.C.R. 351.

committed but for the drink, and even then only when the accused has been so affected by drink as to be unaware of his actings or at least unable to exercise normal self-control.

12.03 ACTIO LIBERA IN CAUSA. Judges who do not wish to give effect to a plea of intoxication sometimes explain their refusal to do so by saying that if intoxication were a valid plea, "if anybody was going to commit a crime all he would need to do would be to take sufficient liquor and commit it, and then say, 'Oh, you can't hold me for this, because I had drink.'"[6] This fails to note that a distinction can easily be made between the man who gets drunk and then decides to commit a crime, and the man who decides to commit a crime and then gets drunk to give himself Dutch courage. The latter situation is described in some jurisdictions as one of *actio libera in causa*.[7] It is clear that in such a situation the accused is guilty of an intentional crime, since he formed a sober intention of committing the crime. If A decides to kill B and then takes drink in order to steel himself to commit the deed, he is guilty of murder whatever his state of intoxication at the time of the killing.[8]

The concept of *actio libera in causa* can also be applied in relation to negligence so that where the ultimate crime is one that can be committed negligently the accused will be guilty of its negligent commission if it was foreseeable that his becoming drunk would lead to the crime. If A ought to know that he will become violent when drunk — if, for example, he has done so on prior occasions — but nonetheless gets drunk and kills someone he will be guilty of culpable homicide or of murder, depending on whether he is regarded as negligent or as reckless.[9]

The law of Scotland

12.04 *Chronic and acute alcoholism.* The effect of the law is to distinguish between chronic and acute alcoholism, and a brief description of these states may be helpful. The distinction is the same as that between what are sometimes called industrial and convivial drinking.[10] The chronic alcoholic gradually drinks himself to death or madness over a period of years, without necessarily ever being at any time drunk in the ordinary sense of the word; acute alcoholism is just the ordinary state of drunkenness. The man who gets "mad drunk" on occasions but is quite normal otherwise is a convivial drinker; the man who is never "mad drunk" (or only so very rarely that this can be discounted in an analysis of his condition), but is an alcoholic who is never wholly sober and who

---

[6] *Kennedy v. H.M. Advocate*, 1944 J.C. 171, Lord Carmont at 172.

[7] This applies, *e.g.*, in South Africa: see E.M. Burchell and P.M.A. Hunt, *South African Criminal Law and Procedure*, Vol. 1, *General Principles of Criminal Law* (3rd ed. by J.M. Burchell, Cape Town, 1997) pp.44–45, where it is noted that actio in libera causa is a contracted form of *"actio non in se, sed tamen in sua causa libera"*.

[8] *Attorney-General for Northern Ireland v. Gallagher* [1963] A.C. 349. *Cf.* Law Commission, Consultation Paper No. 127, *Intoxication and Criminal Liability* (1993), at para. 2.23: "It is, however, remarkably difficult to envisage a case where the defendant has sufficient and sufficiently directed motor control to carry out a *pre-arranged* plan, but was so intoxicated as to lack intention or awareness in relation to that plan. So far as we are aware, there is no example, anywhere in the common law world, of such a case actually occurring." A. Ashworth, *Principles of Criminal Law* (3rd ed., Oxford, 1999) at p.218 makes a similar comment.

[9] See *Brennan*, 1977 J.C. 38, *supra*; *infra*, para. 12.12.

[10] W.C. Sullivan, *Crime and Insanity* (London, 1924), p.59.

cannot live without drink, is an industrial drinker. The state of the insane industrial drinker may be taken into account when he is charged with a crime; but that of the convivial drinker who commits a crime in one of his drunken moments is irrelevant, unless perhaps he is so drunk as to be wholly lacking in *mens rea*.[11] The insane chronic alcoholic is not responsible for any insane intention he may form, but the convivial drinker who forms and carries out a drunken intention is responsible for it. This distinction is due at least in part to the fact that the chronic alcoholic is usually not "drunk" when he commits his crime, and it is drunkenness itself rather than the long-term effects of drink which the law abhors.

The distinction appeared very clearly in the American case of *U.S. v. Drew.*[12] D. was a sailor who while suffering from *delirium tremens* killed a man five days after all the alcohol on the ship had been thrown overboard. Story J. said,

> "In general, insanity is an excuse for the commission of every crime, because the party has not the possession of that reason, which includes responsibility. An exception is, when the crime is committed by a party while in a fit of intoxication, the law not permitting a man to avail himself of the excuse of his own gross vice and misconduct, to shelter himself from the legal consequences of such crime . . . But the crime must take place and be the *immediate* result of the fit of intoxication, *and while it lasts*; and not, as in this case, a remote consequence, superinduced by the antecedent exhaustion of the party, arising from gross and habitual drunkenness."[13]

Lord Deas made a similar distinction in discussing the Case of *Alex. Dingwall*[14] in the case of *John McLean.*[15] He pointed out that although Dingwall's diminished responsibility was the result of alcoholism he had been sober at the time of the crime, and that had he been drunk that would have afforded neither excuse for nor palliation of his crime.

Insanity caused by alcoholism. It is accordingly clearly recognised that **12.05**
insanity caused by drink is as good a defence to a criminal charge as any other insanity. "If the mind is diseased . . . then that is insanity, which will take away criminal responsibility. If there be such insanity, it matters not . . . what was the exciting cause . . . It may be drunkenness — or it may be indulgence in any other vicious propensity — it is of no consequence which it is, if insanity is actually produced and is present at the time."[16] The reason for the rule was given by Lord Justice-Clerk Macdonald as being that "to hold him responsible for that which he does when his mind is overthrown by disease would be to visit him with the consequences of an act which he could not estimate when he did it, because the presence of an actual disease prevented his having sane control of his actions."[17]

---

[11] See *infra*, para. 12.12.
[12] (1828) 5 Mason 28; Fed Cas. 14993; Sayre, 521.
[13] Sayre, p.522.
[14] (1867) 5 Irv. 466.
[15] (1876) 3 Couper 334, 338.
[16] *Alex. Milne* (1863) 4 Irv. 301, L.J.-C. Inglis at 344.
[17] *H.M. Advocate v. McDonald* (1890) 2 White 517, 521.

12.06 *Diminished responsibility caused by alcoholism.* Although strictly speaking the analogy with insanity is not exact since insanity is exculpatory and diminished responsibility merely a plea in mitigation, it is presumably the law that if a man drinks himself into a permanent state which is classifiable as a state of diminished responsibility, he is treated as being of diminished responsibility without any regard to the cause of his condition, provided at any rate that he is sober at the time of the offence.[18]

It is now clear that acute intoxication, if self-induced, can not constitute diminished responsibility,[19] whether alone or in combination with some pre-existing condition not in itself amounting to diminished responsibility.[20]

Acute intoxication in homicide

12.07 *The law prior to 1921.* INTOXICATION AS A DEFENCE. Hume states expressly that "that sort of temporary madness, which is produced by excess in intoxicating liquors" is not a defence.[21] He is followed by Alison,[22] and in a number of cases.[23] Acute intoxication cannot operate as a defence even where it produces temporary insanity, and a man who commits homicide while temporarily insane because of the effect of a drinking bout is not entitled to an acquittal on the ground of insanity.[24] *A fortiori* he is not entitled to an acquittal where the effect of the drink is not so great as to render him temporarily insane.

12.08 INTOXICATION AS A MITIGATING FACTOR. The law on drink as a mitigating factor was formerly bound up with the law of diminished responsibility, and was still in process of developing when it was superseded by the adoption of the law of England in *H.M. Advocate v. Campbell*[25] in 1921. Prior to that adoption there were indications that it was the law in Scotland that where acute intoxication produced a mental disease which amounted to diminished responsibility, or to actual temporary insanity, it could reduce murder to culpable homicide, and that it might do so also on the more general grounds that it produced a condition which excluded the malice required for murder, whether or not any recognisable mental disease was involved.

Hume himself, who as has been seen was no friend to the plea of intoxication, appears to have been of the view that in appropriate cases it should lead to a recommendation to mercy.[26] The question was not raised sharply until the case of *Andrew Granger*[27] in 1878. Granger killed a man while he was drunk, and the jury were directed by Lord Deas that although there was no evidence of insanity they could bring in a verdict of culpable homicide. The jury specifically found Granger guilty of

---

[18] *Alex. Dingwall* (1867) 5 Irv. 466; *Thos. Ferguson* (1881) 4 Couper 552.

[19] *Brennan*, 1977 J.C. 38.

[20] *H.M. Advocate v. McLeod*, 1956 J.C. 20; *Carraher v. H.M. Advocate*, 1946 J.C. 108.

[21] Hume, i, 45–46.

[22] Alison, i, 661.

[23] See *Andrew Granger* (1878) 4 Couper 86; *H.M. Advocate v. McDonald* (1890) 2 White 517; *H.M. Advocate v. Kane* (1892) 3 White 386. But see *Wm Douglas* (1827) Syme 184, and *H.M. Advocate v. Aitken*, 1975 S.L.T. (Notes) 86.

[24] *ibid.*

[25] 1921 J.C. 1.

[26] *cf. Jas. Cummings* (1810) Hume, I, 40–41.

[27] (1878) 4 Couper 86.

culpable homicide on the ground that the crime was committed while he was labouring under *delirium tremens.* In rejecting an argument that the verdict amounted to an acquittal on the ground of insanity Lord Deas said that none of the witnesses had said the accused was insane, but that, "For a few days before . . . he had . . . been drinking heavily; and this, on the day libelled brought on an attack of *delirium tremens*. But it had not gone the length of his not knowing what he was about."[28] Lord Deas went on to say, "I have no hesitation, however, in repeating what I said to the jury, that, in a question between murder and culpable homicide, it was not incompetent for the jury to take into account the weak or diseased state of the panel's mind at the time of the act, whether arising from *delirium tremens* not amounting to insanity, or from some other disease or infirmity."[29] In addressing the prisoner prior to pronouncing sentence Lord Deas said that if he had been simply drunk, even so drunk as not to know what he was about, the verdict would have been murder, and that the conviction for culpable homicide was because his drinking had gone "the length of forthwith producing a degree — it may be a considerable degree — of *delirium tremens*."[30] This case may, however, be seen as a case of mental disease brought on by chronic drinking, albeit the disease was transitory.

In *Margaret Robertson or Brown*[31] the accused was a woman "of inebriate habits" who killed her two grandchildren by putting them on the fire during a drunken hallucination. Lord McLaren drew a distinction between acts "under the influence of a sudden access of homicidal mania which passed off immediately after the occurrences," in which case the verdict should be not guilty because of insanity, and acts "under the influence of some momentary hallucination induced by drunkenness", in which case the jury could convict of culpable homicide.[32] The reason for the verdict of culpable homicide was given as being that, "In violent crimes, and where the crime involves malice or criminal intention, intoxication might be a relevant matter to take into consideration, as showing there could be no malicious intention."[33] **12.09**

In *H.M. Advocate v. McDonald*[34] a defence of insanity was lodged on the ground of *delirium tremens* which was rejected by Lord Justice-Clerk Macdonald. Lord Macdonald went on to explain that where, as in the instant case, the weapon used proved that there was a violent assault but not necessarily murderous intent, where "the means adopted were not of themselves likely to lead to bad results, and if there was no malice aforethought here, then the fact that the man was in a drunken state may be considered in determining the question between murder and culpable homicide."[35] *McDonald*[35a] was quoted extensively and approvingly in **12.10**

---

[28] At 107.

[29] At 110–111.

[30] At 111. The sentence was the very lenient one of five years' imprisonment, the leniency being because unlike the accused in *Alex, Dingwall* (1867) 5 Irv. 466, who had been sober at the time of the crime, Granger was not a habitual drunkard, and so could be more quickly reformed.

[31] (1886) 1 White 93.

[32] At 104–105.

[33] At 104. This *dictum* can presumably not stand with *Brennan, infra.*

[34] (1890) 2 White 517.

[35] At 524.

[35a] (1890) 2 White 517.

Brennan v. H.M. Advocate,[36] but this was mainly in connection with its rejection of the argument that acute intoxication could amount to insanity. The fact that culpable homicide was left to the jury (who convicted of murder) was explained by the fact that the modes of assault used were not in themselves likely to lead to bad results, and not to the presence of possible defences of diminished responsibility or of intoxication. The accused was charged with murdering his wife and his lodger by beating them with a piece of wood and a piece of iron. The use of a piece of wood alone was regarded in *Miller and Denovan*[37] as sufficient to justify the judge in withdrawing culpable homicide from the jury, although admittedly the use there was for the purpose of robbery. Lord Macdonald was concerned with the absence of murderous intent, however, and he did seem to think that it might be found to be absent, irrespective of drink. He said,

> "But where a person, drunk or sober, begins smashing about him, it does not necessarily follow that there was at the outset a murderous intent. I am very much afraid that when people pick up a bludgeon without any intent further than to indulge a violent passion, passion often gets so roused that they proceed with intent to kill, or, what is the same thing, with utter recklessness, whether they kill or not; and it is matter for your consideration in this case whether or not the extent of the injuries do not show that intent to have arisen to put these two people to death, or to injure them regardless of consequences."[38]

He then concluded by saying,

> "I have only to add that while drunkenness is no excuse, yet if the means adopted were not of themselves likely to lead to bad results, and if there was no malice aforethought here, then the fact that the man was in a drunken state may be considered in determining the question between murder and culpable homicide. I should have had great difficulty in saying that, but for the fact that I see from the full and clear citation of authorities which we have had, that some of my brethren have taken that view in similar cases. I have some doubts whether or not it is consistent with principle, but if you will keep clearly in view that drunkenness is no excuse for what occurred here, then I am not inclined to set my own opinion against that of the experienced Judges to whom I have referred, and to debar you from considering whether a crime committed in this drunken state, without motive and without preconceived malice, although murder, in the strict sense of the law, may not be viewed by you as falling within the category of a case of aimless violence, not absolutely murderous."[39]

This is all rather confused, and the confusion is not helped by the fact that the authorities cited, apart from *Margaret Robertson or Brown*,[40] were straightforward diminished responsibility cases, or by the consideration that 'aimless violence' is a description of the typical modern

---

[36] 1977 J.C. 38, *infra*, para. 12.12.
[37] Criminal Appeal Court, Dec. 1960, unrep'd, but noted at 1991 J.C. 48; see Vol. II, Chap. 23.
[38] (1890) 2 White at 523.
[39] *ibid.* 523–524.
[40] (1886) 1 White 93; see para. 12.09, *supra*.

murder. It can certainly not be clearly asserted that *McDonald*[40a] rejects the idea that the presence of drunkenness may make a case of diminished responsibility out of that which would not be such a case in its absence. The later case of *H.M. Advocate v. Kane*[41] is perhaps clearer. In that case the accused was charged with murdering his wife by striking her with a hatchet and kicking her, and was convicted of culpable homicide. The case was complicated by evidence that the victim was in a debilitated state by reason of her habits of dissipation to such an extent that her early death was probable, and the jury were told that that was a very important element in considering whether the crime displayed recklessness, as it might be that but for her debilitated state she would have recovered. But so far as drunkenness was concerned, the jury were clearly told that "It is where it comes to be a question of extent of the malice under which he was actuated in what he did — that is to say, whether the thing which he did and which cannot be excused, falls into a very bad category, or into a less bad category — that his state of intoxication might be taken into consideration."[42] His Lordship then repeated the passage from *Macdonald*[42a] last cited above,[42b] and concluded: "You are entitled to take into consideration in the question whether the full guilt of murder has been incurred in this case, the important fact that the man was intoxicated at the time, and to a certain extent using violence perhaps quite unconscious as to the extent of it. Although he is responsible for that, he may not necessarily be guilty of murder in the circumstances."[43] These observations cannot stand with *Brennan.*[43a]

In *H.M. Advocate v. Paterson*,[44] where the accused had at one time suffered from sunstroke, Lord Young directed the jury that if he killed in an ungovernable rage caused immediately by drink he was guilty of murder, but that he could be convicted of culpable homicide if the jury found that because of the effects of the sunstroke he was more passionate and excitable in drink that he might have been otherwise.

In *H.M. Advocate v. Aitken,*[45] Lord Stormonth Darling told the jury that if the accused committed the crime while his mind was not unhinged, "however much it may have been temporarily disturbed by drink or jealousy, or anger", the crime was murder,[46] but the law of intoxication was not gone into in any detail.

On the whole, although the cases are a little confusing, Anderson appears to have been justified in saying that the law was that "Although intoxication is no defence to a crime, the jury may nevertheless take such a condition into account in considering whether a crime is murder or culpable homicide."[47] The law did not accept that acute intoxication could ever relieve an accused entirely from responsibility for homicide, but was prepared to allow it to act as a mitigating factor.[48]

40a (1890) 2 White 517.
41 (1892) 3 White 386.
42 At 388–389.
42a (1890) 2 White 517.
42b *ibid.,* 523–524.
43 At 389–390.
43a 1977 J.C. 38.
44 (1897) 5 S.L.T. 13.
45 (1902) 4 Adam 88.
46 At 95.
47 Anderson, p.149. For a discussion of the nineteenth century law, see J.F. Sutherland, "The Jurisprudence of Intoxication" (1898) 10 J.R. 309.
48 See also Macdonald, p.14.

12.11 *The Beard era.* In 1921, in *H.M. Advocate v. Campbell,*[49] a High Court judge followed the English case of *D.P.P. v. Beard,*[50] and in *Kennedy v. H.M. Advocate,*[51] in 1944, a Full Bench adopted the principle of *Beard*[51a] as representing the law of Scotland. *Beard*[51b] itself was complicated by the old English rule of constructive malice, and by the notion of crimes of specific intent. Its essence, however, so far as Scotland was concerned, was that where a person was by reason of intoxication incapable of forming the intention necessary to commit murder, he could not be convicted of murder. As Lord Justice-General Normand put it, *Beard*[52] required that "not only shall there be evidence of intoxication, but also that there shall be evidence relevant to infer a present state of incapacity to form the intent at the time when the crime was committed. The essence of the thing is, not the intoxication, but the resulting incapacity to form the intent."[52a] *Kennedy*[52b] accepted the further rule in *Beard*[53] that where such incapacity was present the appropriate verdict was one of guilty of culpable homicide.[53a]

12.12 *Brennan v. H.M. Advocate.* A Full Bench of seven judges overruled *Kennedy*[53b] in the case of *Brennan v. H.M. Advocate.*[54] They did so, apart from policy considerations, on the ground that *Beard*[54a] depended on the English concept of crimes of specific intent,[55] and therefore had no relevance to Scots law.[56] In particular, it had no application to a crime like murder which required only wicked recklessness and not intention for its *mens rea*. It was said, too, that the court in *Kennedy*[56a] had failed to appreciate that there was no trace in the law of Scotland prior to 1920 of self-induced intoxication being a recognised defence to a charge of murder, and that evidence of the effects of such intoxication, by itself, was not even admitted by our law to be a foundation for a plea of diminished responsibility.[57]

Brennan[57a] upholds, therefore, the older common law rule that self-induced intoxication is not a defence to any criminal charge including

---

[49] 1921 J.C. 1.
[50] [1920] A.C. 479.
[51] 1944 J.C. 171.
[51a] [1920] A.C. 479.
[51b] *ibid.*
[52] *ibid.*
[52a] At 177.
[52b] 1944 J.C. 171.
[53] [1920] A.C. 479.
[53a] It may be noted here that while *Kennedy* talks of capacity to form an "intent", Scots judges sometimes use that word to include recklessness: *cf. Cawthorne v. H.M. Advocate*, 1968 J.C. 32; see Vol. II, Chap. 23. It should be noted that murder cannot be committed recklessly in England, the law there being that an intention to kill or to do serious bodily harm must be shown: see *R. v. Moloney* [1985] A.C. 905; *R. v. Hancock and Shankland* [1986] A.C. 455; *R. v. Nedrick* [1986] 1 W.L.R. 1025. The current English rationalisation of *Beard* rests, however, on much the same lines as *Brennan*: see *R. v. Majewski* [1977] A.C. 443.
[53b] 1944 J.C. 171.
[54] 1977 J.C. 38.
[54a] [1920] A.C. 479.
[55] See para. 12.14, *infra*.
[56] The court emphasised that Scots law had never recognized any distinction between specific and basic intent crimes, a distinction which in any event they regarded as illogical (1977 J.C. at 47). See para. 12.14, *infra*.
[56a] 1944 J.C. 171.
[57] 1977 J.C. at 46. *Cf. supra*, para. 12.10.
[57a] 1977 J.C. 38.

murder. The use of the word 'defence' suggests that the Crown continue to have the ordinary burden of proving the *mens rea* of murder[58]; but if that burden is discharged then any doubt which might be cast upon the existence of *mens rea* owing to the voluntary drunkenness of the accused is to be ignored as irrelevant. Such an uncompromising rule recently found favour with the United States' Supreme Court in *Montana v. Egelhoff*,[59] where a provision of the Montana Criminal Code,[60] that voluntary intoxication was not to be taken into account in determining the existence of a mental state which was an element of an offence, was upheld as constitutional, if not indeed meritorious.[61] The point was taken, however, that the Code provision did not shift the burden of proof from the State, which still required to produce evidence independent of the state of intoxication that the defendant had acted "knowingly or purposely" in relation to the killings in question.[62]

Brennan[62a] goes further than the Montana Code provision, however, in that the court concluded as follows:

> "There is nothing unethical or unfair or contrary to the general principle of our law that self-induced intoxication is not by itself a defence to any criminal charge, including in particular the charge of murder. Self-induced intoxication is itself a continuing element, and therefore an integral part of any crime of violence including murder, the other part being the evidence of the actings of the accused who uses force against his victim. Together they add up or may add up to that criminal recklessness which it is the purpose of the criminal law to restrain in the interests of all the citizens of this country."[63]

Far from merely ignoring voluntary intoxication as any defence or excuse, therefore, it is plain that such intoxication may be used actively by the Crown to discharge the burden it would otherwise have in proving the *mens rea* for murder.[64] This raises the question whether self-induced intoxication is itself a form of general *mens rea*[65] and thus a substitute for whatever mental element the crime in question requires,[66] or whether it is (or, more flexibly, can be) evidence of recklessness in relation to a crime such as murder where a degree of recklessness is a sufficient form of *mens rea*. The whole tenor of the decision, and in particular the contrast which it draws between the Scots and English accounts of the mental element for murder, suggests that the latter is to be preferred. As the court, although admittedly not without ambiguity, put it:

> "If according to our law the *mens rea* in murder may be deduced from the wicked recklessness of the actings of the accused, it is extremely difficult to understand how actings may lose the quality of

---

[58] See Barwick C.J. in *The Queen v. O'Connor* (1980) 54 A.L.J.R. 349 at 351.

[59] 116 S.Ct. 2013 (1996).

[60] Section 45–2–203.

[61] 116 S.Ct. 2013 (1996), Scalia J. at 2020, where various policy considerations in favour of such a rule are narrated with obvious approval.

[62] *ibid*., at 2022–2023.

[62a] 1977 J.C. 38.

[63] 1977 J.C. at 51.

[64] In the U.S.A., this would probably breach a fundamental principle of justice: see *Montana v. Egelhoff*, 116 S.Ct. 2013 (1996), Scalia J. at 2022–2023.

[65] See para. 7.05, *supra*.

[66] *cf. Ross v. H.M. Advocate,* 1991 J.C. 210, L.J.-G. Hope at 214: "In all such cases [where *mens rea* is absent due to voluntary intoxication] the accused must be assumed to have intended the natural consequences of his act."

> such recklessness because the actor was in an intoxicated state brought about by his own deliberate and conscious purpose. In this connection the following passage from the speech of Lord Elwyn Jones L.C. in *D.P.P. v. Majewski*[67] . . . where he is dealing with all crimes in England save those requiring proof of specific intent, is both relevant and instructive: 'I do not for my part regard that general principle [that, with very few exceptions, self-induced intoxication is not a defence to a criminal charge] as either unethical or contrary to the principles of natural justice. If a man of his own volition takes a substance which causes him to cast off the restraints of reason and conscience, no wrong is done to him by holding him answerable criminally for any injury he may do while in that condition. His course of conduct in reducing himself by drugs and drink to that condition in my view supplies the evidence of *mens rea*, of guilty mind certainly sufficient for crimes of basic intent. It is a reckless course of conduct and recklessness is enough to constitute the necessary *mens rea* in assault cases: See *R. v. Venna*[68] *per* James L.J. The drunkenness is itself an intrinsic, an integral part of the crime, the other part being the evidence of the unlawful use of force against the victim. Together they add up to criminal recklessness.' "[69]

The conclusion that voluntary intoxication may itself constitute the wicked recklessness necessary for murder is probably easier to accommodate in Scots law than in English, because the former does not regard recklessness as wholly subjective[70] and does not require proof of a particular mental event at the time of the crime.[71] Nevertheless, *Brennan*[72] poses problems of principle and interpretation, and these will be considered in the paragraphs which follow.

12.13 BRENNAN AND PRINCIPLE. Since *Brennan*[73] finds the *mens rea* for murder in the act of becoming voluntarily intoxicated, the decision itself may appear to be not inconsistent with the axiom *actus non facit reum nisi mens sit rea*.[74] Nevertheless it has been said: "In principle it would seem that in all cases where a person lacks the evil intention which is essential to guilt of a crime he must be acquitted."[75] Scots law also accepts that a person may lack the capacity to form *mens rea*, but

---

67 [1977] A.C. 443, 474–475.

68 [1976] Q.B. 421, 429.

69 1977 J.C. at 50. Although not a homicide case, *D.P.P. v. Majewski* remains the leading authority on voluntary intoxication in English criminal law. It should be noted, however, that it is probably untrue in Scotland that assault can be committed other than intentionally: see *Lord Advocate's Reference (No. 2 of 1992)*, 1993 J.C. 43; *H.M. Advocate v. Harris*, 1993 J.C. 150; and, generally, Vol. II, Chap. 29.

70 It should be noted that the objective account of recklessness laid down in *Metropolitan Police Commr v. Caldwell* [1982] A.C. 341, has become confined to criminal damage under the Criminal Damage Act 1971, and to a small number of statutory offences: see A. Ashworth, *Principles of Criminal Law* (3rd ed., Oxford, 1999), p.191. Otherwise, the subjective interpretation found in *R. v. Cunningham*, [1957] 2 Q.B. 396, is favoured in English law.

71 *supra*, para. 7.60.

72 1977 J.C. 38.

73 1977 J.C. 38.

74 See para. 7.01, *supra*.

75 *Ross v. H.M. Advocate*, 1991 J.C. 210, L.J.-G. Hope at 213.

exceptionally may be convicted in the absence of *mens rea* if his lack of capacity was due to voluntary intoxication at the time he completed the required *actus reus*.[76] Even there, however, the view is taken that in all such exceptional cases, "the accused must be assumed to have intended the natural consequences of his act".[77] The correspondence with the axiom is, therefore, somewhat artificial. There will always be something unsatisfactory in convicting A of murder because he killed someone at his home at midnight as a result of embarking on a drunken spree at a public house hours earlier and miles away, if only because he is at the time of the crime incapable of the necesary *mens rea*, as Lord Normand pointed out in *Kennedy*.[78] If principle requires that the accused be shown to have had *mens rea* at the time of the killing, then the decision in *Brennan*[78a] is to that extent in breach of it. Further, as was pointed out by Barwick C.J. in *The Queen v. O'Connor*,[79] acute intoxication may lead to a condition where a person can no longer be said to be acting voluntarily: but in Scotland, self-induced intoxication is excluded from the factors which permit acquittal on the ground of involuntariness,[80] such that conviction of those who are too drunk to be aware of their actions is acceptable in law. The justification advanced for such departures from principle is the large number of crimes committed by those who are intoxicated, and the consequent need to protect the public by deterring those who are tempted to intoxicate themselves and thereby risk causing harm to others.[81] Public policy and principle, therefore, clash over the proper approach to be adopted towards those who cause harm whilst voluntarily intoxicated.

ENGLISH LAW. English law adopts a solution which favours principle **12.14**
relative to some offences and public policy in relation to the remainder. The general justification for such an approach can be expressed in the words of the Criminal Law Revision Committee as follows: "It is doubtful whether any solution to the problem based solely upon legal principle would be generally acceptable. Policy has to be taken into account. Probably the best that can be done is to follow principle as far as possible without producing a result which affronts common sense. Violent drunks have to be restrained and punished."[82] The leading English case is *D.P.P. v. Majewski*.[83] On one interpretation, it decides that voluntary intoxication (which need not be extreme[84]) is capable of demonstrating that the defendant lacked the special type of intent

---

76 *ibid*., at p.214. *Brennan* was quoted in support of the exception, although it may be noted that the court in *Brennan* did not accept that the appellant had been shown to be incapacitated (let alone suffering from a total alienation of reason) notwithstanding the quantity and type of intoxicants ingested: see 1977 J.C. 38, at 51.

77 *ibid*.

78 1944 J.C. 171; see *supra*., para. 12.11.

78a 1977 J.C. 38.

79 (1980) 54 A.L.J.R. 349, at 353–354.

80 *Ross v. H.M. Advocate*, 1991 J.C. 210.

81 See, *e.g.*, *Brennan v. H.M. Advocate*, 1977 J.C. 38, at 42 and 51; *D.P.P. v. Majewski* [1977] A.C. 443, Lord Elwyn Jones L.C. at 469F.

82 Fourteenth Report of the C.L.R.C., "Offences Against the Person" (1980), Cmnd 7844, para. 2.59.

83 [1977] A.C. 443, HL.

84 See J.C. Smith and B. Hogan, *Criminal Law* (9th ed., 1999, Sir J. Smith (ed.)), p.222; Law Commission Consultation Paper, No. 127, "Intoxication and Criminal Liability" (1993), para. 6.32.

required of a "specific intent" crime. An acquittal can, therefore, result; but this is not so in a crime of "basic" or "general" intent. As has often been pointed out,[85] however, the House of Lords laid down no satisfactory test for distinguishing between specific and basic intent crimes. The Lord Chancellor, for example, at one stage adopted the 'rule' that a crime of basic intent is one in which the *mens rea* for murder does not go beyond the act and its consequences.[86] Since under English law the *mens rea* for murder does not stray beyond the physical act and the subsequent consequential death, murder would thus be an offence of basic intent to which voluntary intoxication would be no answer; but it is accepted in England that murder is a crime of specific intent.[87] A leading English textbook concludes that the distinction "is based on no principle but on policy" and that a crime of specific intent is one actually brought under that title as a result of a particular ruling made by the courts.[88] This, of course, is somewhat unsatisfactory; but there is another possible interpretation of *Majewski*[88a] based on Lord Elwyn-Jones' opinion that voluntary intoxication to the point of casting off "the restraints of reason and conscience" is "a reckless course of conduct and recklessness is enough to constitute the necessary *mens rea* in an assault case."[89] Under this view, a crime to which voluntary intoxication is no 'defence' is one where the *mens rea* element is satisfied by recklessness; and thus the conduct of the accused in voluntarily intoxicating himself is taken to fulfil that element. This may well make sense in Scotland where recklessness is something of an objective consideration; it also explains why that particular part of Lord Elwyn-Jones' opinion was quoted with approval in *Brennan*.[90] It is an odd interpretation, however, to favour in England where recklessness requires a subjective awareness of the risk on the part of the defendant.[91] As Professor Ashworth has put it: "In most cases it is far fetched to argue that a person who is getting drunk is aware of the type of conduct he or she might later indulge in."[92]

12.15 PRINCIPLE IN OTHER JURISDICTIONS. *Majewski*[93] proceeds on the assumption that it is not always acceptable to allow principle to prevail

---

[85] See, *e.g.*, A. Ashworth, *Principles of Criminal Law* (Oxford, 3rd ed., 1999), at p.219; J.C. Smith and B. Hogan, *Criminal Law* (9th ed., 1999, by Sir J. Smith), at p.222.

[86] [1977] A.C. 443, Lord Elwyn-Jones L.C. at p.471A-B, quoting from Lord Simon of Glaisdale in *R. v. Morgan* [1976] A.C. 182, at p.216.

[87] See *D.P.P. v. Beard* [1920] A.C. 479, as interpreted and approved in *D.P.P. v. Majewski* [1977] A.C. 443. See also Smith and Hogan (8th ed.), at p.229.

[88] J.C. Smith and B. Hogan, *Criminal Law* (9th ed., 1999, by Sir J. Smith) at p.222; a list of offences under each classification is given at pp.222–223.

[88a] [1977] A.C. 443, HL.

[89] *D.P.P. v. Majewski* [1977] A.C. 443, at 474H-475A.

[90] 1977 J.C. 38, at 50.

[91] Objective recklessness as laid down in *R. v. Caldwell*, [1982] A.C. 341, has become confined in recent years to criminal damage under the Criminal Damage Act 1971 and similar statutory offences: see J.C. Smith and B. Hogan, *Criminal Law* (9th ed., 1999, Sir J. Smith), at pp.66–67; Law Commission No. 229 ("Legislating the Criminal Code: Intoxication and Criminal Liability", H. of C., 1994–95, No. 153, 1995), at para. 2.16.

[92] A. Ashworth, *Principles of Criminal Law* (Oxford, 3rd ed., 1999) at p.220. He suggests there that the Lord Chancellor in *Majewski* has confused the general, non-legal meaning of recklessness with the technical term which in English law denotes subjective awareness of the risk of the result which in fact happened. Nevertheless, at p.219, Ashworth indicates that, with respect to the decision in *Majewski*, "this rather ramshackle law has proved workable."

[93] [1977] A.C. 443.

over public policy in relation to intoxicated offenders. But this is not an assumption universally shared. In Australia, for example, it has been held that "proof of a state of intoxication, whether self-induced or not, so far from constituting itself a matter of defence or excuse, is at most merely part of the totality of the evidence which may raise a reasonable doubt as to the existence of essential elements of criminal responsibility"[94] (*i.e.*, voluntariness and *mens rea*). Concerns for public safety are said to be met by the very high levels of intoxication which would be necessary to throw reasonable doubt on the existence of those elements and by the correspondingly low percentage of cases where defendants have actually been acquitted on such a basis.[95] The courts in New Zealand[96] and South Africa[97] have taken a similar stance.

In Canada the *Majewski*[97a] compromise was confirmed as Canadian law by a majority of the Supreme Court in *Leary v. The Queen*,[98] although more recently that Court (again by a majority) has accepted a modification such that extreme intoxication, which creates a condition similar to insanity or automatism, may be considered in a general intent crime in order to determine whether the minimal *mens rea* required in such a crime has been proved beyond reasonable doubt.[99] This clumsy expedient has been adopted in order to make the *Leary* rule relative to general intent crimes conform with the Canadian Charter of Rights and Freedoms[1]; but it is significant that the Canadian Criminal Code has since been altered in an attempt to restore a proper balance for public policy considerations in relation to certain general intent offences.[2]

---

[94] *The Queen v. O'Connor* (1980) 54 A.L.J.R. 349, *per* Barwick C.J. at 351–352. This decision, which expressly rejects the approach taken in *Majewski*, applies only to States following the common law. Where a State code exists, it is likely to follow a different line: see, *e.g.*, the New South Wales Crimes Act 1900 (as amended), s.428(B)-(D) which follows the spirit of the specific-basic intent dichotomy of English law but lists the code offences which are to be taken as being of specific intent.

[95] See G. Orchard, "The Law Commission's Consultation Paper on Intoxication and Criminal Liability: (2) Surviving without Majewski — A View from Down Under" [1993] Crim.L.R. 426. *Cf.* S. Gough, "Surviving without *Majewski*?" [2000] Crim.L.R. 719.

[96] See *R. v. Kamipeli* [1975] 2 N.Z.L.R. 610.

[97] *S. v. Chretien*, 1981 (1) SA 1097 (A). Parliament there responded by passing the Criminal Law Amendment Act 1988 (amended in 1997), which makes it a statutory offence for a person to be non-criminally liable for committing an act prohibited by the criminal law because his faculties were impaired by the consumption or use of intoxicating substances, where he knew that such substances had the propensity for such impairment.

[97a] [1977] A.C. 443.

[98] [1978] 1 S.C.R. 29.

[99] *R. v. Daviault* [1994] 2 S.C.R. 63. The minimal *mens rea* referred to seems to relate to the voluntariness of the actings of the defendant.

[1] Section 7 of the Charter reads: "Everyone has the right to life, liberty and security of person and the right not to be deprived thereof except in accordance with the principles of fundamental justice."

[2] Clause 33.1(1) reads that "It is not a defence to an [offence which includes as an element an assault or any other interference or threat of interference by a person with the bodily integrity of another person] that the accused, by reason of self-induced intoxication, lacked the general intent or the voluntariness required to commit the offence, where the accused departed markedly from the standard of [reasonable care generally regarded in Canadian society and is thereby criminally at fault]." Additions in brackets are taken from cl. 33.1(3) and (2) respectively. For a general critique of the current Canadian position, see E.M. Burchell and P.M.A. Hunt, *South African Criminal Law and Procedure*, Vol. 1, *General Principles of Criminal Law* (3rd ed., J.M. Burchell (ed.), Cape Town, 1997), pp.195–197.

12.16 INTERPRETING BRENNAN. *Brennan*[3] decides that self-induced intoxication by itself never amounts to insanity or diminished responsibility in law[4]: to that extent, therefore, such intoxication is never a defence "to any criminal charge".[5] The case also decides that self-induced intoxication is not by itself a factor capable of reducing a murder charge to one of culpable homicide. The case has not been interpreted, however, as a decision confined to cases of homicide.[6] Indeed, it appears to lay down a general rule relative to the way in which intoxicated offenders are to be treated under Scots law. Relative to the types of crime to which it applies, the basic rule may tentatively be stated as follows: a person who voluntarily and recklessly consumes known intoxicating substances (including alcohol and drugs), and who, whilst in a state of consequent intoxication, causes the harm prohibited under the definition of a particular crime, cannot be acquitted if his only answer to the charge of committing that crime is the mental impairment (no matter how gross) resulting from that consumption, the *mens rea* he might otherwise lack at the time of the offence being supplied by the reckless way in which he became intoxicated. Some of the issues which arise from this rule are considered in the paragraphs below.

12.17 (1) *consumes.* As the court in *Brennan*[7] frequently refers to "self-induced" intoxication, the consumption of the intoxicating substance must be voluntary and deliberate. It is probably to be assumed that this includes situations where the accused permits such a substance to be administered to him, without coercion or fraud perpetrated upon him by another person.[8]

12.18 (2) *known intoxicants.* The accused requires to have known that he was consuming a substance capable of causing intoxication, *i.e.* a substance which "might deprive him of his ability to control his actions"[9] or impair his "mental faculties".[10] The accused in *Brennan* was found to have had such knowledge[11]; but it is almost certainly the case that Scots law would assume such knowledge on the part of anyone who voluntarily consumed alcohol or the better known (at least) hallucinatory drugs.

12.19 (3) *purpose of the consumption.* It is not certain whether an accused person should have consumed the substances in order to become intoxicated. Although the accused in *Brennan*[12] was certainly found to

---

[3] 1977 J.C. 38.

[4] *ibid.*, at 46.

[5] *ibid.*, at 47.

[6] See para. 12.23, *infra*. *Brennan* was applied, *e.g.*, in the assault case of *Ebsworth v. H.M. Advocate*, 1992 S.C.C.R. 671, and in the reckless endangerment case of *Donaldson v. Normand*, 1997 S.C.C.R. 351.

[7] 1977 J.C. 38.

[8] *cf. H.M. Advocate v. Raiker*, 1989 S.C.C.R. 149, Lord McCluskey's direction to the jury at 154, where he said that if a person acts under the influence of a drug given to him without his consent which, like hypnosis, puts his will under the control of another, he is entitled to be acquitted. (The accused, one of a number of persons charged with offences committed during a prison riot, gave evidence that he had taken part in the riot because he had been given a drug forcibly and perhaps also by stealth.) *Cf.* also the English Draft Criminal Code (L.C. No. 177, "A Criminal Code for England and Wales", 1989, H. of C., No. 299, Vol. 1), cl. 22(5)(c), under which a person 'takes' an intoxicant not only by consuming it, but also by permitting it to be administered to him.

[9] *Brennan v. H.M. Advocate*, 1977 J.C. 38, at 42.

[10] *ibid.*, at 47.

[11] *ibid.*, at 42.

[12] 1977 J.C. 38.

have done so,[13] it is not clear whether the rule requires there to have been such a purpose. If that is required, then the law will have created the means for drawing a distinction between intentional and inadvertent intoxication.[14] Although such a distinction might in practice be a difficult one to make, it would have the theoretical advantage of more readily identifying those who were willing to place themselves in a situation where loss of control and impairment of mental faculties could lead to unacceptable behaviour: such persons are more readily identifiable as risk-takers and therefore reckless, at least in so far as the consumption of known intoxicating substances is concerned.[15]

(4) *distinction between drink and drugs.* The court in *Brennan*[16] takes **12.20** the view that there is no distinction to be made "between intoxication by drink and drugs". Whilst the knowledge that alcohol has the propensity to intoxicate must be assumed on the part of any normal accused person, the same cannot be said for all drugs. Where particular drugs are not generally known to be intoxicative (or, where they are medically prescribed or taken for a medicinal purpose, and the person consuming them has not been advised of such a propensity or of the conditions under which such a propensity might arise) a distinction may in fairness require to be drawn. This may already be the law, following the decision in *Ebsworth v. H.M. Advocate*,[17] a case concerned with the defence of non-insane automatism but which Lord Justice-General Hope described as indistinguishable from *Brennan*.[17a] The facts of the case reveal that the accused had taken 50 paracetamol and 10 diamorphine tablets. It was accepted that his purpose in doing so was to ease the pain of a broken bone in his leg. During the course of a consequent state of automatism, he assaulted and seriously injured a woman by striking her with a bottle. He appealed against conviction on the basis that the trial judge had wrongly withdrawn the defence of non-insane automatism from the jury, and the importance of the case for present purposes lies in the following passage from the opinion of the Lord Justice-General:

> "[The sheriff's] approach would have been entirely justified if the appellant's evidence had been that he took the drugs deliberately in order to experience a state of mental abnormality or that he was entirely careless as to their effect. But his explanation . . . was that he took them deliberately in order to relieve extreme pain and that the consequences of his doing so were wholly unforeseen by him. Had it not been for the grossly excessive quantity which he consumed and the combination of drugs which he took without medical advice, this would have raised a question of fact which could properly have been left to the jury. This is because, unless the accused's conduct was reckless, the fact that he had a legitimate purpose in consuming the drugs ought not to deprive him of the

---

[13] *ibid.*, at 42.

[14] In *The Queen v. O'Connor* (1980) 54 A.L.J.R. 349, at 353, Barwick C.J. points out that while there are doubtless cases where a person sets out to become intoxicated, there are also cases where "the state of intoxication may be reached by inadvertence, even though the drug . . . may be taken voluntarily, as where a diner does not observe the frequency with which the waiter tops up his glass."

[15] See also para. 12.20, *infra*.

[16] 1977 J.C. 38, at 42.

[17] 1992 S.C.C.R. 671.

[17a] 1977 J.C. 38.

> defence on the ground that, since he consumed them deliberately, the condition was self-induced. In this case, however, the quantities which were consumed in combination were so excessive that no reasonable jury could have concluded that the appellant's conduct was other than reckless. In other words he was bound to foresee that the taking of the drugs in this quantity and combination without medical advice might have unexpected consequences".[18]

It seems, therefore, that a legitimate purpose for the consumption of drugs may prevent the rule in *Brennan*[19] from operating and may provide an accused with a defence of non-insane automatism; but this will be so only where the circumstances of the consumption do not exhibit objective recklessness. It may be that any life-line in terms of purpose cannot extend to the consumption of alcohol, or to any other substance which is generally known to be associated with loss of control and aggression:[20] in any event, 'purpose' seems subordinated by *Ebsworth*[21] to recklessness displayed in the manner of consumption,[22] and such recklessness seems to be a question of fact in each case.

12.21 (5) *Mens rea.* The tentative rule in *Brennan*[23] expressed above[24] specifies that the recklessness exhibited in the manner of becoming intoxicated supplies the *mens rea* for the crime in question. This follows from the Appeal Court's conclusion that self-induced intoxication is "itself a continuing element and therefore an integral part of any crime of violence including murder, the other part being the evidence of the actings of the accused who uses force against his victim. Together they add up or may add up to the criminal recklessness which it is the purpose of the criminal law to restrain".[25] Those words, together with the frequent references to murder in Scotland being a crime satisfied by 'wicked recklessness', suggest that the Court had in mind a form of transferred *mens rea*, the recklessness exhibited in the manner of becoming drunk in the first place being transferred to the killing which is ultimately perpetrated. This is certainly arguable in the case of offences for which recklessness is a sufficient form of *mens rea*; but substitution of the recklessness in becoming drunk for the intent which is required by many crimes is much more difficult to justify, and suggests that some additional fault at the time of the prohibited act may be necessary (although that would significantly weaken the effect of the rule).

---

[18] 1992 S.C.C.R., at 680B-D.

[19] 1977 J.C. 38.

[20] *cf. R. v. Hardie* [1985] 1 W.L.R. 64.

[21] 1992 S.C.C.R. 671.

[22] In *Brennan v. H.M. Advocate*, 1977 J.C. 38 at 46, the court went so far as to say that, "a person who voluntarily and deliberately consumes known intoxicants . . . of whatever quantity . . . cannot rely on the resulting intoxication as a foundation of a special defence of insanity at the time nor, indeed, can he plead diminished responsibility." Although the court was clearly thinking of the situation where vast quantities of intoxicating substances were consumed, such that the accused's resulting condition might resemble some forms of insanity, their words are equally consistent with the consumption of (*e.g.*) very small quantities of alcohol; but it is doubtful if minimal consumption would attract the status of recklessness which the more general rule in *Brennan* seems to require.

[23] 1977 J.C. 38.

[24] See para. 12.16.

[25] *Brennan v. H.M. Advocate*, 1977 J.C. 38, at 51.

12.22 In *Brennan*,[26] the accused stabbed his father in the chest with a knife during the course of a quarrel. This viewed objectively would have been sufficient to show wicked recklessness on the accused's part, if not an actual intention to kill. The question therefore arises whether even a murder charge in relation to an intoxicated accused requires to be supported by evidence of conduct which was objectively reckless at the time of the killing. If such evidence is required, then the lack of it may enable a conviction for culpable homicide to be returned. This seems an unlikely outcome given the court's negative reaction to the second ground of appeal in *Brennan*, namely that the trial judge wrongly directed the jury "that it was not open to them to use the appellant's intoxication and state of mind at the time of the offence as a basis for reducing the crime from murder to culpable homicide."[27] Nevertheless the court, having held that intoxication could constitute neither insanity nor diminished responsibility, and having pointed out that the *mens rea* of murder did not require intent, went on to say[28]:

> "Finally we must dispel any suspicion that what was said in *Campbell*[29] and *Kennedy*[30] was merely an echo of a passage in the charge of the Lord Justice-Clerk in *McDonald*[31] in which he directed the jury that 'if the means adopted were not of themselves likely to lead to bad results and if there were no malice aforethought here, then the fact that the man was in a drunken state may be considered in determining the question between murder and culpable homicide'. The initial hypothesis presented to the jury is of crucial importance: (1) absence of malicious or criminal intent to kill and (2) use of modes of assault not of themselves likely to lead to bad results. The case of *McDonald*[31a] therefore lays down and professes to lay down no general principle of law, and the direction is one related precisely to a particular combination of facts. It might indeed have been argued that without any evidence of drunkenness that combination of facts would have made a verdict of culpable homicide a proper one."

It is not clear whether this passage represents a chink in the armour of the Crown or the last nail in the coffin of the defence. It presumably means that if the drunken accused falls on or over, or stumbles into, someone and causes his death he is not guilty of murder.[32] In such a case the actual conduct is not objectively reckless, although the taking of the drink might have been. The converse position, where the actual conduct is objectively reckless, but the taking of drink was not, seems to be one in which the accused is necessarily guilty of murder.

---

[26] 1977 J.C. 38.
[27] *ibid.*, at 39.
[28] *ibid.*, at 48.
[29] *H.M. Advocate v. Campbell*, 1921 J.C. 1.
[30] *Kennedy v. H.M. Advocate*, 1944 J.C. 171.
[31] (1890) 2 White 517. See *supra*, para. 12.10.
[31a] *ibid.*
[32] *cf.* G. Orchard, "The Law Commission Consultation Paper on Intoxication and Criminal Liability: (2) Surviving without Majewski — A View from Down Under" [1993] Crim.L.R. 426, at p.430: "if a man stumbles into another who suffers injury as a result it is not obvious that there should be criminal liability simply because the stumbler was very drunk."

Acute intoxication in crimes other than homicide

12.23 *Exculpation. Brennan v. H.M. Advocate*[33] deals with murder and the sort of recklessness which suffices as the *mens rea* for that crime. The opinion of the court does offer a wider rule, however, in that the "defence of intoxication cannot be received against any criminal charge."[34] This is qualified on two occasions. Firstly it is said that "self-induced intoxication is not a defence to any criminal charge, at least for an offence in itself perilous or hurtful."[35] This qualification is drawn from Alison[36]; but it is doubtful if this rather vague rider contains any significant restriction. There must be few offences, at least at common law, which do not fall within Alison's description. In the second qualification, self-induced intoxication is said to be "in itself a continuing element, and therefore an integral part of any crime of violence, including murder."[37] As intoxication is associated with aggression, it would make much sense for the *Brennan* rule to apply to assault. There is, however, a conceptual difficulty in so applying it in Scotland since it has been made reasonably clear that assault cannot be committed recklessly.[38] It may be that at the time when *Brennan* was decided, the Appeal Court considered that recklessness was sufficient as the *mens rea* for assault, perhaps out of a sense of deference towards English law.[39] Given that assault requires an intent to injure or create a fear of injury,[40] it is not at all clear how recklessness in becoming drunk can be translated into the necessary intent at the time of the crime. It may be that all intent in Scotland is 'basic intent' after *Brennan*, as Gray has argued,[41] or that assault is taken in this country to be a crime of recklessness for the purpose of the intoxication rule.[42] The latter would at least allow the argument to be developed that a voluntarily intoxicated accused was so drunk that he could not have formed the specific aim or purpose which in the case of some offences it is necessary for the Crown to prove. An example of such an offence would be housebreaking with intent to steal. It was not suggested, for example, in *Mason v. Jessop*[43] that a man who had broken two windows of a church was necessarily to be convicted of housebreaking with intent to steal just because he was

---

33 1977 J.C. 38.

34 *ibid.*, at 41 and 51.

35 *ibid.*, at 47.

36 At i, 661. The actual passage is quoted by the court at p.44.

37 1977 J.C. at 51.

38 See *Lord Advocate's Reference (No. 2 of 1992)*, 1993 J.C. 43, L.J.-C. Ross at 48C-D, Lord Cowie at 51B-C, and Lord Sutherland at 52I-53A; *H.M. Advocate v. Harris*, 1993 J.C. 150, L.J.-C. Ross at 154D-E (quoting from para. 29–30 of the 2nd ed. of this book), and Lord Murray at 156C.

39 This would be somewhat ironic in view of the way in which *Kennedy* was disapproved of in *Brennan* itself. Recklessness has clearly been sufficient for conviction of assault under English law since *R. v. Venna* [1976] Q.B. 421.

40 See Vol. II, Chap. 29.

41 J.W.R. Gray, "The Expulsion of *Beard* from Scotland: Murder North of the Border", [1979] Crim.L.R. 369, at p.379.

42 In the unreported case of *Alexr Winchester*, High Court at Glasgow, October 1955, Lord Hill Watson directed the jury that if the accused had been too drunk to form the intention of assaulting the victim he must be acquitted of assault; but this would be difficult to justify nowadays. (Indebtedness must be expressed to Sheriff A.A. MacDonald, who was defence counsel in the case, for the information about it.).

43 1990 S.C.C.R. 387.

drunk at the time.[44] The same argument may apply in cases of theft and similar offences in view of the element of intent required.

There is also an older Scottish case which supports the application of something like *Beard*[45] outside homicide. In *Jas. Kinnison,*[46] there was a charge against a registrar for making false entries in his register, the defence being that he was drunk at the time. The statute required the false entries to be made "wilfully", and Lord Justice-Clerk Moncrieff told the jury that the question for them was "not whether the prisoner did wrong in being in the state in which he was when he was required to attend to that business; nor that he did wrong in the error which he made in filling up the register, but that when he made these errors he meant not to make a true entry, but meant to make a false entry,"[47] and the accused was acquitted.

Mitigation. There are two old cases in which intoxication was treated as mitigating an offence other than murder. In *Jas. Ainslie,*[48] the accused pleaded guilty to assault, and it was said on his behalf that owing to head injuries he became "furious" when drunk, and had been in that state at the time of the crime: he was sentenced to imprisonment instead of transportation. In *James Alves,*[49] the accused was charged with cursing and beating of parents — then technically a capital offence — but convicted only of common assault, the circumstances being that he had scratched his father's lip while drunkenly waving his arms about. **12.24**

Although *Brennan*[50] rejects the view that drunkenness can ever amount to diminished responsibility, a plea which in any event it describes as limited to murder, it does not, and in practice could not, prevent any judge from treating involuntary intoxication as a mitigating factor.

Error. There is no Scots law on the effect of intoxication on the law of error. It is possible that Scots law will disregard any error caused by self-induced intoxication, even perhaps one which negatives an essential part of the definition of the crime, such as a drunken belief that one is taking one's own umbrella. **12.25**

The English view is that where a statute provides a defence of honest belief, a belief induced by drink is relevant,[51] but that drunken error does not exclude recklessness.[52]

On the other hand an error of fact induced by voluntary intoxication has been held not to be capable of supporting a plea of self-defence,

---

[44] The accused might, however, have been convicted of malicious mischief, since recklessness is sufficient *mens rea* for that crime: see Vol. II, Chap. 22. See also *Donaldson v. Normand*, 1997 S.C.C.R. 351, a case of reckless endangerment where L.J.-G. Hope said at 353C-D: "The fact that he took the drugs in the first place constitutes a reckless act on its own and this is, as the Lord Justice-General put it [in *Brennan*], a continuing element which continues up to the time the alleged offence is committed. Accordingly, where the absence or apparent absence of *mens rea* is attributed to self-induced intoxication, that cannot produce any kind of defence."

[45] [1920] A.C. 479.

[46] (1870) 1 Couper 457.

[47] At 461–462.

[48] (1842) 1 Broun 25.

[49] (1830) 5 Deas and Anderson 147.

[50] 1977 J.C. 38.

[51] *Jaggard v. Dickinson* [1981] Q.B. 527.

[52] *R. v. Woods* (1981) 74 Cr.App.R. 312.

even in a crime of 'specific intent',[53] although such intoxication may still be taken into account in order to determine whether the defendant had the specific intent which the crime requires.[54]

Involuntary Intoxication

12.26 Now that Scots law recognises the defence of non-insane automatism,[55] an accused who claims that his intoxicated state was involuntary may be acquitted of any offence, including murder, which requires *mens rea*.[56] He must, however, bring himself within the defence's rule, which is that an external factor, neither self-induced nor one he was bound to foresee, must have resulted in a total alienation of reason amounting to a complete lack of self-control at the time of the alleged offence.[57] This would be a difficult defence to sustain in the case of an external factor such as alcohol or one of the better-known mind-altering drugs, unless, of course, the circumstances were special.[58] Normally, however, knowledge on the accused's part of the nature of what he was consuming and of its capacity to effect alienation of reason will probably be fatal to the defence, and bring him within the rule in *Brennan*.[59] It is unlikely, for example, that an accused who misjudges the alcoholic strength of the beer he knew himself to be consuming will have any way of avoiding conviction.[60] In *H.M. Advocate v. Raiker*,[61] however, one of a number of

---

[53] *R. v. O'Grady* [1987] Q.B. 995. The English Draft Criminal Code seeks to reverse the effect of both *Jaggard v. Dickinson* (*supra*) and *O'Grady*, and provide instead that where intention or knowledge is an element of the offence the defendant's drunken error should be taken into account in order to determine whether he had that element; but "where an offence requires a fault element of recklessness . . . a person voluntarily intoxicated shall be treated — (b) as not having believed in the existence of an exempting circumstance (where the existence of such a belief is in issue) if he would not have so believed had he been sober." See L.C. No. 177, "A Criminal Code for England and Wales" (1989), H. of C., No. 299, Vol. 1, cl. 22(1)(b) and Vol. 2, paras 8.38 and 8.41–8.42; see also L.C. Report No. 229, "Legislating the Criminal Code: Intoxication and Criminal Liability" (1995), para. 1.34. Other English reform proposals have varied as to whether an objective slant should be given to the defendant's belief — *e.g.* the Butler Committee suggested that no account should be taken of a drunken-induced mistaken belief at all unless the same error would have been made by a sober person (Butler Committee on Mentally Abnormal Offenders (1975), Cmnd 6244, para. 18.57). *Cf.* L.C. Consultation Paper No. 127 (1993) "Intoxication and Criminal Liability", para. 6.31 at 6., where, in the context of the then proposed offence of "Criminal Intoxication", it was suggested that "where the defendant seeks to rely on a defence based on an intoxicated mistake, he may not rely on such mistake unless it was one that, viewed objectively, would have been reasonably made by a person who was not intoxicated . . . but was otherwise circumstanced as the defendant."

[54] *R. v. O'Connor* [1991] Crim.L.R. 135.

[55] *Ross v. H.M. Advocate*, 1991 J.C. 210 — overruling on this point *H.M. Advocate v. Cunningham*, 1963 J.C. 80. See paras 3.18 *et seq.*, *supra*.

[56] *cf. MacLeod v. Napier*, 1993 S.C.C.R. 303, where at sheriff court level non-insane automatism was accepted as relevant to charges of careless driving and driving with excess alcohol in the body, contrary to the Road Traffic Act 1988, ss.3 and 5(1)(a) respectively: the appeal against acquittal in this case was disposed of without the need for consideration of the applicability of non-insane automatism to offences of such a nature.

[57] *Ross v. H.M. Advocate*, 1991 J.C. 210, L.J.-G. Hope at 218.

[58] *cf. Ebsworth v. H.M. Advocate*, 1992 S.C.C.R. 671, where paracetamol and diamorphine were taken voluntarily for a medicinal purpose and where a defence of non-insane automatism might have been left to the jury but for the excessive quantities which had been ingested by the accused: the accused's conduct in taking such drugs to excess was considered to be reckless in the circumstances.

[59] 1977 J.C. 38. See para. 12.16, *supra*.

[60] *cf. R. v. Allen* [1988] Crim.L.R. 698, CA.

[61] 1989 S.C.C.R. 149.

persons charged with offences committed during a prison riot gave evidence that he had taken part in the riot because he had been given a drug forcibly and perhaps also by stealth. Lord McCluskey directed the jury that where a person acts under the influence of a drug given to him without his consent which, like hypnosis, puts his will under the control of another, he is entitled to be acquitted.[62] This serves to emphasise that the alienation of reason must be caused by the external factor, such as the drug the accused has unwittingly or forcibly ingested.[63] If the consequential alienation of reason is less than total, the defence flies off.[64] It seems too that what has to be totally alineated are the accused's mental faculties of reasoning and of understanding what he is doing.[65]

Addiction. The addict creates a special problem. Although his drinking would probably be held by a court to be voluntary, there is much to be said for the view that since it is compulsive and the result of a mental illness — alcoholism — it should be regarded as involuntary. The only time the law recognises the effects of chronic alcoholism is when they have led to a state of permanent insanity.[66] It was assumed in *H.M. Advocate v. Campbell*[67] that the accused, who had been rendered peculiarly susceptible to alcohol as the result of an accident, was able to control his desire for drink. It was not suggested that had the accident made him an addict he could have pleaded that as a defence. It is probably inevitable that the law should treat the addict as a voluntary drinker — the idea even of a sudden irresistible impulse is a difficult one for the law to accept, and the addict's impulse is constant and recurring. **12.27**

Proposals for Reform

As indicated above,[68] the major theoretical problem posed by intoxication which deprives a person of *mens rea* is to reconcile the demands of public policy, public safety and public indignation with the axiom *actus non facit reum nisi mens sit rea*.[69] *Brennan*[70] reduces the scope of the problem for at least some cases of crimes whose *mens rea* is recklessness or wicked recklessness, but the problem remains for other cases.[71] It is submitted that one way of solving the problem, of squaring the circle, so to speak, is as follows. Where a crime is wholly the product of intoxication, *i.e.* where it can be shown that the accused's mind was so **12.28**

---

[62] *ibid.*, at 154.

[63] See *Sorley v. H.M. Advocate*, 1992 S.C.C.R. 396. Expert evidence will normally be required to prove the link between the two.

[64] See *Cardle v. Mulrainey*, 1992 S.C.C.R. 658. *Cf. R. v. Kingston* [1994] 3 W.L.R. 519.

[65] *Cardle v. Mulrainey*, 1992 S.C.C.R. 658, at 668D-G; see para. 3.21, *supra*.

[66] But see *Wm Wylie* (1858) 3 Irv. 218, where Lord Cowan observed in passing that "Drunkenness, caused by his own act, would be no defence. But the peculiarity of the present case, even had such a point been raised by the proof, was, that according to the medical evidence, the prisoner's drinking habits were not the cause, but the effect, of his insanity": at 234. The accused was acquitted on the ground of insanity.

[67] 1921 J.C. 1.

[68] See paras 12.13 *et seq.*, *supra*.

[69] *supra*, para. 7.01.

[70] 1977 J.C. 38.

[71] Even in relation to crimes of recklessness some of their Lordships in *Majewski, supra*, recognised that a legislative solution, of the kind discussed below was preferable to the common law solution of imposing a kind of constructive recklessness which was dictated on policy grounds in both *Majewski* and *Brennan*.

affected by drink or drugs that he lacked the capacity to appreciate or control his actings, or that his behaviour was involuntary, he should be acquitted of that crime, even if he formed some sort of insane or intoxicated intention to act, as where in his drugged state he thought he was being attacked.[72] Where a man is very drunk and his criminal actings have been influenced by drink to a great extent although he has not completely lost control of himself, it should be open to the judge or jury to treat this as an element in mitigation, if in the whole circumstances of the case it seems just to do so.

12.29 *The public interest.* This can be protected in a number of ways.

(1) By making it an offence to drink or drug oneself into a state of irresponsibility and then commit a crime. This would be a specific offence, quite separate from the ultimate crime for which the accused is not responsible.[73] Such an offence has been proposed by the Butler Committee on Mentally Abnormal Offenders, although they would restrict it to cases where the crime was a "dangerous" offence *i.e.* one involving injury to the person or sexual attack, or the destruction or damage of property so as to endanger life. The maximum sentence suggested is one year's imprisonment for a first offence and three for a second or subsequent offence on indictment, and a person could be convicted of the proposed new offence only where he had been tried for the dangerous crime and acquitted for lack of *mens rea* resulting from intoxication.[74]

(2) By making it an offence to intoxicate oneself deliberately to a substantial degree and then cause the harm proscribed by another offence. This would be a specific offence relying for its *actus reus* on the *actus reus* of that other crime, but not requiring that the accused lacked the *mens rea* for that crime. This sort of offence was proposed by the Law Commission in its Consultation Paper on Intoxication and Criminal Liability,[75] and was designed to overcome problems identified in the Butler Committee's approach. As with Butler, the Commission wished to restrict the type of existing crime to which the new offence would be linked; but the Butler concept of "dangerousness" was abandoned. Instead a wider range of offences was envisaged, the range being governed by the criteria of substantial harm to the person, the physical safety of property, and public order.[76] It was thought to be an advantage that the new offence of "criminal intoxication" would be available even though the defendant had the *mens rea* for the existing, qualifying offence. This enabled the new offence not only to be charged per se,[77] but also along with an existing offence, and it was envisaged that a defendant might be convicted of both offences.[78] It would also have been available as an alternative "fall-back" verdict where the defendant was acquitted of an existing, qualifying offence due to lack of *mens rea*.[79] The maximum punishment was to be related to the penalty available for the

---

72 *cf. H.M. Advocate v. Aitken*, 1975 S.L.T. (Notes) 86.

73 Such a crime exists in Germany — StGB Art. 323a. *Cf.* H. Mannheim, *Group Problems in Crime and Punishment* (London, 1955), pp.293–296.

74 Cmnd. 6244, 1975, paras 8.51–18.59.

75 L.C. No. 127 (1993), paras 6.30 to 6.88.

76 *ibid.*, para. 6.38. A tentative list of offences is set out at para. 6.41.

77 *ibid.*, para. 6.83.

78 *ibid.*, para. 6.80.

79 *ibid.*, paras 6.81 and 6.82.

existing, qualifying offence — but perhaps to be two-thirds of it, since intoxication was felt to make the defendant less culpable. An overall maximum of ten years was suggested, however, in view of the fact that homicide was within the range of qualifying offences. The Butler "flat-rate" approach to punishment was rejected as not being sufficiently relateable to the harm actually caused by the defendant.[80]

(3) By making it a crime to be "drunk and dangerous." This is the solution suggested by Glanville Williams[81]; and the analogy with the crime of being drunk in charge of a car is obvious. But such a crime would be difficult to enforce because of the difficulty of proving the accused was dangerous.

---

[80] Consultees emphatically rejected the Commission's suggested approach. The result is that the Commission's final report on the issue abandons the "adherence to principle plus new offence" solution in favour of the existing law (see L.C. No 229, H. of C., No. 163, 1995). The Commission in fact endorses the views of the English Draft Criminal Code (L.C. No. 177, "A Criminal Code for England and Wales", 1989, H. of C., No. 299, Vol. 1), cl. 22, which in turn contains the existing law as modified by recommendations of the Criminal Law Revision Committee in its Fourteenth Report ("Offences against the Person") in 1980. The draft bill attached to the Commission's final report (see Appendix A, thereof) is consequentially complex: for a critique of the Commission's change of heart, see: E. Paton, "Reforming the Intoxication Rules: the Law Commission's Report" [1995] Crim.L.R. 382.

[81] Gl. Williams, para. 183.

CHAPTER 13

NECESSITY, COERCION AND SUPERIOR ORDERS[1]

Introduction

In the context of the criminal law the word "necessity" has rather a loose meaning. The law is concerned only with voluntary actions, and strictly speaking no voluntary action is ever necessary. Where the agent is totally deprived of volition so that his acts are wholly the result of causes other than his will there is no occasion to advance the plea of necessity or coercion, since in such cases there is no "act" at all.[2] The plea of necessity or coercion arises where A does something intentionally and voluntarily[3] which is punishable unless it can be justified or excused by the plea. It applies to acts done in situations where the accused's defence is, "I did it, because I had no alternative"; and where "I had no alternative" means, "The only alternative I had was one I was entitled not to adopt". **13.01**

Choice of alternatives. Necessity is therefore necessity for something. It is not the necessity of physical causality which, for example, makes it necessary that water at a certain pressure will boil at a certain temperature, but it is teleological necessity.[4] In situations of necessity the agent is faced with a choice between two courses of action, and he is required to choose by reference to the relative values attached by the law to the two **13.02**

---

[1] For discussions of the general problem see Gl. Williams, Chap. 17; Gl.Williams, "The Defence of Necessity," 1953 *Current Legal Problems*, 216; J. Hall, *General Principles of Criminal Law* (2nd ed., Indianopolis, 1960), Chap. 12; G.P. Fletcher, *Rethinking Criminal Law* (Boston, 1978), Chap. 10; G.P. Fletcher, "The Nature of Justification" in S. Shute, J.Gardner and J. Horder (Eds.), *Action and Value in Criminal Law* (Oxford, 1993), Chap. 6; J.C. Smith and B. Hogan, *Criminal Law* (9th ed., 1999, Sir John Smith (ed.)), pp.231 *et seq.*; A. Ashworth, *Principles of Criminal Law* (3rd ed., 1999), pp.226 *et seq.*; T.W. Price, "Defence, Necessity and Acts of Authority", Butterworth's S.A.L.R. (1954) 1; P.R. Glazebrook, "The Necessity Plea in Criminal Law" [1972A] C.L.J. 87; M. Wasik, "Duress and Criminal Responsibility" [1977] Crim.L.R. 453; P. Alldridge, "The Coherence of Defences" [1983] Crim.L.R. 665; A. Norrie, "The Defence of Coercion in Scots Criminal Law", 1984 S.L.T. (News) 13; Forensis, "The Excuse of Necessity in Scots Law" (1985) 30 J.L.S.S. 151; P. Alldridge, "Developing the Defence of Duress" [1986] Crim.L.R. 433; A. Brudner, "A Theory of Necessity" (1987) 7 Oxford J.L.S. 339; T.H. Jones, "The Defence of Necessity in Scots Law", 1989 S.L.T. (News) 253; D.W. Elliot, "Necessity, Duress and Self-Defence" [1989] Crim.L.R. 611; K.J.M. Smith, "Must Heroes Behave Heroically?" [1989] Crim.L.R. 622; N.M. Padfield, "Duress, Necessity and the Law Commission" [1992] Crim.L.R. 778; P.W. Ferguson, "Necessity and Coercion in Criminal Law", 1997 S.L.T. (News) 127.

[2] *supra*, para. 3.13.

[3] Voluntariness, relative at least to coercion, can be seen as something rather less than would be implied by free choice. Fletcher refers to "moral or normative voluntariness" as the appropriate term in relation to excuses, where "the actor's freedom of choice is constricted": *Rethinking Criminal Law* (Boston, 1978), at p.802. That term was adopted by Dickson J., in giving the opinion of the majority of the Supreme Court of Canada in *Perka v. The Queen* [1984] 2 S.C.R. 232, at 250. See para. 13.03, *infra*.

[4] *cf.* J. Hall, *General Principles of Criminal Law* (2nd ed., Indianopolis, 1960), p.421.

courses and their results. The essential feature of the situation is the conflict of values; and it is the agent's duty to choose that course of action which will realise the greater value.[5]

13.03 "FREE" ACTION. Attempts have been made to deal with the problem by distinguishing between acts which are "merely voluntary" and acts which are the result of free choice, and regarding only the latter as voluntary actions for the purpose of ascribing responsibility. "A man who is threatened acts 'voluntarily' in the sense that he chooses to do what he does; but he does not act 'freely'; on the contrary the man with the gun obliges him."[6] But many actions done under obligation are regarded as free actions. Orestes was "obliged" to kill his mother by his sense of honour and duty, but his act was surely a free one. Any motive can be spoken of as obliging the agent if it is strong enough, but the fact that an action is motivated does not mean that it is unfree, unless one is to say that no actions are free, in which case the whole discussion becomes meaningless. Even the man who acts under threat of death acts as the result of choice and the choice is free in the sense that he could have chosen otherwise: he could have chosen to die. Some systems of law consider this choice sufficiently free to entitle them to punish a man who chooses to kill another rather than die himself, and it cannot be said that there is anything illogical about their attitude, whatever its social or humanitarian value.[7]

Where the question is whether the agent's conduct was justified the important factor is not the strength of the compulsion under which the agent has to choose but the relative value of the alternatives. The solution is found not by considering the mental state of the agent, but by considering the objective situation, and deciding whether the objective action in this situation is to be regarded as something wrong at all. The agent is regarded as having a free choice, and his duty is to choose the lesser of the two evils before him, and so to preserve the greater value.[8] There may be opposing values involved and the agent must then make a rough calculation and choose that course of action which preserves the greater value — the standard and measure of value being taken as that employed by the person to whom the agent is accountable. The question is not "Was the agent responsible for what he did?" but "Was what he did wrong?"

---

[5] *cf.* Gl. Williams, *op.cit.*; Model Penal Code, O.D., s.3.02(1)(*a*) which makes necessity a defence where, *inter alia*, "the harm or evil sought to be avoided . . . is greater than that sought to be prevented by the law defining the offence charged"; StGB, Art 34: "Wer in einer gegenwärtigen, nicht anders abwendbaren Gefahr für Leben, Leib, Freiheit, Ehre, Eigentum oder ein anderes Rechtsgut eine Tat begeht, um die Gefahr von sich oder einem anderen abzuwenden, handelt nicht rechtswidrig, wenn bei Abwägung der widerstreitenden Interessen, namentlich der betroffenen Rechtsgüter und des Grades der ihnen drohenden Gefahren, das — geschützte Interese das beeinträchtigte wesentlich überwiegt. Dies gilt jedoch nur, soweit die Tat ein angemessenes Mittel ist, die Gefahr abzuwenden." *Cf.* G.P. Fletcher, *Rethinking Criminal Law* (Boston, 1978), pp.770–771.

[6] P.H. Nowell-Smith, *Ethics* (Harmondsworth, 1954), p.209.

[7] This attitude is apparent in modern English law: see *R. v. Howe* [1987] 1 All E.R. 771, HL, where it was decided unanimously that duress by threats was not a defence to murder, irrespective of whether the defendant was the principal actor or an accessory to the crime; to the extent that *Lynch v. D.P.P. for N.I.* [1975] A.C. 653, had allowed such a defence to an accessory to murder, it was overruled. The decision in *Howe* has now been extended to attempted murder: *R. v. Gotts* [1992] 2 W.L.R. 284.

[8] In Scotland, it seems that if the accused acts without thinking, without having considered that there was a dilemma requiring him to choose the lesser evil, he cannot be said to have acted under necessity: see *Dawson v. Dickson*, 1999 S.C.C.R. 698.

THE VALUE-SCALE. Theoretically, the law could lay down a calculus which would enable one to discover which was the greatest value capable of being preserved in any situation, but the law does not in fact do so, and one is left to rely on ordinary moral ideas. There are some cases where the moral answer is clear — life is more valuable than banknotes, a leg more valuable than a toe — but there is no generally accepted hierarchy of values. Relative values change from time to time, and place to place. It is difficult, for example, to accept unquestioningly today the assumption of Isabella in *Measure for Measure* that her chastity was more valuable than her brother's life. Again, values are often incommensurate: how can one measure the policeman's duty to keep order against his life; or equal: one man's life against another's. There is no mathematical solution to these problems, and in practice the answer is not found by calculating values. Rather, some principle is regarded as of overriding value in difficult situations, though it may not be so regarded where the choice is easy. The principle may be a legal one, like that of not taking the law into one's own hands, or it may be a religious one, like that of self-sacrifice or resignation to the will of God. Such a principle can be applied, for example, to decide what is the right action in a situation where a man's only chance of survival is to kill someone else; but it is not likely to be regarded as overriding where the choice before the agent is between committing perjury and sacrificing the life of his child, or stealing a fire extinguisher and seeing his house go up in flames. **13.04**

The principle of self-sacrifice is of special importance when it is used to decide which of two lives is to be saved. It means that from the point of view of the agent his own life is always of less value than anyone else's, though to a third party both lives may be of equal value. On this principle, a person would never be justified in killing another in order to save himself though he might be justified in killing him to save a third party.

Another point of general importance is that the carrying out of a prior obligation, legal or moral, may be itself an important value. If robbers enter a bank and ask a customer to help them and threaten to kill him if he refuses, the customer need only weigh the relative value of his own life and the bank's property (the general duty to obey the law can be discounted here since it applies to everyone). But a bank employee or a policeman in such a situation would also have to consider the value involved in carrying out his duty to his employer or his special duty to maintain the law as a policeman. The distinction between the customer and the bank employee or policeman is a significant and important one; and it is an indication of the advantage of the "choice of value" approach to the problem that it brings out this distinction which would be lost if the only question at issue were the physical or psychological effectiveness of the compulsion involved.

THE NEGATIVE VALUE OF A PRIMA FACIE CRIME. In specifically legal situations the most important general consideration is the negative value of the commission of a crime. Where there are two possible ways of preserving x units of value and one of these is criminal, it is clear that the whole situation constituted by the preservation of x by the commission of a crime is less in value than the whole situation constituted by the preservation of x by a non-criminal act. This is because the commission of a crime is itself regarded as of negative value, so that the whole **13.05** situation constituted by the preservation of x by the commission of a crime will in fact have a lesser value than x — its total value will be the value of x less the negative value of the commission of the crime. Suppose now that an agent is faced with a choice between preserving something valued at x and something valued at $x + y$, and that in order to preserve the latter he would have to commit a crime. Then, if the value of the crime is $-y$, the two courses of action will be equal, and if the negative value of the crime is more than y it will be his duty not to preserve the value $(x + y)$ since in doing so he will create a total situation valued at less than x which is the alternative value which can be preserved without the commission of a crime. It is only where the total situation created by the crime is of greater value than the alternative situation that the "crime" is justified or excused, and so ceases to be a crime. Prima facie it is criminal, and this factor must be included in any calculation of values.[9]

If obedience to the law were regarded as the supreme value, and as an absolute value, there would be no room for the plea of necessity at all, since it would not be possible for a situation involving a breach of the law to be more valuable than the one which did not involve such a breach. It would never be permissible to break the law, because no other value would be as great as the value involved in not breaking the law. It would never, for example, be permissible to borrow unlawfully someone else's car in an emergency to take a sick man to hospital, since even the value of his life would not compensate for the breach of the law. The Kantian version of this situation is familiar — if every imperative of the law is categorical, there can never be any conditions in which it is right to disobey any of them.

There seems to be no good reason for regarding legal rules as categorical, or as being all of equal value — there is no reason why some legal rules should not be regarded as more important than others, or why in some cases other considerations should not allow a legal rule to be broken. The law is not the embodiment of absolute wisdom but merely a means of social control, and it would be socially disadvantageous, for example, to prevent the preservation of a building by action involving the theft of a ladder and fire extinguisher.

13.06 *Necessity and coercion.* Situations of the kind discussed may arise independently of the will of any person whose life or property is involved in the balance of values, or they may be created by one of the persons so involved. Hall describes teleological necessity as implying "conduct in the face of serious danger threatened by the impact of physical forces",[10]

---

[9] The view of L.C.W.P. No. 55 that necessity "should be limited to cases where the impending harm is out of all proportion to the harm done by the defendant": para. 42, may, however, set too high a standard; *Cf.* P.O.D., s.302, which talks only of "greater" harm. By way of contrast, the Law Commission in its Report: *Criminal Law: Report on Defences of General Application*, 1977, para. 4.33, recommended that the defence of necessity should be abolished, on the assumption that such a defence existed at all at common law; whereas in L.C. No. 218 (*Legislating the Criminal Code: Offences against the Person and General Principles* (Cm 2370, 1993)), at para. 27.4, the Commission recommended that necessity should be left for common law development on a case to case basis — again on the assumption that such a general defence exists outwith the much more limited defences of duress by threats and duress of circumstances: see, *e.g.*, the version of these in the Law Commission's *Criminal Code for England and Wales* (L.C. No. 177, 1989, H.C., No. 299), Vol. 1, Draft Code Bill, cls 42 and 43.

[10] J. Hall, *General Principles of Criminal Law* (2nd ed., Indianopolis, 1960), p.425.

but this is too narrow if it excludes situations contributed to by human action or treats them as essentially different from those caused solely by physical forces. Coercion where the choice is forced on the agent by someone whose interests are not involved in the value calculation is essentially the same as necessity occasioned by natural events. When a man has, for example, to choose between his own life and that of others, the situation is governed by the same principles whether it is the result of a natural disaster such as a shipwreck caused by storm, or of the coercive action of a human being.[11] The important distinction is that between situations which can be accepted as "given", because none of those whose interests are threatened is responsible for them, and situations where the person who created the situation is involved in the value-conflict so that it is necessary to take his responsibility into account in balancing the values involved. The typical example of the latter type of situation is the case of self-defence against a criminal attack.[12]

Superior orders. The defence of superior orders is probably a subject in itself, but the situations which give rise to it resemble cases of coercion,[13] and it is sometimes treated as an example of necessity. **13.07**

I — NECESSITY[14]

The plea of necessity in one form or another is fairly generally recognised in Continental Law,[15] and has been for some time.[16] It has **13.08**

---

[11] Some of their Lordships accepted this in *D.P.P. v. Lynch* [1975] A.C. 653, others did not. But all their views were coloured by the likely effect of their decision on *R. v. Dudley and Stephens* (1884) Q.B.D. 273; for the view that *Dudley and Stephens* does not preclude a necessity plea on a charge of murder, see P.R. Glazebrook, *op.cit.*, at p.114; L.C.P.W. No. 55, para. 35. Since the decision of the House of Lords in *R. v. Howe* [1987] 1 All E.R. 771, however, that view seems untenable. In *Howe*, it was decided unanimously that duress by threats was not available in answer to a charge of murder. Lord Hailsham of St. Marylebone said: "There is, of course, an obvious distinction between duress and necessity as potential defences: duress arises from the wrongful threats or violence of another human being and necessity arises from any other objective dangers threatening the accused. This, however, is, in my view, a distinction without a relevant difference, since on this view duress is only that species of the genus of necessity which is caused by wrongful threats. I cannot see that there is any way in which a person of ordinary fortitude can be excused from the one type of pressure on his will rather than the other." Lord Hailsham's view is in general accepted in Scotland: see *Moss v. Howdle*, 1997 J.C. 123, opinion of the Court at 128E-F, *viz.*: "we consider that, where an accused commits a crime in an endeavour to escape an immediate danger of death or great bodily harm, it makes no difference to the possible availability of any defence that the danger arises from some contingency such as a natural disaster or illness rather than from the deliberate threats of another." His Lordship's view is also widely accepted in England and elsewhere: see, *e.g.*, *R. v. Conway* [1989] Q.B. 290, Woolf L.J., at 297–298; *Hibbert v. R.* [1995] 2 S.C.R. 973, Lamer C.J. at 1012–1013. See also P.W. Ferguson, "Necessity and Coercion in Criminal Law", 1997 S.L.T. (News) 127.

[12] See Vol. II, Chap. 24. *Cf.*, *Tudhope v. Grubb*, 1983 S.C.C.R. 360, Sh.Ct, where the need to escape assault was accepted as a defence to a charge of attempting to drive with more than the permitted level of alcohol in one's blood. The situation was essentially one of self-defence, but the prima facie crime was not directed at the assailants. In *Moss v. Howdle*, 1997 J.C. 123, at 127C, L.J.-G. Rodger stated that *Tudhope v. Grubb* was a case involving what is known to English law as "duress of circumstances". See paras 13–17 to 13.19 *infra*.

[13] *e.g.*, Hume, i, 53–55; Alison, i, 672–675.

[14] See P.R. Glazebrook, "The Necessity Plea in Criminal Law" [1972A] C.L.J. 87.

[15] *e.g.* StGB Art. 34.

[16] See, *e.g.*, H. Donnedieu de Vabres, *Traité de Droit Criminal et de Législation Pénale Comparée* (3rd ed., Paris, 1947).

recently been recognised in Scotland[17]; and in England, a limited type of necessity known as "duress of circumstances" has become established.[18] As the law, particularly in Scotland, is still in a state of development, it is proposed first to consider the problem in general, then to deal with the law of England, and finally to consider the position in Scots law.

(1) The General Problem

The limits of the plea

13.09 The plea of necessity is one which is not regarded with enthusiasm by the law. The possibilities of abuse are considerable, and accordingly the plea will be allowed to operate only where it is clear that the otherwise criminal action taken was the only means of preserving the value in question. If there are two courses open each of which would preserve the value in question and one of them is criminal, then the agent must adopt the non-criminal one even if the criminal one is easier or more likely to succeed. The criminal course of action may be adopted only where there is no other way out. Again, the danger must be imminent and considerable. A is not entitled to steal B's gun today because he thinks he may need a gun to defend himself against C tomorrow. In many cases the necessity will be such that A can be said to have acted in the agony of the moment, although even when this is so A's action is justified, not by his agonised state of mind, but by the fact that in a situation of necessity he adopted the legally approved course of action. In other cases there may be room for deliberation and choice.[19] Before the law comes to consider the relative values involved it must be satisfied that the situation truly was one of necessity — that danger was imminent and that no other way of avoiding it was open to the accused. Only after that has been decided does it turn to ask if the accused did the right thing in the situation. If there was no imminent danger and no necessity to commit the crime, no question of conflict of values arises.[20]

---

[17] *Moss v. Howdle*, 1997 J.C. 123.

[18] See *R. v. Willer* (1986) 83 Cr.App.R. 225; *R. v. Conway* (1989) 88 Cr.App.R. 159; *R. v. Martin* (1989) 88 Cr.App.R. 343; *R. v. Pommell* [1995] 2 Cr.App.R. 607. *Cf.*, the English Draft Criminal Code (L.C. No. 177, *A Criminal Code for England and Wales*, H. of C. No. 299, 1989), Vol. 1, Draft Bill, Cl. 42. On the assumption that duress of circumstances and duress by threats may be considered subject to the same limitations, then duress of circumstances does not extend to murder (*R. v. Howe* [1987] 1 All E.R. 417, HL, upholding *R. v. Dudley and Stephens* (1884) 14 Q.B.D. 273) nor attempted murder (*R. v. Gotts* [1992] 2 W.L.R. 284, HL).

[19] *cf. Burns v. Nowell* (1880) 5 Q.B.D. 444, as discussed by P.R. Glazebrook [1972A] C.L.J. 87, 95, and indeed *R. v. Dudley and Stephens* (1884) 14 Q.B.D. 273 itself.

[20] See *Downie v. H.M. Advocate*, 1984 S.C.C.R. 365, where the accused in effect pled necessity in answer to a charge of child-stealing. The sheriff ruled at p.367 that it would only be in dire circumstances that a person could possibly be justified in taking the child away from its parent or guardian without recourse to the normal processes of law, and that no such dire circumstances had been established by the accused. A subsequent appeal against conviction on *inter alia* the ground that the taking had been justified, was refused without a formal opinion being delivered by the Court. It would seem unlikely also that an emergency journey would excuse careless driving: *D.P.P. v. Harris* (1995) 1 Cr.App.R. 170, a case of careless driving of a police vehicle; but *cf.* the view there of Curtis L.J. at 181E, and *R. v. Backshall* [1998] R.T.R. 423, Evans L.J. at 431F. There is a specific statutory provision exempting vehicles used for fire brigade, ambulance and police purposes from speed limits when observance of the limit "would be likely to hinder" their use for these

There are other limitations on the plea of necessity which are difficult to categorise. It probably cannot be used to override the rights of others who are not themselves directly involved in the perilous situation in which the plea arises. It would not, for example, apply to justify an assault on a person who happened to have, or even to be the only person to have, blood of a group necessary to save the life of a dying man.[21]

An English Law Commission Working Party suggested special provision to exclude the plea of necessity where "the defendant has put himself into a position where he must commit one offence in order to avoid another", but their examples of its application were trivial.[22]

The possible situations

Situations of necessity can be divided into three main groups by reference to the concept of value-conflicts. These are (i) where one value is clearly greater than another; (ii) where the values involved are equal; (iii) where the values involved are absolute. **13.10**

(i) In such a situation it should be clear that the agent's duty is to preserve the greater value and where this involves the commission of a crime the crime should be justified by the necessity of preserving the greater value. It should not be a crime, for example, to steal a fire extinguisher in order to save a burning building.[23] Indeed there may be occasions on which there is a legal obligation to commit a prima facie crime in order to preserve a value. If it is accepted that abortion is a lesser crime than homicide, then a doctor who refuses to save a pregnant woman's life by performing an abortion may be guilty of culpable homicide.[24]

(ii) Donnedieu de Vabres sums up his views on necesity as follows: "Le délit nécessaire ne peut . . . être consideré comme un acte antisocial; il a été socialement utile, si le bien sauvegardé était supérieur à celui qui a été sacrifié, et socialement indifférent, s'il était de valeur égale."[25] This, it is submitted, is an appropriate approach, provided that the calculation includes the negative value of lawbreaking in arriving at

---

purposes: Road Traffic Regulation Act 1984, s.87: see *Aitken v. Yarwood* [1965] 1 Q.B. 327; and also one permitting vehicles to drive elsewhere than on roads "for the purpose of saving life or extinguishing fire or meeting any other like emergency": Road Traffic Act 1988, s.34(3). See also *Buckoke v. G.L.C.* [1971] 1 Ch. 655. Section 30(1) of the Fire Services Act 1947 empowers firemen and constables to break into premises where there is a fire, or which it is necessary to enter in order to put out or prevent fire, and they "may deem necessary" to protect the premises or rescue persons or property therein. It has been held in England, however, that duress of circumstances can be a defence to driving whilst disqualified: *R. v. Martin (Colin)* (1989) 88 Cr.App.R. 343. Reference should also be made to s.8(5) of the Criminal Law (Consolidation) (Scotland) Act 1995 which provides that a woman detained in a brothel who takes away clothes she needs to enable her to leave the brothel is not liable to any civil or criminal proceedings in respect thereof. Professor Gl. Williams refers to a case where an alien was convicted of a breach of curfew regulations in war-time London by leaving a house to go to an air raid shelter, but the magistrate indicated that had she left because the house had been set on fire and to escape death, her breach of the regulations would have been justified: see Gl. Williams, *op.cit.*, at p.233. There is specific provision for emergency in relation to the entry of a prohibited area under s.3(3)(a) and (c) of the Protection of Wrecks Act 1973.

[21] *cf.* J. Andenaes, *The General Part of the Criminal Law of Norway*, 169; John Harris. "The Survival Lottery" (1975) 50 *Philosophy* 81.

[22] See L.C.W.P. No. 55, 33, 34.

[23] *cf.* Gl. Williams, p.737.

[24] *cf. R. v. Bourne* [1939] 1 K.B. 687, Macnaghten J. at 693.

[25] H. Donnedieu de Vabres, *Traité de Droit Criminal et de Législation Pénale Comparée* (3rd ed., Paris, 1947), p.224.

the equivalence of values. Where the values are equivalent necessity should operate as an excuse.[26] Any system of law must, however, endeavour to avoid the occurrence of a situation of this kind, and normally the negative value of the crime involved will tip the balance.

13.11 (iii) The most difficult questions arise in the case of absolute values which by definition cannot be related to any other values. Probably the only absolute value is the preservation of life. This means that any lesser crime than homicide will be justified by the preservation of life, but it makes it very difficult if not impossible to allow any circumstances to justify homicide. It may be, as Professor Glanville Williams suggests, that "We need a general rule, and one allowing necessity as a defence to homicide where the minority are killed to preserve the majority is on the whole more satisfactory than the opposite",[27] but such a rule is by no means free from difficulty. It is inconsistent with the idea that each human life is of absolute value, and would offend against the feeling that no human being has a right to decide which of his fellows should survive in any situation. Nor is there any way of determining what preponderance of saved lives is necessary to overcome the great negative value of the crime of murder. At the same time there are situations, such as that of the ship-wreck, in which it would clearly be grossly wasteful to insist that all should drown, and to refuse to allow any to be saved at the expense of the rest.

13.12 The problem is a little easier in two special situations: (a) where the person making the choice has a legal duty towards one or more of the persons whose lives are in danger, and (b) where the particular persons sacrificed would necessarily have died anyway.

(a) Suppose A is in a boat with B, his child, and C, a stranger. If it becomes necessary for one of the three to be sacrificed in order to save the other two it might be permissible for A to sacrifice C in order to perform his legal duty to protect B, even if it would not be permissible for him to sacrifice C in order to protect himself, or to sacrifice B to protect himself or C. That is to say, it may be possible to resolve the conflict of values by means of the value involved in A's performance of his duty to protect B.[28]

---

[26] *infra*, para. 13.13.

[27] Gl. Williams, p.740.

[28] *cf. U.S. v. Holmes* (1842) 26 Fed. Cas. 360, Baldwin J's charge to the jury: "But in applying this law, we must look, not only to the jeopardy in which the parties are, but also to the relations in which they stand. The slayer must be under no obligation to make his own safety secondary to the safety of the others. A familiar application of this principle presents itself in the obligations which rest upon the owners of stages, steam-boats, and other vehicles of transportation. In consideration of the payment of fare, the owners of the vehicle are bound to transport the passengers to the place of contemplated destination. Having, in all emergencies, the conduct of the journey, and the control of the passengers, the owners rest under every obligation for care, skill, and general capacity; and if, from defect of any of these requisites, grievous injury is done to the passenger, the persons employed are liable. The passenger owes no duty but submission. He is under no obligation to protect and keep the conductor in safety, nor is the passenger bound to labour, except in cases of emergency, where his services are required by unanticipated and uncommon danger. Such, said the court, is the relation which exists on shipboard. The passenger stands in a position different from that of the officers and seamen. It is the sailor who must encounter the hardships and perils of the voyage. Nor can this relation be changed when the ship is lost by tempest or other danger of the sea, and all on board have betaken themselves, for safety, to the small boats; for imminence of danger can not absolve from duty. The sailor is bound, as before, to undergo whatever hazard is necessary to preserve the boat and the passengers."

(b) Suppose three men, A, B and C, are climbing a mountain, roped together in that order, with A as leader. A is able to pull only one of the other two up behind him, and therefore B cuts the rope between himself and C, and so kills C. This action may be regarded as justifiable[29] because the only choice is between the deaths of B and C, and "sacrificing" C in order to save B, and because the "choice" of C as the sacrifice is made by the relative positions of the three men. Perhaps the real distinction between this case and that where two shipwrecked men decide to put a third out of a lifeboat which can hold only two people is that in the mountain case it is clear that C will die whatever B does, so that B can be said not to have killed him, but only to have saved himself.[30]

The effect of the plea

It is possible to regard necessity as a justification, as an excuse, or as only a mitigating factor. The words "justification" and "excuse" are often used loosely and interchangeably, but it is proposed to use them to distinguish between factors which deprive an act of its criminal nature, and factors which merely render it unpunishable. **13.13**

A killing which is carried out under a valid judicial order is justified, it is not a crime; a killing committed by a lunatic or by someone under the age of criminal responsibility is a crime, but it is not punishable, it is an "unenforceable crime." The important difference is this: it is lawful to defend oneself or one's property against an excusable act, but not against a justifiable one. It is justifiable self-defence to kill a lunatic in order to save one's life from his attack, but it is murder to kill the public hangman in order to prevent him from carrying out a death sentence.[31]

Necessity should probably operate as a justification wherever the law lays down, or recognises, a clear scale of values. The owner of a fire extinguisher can hardly be justified in preventing someone else from using it to put out a fire which has caught a woman's dress.[32] Similarly, if there is a rule that in a shipwreck sailors must give precedence to women and children a sailor would not be entitled to resist anyone who removed him from a boat in order to make room for a child.[33]

It is submitted that where the law lays down no rule of choice anyone who kills another to save himself should be excused. If the law gives no rules at all for a situation it can hardly blame people for making their

---

[29] *cf.* Gl. Williams, 739.

[30] See also T.W. Price, *op.cit.*, n. 1, *supra*, at p.17: "A driver is thrown into a dilemma, through no fault of his own. He deliberately collides with another car rather than mount the pavement and run down pedestrians. The innocent driver of the other car is killed." Prof. Price regards the killing as justifiable.

[31] See generally G.P. Fletcher, *Rethinking Criminal Law* (Boston, 1978), Chap. 10. The distinction between justification and excuse (and the claimed implications of that distinction) have been the subject of significant criticism: see, *e.g.*, J.C. Smith, *Justification and Excuse in the Criminal Law* (London, 1989), Chap. 1; Miriam Gur-Araye, "Should the Criminal Law Distinguish Between Necessity as a Defence and Necessity as an Excuse?" (1986) 102 L.Q.R. 71.

[32] *cf.* Gl. Williams, 745.

[33] As Baldwin J. said in charging the jury in *U.S. v. Holmes* (1842) 2 Fed. Cas. 360: "When the selection has been made by lots, the victim yields of course to his fate, or, if he resists, force may be employed to coerce submission. Whether or not 'a case of necessity' has arisen, or whether the law under which death has been inflicted has been so exercised as to hold the executioner harmless, cannot depend on his own opinion: for no man may pass upon his own conduct when it concerns the rights, and especially, when it affects the lives, of others."

own rules, and at the same time cannot expect anyone who is picked out for sacrifice not to resist the attack on him. In the classic situation of two men making for a raft only strong enough to hold one of them,[34] if the law can provide no principle of choice, each should be excusable for attacking the other and trying to keep him away from the raft, and each be entitled to protect himself against the other's attempts to drown him.

Such a difficulty cannot arise if the law provides a rule for such a situation — the rule that neither may attack the other, but each must await his fate passively, or sacrifice himself.[35] But there remains the question whether the law ought to lay down or to enforce such a negative rule. The sacrifice demanded by the rule is one which can hardly be enforced by threat of punishment — one cannot make a man into a martyr by threatening him that if he saves himself now at the cost of someone else's life, he may be punished at a future date. As Macaulay points out. "An eminently virtuous man indeed will prefer death to crime; but it is not to our virtue that the penal law addresses itself; nor would the world stand in need of penal laws if men were virtuous."[36] On Benthamite principles, therefore, punishment should not be inflicted in such cases since it would be wholly inefficacious.[37] The law should therefore not enforce the negative rule.

Finally, it should be noted that, since justification is an objective matter, and excusability a subjective matter, a person who acts out of a reasonable error of fact regarding necessity can be only excusable. This can be seen most clearly by reference to a situation of self-defence. If A attacks B under the mistaken belief that it is necessary to do so in order to avert a threatened fatal attack by B, A is excusable but B is entitled to defend himself against A, since in fact B is not about to attack A, and A's actions are therefore not justifiable, nor is B under any duty to submit to them.

13.14 The operation of necessity as a plea in mitigation is quite different from its operation as an excuse or justification. It is submitted that necessity may operate in mitigation in the same way as does provocation — by showing that the accused lacked "malice" and acted under a stress which entitles him to be treated sympathetically.

(2) Necessity in English law

Classic Necessity — The case of the Mignonette[38]

13.15 The classic example of the plea of necessity in a charge of murder is the case of *R. v. Dudley and Stephens*,[39] known also as the case of the *Mignonette*. D., S. and a 17-year-old cabin boy got into an open boat

---

[34] See Gl. Williams, p.738 for differing versions of the "plank case."

[35] *R. v. Dudley and Stephens* (1884) 14 Q.B.D. 273; *R. v. Howe* [1987] 1 All E.R. 771. *Dudley and Stephens* was distinguished in *Lynch v. D.P.P.* [1975] 653; but *Lynch* was overruled by *Howe*. See also *R. v. Gotts* [1992] 2 W.L.R. 284.

[36] Macaulay, p.455.

[37] *cf.* Bentham, *Principles*, XIII, 3.

[38] See also L. Fuller, "The Case of the Speluncean Explorers" (1949) 62 H.L.R. 616. For a full account of this and similar cases, see A.W.B. Simpson, *Cannibalism and the Common Law* (University of Chicago Press, 1984).

[39] (1884) 14 Q.B.D. 273.

after the sinking of the *Mignonette*. After they had been in the boat eighteen days, for seven of which they had been without food and for five without water, D. proposed to S. that one of the three should be killed and eaten by the survivors and that the victim should be chosen by lot. Later, however, it was decided to kill the boy who was likely to have died first in any event. This was done on the twentieth day and the two men ate the boy until they were picked up on the twenty-fourth day.[40] On their return to England they were charged with murder. The jury brought in a special verdict in which they found the above facts proved, and "that there was no appreciable chance of saving life except by killing some one for the others to eat. That assuming any necessity to kill anybody, there was no greater necessity for killing the boy than any of the other . . . men." On these facts the court, in a judgment delivered by Lord Coleridge C.J. held without any doubt or misgiving that the men were guilty of murder.

Dudley[40a] proceeded on the view that "the broad proposition that a man may save his life by killing, if necessary, an innocent and unoffending neighbour . . . certainly is not law at the present day."[41] The suggestion that one could save one's life at the expense of another was said to be "at once dangerous, immoral, and opposed to all legal principle and analogy."[42] The effect of *Dudley*[42a] is that in a situation where only some of a group of people can survive, no one is allowed to sacrifice anyone else, and all must let matters take their course.

The decision, which in Scotland is only of persuasive authority, is weakened by two considerations. The first is that in fact the accused were not hanged but only imprisoned for six months, and that the court know that they would not be hanged.[43] The second is that the court may have been influenced by the view that necessity had not been proved, the accused being unable to show that they knew that killing the boy was either necessary or sufficient to save them.[44] The case has nevertheless been open to criticism, mainly because it proceeded on moral and religious, and not on legal, considerations. The court appear to have assumed that the law must enforce the same high standards as are laid down by the Christian religion, and accepted that "We are often compelled to set up standards we cannot reach ourselves, and to lay down rules which we could not ourselves satisfy."[45] But even if it is ethically or religiously right to insist on self-sacrifice and on that "moral necessity not of the preservation, but of the sacrifice of their lives for others, from which in no country, least of all, it is to be hoped, in England, will never ever shrink,"[46] it does not follow that the law must enforce the same standards as those of morality. The decision also fails to take into account the unlikelihood of anyone being persuaded to accept such standards by means of the threat of legal punishment. To try

---

[40] There was another man in the boat but he refused to agree to what was done although he also ate the boy's flesh.

[40a] (1884) 14 Q.B.D. 273.

[41] (1884) 14 Q.B.D. 273, Lord Coleridge C.J. at 286.

[42] *ibid*. at 281.

[42a] (1884) 14 Q.B.D. 273.

[43] Gl. Williams, p.741.

[44] L.C.W.P. No 55, para. 35.

[45] (1884) 14 Q.B.D. 273, Lord Coleridge C.J. at 288.

[46] *ibid*. 287. Lord Coleridge has been not unfairly described as "influenced by emotion to a certain extent": *S. v. Goliath*, 1972 (3) S.A. 1, 15H. The facts were, of course, particularly revolting, involving as they did cannibalism as well as murder.

to prevent crimes like that in *Dudley*[46a] by hanging is probably futile, since the possibility of future hanging will not outweigh the certainty of present death; to try to prevent them by a sentence of six months' imprisonment is merely ludicrous. Nevertheless, the unanimous House of Lords' opinion in the duress case of *R. v. Howe*[47] confirms that *Dudley*[47a] and the philosophy which it entails remain authoritative in English criminal law.

One of the main reasons for the decision in *Dudley*[47b] was the difficulty of answering the questions "Who is to be the judge of this sort of necessity? By what measure is the comparative value of lives to be measured?"[48] It is feared that to allow one man to make such a choice among others is to let people take the law into their own hands, and to invite anarchy. But *Dudley*[48a] fails to face up to the difficulty that there are situations in which people will not in fact remain passive and await their fate with folded hands. By refusing to lay down any rules of action for them it invites a situation in which it will be "every man for himself," and in which no one will be punishable for what he does, or rather will be punishable only to a slight extent because, as was in fact recognised by the way in which Dudley and Stephens were dealt with, his actions will appear as at least excusable. But if there are rules whoever is in charge of the situation will be fortified by the rules and be helped by them to enforce order, and those who disobey the rules will be open to charges of acting wholly unjustifiably. Of course, this will not prevent them so acting if they are determined to do so, but it will give those of them who wish to abide by the law a law by which to abide, and a law which is not wholly negative in character but which will allow some people to be saved.

13.16 In one American case an attempt was made to lay down such a rule. This was *U.S. v. Holmes*[49] which arose out of the wreck of the *William Brown*. Some passengers and all the crew got into two lifeboats. One of these boats, commanded by the mate, was overloaded so that it became necessary to put some people overboard to prevent it sinking. Holmes, who was a member of the crew who had helped to put sixteen male passengers overboard under the mate's orders, was convicted of manslaughter, the Grand Jury having refused to indict him for murder. The defence of necessity which he pleaded was not rejected out of hand; the court accepted the principle but held that the choice of victims had been wrongly made. It was held that passengers should have been preferred to sailors, and only as many seamen saved as were required to sail the boat. As among the passengers it was held that the victims should have been chosen by lot, that being the fairest method and "in some sort, an appeal to God".

[46a] (1884) 14 Q.B.D. 273.
[47] [1987] 1 All E.R. 771.
[47a] (1884) 14 Q.B.D. 273.
[47b] (1884) 14 Q.B.D. 273.
[48] (1884) 14 Q.B.D. 273 at 287.
[48a] (1884) 14 Q.B.D. 273.
[49] (1841) 26 Fed. Cas. 360, No. 15,383; J. Hall, *General Principles of Criminal Law* (2nd ed., Indianopolis, 1960), pp.427 *et seq*. See A.W.B. Simpson, *op.cit.*, Chap. 7.

The preference given the passengers is an example of the application of a recognised rule, referred to in *Dudley*[49a] as an example of self-sacrifice, and described by Glanville Williams as the "etiquette of the sea".[50] Its foundation may be the sailor's contractual duty to look after his passengers, but at the same time it is a rule of law that this duty involves the further duty to sacrifice himself for the sake of the passengers. After all, the sailor does not explicitly contract to sacrifice his life if necessary for the safety of the passengers, and even if he did that in itself would not matter, since no one can consent to be killed so as to free his killer from punishment. A captain who forcibly removed an unwilling sailor from a boat to make room for a passenger would not be guilty of homicide if the sailor was drowned as a result, but this would not be because of the sailor's implied consent to be drowned, but because of a rule of law governing the choice of victim in situations of shipwreck. That there is an "etiquette of the sea" shows that it is possible to construct rules for choice of victim despite the moral and religious difficulties involved; and shows also that where a situation occurs often enough rules will be created. One reason the law manages to do without rules for situations like that in *Dudley*[50a] is that such cases rarely occur. Were they frequent the law might well find that its negative attitude was unworkable and produced undesirable results, and set about trying to lay down and enforce rules.

U.S. v. Holmes[50b] was summarily dismissed in *Dudley*[50c] as unsatisfactory because of the suggestion of a lottery. It might seem wrong, or frivolous, to decide such a matter by lot — it might, for example, be better to apply the convention of women and children first, or to give the young preference over the aged, and so on — but in the absence of any other principle of choice a lottery does prevent an unseemly scramble for survival which can lead only to the survival of the physically strongest. The lottery can also be regarded, as it was in *Holmes*,[51] as an admission that the situation has got beyond the power of human judgment; it is as much a committal of the matter into the hands of a higher power as is the fatalistic inactivity required by *Dudley*[51a] and has the advantage of making possible the survival of some of the persons involved. It has the further advantage that it would often be difficult to reach agreement on any alternative mode of selection, while in the absence of agreement drawing lots, or spinning coins, or picking cards, or any other such method seems an obvious, if a last, resort. The most important thing about *Holmes*,[51b] however, is that it recognises that there should be some rules, and that it is the function of the law to decide what they should be. Until that much is recognised, and it is not recognised in *Dudley*,[51c] one cannot go on to decide what the rules ought to be.

[49a] (1884) 14 Q.B.D. 273.
[50] Gl. Williams, p.741.
[50a] (1884) 14 Q.B.D. 273.
[50b] (1841) 26 Fed. Cas. 360, No. 15, 383.
[50c] (1884) 14 Q.B.D. 273.
[51] (1841) 26 Fed. Cas. 360.
[51a] (1884) 14 Q.B.D. 273.
[51b] (1841) 26 Fed. Cas. 360.
[51c] (1884) 14 Q.B.D. 273.

Duress of circumstances

13.17 'Classic' necessity, with its difficult requirement of balancing the values at stake[52] and its implication that the actor who successfully argues the defence must be taken to have been justified in what he did,[52a] has not proved attractive to English (or indeed Scottish[53]) judges. Instead of necessity as described above, therefore, the English courts have recently developed an alternative rule-based (as opposed to value-based) defence where such necessity might otherwise have been applicable. This limited version of necessity has affinities, and shares rules, with duress by threats.[54]

13.18 That there is no general defence of necessity in English law has been affirmed in several cases,[55] and it is now clear that there is a defence, analogous to duress by threats, where there is a threat from objective dangers.[56] This analogous defence has become known as "duress of circumstances",[57] but the circumstances have to be extreme,[58] in that the defendant must have acted to avoid a threat of death or serious injury to himself or another.[59] The circumstances in which the defence has been held to apply have been very varied: for example, it has been held sufficient that the defendant's wife threatened to kill herself; that the defendant was attacked by some 20 or 30 youths who announced their intention to kill him; that the defendant had taken a firearm from a person who had intended to shoot someone else with it; and, that the defendant believed that he was being approached by assassins.[60] It has been said that the defence is subject to the same limits as apply to duress by threats,[61] and that there are two questions to be put to a jury in a case where there is evidence to support duress of circumstances.[62] These two questions, adapted from Lord Lane's opinion in *R. v. Graham*,[63] were set out by Simon Brown J as follows:

> "(a) Was the accused, or may he have been, impelled to act as he did because as a result of what he reasonably believed to have been the

---

[52] See paras 13.04 and 13.05, *supra*.

[52a] This view, that the actor must have been acting not unlawfully, even commendably, in society's interests, does not necessarily follow: see G.P. Fletcher, *Rethinking Criminal Law* (Boston, 1978), at pp.759 *et seq*., esp. at pp.823–7, where he suggests that necessity, when considered as an excuse rather than a justification, has advantages from the point of view of judicial acceptability, especially in a case such as *Dudley*: the conduct of the actor would then remain wrong and unlawful, although the actor is personally excused from criminal responsibility. See also *Perka v. The Queen* [1984] 2 S.C.R. 232, Dickson J. at 245–250.

[53] See para. 13.22, *infra*.

[54] See A. Ashworth, *Principles of Criminal Law* (3rd ed., 1999), at p.227

[55] See, *e.g.*, *R. v. Pommell* (1995) 2 Cr.App.R. 607, Kennedy L.J. at 613G; *R. v. Rodger & Rose* [1998] 1 Cr.App.R. 143, following *Pommell* on this point. See also the doubts expressed in *R. v. Willer* (1986) 83 Cr.App.R. 225, Watkins L.J. at 226.

[56] *R. v. Martin* (1989) 88 Cr.App.R. 343, Simon Brown J., at 345–346.

[57] The title was adopted in *R. v. Conway* [1989] 1 Q.B. 240, at 296G.

[58] *R. v. Martin*, *supra*, Simon Brown J., at 346.

[59] See *R. v. Conway* [1989] 1 Q.B. 290, at 297; *R. v. Pommell* [1995] 2 Cr.App.R. 607, at 614F.

[60] See *R. v. Martin* (1989) 88 Cr.App.R. 343; *R. v. Willer* (1986) 83 Cr.App.R. 325; *R. v. Pommell* (1995) 2 Cr.App.R. 607; and, *R. v. Conway* [1989] 1 Q.B. 290, respectively.

[61] *R. v. Conway* [1989] 1 Q.B. 290, at 297G.

[62] The evidential burden is laid on the defendant: *R. v. Pommell* [1995] 2 Cr.App.R. 607, at 611–612.

[63] [1982] 1 All E.R. 801, at 806e-f.

situation he had good cause to fear that otherwise death or serious physical injury would result? [and] (b) [If so] may a sober person of reasonable firmness sharing the characteristics of the accused, have responded to that situation by acting as the accused acted?"[64]

These questions encapsulate the essentials of the defence, and are couched in objective terms. Recently, however, it has become clear that in accordance with developments elsewhere in English criminal law, what the defendant honestly believed to be the case is acceptable even if there is no factual basis for that belief.[65] The accused must be "wholly driven" by the force of circumstances into committing a crime to avoid the danger which confronts him[66]; but once that danger has ceased to apply, the rationale for committing or continuing to commit the offence flies off.[67] The circumstances which create the danger must also be external to the defendant, such that a prisoner's own suicidal depression, consequent to his learning that his prison sentence was to be lengthened, was not sufficient for the defence to apply.[68]

It would seem from these complex, detailed rules that duress of **13.19**
circumstances is very far removed from "classic" necessity, and that a balancing of values, so that the lesser evil can be identified and preferred, has little relevance. But it has been emphasised that a defendant faced with a situation of danger of death or serious injury must respond reasonably and proportionately[69]; and indeed it has been held that the defence will be lost if the defendant does not consider any alternatives which there may be to the commission of a crime, and does not avail himself of a reasonable legal alternative when such presents itself.[70] The defence is, however, available to all crimes in England except murder, attempted murder and certain forms of treason[71]; it may also be excluded from statutory offences which either directly or impliedly exclude it, or are incompatible with it.[72] The defence as described would not apply, for example, to the theft of a fire extinguisher in order to safeguard an uninhabited but valuable building which had caught fire, as a true defence of necessity probably should: but English law does not require duress of circumstances to apply to such situations, since these are catered for elsewhere in the law.[73]

---

[64] *R. v. Martin* (1989) 88 Cr.App.R. 343, Simon Brown J. at 346. Which characteristics of the defendant should count for this purpose has proved very troublesome for the English courts, the rule having been borrowed from the English view of provocation: as it now appears that any characteristics are relevant for provocation, it seems that a similar relaxation of the law will apply to duress, see *R. v. Smith (Morgan)* [2000] 3 W.L.R. 654, HL.

[65] *R. v. Cairns* (1999) 2 Cr.App.R. 137.

[66] *R. v. Willer* (1989) 83 Cr.App.R. 225, Watkins L.J. at 227.

[67] See, *e.g.*, *D.P.P. v. Jones* [1990] R.T.R. 32.

[68] *R. v. Rodger and Rose* (1998) 1 Cr.App.R. 143.

[69] *R. v. Martin* (1989) 88 Cr.App.R. 343, Simon Brown J. at 346.

[70] See *D.P.P. v. Harris* (1995) 1 Cr.App.R. 170.

[71] *R. v. Pommell* (1995) 2 Cr.App.R. 607, Kennedy L.J. at 615. *Cf.*, the English Draft Criminal Code (Law Commission No. 177, *A Criminal Code for England and Wales*, H.C., No. 299, 1989, Vol. 1), cl.43, where the Commission were undecided whether duress of circumstances should be available to all crimes.

[72] See *D.P.P. v. Harris* (1995) 1 Cr.App.R. 170, which left the applicability of the defence to careless driving uncertain; but see the later case of *R. v. Backshall* [1998] R.T.R. 423, Evans L.J. at 431F.

[73] See Theft Act 1968, s.2, relative to the theft mentioned in the text above. As to the destruction of property in a situation of necessity, see J.C. Smith & B. Hogan, *Criminal Law* (9th ed., 1999, Sir J. Smith (ed.)), p.694, which refers to the Criminal Damage Act 1971, s.5(2)(b).

(3) Necessity in Scots Law

13.20 Hume deals with the defence of necessity only in connection with the old plea of Burthensack. He interprets the law of Burthensack as meaning that the theft of as much meat as a man can carry on his back is not capital: *i.e.* that the defence of want or necessity may mitigate the punishment of theft. Hume rejects even this restricted operation of the plea of necessity because of the difficulty of calculating "the due measure of distress", of distinguishing genuine cases from those of "pretended necessity," and because such a rule would make every man the judge of his own needs.[74] In spite of Hume's views, a defence of necessity has been recognised in modern times — although that defence bears close affinities to the Scots law of coercion, and appears to be subject to many of the limitations (if not the actual rules) evolved by the English courts for "duress of circumstances".[75]

13.21 The Appeal Court decided in *Moss v. Howdle*[76] that there was a defence of necessity in Scots criminal law,[77] but that the defence (as with coercion) had to be kept within narrow bounds to prevent its abuse. There were, therefore, strict rules to be met before the defence could be successful. In particular, the accused had to be shown to have acted criminally at the material time in order to avoid or escape from an immediate danger of death or great bodily harm to himself or another.[78] This was the minimum requirement.[79] The circumstances causing that danger could range widely, and included natural disasters, medical emergencies[80] and the actings of third parties;[81] but the danger must have dominated the mind of the accused. As Lord Justice-General Rodger said: "[T]he defence cannot apply where the circumstances did not in fact constrain the accused to act in breach of the law."[82] Thus, it seems, if the accused did not think about the dilemma he in fact faced, but acted as he would in any event and thereby committed a crime, he cannot take advantage of the defence notwithstanding that the situation was indeed one of immediate danger of death or great bodily harm.[83] On the other hand, if the accused had a reasonable belief in the existence of the required type of necessitous circumstances, that will suffice even

---

[74] Hume, i, 55; Alison, i, 675.

[75] See paras 13.17 to 13.19, *supra*.

[76] 1997 J.C. 123. See P.W. Ferguson, "Necessity and Coercion in Criminal Law", 1997 S.L.T. (News) 127; M. Christie, "The Mother of Invention? Moss v. Howdle" (1997) 4 E.L.R. 479.

[77] There had been a previous sheriff court case where necessity had resulted in an acquittal: *Tudhope v. Grubb*, 1983 S.C.C.R. 350.

[78] *Moss v. Howdle*, 1997 J.C. 123, L.J.-G. Rodger at 126E-F; 127C; 128I-129A.

[79] *ibid.*, 126G. The Court acknowledged that this sort of defence was known as duress of circumstances in England, and that the earlier case of *Tudhope v. Grubb*, 1983 S.C.C.R. 350, Sh.Ct was a case involving such a defence.

[80] For pre- *Moss v. Howdle* cases which might have contained qualifying medical emergencies, see the fact situations in *Graham v. Annan*, 1980 S.L.T. 28 (disqualified driver having to drive, since his pregnant wife had taken ill while she was driving), and *Watson v. Hamilton*, 1988 S.C.C.R. 13 (person who had been drinking having to drive to hospital a woman suffering a possible miscarriage).

[81] As in *Tudhope v. Grubb*, 1983 S.C.C.R. 350, Sh.Ct; see *Moss v. Howdle*, 1997 J.C. 123, at 127H.

[82] *Moss v. Howdle*, 1997 J.C. 123, at 129G.

[83] See *Dawson v. Dickson*, 1999 S.C.C.R. 698.

though no such circumstances actually existed in fact.[84] In *Moss v. Howdle*[84a] itself, the accused had been driving on a motorway accompanied by a passenger who suddenly cried out in pain: the accused thus reasonably believed that his passenger had been struck by some serious ailment, and that a medical emergency had arisen.[85] It was claimed that this, therefore, provided the accused with a defence to the motoring offence he then committed — *i.e.* driving at well above the permitted speed limit until the nearest service area was reached. But the accused in *Moss*[85a] fell foul of another rule. Although the necessitous circumstances must dominate the mind of the accused, the defence must be tested by enquiring whether or not there was any reasonable and legal alternative to the commission of a crime; and in *Moss*[85b] the accused had thought of stopping at the side of the road to see what was wrong, but said that he realised that if he required to use it, his mobile telephone was not in working order. As the trial court had found that it would have been possible and reasonable for the accused to have stopped to make enquiries as to his passenger's state of health, there had been a legal alternative, and the accused had failed to take it. That was sufficient to prevent his taking advantage of the defence. This, of course, raises the issue of whether an accused's honest, but mistaken, belief in the absence of any reasonable alternative would be sufficient for necessity to be considered in his case: this matter was not tested in *Moss*[85c] since the accused admitted that an appropriate alternative had indeed occurred to him; but it is doubtful whether a mere honest belief would be considered adequate under Scots law, which tends to favour objectivity in such matters. An accused must, therefore, take any reasonable alternative to the crime he proposes in order to avoid or escape from the danger of death or serious injury — or forfeit the use of the defence.[86] Even where there is no reasonable alternative to the commission of a crime to avoid the danger, but in cases where that crime is of a continuing nature — *e.g.*, driving for more than an insignificant distance whilst disqualified or after drinking significant quantities of alcohol — then the criminal conduct must be brought to an end as soon as the necessitous circumstances have ceased to be applicable: if that is not done, the defence will cease to apply and its benefits will be lost.[87] The benefits may also be lost *ab initio*, of course, if there are statutory provisions which make specific rules for emergency situations.[88]

The basis for the defence of necessity in Scots law. The court in *Moss v. Howdle*[89] declined to enter into discussion as to the juridical basis of defences of coercion or duress,[90] but did state that duress and the form **13.22**

---

[84] An honest, but unreasonable belief, sufficient under English law (see para. 13.18, *supra*), is unlikely to be acceptable in Scotland.

[84a] 1997 J.C. 123.

[85] In fact, his passenger was merely suffering from a temporary attack of cramp.

[85a] 1997 J.C. 123.

[85b] *ibid.*

[85c] *ibid.*

[86] See *Moss v. Howdle*, 1997 J.C. 129G. Even where the defence fails, however, the circumstances of necessity might still be useful in mitigation: see, *e.g.*, *Morrison v. Valentine*, 1990 S.C.C.R. 692; *Graham v. Annan*, 1980 S.L.T. 28; *MacLeod v. MacDougall*, 1988 S.C.C.R. 519.

[87] See *Ruxton v. Lang*, 1998 S.C.C.R. 1; *cf.*, *MacLeod v. MacDougall*, 1988 S.C.C.R. 519.

[88] See, *e.g.*, *Downie v. H.M. Advocate*, 1984 S.C.C.R. 365.

[89] 1997 J.C. 123.

[90] *ibid.*, L.J.-G. Rodger, at 129G.

of necessity recognised in the case were simply species of the genus of necessity.[91] This suggests (but no more) acceptance of a wider form of necessity, to be developed perhaps by the courts in Scotland at some later date as the occasion demanded: but there is little sign of such development.[92] It seems that necessity in Scots law is similar to the defence of duress of circumstances found in the law of England:[93] both defences are rule, rather than value-based. Since in both jurisdictions the defence covers a wide range of crimes[94] including offences of strict liability,[95] it cannot be the case that necessity (or coercion for that matter) prevents the formation of *mens rea*. It must, therefore, either be a defence *sui generis* or have some effect on the voluntariness of what was done by the accused, the latter being the preferred option of Dickson J. in the Canadian case of *Perka v. The Queen*[96] — a case much referred to in *Moss*.[96a] Dickson J. accepted that there were two possible approaches to cases of necessity. First there was the humanitarian approach under which, once the elements of the crime had been proved against the accused, the breach of the law might be excused by virtue of the emergency situation the accused had faced. The other approach was the utilitarian one of weighing up the competing interests in order to assess whether the criminal conduct of the accused was justified as having secured a greater good or a lesser evil than the one avoided. Dickson J. was sceptical of the latter approach, since a discussion in terms of higher social values "imports undue subjectivity into the law".[97] His preferred view was as follows: "Relating necessity to the principle that the law ought not to punish involuntary acts leads to a conceptualisation of [necessity] that integrates it into the normal rules for criminal liability rather than constituting it as a *sui generis* exception and threatening to engulf large portions of the criminal law."[98] A true situation of necessity, therefore, where the accused had no reasonable option but to commit a crime in order to prevent death or serious injury, was one which claimed that the accused's conduct had not been fully voluntary in the sense categorised as "normative or moral involuntariness" by Fletcher,[99] by whose published work Dickson J. had been much influenced.

Dickson J.'s rationalisation of necessity does not avoid the need for proportionality, however, in that the defence could hardly be accepted in cases where the commission of the crime in question did not secure a

---

[91] *ibid.*, 128A-B. The Court, there, also agreed with Lord Hailsham in *R. v. Howe* [1987] 1 All E.R. 771, at 777h-i, that there was no real distinction to be drawn in law between necessity and duress.

[92] See, *e.g.*, *John v. Donnelly*, 1999 S.C.C.R. 802, where it was argued that the accused had chosen the lesser of two evils by destroying part of the perimeter fence round a naval base where nuclear weapons were believed to be stored. Even if it had been possible to show that possession of such weapons was an offence against humanity in international law, the court indicated that the proposition that it was acceptable to commit a lesser crime to prevent the commission, or continued commission, of a greater one was unsound (see the opinion of the Court at 804F).

[93] See paras 13.17 to 13.19, *supra*.

[94] Although it is currently unknown whether necessity is or is not a defence to murder.

[95] *Moss v. Howdle*, 1997 J.C. 123, itself, for example, dealt with speeding under the Road Traffic Regulation Act 1984.

[96] [1984] 2 S.C.R. 232. See also *Morgentaler v. The Queen* [1976] 1 S.C.R. 616.

[96a] 1997 J.C. 123.

[97] *ibid.*, at 248.

[98] *ibid.*, at 250.

[99] See G.P. Fletcher, *Rethinking Criminal Law* (Boston, 1978), pp.802–803.

lesser harm than the one sought to be avoided (although it does seem that if necessity is a concession to human frailty — an excuse in cases where the accused could not have been expected to obey the law — it is not entirely clear why proportionality should be insisted upon). In the absence of any judicial pronouncement, it is speculative to suggest that the Court in *Moss v. Howdle*[1] took the view that the juridical basis for necessity was that favoured by Dickson J. in *Perka v. The Queen*[1a]; but Dickson J.'s approach is an attractive one and worthy of consideration; and as long as the involuntariness theory is confined to "moral or normative involuntariness" there should be no danger of self-induced conditions having any bearing on the defence.

Surgical operations. Surgical operations involve what are, prima facie, assaults of a kind which probably cannot be rendered non-criminal by the consent of the patient. That they are not criminal may be due in part to the operation of a principle of necessity, but they are very much a class of their own and not an example of the legal effect of necessity as such.[2] **13.23**

II — Coercion[3]

Coercion was definitively accepted as a defence by the High Court in Scotland in *Thomson v. H.M. Advocate*[4] following the position adopted by Hume.[5] It is probably proper for the law to recognise the defence because the typical situation in coercion — where A is forced to commit a crime at the point of a gun — is similar to the situation in which he is altogether deprived of volition, as when a knife is put into his hand and forcibly guided into the victim's body. Another reason for the acceptance of the defence of coercion is that coercion is often thought of as involving the overpowering of A's will by the force of the threats made against him. There is here an analogy with the case in which a man's will is completely overpowered, a situation in which, if it can ever occur, his actions would clearly not be voluntary. But in such situations, as in that of the man who is physically propelled by a stronger force, there is no need to invoke the defence of coercion, since there is no criminal conduct at all on the part of the accused. Coercion, like necessity, is concerned with situations in which A chooses to commit a crime because he prefers to do so rather than to submit to the threatened alternative. As Lord Kilbrandon has put it: **13.24**

> "The effect of a threat upon its recipient may be said to be to reduce his constancy, so that he is forced to do what he knows to be wrong and would not have done unless he had been threatened. He is not like the infant or the insane, who are disqualified or disabled from forming a criminal intention. He has decided to do a wrong thing, having balanced in his mind, perhaps unconsciously, the

---

[1] 1997 J.C. 123.
[1a] [1984] 2 S.C.R. 232.
[2] See Vol. II, Chap. 29.
[3] For a general discussion of coercion see J.Ll.J. Edwards, "Compulsion, Coercion and Criminal Responsibility" (1951) 14 M.L.R. 297.
[4] 1983 S.C.C.R. 368, at 381.
[5] See Hume, i, 52–53.

consequences to himself of refusal against the consequences to another of acquiescence."[6]

Whether or not the defence of coercion succeeds, assuming the threat to have been sufficiently serious to create a situation of necessity, will depend on whether or not the law approves of A's choice of action. It is this objective choice which is important. To prefer treason to imminent death is justifiable, to prefer it to the destruction of one's property is not[7]: and it would not make any difference if the particular accused preferred the preservation of his property to that of his life so that a threat to the former would be more likely to affect his mind than a threat to the latter.

13.25 The same considerations which make punishment futile in certain situations of necessity apply equally to coercion.

> "A man who refuses to commit a bad action, when he sees preparations made for killing or torturing him unless he complies, is a man who does not require the fear of punishment to restrain him. A man, on the other hand, who is withheld from committing crimes solely or chiefly by the fear of punishment, will never be withheld by that fear when a pistol is held to his forehead or a lighted torch applied to his fingers for the purpose of forcing him to commit a crime."[8]

13.26 Whereas in theory necessity might be considered as either a justification or an excuse, coercion can operate only as an excuse. The reason for this is as follows. The man who commits a crime under coercion does so as the agent, albeit the innocent agent, of the criminal who is coercing him. Anyone, therefore, who defends himself against him is defending himself against a crime — the crime committed by the coercer through the agency of the coerced person. It is unlikely that this right of defence against a crime can be taken away from the victim merely because the criminal operates by way of coercing another person into committing the crime rather than by committing it himself. The defence is special to the coerced person, and does not affect third party rights, so to speak, and accordingly coercion can operate only as an excuse, and not as a justification.

Public compulsion

13.27 Hume deals with coercion under two heads, which he calls called public and private compulsion.[9]

---

[6] *D.P.P. v. Lynch* [1975] A.C. 653 at 703 B-G.; See also Lord Wilberforce at 697–680; Lord Simon of Glaisdale at 689–690.

[7] *R. v. Alex. McGrowther* (1746) 18 St.Tr. 391, Lee C.J. at 393–394; *cf. R. v. Purdy* (1946) 10 J.C.L. 182.

[8] Macaulay, p.455.

[9] Hume, i, 51–52; Alison, i, 672 merely follows Hume. Hume also deals with what he calls the defence of subjection — that the accused acted under the influence of someone to whom he stood in the relation of wife to husband, child to father, or servant to master. Hume accepts the possibility of such a plea being successful in the case of a child instigated to a minor crime by a parent, but rejects it in any other relationship except where in addition to the relationship there is an actual threat of violence, and except the special case of a wife harbouring her husband which he does not regard as a crime, being required by "the feelings of nature and duty" and, he adds, "it is not to be presumed that she has it in her power if she were so disposed, to refuse him this assistance." The case of reset — see Vol. II, Chap. 20 — is also special. The plea of subjection thus becomes an instance of coercion: see Hume, i, 47–51.

Public coercion arises in situations where A's actings are almost involuntary — as where he is forced by a mob to join them. In such a case he will not be responsible for being part of the mob, or even for taking part in their activities, while he was in their power. If he remains with them after he could have made his escape, his further actions will be treated as voluntary and criminal. In *Robert Main*[10] the court found the defence:

> "That he was forced to take a gun by the disorderly people who were running that way, and who threatened to knock him down if he would not take it, relevant to exculpate him as to his being in arms, by having the said gun in that place where he was so forced, but not relevant as to his having the gun in any other place, unless the force was so continued, that he could not with safety lay his gun aside, or withdraw from the company who forced him."

This reasoning is the same as that of Lee C.J. in *R. v. MacGrowther,*[11] a charge of joining the rebel army in 1745, where he said that force and fear alleged as a defence "must continue all the time the party remains with the rebels. It is incumbent in every man, who makes force his defence, to shew an actual force, and that he quitted the service as soon as he could."[12]

In such a case, as in the case of a man pressed into the service of pirates,[13] or even complying with the orders of a rebel army when living in an area under their control, there is an element not merely of threats but of actual physical compulsion. Indeed, the admission of compulsion as a defence to treason may be due to the fact that members of rebel armies were frequently pressed into service and it was thought unfair to punish them in such circumstances.

Private compulsion

Hume takes the view that such situations — where a man is coerced into doing a particular act by threats of one or more individuals, and not merely caught up in a mob or pressed into service — are unlikely to occur in a society where law enforcement is effective. He gives, however, an example of such coercion being accepted in defence to a charge of robbery, although the facts of the case seem to lie somewhere between public and private coercion. The case is *James Graham*[14] who was forced to join Rob Roy's gang and take part in a robbery, under threat of violence. He was dragged out of his house by the gang, and threatened with a pistol and other weapons, threats which were repeated when he tried to escape. The jury found "That he was present in arms along with Roy and others at the time when the robbery was committed, but that he was forced into the service in manner mentioned, and that he was not possessed of arms to make resistance at the time," and he was acquitted. **13.28**

Although Hume seems to accept the authority of this case he goes on to state his own views as follows:

[10] (1725) Hume, i, 52.
[11] (1746) 18 St.Tr. 391 at 394.
[12] *cf. R. v. Crutchley* (1831) 5 C. & P. 133.
[13] *cf.* Hume, i, 52
[14] (1717) Hume, i, 52–53.

"But generally, and with relation to the ordinary condition of a well-regulated society, where every man is under the shield of the law, and has the means of resorting to that protection, this is at least somewhat a difficult plea, and can hardly be serviceable in the case of a trial for any atrocious crime, unless it have the support of these qualifications: an immediate danger of death or great bodily harm; an inability to resist the violence; a backward and an inferior part in the perpetration; and a disclosure of the fact, as well as restitution of the spoil, on the first safe and convenient occasion."[15]

The Modern Law

13.29 The court in *Thomson v. H.M. Advocate*[16] accepted Hume's views as broadly correct, save that the critical issues in his account of coercion were identified as being, first, that, in a serious crime at least, the type of threat should be one of death or serious injury to the actor (or another) and that it should immediately[17] be capable of implementation, and, second, that the actor should have been unable to resist the threats.[18] The other criteria quoted by Hume were considered to be evidential rather than substantive. Although the Court appears to give the impression that Hume had restricted the defence to "atrocious crimes", it is clear[19] that what Hume meant was that the most serious crimes required the strictest of conditions in view of the facile nature of the plea.[20] This, however, leaves open the approach to be taken in relation to non-serious offences: neither Hume nor the courts have made clear what conditions should then attach; and it is equally unclear in Scotland whether the defence is open where the charge is one of murder.[21]

Perhaps clearer is the principle which informs the defence and confirms the way in which it operates. That principle is that an involuntary act is not punishable. As Lord Hunter, the trial judge, said in *Thomson*[21a]: "a defence of coercion in order to be successful requires that the danger must be immediate and that the will and resolution of

---

[15] Hume, i, 53.

[16] 1983 S.C.C.R. 368.

[17] *cf.*, the English case of *R. v. Hudson* [1971] 2 Q.B. 202, where the emphasis was placed on the effectiveness of the threats on the persons to whom they had been directed, even though these threats could not immediately be implemented: that this is still the law in England is shown in *R. v. Lewis* (1993) 96 Cr.App.R. 412.

[18] 1983 S.C.C.R. 368, L.J.-C. Wheatley at 380.

[19] See *Moss v. Howdle*, 1997 J.C. 123, L.J.-G. Rodger at 126D-E.

[20] See *Thomson v. H.M. Advocate*, 1983 S.C.C.R. 368, L.J.-C. Wheatley at 381.

[21] *cf.*, Lord Allanbridge in *Collins v. H.M. Advocate*, 1991 S.C.C.R. 898, where he said in his charge to the jury: "It is because of the supreme importance that the law affords to the protection of human life [that coercion should as a matter of law be denied to those charged with murder]. It is repugnant that the law should recognise in any individual in any circumstances however extreme the right to choose that one innocent person should be killed rather than any other person including himself." This accords, at least in part, with the reasons given in England for refusing the defence of duress by threats to those who are charged with murder or attempted murder, whether as principals or accessories: see *R. v. Howe* [1987] 1 All E.R. 771; *R. v. Gotts* [1992] 2 W.L.R. 284. Some of the difficulties with which the House of Lords wrestled in respect of attempted murder and duress — *e.g.*, that there must be an actual intent to kill in attempt to murder, whereas murder itself need be satisfied by a mere intention to do serious bodily harm — would not be of much concern in Scotland: see *Cawthorne v. H.M. Advocate*, 1968 J.C. 32. It might be noted, however, that Hume did include murder amongst his examples of "atrocious crimes" (see i, 47). *Cf.*, the effect, if any, of Art. 2 ("Right to life") of the European Convention on Human Rights; see, *e.g.*, *McCann v. United Kingdom* (1996) 21 E.H.R.R. 97.

[21a] 1983 S.C.C.R. 368.

the accused must have been overborne by threats which he believed would be carried out so that he was not at the time acting of his own free will."[22] It is submitted that this means that the accused chose to commit the crime and did so with full *mens rea* (if required by the crime in question) but with a voluntariness which was constrained by the operation of the threats. As Chief Justice Lamer said in *Hibbert v. The Queen*: "As a matter of logic, the issue of whether an accused can invoke an excuse or justification arises only after the Crown has proven the existence of all the elements of the offence, including *mens rea*."[23] An approach in terms of an absence of full voluntariness[24] would also help to explain why coercion is believed to be ruled out where the accused voluntarily joined a criminal organisation (or perhaps less formally became involved with organised criminal wrongdoing) where he knew, or perhaps should have realised, that membership or involvement carried with it the likelihood that he might be subjected to violent threats during the course of that membership or involvement.[25]

The Court in *Thomson v. H.M. Advocate*[25a] did, however, accept that Hume's account of coercion related to the situation of a well regulated society where everyone was assumed to have ready access to protection from the forces of law and order, and where that assumption could be made to justify the strict conditions which limited the defence's ready exercise. In the rare situation where that assumption could not be made,[26] the Court considered that a case-by-case approach would have to be adopted where presumably the usual strict criteria would have to be relaxed in accordance with realities.[27]

---

[22] 1983 S.C.C.R. 368, at 374. It seems that the threats must dominate the mind of the accused, such that his criminal conduct is caused by that domination: *ibid.*, L.J.-C. Wheatley, at 382. In England it has been stated that it was not wrong for a trial judge to direct a jury that the criminal acts of the defendant had to be solely due to the threats he had received, if the defence of duress was to be accepted by them, since it was "difficult to conceive of a situation where a man could reasonably say that he committed a criminal act because his will was overborne by the threats made to him and also because he wanted to make money": see *R. v. Ortiz* (1986) 83 Cr.App.R. 173, Farquharson L.J., at 176.

[23] [1995] 2 S.C.R. 473, at para. 38. In *H.M. Advocate v. Raiker*, 1989 S.C.C.R. 149, at 154B-C, Lord McCluskey, wrongly it is respectfully submitted, referred to coercion as showing that the accused had no evil intention.

[24] *i.e.,* the moral or normative involuntariness referred to by George P. Fletcher, *Rethinking Criminal Law* (Boston, 1978), at 802–803, *viz.*: "Another way to approach the rationale of excusing conditions is to start with the premise that law should punish only in cases of voluntary wrongdoing. Excuses arise in cases in which the actor's freedom of choice is constricted. His conduct is not strictly involuntary as if he suffered a seizure or if someone pushed his knife-holding hand down on the victim's throat. In these cases there is no act at all, no wrongdoing and therefore no need for an excuse. The notion of involuntariness at play is what we should call moral or normative involuntariness."

[25] See *Thomson v. H.M. Advocate*, 1983 S.C.C.R. 368, Lord Hunter (trial judge) at 373. In England, such a restriction of the defence of duress is well established: see *R. v. Sharp* [1987] 3 All E.R. 103; *R. v. Shepherd* (1988) 86 Cr.App.R. 47; *R. v. Baker and Ward* (1999) 2 Cr.App.R. 335: *cf. R. v. Lewis* (1993) 96 Cr.App.R. 412.

[25a] 1983 S.C.C.R. 368.

[26] *cf.*, for example, the situation in *R. v. Lewis* (1993) 96 Cr.App.R. 412, where a prisoner had been seriously assaulted by a fellow prisoner, and former companion-in--crime, in the prison yard, and it was accepted that the authorities could not fully protect him from the threat of future injury from his assailant and his associates within the prison community.

[27] *Thomson v. H.M. Advocate*, 1983 S.C.C.R. 368, L.J.-C. Wheatley at 382.

III — Superior Orders

The scope and basis of the defence

13.30 This defence is dealt with by Hume as a form of compulsion or subjection, the subjection of soldiers to officers, or of law-enforcement officers to magistrates.[28] What is involved is not, strictly speaking, coercion, but the right or duty of a soldier to carry out his orders without thereby incurring liability under the criminal law. The soldier who kills someone in pursuance of an order by a superior officer does not have to show that he was in fear that if he failed to carry it out he would himself be shot or undergo some commensurate punishment; he has only to show that he acted under a lawful order, or rather that he believed he was so acting. He does not even have to point to a specific order to kill the deceased; it is enough if he can show that he was acting according to normal military practice when he killed the deceased.[29]

Hume considers the defence in relation to magistrates and judges executing bad laws, such as those against witches; in relation to soldiers carrying out orders; and in relation to officers of court executing orders or killing persons who resist them in the execution of their duty.[30] The only category of importance at the present day is that of the soldier.[31]

The basis of the defence is probably public policy, and that would explain why an order may be lawful according to the municipal law of a particular country and yet be unlawful according to international law. Policemen, messengers-at-arms, and soldiers, act as instruments of the law and of the state, and it would be impossible for the state to punish them for so acting. A public executioner cannot be charged with the murder of the condemned man, or a sheriff-officer with theft or embezzlement of goods which he poinds and sells under a court order. In acting as they do these officials are carrying out the law, and the law can hardly punish them for doing so. Nor can a soldier be convicted of murder when he kills an enemy soldier according to the usages of war, since he does so on the command of the state. Even if he acts contrary to the usages of war his own state can hardly prosecute him if it authorised his action.

This protection extends beyond specific acts done in pursuance of specific orders; it extends to anything done in the course of the accused's duty. A soldier or a policemen must be allowed a certain discretion in carrying out his duties — his every move cannot be specifically ordered by a superior authority. So long therefore as he acts in the ordinary course of his employment and within the general rules laid down for his conduct he is acting as an instrument of the state, and is entitled to protection even if, on occasion, he is overzealous. The protection may even extend to acts which are not strictly legal, in the sense that they have not been explicitly or implicitly authorised by any lawful order.

---

[28] Hume, i, 53–55.

[29] *cf. Hawton and Parker* (1861) 4 Irv. 58.

[30] Hume, i, 53–55, 195–217.

[31] Hume also deals with homicide committed by soldiers on duty as a form of justifiable homicide, but he there treats the case as a form of self-defence to which more lenient rules apply than in the normal case: Hume i, 205 *et seq.*; see also Alison, i, 39 *et seq.*; Burnett, pp.71 *et seq.*; Macdonald, pp.105–106; see Vol. II, Chap. 23.

It may also extend to actings in pursuance of an illegal order, for it is necessary for the proper functioning of bodies like the police and the army that they be disciplined and obedient — theirs not to reason why. They will therefore be excused for obeying any order which is in fact illegal, provided that it is not blatantly so. It is bad public policy to encourage soldiers to disobey orders because they think them improper. And looked at from the point of view of the individual soldier or policeman it is unfair to train a man in automatic obedience, and then to penalise him for acting in the way the state itself has trained him to act.[32] **13.31**

Hume suggests that someone who carries out an unlawful order is excused because he is "entitled to repose in confidence of the skill and attention of his superior," and because "He intended to do a lawful act, and was justifiable in thinking it such: The error in that respect is thus, as to him, an error in point of fact only; and it ought therefore to excuse him, as that sort of error does in other cases."[33] This seems, however, to be a very strained application of the law of mistake — to believe wrongly that an order is lawful is surely an error of law. Nonetheless, it may be of importance to show that the soldier believed, and was justified in believing, that the order he was carrying out was lawful. A soldier might not be justified (or even excusable) in carrying out an order known to him to be unlawful, for example, an order by a junior officer which he knew to be contrary to the order of a superior, unless he acted under actual coercion. But the limits of the defence are by no means clear.

The cases

It is submitted that the above statement of the law is borne out by the 19th and 20th century cases, which must now be considered. **13.32**

The first is *Hawton and Parker*.[34] A boatswain of the Royal Navy, Hawton was sent out on a dark night in a boat with a crew of seamen and one marine, Parker, in order to intercept a trawler. Hawton had a revolver and Parker a rifle; the seamen had cutlasses. The boatswain ordered the marine to fire on the trawler. He fired blank shots first and then fired live shots intended to go wide of the trawler; in fact one of them killed a member of the trawler's crew. The boatswain and the marine were charged with murder, but the Crown asked for a conviction of culpable homicide only.

The marine pleaded that he had acted under the boatswain's orders, and the boatswain pleaded that he had acted in accordance with normal navy practice. It was argued that the marine was absolutely bound to obey the boatswain unless he was ordered to do something obviously grossly criminal, and that the boatswain's order was not obviously criminal, since it was in accord with naval practice. Lord Justice-General McNeill told the jury:

> "[S]ubordinate officers or privates were not persons who were entitled to consider whether the rules to which they had been accustomed were imported into this duty [of suppressing trawlers], unless that were explained to them by their superior officers. One of the prisoners in this case had a certain command, the other was in

---

[32] *cf.* Hume, i, 54–55. He may, however, be liable to be dealt with by an international court.

[33] Hume, i, 54.

[34] (1861) 4 Irv. 58. An earlier case with similar facts is *Henry Lloyd* (1810) Hume, i, 209.

> the position of a subordinate; and it was the duty of the subordinate to obey his superior officer, unless the order given by his superior was so flagrantly and violently wrong that no citizen could be expected to obey it. But that principle extended also to the other prisoner, the officer then in command, because he was there also as a subordinate to fulfil the duty entrusted to him according to the rules of the service. And, therefore, if, when the prisoners fired the shots with the view of making the fishermen yield to legal authority, they were acting in accordance with the usage of the naval service, they were not guilty of any violation of the law."[35]

His Lordship added that if the jury thought the accused had deviated from the rules of the service, or that "in acting according to the rules of the service, they had failed to use due caution",[36] they should convict. The question of negligence arose because the shots had been intended to go wide of the trawler, and it was by accident or carelessness that they had instead hit a member of the trawler's crew. This aspect of the case was to some extent subsumed in the general question of naval practice. Presumably if the accused had acted recklessly it might have been said that they were not acting in accordance with practice, but it may have been assumed that if naval practice authorised firing it would be very difficult to convict the accused on the ground that only careful and accurate firing designed not to injure anyone was authorised. If a man is justified in doing an inherently dangerous act he can hardly be convicted because the act causes harm, unless it can be shown that he did the act in a manner more likely to cause harm than the normal approved manner of acting.

13.33 The case of *H.M. Advocate v. Macpherson*[37] suggests that a soldier who exceeds his orders and acts recklessly may be protected if he acted honestly and with the intention of carrying out what he believed to be his duty. Macpherson was on leave and drunk when he saw a car during an air raid alert which he thought was travelling too quickly with its lights insufficiently dimmed. He called on it to stop, and when it failed to do so he fired at it, killing the occupant who was the Assistant Chief Constable of Edinburgh. The case was treated as one of simple culpable homicide on the issue of recklessness and not of military duty, since Macpherson was not in fact on duty at the time of the shooting. Indeed, Lord Justice-Clerk Aitchison told the jury that there was no question of justifiable homicide in the case. But he went on to say: "Even in a case where the soldier was on leave and had no specific duty to perform, if you are able to say that the accused acted under a mistaken sense of duty and that he had some reasonable cause for what he did, you would be entitled to acquit him."[38] These observations appear to have been based on the general law of mistake — a man who reasonably believes that he is acting under orders or in accordance with proper military practice is entitled to be treated as if he were in fact so acting. As Lord Aitchison said:

---

[35] At 71–72.

[36] At 73.

[37] High Court at Edinburgh, Sept. 1940, unrep'd — see *H.M. Advocate v. Shepherd*, 1941 J.C. 67, 69.

[38] See 1941 J.C. 67 at 70.

> "It won't do for a soldier on leave to discharge a loaded rifle in the public street and take human life and then seek to evade the responsibility by saying that he thought he was doing his duty. You must ask yourselves whether there were any reasonable grounds, such as might influence a man in his sober senses, for the accused acting as he did."[39]

The mistake here is of course an error of fact, and distinguishable from the case of a soldier acting under an order he wrongly believes to be lawful. The legality of a practice of shooting at cars which did not stop when challenged does not appear to have been considered in *Macpherson*.[39a]

The question of homicide committed in pursuance of an illegal order was considered in *H.M. Advocate v. Shepherd*,[40] The accused was a private in an escort under the immediate command of a lance-corporal which was taking a British deserter from one camp to another. The lance-corporal left the accused alone with the prisoner for a short time in a railway station, having warned him to stand no nonsense and to shoot if necessary to prevent the prisoner escaping, as the prisoner had previously tried to escape. The prisoner tried to escape and the accused killed him. He was charged with culpable homicide, and succeeded in the defence that he was acting in the course of his duty. Lord Robertson told the jury that they could take the view that, **13.34**

> "[I]f the circumstances were such as to require the accused, for the due execution of his duty, to shoot in order to keep this man in custody, then the homicide was justifiable . . . It would be altogether wrong to judge his actings, so placed, too meticulously — to weigh them in fine scales. If that were to be done, it seems to me that the actings of soldiers on duty might well be paralysed by fear of consequences, with great prejudice to national interests."[41]

The Crown sought to prove that the accused had been ordered not to shoot British prisoners, in that general orders of that nature had been posted in his camp. They also produced an Army Council Instruction of later date than the shooting, to show that it was not army practice to shoot British prisoners. If they had succeeded in proving the accused's knowledge of such an order or practice he might have been convicted, since it would probably have been unreasonable for him to prefer the order of an absent lance-corporal to a general order from his headquarters, especially in a question of shooting someone. But had he been ordered to shoot by a senior officer he might still have been excused for doing so, even if he had known that the order was contrary to a general order. The matter may resolve itself into one of degree, depending on the circumstances, and in particular on the rank of the officer who gives the illegal order. The question becomes one whether the accused could reasonably consider himself bound to obey the order last given by an officer on the spot, and whether he could be reasonably expected to risk the consequences of disobedience. Such a situation approaches one of

---

39 *ibid.* at 69.

39a High Court at Edinburgh, Sept. 1940, unrep'd. — see *H.M. Advocate v. Shepherd,* 1941 J.C. 67 at 69.

40 1941 J.C. 67.

41 At 71.

true coercion, since the soldier would be placed in a dilemma in which it would be unreasonable to saddle him with responsibility for his superior's illegal orders, and in which he might be said to have been "coerced" by his superior orders.[42]

Private orders

13.35 In *Calder v. Robertson*[43] a farmer who had no right to shoot rabbits on his land sent his servant to do so and the latter was charged with poaching. The sheriff-substitute acquitted him on the ground that he was "acting under the orders of his master the tenant therein", and the High Court upheld the acquittal. Lord Young said that the sheriff had acted consistently with law and common sense, and that the servant could not turn round and ask to examine his master's lease. *Calder*[43a] is special in that tenants are entitled to kill rabbits except when that right is excluded by their lease, and in any event appears to have been decided on the ground that the accused lacked *mens rea* and acted in error. However that may be, there is no warrant for any general proposition that the orders of a private master can in any way form a defence to a criminal charge, and ample authority to the contrary.[44]

---

[42] The case of *Ensign Maxwell* in 1807 (Buch., Pt. II, 3) may be noted in this connection. The accused was an officer at a prison where prisoners of war were detained. There were orders issuing from the Adjutant General allowing prisoners to be killed if they tried to escape, and setting out certain other rules which were to be enforced. The commander of the prison instituted a system whereby force might be used by an officer on a report by a sentinel that the prisoners were creating a disturbance or had ignored an order to put their lights out. The accused ordered a private to shoot into the prisoners' room, apparently following this practice. The private refused at first because he did not think the circumstances justified such an order, but eventually he obeyed, and one of the prisoners was killed. The private was not charged, but the accused officer was charged with murder and pleaded justification, a plea in which he failed, partly at least because of evidence that the prisoners had not been disobeying any rules. In the course of his charge, Lord Hope said that the shooting would be justifiable if the accused acted under specific orders, or if "in the general discharge of his duty, he was placed in circumstances which gave him discretion, and called upon him to do what he did": at 58. On the question of acting under orders Lord Hope said, "be these orders right or wrong, he was bound to obey . . . There is some restriction, however, even upon this; because if an officer were to command a soldier to go out to the street, and kill you or me, he would not be bound to obey. It must be a legal order given with reference to the circumstances in which he was placed; and thus every officer has a discretion to disobey orders against the known laws of the land": at 58, which, like the more modern statements leaves the matter to be dealt with according to the circumstances of each case. See also *William Inglis* (1810) Burnett, p.79.

[43] (1878) 4 Couper 131.

[43a] *ibid.*

[44] See Alison, i, 672; Hume, i, 50–51; *Richardson v. Maitland* (1897) 2 Adam 243; *Gordon v. Shaw* (1908) 5 Adam, 469. Lord Young did, however, repeat the views he expressed in *Calder v. Robertson, supra*, in the later case of *Jack v. Nairne* (1887) 1 White 350. For an example of a statutory defence of superior orders see the Food and Environment Protection Act 1985, s.22(2)(a).

INDEX